D1283072

North American Exploration

North American Exploration

VOLUME 1

A NEW WORLD DISCLOSED

JOHN LOGAN ALLEN, EDITOR

UNIVERSITY OF NEBRASKA PRESS   LINCOLN AND LONDON

"Imagining the Indies" (p. v) from *The Double Reckoning of Christopher Columbus* by Barbara Helfgott Hyett. Copyright 1992 by the Board of Trustees of the University of Illinois. Used with permission of the author and the University of Illinois Press.

Chapter 4 © 1997 by Robert H. Fuson

© 1997 by the University of Nebraska Press

Library of Congress Cataloging-in-Publication Data

North American exploration /
John Logan Allen, editor.
p.   cm.
Includes bibliographical references and index.
Contents: v. 1. A new world disclosed—
v. 2. A continent defined—
v. 3. A continent comprehended.
ISBN 0-8032-1015-9 (cloth : alk. paper).—
ISBN 0-8032-1023-x (cloth : alk. paper).—
ISBN 0-8032-1043-4 (cloth : alk. paper)
1. North America—Discovery and exploration.
I. Allen, John Logan, 1941–
E45.N67   1997
917.04—dc20   96-33025
CIP

Imagining the Indies

This day we completely lost sight of land and many men sighed and wept for fear that they would not see it again for a long time. I comforted them with great promises.   Christopher Columbus, *Diario*, Sunday, 9 September 1492

All things in the Indies overflow.
Blue cranes throng the marshes. The rivers and lakes
are lustrous with swans. Along the quays, men fish
with gigantic poles and silk. None of the shoals

is dangerous. Ships take the coves like streams.
Musk and lichens swell in the cedar forests;
and past the plains and mountains: crystal and dome.
Each palace shines. Each city is a new city.

Every person lives in an honest fashion,
and the king is sympathetic as the moon.
The Indies are the Earthly Paradise
where even the snakes that crawl are undisguised.

The whole land is fluvial. Red fruit
fattens beneath the canopy of palms.
Wheat as it ripens speaks more softly;
the sea is sweet to drink. The sun ascends

to its most majestic height and every hill
it touches wears a purple crown. Tall grasses
bend before the scythe in every valley
and all the dust that sifts through stones is gold.

Barbara Helfgott Hyett, from *Double Reckoning*

Contents

Illustrations

Maps

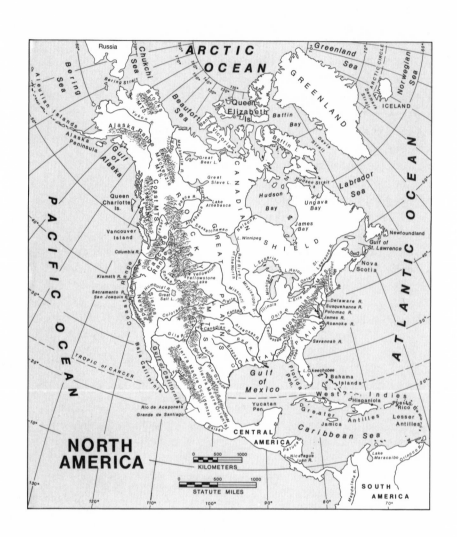

Preface and Acknowledgments

The literature of the exploration and discovery of North America is massive, and with the recent upsurge of interest in exploration and the subsequent reeditions of explorers' journals and the publication of other works stimulated by the Columbian Quincentennial, it promises to become even more so. Why, then, is there a need for such an effort as that presented in the three volumes of *North American Exploration*, for another research project and publication dealing with the exploration of North America?

The best among many good answers to this question is quite simple: there has not been, since late in the nineteenth century, an undertaking of similar scope. Extremely valuable collections of original documentary materials have been compiled, explorers' journals have been reedited and reissued, and major interpretative works by single or small groups of scholars have been produced. But a collaborative, comprehensive study and overview devoted exclusively to the topic of North American exploration has not been undertaken. In this sense, the project that culminates in these three volumes is long overdue. The contributing authors whose works are presented in these volumes have, of necessity, written chapters that are partly synthetic—that is, they build upon existing erudition. But each of these chapters is also a work of original scholarship, bringing new perspectives and approaches to the story of the exploration of the North American continent. The authors have considered new approaches, explored new ideas and new facts, developed new questions, and newly examined previous works. They have written chapters that are both interpretative and synthesizing, accurate in detail of facts both spatial and temporal, and well-documented from both primary and secondary source materials. They have produced a body of scholarship that, in addition to its historical and geographical content, is replete with historiographical references to the literature of exploration, with commentary on the political and economic and social aspects of exploration and with analyses of the consequences of exploration for other human endeavors.

The editor has chosen to preserve British, Canadian, and American usages in spelling and form. We hope that this internationally flavored (or flavoured) *North American Exploration* will play a pivotal role in the scholarly assessment of exploration for years to come. And we more strongly hope that the work will serve as a fitting memorial for the generations of explorers, cartographers, diplomats, scientists, and artists who, in the years after Columbus, brought forth a new continent. It is much more than symbolic that the completion of the writing phase of this massive work occurred in 1992, when we celebrated not only the Columbian Quincentennial but also the launching of NASA's *Mars Observer*, the first in a new wave of exploration that may carry new generations of explorers to worlds that are new in an even broader sense than was the North American continent five hundred years ago.

Like other collaborative projects, this one owes both its inception and its completion to so many different people that acknowledging them all is a perilous process. With the understanding that some people to whom I and the contributing authors owe thanks do not appear in my accounting, there are a number of individuals and institutions that must be singled out for their extraordinary assistance in this immense undertaking.

First and foremost, I would like to acknowledge the editorial board that has advised and guided me from the very beginning of this project, five years before the onslaught of the Quincentennial. These scholars, whose names are listed on a preceding page, assisted with the compilation of the basic outline upon which the research project was based; they aided in the selection of contributing authors (indeed, some of them even agreed to serve in that capacity); they provided a valuable sounding board for me as I was preparing research grants requesting funding for the project; they served as readers of and commentators on the individual chapters and made my job as editor appreciably easier. This project could not have been completed without their assistance, and they deserve special recognition. I would like particularly to single out my good friends and editorial board members Dr. James P. Ronda and Dr. Richard I. Ruggles. Both of these scholars were extraordinarily helpful in providing guidance and assistance and moral support to a harried editor who, due to unforeseen circumstances, had to step in and become an author for chapters 16 and 17. I could not have completed those chapters without their help.

I would also like to pay a special tribute to another member of the editorial board, Dr. J. Brian Harley, former professor of geography at the University of Wisconsin–Milwaukee and coeditor of *The History of Cartography*. Tragically, Brian passed away just as the work on the project was coming to a close. He had served as more than an adviser on the project; he also offered a shoulder for me to cry upon. His own vast editorial experience stood me in good stead time after time. We shall all miss you, Brian. May you find fair winds and a good harbor.

In addition to the above scholars, thanks are owed to Dr. William S. Coker, professor of history and chairman of the Department of History in the University of West Florida, for his very helpful suggestions on and review of the La Florida and southeastern U.S. portion of chapter 9. A debt of gratitude is also owed Clive Holland, of the Scott Polar Research Institute, Cambridge, England, who read the first draft of chapter 19 and provided helpful suggestions. Peter Kerr and Gail Strachan, of Wilfred Laurier University, provided research assistance for chapter 18, and Maria Mantica (chapter 9), Lynda Raymond (chapter 18), and Jean Horosko (chapter 21), contributed careful and thoughtful manuscript preparation for individual authors.

A number of institutions and individuals have been incredibly helpful in providing a variety of types of assistance, especially with the illustrative material that accompanies the chapters in the three volumes of *North American Exploration*. Among the host of libraries, museums, and people who were extraordinarily helpful with illustrative material (and who are listed in various figure captions), I would like to acknowledge the following: Mr. Richard Schimmelpfeng, of the Special Collections Department of the Babbidge Library, the University of Connecticut, has been—as always—an unfailing source of guidance and support in the acquisition of rare and fragile materials for photographing; Mr. William Breadheft and the staff of the University of Connecticut Photographic Services and Mr. Alec Bothell, of the Center for Instructional Media and Technology, endured, with grace and promptness and high professionalism, my importunate requests for delivery of photographic work; Edward H. Dahl, Early Cartographic Specialist of the National Archives of Canada, was of tremendous assistance in locating rare French and English maps at a most trying time for him and the Canadian Archives following the tragic destruction of some of their holdings; Mr. Peter Hassrick, former director of the Buffalo Bill Historical Center, Cody, Wyoming, was most helpful in providing illustrative material from the Center's remarkable Whitney Gallery of Western Art; the staff of the Joslyn Art Museum, the Internorth Foundation, Omaha, Nebraska, were most cooperative in securing quality prints of paintings from their collection. For permission to reprint portions of copyrighted material, specifically a section of Barbara Helfgott Hyett's remarkable epic poem about Columbus, *Double Reckoning*, I am deeply grateful to my former publisher, the University of Illinois Press.

Special financial support for portions of the volume came from Wilfrid Laurier University and the Social Sciences and Humanities Research Council of Canada, which funded much of the research for chapter 18, and from the President's Social Sciences and Humanities Research Council of Canada Fund, which supported the research for chapter 21. For generous and continuing financial support of the editorial part of the North American Exploration project I am profoundly in the debt of the University of Connecticut Research Foundation (UCRF). For a period of five years, UCRF provided me virtually unrestricted funds for postage, parcel delivery, copying, and other miscellaneous and "incidental" expenses that I didn't even know I would incur. The freedom this support gave me in terms of copying large manuscripts and shipping them to faraway places with strange-sounding names is vastly appreciated. The members of the Foundation never questioned why they were getting annual support requests for a project that, it must have seemed to them (it certainly did to me), would go on forever; they simply supplied me with the support needed.

Of all the individuals and institutions that have provided assistance to the North American Exploration project, none played as large a role as the National Endowment for the Humanities (NEH). Its generous financial support allowed the project to move from a gleam in my eye to these volumes. The substantial research grant from the NEH, which funded virtually all major expenses of the research project, was provided under its Columbian Quincentenary incentive program. I can only hope that the end result of this five-year project justifies the investment in scholarship made by the NEH.

Finally, I thankfully acknowledge a number of my colleagues at the University of Connecticut for their assistance and support during the five years of the project. Dr. Frank Vasington, former dean of the College of Arts and Sciences, graciously provided me with release time during part of the editing process so that I might devote a larger portion of my time to that effort and less time to teaching undergraduates. Dr. Judith W. Meyer, former head of the Department of Geography, was most cooperative in working my teaching schedule around the needs of the project and provided much more than just moral support throughout the duration of my editing efforts; since I served as department head myself at the beginning of the project, no one knows better than I what kinds of departmental adjustments she had to make to allow me to work nearly unfettered, and I am very grateful to her. My other present and past departmental colleagues—Dr. Robert Andrle, Dr. William Berentsen, Dr. Ellen Cromley, Dr. Robert

Cromley, Dr. Michael Folkoff, and Dr. Dean Hanink—have often taken up the slack for me in departmental committee responsibilities and have, in many other ways, been encouraging and supportive, particularly during times when it appeared as if I were going to be editing *North American Exploration* for the remainder of my academic career. A special thanks is due to the other "old guy" in my department, Dr. Peter Halvorson, for offering continual encouragement and for listening sympathetically to my griping and carping about everything, ranging from state bureaucracies to recalcitrant computers. Mrs. Carolee Tollefson, former departmental secretary, served as the bookkeeper and administrator of the various research grants that supported the project, and she handled an incredible amount of state and federal paperwork with efficiency and grace. Mr. John Diniz, my cartographer who began the project as a graduate student and completed it after he had received his postgraduate degree, handled not only outrageous requests for changes at the last minute but also a mass of bewildering cartographic detail, all with extraordinary aplomb and professionalism.

The greatest acknowledgment is deserved by my wife, Anne, who was remarkably patient with me during a long and often grueling time of reading and writing and editing. During much of this process, I was "away" even when I was home, and she put up with more than any person should have to, nevertheless managing to keep her sense of perspective and humor.

All of these people have my deepest gratitude for their support—moral and otherwise. This project could not have been completed without them, and they should share whatever credit exists for its successful completion. None of them, however, need take credit for any of the deficiencies in these volumes—those belong solely to me.

John L. Allen
Storrs, Connecticut

A New World Disclosed

Introduction to Volume 1

A little more than a century ago, the four hundredth anniversary of the discovery of the New World by Christopher Columbus was celebrated by an American public in a mood to embrace heroes who glorified the American past. The watershed of the Civil War, followed by the patriotic passion of the Republic's centennial celebration and by a period of brilliant economic growth and expansion, had stimulated the process of inventing traditions, of creating a shared view of the past as most would like it to have been rather than as it was.[1] Critical to the process of inventing tradition is the development of iconographic figures, cast larger than life and playing key roles in the American past. Christopher Columbus was such an iconographic figure, and a major exhibit at the Chicago World Columbian Exposition was fashioned around the theme of the Columbian voyages, a theme that served as the *raison d'être* for the Exposition itself. In the streets fronting the crowded immigrant tenements of New York City's East Side, the small-but-growing Italian population danced and marched and sang in honor of their celebrated countrymen Columbus and John Cabot and Giovanni da Verrazzano. And scholars from America's finest and most prestigious universities, secure in their study of heroes and unafraid to enthuse over adventure and romance, wrote new works about Columbus and those who followed him and edited collections of exploratory accounts the primary purposes of which were to portray discovery and discoverers as symbols of progress and, thereby, to both invent and glorify the American past.

What a difference a century makes! The occasion of the five hundredth anniversary of the landing of Columbus on an obscure island off the American mainland was greeted not by a world's fair but by a storm of controversy, and although the 1992 Columbus Day parades in cities like Boston and New York were celebrated by a large Italian-American community with more than their usual fervor, there were more rallies designed to denounce the discovery than to celebrate it. From the base of a quarter century of disillusionment, Americans in 1992 were disposed to invent new traditions, ones in which Columbus and his contemporaries were not heroes but villains and in which the events of discovery and the processes of exploration were symbols not of past glories but of past shame. Scholars, however, are perhaps more consistent than the general public, if no less fickle, and like the Quadricentennial, the Quincentennial occasioned a remarkable array of publications devoted to the Columbian voyages and related topics. Although many of these publications were cynical attempts to climb on the bandwagon of politically correct Columbus-bashing, at least as many were serious contributions to the literature of the history of geographical discovery and exploration. These publications of the Quincentennial obviously differed from their antecedents of a hundred years ago in tone and approach; they were more willing to see the warts on the nose of Euro-American "progress" and were more sensitive to the fact that explorations by Columbus and by his predecessors, contemporaries, and successors were events that took place on two sides of a cultural divide. Whereas the scholarly works of the late nineteenth century had cast discoverers and explorers in the heroic mold, late-twentieth-century scholarship has cast them in the mold of conquerors, representatives of the European invading powers that vanquished the peoples and landscapes of a New World Arcadia.

Neither the heroic nor the conquest model of exploration is truly satisfactory because both models, as demonstrated by the bulk of the Quincentennial publications, lack breadth and depth of content and purpose. There were publications aplenty that dealt with the events of discovery, but there were none that focused on the process of exploration. This gap in the literature, this lack of a comprehensive treatment of the process of exploration, is now filled, with the publication of *North American Exploration*, a broadly conceived project begun as part of the Quincentennial commemoration. In these three volumes, the full scope of the exploration of the North American continent and its oceanic margins from before Columbus down to the end of the nineteenth century is appraised. More than just an assessment of "discoveries" and other historical events, however, these volumes are an attempt to portray exploration in its broader context as a "planned effort to fit the facts of discovery into larger patterns of meaning."[2] Although none of the authors contributing to this collective effort can forget the glamour and romance of exploration that so attracted our predecessors at the four hundredth centenary, all of us recognize that exploration, as a human activity, is a great deal more than just an adventure story. No exploration, and that includes the first voyage of Columbus, takes place in a vacuum. Rather, all explorers are conditioned by the time and place and circumstance of their exploration; such conditioning is a determining factor in the establishment of exploratory objectives, in the behavior of explorers as they engage in their explorations, and in the consequences of exploration for the future.

Our intent in these volumes is to place the subject of North American exploration in just that context. We have made the effort to weave the threads of North American exploration into the whole cloth of exploration studies in general and, in particular, to reweave the various strands unraveling from the Quincentennial—knowing full well that the Columbian Quincentennial commemoration took shape along lines very different from those originally intended by the Columbian Quincentennial Jubilee Commission.[3] Columbus himself, for example, was transformed from the hero of our childhood history texts into a villain whose chief contribution to the world was to set in motion the chain of events that led to the exploitation and destruction of the environments and native peoples of the New World. His remarkable accomplishments were condemned as "an invasion and colonization with legalized occupation, genocide, economic exploitation and a deep level of institutional racism and moral decadence."[4] The exploration of North America became, for some scholars, something that had "meaning only in terms of European ignorance, not in terms of any contribution to universal knowledge."[5] And "discovery" (always now written in quotes, if you please) became a word to describe Europeans' bemusingly foolish and pretentious belief that they had done something noteworthy in crossing the Atlantic and reestablishing contact between two long-separated culture regions.

There is at least some justification for the belief that commemoration of the Columbian Quincentennial was more appropriate than celebration, but somewhere along the way things went terribly wrong. Critics of Columbus and his contemporaries have made the mistake of attempting to interpret the sixteenth-century mind as if they were dealing with a twentieth-century mind.[6] Columbus was almost certainly not the hero we remember from our grammar-school histories; but—within the context of his time—neither was he quite the villain that much of the new and somewhat selective Quincentennial scholarship made him out to be. It was equally wrong to suggest that the exploration of the New World had no meaning in the context of global knowledge. For better or worse, that knowledge was largely written and articulated by the European and Euro-American world, and to deny the process of exploration its important place in the broader epistemological process of how we know and understand the world is contentious. To suggest that "discovery" has meaning *only* in a universal context is just plain silly. The word *discover* means to find out about, to realize, to see—and that realization or divulging must be placed in the context of the discoverer and the discoverer's cultural and intellectual milieu. Major discoveries—whether they are geographical or not—are made by people who recognize data that do not conform to their preexisting worldview. Thus Columbus did indeed "discover" something in the western Atlantic: it was unknown to him and to his cultural contemporaries. Had Native Americans sailed eastward across the Atlantic and arrived on European shores that were not previously part of their worldview, they too would have achieved "discovery."

Work on these volumes began with the admission that the critics of exploratory studies who argued against the "glorification" of explorers, and against the ethnocentrism of the concept of "discovery," were at least partially correct. A substantial portion of the literature of geographical discovery and exploration is antiquarian in nature: romanticized, ethnocentric, fantastic, and even racist—or at least biased in favor of a particular point of view, that of white male historians. But the central problem—and it is the problem of the critics and their selective scholarship—is that those who castigate earlier scholars of exploration often have not been reading the right kind of literature pertaining to exploration and discovery. In particular, they have not closely examined a body of literature that views exploration as a subjective process both depending on and creating geographical images or patterns of belief about the nature and content of the world or any of its regions, a body of literature that builds into that view considerable analyses of indigenous peoples and the environments they occupied and modified. Nearly a half century ago John K. Wright, a geographer, described a geographical approach to the study of exploration that, had it been adopted as a basic paradigm of historical scholarship, would have led to a body of literature that would have been much more palatable to current critics than is, say, the work of Samuel Eliot Morison.[7] It was not adopted, but a number of studies of exploration by geographers and others *have* followed Wright's nonantiquarian, systematic, and integrative approach. Yet in the critical evaluations of the literature of exploration there is little evidence that either Wright's pioneering work or those studies based on it have even been read by the critics. Similarly, the works of Bernard DeVoto—an essayist and popular historian who also dealt with subjectivity in the exploratory process—have not been given their proper due by the critics of the literature of exploration and discovery.[8]

In 1943 Wright had suggested that the history of exploration should focus on the role of geographical knowledge in exploration. Wright argued, along with the Mexican historian Edmundo O'Gorman, that America was not so much discovered or explored as it was "invented," with the "invention" being the result of the attempt to reconcile the worldview that preceded the events of 1492 with the expansion and change in geographical knowledge that followed the first landing of Columbus.[9] When Wright spoke of geographical knowledge, he was thinking not only of European or Euro-American geographical knowledge but of geographical knowledge from any or all points of view, covering (in his words) "the geographical ideas, both true and false, of all manner of people—not only geographers, but farmers and fishermen, business executives and poets, novelists and painters, Bedouins and Hottentots."[10] For this reason, geographical knowledge, as Wright defined it, necessarily concerns highly subjective conceptions. Similarly, DeVoto, writing in 1952, proposed that scholars studying North American exploration should examine the ideas that explorers had about geography, the misconceptions and errors in those ideas, the growth of geographical knowledge following exploration, and "the relationship to all these things of various Indian tribes that affected them."[11] Like Wright, DeVoto stressed the subjective elements in exploration. DeVoto could also well have agreed with Wright that the process of North American discovery and exploration incorporated the "invention" of geographical knowledge and regional images as much as it did the accumulation and accretion of lore.

There are three common elements in Wright's and DeVoto's work: a belief in the importance of geographical knowledge, particularly its subjective nature; a belief in the significance of the relationship among the natural environment, indigenous peoples, and European and Euro-American explorers; and a belief in the subjective influence of the exploratory process on later historical events. These three elements serve as a model for the study of North American exploration and discovery in these volumes. It is our hope that this model not only will be productive in terms of our understanding of the continent but will provide links between North American exploration and the broader process of exploration and the shaping of geographical knowledge in general.

Our volumes on North American exploration, therefore, focus on the three key elements of the exploratory process: the relationship between preexisting and preconceived geographical lore and the development of exploratory goals; the links between that previous lore, along with new data obtained in the field during a journey of exploration, and the decisions made by explorers during the course of their exploration; and the connections between the preexploratory lore of an area, the data obtained through exploration, and the resultant geographical images of newly explored territory. Put another way, this work emphasizes the role of the human imagination in exploration as much as it features observation and experience. The reader should be cautioned that "imagination" does *not* mean "imaginary." Rather, imagination is the process whereby people create "images" or patterns of belief about the nature and content of a portion of the earth's surface. In those images there may be, to be sure, much that is "imaginary," but there will also be much that is real. In the images of North America, before and after Columbus, there were, then, both "imaginary" elements such as the Straits of Anián or the Seven Cities of Cíbola and "real" elements such as Chesapeake Bay or the Rocky Mountains. The central point to remember is that before conclusive exploration of an area takes place, it is impossible to separate what is "imaginary" from what is "real"; therefore, both factual and fictitious geographical elements may be given equal weight in the formation of geographical images.

Before 1492, attempts had been made to define, describe, and classify all the regions of the earth and their particulars. For the *oikoumene*, or the known world (the "Old World"), the portion of the globe within the scope of human experience and observation, these attempts at definition and description were based on what scholars "knew" about a region as learned through experience and observation. But when efforts were made to describe terrae incognitae—unknown lands—extrapolations from the known became confused with the believed, the conjectured, or the desired. According to some, after 1492 the white light of knowledge derived from the Columbian and subsequent discoveries dispelled the shadows that had hidden the unknown lands from the sight of humanity. But the geographical knowledge obtained through exploration is no more a pure "white light" than is preexploratory lore—rather, it is a spectrum with wave lengths of differing sizes and intensities. And in analyzing the spectrum it is difficult to separate what is truly known from what is thought to be known. Thus, it is not just observation and experience that combine to create the images of the world's regions; the transcendent force of the imagination blends with observation and experience, often overshadowing them in the images of unknown or recently discovered regions.

When exploration is viewed as a process rather than as a series of distinct events, its major components—establishment of objectives, performance of operations to implement them, and the consequences of those operations—are clearly related to the imagination. No exploratory venture begins without objectives based on the imagined nature and content of the lands to be explored. Imagination becomes a behavioral factor in geographical exploration as courses of action are laid out according to preconceived images; later decisions based on field observations may be distorted by these images. The results of exploration are modified by reports that have been written and interpreted in the light of persistent illusions and by attempts to fit new information into partly erroneous systems and frameworks of geographical understanding. Since the process of exploration is conditioned by the imagination, it follows that the study of exploration should include an examination of the influence of imagination. The exploration of North America through the end of the nineteenth century gives us a perfect laboratory to do just that. In the great process of exploration that began even before 1492, we find ample evidence of the role of the imagination in the establishment of exploratory objectives, in the field behavior of explorers, and in the consequences arising from exploratory events. For North America was not just discovered (exposed to initial contact) and explored (experienced); it was also created or imagined.

Discovery, exploration, and imagination are themes found in each of the chapters of the first and subsequent volumes of *North American Exploration*. The first volume, in particular, relies heavily on the role of the imagination in telling the story of the exploration of North America from the entry of the first Pleistocene hunters into the continent, via the land bridge from Asia, some twenty thousand years ago, through the period of pre-Columbian exploration, the rediscovery of the New World in 1492, and the coastal explorations and continental penetrations of the early years of the seventeenth century. Although the chapters in this first volume differ from each other in tone and approach, each of them tells part of the remarkable story of North American exploration in its formative years, when the continent was still, in the words of James Russell Lowell, that "strange New World, that never yit wast young."

The first two chapters—"The Pre-Columbian Discoveries and Exploration of North America" by Alan G. Macpherson and "Native North Americans' Cosmological Ideas and Geographical Awareness: Their Representation and Influence on Early European Exploration and Geographical Knowledge" by G. Malcolm Lewis—set the stage for the events that followed the "great event" of 1492. Macpherson describes the nature of both real and imaginary pre-Columbian contacts between the Old World and the New, discussing such probably apocryphal explorations as those of the

Irish cleric Brendan and the Welsh prince Madoc. But the bulk of Macpherson's chapter deals with the known pre-Columbian contacts: those of the Norse in the tenth and eleventh centuries. Noting that the Norse discovery of the New World did nothing to detract from Columbus's epochal first voyage, Macpherson nevertheless points out that Columbus was engaged in the rediscovery of a New World whose knowledge had been lost to Europe. Buttressing his argument with the most recent archaeological and historical scholarship, Macpherson presents what may be the most convincing case yet for the pre-Columbian discovery of North America by Norse voyagers. Lewis, in his far-ranging discussion of Native American exploration and cosmology, places the Columbian discovery in an even more logical context by pointing out that much of the past Eurocentric scholarship of North American exploration has "forgotten" two critical elements: first, that European explorers arrived on a continent already populated by peoples with rich cultural traditions of their own; and second, that much of the success of European exploration may be attributed to the geographical awareness of Native Americans, who provided much of the exploratory data that would work their way onto European maps during the entire time span of four centuries covered by these volumes.

The following three chapters—"The Columbian Voyages" by Robert H. Fuson, "Early Spanish Exploration: The Caribbean, Central America, and the Gulf of Mexico" by Robert S. Weddle, and *"Hacia el Norte!* The Spanish *Entrada* into North America" by Dennis Reinhartz and Oakah L. Jones—all deal primarily with the very earliest stage of European exploration of North America, one in which Spanish explorers were the primary actors. Fuson's chapter on the Columbian voyages presents new and intriguing ideas on the state of European geographical knowledge on the eve of the first Columbian voyage and describes Columbus's efforts as an explorer within the broader context of his "Grand Design" for exploration. Fuson does not hesitate to make bold pronouncements regarding the location of Columbus's "San Salvador," the first New World landfall of a European voyager since the Norse "Vinland." Fuson's work is the result of the most recent scholarly efforts to illumine the process of exploration that began with Columbus. Like Fuson's chapter, Weddle's work is reflective of the most recent scholarship on the early Spanish exploration. Erecting his chapter's central arguments upon the events of the Columbian voyages, Weddle describes the process of Spanish explorers' incremental awareness of the existence of a North American continent. He discusses explorations and explorers that were, in at least some cases, contemporaries of Columbus. From Weddle we learn of the earliest European penetrations of Mexico and Central America as Spanish voyagers first sought a strait through what they gradually came to view as a continental barrier between Europe and the Orient and as they subsequently sought to locate and subdue the brilliant Native American civilizations in regions adjacent to the Gulf of Mexico. Reinhartz and Jones carry the story of Spanish exploration in the early sixteenth century to the great *entradas* of the 1540s: the North American explorations of Francisco Vázquez de Coronado in the Southwest and of Hernando de Soto in the Southeast. Reinhartz and Jones place Coronado and Soto into the temporal context of Spain after the Mexican conquest, when Spanish explorers—having located the rich Mexican and Central American native civilizations—quite logically looked for counterparts of those civilizations farther north. In so doing, both Coronado and Soto advanced the state of geographical knowledge of the continental interior of North America more than almost any other explorers until the early nineteenth century. Taken together, the chapters by Weddle and by Reinhartz and Jones present a remarkable picture of the role of the imagination in the establishment of exploratory objectives as Spanish explorers searched for mythical straits and imaginary kingdoms.

The final three chapters in volume 1 deal with European exploration of the North American margins during the sixteenth century, a process that resulted in a continent of reasonably well-known proportions and outlines by the early seventeenth century. In "The Northwest Passage in Theory and Practice," David Beers Quinn describes both a geographical idea—the theoretical water passageway around or through North America—and the explorations devised to attempt its discovery. Certainly the search for the Passage is one of the most remarkable tales in North American discovery, and Quinn illustrates not only the process of exploration but also the conceptual foundations of theoretical geography and cartography on which it was based. From Quinn we learn much about the increasingly accurate geographical image of the northern portions of the continent, a process of growth in geographical awareness that resulted from the search for something that was never there. In "A Continent Revealed: Assimilation of the Shape and Possibilities of North America's East Coast," Karen Ordahl Kupperman not only provides an excellent thematic and chronological treatment of the major explorations of the Atlantic Seaboard in the sixteenth century but also describes the interlocking of the process of exploration with that of "plantation" or settlement of European populations on North American shores. Kupperman's work provides significant evidence that much of North American exploration, as scholars such as Daniel Boorstin have long maintained, was indeed accompanied (and even sometimes preceded) by the establishment of European colonial footholds on the North American continent. Finally, W. Michael Mathes describes the sixteenth- and seventeenth-century explorations of the Pacific coastal region, explorations that had as their goals the establishment of termini for the Philippine-Mexico sailing routes, the definition of the "pearl-ringed Island of California," and the discovery of the Straits of Anián—a North Pacific counterpart of the Northwest Passage in the North Atlantic. Many of the actors in Mathes's chapter are, again, Spanish—in contrast to the English and French and Dutch explorers and settlers discussed by Quinn and Kupperman—and the culmination of this initial period of Spanish exploration along the Pacific coast was both the extension of the Spanish colonial empire northward almost to Alaska and the delineation of many of the key features of North America's Pacific shores.

By the end of the initial phase of exploration discussed in volume 1, North America—although still far from "known" by Europeans and even farther from being understood—was no longer a blank area on European maps. The outlines, from the Gulf shores and the Florida peninsula to the coast of Hudson's Bay and from the Chesapeake to San Francisco Bay, were reasonably accurately portrayed. No longer viewed, as it had been during the earliest years of European contact, as an extension or peninsula of Asia, North America had at least a continental outline and an identity. A New World had been disclosed to European science.

In the collaborative research project that begins here with volume 1, the role of the imagination in the exploration of North America is the integrating theme. Although coming from differing academic traditions and disciplines, the authors share the perspective that image has been as important as reality in that great historical and geographical process that began even before 1492. This common perspective provides unity to *North American Exploration* and lends coherence to a project that is grand and broad in scope. The common perspective also enables the first and the subsequent volumes to integrate the other themes of North American exploration both with the role of the imagination and with each other. When Columbus discovered a New World that was unknown to European science—although it was known, in a visceral way, to the European mind, which had long imagined lands to the west in the Ocean Sea—he set in motion a chain of events that quite literally have molded the modern world in political, economic, scientific, social, and philosophical terms. The chapters in these volumes attempt to illumine this critical chain of events, this exploratory process, in all its complexity. But in this attempt at illumination, the foundation of the research upon which these volumes are based is the complex of images and ideas that shaped the process by which the terrae incognitae of North America became known.

1 / Pre-Columbian Discoveries and Exploration of North America

ALAN G. MACPHERSON

In March 1493 Christopher Columbus triumphantly returned from his first transatlantic voyage. After docking in the port of Lisbon and reporting his success to the king of Portugal (who had declined to support Columbus's appeal for funding a year earlier), Columbus wrote a dramatic letter to the monarchs of Spain, who had sponsored his initial attempt to reach the Orient. In this first document of a new European age, Columbus gave his account of the discovery of "very many islands, filled with people innumerable," far westward across the "Ocean Sea."[1] Columbus could verify what he said he had done, for accompanying him on his return to Europe was a group of Taino people, the first Native Americans to be captured by European explorers and exhibited to the curious Europeans. Columbus's simple act of discovery, coupled with his transportation of New World people to the Spanish court, set in motion five centuries of exploration, exploitation, and settlement of the Americas by people of non-American origin.

Discovery of the lands Columbus dubbed "the Indies" and of the people he called "Indians," in the mistaken but stubborn belief that he had reached the outer fringe of Asia, ignited a controversy that occupied European scholars of the late fifteenth and early sixteenth centuries: who were these native peoples of the Indies? As European exploration determined that what Columbus had discovered in 1492 was not really the Orient at all but an entire "New World," the controversy was enlarged to include questions of the origins of the native peoples of the Americas: if they were not Asians or Africans or Europeans, where had they come from? And as European political rivalries grew in the decades following Columbus, still another level of complexity was added to the debate: since the New World reached by Columbus was inhabited, had its inhabitants originated in a known part of the Old World or been visited by representatives of Old World cultures before 1492? Could such discovery be used to justify, for example, an English claim to New World territory? Such questions were not easily answered by scholars of Columbus's time. Nor have they been easily answered by scholarship since, although the search for answers has been responsible for an enormous speculative literature. And though much of modern scholarship is still conjectural, better answers exist now for the critical questions: what were the origins of the native peoples of the Americas, and did they have contacts with the Old World before Columbus? Cautious scientific inquiry on the part of scholars in the natural sciences, the social sciences, and the humanities has mostly resolved what Columbus and his contemporaries could not. We can now make statements that, if not definitive, are at least informed about the origins of the native North American population and about the questions of pre-Columbian contact with those peoples and the continent they occupied.

Aboriginal Exploration of North America

Although there is still controversy concerning the origins of the native peoples of North America, and despite arguments that have been advanced for the ancestry of American indigenes in ancient Carthage, dynastic Egypt, Plato's lost continent of Atlantis, or even the Lost Tribes of Israel, there is consensus among archaeologists, human geneticists, and linguists. Their conclusion is that the Americas were first colonised by migrations out of northeastern Asia across a late-glacial land bridge now covered by the Bering Sea. The members of the first party to cross into what is now Alaska may have had no sense of discovery, for no water crossing was involved. They were simply extending their hunting territory into the unglaciated parts of northern Alaska, north of the main ice sheets.

Penetration south of the ice sheets was effected about 11,500 years ago when parties of hunters passed through an ice-free corridor that opened between the glaciers flowing down the eastern slopes of the Canadian Rockies and the western lobes of the major continental ice sheet over Hudson's Bay.[2] This represented the real beginning for aboriginal America, with the arrival of the Paleo-Indian people of the Clovis culture (a microblade technology shared with northern Alaskan-Yukon and northeastern Asian homelands). From near present-day Edmonton, Alberta, Paleo-Indian populations spread rapidly through the Americas, passing through the Central American isthmus about 11,000 years ago and reaching the southern limits of South America 500 years later. The Americas were first explored—and their resources first exploited—by palaeolithic hunters of northeastern Asian origin during the period of a single millennium, their success leading to the rich diversity of languages and cultures found by Columbus and his successors.

Genetic and linguistic evidence indicates that although most of the American Indian population is derived from the Paleo-Indian Clovis culture, parts of North America have been "discovered," explored, and colonised by waves of more recent arrival. Athabaskan-speakers have been recognised as belonging to a distinct linguistic family, but genetic differentiation also suggests their arrival 2,000 years after the first wave of Paleo-Indians. As the Na-Dene peoples, they have spread into the northwestern quarter of North America since 600 B.C., the Navajos and the Apaches representing their deepest penetration of the continent. Aleut-Eskimo people formed the third wave—probably moving across the land bridge shortly after the ancestors of the Na-Denes—and developed into the Aleuts and the Paleo-Eskimos, the latter carrying the Dorset culture across the Arctic as far east as Greenland and as far south as Northern Labrador in six to eight generations, beginning around 2000 B.C. Their experience was repeated between A.D. 1000 and 1400 by the people of the Thule culture, ancestral to the modern-day Inuits of Alaska, Canada, and Greenland. Therefore the Americas were entered from Asia and the land bridge by groups of newcomers on no less than four occasions during the prehistoric period. On each occasion frontiers of population expansion and resource exploitation ensued, involving a rapid exploration of all the environmental niches available, including the tundra of the Arctic islands.[3] The anonymity of the men and women who carried out each stage of the process does not detract from their achievements. The real discovery and exploration of North America by these anonymous Americans deserves recognition.

Spurious Claims to Pre-Columbian Discoveries

It is not known when European myth and legend first began to describe the discovery of lands west of Europe. There were widely told stories of wayfarers who had traveled into the western Atlantic shortly before the departure of Columbus and who, it is alleged, provided him with information.

Saint Brendan the Navigator

The story that an early Irish saint, Brendan, discovered the continent of America in the sixth century was first advanced in 1580, when John Dee's *Title Royall* listed him with Madoc of Wales as the basis for Queen Elizabeth I's right to break the monopoly of the Portuguese and the Spaniards and to establish English colonies in the New World. The claim was based on two Latin texts, *Vita Sancti Brendani* (Life of Saint Brendan) and *Navigatio Sancti Brendani Abbatis* (Voyage of the Abbot Saint Brendan), the former based in part on an Irish Gaelic text, *Betha Brenainn*. Manuscript copies of both *Vita* and *Navigatio* have been found in libraries all over Europe, and translations—most notably in English, French, and German—were popular in the later Middle Ages. The earliest of the Latin manuscripts date from the late tenth century, and they may be based on a composition of about A.D. 800. If so, their contents predate the Viking invasions of the British Isles and Norse exploration of the North Atlantic.

Both *Vita* and *Navigatio* present accounts of maritime adventure in which Brendan and his companions visited islands in the ocean, many of which were already inhabited by Irish hermits and monastic communities. Exploration of a vast island-studded Atlantic in a large curragh, built with materials and to a design still traditional in Ireland (and once so in Britain) and the discovery of an "island" of continental proportions were features of *Navigatio* that were bound to appeal to post-Columbians. But why did John Dee and his successors pick Brendan as the discoverer when *Navigatio* makes it clear that Abbot Mernóc had preceded him to the Promised Land of the Saints?

Saint Brendan, like Christopher Columbus, was a historical personage.[4] Born at Fenit on Trales Bay around A.D. 484 into a leading family, he was ordained in 512 and founded monasteries at Ardfert, near his home, and at Inis da Dromand, an island in the estuary of the Shannon River. Later he founded a third monastery at Clonfert in Galway of Connacht, and later still—after 563 when he was about eighty years old—he visited Saint Columcille, Columba of the Cells, at Iona in the Hebrides. *Vita* and *Betha Brenainn* indicate that he also made sea journeys to the monasteries of Llancarfan in South Wales and Rhuys in Brittany and possibly to the Orkneys and Shetlands. He died sometime between 570 and 583.

The first notice of Saint Brendan occurred in *Vita Sancti Columbae* (Life of Saint Columba), written between 679 and 704 by Saint Adamnan, abbot of Iona. The first recognition of his fame as an ocean voyager appeared in *Martyrology of Tallaght*, which was written in the ninth century and which

1.1 The first three images are woodcuts from the Navigatio Sancti Brendani Abbatis, *printed at Ulm in 1499. They depict the voyages of Saint Brendan and show a siren (upper left), a holy man (upper right), and a "sea monster" on which Brendan's boat came to rest (lower left). The fourth image, also depicting European views of the northern Atlantic, is of a walrus and is from* Historia de gentibus septentrionalibus *by Olaus Magnus (Rome, 1555). By permission of The British Library.*

commemorates the setting forth of Brendan's "family" of voyagers. Bili the Deacon's *Life of Saint Machutus* (Saint Malo of Brittany), written around 870, associated Saint Malo with Saint Brendan in a voyage from Llancarfan in Wales in search of Yma, the Isle of the Blest, a variation reflected in the cartography of the later Middle Ages. The Hereford *mappamundi*, or world map, drawn by Richard de Bello, treasurer of Lincoln Cathedral between 1276 and 1283, bears a label attached to the Canary Islands off the northwestern coast of Africa: "Fortunate insulee sex sunt insulae sct brandani" (The six blessed isles are the islands of Saint Brendan).[5] On the Pizzigano map of 1367 the same group is similarly labeled. Once Madeira and the Azores were discovered, such labels shifted out into the Atlantic, as on Battista Beccario's charts of 1426 and 1435 and Andrea Bianco's map of 1448.[6]

Some modern-day scholars have accepted these accounts as based on fact and have put them to the test. Between 1973 and 1975 Timothy Severin had a large curragh built to the same specifications and with the same materials as Saint Brendan's. In the summers of 1976 and 1977 he sailed it up the western coasts of Ireland and Scotland, to the Faeroes and Iceland, and eventually to the eastern coast of Newfoundland—making his first New World landfall only a few short sea miles from an island community in Bonavista Bay called Saint Brendan's! The voyage demonstrated that a sixth-century Irish curragh would have had the capability and the seaworthiness required to sail across the Atlantic. Moreover, many of the observations made on the voyage appeared to match occurrences noted in *Navigatio*.[7] Demonstration of a capability, however, is no proof of an actual event.

Vita Sancti Brendani and *Betha Brenainn* can be accepted—albeit with caution—as biographies containing a basis in historical fact. Modern scholarship, on the other hand, views *Navigatio Sancti Brendani Abbatis* as a visionary quest for the lost paradise, for the promised land, a kind of "pilgrim's progress" laced with exhortatory dialogue. It is also within the tradition of the *immrama* genre in early Irish literature, the heroic tales of sea voyages. A third element in *Navigatio* is the portrayal of the ascetic tradition, which in its Irish manifestation involved the solitude of prayer and self-mortification on uninhabited islands. The practitioners of this asceticism, a form of exile, were known as anchorites, as *peregrinari*, and—by the Norse, when they found these ascetics in the Faeroes and Iceland—as *papar*.[8] There is evidence of actual maritime experience in *Navigatio*, but a cautious interpretation is that this refers to the coasts of the British Isles and Brittany.[9]

Prince Madoc of Wales
The legend of discovery of North America in A.D. 1170 by Prince Madoc of Wales has been the most persistent of such claims since the rise of Elizabethan England in the last quarter of the sixteenth century. It was invoked to explain the existence of the native Mayan, Aztec, and Inca civilisations of the Americas. For the United States, it became an incredibly elaborate historical myth, potent in its ability to send explorers in quest of Welsh-speaking Indians from Virginia to the Mandan villages of the upper Missouri River and from there to the shores of the Pacific. It was still respectable in the Smithsonian Institution and the American Ethnological Society in the 1860s and found a place in American schooltexts into the twentieth century. As late as 1947 the Associated Press carried a story that the Kutenai Indians of southern British Columbia had been finally identified as descendants of the Madoc colony.[10] Born of Welsh contributions to Elizabethan co-

lonial ambitions, the myth was fueled by Welsh nationalism on both sides of the Atlantic for almost three centuries and was not challenged until Thomas Stephens's critical essay "Madoc" in 1858. Even then, the weight of Welsh scholarship declared his essay ineligible, as in error, and delayed its publication till 1893.

The claim that Madoc was the discoverer of America can be dated precisely to 3 October 1580, when the Welsh polymath John Dee presented the court of Queen Elizabeth I with a map listing her rights overseas. According to the first of these, "Circa an. 1170: The Lord Madoc, sonne to Owen Gwynedd, Prince of North Wales, led a Colonie and inhabited in Terra Florida or thereabowts."[11] Next, in the aftermath of Sir Humphrey Gilbert's disastrous attempt to establish an English Catholic colony in Norumbega (New England) and immediately before the first expedition promoted by Sir Walter Raleigh to settle Virginia, came Sir George Peckham's *True Reporte* in November 1583. To "restore to her Highnesse auncient right and interest in those Countries," Peckham stated, "a noble and woorthy personage, lyneally descended from the blood royall, borne in Wales, named Madock ap Owen Gwyneth, departing from the coast of England, about the yeere of our Lord God 1170 arrived [into those Countries] and there planted himselfe, and his Colonies, and afterward returned himself into England, leaving certain of his people there, as appeareth in an auncient Welch chronicle."[124] This is the first mention of Prince Madoc of Wales in print; his father Owen Gwynedd (d. 1169 or 1170) was the leader of the first Welsh resurgence against Norman rule.

True Reporte supported this extraordinary claim with linguistic and place-name evidence allegedly gathered among the Eastern Woodlands Indians by David Ingram, a survivor of Sir John Hawkins's expedition into the Gulf of Mexico in 1568, and by reference to the Aztec Emperor Moctezuma's speech before Hernán Cortés in 1519, in which he stated that his "forefathers came from a farre countrie and their King and Captaine who brought them hitcher [hither], returned againe to his natural countrie, saying that he would send such as should rule and govern us."[13] Moctezuma was equating Cortés with the god-king Quetzalcoatl, identified by the Spanish Catholic missionaries as Saint Thomas the apostle. Peckham was placing Madoc in competition with the Mexican god-king and Thomas the Doubter.

Peckham's *True Reporte* was followed by Richard Hakluyt's *Discourse of Western Planting*, in 1584. Under the caption "That the Queene of Englandes title to all the West Indies, or at the leaste to as moche as is from

Florida to the Circle Articke, is more lawfull and righte then the Span-
iardes, or any other Christian Princes," it claimed:

> One Madock ap Owen Guyneth, a Prince of North Wales, beinge
> wearye of the civill warres and domesticall dissentions in his contrie,
> made twoo voyadges oute of Wales, and discovered and planted
> large contries which he found in the mayne ocean south westwarde
> of Ireland, in the yere of our Lorde 1170. . . . this is confirmed by the
> language of some of those people that dwell upon the continent be-
> twene the Bay of Mexico and the Grande Bay of Newfoundelande,
> whose language is said to agree with the Welshe in divers wordes
> and names of places, by experience of some of our nation that have
> bene in those partes. By this testimonie it appereth that the West
> Indies were discovered and inhabited 322 yeares before Columbus
> made his first voyadge.[14]

Hakluyt gave his authority as "the booke sett furthe this yere of the Princes
of Wales," identified as *The Historie of Cambria* (1584), David Powel's version
of Humphrey Llwyd of Denbigh's manuscript original, allegedly based on
a chronicle of Wales by Caradoc of Llancarfan, finished in 1559 but subjected to annotation and "correction" before 1580 by John Dee. With respect to Madoc, this would seem to be the source for John Dee's *Title Royall*,
Sir George Peckham's *True Reporte*, and Richard Hakluyt's *Discourse of Western Planting*. It deserves careful comparison with the preceding passages:

> Madoc [one] of Owen Gwyneth his sonnes left the land in contention
> betwixt his brethren, and prepared certaine ships with men and mu-
> nition, and sought adventures by seas, sailing west, and leaving the
> coast of Ireland so far north, that he came to a land unknowen, where
> he saw manie strange things. . . . Of the viage and returne of this
> Madoc there be manie fables fained, as the common people do
> use. . . . And after he had returned home and declared the pleasant
> and fruitful countries that he had seen without inhabitants . . . he
> prepared a number of ships and got with him such men and women
> as were desirous to live in quietnes, and taking leave of his freends
> tooke his journie thitherward againe. . . . But bicause this people
> were not manie, they followed the maners of the land they came
> unto, and used the language they found there.[15]

Powel's text contains the speculation—probably incorporated by Dee—
that the land settled by Madoc was "some part of Nove Hispania or Florida." Hakluyt interpreted these vague geographical terms to extend from

the Gulf of Mexico to the Strait of Belle Isle (his "Grande Bay of New-foundelande").

Five years later Llwyd's text was incorporated into Hakluyt's *Principall Navigations, Voiages, and Discoveries of the English Nation* (1589), with the addition that Madoc, "taking leave of his friends, tooke his journey thitherward againe. . . . This Madoc arriving in the Westerne country, unto the which he came in the yere 1170, left most of his people there, and returning backe for more of his own nation, acquaintance and friends to inhabit that faire and large countrey, went thither againe with ten sailes, as I find noted by Gutyn Owen."[16]

Gutyn Owain was a Welsh poet, genealogist, and chronicler whose writings date from 1470–98; nothing of his that is extant mentions Madoc. Caradoc of Llancarfan is believed to have died in 1156, too early to have recorded Madoc's discovery. The only pre-Columbian reference to Madoc and Owen Gwynedd appears in a poem of Maredudd ap Rhys, quoted by Hakluyt in 1589 as received in the Welsh original and an English translation and ascribed to 1477:

Madoc I am the sonne of Owen Gwynedd
With stature large, and comely grace adorned:
No lands at home nor store of wealth me please,
My minde was whole to search the Ocean seas.

Another translation suggests a date around 1440 for the poem.[17] The poem says nothing of discovery.

There are hints of Madoc in Flemish romance literature of the mid–thirteenth century, and a fourteenth-century fragment in French refers to him as a Welshman of noble birth with Viking ancestry and fame as a sailor, who went as a secret emissary to the French court. Later he sailed to search for the Fountain of Youth and to establish a new kingdom of love and music.[18] The *Madoc* romance falls within the troubadour tradition, but the motifs are reminiscent of Saint Brendan's *Navigatio*. Like *Navigatio*, it reflects medieval concepts of the geography of the Atlantic.

Estotiland and Drogeo: The Zeno Map
In 1558 Nicolo Zeno, of a distinguished Venetian family, published a collection of travels allegedly undertaken by his ancestors in the fourteenth and fifteenth centuries, part of which was entitled *Dello scoprimento dell' isole Frislanda, Eslanda, Engroueland, Estotilanda, & Icaria, fatto per due fratelli Zeni M. Nicolo il Cavaliere, & M. Antonio . . . col diseqno di dette isole* (The discov-

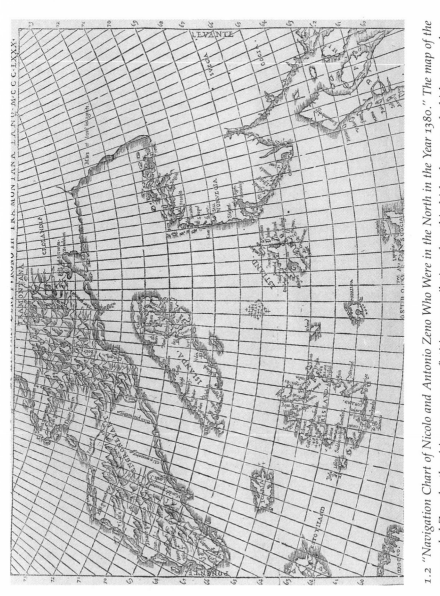

1.2 "Navigation Chart of Nicolo and Antonio Zeno Who Were in the North in the Year 1380." The map of the apocryphal Zeno brothers' journeys was a fictitious compilation of mythical islands, none of which appeared on pre-Columbian maps. From Nicolo Zeno, Commentarii (Venice, 1538). Courtesy The Newberry Library.

ery of the islands of Frislanda, Eslanda, Engronelanda, Estotilanda, and Icaria by two brothers of the Zeno family, viz. Messiore Nicolo the Chevalier, and Messire Antonio . . . with a map of those islands). The account of the discovery of these islands in the North Atlantic during the latter half of the fourteenth century purports to have been drawn from old family letters and to have been based on "a sailing chart . . . rotten with age" found among the family records.[19]

As early as 1898, the narrative of the Zeno brothers' voyages was shown to be a compilation of earlier printed works of the sixteenth century.[20] There are echoes of medieval accounts of Norse Greenland, of the conquest of Mexico and the Spanish expeditions north of the Gulf of Mexico between 1528 and 1543, and perhaps of Giovanni da Verrazzano's French expedition of 1524, which explored the shores from Cape Fear to Cape Breton, but these indicate a post-Columbian provenance.

The Zeno map, entitled "Carta da navegar de Nicolo et Antonio Zeni furono in tramontana lano M.CCC.LXXX" ("Navigation chart of Nicolo and Antonio Zeno who were in the North in the year 1380"), despite its claim of pre-Columbian origin, was a cartographic amalgam derived from maps drawn by Claudius Clavus in Italy between 1424 and 1430 and by Olaus Magnus in 1539, with fictitious islands and mainland (Drogeo) added. Its importance lies not in its claim to be a sea chart of the late 1300s but in its influence on later cartography. From the Venice Ptolemy map of 1561 to Gerardus Mercator's world map of 1569 (which identified Estotiland with Baffin Island) and Richard Hakluyt's map of 1598 showing John Davis's discoveries in 1585–87, to Hans Poulsen Resen's "Map of the North" (1605) and Gudbrandur Thórlaksson's map of 1606, Estotiland was identified with the Norse Helluland and placed in Northern Labrador.[21] Fictitious islands such as Frislanda continued to appear on maps of the North Atlantic as recently as the nineteenth century.

Columbus's "Informants"

Claims that individuals, on the basis of pre-Columbian discoveries, were able to guide the Great Navigator fall into a special category. In 1609 it was claimed that Alonzo Sanchez de Huelva, a pilot on the Spain-Canaries-Madeira run, was driven west for twenty-nine days in 1484 and reached an island—Santo Domingo (Hispaniola) is suggested—before making it back to Terceira in the Azores, where survivors lodged with Columbus, told their tale, and promptly died. In 1488, it is said, Cousin of Dieppe was blown off course from the African coast and arrived at the mouth of a great river, duly reported to Columbus by one Pinzon, a mutinous member of Cousin's crew who later accompanied Columbus in 1492. A similar tale is told of the Basque pilot from St. Jean de Luz, who also died in Columbus's house, a tale that may be the basis for King Charles IX's statement to the Spanish ambassador in 1565 that French fishermen had made discoveries near the Grand Bank of Newfoundland before 1465.[22] No fifteenth- or sixteenth-century Basque ever claimed to have discovered America, and neither Estaban de Garibay nor Lope de Isasti—Basque historians born in the sixteenth century—mentioned any such event.[23]

Further, no evidence exists to substantiate claims for crossings of the Atlantic by Bronze Age Europeans, biblical Hebrews, classical Carthaginians and Romans, early Christians, Jews and Moslems, West Africans, or any others.[24] The strongest argument against such claims is that the mid-Atlantic islands—the real ones—were among the last parts of the habitable earth to be populated and settled: Iceland, in 874; Madeira, after 1420; the Azores, about 1432; the Cape Verde group, after 1460; Ascension, discovered in 1501, not settled until 1815; Saint Helena, discovered in 1506, not inhabited until 1816.

The Norse Discovery of North America

None of the apocrypha of the pre-Columbian voyages of Brendan, Madoc, the Zeno brothers, or others should be allowed to cast a shadow on the fact that there was, indeed, a European contact with North America before the Columbian voyage of 1492. This contact can be documented by both historical and archaeological evidence. Unfortunately for the early acceptance of the validity of the claims of the Norse discovery of the New World, however, the true history of Norse exploration has until recently been subject to scholarly skepticism. This skepticism has existed largely because of the many "discoveries" of bits and pieces of "evidence" that purported to prove the existence of pre-Columbian Norse contacts but that were eventually proven to be honest mistakes, historical and linguistic misinterpretations, or downright hoaxes.

"Viking Artifacts" in North America

The recognition that Columbus had been preceded to America by people from Iceland and Greenland, as described in their sagas, must have dawned slowly on the Icelanders during the sixteenth century. The voyages of Martin Frobisher in 1576–78 and of John Davis in 1585–87 in search of a Northwest Passage found cartographic response in Sigurdur Stefánsson's map of 1590 and, more particularly, in Hans Poulsen Resen's map of 1605 and Bishop Gudbrandur Thórlaksson's of 1606. This Icelandic cartography was related to interest in rediscovering Greenland by the Danish-Norwegian state in the first decade of the seventeenth century,[25] which also marked the beginning of the serious collection of Icelandic manuscripts. Printed versions of the sagas, in Latin translation, appeared in Denmark and Sweden during the 1660s and from the Skálholt press in Iceland in the 1680s,[26] resulting in the publication of *Historia Vinlandiae antiquae, seu partis Americae septentrionalis . . .* by Thormod Torfeson (Torfaeus) in 1705. The English-reading world learned of the Norse claim when Paul Henri Mallet's *Northern Antiquities* was published in London in 1770 and when Johann Reinhold Forster's *History of the Voyages and Discoveries Made in the North* appeared in translation from the German in 1786. In 1805 David Macpherson, in *Annals of Commerce, Manufactures, Fisheries, and Navigation*, speculated whether "a tribe of people in the interior part of Newfoundland . . . may not improbably be supposed the remains of the Icelandic colony. Whether those people are of Norwegian origin or not, may be very easily ascertained by their language, which to a proper judge must appear, through all the fluctuations of eight centuries, to be radically Norwegian, if they are the remains of a Norwegian colony, though they may have lost all traditional knowledge of their ancestors." He added, "Such an enquiry I have myself set on foot, but hitherto without success."[27] Macpherson's theory that the native Beothuks of Newfoundland were descended from Icelanders was tested in 1811 when Lieutenant David Buchan of the Royal Navy, accompanied by Norwegian-speakers from his crew, made contact with the tribe. The results were negative.

The late nineteenth century also saw claims for "Norse" artifacts of a more material nature. A stone tower supported by pillars, standing above Newport, Rhode Island, was accepted as a legacy of medieval Norse settlers and became the basis of a large literature in support of the claim. Archaeological excavations in the 1940s, however, indicated that it was built in the early colonial period, as a windmill or a watchtower. First mentioned in 1677, it is now known to have been built by a patrilineal ancestor and namesake of Benedict Arnold.[28]

In 1898 a Swedish immigrant found the Kensington runestone, allegedly unearthed in tree roots near Alexandria, Minnesota, an area heavily settled by Scandinavian farmers. Transliterated and translated, it bore

an astonishing message: "8 Goths [Swedes] and 22 Norwegians on an expedition from Vinland to the West. Our camp was by two skerries one
day's journey north of this stone. We went fishing one day. When we came
home found ten men red with blood and dead. AVM deliver us from evil.
Have ten men by the sea to look after our ship 14 days' journey from this
island. 1362." If authentic, it meant that the Vinland of the sagas had survived into the mid–fourteenth century and that it was a base for exploration into the interior of the continent. The improbability of this—particularly since the settlement in Greenland was in decline in 1362—brought
denunciation as a hoax, a judgment confirmed when expert philologists
found the runic text wanting.[29]

A similar "find" on a mining claim near Beardmore, a way station on the
Canadian National Railway east of Lake Nipigon in northern Ontario, involved genuine eleventh-century Viking artifacts—a broken iron sword,
an ax blade, and fragments of what may have been a shield boss—alleged
to have been found in a Viking grave in 1926 or 1930. The find has since
been dismissed as a hoax perpetrated by a Norwegian settler.[30] In the 1960s
Canadian archaeologists working on the western shores of Ungava Bay
near Payne Bay and on Pamick Island found stone longhouses, shoreline
stone beacons, and sunken stone "boxes" that, despite the absence of
Norse artifacts, were initially interpreted as of Norse provenance but were
later proved to be Dorset Eskimo in origin.[31]

At about the same time as this last mistakenly identified archaeological
find, however, another excavation was taking place in Newfoundland, an
excavation that would provide incontrovertible proof of a Norse discovery
of North America before the Columbus landfall of 1492 and that would alter
the terms of the debate over pre-Columbian European experience of North
America. In 1960 Helge Ingstad, a Norwegian writer interested in Norse
discovery and exploration, arrived at the Newfoundland fishing village of
L'Anse aux Meadows and was directed to a site at the mouth of Black Duck
Brook, about a mile from the village, where local people had long known of
features in the vegetation indicating former house sites.[32] Excavation of the
site followed, under the direction of Helge's archaeologist wife, Anne Stine
Ingstad. In 1968, administration of the site came under the jurisdiction of
Parks Canada and further excavation was conducted between 1973 and
1976. In 1977 the site became the centre of a National Historic Park of some
eight thousand hectares of land and adjacent ocean, and in 1978 it became
the first site on UNESCO's World Heritage List.[33]

The L'Anse aux Meadows site, consisting of three house groups and

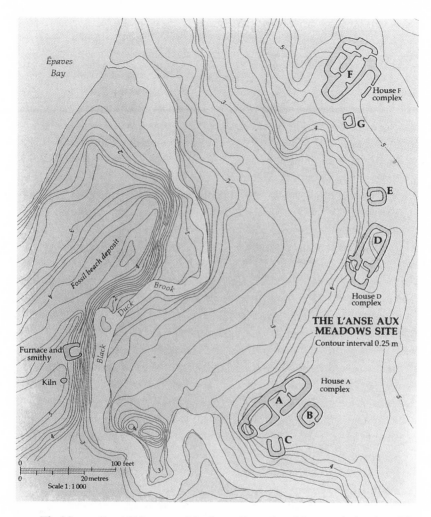

1.3 The Norse site at L'Anse aux Meadows. Reproduced by permission from The Historical Atlas of Canada *(University of Toronto Press, 1987).*

other buildings (including a smithy), has been interpreted as a way station between a Norse colony in Greenland and another Norse settlement (not yet discovered) in the southern part of the Gulf of Saint Lawrence.[34] The more conservative interpretation is that it was an overwintering station for parties from Greenland and served as a base for limited exploration. There are strong indications that the settlement was occupied for a very short period of time, probably less than two decades. Radiocarbon dating for the site suggests an occupance somewhere between A.D. 975 and 1020, weighted toward the later date, while AMS dating provides a more precise date of A.D. 997 plus or minus eight years.[35] The consensus since excavations began in 1961 is that the site is Norse. The Norse site at Black Duck Brook near L'Anse aux Meadows is the only representation of Norse settlement on the American side of the Atlantic. Its significance can be understood only in the context of medieval Norse settlement in Norway and the British Isles and more particularly in the Faeroes, Iceland, and Greenland. Of the Norse settlements westward into the Atlantic, Norse Greenland stands alone, known only from its archaeology and its appearance in Icelandic literature. In the transatlantic pattern of Norse settlement, it stood as "nearest neighbor" to the site at Black Duck Brook.

The primary settlement of Norse Greenland occurred in the closing years of the tenth century (A.D. 986–1000) with the arrival of colonists from Iceland. They were preceded by Eskimo people of the Dorset culture, who had withdrawn from the fjords and islands of southwestern Greenland shortly before the Norse arrival.[36]

Pre-Columbian Discoveries and Exploration by the Norse
From the beginning, Norse settlement of Greenland took place in two districts centred on the modern settlements of Julianehåb and Godthåb: the former consisting of some dozen major fjords along an island-studded coast about 160 miles long, some of which penetrate the land for about 70 miles (100 km), and the latter a ramification of fjords that converges in the vicinity of Godthåb and penetrates about 100 miles (150 km) from the coast. The archaeological sites of the colony are located almost exclusively within the fjords, where settlers and livestock could enjoy a milder climate well away from the more exposed sites along the outer coast. On these sites, the Norse settlers built Scandinavian longhouses, outbuildings, and fire pits; smithies with charcoal-fired forges for the manufacture and repair of iron goods were also numerous.[37] From the beginning, as the Icelandic literature indicates, the Greenland colony was visited by merchants, including some of the more influential of the colonists themselves, in large trading ships *(hafskip)* from Iceland, Norway, and the British Isles.

By the twelfth century the colony had probably reached an optimum stage of development with some three hundred settlement sites, mostly pastoral farms with summer grazings *(saeters)* in the glens under the glaciers. The original Icelandic colonists had been half-Christianised, as indicated by the chapel excavated at Brattahlíd in 1961–62 and identified as

"Thjodchild's Church," which stood within a small, circular, diked grave-yard containing some sixteen graves oriented in Christian fashion.[38] At its height, the more populous southern district had twelve parish churches, a diocesan cathedral (established in 1126, excavated in 1926), an Augustinian monastery, and a Benedictine nunnery. The northern district had four parish churches, one of which probably served as a cathedral for a short time before 1126.[39]

Norse occupancy was not limited to the two settled districts but extended northward along the western coast at least as far as 73° north, giving access to the *nordsetur*, or northern hunting grounds, from which live polar bear cubs, Greenland falcons, and walrus and narwhal ivory were exported to Europe. The hunt and the related trade were essentially under the control of the Church, at least until the abandonment of the northern district—the "Western Settlement"—in 1342.[40]

After 1410 all trading and ecclesiastical contact with Bergen and Rome was lost, the farm economy declined,[41] and the settlement in the southern district—the "Eastern Settlement"—shriveled away. By 1500 Norse Greenland was gone, its demise hastened by climatic and environmental change, by the southward advance of the Inuits, and perhaps even by attacks from English fishing ships straying from their traditional grounds off Iceland.

The principal source for the history of Norse expansion to the shores of North America is *Landnámabók*, the "Book of the Land Takings or Colonisation of Iceland and Greenland." It was probably compiled by priest Ari Thórgilsson (1067–1148), author of *Islendingabók*, between 1123 and 1132. He was aided in the task by descendants of the original settlers in Iceland.

The two sagas that recount the discovery of lands identifiable with parts of North America are less authoritative than *Landnámabók* and can be understood only in the context of the earlier work; the authorship of neither is known. *Grænlendinga saga* (Saga of the Greenlanders) was written before 1200, probably in the North Quarter of Iceland in Skaga Fjord, whereas *Eiríks saga Rauda* (Erik the Red's saga)—also known as *Thórfinns saga Karl-sefnis Thórdarson* (Saga of Thórfinn Karlsefni Thórdarson)—was written after 1263, possibly on Iceland's Snaefelsnes peninsula or elsewhere in the West Quarter of the island. Though the two are collectively known as the Vinland sagas, neither appears to owe anything to the other, and both show discrepancies in their accounts that are irreconcilable. Nevertheless it has been accepted that they had a common origin in the folklore of Iceland and Greenland and were rooted in real events. The discovery of the L'Anse aux Meadows site seems to confirm this and enhances their credibility. Value is also accorded *Saga Thórsnesinga ok Eyrbyggia*, concerned for the most part with events on the Snaefelsnes peninsula between 981 and 998 but also containing material that can be related to the Norse colonisation of Greenland and the discovery of North America.

The nature of the Norse advance across the Atlantic to North American shores, as it emerges from an analysis of *Landnámabók* and the Vinland sagas, differs in several important respects from that of Columbus. The voyage of 1492 was based on preconceived ideas about cosmography as understood by Columbus. It was a geographical experiment based on a theory. It was also motivated by zeal to convert the heathen and desire to find silver and gold and a shorter and safer route to the Orient than through Central Asia. The advance from Europe to the Americas was effected by the success of a single voyage. The Norse advance, on the other hand, was a protracted process covering three centuries, in which accidental events were crucial in launching numerous voyages of exploration and colonisation. It represented a number of folk-migrations, the underlying motive for which was acquisition of land suitable for the traditional high-latitude and mountain pastoralism of medieval Norway. Flight—from the centralising power of the Norwegian Crown, from resurgent nativism in the British Isles, and from the law—was also a factor. Freehold landholding, pastoralism, and maritime trade were principal elements in the folk culture and were dominant characteristics of the Norse frontier as it moved across the Atlantic. It was the failure of these elements to take root on American shores that ultimately forced that frontier to retreat.

The Norse frontier can best be understood as a series of overlapping cycles of events of discovery, exploration, and colonisation. Each of these cycles—Britain, the Faeroes, Iceland, Greenland, Vinland, and Hvítra-mannaland—consisted of an initial episode of accidental discovery, followed by deliberate exploration and subsequent colonisation. The recurrence of this sequence of events and the overlapping of cycles suggest that the advance of the Norse frontier of settlement—an advance culminating in the settlement at L'Anse aux Meadows and, possibly, elsewhere—was a coherent process through time and space despite the duration and distances involved.[42]

The Early Cycles: Britain, the Faeroes, and Iceland

The Norse "discovery" of Britain began in A.D. 789 when three ships from western Norway attacked Portland on the Dorset coast in southern England.[43] In 793 the monastery of Lindisfarne on the Northumbrian coast

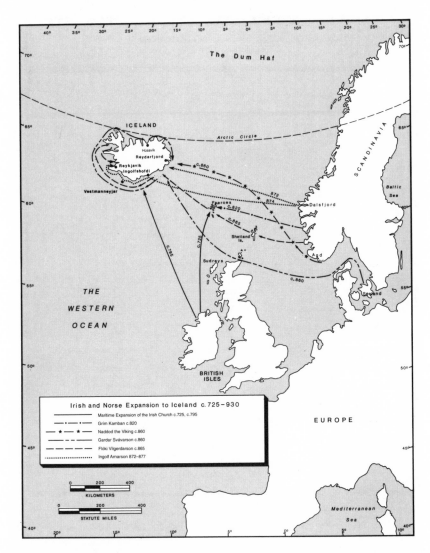

Map 1.1 Irish and Norse Expansion to Iceland, c. 725–930.

was looted; in 794 the monastery at Jarrow, a few miles to the south, was attacked; and in 795 the monastic settlements of Iona on the western coast of Scotland, Lambey Island near Dublin, and Llancarfan Morganwg in South Wales were all ravaged. This sudden and apparently coordinated descent on the British Isles and its monastic centres, most of which were founded by Irish missionaries, eventually provided the Norsemen with

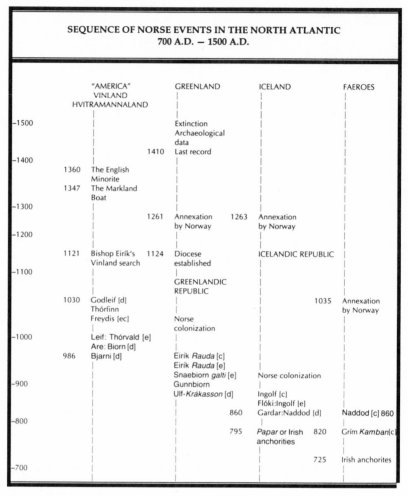

Key: [d] – discovery [e] – exploration [c] – colonization

1.4 Sequence of Norse Events in the North Atlantic, A.D. 700–1500.

knowledge of the Faeroes and, possibly, Iceland. Norse colonisation of Britain and Ireland proceeded vigorously for the next two centuries and played a major role in the evolution of the English, Irish, Welsh, and Scottish peoples. Its success established the British Isles as a base for the subsequent discovery and colonisation of the Faeroes and Iceland.

The Norse discovery and exploration of the uninhabited Faeroe Islands occurred in the period between the initial raids on the British Isles and the arrival of the first Norse settler, around A.D. 820.[44] The date fits well with

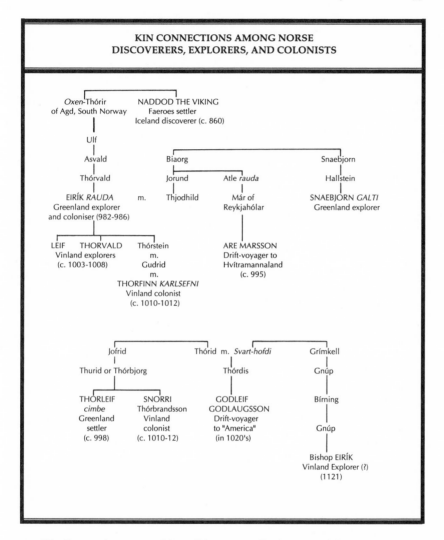

KIN CONNECTIONS AMONG NORSE
DISCOVERERS, EXPLORERS, AND COLONISTS

1.5 Kin Connections among Norse Discoverers, Explorers, and Colonists.

the 825 account of Dicuil, an Irish monk, of Norse pirates replacing Irish hermits in the Faeroes. The colonisation stage of the Faeroes continued until 860, when Naddod the Viking sailed from the Agd district in southern Norway to settle in the islands.

Naddod's voyage represented the end of the colonisation stage in the Faeroes. It also represented the opening stage of accidental discovery in Iceland. His ship was storm-driven westward and made landfall at Reydarfjord on the eastern coast of Iceland. Naddod and some of his crew "walked up a high mountain . . . and looked far and wide to see if they could see smoke or any token that the land was settled, but they saw none; They went back at harvest-tide to the Faeroes, and as they sailed from the land there fell great snow upon the hills, wherefore they called the land Snaeland; They praised the land much."[45]

Naddod's discovery was shared at about the same time by Gardar Svávarson, a Swede who owned land in Denmark, on a voyage from Sjælland to the Sudreys (Hebrides), where his wife had an inheritance. After a gale drove his ship out of the Pentland Firth between the northern tip of Scotland and the Orkneys, he made landfall east of the Eastern Horn of Iceland. He then circumnavigated Iceland clockwise and overwintered at Húsavík on the Arctic coast, naming the island "Gardarsholm."[46]

The exploration stage was represented by Flóki Vilgerdarson, sailing from the old western Norwegian districts of Hordaland and Rogaland via the Shetlands and Faeroes to make landfall at the Eastern Horn of Iceland, close to Gardar's landfall; Flóki coasted west along the southern coast, turned the Reykjanes and Snaefelsnes peninsulas, and overwintered on the Bardarstrand, the northern shore of the Breidafjord, and again in Hafnarsfjord in the Faxaflói before returning to Norway. His perceptions were that the large rivers of the region denoted a large country, that inshore waters were rich in marine resources, that the winter was too cold for cattle to survive by foraging, but "that butter dripped out of every blade of grass" in the summer and that the northwestern fjords such as Isafjord could fill with floe ice in the spring—hence the name "Island" (Iceland). Another voyage, that of the cousins and foster-brothers Ingolf Arnarson and Hiaor-Leif Hrodmarsson, who sailed in about 872 direct to the South Alftafjord in the Eastfirths, revealed that the land was better south than north in the direction of Reydarfjord, Naddod's landfall.

Serious colonisation of Iceland began in 874 when Ingolf and Hiaor-Leif returned, Ingolf progressing westward along the southern coast in a series of overwinterings before finally settling at Reykjavik in the southwest in 877. Landnámabók characterises him as "the most famous of all the settlers for he came here to an uninhabited land and was the first to settle the land." It then describes in detail the settlement of Iceland clockwise from Reykjavik—coast by coast, Quarter by Quarter, estate (landnám) by estate, by some four hundred leading settlers—and concludes by noting that within sixty years the land was fully settled. The colonisation phase of the Iceland cycle was complete, therefore, by the 930s. Landnámabók reveals that many of the principal colonists in the West Quarter—and in the western half of the island generally—were Vestmenn and Irskr, West Vikings from the British Isles, particularly from Ireland and the Hebrides and the Isle of Man, rather than direct from Norway or other parts of Scandinavia. This fact, which has largely gone unnoticed, has bearing on the colonisation of Greenland and the exploration of Vinland in that much of that process was undertaken by neighbors and members of kin-groups, many of whom knew one another and among whom geographical information was shared.

The Greenland Cycle

The Greenland cycle began around A.D. 900, halfway through the primary settlement of Iceland, when Gunnbiorn Ulf-Krákasson, an Icelandic settler at Saxahvál on the point of the Snaefelsnes peninsula, made an accidental discovery of skerries off the eastern coast of Greenland. These small islands, which are generally thought to be those in latitude 65° north near Angmagssalik on the eastern coast of Greenland and due west of Snaefelsnes, were known in Iceland as "Gunnbiarnarsker," Gunnbiorn's skerries. No details of this voyage were known to the compilers of *Landnámabók*, but it is probable that it was a voyage to explore the deeper recesses of the fjords of northwestern Iceland, particularly the potential for settlement at Laugardal near the head of Isafjord, where Gunnbiorn's sons, Gunnstein and Halldór, eventually settled.

The original idea for the exploration of Greenland may well have originated in Isafjord, at Vatnsfjord, the Icelandic estate adjacent to Laugardal. The exploration stage in the Greenland cycle opened with a large expedition of some two dozen men led jointly by Snaebiorn Holmsteinsson of Vatnsfjord and Hrólf Thórbiarnarson of Raudasand. Their voyage, which began in Borgarfjord in the Faxaflói district, set out to rediscover Gunnbiorn's skerries. There may have been another motive in Snaebiorn's exile for manslaughter. Nothing is recorded of the success of this expedition beyond the fact that it overwintered—presumably somewhere on the ice-bound eastern coast of Greenland—under heavy snow conditions.

In the summers of 982–85, successful exploration of Greenland was carried out by Eirík Rauda Thorvaldsson ("Erik the Red"), sailing out from the islands in the entrance to Hvammsfjord on the northern side of the Snaefelsnes peninsula to search for the land seen by Gunnbiorn when he was driven west of Iceland to Gunnbiarnar-sker. During the summer of 982, Erik sailed west, using the ice-cap glacier on Snaefelsnes as a land-

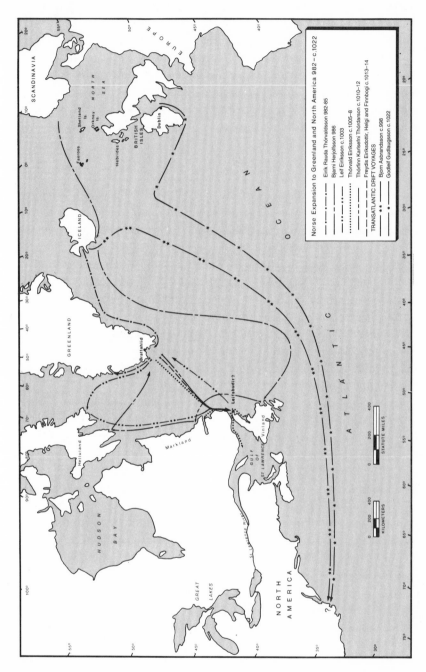

Map 1.2 *Norse Expansion to Greenland and North America, 982–c. 1022.*

Norse Expansion to Greenland and North America 982–c.1022

Eirik Rauda Thórvaldsson 982-85
Bjarni Herjolfsson 986
Leif Eiriksson c.1003
Thórvald Eiriksson c.1005-8
Thorfinn Karlsefni Thórdarson c.1010-12
Freydis Eiriksdóttir, Helgi and Finnbogi c.1013-14

TRANSATLANTIC DRIFT VOYAGES

Bjorn Asbrandsson c.998
Godleif Gudlaugsson c.1022

mark astern; he made landfall at Bláserk and sailed south along the coast to determine whether it was inhabitable, then sailed west of Hvarf (Cape Farewell)—perhaps using the relative shelter of Prince Christian Sound—and up the deeply fjorded coast of southwestern Greenland. Over the winter of 982–83, he and his men wintered at Eiríksey in the middle of what became the Eastern Settlement (Eystrebygd) of Greenland. In the spring and summer of 983 he explored Eiríksfjord, built a homestead (which may have been Brattahlíd), and sailed north to what became the Western Settlement (Vestrebygd), naming features of the land as he went. The following winter was spent at Eiríksholm near Cape Farewell. Summer 984 saw Erik sailing far north and later exploring Hrafnsfjord south of Eiríksfjord. The winter of 984–85 was spent at Eiríksey in the opening into Eiríksfjord. The following summer Erik sailed back to Iceland.

It has been suggested that one of his expeditions northward was along the eastern coast of Greenland, but this seems unlikely after his coasting on the outward voyage. It has also been suggested that his exploration of the western coast extended as far north as Disco Island in latitude 70° north. What is certain is that he and his comrades explored the fjords from Cape Farewell to Isafjord (north of Eiríksfjord) and identified potential sites for settlement in the inner reaches of the fjords. The expedition from Eiríksfjord in the summer of 983 to explore the labyrinth of fjords that were to provide the future site of the Western Settlement involved a voyage northward of some three hundred miles (480 km) beyond Eiríksfjord on the open sea. Further penetration of the north to Disco Island would have added another four hundred miles. The minimum sea distances involved in Erik's exploration of Greenland add up to a round trip of some thirty-three hundred miles, to which must be added at least another one thousand miles navigating the inner reaches of the fjords, making it one of the most impressive feats of exploration known.

Erik's return to Iceland was immediately followed by the departure of a colonisation fleet of some twenty-five ships from Breidafjord, Borgarfjord, and the Reykjanes peninsula in the summer of 986; fourteen of these ships succeeded in reaching Greenland. *Landnámabók* lists the principal settlers of the Eastern Settlement and their *landnáms* in the order in which, presumably, they dropped out of the fleet as it passed northward from Cape Farewell. By the time Erik entered Eiríksfjord to settle at Brattahlíd, only four ships remained. These continued up the coast for another three hundred miles to enter the fjords of the Western Settlement. One of them was commanded, perhaps, by Thórstein the Black, who appears in *Grænlen-*

dinga saga as the settler in Lysufjord. Of the Greenland pioneers, only Herjolf Bárdarson of Drepstokk and Snorri Thórbrandsson of Alftafjord can be identified, with Erik, in *Landnámabók*. The achievement of these settlers and their countrymen in establishing a Norse presence on the southwestern coast of Greenland, facing across Davis Strait, provided the base for the advance to the North American continent.

The Vinland Cycle

According to *Grænlendinga saga*, the Vinland cycle of events began with a drift voyage and a series of accidental landfalls that were the immediate result of Herjolf Bárdarson's departure from Iceland to join Erik's fleet of Greenland colonists in the summer of 986. His son, Bjarni Herjolfsson, an experienced deep-sea merchant-adventurer who spent alternate winters in Norway and Iceland, was preparing to sail from Norway as his father sailed for Greenland. Bjarni arrived in Iceland to find his father's estate abandoned, and he decided to follow the fleet to the new colony. None of his crew had experience navigating Greenland waters, and all that Bjarni had learned was that the coastal districts of Greenland were mountainous and were backed by large glaciers. With this information, he and his crew sailed west into the Greenland Sea for three days with a following wind but then encountered north winds and fog, which continued for many days. The ship was presumably well south and west of Cape Farewell when they emerged from the fog and got their bearings. Their first landfall was a shore backed by low forest-covered hills. Two days' sail to the north brought them to a second landfall and a shore that was level and heavily forested. Three days' sail before a southwest wind and a third landfall presented them with a high and rugged land, covered by glaciers, which proved to be an island. Bjarni rejected this landfall as unsuitable, presumably because it showed no potential for a pastoral economy, although it matched his expectations in every other respect, and he ordered the ship about. If this series of landfalls on shores west of Greenland represented a navigational strategy to find the latitude appropriate for an intended landfall somewhere in one of the Greenland colonies, it seems to have been successful. Four days' sail with a southwest wind brought them to a landfall that Bjarni was satisfied was Greenland and eventually to his intended destination at Herjolfsness. His descriptions of the three landfalls to the northwest and southwest represent the first historical reports of North American shores.[47]

Grænlendinga saga indicates that Bjarni Herjolfsson made a later voyage

to Norway "to see Earl Eirík," presumably after Eirík Hakonárson had defeated and killed King Olaf Tryggvason at the sea fight at Svold in the summer of 1000 and had become ruler of Norway. This would place Bjarni with
Earl Eirík, at the earliest, in 1001 and back in Greenland in 1002. If this date
is correct, it can serve as the basis for the chronology of events in *Grænlendinga saga*.[48]

Bjarni Herjolfsson's return to the Eastern Colony of Greenland appears
to have provoked "much talk of voyages of discovery," probably over the
winter of 1002–3. Serious exploration was undertaken by Leif Eiríksson of
Brattahlíd, the eldest son of Erik and the principal man of the Norse colony,
who acquired Bjarni's ship and perhaps some of his crew for the purpose.
Leif's voyage, which probably took place in the summer of 1003, was essentially a reconnaisance to retrace Bjarni's landfalls in reverse order. With a
crew of thirty-five men, Leif sailed up the western coast of Greenland and
across the strait to the third landfall. Their observations as recorded in
Grænlendinga saga confirmed Bjarni's description: "no grass; the hinterland
was all great glaciers, and right up to the glaciers from the sea as it were a
single slab of rock; the land impressed them as barren and useless." Leif
named it "Helluland" (Flatstone Land). Leif's visit to Bjarni's second landfall confirmed that it was "flat and wooded" and added the navigational
detail that it was bordered by "white sandy beaches wherever they went,
shelving gently down to the sea." He gave it the name "Markland" (Forest
Land).

Bjarni's first landfall was reached in two days' sail with a northeast
wind. It proved to be a promontory pointing north with a grassy island offshore, to the west of which were extensive shallows and a river issuing
from a lake, into which they towed their ship. "There was no lack of salmon
in the river or the lake, bigger than they had ever seen. The country
seemed so kind that no winter fodder would be needed for livestock; there
was never any frost all winter and the grass hardly withered. Day and
night were of more even length than in either Greenland or Iceland. On the
shortest day of winter the sun was visible in the middle of the afternoon
[about 3.00 pm.] and at breakfast-time [about 9.00 am.]."[49]

After constructing temporary shelters, the men decided that they should
overwinter and explore the neighborhood, and more substantial houses
were built to accommodate the crew. Grapes were found, and Leif ordered
the crew to divide work between felling trees and gathering grapes to take
back to Greenland. "The tow-boat was filled with grapes. They took on a
full cargo of timber; and in the spring they made ready to leave and sailed

away. Leif named the country after its natural qualities and called it *Vinland*. They put out to sea and had favourable winds all the way until they sighted Greenland and its ice-capped mountains."[50] They sailed for Eiríksfjord until they reached Brattahlíd, where they discharged their cargo.

Leif Eiríksson's reconnaissance expedition returned to Eiríksfjord in Greenland in the spring of a year no earlier than 1004. A second expedition was launched in the autumn of 1005 under the leadership of Leif's brother, Thórvald Eiríksson, with the purpose of carrying out more extensive exploration. The same ship was used, but with a slightly reduced crew of thirty men. *Grænlendinga saga* states, "There are no reports of their voyage till they came to Vínland, to Leifsbúdir, where they saw to their ship and stayed quiet over the winter [1005–6?], catching fish for their food." Thórvald Eiríksson's party spent three winters at Leifsbúdir and spent the summers exploring by ship and boat. The first summer (1006?) was devoted to exploration to the west: "It looked to them a beautiful and well-wooded land, the woods scarcely any distance from the sea, with white sands and a great many islands and shallows. Nowhere did they come across habitation of man or beast, but on an island in the west they found a wooden grain-holder. They found no other work of man, so returned and reached Leifsbúdir that autumn."[51]

The second summer (1007?) was devoted to exploration eastward and northward; their ship was driven ashore near a headland in a gale and suffered extensive damage to the keel, requiring them to remain as long as was needed to repair the vessel. Thórvald marked the event by naming the headland Kjalarness (Keelness). They then sailed eastward along the coast and discovered a heavily wooded promontory where two fjords met, which so impressed Thórvald that he considered it a possible *landnám*. Natives, referred to by the Norse as Skrælings, were first encountered in skin-boats at this place, and Norse aggression and native hostility ensued, during which Thórvald was mortally wounded. He was buried on the headland at his own request, naming it Krossanes (Crossness) as a mark of his Christian faith. The ship's party rejoined the rest of the expedition at Leifsbúdir, where they spent the third winter—gathering grapes for a cargo—before returning to Eiríksfjord in Greenland in the spring. The year was probably no earlier than A.D. 1008.

The Vinland cycle was completed, according to *Grænlendinga saga*, when Thórfinn Thórdarson, a merchant-trader from Skagafjord in the North Quarter of Iceland overwintering with Leif Eiríksson at Brattahlíd (1009–10?), was persuaded to undertake a voyage to establish a permanent colony at Leifsbúdir in Vinland. With antecedents among the leading set-tlers in both the North and the West Quarters of Iceland, and with more re-mote ancestry among the Viking kings of York, Dublin, and the Hebrides, Thórfinn Thórdarson was well qualified to command such an expedition. His ship was a large one, capable of taking a company of sixty men and five women, besides livestock (including a bull!), sufficient for colonisation. On the other hand, *Grænlendinga saga* is careful to note that the colonisers required Leif Eiríksson's permission to use the property at Leifsbúdir as their base, indicating that he retained the right of first land-taking there and regarded the vicinity of Leifsbúdir as his own estate. Thórfinn also en-tered into an agreement with his shipmates that they should share equally in the profits of the voyage, an arrangement among maritime traders that indicated that colonisation was motivated by the hope of trade. The year was probably 1010.

The saga related that a large rorqual whale beached itself shortly after they arrived, ensuring an adequate supply of meat through their first win-ter. "[Thórfinn] had timber felled and dressed for his ship's cargo, laying it out to season on a rock. They took every advantage of the resources the country had to offer, both in the way of grapes, and all kinds of hunting and fishing and good things."[52] During the first summer (1011?) a large body of native Skrælings appeared out of the forest to trade furs—"grey furs, sables, skins of all kinds"—in exchange for arms. This was denied, and milk was offered instead. Thórfinn, whose wife had recently given birth to a son, Snorri, ordered his men to build a strong wooden palisade or stockade to be erected around Leifsbúdir in anticipation of a second visit from the natives. This visit came at the beginning of winter, when a larger body arrived and similar trading occurred, the Skrælings throwing their bales of pelts over the palisade, the Norse women taking out supplies of milk in exchange. It must have been clear to the Norse that the natives were more eager to acquire steel axes and other weapons. In anticipation of a third and hostile visit, a battle plan was devised that resulted in the rout of a Skræling attack. "In the spring [1012?] [Thórfinn] announced that he would be staying there no longer, and that he wanted to go back to Green-land. They made ready for the voyage, and fetched away with them many valuable commodities: vines, grapes and furs."[53]

A second and equally abortive attempt to colonise Vinland at Leifsbúdir was made in the following summer (1013), according to *Grænlendinga saga*. The leading spirit of this enterprise was a woman, Freydis Eiríksdottir of Gardar, a daughter of Erik the Red. With her husband, she owned a ship in which they took thirty-five men and a small number of women, presumably all Greenland Norse. A second, somewhat larger ship with thirty men and five women, presumably all Icelanders and Norwegians, was commanded by Helgi and Finnbogi, merchant brothers from the Eastfirths of Iceland, who had arrived the year before from Norway and had been persuaded to join the expedition. Again, Leif Eiríksson stood on his *landnám* rights at Leifsbúdir.

The joint expedition was marked by ill-will from the moment it reached Leifsbúdir. The Icelanders arrived first and took possession of Leif's houses until ordered out by Freydis, whereupon "they built their own hall, siting it further away from the sea by the lakeside." The Greenlanders felled a cargo of timber. The Icelanders assessed the land as "good and fruitful." During the winter the two parties became estranged, and the expedition ended with a massacre of the Icelanders, whereupon Freydis and the Greenlanders returned to Greenland in Helgi and Finnbogi's ship: "They sailed to sea, had a good passage, and brought their ship to Eiríksfjord early in the summer [1014?]."[54] *Grænlendinga saga* closes the account of this expedition by noting: "[Thórfinn] was still there and had his ship ready and was waiting for a favorable wind to put to sea. It is said that no ship has ever sailed from Greenland more richly laden than the one that he commanded. He had a good crossing, reached Norway safe and sound, stayed there over the winter, and disposed of his cargo. Next spring [1015] he made his ship ready for Iceland, sailed to sea and brought his ship to Skagafjord in the North Quarter. In the spring [1016] he negotiated for Glaumboejarland and lived there for the rest of his life."[55]

Thórfinn Thórdarson's gray furs constituted the first cargo of North American resources to reach a European market, and his purchase of Glaumboejarland represented the first investment in the Old World of profits from the New World. His last act before he sailed from Norway was to sell a *húsasnotra*—either a ship's figurehead or a house-gable decoration—carved from *mosurr* wood, generally taken to be maple, brought from Vinland. The buyer was a German from Bremen.

The story of the Vinland voyages as told in *Eiríks saga Rauda* differs significantly from that related by *Grænlendinga saga*. There is no mention of Bjarni Herjolfsson's drift voyage and western landfalls in the summer of 986. Instead, the saga presents Leif Eiríksson as the merchant-trader who made the original discovery when he was storm-tossed while returning to Greenland from Norway, allegedly on a mission from King Olaf Tryggvason to Christianise the Greenland colony. The year A.D. 1000 is usually identified with this event, the year of King Olaf's death. No details of Leif's drift voyage are given, no landfalls are described, and there was no overwintering and consequently no settlement, no Leifsbúdir. Description of the land is confined to a statement that there were fields of self-sown wheat, grapevines, and the maple trees the Norse called *mosurr*, prized because of the beauty of the wood. The implication is that, unlike Bjarni Herjolfsson, Leif turned his discovery into exploration and investigation of potential resources. The discussions that ensued at Brattahlíd during the winter revolved around the question of the exact location of Vinland—the name that Leif, by implication, gave to the new land where, it was reported, there was excellent land to be had.

The second, third, and fourth voyages of *Grænlendinga saga* are conflated in *Eiríks saga Rauda* into a single expedition in which Thórfinn Thórdarson, Thórvald Eiríksson, and Freydis Eiríksdottir all participated. The Icelanders were represented by Thórfinn and Snorri Thórbrandsson of Alftafjord[56] in partnership in a trading vessel with forty men and by Bjarni Grímolfsson of Breidafjord and Thórhall Gamlason from the Eastfirths in a second ship with a similar crew. The Greenlanders were also in two ships, the first commanded by Thórhall the Hunter, one of Erik the Red's henchmen, and the other by Thórvard, Freydis's husband, and by Thórvald Eiríksson. The conflation greatly shortens the chronology of events to the years 1003–6, compared with *Grænlendinga saga's* three separate expeditions that cover the period 1005–15. The total complement of the expedition was 160 persons; Freydis and Gudrid (Thórfinn's wife) are the only women mentioned.

Eiríks saga Rauda has the joint expedition under Thórfinn's general command reenact Leif Eiríksson's voyage of rediscovery as described in *Grænlendinga saga*: up the West Greenland coast to the Western Settlement and beyond to the Bjarneyjar or Bear Islands and then cross with a north wind for two days to reach a shore of large flat stones, which Thórfinn named "Helluland." There is no mention of glaciers, but foxes suggest a tundra landscape. After another two days the north wind put them at an island they called Bjarney (Bear Island), lying off a forested mainland that had many animals and that received the name Markland.

A third leg of two days' sail found them tacking off a coastline with features that added a good deal to the Norse record of geographical observation: "After two days they sighted land again and held in towards it; it was a promontory they were approaching. They tacked along the coast, with the land to starboard. It was open and harbourless, with long beaches and extensive sands. They went ashore in boats and found a ship's keel on the headland, and so they called the place *Kjalarnes*. They called this stretch of coast *Furdustrandir* [Marvel Strands] because it took so long to sail past it. Then the coastline became indented with bays."[57] This valuable description is followed by yet another reference to grapes and wild wheat.

The expedition sailed on until it found a fjord with an island in its mouth, the home of a large bird colony, with strong currents around it. The island they called Straumey, the fjord Straumfjord; there were mountains there and tall grass, and this they made their base. The autumn was spent exploring the locality, and Thórfinn's wife, Gudrid, gave birth to their son Snorri. The saga says nothing about building houses, but the livestock were put ashore and thrived, despite the severity of their first winter. They overwintered on Straumey, where they found a stranded whale, of a species unknown to them; they successfully fished from the island. In the spring they returned to Straumfjord to collect "game on the mainland, eggs on the island, and fish from the sea." A decision was made to explore both northward and southward: Thórhall the Hunter sailed north with ten men "to search for Vínland" beyond Furdustrands and Kjalarnes but was swept across the Atlantic and enslaved in Ireland; Thórfinn and Snorri Thórbrandsson, accompanied by Bjarni Grímolfsson, sailed south along the coast and arrived at an estuary where a river "flowed down into a lake and from the lake into the sea. There were extensive sandbars outside the river mouth, and ships could only enter it at high tide. . . . Here they found wild wheat growing in fields on all the low ground and grape vines on all the higher ground. Every stream was teeming with fish. They dug trenches at the high-tide mark, and when the tide went out there were halibut trapped in the trenches. In the woods there was a great number of animals of all kinds."[58] They named this place Hóp (Landlocked or Tidal Bay), put their livestock ashore, and built houses near the lake to overwinter.

It was at Hóp during this first summer that they were visited by a party of natives, Skrælings, in nine skin-boats. *Eiríks saga Rauda* provides the first ethnographic description: "They were small and evil-looking, and their hair was coarse; they had large eyes and broad cheekbones." The visitors departed to the south, and the Norse settled in for their second winter. This proved to be clement, without snow, and the livestock stayed outdoors to forage for themselves. In the spring the Skrælings returned from the south in large numbers, and trading began: gray furs for red cloth, though the natives would have preferred weapons. It ended when the Skrælings were frightened by the bellowing of a bull that suddenly appeared from the forest. Three weeks later they reappeared, and hostilities occurred, during which two Norsemen were killed, and Freydis made a dramatic and heroic first appearance in the saga by taking part in the battle. The encounter caused Thórfinn to abandon Hóp and retreat north to Straumfjord: "[Thórfinn] Karlsefni and his men had realised by now that although the land was excellent they could never live there in safety or freedom from fear, because of the native inhabitants."[59] Sailing north, they killed five skin-clad Skrælings, whom they found with containers full of deer marrow mixed with blood. They passed a headland frequented by deer in the winter and covered with their dung.

At this point in the saga an alternative version of the expedition to Hóp is inserted: "It is some men's report that Bjarni and Freydis [one manuscript source says Gudrid] had remained behind at Straumfjord with a hundred men, and had proceeded no further, while [Thórfinn] Karlsefni and Snorri had travelled south with forty men, yet spent no longer at Hop than a bare two months, and got back again that same summer."[60] This would imply that there was no overwintering at Hóp and that all encounters with the Skrælings occurred during the first summer of exploration, possibly at Straumfjord rather than Hóp.

From Straumfjord, during the second summer, Thórfinn and Thórvald Eiríksson (making his first appearance in the saga) sailed north past Kjalarnes and headed west, "with the land on the port beam. It was a region of wild and desolate woodland." Eventually they came to a river flowing into the sea from east to west, where they encountered a one-legged manbeast, or *uniped*, who mortally wounded Thórvald Eiríksson with an arrow. They sailed farther north and observed mountains: "They reckoned that the mountains they could see there roughly corresponded with those at Hóp and were part of the same range, and they estimated that both regions were equidistant from Straumfjord."[61] The third winter was spent at Straumfjord.

The return voyage to Greenland involved a visit to Markland, where they captured two Skræling boys who provided information that although their own people lived in caves or holes in the ground, there was a country nearby where the inhabitants went about in white clothing, uttering loud cries and carrying poles with patches of cloth attached. The saga writer associates this country with Hvítramannaland. After overwintering two more years in Greenland with Erik the Red, Thórfinn returned directly to Reynisnes in the North Quarter of Iceland, to end the saga.

Although the two sagas differ in many respects, they both draw on memory of the same events. They deal with the same cast of actors, though not always in the same roles. They both describe the landfalls and the naming of Helluland, Markland, Kjalarnes, and Vinland. They both indicate that the parties involved in the expeditions overwintered and that women and "livestock," including a bull, were elements of the initial colonisation attempt. Both sagas describe three visits from parties of natives, visits that led to fur trading followed by hostilities. Both record the killing of Skrælings taken by surprise. Both mention stranded whales and *mosurr* wood—usually translated as maple—and mention grapes and vines.

The two sagas also diverge in their accounts of exploration, establishment, and location of the short-lived North American settlements. In *Grænlendinga saga* Leif Eiríksson's explorations seem to have been confined to local excursions conducted daily from Leifsbúdir. Regional exploration was carried out by his brother Thórvald in three directions. In the first summer, the men headed westward along the coast of a beautiful and well-wooded land, with forests growing down to the water's edge. The beaches were of white sands, and the shoreline included many islands and shallows but virtually no evidence of human habitation. In the second summer, exploration proceeded eastward and northward along the coast to Kjalarnes; and then eastward along the coast to Krossanes at the entrance to a double fjord, where they encountered hostile Skrælings. Each of the three winters was spent at Leifsbúdir. Nowhere is there mention of self-sown wheat.

Eiríks saga Rauda, on the other hand, makes no mention of Leifsbúdir; instead, Thórfinn's expedition based itself at Straumfjord, the vicinity of which was thoroughly explored before the onset of their first winter. In the first summer two expeditions were organised: one proceeding north by way of Furdustrandir and Kjalarnes to look for Vínland (which makes no geographical sense), the other traveling south and east along the coast to Hóp, where the Skrælings were encountered, where the Norse may have overwintered, and where fur trading occurred and hostilities ensued before they returned to Straumfjord. In the second summer a single expedition sailed north past Kjalarnes and then west with the coast on the left, past a region of wild and desolate woodland, with little cleared land, and then north to a region of coastal mountains. There is no equivalent of *Grænlendinga saga*'s expedition to the west or of its eastward expedition to Krossanes; in place of the latter, *Eiríks saga Rauda* introduces the expedition southward to Hóp; both sagas include expeditions northward at least as far as Kjalarnes in Markland, but *Grænlendinga saga* has no extension of such an exploration west and north to a region of coastal mountains.

Attempts to reconcile the two sagas have been forced to focus on the settlements that served as bases for exploration and colonisation. A comparison of Leifsbúdir with Straumfjord and Hóp reveals that Straumfjord and Hóp represent different aspects of Leifsbúdir, in terms of physical geography, biogeography, and human geography. The discovery of the Norse site at Black Duck Brook near L'Anse aux Meadows in 1960 made it possible, for the first time, to compare the saga accounts with an actual site—and so far the only site—that has been identified as Norse. Its general location just inside the entrance to the Strait of Belle Isle, the Gran Baia of the Basques—a sea gate of strong currents, with Belle Isle in its midst and Great and Little Sacred Islands closer inshore—matches Straumfjord and Straumey; the north-pointing "peninsula" of Quirpon Island that terminates at Cape Bauld, with the shallows of Epaves Bay and others to the west, conforms to Leifsbúdir and Hóp. Its site, however, does not offer the feature of a river issuing from a lake into which the Norse ships could be drawn. That aspect of Leifsbúdir is missing. The absence of mountains in the vicinity favors Leifsbúdir against both Straumfjord and Hóp.

Despite valiant attempts to reconcile these discrepancies, the difficulties of interpreting the geographical context in terms of latitude, coastlines, environmental conditions, natural resources, and ethnography have always raised problems. Despite mention of wind directions and days of sailing, the general lack of information about distances and bearings deprives the saga accounts of any sense of scale. The result has been a plethora of suggestions for the location of the Norse settlement in North America, ranging from the high Arctic to Florida and from Newfoundland to Minnesota. However, if we accept that the site at L'Anse aux Meadows conforms generally to the saga descriptions of Straumfjord-Leifsbúdir, much falls into place.

A reconstructed sequence of events, combining elements from both sagas, includes at least four separate expeditions. The expedition to the west probably followed the northern shore of the Gulf of Saint Lawrence (rather than the islandless western shore of Newfoundland's Northern Peninsula). The exploration northward was probably retracing the route down the Labrador (Markland) coast, where the fjorded coast of southern Labrador gives way to the forty-mile sand beaches (Furdustrandir) associated with Cape Porcupine (Kjalarnes) and then to the entrance to Hamilton

Inlet, which was penetrated for some considerable distance; the mountains at the furthest point of this expedition would correspond, perhaps, to the deeply dissected edge of the Labrador Plateau, standing two thousand feet above the northern Labrador shore from Cape Harrison northward. The expedition eastward to the double fjord and Krossanes *(Grænlendinga saga)* and the expedition southward to Hóp *(Eiríks saga Rauda)*—may indicate exploration down the eastern side of Newfoundland's Northern Peninsula at least as far as Canada Bay (the double fjord of Chimney Bay and Bide Arm?) and possibly into Notre Dame Bay. Helluland, in terms of arctic fox terrain, could be the Torngat Mountains shore of northern Labrador or the southern tips of Baffin Island, whereas its identification with coastal glaciers would place it farther north, in the vicinity of Cape Dyer. Cape Dyer, on the Arctic Circle, marks the narrowest part of the Davis Strait (300 km) and an appropriate landfall for ships taking advantage of the West Greenland and Labrador Currents on voyages from Greenland to Markland and Vinland.

The interpretation of the geographical situation of Leifsbúdir/Straumfjord as the base for Norse exploration is conservative when compared with the claims that fill speculative literature. It is supported by the fact that exploration to the west encountered no native populations. The expedition to the east and south, whether it involved overwintering or not, may have been an attempt to relieve some of the pressure of numbers at the main base during the winter. It would not have involved great distances between the main base and the secondary camp.

The first appearance of Vinland in the geography of the North occurred in "Descriptio insularum aquilonis" (Description of the northern islands), the fourth chapter of Adam of Bremen's *Gesta Hammaburgensis ecclesiae pontificum*, written between 1072 and 1081 in the cathedral school at Bremen. His informant was King Svein II Estridsson of Denmark, a monarch who had considerable contact with the Archbishop of Hamburg-Bremen up to his death in 1074. His information was that there was "another island, discovered by many in that ocean, which is called Wineland from the circumstance that vines grow there of their own accord, and produce the most excellent wine. While that there is an abundance of unsown corn there we have learned from . . . the trustworthy report of the Danes."[62]

This is the only pre-Columbian reference to Vinland that identifies the land explicitly as an island, in contrast with the later references in *Landnámabók* and the sagas, and may reflect medieval cosmology that all landfalls in the western ocean were necessarily islands. If "the report of the

Danes" was trustworthy, the reference to corn may well have been based on the large lyme grass *(Elymus* or *Leymus arenarius)*, common in sandy coastal environments in Iceland, where it was used as a substitute for barley, and present in both the modern vegetation and the medieval pollen found at L'Anse aux Meadows. The same pollen record shows no signs of grape species *(Vitis)* in the fossil vegetation.[63]

The saga references to "grapes and vines" have been a most vexing problem in the quest to locate Vinland. In *Grænlendinga saga* they are mentioned as occurring only at Leifsbúdir; vines as well as grapes were harvested, and always in springtime, by three of the expedition parties returning to Greenland. In *Eiríks saga Rauda* they appear in the vague description of Leif's brief initial visit, in an account—generally regarded as apocryphal—of an excursion to explore the hinterland of the indented coast south of Markland and north of Straumfjord, and in the extraordinary description of the country round Hóp south of Straumfjord. There is no mention of them at Straumfjord itself, and there is no mention of their forming part of a return cargo. Sceptics have pointed to Adam of Bremen, to *Navigatio Sancti Brandani Abbatis* (tenth century), to Isidore of Seville (c. 560–636) and his *Insulae fortunatae*, and to the Pentateuch (Numbers 13:17–27) as literary sources for the saga grapes.[64] In attempts to retain the grapes, scholars have invoked various species of wild berries as a possible explanation, and locations far up the estuary of the Saint Lawrence and in southern New England, where native vines are part of the natural vegetation, have been suggested for Vinland.[65] Neither explanation is warranted by the saga accounts, and both present new difficulties.

Removal of grapes and vines from Leifsbúdir/Straumfjord and Hóp—not to mention southern Markland—has the virtue of allowing the rest of the data in the sagas to make complete sense for L'Anse aux Meadows. Unfortunately, it leaves the meaning of the descriptive place-name "Vinland" in doubt. Those who argue for the retention of the grapes and vines tend to insist on the name as it appears in the sagas and *Landnámabók*: Vínland, meaning "Wineland." Those who prefer to dismiss the grapes have argued for an etymological alteration in the name to Vinland (with a short "i"), meaning "Grassland." Such a change makes a good deal of sense and fits the cultural background and pastoral preoccupations of the Norse.[66]

Helluland and Markland appear briefly with Vinland in a geographical treatise written around 1300: "To the south of Greenland lies Helluland, and then Markland, and from there it is not far to Vinland, which some people consider extends from Africa."[67] A confused version of Vinland and

Helluland's place in the geography of the northern lands and seas west of Europe appeared in *Gripla*, a lost pre-Columbian collection, a part of which has been preserved in the *Grænlands annál* of 1623: "Opposite Greenland lies . . . Furdustrandir. There the cold is so intense that so far as men know it is uninhabitable. South [*sic*] of it lies Helluland, which is called Skrælingaland. From there it is only a short distance to Vinland the Good, which some maintain is a projection of Africa."[68]

Furdustrandir here is clearly a surrogate for Markland, whereas the identification of Helluland with the Skrælings is an innovation that may reflect early Norse observations of the advancing Thule Eskimos around the shores of Baffin Bay. The latter can be traced back to a statement incorporated in the *Historia Norveqiae*, compiled between the 1160s and the end of the twelfth century, which again brings Greenland, Africa, and the Skrælings into conjunction: "Greenland, discovered and settled and fortified with the Catholic Faith by the Icelanders, is the westernmost bound of Europe, extending almost as far as the Isles of Africa, where the refluent streams of Ocean flood in and over. Beyond Greenland, still further to the north, hunters have come across people of small stature who are called *Scraelinga*. When they are struck their wounds turn white and they do not bleed, but if they are hurt to death they bleed and bleed almost endlessly. They do not know the use of iron, but employ walrus tusks as missiles and sharpened stones in place of knives."[69] Vinland, Markland, and Helluland —the northeastern margins of North America—are represented by "the Isles of Africa," a medieval myth that joins strangely with the accuracy exhibited in the description of the Eskimos.

The literary tradition of Adam of Bremen's *Descriptio insularum aquilonis*, along with that of *Historia Norvegiae, Gripla*, and the "Geographical Treatise," was continued in the speculative Icelandic cartography of the early post-Columbian period. Sigurdur Stefánsson's map of the "hyperborean lands" (1590) incorporates "Helleland" (*reqio petrosa*, "stony region"), "Markland," "Skrælinge Land," and "Promontorium Winlandiae" to denote lands west and southwest of Greenland ("Gronlandia"), the southern tip of which he labeled "Herjolfsnes"; his accompanying text refers to "Vinlandia" and equates "Skrælinge Land" with shores reached by the English (*A. Hi sunt ad quos Angli pervenerunt*). This has been interpreted as a reference to Frobisher's two voyages to Baffin Island in 1576 and 1577,[70] but it might be referring to John Cabot's initial landfall in 1497 in the latitude of Dursey Head in Ireland (i.e., Cape Bauld, the northern tip of Newfoundland, or on the southern Labrador coast, between 51° and 52° north) or—

more probably—to Frobisher's initial landfall on the Labrador coast in 1576. "Helleland," "Markland," "Promontorium Vinlandiae," "Vinlandia," and "Skrellinger" also appear on Bishop Hans Poulsen Resen's map of the northern lands between northwestern Europe and northeastern North America, a map drawn in 1605 in support of King Christian IV of Denmark's expeditions in search of the lost Greenland colonies. Each is accompanied by Latinised descriptions drawn from the sagas.[71] Stefánsson and Resen's maps place Helluland, Markland, and Promontorium Vinlandiae firmly between latitudes 63° and 52° north, matching the zone between the southern tip of the Hall Peninsula of Baffin Island and the base of Newfoundland's Northern Peninsula.[72]

The Hvítramannaland Cycle

When Bjarni Herjolfsson arrived in the Greenland colony in the summer of 986, after his eventful drift voyage and discovery of western landfalls, he not only initiated the Vinland cycle but also, as an itinerant merchant and would-be-settler, opened the sea lanes from Iceland to the new colony for others. Icelander Thórbjorn Vífilsson of Laugarbrekka on Snaefelsnes, the father of Gudrid, who married Thórfinn Thórdarson at Brattahlíd and bore the first European child born in the New World, was a supporter of Erik the Red in the feud that sent Erik into exile; his stormy voyage to join Erik in Greenland, his overwintering at Herjolfsnes, and his settlement at Stokkanes in Eiríksfjord are described in *Eiríks saga Rauda*. Thórgisl Thórdarson of Tradarholt and Iostein of Kalfaholt in the South Quarter were other estate owners who responded "when the ships began to go between [Green]land and [Ice]land, and there came messages from Greenland that Eirík *rauda* asked Thórgisl to come out to Greenland, making him the best offer that he was able to."[73] Thórfinn and the partnerships of Bjarni Grímolfsson of Breidafjord and Thórhall Gamlason of the Eastfirths and of the brothers Helgi and Finnbogi of the Eastfirths in Iceland all represent itinerant merchants seeking trade in the new colony, and there were undoubtedly others.

The experiences of Bjarni Herjolfsson and Thórbjorn Vífilsson in being storm-driven between Iceland and Greenland were by no means unique. The voyage of Thórgisl Thórdarson toward the west was bedeviled by stormy conditions and ended with shipwreck and five winters in the ice-bound fjords of eastern Greenland before he reached Eiríksfjord; his return voyage to Iceland was also delayed by storms. If Greenland-bound mariners encountered such conditions with normal frequency, Bjarni Herjolfsson's experience of being blown beyond Greenland to far western landfalls could hardly have been unique. Indeed, *Landnámabók* and *Eyrbyggia saga* provide evidence and accounts of three such drift voyages. Two of these occurred within the period when the primary Norse settlement of Greenland was under way, before the exploration and attempted colonisation of Vinland.

The first of these voyages—dated by the Icelandic historian Gudbrandur Vigfusson to 995–1000, although it could have occurred anytime after 986—was that of Are Mársson of Reykjahólar, a settler on the northern shore of Breidafjord and a direct ancestor of Ari Thórgilsson, the historian. *Landnámabók* relates that Are

> was drifted by the sea to *Hvítra-manna-land*, which some call *Irland et Mykla*, Ireland the Great. It lies west in the ocean near *Vínlande eno Goda*, Vinland the Good. It is said to be six days' sail west of Ireland. Are could not get away from there, and he was baptized there. The first who told this story was Hrafn *Hlymreks-fare* [Limerick-farer], who had long been in Limerick in Ireland. Thórkell Gellisson said that an Icelander told him that he had heard from Thórfinn, jarl in the Orkneys, that Are had been recognised in *Hvítra-manna-land*, but could not get away thence, although he was held in great esteem there.[74]

Hrafn Hlymreks-fare Oddsson was a Breidafjord merchant of the mid–eleventh century whose maternal grandfather was second cousin to Are Mársson; Thórkell Gellisson was one of Are's great-grandsons. The story told by Jarl Thórfinn Sigurdsson of the Orkneys—himself a distant kinsman of Are Mársson—must have been heard by Thórkell's informant before Thórfinn's death in 1065. Both Hrafn and Thórkell had kinship reasons to be interested in Are Mársson's fate.

Cristne saga, the saga that relates the story of the conversion of Iceland to Christianity, lists Are Mársson as one of "the mightiest chiefs" in the West Quarter of Iceland in 982 when the first missionary arrived at the island—the same year that Erik sailed out of Breidafjord to explore Greenland. Although he does not appear in the record of Erik before 982, Are Mársson must have been interested in Erik's discoveries and his plan to colonise Greenland. Are Mársson was second cousin to Leif and Thórvald Eiríksson, the later explorers of Vinland. The circumstances of his departure from Breidafjord are unknown, but his personal relationships make it possible that he disappeared on a voyage to Eiríksfjord in Greenland.

The second drift voyage that made a far western landfall was that of Biorn Breidavíkinga-kappe, as related in *Eyrbyggia saga*. Vigfusson dates this voyage to about 998, although, again, it could have taken place soon after Erik the Red's colonisation fleet sailed for Greenland in 986. The saga record is brief: "Biorn rode south to Hraunhaven to a ship, and took a berth to go abroad that summer. And they were rather late getting ready for sea. They got a north-east wind, and it blew for a long time that summer, and this ship was not heard of for a long time thereafter."[75]

Biorn's fate was unknown until "late in the days of King Olaf the Saint," who ruled Norway between 1015 and 1030. The story is told in *Eyrbyggia saga* on the authority of Godleif Godlaugsson of Borgarholt, the third of the drift voyagers to the west. Godlief appears briefly in *Landnámabók*, and *Eyrbyggia saga* introduces him as "a great merchant-trader who had a big ship." The saga relates his transatlantic experiences as follows:

> Godleif went on a trading voyage west to Dublin [from Norway?], and when he sailed from the west he was bound to Iceland. He sailed west about Ireland, and he got easterly and north-easterly winds, and they were driven far west into the sea, and into the south-west, so that they did not know where the land lay; and now much of the summer was past, and they made many vows to get off the sea, and now it came about that they got sight of land. It was a big land, but they did not know what land it was. Godleif and his men took this plan, to sail to the land, because they were tired of striving any longer against the might of the ocean. They got a good harbour there, and when they had been off this land a little while, there came men to see them. They knew no one, but they rather thought they were speaking Irish. Soon there came to them such a great gathering that it came to many hundreds. They laid hands on them all and bound them, and drove them up into the country. Then they were brought to a moot, and judgment given them. They understood that some men wished them to be slain, but some wished that they be sent to divers quarters to become slaves.

They were saved from either fate by the arrival of "a big and soldierly man, but much stricken in age and white of hair," to whom the people deferred. He spoke to the captive Icelanders in the Northern tongue and "asked minutely after every great man in Borgarfjord and Breidafjord" in such a manner as to convince Godleif that this was indeed the long-lost Biorn Breidavíkinga-kappe.

> Meanwhile, the people of the country were calling upon him to make a decision on the ship's crew, upon which he left them and called out by name twelve of his men, and sat a long while talking. Returning,

he spoke to Godleif and those that were with him: "We men of this country have talked over your case a good deal, and the men of this country have given over your case to my ruling. Now I will give you leave to go wherever you wish, and though you may think a greater part of the summer gone, yet I will give you this counsel to get away, for the people here are faithless and ill to deal with, and they deem the law is already broken in your case. . . . There are here in this country mightier men than I, that would give small quarter to strangers, though they are not living near where you have come. . . . I forbid any man to come to see me, for it is the worst voyage unless you take the way by good luck and land where you landed. And this land is also bad in harbours, and war certain to all kinds of aliens, save it happens as it has happened on this occasion." Then this man had their ship made ready for them, and stayed with them till the wind came fair and favourable for them to put to sea. Godleif and his men made it to Ireland late at harvest-time, and were in Dublin through the winter; but in the summer they sailed to Iceland.[76]

Scholars have generally treated the stories of Are Mársson's, Biorn Breidavíkinga-kappe's, and Godleif Godlaugsson's drift voyages to far western landfalls with great caution, pointing to literary motifs to justify suspicion of the collective historicity of the tales. Placed in the locational and temporal context of the colonisation of Greenland and the series of events that constitute the Vinland cycle, however, the drift voyages invite serious examination. The distance between Ireland and Hvítramannaland in terms of "six days' sail west" falls into the miraculous category, but if the direction was valid, Are Mársson's landfall should have been on the coast of southern Labrador, the part of Markland where Thórfinn Karlsefni learned of Hvítramannaland from the young Skræling captives, according to *Eiríks saga Rauda*.

The accounts of the drift voyages of Biorn Breidavíkinga-kappe and Godleif Godlaugsson in *Eyrbyggia saga* both mention prolonged periods of easterly and northeasterly winds, suggesting weather patterns of persistent zonal flow similar to those that affected Naddod the Faeroese and Gardar Svávarson in the first stage of the Iceland cycle, but over much greater distances. The notion that such winds would lead to far western landfalls is remarkable in a thirteenth-century saga. There are no hints of an encounter with an earthly paradise or with angels with flaming swords in Godleif's account; instead, it has the laconic style of the early sagas, with the ring of a ship's log to it.

The ethnographic descriptions in *Eyrbyggia saga* have received less attention than similar material in the Vinland sagas. There is no mention of Hvítramannaland in Godleif's account of his and Biorn's coincidental landfall, but his speculation that the natives were speaking Irish (Gaelic) parallels the association of Are Mársson's Hvítramannaland with Ireland the Great. Whether these were echoes of the *papar* in the Norse mind or were reflections of Hrafn Hlymreks-fare Oddsson's and Godleif Godlaugsson's connections with trading centers in Ireland remains undetermined. But Godleif's notion of Gaelic-speaking natives is reminiscent of John Dee's Welsh-speaking Indians and David Macpherson's Icelandic-speaking Beothuks.

The deference with which Biorn was treated by the native people bears a striking parallel with the "great esteem" in which Are was held. Godleif's description of the "moot" where their fate was to be decided and his statement that Biorn "called out by name twelve of his men, and sat a long while talking," have the marks of an Indian council. The portrait of European castaways being held against their will, possibly enslaved, identifying with their captors, assimilating culturally, and rising to power and influence among them is common in post-Columbian history.

Godleif Godlaugsson's voyage, if it happened, must be regarded as a major feat of North Atlantic navigation, involving a double crossing of the ocean, from and returning to Dublin without intervening landfall. Both Bjarni Herjolfsson and Thórfinn Thórdarson had already sailed between Vinland and Norway, but with intervals in Greenland, and possibly Iceland, on the way.

Finally, it should be noted that the Hvítramannaland cycle never progressed beyond the stage of accidental discovery. No subsequent exploration took place, and if *Grænlendinga saga* and *Eyrbyggia saga* are to be taken seriously, the reason would seem to lie in the fact that the western shores of the Atlantic were perceived to be inhabited by people capable of thwarting attempts to colonise by small and unsupported parties. That, at least, was the advice of Biorn Breidavíkinga-kappe and the conclusion of Thórfinn, who made an attempt and withdrew. In effect, the Vinland cycle, though completed, was abortive. Hvítramannaland, apart from its brief appearances in *Landnámabók* and *Eiríks saga Rauda*, played no part in the geographical lore of the North.

Eirík, the Greenlanders' Bishop
A century passed before anything more was heard of Vinland or other lands west of Greenland. Then in 1121, according to the fourteenth-century

Annals of Iceland, Eirík the bishop voyaged west to search for Vinland. Some have erected on this brief statement theories of a search for a lost colony of Norsemen and a mission to convert the heathen, but all that is known positively about Bishop Eirík is that he was a native Icelander and is listed in *Landnámabók* as Eirík Gnúpsson, the Greenlanders' bishop, and that he went to the Greenland colony in 1112 or 1113.

Inspiration and authority for Eirík the bishop's voyage began during the incumbency of Gizur Isleifsson as bishop of Iceland (1082–1118), who was responsible for establishing the diocese at Hólar in 1106 by carving off the North Quarter, the most populous part of Iceland. He may have been responsible for dispatching Eirík Gnúpsson to Greenland on a similar mission.

Whatever the result of Bishop Eirík's voyage in search of Vinland—there is no record of his return—it was soon followed by a session of the Greenland parliament, called by Sokki Thórisson of Brattahlíd, the principal man of the colony, to announce that he wanted his compatriots to contribute funds for the establishment of a bishop's see.

The statement that Bishop Eirík Gnúpsson sailed "in search of Vinland" implies that the Norse Greenlanders of 1121 had no recent experience of Vinland, that his enterprise was a voyage of rediscovery and exploration, with no men in his crew that had been there before. Lack of a Norse Greenland presence at Leifsbúdir/Straumfjord between 1013 and 1121 is confirmed by the archaeological evidence, which indicates that the bishop's expedition never reached its destination.

The Markland Ship

Eirík Gnúpsson's attempt to rediscover Vinland in 1121 is the last mention of Vinland as a practical objective for Norse exploration. It also indicates a century of inactivity since the attempt to colonise Leif Eiríksson's *landnám* in the New World. But the arrival of a small Greenlandic vessel at a haven on the southern side of the Snaefelsnes peninsula in 1347 provides indications of a continuing knowledge of western shores identifiable with Labrador and of the navigation required to reach them more than three centuries after the voyages of the Eiríkssons and Thórfinn Thórdarson. The record appears in two versions of the Icelandic annals. From *Flateyjarannáll*, "At this time came a ship from Greenland, which had made a voyage to Markland, and had eighteen men on board." From *Skálholtsannáll hinn forni*, "There came also a ship from Greenland, smaller in size than the small Icelandic boats; she came into the outer Straumfjord, and had no anchor. There were seventeen men on board. They had made a voyage to Markland, but were afterwards storm-driven here."[77]

Vestrebygd, the Western Colony established by Erik the Red in Greenland, had been overrun by the Inugsuk bands of the Thule or proto-Inuit culture by 1342, five years before this drift voyage occurred. The crew of the Markland ship must, then, have been from the Eystrebygd, or Eastern Colony. This is significant because it indicates that the Greenland Norse had maintained interest in the territory to the west and southwest across the Greenland Sea (Davis Strait). That interest has been generally accepted as focused on the acquisition of timber for subsistence and furs for European markets.

Timber was a necessity for shipbuilding, and the forests of Markland/Labrador were more accessible and more dependable than those of distant Scandinavia. Cargos could have been obtained by sending logging crews for short spells to minimise hazards of encounters with natives. Shipbuilding in Markland, as well as fur trapping, would probably have been too risky. Fur trading with natives, on the other hand, might have been possible, in which case the occasional small ship, such as the Markland vessel, might well have been built on the spot. Whether such ventures were frequent or occasional and whether they occurred throughout the three centuries since the discovery of Markland are moot questions. Markland, after all, might have been "lost" and rediscovered on several occasions during that interval of time, as seen in Bishop Eirík's voyage "in search of Vinland." The answers were known at the time in Greenland and to Icelanders and at Bergen in Norway, for—according to *Gottskálksannáll*—the crewmen of the Markland ship "were brought the next year [1348] to the King's court at Bergen by a prominent Icelander."[78]

That the Greenland Norse made occasional visits to the Markland/Labrador coast before 1347 may suggest an explanation for an entry in Bishop Gisli Oddsson's annals, written in the 1630s but probably based on records from the cathedral at Skálholt: "1342: The inhabitants of Greenland of their own will abandoned the true faith and the Christian religion, having already forsaken all good ways and true virtues, and joined themselves with the folk of America. Some consider too that Greenland lies closely adjacent to the western regions of the world. From this it came about that the Christians gave up their voyaging to Greenland."[79]

The reference to "America"—a name first applied to North America by the cartographer Gerardus Mercator in 1538—is anachronistic and must represent a translation of the Icelandic "Skrælinga" or a similar term. Did the original source refer to the Thule Eskimos, who had been encroaching on Norse Greenland since 1200 and were probably thought to have originated in the west? Or did it refer to people encountered in those western lands, particularly in Markland? Perhaps the Markland ship represented some form of free-trading in defiance of the trade monopoly held by the late medieval church, necessitating some accommodation to the culture of the Markland Eskimos. This, at least, would help to explain the ecclesiastical condemnation in the annals. It might also explain the disruption of authorised ventures from Europe, implicit in the last sentence of the entry.

The English Minorite

The appearance of the Markland crew at the court in Bergen apparently revived, for a time, official Norwegian interest in the western Atlantic. In October 1354 Magnus Eriksson, king of Norway and Sweden, ordered Poul Knutsson to take the royal *knorr* and sail for Greenland "for the sake of our predecessor who established Christianity in Greenland . . . and which we will not let perish in our day."[80] There is no evidence that this voyage was ever undertaken, but the royal *knorr* has been associated with the report that "in A.D. 1360 there had come to these Northern Islands an English Minorite from Oxford, who was a good astronomer etc. Leaving the rest of the party who had come to the Islands, he journeyed further through the North etc., and put into writing all the wonders of those islands, and gave the King of England [Edward III] this book which he called *Inventio fortunatae*, which book began at the last climate, that is to say latitude 54°, continuing to the Pole."[81]

John Dee, to whom we are indebted for the preservation of this report, believed that the "Northern Islands" included Greenland as well as fictitious islands within the seventy-eighth degree of latitude. His immediate source was Gerardus Mercator, who wrote to him in 1577 in response to a request for information about the sources used for "that strange plat of the Septentrionall Ilands," Mercator's map of the Arctic region from 70° north to the Pole, which appeared on his world map of 1569. Mercator gave *his* source as one Jacobus Cnoyen van Tsertoghenbosche, who, he says, "travelled the world like Mandeville but described what he saw with better judgment." Cnoyen, writing in Flemish, gave *his* sources as *Gestae Arturi* (Exploits of Arthur), of unknown authorship, and *Inventio fortunatae*, written by the English Minorite between 1360 and 1377, the last year of the reign of Edward III, the English king who revived the cult of King Arthur. Cnoyen, who appears to have been a contemporary of the English Minorite and who may have been in the service of Edward's Flemish queen, Philippa of Hainaut, also quoted a priest from the "Northern Regions" whom he had met at the Norwegian court in 1364 as his source for the information about the arrival and activities of the Minorite in the "Northern Islands." The priest possessed an astrolabe obtained from the Minorite.[82]

Gestae Arturi, the Minorite's *Inventio fortunatae*, and Cnoyen van Tsertoghenbosche's *Itinerarium* are all lost medieval texts. The information in Mercator's letter—in contrast with the sources of Bishop Eirík's voyage of exploration and the arrival of the Markland ship in Iceland—is unverifiable. Mercator's "strange plat" is accompanied by a legend that repeats his sources and that was translated into English by Richard Hakluyt. The Minorite is described as "a certain English Frier, a Franciscan ["Minoritam," in Latin], and a Mathematician of Oxford [who] came into those Islands in the yeere 1360, who leaving them, & passing further by his magical Arte, described all those places that he sawe, & tooke the height [i.e., latitude] of them with his astrolabe, according to the forme that I have set down in my map, and as I have taken it out of the aforesaid Jacob Cnoyen."[83]

The identity of the English Minorite has been a matter of discussion since 1577, the best suggestion being Hugh of Ireland, a widely traveled Franciscan who was "said to have flourished in 1360 A.D. in the reign of King Edward III" and who "committed to paper whatever he saw on his journey with the greatest care, . . . wrote a certain journey in one volume . . . now [earlier than 1557] nothing remains of his unrewarded labours."[84] There is only a hint that his "one volume" might have been the missing *Inventio fortunatae*. Mercator and Dee were fortunate to have Cnoyen's *Itinerarium* as a secondary source.

Interest in *Inventio fortunatae* and the English Minorite focuses primarily on Cnoyen's assertion that the description of the "Northern Regions" began at 54° north, well below the bounding parallel of Mercator's "strange plat" (70° north) and considerably below the southern tips of Iceland (63° north) and Greenland (60° north). On the European side of the Atlantic this parallel cuts through the northern parts of Ireland and England, and on the American side it enters the continent at Cape Porcupine—Kjalarnes and the Furdustrandir in Markland of the sagas—just south of the entrance to Hamilton Inlet and Lake Melville. If the English Minorite did visit the Eystrebygd, the principal Norse colony in Greenland, the reference to the fifty-fourth parallel could indicate a journey north round Baffin Bay to Helluland and down the saga route as far as Markland on the southeastern (Labrador) shore of Davis Strait.[85]

If such was the case, the bizarre features of Mercator's concept of the high Arctic—the encompassing mountain range "almost all rock bare of vegetation," the indrawing sea "all ice from October to March," a climate of "almost always misty and dull weather," channels through the mountain rim "some two, some one, some three kennings wide" (20–60 nautical miles), a country where "beyond 70 or 78 degrees of latitude there is no human habitation" but where "ship's planking and balks which had been used in big ships" were found "further inland," indicating "with certainty that there had formerly been habitation there but the people had now gone" (Vestrebygd?), and where natives "not above 4 feet tall" (Mercator's "pygmeys") were met—these features might well be reflections of the shrinking world of the Greenland Norse.[86] But if this speculation concerning the northern explorations of the English Minorite in the early 1360s is dismissed, the Markland ship of 1347 marks the last contact of medieval Europe with the North American mainland.

Mercator, however, was not the first geographer to interpret the work of the English Minorite cartographically. Martin Behaim imposed it on his famous Nuremberg globe in 1492, and Johann Ruysch—claiming to have read *Inventio fortunatae*—produced an equidistant conic projection of the Arctic region, inset on his "World Map" of 1508, which was evidently used as a model by Mercator. Greenland ("Gruenlant") and "Terra Nova" both appear on Ruysch's map as eastern extensions of Asia, the latter between 42° and 51° north; between them lies the "Sinus Gruenlant" (Greenland Gulf), which contains an island at 56°–58° north inhabited by people called "Arumfeie." A similar term, "Aronphei," appears on one of Ruysch's fictitious Arctic islands. Mercator, following the model, inscribed one of his Arctic islands with a legend: "Here live pygmies, at most 4 feet tall, who are like those in Greenland called *Screlinger*." He placed the same Icelandic term, "Screlingers," on Greenland, where it appears on his principal map, drawn on his famous projection. The term, which does not appear in his letter to John Dee, was probably derived from *Historia Norvegiae*, but it is also possible that he obtained it from Cnoyen's *Itinerarium* and ultimately from the English Minorite or the priest with the astrolabe.[87] Combined with Ruysch's earlier version, this would be the strongest indication that the English Minorite had indeed carried his astrolabe from the Eystrebygd to Markland and had encountered Thule people on both sides of the Davis Strait.

Norse Frontier Cycles and Climatic Fluctuations
The Markland ship and the English Minorite close the book on Greenland Norse contact with North America. When Norse discovery, exploration, and colonisation in the North Atlantic is placed in the context of what is known about the climatic history of the region, a remarkable fit is observed, suggesting that part of the explanation for the series of successes and failures of the Norse lies in climatic change. The historical data correlates nicely with scientific evidence of variations in mean temperature found in ice cores taken from the Greenland ice cap.[88]

The activities of the Irish missionary-saints, such as Brendan and Columba, in the waters around the British Isles occurred during a long warm phase that ended in the middle of the seventh century. The hazardous curragh voyages of the Irish monks to the Faeroes and Iceland between A.D. 725 and 820 coincided with the longest and warmest phase, at the peak of which the Viking raids on the British Isles began (793). Of the Norse cycles of activity, the Faeroes cycle, between 820 and 860, opened at the end of the long warm phase and closed in the middle of the short cold phase that followed. The Iceland cycle began in the middle of the cold phase, its colonisation period correlating with the onset and peak of the next warm phase (874–935). The next warm phase, which peaked around 1000, embraced the exploration and colonisation of Greenland, the Hvítramannaland drift voyages, and the Vinland cycle of events (986–1025). Bishop Eirík Gnúpsson's Vinland voyage in 1121 occurred at the peak of a short warm phase around that date. All of these phases fell within the Little (Medieval) Optimum, which came to an end in the middle of the thirteenth century. The voyage of the Markland ship in 1347 and the Minorite's exploration of the inner recesses of Baffin Bay and coastal Labrador in the early 1360s coincided with the coldest phase of the ensuing Little Ice Age. It is difficult to avoid the conclusion that temperature trends had some bearing on the successes and failures in the Norse record of colonisation.

The Portuguese, Danish, and English Experience before Columbus

As the curtain fell on the historical record of the Greenland colony in 1410 it rose on the record of the maritime enterprises of European countries in the North Atlantic. Although relatively little is known of these activities, there

CLIMATIC CHANGE

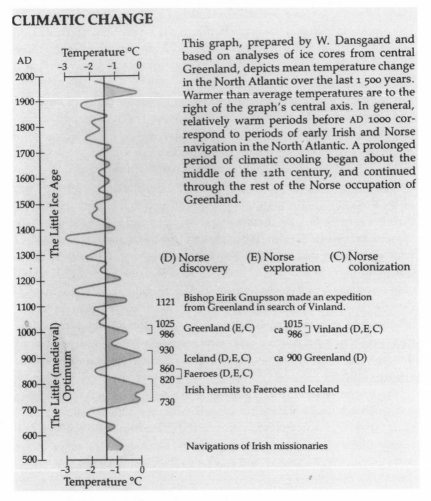

This graph, prepared by W. Dansgaard and based on analyses of ice cores from central Greenland, depicts mean temperature change in the North Atlantic over the last 1 500 years. Warmer than average temperatures are to the right of the graph's central axis. In general, relatively warm periods before AD 1000 correspond to periods of early Irish and Norse navigation in the North Atlantic. A prolonged period of climatic cooling began about the middle of the 12th century, and continued through the rest of the Norse occupation of Greenland.

(D) Norse discovery (E) Norse exploration (C) Norse colonization

1121 Bishop Eirik Gnupsson made an expedition from Greenland in search of Vinland.

1025 / 986 Greenland (E,C)   ca 1015 / 986 Vinland (D,E,C)

930

Iceland (D,E,C)   ca 900 Greenland (D)

860 / 820 Faeroes (D,E,C)

Irish hermits to Faeroes and Iceland

730

Navigations of Irish missionaries

1.6 Climatic Background to the Irish and Norse Experience in the North Atlantic. Reproduced by permission from The Historical Atlas of Canada *(University of Toronto Press, 1987).*

is sufficient evidence that Portuguese, Danish, and English sailors were active in the North Atlantic; in addition, there is speculation that some of these (particularly the Bristolmen sailing out of Bristol, England) may have made contacts with North America before the Columbian landing in 1492.

The fifteenth century, although it ended with the Spanish triumph in the Caribbean, was essentially Portugal's century in ocean exploration.

The Portuguese capture of Ceuta on the African shore of the Straits of Gibraltar, in which Prince Henry the Navigator participated, was followed in 1418–25 by the settlement of Porto Santo and Madeira, both uninhabited. It was the first state-sponsored colonisation for Portugal and initiated a long process of exploration in two directions.

A spasmodic and painful advance southward down the Atlantic shores of continental Africa began under Prince Henry, after he instituted his school for navigators and geographers at Sagres in the Algarve, and reached Sierra Leone in 1460, the year of his death. It continued with the "African Contract" held by Fernão Gomes, a merchant adventurer of Lisbon, between 1469 and 1475 and reached the islands of Fernando Póo, Príncipe, and São Tomé in the Gulf of Guinea, just north of the equator. In 1487–88 Bartolomeu Dias passed beyond the southern tip of Africa and reached the vicinity of the Great Fish River, preparing the way for Vasco da Gama's opening of the trade route across the Indian Ocean to India and the Spice Islands.[89]

Exploration to the west and northwest—the other direction in which Portugal looked during the fifteenth century—was a by-product of the thrust down the African coast. As such, and despite its initial success, its hypothetical nature—as distinct from the reality of Africa—was less attractive to Portuguese adventurers and never drew the strong official support enjoyed by the exploration to the south. Portuguese interest in the Spanish Canaries may have led to the discovery of the Madeira group in latitude 32°–33° north some 360 miles out from the northwestern coast of Africa and some 240 miles due north from Tenerife in the Canaries. Seeking the latitude on which one's destination lay was an old navigational practice, but in this case it would have given the pilot the added advantage of cutting across the southward sweep of the Canary Current until the midlatitude westerlies were gained for the run into the Portuguese coast. Instead of arduous short-tacking upcurrent, the technique that developed from this experience involved a long tack out into midocean.[90]

Once the colonisation of the Madeiras was under way in the 1420s, the adoption of a "Madeira tack" to the northwest as far as latitude 38° north led to the midocean discovery of Santa Maria and São Miguel in the Azores, in 1427. The discovery has been attributed to Diogo da Silves based on a sea chart drawn in 1439—the first to show the new archipelago in true geographical position. Colonisation began in 1431–32 under the direction of Frei Gonçalo Velho, one of Prince Henry's sea captains on the African coast and a candidate for the Azorean discoveries of the following year.[91]

The discovery of Terceira, Graciosa, São Jorge, Pico, and Faial—the central Azores—followed within the next few years. The archipelago took final shape in 1452 or shortly before, when Diogo de Teive, sailing from the still uninhabited Faial, discovered the western islands of Corvo and Flores.[92] On the African coast, exploration—now equipped with Prince Henry's revolutionary caravels, which were replacing the old square-rigged *varinels* and *barcas*—had barely reached the mouth of the Gambia and had yet to enter the Gulf of Guinea.

In 1563 António Galvão's *Tratado dos descobrimentos* (Treatise of the discoveries) introduced an account of the discovery of the legendary island of Antillia in 1447: "In this year [1447] . . . there came a Portugall ship through the streight of Gibraltar; and being taken with a great tempest, was forced to runne westwards more then willingly the men would, and at last they fell upon an island which had seven cities, and the people spake the Portugall toong, and they demanded if the Moores did yet trouble Spaine, whence they had fled for the loss which they had received by the death of the king of Spaine, Don Roderigo."[93]

Galvão equated this with the true Antilles despite the fact that no Portuguese-speaking natives had been found in the Spanish colonies up to 1563. His reference was to the potent legend of the Island of the Seven Cities, colonised from Oporto in A.D. 743 by seven Spanish bishops and their following, in flight from Moorish conquest, and a prominent feature in the late-medieval cartography of the Atlantic. Like Prince Madoc's Welsh-speaking Indians, the mythical Seven Cities retreated westward as the European frontier in the New World advanced and were last sought, as the Seven Golden Cities of Cíbola, in what is now the American Southwest. Columbus, as reported by Bartolomé de Las Casas in his *Historia de las Indias* (c. 1559–60), knew of a version of the voyage of 1447 that differed from Galvão's account in a number of details, including its departure point at Oporto—which suggests that it was but sailors' folklore.[94] A ship storm-driven into the Atlantic, whether from the straits or Oporto, does not fit the pattern of Portuguese exploration that led to the discovery of the Madeiras and the Azores.

The emergence of first the Madeira group and then the Azores must have impressed Prince Henry and the members of the Sagres school as a promising feature of their program of exploration. Prince Henry is reported—by Diogo Gomes, one of his last sea captains, to Martin Behaim in 1484—to have expressed interest in knowing "the distant regions of the western ocean if by chance there might be islands or *terra firma* beyond what Ptolemy described" and, accordingly, to have sent out caravels "in search of lands."[95] Whether this was true or not, the Azores, and particularly the island of Terceira, became the base for exploration in the western Atlantic during the latter half of the fifteenth century. Mercantile contacts between the Azores and the Port of Bristol, and dynastic connections among the royal families of Portugal, England, and Denmark,[96] appear to have led to some level of international collaboration.

Didrik Pining is on record as governor or chief magistrate *(hirdstjore)* of Iceland for the Danish Crown in 1478,[97] but a report of a voyage by him and Hans Pothorst in 1472 or 1473 is found only in a letter from Carsten Grip, burgomaster of Kiel, to King Christian III. The letter, dated 3 March 1551, refers to "the two admirals [*sceppere*] Pyningk and Poidthorsth, who were sent out by your majesty's royal grandfather, King Christiern the First [1448–81], at the request of his majesty the king of Portugal [Afonso V, 1438–81, nephew of Prince Henry] with certain ships to explore new countries and islands in the north, have raised on the rock Wydthszerck [Hvítserk], lying off Greenland and towards Sniefeldsiekel [Snaefelsjokul] in Iceland on the sea, a great sea-mark on account of the Greenland pirates, who with many small ships without keels fall in large numbers upon other ships."[98]

Burgomaster Grip's reference to liaison between Denmark and Portugal for ocean exploration has become the basis for speculation that Afonso V's emissary to the Danish court was João Vaz Côrte-Real of Terceira and that Côrte-Real may have accompanied Pining and Pothorst on their voyage of discovery. It has also been suggested that their pilot may have been John Skolp. There is nothing in the Portuguese, Danish, or Icelandic records to support this conflation of voyages, which, in any case, are hypothetical. João Vaz Côrte-Real is recorded as having held a captaincy on Terceira, later on São Jorge, between 1474 and his death in 1496, but the basis for his alleged voyage of 1474—on which he is supposed to have discovered Newfoundland—first appeared in Gaspar Fructuoso's *Saudades da terra*, written about 1590. The tale that he was accompanied by Alvaro Martins Homem dates from 1717.[99] As for a voyage by Johannes Scolvus (John Skolp) in 1476, the only evidence is an inscription on one of the globes made by Gerardus Mercator in 1537: "Quij populi ad quos Joes Scoluss danus pervenit circa annum 1476" (The Quij people, reached by the Dane Johannes Scolvus about the year 1476).[100] The inscription was placed on one of the hypothetical polar islands northwest of Greenland, which may account for its later appearance in association with Helluland of the sagas and Frobisher's Baffin Island on Hans Poulsen Resen's "Map of the North" of 1605.[101] The suggestion that Scolvus the Dane may have been associated with Côrte-Real the Azorian relies on the notion that Gemma Frisius's globe reflected Portuguese influence.

Until 1778 the view of English historians was that England entered the competition for ocean discovery and exploration abruptly in 1497 with King Henry VII's letters-patent, dated 5 March 1496 [1497], to John Cabot (Giovanni Caboto) the Venetian.[102] In 1778 James Nasmith of Cambridge published his *Itineraria Symonis Simeonis et Willelmi de Worcestre*, including William Botoner of Worcester's manuscript from Corpus Christi College, which indicated that the first attempt was made in 1480, in the last years of the reign of King Edward IV (1461–83). In translation it read: "1480, on July 15, the ship . . . of John Jay the younger, of the burden of 80 tons began a voyage from the port of the Kingrode of Bristol to the island of Brasylle beyond the western part of Ireland, to traverse the seas . . . and Thlyde [John Lloyd] is the most expert shipmaster in all England; and news came to Bristol on Monday the 18th of September that in the said ship they sailed the seas for about nine months [*sic*, weeks], and did not find the island, but were driven back by storms to a port . . . in Ireland for the refreshment of the ship and the men."[103]

The Welsh shipmaster John Lloyd had made a number of appearances in the customs ledgers of Bristol between 1461 and 1479, but the ledger entries for 1480 are missing. The records of the Commission of the Exchequer for 1483, however, contain an account of an examination held in Bristol into a planned voyage by Thomas Croft for "the intent to serch and fynd a certaine Ile callid the Isle of Brasile."[104] "Brasil" was one of the legendary islands of the cartography of the North Atlantic, put variously west of Ireland and west of Cape Saint Vincent at the southwestern corner of Portugal and sometimes appearing at both locations on the same map.[105]

Taken alone, the English voyages of 1480 and 1481 indicate only that Bristol merchants such as John Jay the Younger and Thomas Croft were willing to sponsor exploratory voyages, much as the recipients of Portuguese grants were expected to undertake. Their relevance to the discovery—or the rediscovery—of North America lies in documents of 1497 and 1498 commenting on John Cabot's successful voyage of the earlier year. A letter written to the "Lord Grand Admiral" of Spain (probably Christopher Columbus) in the winter of 1497–98 by John Day, an English merchant in Andalusia, refers to Cabot's landfall as "the cape nearest to Ireland . . . 1800 miles west of Dursey Head which is in Ireland" (51.5° north). Day then

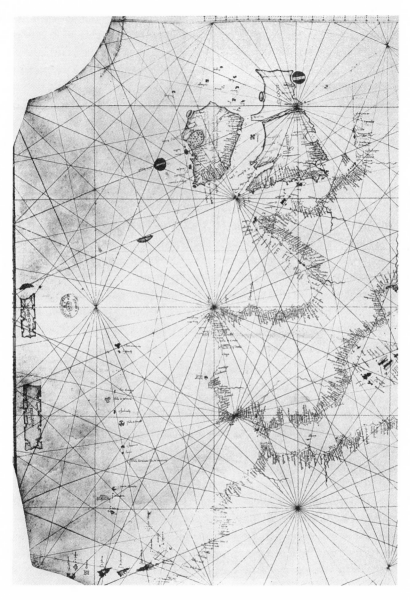

1.7 "Islands of the Western Ocean" (Andrea Benincasa, 1470). Benincasa's map shows several Atlantic islands, most notably the isles of Hy Brasil (off the Irish coast) and Antilla (in the southwestern Atlantic). By permission of The British Library.

makes a remarkable statement: "It is considered certain that the cape of the said land was found and discovered in the past by the men of Bristol who found 'Brasil' as your Lordship well knows. It was called the Island of Brasil, and it is assumed and believed to be the mainland that the men from Bristol found."[106]

Such discovery must have occurred after 1481 and before 1496, the year of Cabot's aborted voyage—also known only from Day's letter. The only source that casts any further light on Day's claim—that John Cabot's discovery of North America had been preempted by an earlier Bristol voyage—is a report from Pedro de Ayala, the Spanish ambassador at the Tudor court, to the Spanish monarchs, Ferdinand of Aragon and Isabella of Castile. Dated 25 July 1498, this report alleged, "For the last seven years the people of Bristol have equipped two, three, four caravels to go in search of the island of Brazil and the Seven Cities [Antillia] according to the fancy of this Genoese."[107] Ayala seems to confirm that the Bristol merchants explored the North Atlantic for discovery and trade. But he gives no support to John Day's claim that a discovery had actually been made. Ayala, however, was a newcomer to the Tudor court, recently arrived from his post as Spanish ambassador to Scotland, and his intelligence may have been defective.

Day's letter, which emerged from the archives in 1956, has an air of greater authority than Ayala's report in reference to the Island of Brasil. If true, it requires reinterpretation of Ayala's statement. It also invites reconsideration of Robert Thorne the Younger's statement concerning his father, Robert Thorne, in a plan for Arctic exploration submitted to the English ambassador to Spain in 1527: "My father . . . with an other Marchaunt of Brystow named Hughe Elliot were the discoverers of the Newfound Landes, of the which there is no dowt . . . yf the mariners wolde then have bene ruled & followed their Pylots mynde, the Land of the Indians from whence all the Gold commeth had bene ours: for all is one Coaste."[108] The elder Robert Thorne was a merchant-trader between Bristol and Portugal for almost thirty years beginning in 1479 and was particularly active in 1492–93; he died in 1519, the year Hugh Eliot first appeared in the Bristol customs records.[109] Thorne could have had a share in John Jay's enterprise in 1480 or Thomas Croft's in 1481; both he and Eliot could well have been involved in voyages of discovery in the early 1490s, as suggested by Ayala.

In 1580 John Dee listed this claim, in Queen Elizabeth I of England's *Title Royal* after Prince Madoc: "Circa An. 1494. Mr Robert Thorn his father, and Mr Eliot of Bristow, discovered Newfound Lande." Dee's ascription of an approximate date for the Thorne-Eliot discovery is not supported, however, by any of the four surviving versions of the 1527 plan,[110] and it is difficult to determine from the text of the younger Thorne's statement in 1527 whether his intention was to refer to an event before Columbus's voyage (1492), Cabot's voyage (1497), or Cortés's conquest of Mexico (1519). The simplest and most probable solution, in the absence of solid documentation, is to assume that Thorne and Eliot were leading merchants in the group backing Cabot and that they accompanied him in 1497 or 1498.[111]

The Day, Ayala, and Thorne statements have been subjected to numerous attempts to reconcile them.[112] Connections to Portuguese exploration, to Bristol trade with Iceland and possibly with Greenland, to the development of an early English fishery at Newfoundland, and to John Cabot and later voyages have been debated, but English exploration between 1481 and 1496 left no legacy in the emerging cartography of the eastern shores or in the archaeological record of North America. No descriptions survive from whatever successes may have been achieved. Only the aboriginal peoples and the Greenland and Iceland Norse can demonstrate a claim to have preceded Columbus.

No credence can be placed on post-Columbian claims for legendary discoveries and colonisations of the Americas in pre-Columbian times, nor is there any evidence for Portuguese, Danish, or English discoveries in the latter half of the fifteenth century. This situation could change dramatically—as it did with the identification of the L'Anse aux Meadows site—if such evidence ever emerges.

The exploration of America, in its most dramatic form, belongs to the so-called aboriginal peoples of the two continents, overwhelmingly to the ancestral Clovis people and their American Indian descendents and, in the Arctic, to the Paleo-Eskimo/Dorset pioneers. The terminology of the archaeologist and the prehistorian obscures the fact that particular explorations were carried out at particular times and in particular places by individual men and women whose names and personal histories are lost. In this record, the short-lived intrusion of the Norse can be seen only as peripheral and irrelevant, its impact minimal.

The Norse experience on the western shores of the Atlantic was also peripheral to European culture, in both time and place. The exploration of the western shores of Davis Strait, from Cape Dyer to points south and west of L'Anse aux Meadows, came when the Greenland colony was still in its infancy and incapable of sustaining colonisation over such extended distances. This must have been obvious to the would-be colonist Thórfinn Thórdarson, when he decided to withdraw from Leifsbúdir in the face of native hostility. Native hostility of a more sophisticated kind was ineffective in deterring his Viking ancestors from imposing themselves on Britain, Ireland, and the powerful Carolingian empire, but Greenland was far from Norway.

That Norse Greenlanders continued to visit North American shores for three and a half centuries, as indicated by the little Markland ship, seems to be undeniable. But the lack of evidence for any impact on the landscape or people of the new continent, the absence of any indication that trade goods reached the farms, churches, or monasteries of Greenland or were transmitted to European markets, argues that such visits were extremely infrequent—perhaps, as in the case of Bishop Eirík's search for Vinland, generations apart. There is little evidence for any degree of continuity in whatever contacts may have occurred. The Dorset and Indian "smelted metal" sites argue, perhaps, for limited contact in the "Ramah chert" region of Northern Labrador, just as the similar Thule sites argue for contact in Greenland. The onset of the Little Ice Age and its impact on the subsistence economy of the Greenland Norse, the loss of the Western Settlement by 1342, and the lack of commercial and ecclesiastical contact with Europe after 1410 removed any chance of renewed American exploration on the part of the beleaguered and ultimately doomed colony.

2 / Native North Americans' Cosmological Ideas and Geographical Awareness: Their Representation and Influence on Early European Exploration and Geographical Knowledge

G. MALCOLM LEWIS

If the earth's surface were homogeneous in every respect and all peoples were cognitively and culturally the same, there would be one earthwide environment and a simple set of recurring spatial relationships. There would then be no need for exploration or for geography. Indeed, geography would be inconceivable in that it would have no basis in reality. In fact, of course, the earth's surface, at whatever scale it is considered, is heterogeneous. Man's environments and the characteristics of particular places are diverse. Likewise, the spatial relationships between these environments are incredibly complex. Such diversity and complexity compel awareness by individuals. That awareness, when shared between them, may become formalized, institutionalized, and given a name: in the Graeco-Roman tradition, *geography*; in the Chinese tradition, *ti li*; in the much later Germanic tradition, *erdkunde*; and so on. In intellectually less developed cultures such awareness lacks a formal status but exists as part of uncategorized lore. Since people occupy different parts of a heterogeneous earth surface, exhibit a range of cognitive styles, and have achieved a diversity of cultural conditions, the content and structure of their awareness differs.

Inevitably, therefore, there are and always have been many geographies: different in content; different in structure; and different in the balance and relationship between components obtained through direct experience, those that are communicated by others and those that are derived by inference, based on supposition, or enshrined in myth. Regrettably, as our formal geography has become increasingly standardized, we in the Graeco-Roman–Euro-American tradition of knowledge have, until recently at least, consistently overlooked these intercultural differences in geographical epistemology, and for the most part, we continue to ignore their consequences.[1] Yet these consequences have been significant in several contexts, not the least during the so-called Age of Discovery when, in attempting to accelerate the process of obtaining information about areas until then unknown or little known to them, Europeans repeatedly sought and received information from preliterate native peoples. They integrated the received information into their emerging geographies of the newly faced *terrae semicognitae* (semiknown lands) on the assumption that native geographies were inferior in detail and precision but similar to their own in structure, metrics, and the categorization of phenomena. The converse assumption would have been truer. Although preliterate peoples possessed well-developed senses of geographical awareness and shared that awareness with most others within the group, the epistemologies whereby they knew and, in many cases, still know the earth's surface differed, often quite markedly, between neighbouring groups of natives and, even more radically, between the natives and the intrusive Europeans.

Place, space, and environment are three closely related and overlapping ways through which modern-day peoples categorize their world: modes by which they organize and structure much of the information received through the senses. A basic awareness of these modes is vital for survival, and their fuller appreciation is a necessary basis for much intellectual and aesthetic development. Such awareness is a product of cognition mediated by culture and, as such, is the focus of research by environmental and cultural psychologists. Awareness, however, is also important in that it manifests itself in behaviour. Man's awareness of space, place, and environment is reflected in such activities as hiding, shelter-seeking, procreating, fighting, hunting, herding, trading, settling, migrating, and, central to this chapter, exploring. These basic but nevertheless sophisticated forms of group behaviour would, of course, be impossible if awareness were entirely a cerebral process, locked in the minds of insular individuals. Within each human society, however, awareness is more or less shared between most sane and sentient adult members of the group. This sharing is by means of representations: gestures, dance, graphics, three-dimensional models, music, number, speech, and, in many but not all societies, writing. Through many generations, representations of their awarenesses

have enabled individuals operating in groups to achieve approximate consensus about what exists and what is supposed to exist. Between groups
characterized by different cultures, the degrees of consensus are, of
course, less—indeed, often markedly so.

Very occasionally, in the course of early contacts, differences between
the native and the European awareness of space, place, and environment
were recognized, at least by perceptive Europeans. In 1736, for example,
Cadwallader Colden, surveyor general of the province of New York, was
sent to "Survey several Tracts of Land" near Albany, land that had been
purchased by settlers from Mohawk Indians only a few months before.
Once he was in the field, Indians began to obstruct his work, protesting
that the boundaries he was pegging out on the ground in accordance with
the signed deeds were not always those to which they felt they had agreed.
He was sympathetic to the Mohawks and, in a memorial to the lieutenant
governor of the province, ascribed their protestations only in part to their
failure to comprehend the English language, in which the negotiations had
been conducted and the deeds written. Much of the misunderstanding was,
he felt, more fundamental, arising because "the Boundaries of the Land
said to be purchased are in several cases expressed by points or Degrees of
the Compass & by English Measures which are absolutely unknown to the
Indians."[2] The principles of Euclidean geometry whereby educated Europeans had for several generations delimited landholdings were not merely
strange to the Indians: they were incomprehensible. So were the principles
of surveying, whereby that geometry was imposed on the land. At the beginning of the eighteenth century, in what is now the upper Middle West,
the French explorer Baron Lahontan reported that the Indians considered
his graphometer to be "Divine, being unable to guess how we could know
the distance of places without measuring them [on the ground] by Cords
or Rods without there were some Supernatural Assistance."[3]

For every time that Europeans explicitly recognized the incongruity of
European and native geographies, there were many more times that they
recorded and interpreted information without appreciating that the epistemologies in which it had originated were different from their own. Itinerary—loosely speaking, distance—measure affords many examples. In Europe there were two coexisting but conceptually different types of metric
units: long-established time-distance units, defined in terms of distance
traveled in a period of time; and newer geodetic units, defined in terms of
degrees of the great circle. Although by the sixteenth century there was
still a diversity of leagues and so forth in use in western Europe, absolutes

2.1 "Europe, Asia, Africa, and America Bringing Intelligence to the Genius of the London Magazine." The London Magazine or Gentleman's Monthly Quarterly, *vol. 47 (1778). The illustration shows Europe obtaining information from natives of the four continents. The Native American informant is fourth from the left. Reproduced by permission of the Trustees of the National Library of Scotland.*

had been established for several of the smaller units of length. Further-more, scientists were beginning to develop a precise idea of the earth's dimensions, to redefine traditional units of linear measure on geodetic principles, and hence to calculate conversion factors between the still-numerous traditional units.[4] Native North Americans, however, used and have for the most part continued to use time-distance units of itinerary measure. Furthermore, these were not defined by the aggregation of stan-dardized smaller units equivalent to, for example, the European *pied, pas, pasos*, or several kinds of feet. Distances were expressed solely in terms of intervals of travel time: moons; days; overnight camps; pauses for smokes. Rarely were these measures qualified in terms of mode of travel, physique of the weakest member of the group, traversability of the terrain, direction of stream flow, weather conditions, or degree of urgency. Furthermore, in the absence of surveyed maps, Europeans could not take into account the planimetry of the routes and linear features such as rivers and coasts, for which time distances were specified, in trying to establish true distances.

Yet Europeans soon began and long continued to try to incorporate this kind of information, as received from Indians, in constructing their own geographies of North America. In 1587 Jacques Noel, who had been up the Saint Lawrence River with his uncle Jacques Cartier, indicated that it was "ten dayes journey from the Saults [above present-day Montreal] into the Great Lake" but regretted that he knew "not how many leagues they make to a dayes journey."[5] In the early 1540s, Hernando de Soto had considered a distance described as a ten-day journey by Indians in the lower Mississippi Valley to be "about eighty [presumably Castilian] leagues."[6] Pierre Radis-son, on entering Lake Ontario from the Saint Lawrence River, noted in consecutive sentences of his journal for 1656 that the Iroquois reckoned distance "by their [number of] days' journey" and that the lake was "above a hundred leagues in length and thirty in breadth."[7] In these instances, as in most others, the basis for conversion from native to European linear measure was not given. Neither was the European unit of distance de-fined. Radisson's league was presumably the *lieue commune*, "used by ex-plorers working in the name of France during the 1500s and early 1600s," in which case Lake Ontario was supposedly more than 276 English miles long and, at its widest, 83 English miles across. These distances are approx-imately 1.36 and 1.66 times greater, respectively, than those later estab-lished by precise survey. In 1657 Guillaume de l'Isle noted that in what is now eastern Canada, journeys by canoe averaged seven to eight *lieues* per day upstream but fifteen *lieues* per day downstream.[8] Such qualifying statements were not, however, generally given until much later.[9] For example, in 1841 Pierre de Smet, on the basis of his experiences in the Rocky Mountains in present-day Montana, Idaho, and Washington, reported that when "an Indian travels alone, his day's journey will be about fifty to sixty English miles but only fifteen or twenty when he moves with the camp."[10]

Recent estimates of the population of North America at the time of Columbus vary between 4.4 million and 18 million.[11] There were approximately two thousand mutually unintelligible languages and fourteen fundamentally different language groups.[12] Not surprisingly, therefore, in the early contact period, mistranslations and noncommunication of information transmitted by native peoples were common. In 1528, for example, Alvar Núñez Cabeza de Vaca advised against leaving the Gulf of Mexico for the interior because, in addition to other risks, it would not be possible "to communicate with the [unknown] Indians by use of speech." He feared that he and his companions would learn "but poorly" what they "desired to know of the land."[13] On this occasion, as on innumerable later occasions throughout the continent, sign language was used, but at best it was imprecise, particularly so in communicating spatial and qualitative information. Furthermore, although the elements of sign language are, at their purest, natural and almost universal, in practice native North American sign language had by the time of contact become conventionalized, increasing its utility between initiates but having the opposite consequences for strangers.

Failure of communication arising from an inability to translate and from mistranslation, albeit common and widespread, was not as serious as problems arising from fundamental differences between natives and Euro-Americans in the categorization of knowledge. The nature and significance of these differences did not begin to emerge until the development of the ethnosciences in the nineteenth century. Even now, the differences are difficult for both Euro-Americans and native peoples to comprehend. In retrospect, however, something of the enormity of the gap between native and European ways of categorizing the contents of their respective worlds is beginning to be recognized. For example, it seems very unlikely that before the first contact with Europeans in the early 1540s, the relatively culturally advanced Zuni Indians in present-day western New Mexico "could have conceptualized humans as opposed to animals, or could ever have conceived of the exploitation of nature by man; for the categories human, animal, nature, and man were all alien to the native classification of the universe insofar as this is known to linguists."[14] To a considerable extent, the Euro-American categories *real* and *mythical* would appear to have been alien to the Zunis or the Yuroks. "One can scarcely find a better illustration of the Indian concept of the mythical world that is blended with the actual physical earth than in the world map of the Yurok [Indians of northern California]. The small bounded earth known to the Yurok is there—the land with the Klamath River flowing across it, and the edge [the Pacific coastline] of the great saltwater ocean. For the rest it is all mythical, but in the Indian mind as real as the palpable earth," a circular "edge of the sky" at the outer edge of the saltwater ocean, breached by a "sky hole" that leads to an outer "ocean of pitch," near the outer edge of which in one direction is further good land, the home of certain myth characters. The ocean of pitch and the good land end at the circular edge of the universe.[15]

Even today, some maps made by Indians are, in Euro-American terms, almost entirely mythical in content. In the late 1970s, for example, at an official hearing on the proposed construction of a natural-gas pipeline across the Beaver Indian Reserve in northeastern British Columbia, the native people presented as evidence two kinds of maps. The first were land-use biographies. Using a topographic map as a base, each Indian plotted the limits of the areas he traditionally used for hunting, berry picking, fishing, and so forth. The second type of map was a much revered and rarely opened "dream map." Made on moosehide and carefully folded in a bundle, it had been derived in dreams. Among other things, it represented the trail to heaven. A corner of the map was missing, having been buried with someone who, it had been felt, might not otherwise have been able to find his way. Not surprisingly, the white officials, who do not appear to have been in any way confused by the land-use biographies, were at a loss to comprehend the content or the significance of the dream map.[16]

This chapter is ultimately concerned with the role and consequences of natives' geographical awareness for the European discovery and the Euro-American exploration of North America: important topics that have hitherto received remarkably little scholarly attention.[17] Before investigating these subjects, however, it is important to try to establish something about the native peoples' indigenous awareness and representation of space, place, and environment in the pre-Columbian and early colonial periods; to recognize differences therein between different groups of natives; to understand how Euro-Americans solicited geographical information from the natives; to appreciate how the natives communicated their replies; and to consider how these replies were interpreted and assimilated by the aliens.

Early Native Cosmologies and Geographies

The discovery of the Americas by Europeans, the coastal colonizations, and the exploration and settlement of the interior composed the most recent of at least four major cultural invasions from Eurasia.[18] These were spread over approximately forty thousand years. Whereas the last invasion originated in western Eurasia and came via the Atlantic Ocean, the three previous ones had each come from eastern Eurasia via what used to be called the Bering land bridge but is now often referred to as Beringia; this terrestrial connection between Siberia and Alaska had existed at least three times during the previous forty-five thousand years and was caused by the lowering of the sea level after the accumulation of water in ice caps during the colder phases of the Wisconsin glacial period.[19] The mechanisms, routes, chronologies, and consequences of the three earlier invasions were very complex, and it will take a long time for ethno- and earth-scientists to reconstruct them exactly. It is, however, already clear that when Europeans began to discover the Americas in the fifteenth and sixteenth centuries, the native peoples were more diverse than was then generally recognized. Occasionally, real or supposed differences were observed between adjacent tribes. For example, in an account of the Spanish conquest of Florida in 1565, the natives in the area between present-day Savannah, Georgia, and Charleston, South Carolina, were said to be "of good intelligence and . . . not as rustic or savage" as those along the coast to the south.[20] It would be a long time, however, before the broad regional ethnological patterns began to become apparent.

A recent bold and still controversial synthesis claims that there were distinct regional patterns of culture and that these were the consequences of the three pre-Columbian invasions. The earliest, some thirty thousand to forty thousand years before, had eventually led to the first settlement of much of the American continent by *Homo sapiens*. Except in eastern South America, the second group of settlers effectively displaced the first as a living culture and probably led to the settlement of some areas not occupied by the first-wave peoples. At the time of Columbus, the culture associated with descendants of the second-wave peoples characterized much of North America, excluding the Arctic fringe, parts of the Southeast, the middle Mississippi Valley, and parts of the Southwest. In the latter areas, second-wave cultures had in turn been displaced by cultures introduced in the third wave.

Adopting a broad circum-Pacific perspective, a recent bold attempt to explain the origins of pre-Columbian art has claimed that the first-wave cultures of eastern South America had much in common with the cultures of the Australian aborigines; the second-wave cultures, which characterized much of North America, had strong affinities with the cultures of Melanesia and New Guinea; and the third-wave cultures of the Andes, Meso America, and the southeastern, south-central, southwestern, and northern peripheries of North America had remarkable parallels in Indonesia, South Asia, much of China, Japan, and northern Siberia.[21] For the wrong reasons and in this sense only, Columbus's contemporaries were correct in assuming that he had discovered Asia.

The earliest generations of first-, second-, and third-wave peoples to enter the Americas walked or coasted in via Beringia. Like all preliterate peoples, but unlike so many modern-day men and women, pre-Columbian Americans, in order to have survived and diffused, must have had a well-developed awareness of both environment and earth space, together with the facility to navigate in wild terrains. This cannot be established conclusively for the pre-Columbian period, but in North America during the early contact period, Europeans occasionally noted superb navigational skills among what can now be thought of as the descendants of second- and third-wave peoples. Some of these observations, however, contained Eurocentric reservations. For example, having lived among the Micmac Indians of the Gaspé Peninsula from 1675 to 1677, Chrétien Le Clercq observed: "Provided they have the sun in view, they never wander from their route. . . . But when night overtakes them, or when clouds hide the sun, then they would be really embarrassed were it not for some natural signs which they find upon certain trees—some moss or branches which incline to the north side and which serve them as guides on their voyages in default of the sun. But as soon as the darkness comes they are at their wits end."[22]

Father Joseph Lafitau, on the basis of close observation of the Iroquois Indians between 1711 and 1717 and extensive reading of the *relations* (written reports) of his Jesuit predecessors, made no such reservations, observing that they had "an excellent sense [of direction]. It is a quality which seems born in them. A child would be able to orient himself naturally . . . in (respect to) the places where he has been, or of which he has heard. In the thickest forest and at the darkest times, they do not lose, as they say, their star. They go straight where they wish to go, even in unchartered wilderness and where no paths are marked."[23]

Writing in 1819 about the Delaware and other Indians who had formerly occupied eastern Pennsylvania, John Heckewelder, who had lived with them as a Moravian missionary for more than twenty years, was equally emphatic about their navigational abilities but more specific about the methods used.

They can steer directly through the woods in cloudy weather as well as in sunshine to the place where they wish to go, at the distance of two hundred miles or more. . . . There are many who conjecture that they regulate their course by certain signs or marks on the trees, as for instance, that those that have the thickest bark are exposed to the north, and other similar observations, but those who think so are mistaken. The fact is that the Indians have an accurate knowledge of all the streams of consequence and the courses which they run; they can tell directly while travelling along a stream, whether large or small, into what larger stream it empties itself. They know how to take the advantage of dividing ridges, where the smaller streams have their heads or from whence they take their source, and in travelling on the mountains, they have a full view of the country round and can perceive the point to which their march is directed.[24]

With widely spaced watering places, the almost featureless short-grass plains of what is now northwestern Texas presented the Teyas (probably a Caddoan-speaking tribe)—met by Francisco Vázquez de Coronado in the early 1540s—with a quite different navigational problem from that faced by the Indians of the northeastern forested hills. Unwittingly applying principles of Euclidean geometry, they solved the problem of maintaining constant direction as follows: "Early in the morning they watched where the sun rose, then, going in the direction they wanted to take they shot an arrow, and before coming to it they shot another over it, and in this manner they traveled the whole day until they reached some water where they were to stop for the night. By this method, what had taken them thirty-seven days to travel they now covered on their return in twenty-five, hunting cattle [bison] on their way."[25]

Artifacts afford indirect evidence that these way-finding skills were well developed in prehistoric times. Native North Americans engaged in long-distance trade and had established macro trade networks for certain materials and goods long before Columbus. For example, marine shells from central California were being traded some six hundred miles across the Coast Range, the Sierra Nevada, and the Great Basin to the Great Salt Lake region more than six thousand years earlier.[26] On the northern shore of Lake Superior, obsidian was being obtained from the Rocky Mountains in present-day Wyoming, some twelve hundred miles across the interior grassland to the southwest, at least one thousand years before Columbus.[27] At approximately the same time, peoples in the Middle West were obtaining obsidian from the same source, as well as conch shells from the Gulf coast, some one thousand miles to the south.[28] A century or so before Columbus, the Thule peoples of the eastern Arctic Archipelago possessed items of European origin, and at much the same time similar peoples of the western Arctic Archipelago may have been using objects made from Siberian iron.[29] Some of the Indians in the Southwest had trade links with Mexico in the centuries immediately before Columbus.[30] Quite clearly, trade over distances of one thousand miles and more was, and in some cases for long had been, practiced within and even beyond the North American continent. Much of this trade may have been multistaged, and individual traders may not have traveled these distances. Nevertheless, its existence manifested a macro view of earth space on the part of some individuals and groups. Furthermore, the associated exchange of information must have done much to improve the content and accuracy of geographical knowledge beyond the worlds of direct experience.

Even at first contact, therefore, some native North Americans were, potentially at least, good guides and reliable sources of information about distant as well as local places and conditions. Their worldviews, however, made them far less reliable as informants than might otherwise have been the case. Whereas first-wave peoples had been concerned almost exclusively with the "immediate environment," the descendants of the second-wave peoples, who, in North America at least, had effectively replaced them, were in addition concerned "with regions beyond actual perception which could be described only imaginatively—beyond the horizon, below the surface of the earth, and in the heavens." They attempted "to represent the inhabitants from those surrounding regions, to give them personalities and explain how they might be influencing events in the known world at the center."[31] Their world was centred at a tree or pole that had phallic or axial connotations. It was not, however, merely the centre of the real world. It was also the centre of the unknown but imagined world beyond. The latter was usually conceived as circular. For example, in 1607 John Smith, during his captivity among Algonquian-speaking peoples of tide-

2.2 *Inset from an illustrative panel surrounding "A description of part of the adventures of Cap. Smith in Virginia" in* The General Histoire of Virginia *(London, 1624). The fire symbolizes the center of the Indians' world. Smith is seated on the pile of sticks representing the British Isles. From the American Geographical Society Collection, University of Wisconsin–Milwaukee Library.*

water Virginia, was entertained in a long house "with strange conjurations." First a fire was made to represent the centre of the Indians' world. This was circumscribed by three concentric circles, the inner one of meal and the other two of unground maize. The ceremony, which lasted three days, was conducted to establish whether the Englishmen intended good or ill. Smith explains that the inner circle signified the limits of the Indians' country, the second circle the coast of the American landmass, and the outer circle the edge of the ocean-girt world, which they imagined "to be flat and round like a trencher, and themselves in the midst."[32] A pile of small sticks placed between the second circle and the outer circle was intended to represent the land from which the Englishmen had come.

The outer world was often populated with mythical beings. A Yurok "good land," for example, was located beyond the Yurok Indians' "ocean of pitch" and was the shared home of a presiding genius associated with gambling, of a being who had once cleared the known world of monsters and evil beings, of the dentalium shell that served as the Yuroks' medium of exchange, and of a culture hero who had earlier been taken from the real world on the back of a skate who had tricked him by dressing as a woman.[33]

Not surprisingly, early Europeans were rarely in a position to distinguish between native reports of real and mythical features, creatures, and conditions. In 1512, in the course of a voyage intended to settle Florida, Juan Ponce de León wasted time sailing to and fro between the islands to the north of Cuba in search "of the fountain which rejuvenates or makes old men young." Its existence had been "confirmed by the Indians of these parts"; nevertheless, the search brought forth "mocking" from them.[34] Samuel de Champlain, whose accounts were in general much more objective than those of other early European explorers, appears to have believed the Indians who told him that off the coast of what is now New Brunswick, near Chaleur Bay, was "an island where makes his abode a dreadful monster, which the savages call *Gougou*." The monster was hideous, had the form of a woman, was taller than the masts of the French ships, made terrible noises, and on catching Indians, put them in its pocket before eating them.[35] In 1604–5, Juan de Oñate, traveling westward from present-day New Mexico down the Colorado River toward the Gulf of California, was told by Indians about people with "so large and long ears that they dragged on the ground," about men with "virile members so long that they wound them four times around the waist," and about a variety of other people, some with one foot, others who slept under the waters of a lake, and a group who nourished themselves solely by the smell of food. These and other "monstrous" peoples each had a name and a region in which they lived—much like the beings in the outer zones of Yurok and other cosmologies. In a diary of the expedition, Father Escobar expressed some doubt, but he implied that if these peoples existed at all, they were only "twenty-five or thirty leagues away": some sixty to seventy-five miles.[36]

The idea of an earth island, centred in a world ocean that extended to the edge of a flat universe, may have been responsible for at least some of the early reports of a salt sea not far to the west of the Appalachians. Given the known geography of the Atlantic coast, some Indians may have been referring to a real coast beyond the mountains to the west. Some of these reports doubtless had one or another of the two eastern Great Lakes as their referents, and one or two may even have referred to the Gulf of Mexico. A minority, however, seem unlikely to have referred to either. For example, on the basis of his residence in the Virginia colony in 1610–11, William Strachey reported that from the hills at the source of the James River, near the present-day boundary between Virginia and West Virginia, "the people [Indians] say they see another Sea, and that the water is there salt; and the Journye to this Sea from the Falls [at what is now Richmond, Virginia] by their accompt should be about 10 dayes, allowing according to a March, some 14 or 16 myles a day."[37] This was almost certainly the same source of information that in 1612 caused John Smith to include the north-south-oriented eastern shore of a large, unnamed, and unexplained body of water at the northwestern edge of his now famous "Map of Virginia," even though, in 1608, Chief Powhatan had told him personally, "The relations you have had from my people . . . [of] salt water beyond the mountaines . . . are false."[38]

Powhatan's Algonquian-speaking Indians were almost certainly descendants of second-wave peoples. From the more or less equal participation of all people in spiritual life, a practice that had characterized the first wave, they had developed a high degree of spiritual and organizational specialization. Perhaps the ordinary Indians accepted as fact what their spiritual and temporal leaders recognized to be tentative cosmologies, much in the same way that many Euro-Americans today accept as fact the black holes of the astronomer, the particles of the nuclear physicist, and the models of the social scientist. If so, in relation to information about distant features, Europeans may have been at greater risk of being misinformed by friendly but ordinary natives than by equally friendly spiritual and temporal leaders.

> The third-wave cultures were characterized by a new preoccupation with the celestial realm and the development of orderly systems for understanding and recording its phenomena. . . . The ancient symbol of the circle, which for millennia had represented the earth, was seen by Third Wave people as more appropriate to the sky, which spins around the celestial poles. The directions established by the poles and the paths of the sun, moon, and planets were taken from the sky and applied back to the earth as its new symbol, the four directions or the square. But the real world was in the heavens where the gods lived, visible as the sun, moon, planets, stars and every other celestial phenomenon. Events on earth took on meaning only by reflection from the heavens.[39]

Spatial diagrams (cosmological maps) were squares or rectangles. A somewhat debased form of such a diagram was used by a Delaware Indian in 1762 in preaching to members of his tribe who, in the years immediately before, had been relocated in the upper Ohio Valley. Copies of the diagram were made on skin and offered for sale to the congregation, presumably to serve as mnemonics for a partly spiritual and partly political message. The preacher "had drawn, as he pretended, by the direction of the great Spirit, a kind of map on a piece of deer skin, somewhat dressed like parchment. . . . This, he said, he had been ordered to show to the Indians, that they might see the situation in which the Mannitta [i.e., manitou, that great spirit common to the religions of many of the eastern Indians] had originally placed them, the misery which they had brought upon themselves by neglecting their duty, and the only way that was now left them to regain what they had lost. This map he held before him while preaching, frequently pointing to particular marks and spots upon it, and giving explanations as he went along."[40]

Heckewelder gives a detailed description of the content of the map. Essentially, it consisted of a square positioned symmetrically within a larger square. The edge of the larger square represented the shores of the known and the supposed lands of the real world, including that recently settled by the Delaware Indians and that from which they had recently been displaced by the Europeans. The inner square represented their home in the afterlife, with a previous point of entry that had recently been blocked by the Europeans and a new point of entry that had been opened up for them by the "great Spirit."[41] The new entry, however, was dangerous, involving jumping over "a large ditch" at which Indians were at risk of being captured by an evil spirit, who would take them to his (by implication) lower region of poverty and drought, where they would be transformed into horses or dogs.[42]

In the Southwest, the Spaniards came into contact with peoples exhibiting either better-developed or less-debased third-wave-type cultures than in the East. The celestial realm is represented in much pre-Columbian rock art, and in recent years progress has been made in interpreting some of the representations.[43] A pre-Columbian celestial event authentically recorded elsewhere in the world affords the basis for the best of these interpretations. Chinese records from the Sung Dynasty describe the sudden appearance of a bright object in the constellation Taurus on 4 July 1054 (Julian calendar). It was visible in China for 23 days and for 653 nights and, except for the sun, was probably the brightest object seen in the sky in human memory. This supernova, although apparently not observed in Europe, theoretically should first have been visible in southwestern North America just before dawn on 5 July, when it would have been observed by any celestially aware natives. It would have been noteworthy to them for two reasons: its extreme brightness and its very close juxtaposition to a crescent moon. Examples of a closely juxtaposed crescent (moon) and circle (supernova) have to date been found at more than fifteen rock-art sites in Arizona, New Mexico, Texas, Utah, and Baja California. At least some of these appear to be representations of the outburst of the supernova, though confirmation of particular cases must await the development of precise techniques for dating rock art.[44]

Canyon de Chelly, in northeastern Arizona, contains nearly one hundred places still sacred to the local Navajos—undoubtedly descendants of third-wave peoples. Of these places, at least fourteen are star-ceiling sites: representations of stars "precisely painted on the roofs of high overhangs or on the roofs of cave-like rock shelters. So-called planetarium sites, some undoubtedly depict constellations."[45] Likewise, several rock-art sites in the Southwest almost certainly depict meteorites.[46]

Prehistoric stone patterns known as medicine wheels are fairly common on the high western plains of Alberta, Montana, and adjacent areas. The typical medicine wheel consists of a small ring of stones, from which lines of stones radiate out at irregular angular intervals. Their original function was long debated, but it now seems probable that they were solar observatories, used in particular for solstice marking in connection with ceremonies held as much as two thousand years ago.[47] Observing, recording, and behaving according to the stars continued to be characteristic of some Plains Indians until contact times. By the late nineteenth century, members of the Skidi band of the Pawnees could recognize only two stars. Yet a sky chart on buckskin, which had been kept in one of their sacred bundles until some date before 1906, shows hundreds of four-pointed stars, drawn according to four different magnitudes, representing eleven constellations plus the Milky Way.[48]

The importance of stars as controlling influences on society was, and in a few cases still is, exemplified among the descendants of presumably third-wave peoples. When, at the beginning of the twentieth century, the Skidi sky chart was collected in northeastern Oklahoma, a few old Pawnees could still remember the tribe's former home in what is now central Nebraska. There had then been four bands of Pawnees. The Skidi band had been one, and it had always built its villages to the west of the other bands. The Skidi band had itself been divided into approximately twenty-two separate villages. With only two exceptions, each of these had possessed sacred symbolic articles believed to have been given to it by its particular star. Each village was named after its star, and the relative locations of the villages on the prairie reflected the positions of the stars in the sky. The status and role of each village, especially its ceremonial role, was determined by its star. The star cult was also manifest in the construction of the earth lodges. The circular floor represented the earth. The four posts supporting the roof represented the leading stars and were painted in their respective colours. The position of the shrine within the lodge was in accordance with the star of the west, and the dome-shaped roof was the arching sky. According to one Indian informant, "The Skidi were organized by the stars; these powers above made them into families and villages, and taught them how to live and how to perform their ceremonies." Though by the end of the nineteenth century the Skidis could recognize only two stars in the sky, until sometime earlier in the century they had preserved "traces of an ancient and deeply rooted cult."[49] That cult was almost certainly a late manifestation of a third-wave culture.

The importance of the celestial world is even more apparent among some of the Indians of the Southwest. Representations of celestial phenomena are important components of many sand paintings (also called ground or dry paintings)—symbolic pictures made from memory at special places in the course of ceremonies. Varying in size and complexity, these paintings are made on the ground by the chanters, the leaders of the ceremonies, who trickle coloured sands, pulverized charcoal, and the like through their fingers. Among the Luiseño Indians of southern California, for example, the paintings were almost always circular. They were made at initiation and death rites, after which they were destroyed. Most of them represented aspects of the celestial world—the Milky Way, selected constellations according to form, the sun and the moon—together with sacred and mythical beings and some specific geographical features. Somewhat surprisingly, such nearby conspicuous features as the San Bernardino mountain range, southeast of present-day Los Angeles, and the Coronado and Santa Catalina Islands, off the coast of southern California, were positioned at the periphery of the world as represented in the paintings, beyond the celestial features and mythical beings at the centre. Such sand paintings were still occasionally being made by the Luiseños in the 1970s.[50]

Like the Skidis, Indians in the Southwest often continue to mirror on earth their conceptions of the cosmos. For example, the Navajos of northwestern New Mexico think of the cosmos as a circle in which the sky meets the earth. Four sacred mountains, four precious stones, four kinds of birds, and four different colours are associated with the four cardinal directions. Much of this is reflected in Navajo ritual. Chants take place in a traditional dwelling, called a hogan, that is circular, like the horizon. Movement during a curing ceremony is always clockwise (i.e., in the direction of the sun's movement), and many other aspects of the chants are determined by the cardinal directions.[51]

A further third-wave characteristic found among many native North Americans was the belief in a multilayered universe. Modeled most spectacularly in some of the temple architecture of the Indian subcontinent and in the pyramidal temples of Mesoamerica, the antecedent stage involved the use of natural mounds and caves to symbolize the multilayered cosmos.[52] North America lacks such grand architectural manifestations of third-wave cosmology, but the approximately one-thousand-year-old temple mounds of the middle Mississippi Valley may have had similar symbolic roles, and some native North Americans still incorporate a multilayered universe in their belief systems. The Hopi Indians of northeastern Arizona, for example, believe in an upper world of the dead.[53] Their southeastern neighbours, the Zunis, believe in a nine-level world, with four levels below and four above the earth itself. Each level is supposedly the domain of a specific tree or bird: the ponderosa pine, Douglas fir, aspen, and cottonwood below; and the crow, Cooper's hawk, nighthawk, and eagle above.[54] The Fox Indians of the Upper Mississippi Valley believe in a three-layered universe. The upper layer, ruled by the "Great Manitou," contains lesser manitous, or spirits, as well as a culture hero known as *wisahke-ha*.[55] In many cases, the movement of beings between levels is considered normal. Indeed, as in second-wave cultures, mythical beings could be residents of or visitors to the earth's surface. Many were nonhuman, with dwarfs, giants, cannibals, and culture heroes common throughout most of North America. Other beings were almost human but were deformed or anatomically deficient in some way.

To the Indians, these other worlds and their occupants were—and in many cases remain—very real. Although difficult to prove, Indian accounts of them almost certainly confused European explorers, who for the most part failed to distinguish between the geographies and the cosmologies of the native informants. Indeed, most of the explorers would have failed to appreciate the basis of that distinction even if it could have been pointed out to them, for in Europe the "general medieval picture of the world [had] survived in outline into the Elizabethan age."[56] With its heaven and hell, it too was multilayered. With one or more devils and many angels, these layers were likewise peopled with other beings. All Eu ropean languages had nouns for dwarf, giant, fairy, elf, and so forth to denote beings supposedly existing, and even occasionally reported to have been seen, on earth. Indeed, although commerce and the emerging new science were together powering the exploration and settlement of the Americas, "the greatness of the Elizabethan age was that it contained so much of the new without bursting the noble form of the old order." The "educated Elizabethan had plenty of textbooks in the vernacular instructing him in the Copernican astronomy, yet he was loath to upset the old order by applying his knowledge."[57] It was not until "the closing years of the seventeenth century [that] a new order of things began its course" in Europe.[58] This was approximately two hundred years after Columbus had sailed from Spain and one hundred years after Champlain had reported a monster off the New Brunswick coast and Oñate had reported monstrous peoples near the lower Colorado River. In retrospect, it seems almost certain that Champlain's *gougou* was *cenu*, the cannibal giant of the Micmac Indians, a local case of the *windingo*, a malevolent monster common to the cosmologies of many tribes in northeastern North America.[59] Likewise, of Oñate's nations of monstrous peoples, those who slept beneath the waters of a lake were almost certainly one of the forms of water sprites so characteristic of the lore of several Great Basin tribes. Indeed, some Washo Indians still believe that sprites live at the bottom of Lake Tahoe at the eastern foot of the Sierra Nevada, and the Owens Valley Paiutes to the south call the sprites *paco ana*, a name very similar to *anpacha*, the name reported by Oñate.[60] The latter's nation of people with only one foot still exists in the one-legged monsters of Washo lore.[61] Likewise, Oñate's nation of people who sustain themselves solely on the odour of food survives in Kawaiisu lore as the people who feed by inhaling the smoke of frying meat, the only difference between them being that those reported by Oñate had no anuses, whereas those in Kawaiisu lore have no mouths.[62]

More than a hundred years after Columbus, Europeans had barely begun to distinguish myth from reality or cosmology from geography in the information they received from native North Americans. Indeed, except in relation to immediate matters of local geography and strategy, they for the most part lacked an awareness of the need to do so. As the seventeenth century progressed, however, the European mind changed, at first very slowly and then, toward the end of the century, very rapidly. In North America the change began to make manifest to explorers and settlers from Europe the differences between their worldview and the worldview of the native peoples. An important consequence of this was that information ob-

2.3 Amerigo Vespucci introduces European science—symbolized by his sea astro-labe—to the Indians. The Indian and the increasingly scientific European world-views were never accommodated successfully. From Theodor Galle, L'Amerique historique (Paris, 1638). From the American Geographical Society Collection, University of Wisconsin–Milwaukee Library.

tained from natives began to be evaluated more critically. Even so, the sharpening of the evaluation process was to be slow. As exploration and settlement began to penetrate into the interior parts of the continent, information obtained from native peoples was more important than ever. Yet the solicitation, evaluation, and assimilation of that information have received far less attention than their importance merits.

The Communication of Native Geographical Information

Opinions about Indians differed considerably between those Europeans who had direct experience with Indians and those who did not and between those Europeans who perceived Indians primarily as potential converts to Christianity and those who considered them as exploitable resources. Opinions also varied according to current moral and public attitudes.[63] The earliest moral opinions on the nature of Indians stemmed from Aristotle's then recently rediscovered doctrine of natural slavery. In its extreme form, this categorized the Indian as something between semi-animal and subhuman: grossly inferior to Europeans, savage, ignorant, and born to be exploited. A somewhat less extreme variant of this position equated Indians with the mass of people at the bottom of European society, who likewise had supposedly been born to serve and to be exploited. Though persisting into the nineteenth century, these extreme attitudes were opposed by an increasing minority of Europeans who saw Indians as noble and educable and as potential converts to Christianity. These polarized opinions gradually gave way to the relativistic position that Indians were somewhat below Europeans on a hierarchical scale of cultural achievement. Furthermore, some groups of Indians were lower down on that scale than other groups, and some individual Indians were higher up than others in their group.

Notwithstanding these changing and often conflicting currents of opinion concerning Indians, from the time of earliest contact Europeans used them as informants, particularly when seeking information about conditions and recent events in nearby terrae semicognitae and more remote terrae incognitae. Even so, the information-eliciting process reflects the Europeans' doubts about the integrity of the informants and the efficiency of the modes of information exchange. Perhaps not surprisingly, given the late emergence of epistemology within European philosophy, recognition of the consequences for information exchange of different modes of knowing and representing the world came late.[64] More surprisingly, there appear to be no previous attempts to evaluate the role of Indians as sources of information, the modes of Indian-European information transfer, or the consequences of the transfer processes for the information received by Europeans.

With a few notable exceptions, the European experience of North America during the presettlement period was transitory, fragmented, and geographically peripheral. Furthermore, probably fewer than one hundred thousand persons participated in the 120-year experience, and of these, most were illiterate, uneducated, and hence incapable of sharing this experience at a significant level with other Europeans. Spain, France, and England were the dominant participants, but their objectives and activities were uncoordinated and erratic. By the early seventeenth century fewer than five thousand Europeans and first-generation Euro-Americans lived in the twenty or so widely separated forts, missions, and fishing communities that, with the exception of Santa Fe, lay on the eastern edge of the

2.4 *King Ferdinand of Spain apparently directing Columbus's first contact with the* *Indians. In reality, European control of relations with native peoples was never very* *effective and had to be worked out on the ground. From Guiliano Dati,* La lettera d'ellisole che ha trouato nuouamente il Re dispangna *(Florence, 1493). Photo courtesy Edward E. Ayer Collection, The Newberry Library.*

continent. The existence of these settlements reflected a number of often short-lived initiatives, of which appraising the resources, exploiting the resources, and Christianizing the native populations were the most important. Intermittently, searching for a westward route from Europe to China had also been an important factor in bringing Europeans to the continent. Occasionally there had also been naval and military skirmishes between the Europeans. The European powers, however, had each tended to focus on different parts of the continent's periphery, and on the whole, international contacts on it were less significant than interracial ones. Explorers, soldiers, missionaries, and their retinues inevitably, and for the most part deliberately, made contact with native North Americans and quickly began to exploit them, particularly as coastal pilots, guides, and informants.

Learning how to communicate with the natives was an important part of the information-seeking process. At its simplest, this involved the interpretation of spoken and sign languages, but interpretation was only part of a much more complex information-exchange process involving eliciting, verifying, and evaluating the information. Furthermore, to be of significance, the received information had to be accommodated into the worldviews of at least some of the influential recipients. Given the ignorance of Europeans concerning the geography of even the proximate parts of the continent and the need to survive for months or even years, much of the required information was about phenomena—food, minerals, fresh water —or strategic considerations such as terrain, routes, and characteristics of other natives, almost always, however, in the context of place, space, and environment.

At the beginning of the sixteenth century the Spaniards, in particular, viewed native North Americans as potential slaves, but very quickly they and other Europeans began to use the natives as pilots and guides. In 1572, for example, the party of Pedro Menéndez de Avilés proposed to keep an Indian boy. He had come into their hands on Chesapeake Bay, when they had recovered a Spanish boy who had been held by Indians long enough to learn the local Algonquian dialect and to almost forget his Spanish. The proposal had two objectives. The young Indian would help the young Spaniard retain his command of the Algonquian language and at the same time would be taught Spanish.[65] Communication was essential for the immediate purposes of piloting and being piloted through coastal and estuarine waters and of guiding and being guided along trails. And communication was equally necessary, if not more so, for establishing what lay ahead, where to find essential or highly prized resources, which of several alternative routes to select, whether nearby Indians were likely to be friendly or unfriendly, what the environmental conditions were at other times of the year, and whether other Europeans were known to have been in the region and, if so, when they were there and what they were like. As a mode of communication, however, the spoken language was inherently difficult and very unsatisfactory. Early-sixteenth-century reports frequently refer to the unintelligible speech of natives. In 1504, for example,

after two years of residence in England, two Indians presumed to be Beothuks from Newfoundland were said to be indistinguishable in appearance from Englishmen except "for speech . . . noon of theym uttyr oon
word."[66] Several different strategies were used to try to overcome this serious barrier to communication, but with so many different native spoken
languages, this was a never-ending and almost impossible task. A set of instructions written in 1582 or 1583 for the captain of a reconnaissance expedition that probably never took place reflects the awareness of and importance of this problem. The thirteenth instruction given to the captain
ordered him to appoint a man specifically to "note the dyversitie of their
[i.e., Indian] language and in what places their speache beginnethe to alter
as nere as you can both in the Jornall & [on the] platt [map or chart]. . . . the
same man to Carry with him an Englishe dictionarie with the Englishe
wordes before therein to sett downe their language."[67]

We now know that there were fourteen major and fundamentally different language families in North America and that within a few decades Europeans had made contact with examples from all but perhaps two of
these. In 1612, for example, the governor of Florida, in a letter to King Philip
III of Spain, gave three reasons for having failed repeatedly to satisfy requests from the Council of War of the Indies for information "by land"
about Virginia to the north: intervening riverine and terrain barriers to
transport; wars between some of the several groups of intervening Indians; and the fact that the Indians "speak different languages."[68] Strategies for minimizing the language barriers included compiling vocabu-
laries, teaching a European language to captured natives (sometimes
during enforced exile in Europe), rescuing Europeans who had learned native languages during periods of captivity, and, particularly in the case of
missionaries, actually learning a native language. None of these strategies,
however, overcame the problem that the native languages were gram-
matically different from the European ones. In particular, they were less effective in expressing relationships, especially spatial relationships, which
were important in the context of the Europeans' information needs. Inevitably, therefore, supplementary or alternative strategies had to be used in
communicating with the natives. Particularly important among these were
sign language, graphics, and the use of specimens when asking for information about mobiliary objects such as smaller plants, minerals, and precious stones and metals.

Sign language was the lingua franca of native North Americans. Widely
used in protohistoric times, and probably much earlier, this well-devel-

oped mode of communication was soon learned by Europeans as well.[69] In 1524, for example, Giovanni da Verrazzano, probably on the coast of the Carolinas in his first contact with Indians, "reassured them with various signs." They, in turn, showed him "by various signs where [he] could most easily secure the boat."[70] Later, however, on the coast of Maine or Nova Scotia, signs proved useless in trying to establish "how much religious faith" the Indians possessed.[71] The two-way use of signs was used a few years later by Pánfilo de Narváez in attempting to reach the Apalachee Indians in what is now northwestern Florida. En route, he managed to communicate, by signs to an Indian chief, where he wanted to go; the chief, likewise, indicated that he was willing to accompany Narváez there.[72] Although the limitations of sign language were frequently referred to, at the first contacts between particular groups of Indians and Europeans sign language generally appears to have been more effective than spoken language. Coronado, in his search for Quivira, reported that the Plains Apaches in what is now northwestern Texas "were so skillful in the use of signs that it seemed as if they spoke. They made everything so clear that an interpreter was not necessary."[73] By this mode they gave Coronado information about the route he should follow. At approximately the same date, Juan Rodríguez Cabrillo had mixed success in seeking information by sign from the coastal Indians of northwestern Mexico and southern California. He reported that some "could not make out anything . . . even by signs," whereas others "explained by signs that they did not live there [on the coast, where Cabrillo had met them] but inland, and that there were many people [there]." They also indicated by signs "that they had seen other men like them [i.e., Cabrillo's band of Spaniards] that were five days journey from there and also that there were many Indians [who] had much maize and many parrots."[74] In 1562, René Goulaine de Laudonnière, at the French settlement of Charlesfort, on the coast of what is now southern South Carolina, was shown by "signes, that farther towards the North, there was a great inclosure or city, where Chiquola dwelt." Another Indian showed Laudonnière "with his hands the limits of his habitation [territory]."[75]

Reports are frequently unclear whether information was received from Indians by spoken or by sign language. Even when sign language was indicated, it is usually unclear whether the signs were purely gestural or involved the use of graphics or models. Drawings and paintings were occasionally used to establish what existed beyond the geographical range of Europeans' experience. In 1540, for example, Coronado asked Zuni Indians "to have a cloth painted" for him "with all the animals that they know in that country, and, although they are poor painters, they quickly painted two . . . , one of the animals and the other of the birds and fishes."[76] This was a useful procedure for establishing preliminary inventories of phenomena occurring in particular neighbourhoods or regions. Sometimes, as in this example, painting was done explicitly by request. On other occasions the representation already existed. For example, one of the earliest indications of the vast herds of bison on the southern Great Plains was a "picture which one of the Indians had painted on his body."[77]

The spatial distribution of phenomena was, likewise, often communicated by means of a category of drawings, paintings, or models usually referred to at the time as maps or charts.[78] For example, in 1540 on the lower Colorado River, Hernando de Alarcón asked an elderly Indian to set "downe in a charte as much as he knew concerning that River, and what maner of people those were which dwelt upon the banckes thereof on both sides: which he did willingly."[79] This was one of the earliest accounts of native North Americans making maps in order to communicate geographical intelligence to Europeans. They had, however, almost certainly made maps indigenously during prehistory, though it is inevitably speculative to say that surviving maplike petroglyphs and rock paintings were indeed made to serve some of the functions of maps. For the historic period there is abundant evidence that native peoples in most parts of North America made maps for at least four purposes: as aids in the interactive planning of journeys and wars; as guides, by the experienced and informed, in briefing the uninitiated about to embark on journeys and wars; as ephemeral messages left at bifurcation points along routes for the benefit of those following behind; and as semipermanent records of important real and mythical events involving spatial activity. In 1541, Jacques Cartier received the first clear information about the rapids on the Saint Lawrence River above what is now Montreal from Indians who made a model of the river thereabouts "with certaine little stickes, which they layd upon the ground in a certaine distance, and afterwards layde other small branches betweene both, representing the Saults [rapids]."[80] Sometimes such modeling and mapping was interactive between Europeans and Indians. Champlain, for example, sailing in 1605 down the coast of present-day New England, anchored near Cape Ann, where he met some local Indians. "[I] made them understand, as well as I could, that they should show me how the coast trended. After I had drawn for them with a charcoal the bay and the Island Cape, where we then were [Cape Ann], they pictured for me with the same charcoal another bay which they represented as very large. There they placed six pebbles at equal intervals, giving me thereby to understand that each one of these marks represented that number of chiefs and tribes. Next they represented within the said bay a river which we had passed, which is very long and has shoals."[81]

The large bay, which Champlain had not yet seen, was Massachusetts Bay, and the long river, which he had passed but not seen because of the bar at its mouth, was the Merrimack River. The pebbles represented the settlements of Massachusett Indians on the shore of the bay, which was later named after them. In May 1602, Captain Bartholomew Gosnold met a group of Micmac Indians somewhere on the coast of what is now southern Maine. From aspects of their dress and a few of the words they spoke, they appeared to have had some previous contact with Europeans. Indeed, they could name Placentia, the bay more than eight hundred miles away in Newfoundland, which was already serving as a land base for European fisheries. It is unlikely, however, that Europeanization caused them to describe "the Coast" of southern Maine "with a piece of Chalke."[82] Ferdinando Gorges, commander of the harbour at Plymouth, England, described retrospectively how in 1605 George Waymouth brought back with him from coastal Maine five Indians (probably Eastern Abenakis). He kept them in his custody for a "full three years," learning from them of their homeland with its "goodly Rivers, stately Islands, and safe harbours." Furthermore, he got them to set "downe what great Rivers ran up into the Land, what Men of note were seated on them, what power they were of, how allyed [and] what enemies they had."[83]

The oldest extant map made by a North American Indian dates from 1602. The Spaniards had captured an Indian in what is now eastern Texas, had named him Miguel, and had taken him back with them to Mexico City. There he drew a map in the course of an officially conducted interrogation. It showed the rivers, trails, and, by means of circles, native settlements of his part of North America. Its most distinctive feature is a key, apparently showing—by means of approximately proportional circles—the relative sizes (populations) of four northern Mexican towns through which his captors had brought him en route to Mexico City. By implication, these were intended to indicate to his interrogators the relative sizes of twelve native settlements in a very large, but as yet undetermined, part of what is now the southern United States.[84]

Maps were not the only means for communicating spatially arranged information. The use of gesture, either with or without speech, was very common. The exact procedures, however, were only occasionally described. António de Espejo, reporting on his expedition of 1582–83 to the Pueblo Indians of present-day western New Mexico, provides a relatively rare example. Regretting that he was unable to visit all the pueblos, he explained how he and his party attempted "to see and understand everything, learning the facts through interpreters where there were any, or by signs where there were none, the Indians of those provinces showing us by lines which they made on the ground and by their hands [gestures] the number of days' journey from one province to another and the number of pueblos in each province," adding significantly, "or at the best means at our command for understanding."[85] Pointing, using other forms of body language, indicating distances by travel time, making maps, referring to the day and night skies, and using limited speech were doubtless all included within "the best means," not only by Espejo but, on many occasions and in every part of the continent, by many other Europeans.

Sometimes, in retrospect, the information concerning a European's terra incognita can be seen to have been remarkably good. The expedition of Champlain to the Gaspé Peninsula and Saint Lawrence Valley in 1603 affords several excellent examples. Montagnais Indians reported to him that, in the course of their trading contacts with the Indians farther north (probably the Eastern Crees), they had heard of a northern "sea which is salt."[86] This was doubtless a report of what was later to be named James Bay, which would not be reached by Europeans until Henry Hudson wintered there seven years later. Champlain's account of an Indian report of the route southward from the region of present-day Montreal to the Atlantic seaboard is particularly detailed and readily reconstructible in relation to the geography and toponymy of the region as now known.

The savages say, that some fifteen leagues from where we had been [i.e., the southern limit of French exploration up the Richelieu River], there is a rapid [Saint Louis Rapid at Chambly] which descends from a much higher level, to pass which they carry their canoes about a quarter of a league, and there enter a lake [Lake Champlain] at the entrance of which are three islands [Isle La Motte, Long Island, and La Grande Isle]. This lake is some forty or fifty leagues in length [actually, nearer thirty-five, assuming the league referred to was the *lieue commune*], and some twenty-five leagues in breadth [a gross exaggeration, whatever type of league was being used], and into it fall a number of rivers, as many as ten, which are navigable for canoes a long way. Then when they come to the end of this lake, there is another rapid [above Ticonderoga], and they enter another lake [Lake George], which is as large as the former [the second major error: it is less than half as long], and at the extremity of this are lodged the Iroquois [almost certainly the Mohawk Indians, the easternmost of the five confederate tribes forming the League of the Iroquois and, therefore, the first to be met along this route]. They say, moreover, that there is a river [the Hudson River, passing within two or three miles of Lake George], which leads down to the coast of Florida [New Amsterdam, now New York, near the mouth of the Hudson River, would not be established for another eleven years; the Indians would not have considered this to be part of Florida, but it did mark a stage on the route to the culturally quite different Indians beyond Chesapeake Bay, in what was still Spanish Florida].[87]

Champlain's account of his 1603 expedition also contains excellent examples of Indians communicating information by means of what might now be called the comparative method: comparing—or contrasting—features and conditions in areas unknown to the French with those in areas already known to them. When Champlain, in his little skiff, failed to proceed up the Saint Lawrence River beyond the "first [Lachine] rapid," Indians informed him that he would encounter ten more rapids further upstream before reaching "a lake . . . so vast that they [the Indians] will not venture to put out into the same, for fear lest some storm or gale should surprise them [this was almost certainly what was to become known as Lake Ontario]." This information was communicated with the aid of a specially made drawing or map, but it was supplemented by an important comparative statement: "None of all these rapids is so hard to pass as that [the Lachine] we had seen."[88] A conceptually more complex example involved a comparison by Algonquin informants of their own territory, essentially in the Ottawa River valley to the northeast of Lake Ontario, with that of the Iroquois Indians on the northern edge of the Allegheny Plateau, some "fifty or sixty leagues" to the south. Both territories covered tens of thousands of square miles. At the time, the French lacked firsthand experience of either, but in retrospect the contrast can be seen to have had considerable validity and to have involved generalizations about important environmental characteristics: terrain, vegetation, climate, and soil fertility. "All the territory of the Algonquins is low land, thinly wooded: while the Iroquois country is hilly, but nevertheless very good and fertile, and better than any region they [the Algonquins] had seen."[89] Champlain recorded that this report differed "but very little from the account" by a previous group of Algonquins, who, however, had also managed to indicate, presumably in relation to the climate in their own territory, that the Iroquois country was "temperate, without much winter, nay, very little."[90] A third group of Algonquins further supplemented this contrasting description by indicating that in the "country of the Iroquois . . . is grown a quantity of Indian corn [maize] and other products which they have not in their own country."[91] In retrospect, including that provided by archaeology, the image is confirmed of a country that was hillier, better forested, milder in winter, and agriculturally richer than that of the Algonquins.

Europeans frequently wanted to find out or confirm whether particular resources or peoples existed beyond areas or routes with which they were already familiar. On these occasions specimens were commonly used to elicit information. Jacques Cartier stated the principle succinctly in 1534, on the basis of his experience with Micmac and Stadaconan (Saint Lawrence Iroquoian) Indians on the Gaspé Peninsula and in the lower Saint Lawrence Valley: "If one shows them something they have not got and they know not what it is they shake their heads and say, *nouda*, which means, they have none of it and know not what it is. Of the things they have, they showed us by signs the way they grow and how they prepare them."[92] In 1528, Cabeza de Vaca, probably not far inland from present-day Galveston, Texas, "captured four Indians [and] showed them maize, to see if they had knowledge of it, for up to that time [the Europeans] had seen no indication of any." He reported, "They said they would take us where there was some; so they brought us to their town near by at the head of the [Galveston?] bay, and showed us a little corn not yet fit for gathering."[93]

It was April and early in the growing season, even for southern Texas, but the means of communicating was probably not capable of expressing such distinctions as growing versus harvested or as maturing versus ripe. Eleven years later, Fray Marcos de Niza used the same procedure in attempting to establish the existence and locations of precious resources. On his expedition from Mexico City to what is now the southwestern United States, he took with him pearls to be used "for a show." On showing them to Indians from islands in the Gulf of California who "had about their necks many great shells which were mother of Pearl," he was informed "that there were in the Islands great store of them, and those very great." Likewise, he took with him metals "to learne what riche Metals were in the Lande [and] they [the Indians] tooke the mineral of Golde and tolde [him], that thereof were vesselles among the people of that plaine [probably Sonora in northwestern Mexico] . . . and that they have certaine thinne plates of that Golde, wherein they scrape off their sweat, and that the walles of their Temples are covered therewith, and that they use it in all their household vessels."[94] Sometimes the response was negative, as when, in 1540, Alarcón, on being presented with maize by Indians on the lower Colorado River, "shewed unto them Wheate and Beanes, and other seedes, to see whether they had any of those kindes: but they shewed [him] that they had no knowledge of them."[95] The same procedure was also used to establish cultural information about unknown or little-known areas. In the early 1540s, for example, Luis de Moscoso Alvarado found at the native settlement of Guasco, in what is now eastern Texas, "some turquoises and cotton blankets which the Indians gave them to understand by signs were brought from the west; and if they took that way, they would reach the land of the Christians."[96] This information probably referred to one or more of the Spanish expeditions into the Southwest led by Niza, Coronado, or even Alarcón, almost certainly all unknown to Moscoso because they had been mounted from Mexico City after Soto and he had sailed from Spain for Florida via the West Indies. Since there were no Christian Indians in the Southwest by that date, the Christians referred to had to be Spaniards. Turquoises were widely traded, but most were mined at the village of Cerrillos in the Rio Grande valley of central New Mexico. Likewise, cotton goods were widely traded, but the nearest cultivation of cotton was in the extreme Southwest, and the nearest source of cotton goods was the pueblos of New Mexico.

On some occasions the use of specimens in establishing partial inventories of phenomena characterizing particular places or areas almost certainly lessened a problem that must have arisen frequently, though without necessarily being recognized at the time, whenever attempts were made to communicate by speech—the problem of the fundamental differences between European and native North American languages both in the semantic categorization of phenomena and in the structure as determined by grammar. In sixteenth- and seventeenth-century Europe, the nomenclatures of plants, animals, and other natural phenomena were still volatile, varying regionally even within given language areas. Furthermore, there were no generally agreed-upon classifications of natural phenomena.[97] There was, however, a considerable consensus concerning the basic components of the natural world. In short, nomenclatures may have been chaotic and classifications rudimentary, but typologies were generally agreed upon. This consensus was not, however, shared between Europeans and native North Americans. Today, Indian and Inuit languages frequently subdivide—and just as frequently aggregate—the basic elements of the Europeans' world. Furthermore, the semantic categories of native North American languages tend to be much more fluid than those of European languages. These differences are in some cases so fundamental that they are difficult for a European to comprehend without having shared for a long time the native way of life, thought, and speech. Edmund Carpenter, an anthropologist who lived and worked among the Inuits of the Canadian Arctic, expressed some of these differences: "The Eskimo seem to be saying that nature is there, but man alone can free it from its dormant state; that it requires a creative human act before the world explored becomes a world revealed; that the universe acquires form, 'existence,' only through man the revealer: he who releases life inherent in nature and guides its expression into beautiful forms. Eskimo isn't a nominal language, it doesn't name things which already exist, but brings things/action (noun/verbs) into being as it goes along." And he added: "Language is the principal tool with which the Eskimo make the natural world a human world. They use many 'words' for snow which permit fine distinctions, not simply because they are much concerned with snow, but because snow takes its form from the actions in which it participates: sledding, falling, igloo-building. Different kinds of snow are brought into existence by the Eskimo as they experience their environment and speak; words do not label things already there. Words are like the knife of the carver: they free the idea, the thing, from the general formlessness of the outside."[98]

Historical comparative linguists are unlikely ever to establish precisely the differences between European and native North American languages in early contact times. It can be assumed, however, that for some native languages at least, the differences then were much as there were in the recent, relatively well studied past. If so, these differences could explain some of the grosser errors in European representations of the geography of areas that, to them at the time, were terrae semicognitae or even terrae incognitae. Their maps of such areas, for example, frequently contained representations of drainage systems that were not merely wrong but, seen in the light of modern fluvial hydrology, unnatural. Stream channels diverged into two or more channels; drainage systems now known to be separate were cross-linked; and single systems often had two or more estuaries. Such drainage systems did not exist in Europe, and it is inconceivable that European mapmakers would have spontaneously filled in otherwise empty spaces with such improbable networks. Much more likely, the patterns were based on native information. Boats of one kind or another were almost universal modes of transport among the natives. The bark canoe of the northern half of the continent was particularly important. Eminently portable, the canoe could be carried across portages, often in the course of long journeys involving crossings between two or more drainage systems. To the natives, therefore, a mix of river channels, lakes, portages, *detroits*, and land trails was often experienced as a single route system rather than as several separate drainage networks linked by one or more roads, physically different elements integrated experientially by the Indians into single systems. When represented by them in this way, the systems were easily misinterpreted by Europeans.

Giacomo Gastaldi's "Tierra Nueva" of 1547–48 affords an early example, which may in part have been derived from information given to Cartier by Indians on his return down the Saint Lawrence River in 1536. The map shows four channels coming from the interior and entering the Atlantic Ocean between 49° north and 55° north; however, these are all joined by one interconnecting channel.[99] This could be an incorporation of information given by Indians to Cartier in map form. Alternatively, it could be Gastadi's attempt to represent, cartographically, native information as reported by Cartier in words. The latter's report certainly contains a native description of a very large "island, which is encircled and surrounded by rivers."[100] Samuel de Champlain's "Carte geographique de la Nouvelle Franse . . ." of 1612 contains an equally good example, one that, however, is easier to explain.[101] It represents six waterway cross-links between the approximately parallel Saint Lawrence and Ottawa Rivers above their actual confluence a little upstream from present-day Montreal. Through waterways across what is now eastern Ontario never, of course, existed. What Champlain was unknowingly representing were the stream-lake-portage-*detroit*-trail routes between the Algonquin Indians of the Ottawa Valley to the north and the Iroquois Indians to the south of the upper Saint Lawrence and Lake Ontario.

Semantic differences may also have been responsible for some of the early reports of a sea to the west of the Appalachians. It is quite possible that the native peoples of northeastern North America had no particular need to distinguish carefully between the chemical characteristics of the waters along the Atlantic and the Great Lakes shorelines. Indeed, in many respects, from their point of view the waters had much in common. Compared with the tens of thousands of other lakes in the region, the five Great Lakes were enormous, developed tremendous waves, and occasionally experienced sudden changes in water level. For Indians in a canoe, they could be almost as dangerous as Atlantic inshore waters. That the Great Lakes water had saline concentrations less than one-hundredth that of seawater was not locally as important as the fact that, especially in the coastal zones of Lakes Ontario and Erie, it was brackish in comparison with that of most nearby lakes and streams. Furthermore, no Indian tribes had territories or resource areas embracing both maritime and Great Lakes environments. On the other hand, in 1598, Zuni Indians, in explaining to Marcos Farfan a map of a very large drainage system that they had modeled on the ground for him, noted that the main river eventually entered "the sea, which they showed to be salty by dissolving a small quantity of salt in water in order to demonstrate the condition of the sea water."[102] Farfan's account is vague, but the "sea" was probably the head of the Gulf of California at the outflow of the Colorado River. Possibly, but far less likely, the sea could have been the Salton Sea in southern California. In either case, the saltiness was relative to the freshness of the streams and springs of the Zunis' immediate environment. These were fed by meltwater from the snowfields of the nearby Zuni Mountains and by runoff from occasional summer cloudbursts. To the Zunis the freshness of these two types of water was vital to their agricultural economy, in what was otherwise a subhumid to semiarid environment. Their water was a fundamentally different liquid from the saltwater of the desert basins and the ocean. Its importance to them is still reflected in aspects of their religious beliefs and ceremonies: rain and snow priests, who take on the form of clouds, rainstorms, fog, dew, and snow; "bow priests," who make lightning and thunder; and six "water-bringing birds."[103]

When significant to their way of life, Indians could and still do distinguish in language between what to Europeans must have seemed very subtle differences in environment. The Inuit categorization of many kinds of snow is paralleled on the desert plateaus of southern Nevada and adjacent parts of Arizona and California by the Southern Paiutes' remarkably large repertoire of precise nouns for a considerable number of subtly differentiated topographic features.[104] These features are of vital importance to the Paiutes in locating water, edible plants, small ground animals, and shelter, each in the context of season. Conversely, Europeans could be equally surprised by Indian tendencies to aggregate what Europeans have intuitively separated for millennia. For example, several Indian languages have a single word for sun and moon; the differences between the two visually largest bodies in the sky emerge only in the context of day, night, season, and so on.[105]

Appraising Native Geographical Information

Quite clearly, even those sixteenth- and early-seventeenth-century Europeans with direct experience had little or no understanding of the Indians'
relativist—indeed, almost existentialist—perspective on nature or of the
ways and extent to which that perspective differed from their own. They
were, however, preoccupied with two closely related practical concerns:
appraising the integrity of their native informants; and ensuring and verifying the reliability of information that they received from these natives.

Reports of early attempts to assess the integrity of the natives are quite
numerous. In retrospect, however, they do not present a consistent impression, though as the sixteenth century progressed, Europeans would
seem to have become more rather than less suspicious. Repeated examples
of apparent proof that false information had been received from natives
were assumed to reflect deliberate falsehoods rather than the inefficiency
of the intercultural transmission and reception systems. In 1540, for example, in the course of Coronado's expedition to the Pueblo Indians of New
Mexico and Arizona, Pedro de Castañeda described what at the time was
believed to be a "reliable report of a province named Topira, which touched
Caliacán on the north." Coronado "set forth at once . . . to discover it." The
expedition produced few results, and Castañeda recorded that, in part at
least, this was because "the information they had received was untruth-
ful." Thereafter, Coronado was reluctant to accept further information
from the Indians because "they had already been caught in several lies."[106]
Champlain, in the course of his experiences with Indians in and around
Quebec in 1608–9, and influenced no doubt by his earlier involvement with
natives elsewhere in the Saint Lawrence Valley, the Maritime Provinces,
and New England, stated his opinion: "There are many of them who have
good judgement, and reply pointedly to the questions put to them. But
they have bad points: they are revengeful and awful liars, people whom
one must not trust too far, but rather judiciously, and with force in one's
hand. They promise readily, but perform badly."[107]

Dishonesty concerning geographical intelligence was certainly involved in the course of the first European experience of the inhospitable
and potentially dangerous southern Great Plains. Coronado, on his expedition of 1541 eastward or northeastward from the Pecos Valley in present-
day New Mexico, took with him as a guide a slave of the Apaches. The
guide appeared to be well qualified for the task because his original home
had been somewhere to the east, in what is now the south-central part of

the United States. At first he was believed because of "the directness with which he told his story." After more than eight days, however, the Spaniards realized that he had guided the party away from their route. "[He] had led us over the plains as he did in order that we should exhaust our food, and without it both we and our horses would become weak."[108] On some occasions, natives admitted their duplicity, especially when implicated in the tensions between European powers. In July 1580, for example, an Indian in what is now northeastern Florida brought information to the Spanish governor, Pedro Menéndez Marques, near the mouth of Saint Johns River, concerning the arrival nearby of a French ship. The Indian said that

> he had spoken with them [the French], and been aboard their ship, and that the French asked him how many people there were in this [the Spanish] fort, and if there were any vessels in the fort [the Spanish harbour]. And the Indian said that he answered them that there were no ships whatever in the harbour, except two [small] launches, and that there were few [Spanish] people in the harbor [fort] and those were very sick. The general asked the Indian why he had told them [the French] that the [Spanish] people were few and sick, since he knew that there were two large frigates in the harbor. The Indian replied that he and the others thought they would deceive the French, so that they would land, and there [the Indians] would kill and despoil them.

Although Marques valued the unsolicited intelligence, he was at the same time suspicious of a double duplicity and ordered a Spaniard "to go on horseback that night to San Mateo, a distance of twelve leagues, arriving there at dawn, when he would look and see if there were more than one ship."[109] This was verification of military intelligence, but such actions were frequently just as important to verify geographical information, and the strategies adopted for doing so were quite diverse.

The verification process was, in modern terminology, concerned with quality-of-information control. It involved establishing and, when it was recognized to be necessary, correcting for two closely interrelated aspects: the veracity of the native informants; and the quality of the information as received and interpreted by the Europeans. As already demonstrated, information honestly transmitted by Indians and Inuits according to their own mores could be very misleading because, at the time, it was often very difficult for Europeans to interpret—in the fullest sense of that word—that information correctly. Europeans were generally more aware of the need to ensure the reliability of the informants than of the need to assess the quality of the information received.

Several strategies were adopted to ensure veracity. These included using fear and force, interrogating in European-controlled rather than native environments, making gifts, offering assistance, developing amicable relationships, training natives (especially in European languages), and deploying genuinely friendly natives as intermediaries. Force and fear were used mainly, though not exclusively, by the Spaniards. In the early 1540s, for example, Moscoso ordered to be "hanged from a tree" three Indian guides who had led him east when he had wanted to go west and who had gone through dense forest when they should have followed an established trail. Soon afterward, another guide was tortured for leading the party "off the road for two days." When the guide later admitted having done so in response to a prior instruction from his chief, Moscoso gave instructions that he be "thrown to the dogs."[110] Known as *aperrear*, this practice was then quite common in the Indies. Conquistadores regularly took with them "Irish greyhounds and very bold, savage dogs" for this purpose.[111] There are indications that some Indians responded to the threat of force. In 1565, for example, Indians promised to lead the Frenchman Jean Ribault from La Caroline, on the Atlantic coast of what is now northeastern Florida, to the "mountaines of Apalachy," approximately 250 miles inland; the Indians volunteered to be "cut in pieces" if they "performed not their promise." In part, however, their promise was in anticipation of receiving from Ribault "merchandise that hee had brought with him to be delivered them."[112] The carrot may have been more powerful than the threat of a stick.

The giving of gifts and the cultivation of friendships were almost certainly more frequent and probably more effective than the engendering of fear or the actual use of force. In 1540 on the lower Colorado River, Alarcón, on meeting an Indian with whom the interpreter could converse, persuaded him to enter their boat and "made very much of him and gave him the best entertaynement" before asking many questions about the geography and peoples of the areas farther up the river. Alarcón wanted to know "whether hee had ever seene any men like us, or had heard any report of them . . . whether hee knewe a place called Cevola, and a River called Tontonteac, whether they helde that there was one God, creator of heaven and earth, or that they worshipped any other Idol . . . whether they had any Lorde, . . . whether they had any warre, and for what occasion . . . [and] what they did with those men which they killed in battel."[113] On this occa-

2.5 Aperrear *was one of the forms of threat used by the Spaniards to ensure—among other things—the veracity of geographical information received from Indians. From Theodor de Bry,* Historia America, *part 4 (Antwerp, 1594). From the American Geographical Society Collection, University of Wisconsin–Milwaukee Library.*

sion, as on many others, questions about people were at least as important as those about places, regions, and environments. In 1564, René Goulaine de Laudonnière's French lieutenant at La Caroline tried to establish friendly relations with the nearby Indians, "hoping by this meane to discover dayly some new thing, & especially the certain course of the [Saint Johns] River." On returning to the fort he deliberately left a "souldier [alone] with the Indians to enforme himselfe more of such things he might discover more at leasure."[114] Two years later, and some 350 miles or so to the south, Menéndez de Avilés, the Spanish *adelantado* of Florida, instructed the captain of a group of soldiers to settle at a village of Calusa Indians toward the southern end of the peninsula. There they were to set a

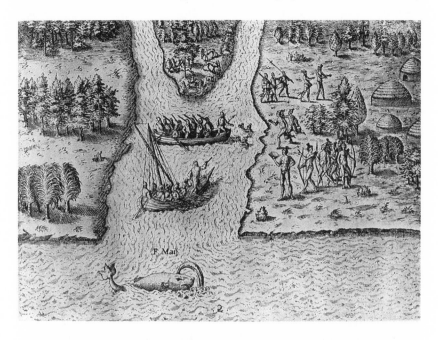

2.6 René de Laudonnière establishing friendly relations with the Indians on the River of May (Saint Johns River) in 1564. From Theodor de Bry, Great Voyages *(Antwerp, 1591). From the American Geographical Society Collection, University of Wisconsin–Milwaukee Library.*

good example by worshipping regularly, Avilés hoping thereby to "indoctrinate" the natives and to cultivate friendly relations. Through "their friendship with the Indians they were to try and find out if a river which was 2 leagues from there, went into the Lagoon at Maymi [Miami], and what the distance was in leagues." The information was being sought to complete the Spaniards' knowledge of the lagoonal waterway system along that part of the coast of southeastern Florida. Avilés "already knew how many *leagues* there were from that [Maymi] lagoon to Macoya, and that there was a passageway; and within 3 or 4 months he would go to see if he could travel by that river to San Mateo and St. Augustine."[115] In this case, therefore, a deliberate attempt was being made to cultivate friendly relations with Indians in order to fill a strategically important information gap in the emerging Spanish understanding of the coastal waterways.

Shorter-term goodwill was often achieved by means of gifts. Only a few years before Avilés was in Florida, soldiers at the first French settlement at Charlesfort had given an Indian chief "certaine trifles" in exchange for having received a "number of exceeding faire pearles, & two stones of fine Christal and certaine silver oare." In giving the trifles, the soldiers asked to be told of "the place whence the silver oare and the Christall came." In response, the chief indicated that it came "ten dayes journey from his habitation up within the countrey: and that the inhabitants of the countrey did dig the same at the foote of certaine high mountaines, where they found of it in very good quantitie."[116] Similar exchanges of material gifts for geographical information were made on many occasions and in all parts of North America. Sometimes, however, gifts were given as acknowledgments rather than incentives, as when, in 1609, Fernández de Ecija, in the course of trying to sail up the Atlantic coast as far as the mouth of the James River, sent men onshore to talk with the Guale Indians near present-day Charleston, South Carolina; Ecija received one of them onboard the ship, obtained unspecified information from him, and then "regailed him and six [other] Indians who had come with him with food and drink and beads and other things."[117]

The most serious attempts to ensure the reliability of information involved one or more of three often closely related strategies: teaching natives a European language; Europeanizing selected natives; and using acculturized natives to elicit information from their former friends and associates. In 1513 in Florida, for example, Ponce de León captured an Indian both so that he could serve as "a pilot and so that he might learn the [Spanish] language." This was an early example of what was to become quite common. It is not known how much Spanish the Indian learned, but he was probably one of those who, a few weeks later, informed the Spaniards of "some islands" (probably in the Bahaman group) that they had not seen on their outward voyage to Florida.[118] When, in 1525, Esteban Gómez returned to La Coruña in northwestern Spain after a voyage along the coasts of what are now New England and the Maritime Provinces, he brought back with him as slaves fifty-eight Algonquian-speaking Indians. Some of these were taken to Toledo. It is not known how much Spanish they learned there, but an almost contemporary account from that city records, "Judging by what the Indians say, they have silver and copper."[119] Similarly, in 1536, at the end of his second voyage to the Saint Lawrence River, Cartier took back with him to France three Indians. One of them, Donnacona, was the headman of the Stadacona villages, settlements of Iroquoian-speaking Indians near the present-day city of Quebec. Donnacona remained in France for several years, presumably learned some French, and was considered a sufficiently reliable informant to be interviewed by King Francis I. Afterward, Francis said that Donnacona had "told him [that] there is a large city called Sagana [Saguenay], where there are many mines of gold and silver in great abundance, and men who dress and wear shoes like we do; and that there is an abundance of clove, nutmeg and pepper." On being asked for his opinion of Donnacona's integrity, Francis said that the Indian "spoke strict truth," noting the fact that Donnacona "was questioned on coming on board [at the Stadacona villages], and the Notary took it down, and the Captain again questioned him at times [on the voyage back to France], and the King also after his arrival, and he always said the same, and he had never been found in error." It was suggested to Francis that Donnacona might "be like him who tempted Christ who said '*haec omnia tibi dabo,*'" so as to return to his own land. "The king laughed and said that the Indian . . . was an honest man."[120] It seems unlikely, therefore, that Francis had been informed of Donnacona's earlier account of a region "where the people, possessing no anus, never eat nor digest, but simply make water through the penis" and of "another country whose inhabitants have only one leg."[121]

Asking one Indian or one group of Indians the same question at different times was a common verification procedure, as indeed was asking the same question of two or more different and preferably unrelated Indians or groups of Indians. In 1605, for example, Father Escobar of Juan de Oñate's expedition believed the report by a chief named Otata of occurrences of tin and gold on a "little island" in the Gulf of California because this Indian "and many others again told us the same things that they had said before, without contradicting themselves, in any detail, even though forty days had passed since they had [first] furnished us this information." Escobar added, "Many other Indians corroborated these reports; some of them were from the island and had come to see us." This corroboration of Otata's report caused Escobar to accept the chief's other account of "the people who live on the Buena Esperanza river, up to its source, indicating that this was near to the sea to the northwest . . . [and] making a sketch of the land on a piece of paper, in which he indicated many nations of people so strange that only at risk of not being believed do I venture to report them."

Quite clearly, Escobar had doubts, but the supposed honesty of Otata in giving geographical intelligence about one area led to the Spaniard's somewhat incredulous acceptance of information about people with large ears, others with one foot, men with enormous penises, and people who slept underwater.[122] Sometimes, however, native information concerning distant places can be seen in retrospect to have been remarkably good. One of the earliest Spanish accounts of the pueblo settlements of Cíbola (Zuni) is contained in a letter written by Melchior Díaz in 1540, when he was somewhere near the Gila River in what is now southern Arizona, three hundred to four hundred miles to the southwest of the settlements themselves. This was the closest he was to get to the pueblos, but he heard of them "in many diverse ways, questioning some Indians together and others separately," and found that they all seemed to agree. Thus obtained, his approximately nine-hundred-word account incorporates many of the distinctive characteristics of what were to become known as the Zuni and Hopi pueblos: dwellings several stories high and entered by means of ladders; the manufacture of textiles and the use of turquoises as ornaments; the cultivation of maize, beans, and squash; the critical nature of the water supply; and the nearby availability of timber.[123]

Friendly and partly Europeanized natives were quite frequently used to assess or ensure the reliability of information received from other Indians. In 1603, for example, François Gravé du Pont took with him to the Saint Lawrence River two Indians who had spent some time in France. Within three days of anchoring at the mouth of the Saguenay River, he "sought the [Algonquian-speaking] savages" located just a league away, taking along with him "the two savages . . . brought to make report of what they had seen in France, and of the good reception the King [Henry IV] had given them." The "grand Sagamore" and "some eighty or hundred of his companions" received the French "very well" and, when assembled, were addressed by one of the two Indians who had been brought back. He told them about France, its king, the people, and their way of life and was listened to "attentively" and "with the greatest possible silence." His "oration" marked the beginning of a long and friendly ceremony and must have been an important factor in establishing the amicable relationship that during the next few days led, among other things, to information being received from the local Indians about the source of the Saguenay River.[124]

Europeans who had been "nativized" were probably even more reliable as informants than natives who had been Europeanized. For example, in 1566, while sailing north up the Atlantic coast of Florida to attack the French at La Caroline, the Spaniards met a "solitary" fellow countryman "who had escaped a shipwreck twenty years before." They "gave him hospitality and enquired whether he had heard anything of the French and the location of their settlement." He replied that "he knew nothing but what he had heard from the natives; that they were located fifty leagues to the north of the place where" the Spaniards had just landed; his information proved to be essentially correct.[125] As the number of Europeans increased in North America, as their settlements grew, and as Euro-Americans and Canadians later began to diffuse into previously unsettled areas, the native peoples inevitably tended to become alienated, physically and spiritually weakened, and hence less reliable informants than the "noble savages" of a few generations before. Conversely, as more whites were captured by or chose to live with native peoples, their role in transmitting geographical information from the natives to the alien intruders was to become increasingly important, especially after the early seventeenth century. The considerable body of "captivity literature" is an indicator of the significance of this type of intermediary, but the captive's role in this context has never been examined systematically.[126]

Verification, modification, and refutation were achieved only when Europeans experienced directly those areas that had previously been represented to them. In 1528, for example, Cabeza de Vaca left Aute, in what is now Georgia or adjacent Alabama, in part because during "forays, which they had made farther inland, the Christians [Spaniards] saw that the land in which they were was not as had been described to them by the Indians."[127] Conversely, the day after the Indians had drawn for Champlain their charcoal-with-pebbles map of Massachusetts Bay, the explorer sailed along its coast for the first time and recorded that he "recognised in this bay everything the Indians . . . had drawn" for him.[128] Although not quite so absolute, verification sometimes involved obtaining reports about a previously unknown area geographically located between two known places, in which the reported information conformed to some rational principle. For example, in 1604, one year after he had been at Tadoussac on the Saint Lawrence River, Champlain, in the course of exploring the Bay of Fundy, went a short distance up the Saint John River. Contact was made with a local Maliseet chief, who described the characteristics of the river valley and reported that his people went "up this river as far as Tadoussac" and in doing so went "overland" (i.e., over the watershed) "only a short distance to reach that place," adding that from "the river St. John to Tadoussac the distance is sixty five leagues."[129] Much later, this was to become the settlers' most important route across New Brunswick. From Champlain's perspective, however, the information concerning intervening features and distance was akin to a surveyor's backsight. It evidently satisfied his verification standards: it was represented—albeit somewhat schematically—on his influential printed map of 1612, "Carte geographique de la Nouvelle Franse en son vray meridiein."[130] Sometimes, however, the process involved excessive European extrapolation and inference. Coronado's guides, for example, correctly informed him that the Cicuye (Pecos) River, which he knew, joined the Tiguex River (Rio Grande), which he also knew, but noted that the joining was twenty days' travel downstream, well beyond the limits of his own experience. Below that, they reported, the Tiguex flowed east, whereas its true direction to the Gulf of Mexico is closer to southeast. The Spaniards, however, later assumed that it emptied into the "mighty Espiritu Santo [Mississippi River] which Don Hernando de Soto's men [had] discovered in Florida" at about the same time.[131] Working in Venice, the Genoese geographer Battista Agnese either did not know of or disagreed with this assumption, because on his 1557 map of the southern part of North America he represented the Tiguex River even more erroneously, as flowing south into the head of the Gulf of California.[132] In this case a European mapmaker, in part, though indirectly, using native information, made a very serious error. There were to be many more examples of such geographical mistakes during the next three hundred years.

Native North Americans not only played an important role in the exploration of their continent by Europeans and, later on, by Americans and Canadians. Unknowingly, they also helped to shape the alien cultures' formal geographies of it. Almost always, the critical stage in that shaping occurred in places far removed from direct involvement with or by natives, often by geographers and mapmakers with no direct experience of the areas involved and little or no understanding of the processes reviewed in this chapter. Not surprisingly, the errors were often very serious and usually persisted for decades before being corrected. Surprisingly, until recently, scholars have shown relatively little interest in examining the origins and consequences of these errors.

The Influences of Native Geographical Information

Early Native American influences on European thought, art, and activities have been the focus of much scholarship. Fredi Chiappelli's First Images of America is one major synthesis of what is known about the early impact of the New World on the Old World. Yet, notwithstanding the book's theme, the otherwise authoritative section on "The New Geography" contains no indication that native North Americans helped to shape Europeans' images of the geography of the continent.[133] The omission is typical. In part it reflects a lack of understanding of the ways in which geographers and cartographers obtained and processed information before incorporating it into texts and onto maps.

In one respect, sixteenth- and early-seventeenth-century geographers had been well provided with information about North America. Some officials and explorers published accounts of their voyages along the coasts and their travels on the land; letters and manuscript logs and journals were copied and exchanged in European capitals and ports; and collections of these were compiled for publication. Pioneered by the several compilations of Spanish and Portuguese voyages published by Pietro Martire d'Anghiera (Peter Martyr) between 1516 and 1534, the collections later included Giovanni Battista Ramusio's three-volume *Navigationi et viaggi*, published between 1550 and 1559, and Richard Hakluyt's *Principal Navigations*, published between 1598 and 1600. Together these were perhaps the most important component of the geographical information system at that time.[134] The last of Hakluyt's three volumes was, and remains, particularly important in a North American context. This body of widely available literature contained much firsthand evidence concerning the role of native North Americans as informants. That this role was not generally recognized at the time in Europe and has only recently begun to be recognized by scholars is probably a consequence of the limited access to the complementary chart and map evidence. Manuscript maps were, of course, made by most of the explorers, but they tended not to be generally available. Some maps were published, but for reasons in part related to printing technology, they were very generalized. Woodcut maps did not begin to be replaced by intaglio maps until after 1550, and the detail on the latter did not approach that of their late-seventeenth- and eighteenth-century successors. Furthermore, information sources were rarely acknowledged on maps, and accounts of map compilation procedures were virtually nonexistent. The era of explanatory map memoirs did not begin until the late seventeenth century. Hence, only in the fairly recent past, with relatively easy access to great public map collections and even easier access to large numbers of good-quality facsimile maps and the availability of a new generation of scholarly editions of many of the early voyages and travels, has it become possible to readily relate source information to map content. Furthermore, such relating can now be done with the benefit of insights from fields as diverse as archaeology, cultural anthropology, traditional cosmology, and psychology, together with detailed information on environments as they now are—the latter essential for reconstructing environments as they formerly were. Given these new perspectives and the assembly of hitherto dispersed evidence, it is possible to begin for the first time to assess the role of native North Americans in shaping early Europeans' geographical images of North America.

By circa 1612, Europeans had some firsthand experience of approximately 60 percent of the coastline of North America but had seen much less of the continent's surface and had settled less than 1 percent of it. Yet they had represented much of it on maps that showed rivers, lakes, mountains, aspects of vegetation, and native settlements, often with names. In some cases, features may have been inferred on the basis of general geographical concepts, as with the clusters of hill symbols that commonly occurred around the catchments of rivers and the lines of similar symbols that often separated the lower basins of adjacent rivers. In western Europe, virtually all major rivers do rise in hilly or mountainous areas, but the watersheds between the lower basins are not ridgelike. Yet, even there, the concept of mountain-and-ridge girt drainage basins defied reality until the early nineteenth century.[135] In some cases, information may have been invented by mapmakers to fill gaps. After all, Jonathan Swift's eighteenth-century "geographers, in Afric-maps, [supposedly] with savage-pictures fill[ed] their gaps; And o'er unhabitable downs Place[d] elephants for want of towns." The true terrae incognitae in North America, however, were so extensive that frequent imaginative gap-filling could not have achieved what in retrospect can be seen as a progressive improvement in the quality and quantity of information on early maps of areas beyond the range of direct European experience. Before such experience, the only other explanation for the not inconsiderable amount of approximately correct information on maps is that it was derived from native peoples. Scholars are beginning to realize that for four centuries or more, native peoples did function in this way: as the human precursors of modern remote-sensing technology. The evidence for this is of four types: acknowledgments on maps; inferences from the style of map content; toponymy; and correlations between accounts of geographical information known to have been received from natives and the cartographic representation of essentially identical information.

Acknowledgments on maps of specific information content based on native sources afford the most conclusive evidence but are relatively rare. One of the best-documented examples is John Smith's map "Virginia," of

1612. The mother map for many later ones, it essentially represents the drainage catchment of Chesapeake Bay between the Atlantic coast of the Delmarva Peninsula and the Allegheny Mountains. At, or in most cases some distance below, the source of almost every river and main tributary is positioned a small but conspicuous Maltese cross. The same symbol also occurs at two locations on the coastline. Beyond each cross, the river or coast is represented more schematically than below, incorporating less detail and with less visual weight. The same symbol also occurs on the map at three inland locations between rivers. The "Signification of these markes" (i.e., the key to the map) explains, "To the crosses hath bin discovered what beyond is by relation." The map was published in Smith's *A Map of Virginia with a Description of the Countrey . . .* , and in the text the explanation is even more explicit: "As far as you see the little Crosses on rivers, mountaines, or other places have been discovered; the rest was had by information of the Savages, and are set downe, according to their instructions."[136] Another source contains an account of the setting "downe" of one of these rivers: the Powhatan, now James, River. Some eighteen miles up the river, the English party met eight Indians. One of these "offred with his foote to describe the river to us. So I [a gent. of the Colony: probably Gabriel Archer] gave him a pen and paper (shewing first ye use) and he layd out the whole River from Chesseian [Chesapeake] bay to the end of it so farr as passadg was for boates: he tolde us of two Ilettes in the Ryver we should passe by, meaning that one whereon we were, and then came to an overfall of water [at which Richmond is now centred], beyond that the two kyngdomes which the Ryver Runes by then a greate Distance of[f]." On the following day, the same Indian was asked to draw the map again in the presence of Powhatan, the overlord of Tidewater Virginia, "who in every thing consented to this draught."[137] In this way there appeared toward the upper left corner of Smith's map a spindly extension of the Powhatan River above the falls, paralleled for part of its course by a dotted line that probably represented a trail, interrupted by one "ilette" and passing close to five named Indian settlements.

Although not as well authenticated as Smith's "Virginia," other examples of acknowledgments of native information are known. Of these, the so-called Velasco map of 1611 is one of the earliest examples.[138] It is a contemporary Spanish copy of a map made by an unknown Englishman who had been sent by James I to map the English provinces in North America. He exceeded his brief by embracing far more, but he based his drawing almost exclusively on the maps and writings of others. All the linework is coloured. Of the four colours used, only one is explained on the map itself; a legend indicates, "All the blue is done by the relations of the Indians." The map represents the coast between present-day North Carolina and southern Labrador, including Newfoundland and the Saint Lawrence and Hudson Rivers. There is no indication of how many Indian sources were used, but blue linework is used to represent four different noncontiguous groups of features: Lakes Champlain and George and the upper part of the Champlain River; the Saint Lawrence River above the confluence of the Ottawa River and the eastern part of Lake Ontario; a supposed north-south-oriented coastline to the south of Lake Ontario; and the upper parts of three rivers flowing into the head of Chesapeake Bay (the Susquehanna, perhaps the Patapsco, and certainly the Potomac).

Although not proven, the representations of the upper Saint Lawrence River and Lakes Champlain, George, and Ontario were in all probability based on Indian accounts given to Champlain in 1603 of features he never reached. Lakes Champlain and George, for example, are represented as almost equal in area. In reality this is not so, but Champlain was wrongly told by his Indian guides that the upper lake was "as large as the former."[139] Likewise, the eastern end of Lake Ontario is represented as having one short river flowing into it from the north and another from the south. They are unnamed and unexplained, but Champlain had been told by Algonquin Indians that "about four or five leagues from the entrance [hydrologically, the exit] of that lake [Ontario] there is a river leading northward to the Algonquins, and another leading [southward] to the Iroquois, by way of which the said Algonquins and Iroquois made war upon one another."[140] These are the Trent and the Oswego Rivers, respectively, which are inconspicuous, sometimes unnamed, and even omitted from modern atlas maps. Yet on the Velasco map they locally dominate otherwise empty areas. To the Indians they were strategically important and hence worth mentioning to Champlain. In turn, Champlain reported them in the published account of his 1603 expedition, in which they were perceived to be important by the compiler of the Velasco map. Such compilers were of course selective and, at best, judicious. In this particular case, another reported river flowing into the southern shore of Lake Ontario was wrongly omitted. Hydrologically, the omitted Genesee is more important than the Oswego. Conversely, in representing Lakes Champlain and George at approximately half the linear dimensions given by the Indians, the compiler reduced significantly what would otherwise have been an enormous error.

The representation in blue of the false coastline to the south of Lake Ontario was almost certainly derived from an unpublished earlier version of Smith's map. Ironically, although the compiler reproduced the river systems fairly faithfully from what must have been a prepublication copy of Smith's "Virginia," those rivers south of the Potomac are not in blue, though the upper Potomac is. It will never be known whether the unknown compiler missed or ignored the Maltese crosses or whether they were not included on the version of the map to which he had access. It is clear, however, that he had access to additional information about the Susquehanna River. Though named and acknowledged to be "by relation" of the Indians, it is relatively short on Smith's map. The Velasco map also indicates it as having been "done by the relations of the Indians" but represents it as being far longer than any of the other rivers draining into Chesapeake Bay. The straightness of the river as represented on the map confirms its Indian origin, and a shorter west-bank branch almost certainly signals the existence of either the Juniata or the West Branch Susquehanna Rivers. In reality, the complex course of the Susquehanna contrasts markedly with the essential straightness of the Hudson River to the east. On the Velasco map, however, the latter is represented as the more complex. The Hudson is not, however, "done" in "blue," and the compiler would appear to have been drawing on survey information brought back by Henry Hudson in 1609, after Hudson ascended the river as far as the site of present-day Albany.

In the case of the Smith and Velasco maps, acknowledging and indicating native inputs does not extend to explaining how they were incorporated with the other information. Indians had no concept of latitude, longitude, absolute distance, or absolute direction. Consequently, information received from them could not be automatically incorporated into existing schemas. A Dutch manuscript map of the same period does, however, afford evidence that the problem was sometimes recognized. In 1616, Cornelis Hendricks produced a large and detailed map of the Hudson River, based largely on his own surveys of the previous few years. The map, however, also incorporated schematic representations of the Delaware and the Susquehanna Rivers to the west. From the petition that Hendricks presented to his Dutch patrons and from the general appearance of the map itself, it is clear that the information concerning these two rivers and associated Indian settlements had been obtained from one of three Dutchmen who had lived and traveled with, worked for, and collected information from Mohawk and Mahican Indians. Having incorporated this informa-

tion with his own survey of the Hudson River to make one map, Hendricks
expressed, in a long legend, his doubts about the relationships of the two
components:

> Regarding what Kleytjen and his Companion have told me of the sit-
> uation of the [Delaware and Susquehanna] Rivers, and the places oc-
> cupied by the Tribes, which they found when going inland away
> from the Maquaas [Mohawks] and along the New [Susquehanna]
> river down to Ogehage [Susquehannock?] namely the enemy of the
> aforesaid northern nations I cannot at present find anything but two
> sketches of small [Indian?] maps partly finished. . . . And when I
> think how best to make the one correspond with the rough notes to
> the best of my knowledge I find that the dwelling-places of the Sen-
> necas Gachoos Capitannesses and Jottecas ought to have been indi-
> cated rather more to the west.[141]

Since these tribes were settled on the headwater tributaries of the Susquehanna River, Hendricks was also indicating that they should have been
represented "rather more to the west." He was correct in his revised opinion, though how he reached it is not known.

Sometimes, attempts to incorporate Indian information into a European
schema resulted in enormous errors. More than one hundred years after
Hendricks, the French Canadian explorer Pierre La Vérendrye collected information from several different groups of Indians on and near the northwestern shore of Lake Superior. Basically, this information consisted of
maps of the rivers and lakes of the area between Lake Superior, Lake Winnipeg, and Hudson Bay. Some of this information was incorporated into a
composite map, which, in turn, was differentially rescaled and then integrated into a manuscript version of Guillaume De l'Isle's "Carte D'Amerique . . ." of a few years before. Incorporation into Nicolas Bellin's "Carte
D'L'Amerique Septentrionale . . ." of 1743 resulted in a great river flowing
westward across the continent, almost to the Pacific Ocean, where, according to a legend on the map, the Indians reported that the water began to
rise and fall. The French assumed that this referred to the head of a great
estuary entering into the Pacific Ocean, whereas the Indian informants had
almost certainly been referring to one of several unusual hydrological phenomena in the English-Winnipeg-Nelson River system, some thirteen
hundred miles to the east. The Indians were in no way responsible for it,
but the error was enormous, and its consequences persisted on printed
maps of western North America almost until the end of the eighteenth
century.[142]

Very often, the received information had not been transmitted by the natives in graphical form or, if it had, had been transformed subsequently into a written description. The representation on the Velasco map of Lakes Champlain and George would appear to have been based on such a description in Champlain's *Des Sauvages . . .* of 1603: two lakes connected to each other *en echelon* at corners; each lake rectangular and with similar proportions and dimensions. This was indeed a reasonable reconstruction of the Indian evidence as published by Champlain: "Some forty or fifty leagues in length, and some twenty-five leagues in breadth . . . when you come to the end of this lake [Champlain], there is another rapid, and they [the Indians] enter another lake, which is as large as the former."[143] Champlain's own "Carte geographique de la Nouvelle Franse . . ." of 1612 contains less specific but perhaps more representative examples. Within the interior, and away from the Saint Lawrence itself, very few of the rivers and lakes had by that date been explored by Europeans. The course of several, however, had been described to Champlain by Indians, and the representations of these on the map can be best explained as transformations from words to lines.

Given an understanding of the principles and processes discussed thus far, it becomes possible to develop an iconography of native components of European maps, that is, to recognize probable examples in the absence of direct supporting evidence. Recent work suggests six diagnostic characteristics: straight or gently curved lines to represent complex linear features; symmetrical representations of asymmetrical drainage and route networks; circles and other simple geometrical shapes to represent complexly shaped enclosed spaces, such as lakes; the caricaturization and exaggeration of the shapes of distinctive and culturally important features; the duplication of features, arising from failure to relate independent reports of the same feature; and discontinuities of style, as on Hendricks's map of 1616.[144] The application of these diagnostic principles indicates that native information accounted for a far greater proportion of the content of European and, later in time, American and Canadian maps than has been hitherto suspected.

An as yet unexplained and, until 1970, unknown early-seventeenth-century manuscript map of Virginia consists essentially of three elements: an absolutely straight watershed; straight main rivers; and straight tributary streams that join the main rivers at acute angles. Its provenance is unknown, but even though it is almost certainly a transcript, it has all the hallmarks of having been copied from an Indian original.[145] Symmetrical

representations of asymmetrical drainage systems are quite common. One
of the largest is the lower Mississippi drainage as represented on Jan Jansson's "America Septentrionalis" of 1641.[146] Native topological representations of relatively small, clearly bounded spaces usually paid no regard to
shape. Lakes, for example, are characteristically represented as circles. In
reality, most of the thousands of lakes of the Canadian shield are very irregular in shape and tend to be elongate, with the larger ones located toward
the heads of rivers. In 1632, Europeans had seen very few of these, yet
Champlain's 1632 map "Carte de la Nouvelle France . . ." is full of tadpole-
shaped lakes in the upper part of drainage systems.[147] Since the representation of the drainage is not fundamentally wrong, it is reasonable to suppose that much of it was derived from Indian sources. Indians tended to
caricaturize the shapes of features that were culturally significant. Like the
facial features of politicians in drawings by political cartoonists, significant
features were exaggerated. John Foster's "A Map of New-England" of 1677
is in many respects remarkably good for its time. It is, however dominated
by the representation of one feature: the unnamed present-day Winnipe-
saukee Lake, in what is now central New Hampshire. Not only is it far too
large in relation to the remainder of New England, but also only one of its
several peninsulas is represented, though that very boldly; the whole
tends to be excessively rounded; and twenty or so islands are scattered ran-
domly across its surface. With the lake then located well beyond the frontier of English settlement, its appearance on the map can best be explained
as the consequence of having incorporated a native caricaturization into an
otherwise essentially European map.[148]

A large lake, when reported from fundamentally different locations by
two or more different groups of natives, could result in duplication on European maps. The Velasco map may well contain an example of this. The
representation of the eastern end of lake Ontario is essentially correct, is
certainly incontestable, and as has been shown already, was derived from
Indian sources. But the representation on the same map of the shoreline of
a large but separate sea or lake immediately to the west of the Allegheny
Plateau was derived from quite different Indian sources. The Algonquian
Indians of Virginia could, likewise, have been referring to Lake Ontario,
though Lake Erie seems more likely, and as has been noted earlier, this
could possibly have been the mythical western shoreline implicit in Algonquian cosmology. Jacques Le Moyne de Morgues's "Floridas Americas Provinciae . . . ," based on his experiences between 1562 and 1565, may contain
another example.[149] It depicts two lakes in the interior of the Florida penin-

sula. The larger, northern one is placed at the source of the present-day Saint Johns River, and the smaller one is farther south, with no outlet to the sea. In reality, Lake Okeechobee is by far the largest lake in modern-day Florida, and the southern of Le Moyne de Morgues's lakes could well be a representation of it. The larger lake to the north could be Lake George or one of the many other lakes in the upper catchment area of the Saint Johns River. If so, however, it is represented as far too large in relation to the southern lake. Alternatively, because portages afford an easy route between the upper Saint Johns River and Lake Okeechobee, the northern of the two representations could also have been Lake Okeechobee, that is, this could be a case of duplication. Whether this is a case of duplication or of an inversion of relative sizes, separate Indian sources of information would seem to offer the best explanation. Difficult either to prove or to refute in the absence of detailed contemporary records, similar duplications may explain the appearance and disappearance of large islands on eighteenth-century maps of Lake Superior and, similarly, the coexistence of a Lake Winnipeg and a Lake Assiniboin on eighteenth-century maps of the trans–Great Lakes region. The former could have been a consequence of failure to relate information given by Indians on the northern and southern shores of the vast and dangerous Lake Superior. Likewise, the latter could have arisen as a result of failure to relate information given by Indians to the northwest of Lake Superior with that given by Indians on the western shore of Hudson Bay: the former to the French and the latter to the English.

Further evidence that native peoples were directly or indirectly responsible for a significant proportion of the content of early maps is afforded by toponymic names, especially those of natural features. Even now, after almost four hundred years of active Europeanization, approximately half the natural features of North America are officially known by native names or names of native derivation. Not all native names, however, are descriptive or were native originals. Europeans often named features after the tribes in whose territories they were located; the Susquehanna and Arkansas Rivers, for example, and the Adirondack and Appalachian Mountains.

In all but the driest parts of the Southwest, river systems and coastlines were the matrices of early maps. Lines of latitude and longitude were either absent or grossly inaccurate, and the representations of rivers and coasts formed the "skeleton" with reference to which other features could be plotted. In their essentials, the coasts were known and surveyed first. The rivers, especially those in the interior, "emerged" on maps somewhat later and usually over several decades or more. Some were explored from their estuaries upward, and the larger of these, at least, tended to be given and to retain European names. For example, the name "Saint Lawrence" was first given by Cartier to a small bay. He had discovered it on 10 August 1535, the day of Saint Lawrence of Rome.[150] The use of the name was then extended to embrace the whole of the then unnamed gulf and, thereafter, gradually up the mighty river flowing into it. Seven years before, Cabeza de Vaca and his men had passed the mouth of a great river flowing into the northern shore of the Gulf of Mexico. Although it was probably not recognized as such, the same river was crossed some six years later by Soto and his men. In circa 1544 it was represented on a Spanish manuscript map as somewhat longer than, and with a more complex pattern of catchment streams than, the other ten rivers flowing into the Gulf coast in what is now the southern United States.[151] Its representation was not speculative and must have been influenced—if not determined—by Indian informants. It was named on the map "R. del espiritu Sa[n]to." However, the river was explored upstream not by the Spaniards but, more than a century later, by the French, moving downstream. They and their maps were responsible for introducing the name "Mississippi," derived from the Algonquian name "Messipi," meaning "big river." Other river names were similarly derived: "Ohio," from the Iroquois for "river fine"; "Allegheny," from the Delaware for "most beautiful or best stream"; and "Minnesota," from the Siouan for "water cloudy." These and many other names epitomized from the native perspective the essential characteristics of the rivers as a whole. In other cases, the name of the whole was derived from a characteristic of a culturally distinctive part. "Monongahela," for example, is a Delaware name and probably means "high-banks-falling-down" river, a characteristic of only part of the river flowing through what is now southwestern Pennsylvania. Likewise, the "Yellowstone" River probably derived its name via the French "Roche Jaune," from an Indian name associating the river with a distinctive yellow rock near its mouth. The adjective in the name "Black Hills" was similarly derived from an Indian name. The Sioux described the hills thus because they supported pine trees and appeared dark when seen from a distance, in contrast to the brown and green appearance of the surrounding grassy plains. Occasionally, a translation assumed the form of a transliteration, with serious consequences. For example, the Caddoan name "Canohatino" (for "Red River" because of the colour of its water), for the river flowing from northeastern New Mexico across northern Texas into Oklahoma, became anglicized as the "Canadian River."

In thousands of cases, however, it is reasonable to infer that Europeans or, later, Euro-Americans and Canadians applied or translated native names because the Indians or Inuits had alerted the explorers to anticipate these places, led the explorers to them, or, in the case of some large drainage systems, confirmed that a river already known at one point was the same as that being seen for the first time at another. Although not proven, the idea seems probable that transliterating or translating native toponymy occurred most frequently during periods of rapid exploration and after the waning of the early drive to implant Christian and national signatures on the land.

Retrospect and Prospect

The role of native North Americans in early European exploration has, for the most part, been overlooked by historians. There have been several reasons for this. Whatever the reasons, however, there is no doubt that native North Americans influenced European exploration of their continent in ways and to an extent that, until now, have been unsuspected or, at least, grossly underestimated. Inevitably, therefore, the consequences of these influences have also been overlooked.

Native North Americans communicated to Europeans spatial images of the latter's terrae semicognitae and terrae incognitae. Structured according to native cognition and culture and distorted by the communication and reception processes, these images nevertheless functioned as spatial models: to be tested for content and shape by comparison with one another and to be retested and revised in the course of the European exploratory process. As such, the models facilitated and accelerated that process. Misunderstandings inevitably arose from failure on the part of Europeans both to recognize the essential differences between their own and the natives' geographical cognition and to appreciate the distortions arising in the course of communication. Nevertheless, without these models, the exploration and initial mapping of North America would have been far slower, much harder, and, doubtless, costlier.

The use of native models of lands unexplored by Europeans continued long after the early seventeenth century. Indeed, in the remoter parts of North America they were being used by field scientists and others until well into the twentieth century. The more than four-hundred-year history of this process still has to be researched and written, not only as an overlooked aspect of North American history but also for at least three other important reasons. First, it will lead to a better appreciation of the intercultural misunderstandings concerning the natures of space, place, and environment in the context of treaty negotiations. Second, it should ultimately lead to the feedback of evidence to the cognitive and other sciences, sciences from which, in the short term, history itself should be an unashamed borrower. Finally, it will contribute significantly to the reinstatement of native peoples into North American history, a process that is at long last under way but still has far to go.

The role of Christopher Columbus as the key initiator of the European discovery of the Americas has long been known. Only the details need to be revised from time to time. Conversely, the role of native North Americans as the Columbuses of the European exploration process still has to be investigated and publicized. It is hoped that this chapter will mark the beginning.

3 / The Columbian Voyages

ROBERT H. FUSON

Christopher Columbus made four round-trip crossings of the Atlantic Ocean between the years 1492 and 1504 and discovered in the process the Bahama Islands, the Greater Antilles, most of the Lesser Antilles, Trinidad, South America, and the Caribbean coast of Central America from Honduras to Panama. In spite of these remarkable landfalls, he never reached his destination, Asia, and was totally unaware that he had failed to cross the "Ocean Sea," which supposedly spanned the distance between Europe and Marco Polo's Cathay. Columbus never sailed the Ocean Sea because it did not exist. Yet this single geographical concept—one ocean, one landmass—probably ranks as the most important physical difference between the view of the world then and the view of the world now. The fact that the fifteenth-century notion of a common sea washing the shores of western Europe and eastern Asia lay only in the minds of the believers was (and is) irrelevant. *Belief* in the Ocean Sea provided sufficient validation. Its existence had been confirmed by every test known to philosophy, science, and religion.

Even though the world ocean was universally accepted in the fifteenth century, there was still doubt and debate concerning the relationship of the earth's land and water distribution. Throughout antiquity and the Middle Ages the belief commonly held was that the sea surrounded the world island (Afro-Eurasia), an idea that had its roots in Babylonian geography and represented an evolution of the early Greek concept of a land-girdling ocean-river. By the end of the fifteenth century there had been a reversal of informed opinion regarding the earth's land and water relationship: the land was now perceived as encompassing the Ocean Sea. Both concepts, however, relegated the larger percentage of surface area to land, and in the fifteenth century the centuries-old belief that the land-to-water ratio was six or seven to one still held sway.

Coupled with the erroneous supposition that the earth was mostly land was another misfounded belief, one that underestimated the planet's cir-

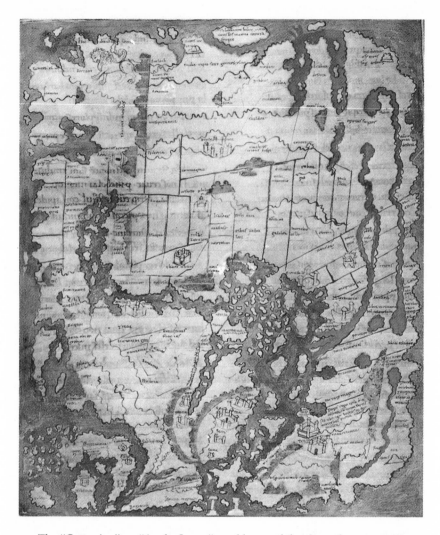

3.1 *The "Cottonian" or "Anglo-Saxon" world map of the eleventh century, illus-trating the World Island concept that was at the heart of Columbus's geographical conceptions. By permission of The British Library.*

cumference. Columbus accepted the Ptolemaic value of 20,400 statute miles, approximately 20 percent less than the correct distance. Before we rush to condemn Columbus for this incredible inaccuracy, it should be pointed out that a correct measurement of a degree of longitude at the equator was not made until 1669–70. Even Sir Isaac Newton, writing at about the same time that the correct degree was calculated, underestimated the earth's circumference by 15 percent.[1]

Although there was disagreement about the size of the earth, there was no disagreement about its sphericity, at least not among cosmographers, geographers, and astronomers. No one schooled in these sciences questioned the fact that one could reach the East by sailing west, *if* the crew did not starve to death or drown in the process. As far as Columbus or anyone else knew, no one had ever sailed due west to the (East) Indies, or to China, or to Japan. The few Europeans who had ventured to India and China in the past had always taken overland routes to the East. Even though many of these travelers, such as Marco Polo, had returned part of the way to Europe from China (beginning in 1292) by ship through the Strait of Malacca and the Indian Ocean, there were still some fifteenth-century cosmographers who believed the Ptolemaic representation of the Indian Ocean as an enclosed sea. Not until Vasco da Gama's 1497–98 voyage around Africa to India was this concept weakened. But Columbus's (and others') inability to find the connection between the Ocean Sea and the Indian Ocean (and no wonder, they were seeking the connection in Central America!) delayed an understanding of the world's oceans. With no comprehension of the Pacific Ocean—or its immense dimensions—they continued to underestimate the size of the earth until the voyage of Ferdinand Magellan (1519–22).

Perhaps it was just as well that Columbus did not know how large the earth really is, for it is almost a certainty that no crew could have been assembled for a voyage of twelve thousand miles. And that would have been the approximate expanse of the Ocean Sea. Even with this information, Columbus still would have remained ignorant of North and South America. There is absolutely no documentation that Columbus ever heard of the Viking voyages, and after Adam of Bremen (1072), there was only *one* mention of Vinland before 1500 and *no* map.[2] Norse tradition made Greenland, and perhaps Vinland, a peninsular extension of Europe through the Arctic. To the Norse themselves and in the minds of those few beyond Scandinavia who may have heard of them, the Norse discoveries were either European peninsulas stretching to the west, or islands. There was never any claim of an Asiatic landfall or of the discovery of a new continent. And even if such a discovery had occurred, the Norse lacked the technology to broadcast the news to the rest of Europe: printing had not been invented.

By 1492, however, printing technology, among a wide range of other innovations, was available. There were now not only the means to announce a successful voyage of discovery but also the means to make such a voyage.

By the fourteenth century the Portuguese had borrowed the Arabic *dhow* and improved it. They had added one or two masts (for a total of three, usually) and a bowsprit and had increased the length to about sixty-five feet. The wide hull that displaced little water was maintained, as was the triangular (lateen) sail. In effect, the Portuguese "invented" the caravel (Arabic, *karib*) over a century before Columbus. The oarlike lateral rudder, a Mediterranean and Middle Eastern standby for centuries, was replaced by a Baltic invention of the middle thirteenth century: the central hinged rudder, fixed to a stern post. The compass came to Europe in the twelfth century and, like the *dhow*, was a contribution of the Arabs, who almost certainly learned of it from the Chinese. Other navigational devices in use by the fourteenth century included the quadrant (forerunner to the sextant), astrolabe (a portable analemma, for determining the sun's angle for any day and place), jack-staffs and cross-staffs (for determining the sun's elevation), and sandglasses (for telling time). Last but not least, some unsung genius of the thirteenth century devised the portolan chart, designed for compass (dead-reckoning) navigation. At first charts were constructed only for the Mediterranean and Black Seas; later the waters of northern Europe were added. As Portuguese activity increased along the western coast of Africa in the fourteenth century, portions of the Atlantic Ocean began to appear on the charts.

All of these elements had to come together in the right place and at the right time before reliable, open-ocean voyaging was practical. Most of the pre-fifteenth-century voyages on the Ocean Sea had consisted of coast hugging, island hopping, or lucky accidents. These were the voyages that provided Christopher Columbus with the maritime lore that may have shaped some of his geographical concepts before 1492.

Maritime Lore of the Middle Ages

The art of printing reached Mediterranean Europe in the latter part of the fifteenth century: Italy in 1465, Spain in 1473, Portugal in 1487.[3] Before then there was little chance for anyone outside of a university, a religious order, or the royal court to study the works of scholars. Inasmuch as no book in Columbus's personal library was published before the 1477 *Historia rerum ubique gestarum*, by Aeneas Sylvius Piccolomini, or was marginally annotated (by either Christopher or his brother Bartholomew) before 1487 or

1488, it may be assumed that any (or at least most) of the knowledge Columbus had about the world before 1477 and probably before 1488 came from either personal experience or hearsay.[4] Columbus did not begin to make a formal, book study of philosophy and the sciences until after he went to Spain (about 1485), and he probably owned few, if any, books before that time.

Every *mappamundi* (world map) and portolan chart of the fifteenth century depicted strange and exotic places, some of which were legendary (based on fact) and some, mythical (fictitious). There were not as many of the latter as one might suppose, for the inability of cartographic historians to identify a place is not prima facie evidence that it never existed. More and more of the so-called mythical places (often islands) are being identified. Legendary places are rooted in truth, but they may have been erroneously positioned, incorrectly drawn (wrong size and/or shape), or misnamed. It is even possible that a place has vanished altogether, as might happen in a volcanic or seismic event.

During the last half of the fifteenth century, there were three dominant island legends in the Ocean Sea: the Island of the Seven Cities, Antilia, and Brazil. The three legends sometimes became intertwined, as is so often the case with enigmas, but in general, Antilia was a southern European product; Brazil was of northern European origin; and the Seven Cities were a shared phenomenon. As an added complication, the northern Europeans (mostly the English) perceived the Seven Cities and Brazil as neighboring places, while southern Europeans (mostly the Spanish and Portuguese) sometimes believed the Seven Cities and Antilia to be one and the same. Although Columbus never mentioned any of these islands by name in his journal of the first voyage, he does make several references to islands in the Ocean Sea.[5] Apparently he planned to visit one or two during his return trip. Columbus not only knew of the legends but regarded their existence as one of many proofs that land lay to the west—and not too far away at that. Further, the testimonies of his son Ferdinand and his staunch supporter Bishop Bartolomé de Las Casas clearly indicate that the "Admiral of the Ocean Sea" knew these stories.

The legend of the Seven Cities probably originated in Portugal, shortly after the Moorish invasion of the Iberian Peninsula in 711. Through the following centuries the legend was entangled with that of Antilia, and both were often associated with Japan (Cipango). The Seven Cities were great wanderers, sometimes appearing as an island, sometimes as seven cities on an island of another name, and sometimes as seven cities on a continental mainland. As a continental feature, they were mapped in Canada (in 1500), in South America, and lastly (1578) in what is now the southwestern United States. As an island, the Seven Cities floated over the Ocean Sea until 1587. Ferdinand Columbus provided this version of the legend in a biography of his father (the *Historie*):

> This island some Portuguese showed on their charts under the name of *Antilia*, but in a different situation from Aristotle, though none placed it more than two hundred leagues due west of the Canaries and Azores. And they hold it for certain that this is the *Island of the Seven Cities*, settled by the Portuguese at the time the Moors conquered Spain from King Rodrigo, that is, in the year A.D. 714. They say that at that time seven bishops embarked from Spain and came with their ships and people to this island, where each founded a city; and in order that their people might give up all thought of returning to Spain they burned their ships, riggings, and all else needed for navigation. Some Portuguese who speculated about this island conjectured that many of their nation had gone thither but were never able to return.[6]

Las Casas spins the same yarn in his *Historia de las Indias* (c. 1559–60), and Martin Behaim placed the following legend next to the little island he mapped as Antilia on his famous *mappamundi* of 1492: "In the year 734 of Christ, when the whole of Spain had been conquered by the heathens of Africa, the above island of Antilia, called Seven Cities, was inhabited by an archbishop from Oporto in Portugal, with six other bishops, and other Christians, men and women, who had fled there from Spain, by ship, together with their cattle, belongings, and goods. In 1414 a ship from Spain got near it without being endangered."[7]

The first documented reference to the Seven Cities is found in a grant, dated 1475, made by Afonso V of Portugal: "Dom Afonso, etc., to all who shall see this charter: I make known that I have made a grant . . . to Fernão Teles . . . of any islands to be discovered by him . . . and it might happen that, in thus sending him out to seek them, his ships or people might find the Seven Cities."[8] It is interesting to note that this authorization for exploration was made *the year before* Christopher Columbus went to Portugal. And of equal interest is another charter that was granted to Fernão Dulmo, captain of the Azorean island of Terceira, by João II, *one year after* (1486) the traditional date given for Columbus's departure from Portugal for Spain (1485). Dulmo was sent "to discover a large island or *mainland* by the coast, which is supposed to be the Island of the Seven Cities."[9] As far as is known, Dulmo made the voyage but found no land.

It is obvious from the foregoing that the Island of the Seven Cities was believed by some (including Columbus, according to his son) to be synonymous with Antilia. Nevertheless, there is no documented evidence that a place called Antilia existed before 1424; if the place did exist, it was known by another name.[10] Antilia first appeared on a Venetian chart drafted by Zuane Pizzigano.[11] There is strong evidence that the 1424 representation of Antilia is the island of Taiwan, mapped by the Chinese Admiral Cheng Ho during the first six of his seven great voyages in the Pacific and Indian Oceans (1405–23).[12] These voyages were made at the behest of the third Ming emperor (Yung-lo, or Ch'eng Tsu), who ruled from 1402 until 1424. By July 1405, Cheng Ho had at his disposal more than a thousand ships, some as long as 440 feet. The first (1405) voyage consisted of 317 ships and 27,800 men and sailed as far west as Calicut, India. The Cheng Ho sailings eventually covered the entire coast of eastern and southern Asia from Shanghai to the Red Sea and all of the eastern African coast from Egypt to Mozambique. The Asiatic islands (Taiwan, Philippines, Indonesia, etc.) were all visited.

Many of the pilots with the Chinese fleet were Arabs, and some of the Chinese were Arabic-speaking Muslims. These people were perfectly capable of supplying a chart, or the information to make a chart, to any of the Venetian middlemen encountered in the trading centers along the way. This is how islands on the western side of the Ocean Sea found their way onto a Venetian chart, located exactly where they should have been: on the western side of the Ocean Sea. It was entirely proper for Columbus to look for some of these islands; indeed he would have been derelict to have ignored them. Mediterranean sailors looked long and hard for the Island of the Seven Cities and for Antilia, never certain if the two places were one and the same or perhaps even Japan. Columbus succumbed to the same confusion.

Sometime between 1424, when Antilia made its first appearance on the Pizzigano chart, and 1492 the shape and the general location of Antilia were cartographically captured by Japan. The real Japan disappeared from the European charts for more than a century, and apparently Taiwan accompanied it. This "new" Japan, shaped like the old Antilia and moved to the tropics, also assumed Japan's offshore position vis-à-vis China—right where Marco Polo had said it should be. But Marco Polo had stated that Japan was five hundred miles east of China, not fifteen hundred miles, as located by some cartographers. The error was a simple one: Polo used the Chinese linear unit *li*, each with a value of one-third mile; European cartographers made a direct *li*-to-mile exchange.

On Behaim's 1492 globe—the oldest globe extant, now in the German National History Museum—Japan is exactly where Cuba should be. On reaching Cuba, Columbus thought he had found Japan. Later on in the first voyage, when Columbus thought Cuba was the Asiatic mainland, the honor of being Japan went to Española (Hispaniola). It is interesting to note that Behaim, borrowing from earlier fifteenth-century cartographers (such as Henricus Martellus, c. 1490, or Fra Mauro, 1459), had the name "Antilia" left over after using that island's form and position for Japan. To solve this problem, he simply invented a new shape and location for Antilia. On the Behaim globe, then, Antilia is not a mythical island—it is a real island in the wrong place! No wonder Columbus could not find it or Japan. The failure of Columbus to find the legendary islands of Antilia and/or the Seven Cities may thus be excused; he was seeking them in the wrong ocean but was totally unaware of that fact. Modern map detectives, however, cannot be forgiven for searching in the same place, and it is astounding to read that Antilia (that is, Taiwan) has recently been called Cuba,[13] the Delmarva Peninsula,[14] an unidentified island between Greenland and Trinidad,[15] and a piece of cartographic fiction.[16]

Northern mariners, on the other hand, did not concern themselves with Antilia. It is possible that most of them had never heard of it. They did expend great effort, however, plowing the Ocean Sea in hopes of finding the Seven Cities and Brazil. Brazil appeared on the charts at least as early as 1325, and Irish legends of *O'Brazil* and *Breas-ail* are much older than that.[17] The English were still seeking the legendary island in 1480: "1480 on the 15th day of July the ship . . . belonging to John Jay, Jr., of 80 tons burden, began a voyage at the port of Bristol from King Road to the island of *Brazil* on the west part of Ireland. . . . The news came to Bristol on Monday, September 18, that the said ship had sailed for about nine weeks but had not found the island."[18] And in 1481 Thomas Croft sailed, with two vessels, for "examining and finding a certain island called the Isle of Brazil."[19]

By the time of the second voyage (1497) of John Cabot (née Giovanni Caboto, a Venetian navigator in the employ of England), the English were reasonably certain that they had found Brazil. In a letter written by the English merchant John Day in late 1497 or early 1498, there is a most interesting sentence: "It is considered certain that the cape of the said land [i.e., the land discovered by Cabot] was found and discovered in the past by the men from Bristol who found 'Brazil.' "[20] In other words, something called *Brazil* was known to the Bristol seamen before 1497. And it was either Newfoundland or Nova Scotia. Cabot was seeking lands *beyond* Brazil—beyond a land already known to the men of Bristol. A document dated 24 August 1497 tells us what Cabot did. Sent anonymously from London to the Duke of Milan, it reads in part: "Some months ago His Majesty sent out a Venetian, who is a very good mariner, and has good skill in discovering new islands, and he has returned safe, and has found two very large and fertile new islands. He has also discovered the Seven Cities, 400 leagues from England, on the western passage."[21] This was the first northern European record of the Seven Cities, and it suggests that the Seven Cities were discovered as an adjunct to the search for Brazil. The Seven Cities may have been Nova Scotia or Maine. Along with twenty-two place-names (given by Cabot?), Juan de la Cosa located the Seven Cities on his famous map of 1500. The Seven Cities seem to be in the interior of what is now Quebec, and to add a little intrigue to the story, the name has been largely erased. Nevertheless, cartographers continued to place the Seven Cities in the Canadian interior until the second decade of the sixteenth century.[22]

These, then, were some of the facts (and fiction) known to Columbus and his contemporaries. There were many other real and imagined islands in the Ocean Sea. John Mandeville, in a fourteenth-century work well known to Columbus, told of a journey made to India and beyond, where there were more than 5,000 islands. Marco Polo went even further, saying that 7,440 islands lay off the coast of Asia. The portolan charts of the fourteenth and fifteenth centuries have liberal sprinklings of islands in the Ocean Sea, and the *mappaemundi* depict hundreds. Behaim's globe affords an excellent summary of late-fifteenth-century geography. Behaim also offers vivid proof that for all practical purposes, the late-fifteenth- and early-sixteenth-century world of Columbus was the world of Ptolemy. Though many astronomers and cosmographers had abandoned large parts of Ptolemaic geography by 1492, Columbus was slavish to the ancient system. We can only speculate what might have happened (or not have happened) if Columbus had rejected Ptolemy's erroneous measurement of the earth's circumference.

Claudius Ptolemaeus—"Ptolemy"—was born in Egypt in about A.D. 75 and died in about A.D. 153.[23] Most of Ptolemy's work was at Alexandria, Egypt, and falls roughly between A.D. 127 and 150. His interests were broad and ran the gamut from music and optics to meteorology and mechanics, but he is best known as a mathematician, astronomer, and geographer. In the present instance we are concerned with Ptolemy's perception of the earth and with his legacy that made such a tremendous impact on Christopher Columbus. Ptolemy was not what one would call an original genius. He borrowed widely and heavily, but he always gave proper credit to his sources. He corrected many errors made by his predecessors, and he committed a number of mistakes in his own right. His theoretical science outstripped his power of applying it practically.[24] It is quite safe to claim that ancient geography culminated with Ptolemy. His *Guide to Geography* contained the latitude and longitude of eight thousand places. With information of this sort, and with a set of instructions on how to use it, one could make a map. There was only one problem in the second century: how could a map be plotted when there were no accurate instruments for measurement and when even the fundamental parallels and meridians were guesswork?

Ptolemy derived his material from three primary sources: Hipparchus (c. 180–c. 127 B.C), Poseidonius (c. 135–50 B.C.), and Marinus of Tyre (fl. c. A.D. 100). From Hipparchus he took the 360° circle, parallels of latitude based on the hours of daylight, and the idea that a map must be constructed from a set of known coordinates. Poseidonius provided Ptolemy with a value for the earth's circumference—about 18,000 nautical miles (20,400 statute miles). This is the figure passed through the centuries to Columbus, instead of the correct measurement of approximately 21,600 nautical miles (25,000 statute miles). A degree at the equator is 60 nautical miles; for Columbus it was 50 nautical miles. In other words, basing his opinion on Ptolemy's geography, Columbus believed the world to be about 20 percent smaller than it really is. Following the reasoning of Marinus of Tyre, Ptolemy placed the prime meridian in the Canary Islands, about 70° to the east of where these islands are actually located. Next he stretched Asia to beyond the present longitude of 160° east (half the distance from China to Hawaii), thereby making Eurasia extend over half the circumference of the earth. Additionally, he enclosed the Indian Ocean by joining southern Africa with what seems to be the Malay Peninsula. These ideas, and others, became part of Columbus's cosmographical baggage. But these unbelievable concepts—unbelievable even by late-fifteenth-century cosmographers—became the database for the Ptolemaic maps that began to appear during Columbus's lifetime. Columbus had been in Portugal for a year when, in 1477, Dominico de' Lapi printed five hundred copies of Ptolemy's *Geography* in Bologna, Italy. Twelve additional editions appeared before 1500. The last edition was printed in 1883![25]

Ptolemy, Marinus of Tyre, and Hipparchus all believed one thing: the planet was not composed of a relatively small continental mass surrounded by the Ocean Sea. It was the other way around: the Ocean Sea occupied only a small portion of the globe. Based on Columbus's calculations (derived from Ptolemy et al.), about one-third of the sphere was occupied by the Ocean Sea between Lisbon and China. This would have been no more than 6,500 nautical miles, possibly less. Columbus was aware of the ancient perception of the earth (i.e., before Ptolemy), from Homer and Hesiod in the ninth and eighth centuries B.C., through the golden age of Greece and Plato and Aristotle, to Pliny and Seneca, near-contemporaries of Ptolemy. It was this theoretical framework, coupled with many years of practical navigation, that provided Columbus with what he felt was sufficient expertise to go where no European had gone before. But where had Europeans gone before, and what impact, if any, did such voyages have on Europeans in general and Columbus in particular?

Exploration before Columbus

In the fifteenth century, European knowledge of the world was derived from five sources: (1) Greek and Roman information that was fifteen hundred years old; (2) reports of Arab travels between the tenth and fifteenth centuries; (3) the sojourn of Marco Polo to China in the thirteenth century; (4) an occasional tale (sometimes partly true) of northern exploits by the Irish, English, and Scandinavians (between the eighth and fifteenth centuries); and (5) voyages by southern Europeans (mostly the Portuguese) in the fourteenth and fifteenth centuries.

Although ignorance about the world increased geometrically for most Europeans as the distance from home increased arithmetically, journeys beyond the Pillars of Hercules (Gibraltar) had been going on for a very long time. The Phoenicians were sailing to England for tin and to Germany for amber more than a thousand years before the time of Christ. If Herodotus is to be believed, King Necho II of Egypt sent out a fleet to circumnavigate Africa in about the year 595 B.C. Within a century, more or less, Hanno departed from Carthage (in modern-day Tunisia) and led sixty ships and several thousand people as far south as Sierra Leone on the coast of West Africa. Pytheas, journeying from the city that is now Marseilles, France, went to northern Europe in 275 B.C. and possibly reached Iceland.

Saint Brendan of Ardfert (c. A.D. 484–577) may or may not have done all of the things attributed to him, but the Irish accumulated enough maritime information before the Vikings to prove that a number of voyages of exploration were made by the eighth century. In fact, it was the Irish who discovered and settled the uninhabited island of Iceland in 795—sixty-five years before the Vikings even saw that island and seventy-nine years before a Norse colony was established there (874). According to one thread running through the fabric of northern mythology, the Irish made their way westward to Greenland after their Icelandic settlement was abandoned, but this is a very fine thread. There is no evidence that anyone had ever seen Greenland before Gunnbjörn Ulfsson discovered that giant island in the year 900. His discovery came about by a simple navigational error: he missed Iceland. History usually accords the Greenland discovery to Erik the Red, in 986, but that is when Erik founded the first Greenland colony. Nevertheless, the Irish had a little more than a century between the Viking discovery of Iceland and the settlement of Greenland to have pushed farther west. And they *may* have ventured all the way to North America.

Unlike the voyages in the Irish myths, the Viking expeditions to North America are fairly well documented, and they are supported by archaeological remains. Bjarni Herjolfsson, in 987, was the first European *known* to have sighted the North American mainland, and he accomplished the feat by borrowing from the navigational expertise of Ulfsson, the discoverer of Greenland: Herjolfsson, on his way to visit his father in Erik's Greenland colony, missed the island altogether. Leif Eriksson (Erik's son) did not reach America until 1003, landing somewhere between Cape Cod and Labrador and calling the region "Vinland." The last known voyage to Vinland was in 1347; the Greenland Western Settlements vanished by 1350; the last ship to visit the Greenland Eastern Settlements was there in 1410. By the fifteenth century, Greenland was on the European charts.

The debate still rages about the first mapping of continental America.[26] Although North America was visited off and on for 350 years by the Norse, there was little interest in these voyages by anyone outside the region. In fact, there is no evidence that Iberian navigators had even heard of them before the fifteenth century. By this time, however, there was a great deal of activity in the rich fishing zones of the North Atlantic, and the Newfoundland Banks were rediscovered by the Basques, Bretons, Portuguese, and English. To these European fishermen, the western lands that we now know as Labrador, Newfoundland, and Nova Scotia were merely either peninsular extensions of Europe or large islands; there was nothing to indicate that they were eastern extensions of Asia, and no one filed a claim on a new continent. It is possible that all of this northern maritime activity—especially the long pursuit of whales—was responsible for the discovery of the Azores and Madeira Islands as early as the fourteenth century, for by 1339 the Catalán cartographer Angelino Dulcert had charted them.[27]

The northern and southern probes of the Ocean Sea were, in general, separate and distinct. Nevertheless, they evolved along similar patterns, involving both island-hopping and coast-hugging operations at first. In the north, for example, there is only one segment of the Viking route from Norway to Canada that takes a ship more than 150 miles from land. That stretch is found between the Faeroe Islands and Iceland, a distance of 175 miles. Because of the great elevation of most of the islands on the northern route (islands formed by volcanos or ice), one island is in sight almost as soon as another is left behind. The great problem facing the northern sailor was the weather, especially fog, which probably accounted for the bypassing of some islands and the discovery of new ones. In the south, exploration also began with the familiar; knowledge of the Canary Islands dates from at least the time of King Juba of Mauritania (c. 50 B.C.–c. A.D. 24).[28] The islands of Lanzarote and Fuerteventura lie only sixty-five miles west of Morocco, and both may be seen from the mainland. Surely the seven islands of the Canaries were the same islands known to the ancients as the Fortunate Islands and/or the Islands of the Blessed. The Genoese probably reached the Canaries in 1291, when Ugolino and Vadino Vivaldi sailed from Genoa for India with the intention of circumnavigating Africa. Although this attempt failed, a fellow countryman, Lancellotto Malocello, definitely arrived in the islands in 1312. The name for one of the islands, Lanzarote, is a corruption of "Lancellotto." From that date forward, there was never a serious interruption in European visits to the Canaries.

In 1314, King Dinis of Portugal began construction of a navy and chose a Genoese, Emmanuele Pessagno, as its first admiral, making the office perpetual and hereditary. The new admiral brought many Genoese seamen to Lisbon, and for many years they were to play a major role in Portuguese exploration. By 1341 Portugal was sending out exploratory expeditions, and the first—to the Canary Islands—was led by a Genoese, Niccoloso da Recco, and a Florentine, Angiolino del Tegghia dei Corbizzi. It is probable that one of the post-1341 voyages visited Madeira and Porto Santo and assigned the Italian names, which appeared on charts as early as 1375. Although the Portuguese got off to an early lead in Atlantic Ocean exploration, much of it was an accidental spin-off of their activity in North Africa. The Canaries were neglected, except for brief flurries when it seemed as though the French and the Spanish (Castilians, Aragonese, Catalans) were about to gain the upper hand. The official discoveries of Madeira, Porto Santo, and the Azores were actually rediscoveries, made between 1419 and 1427 by vessels returning to Lisbon from northwestern Africa. By sailing northwest of the Canaries to pick up favorable winds, these vessels made the so-called discoveries. Even then there was a reluctance to settle those islands until it was believed that either the French or the Castilians would.

The Portuguese were obsessed with three objectives: (1) driving the Muslims from North Africa; (2) locating the legendary Christian kingdom of Prester John, thought to occupy a region south of the Muslims and to extend from the Atlantic Ocean to the Indian Ocean; and (3) locating the sub-Saharan source of the Muslims' gold. These were goals that dated at least as far back as King Dinis (1279–1325); they were the principal reason he constructed a fleet. By 1415, during the reign of João I, the Portuguese had captured Ceuta, in Morocco, and one of João's sons, Prince Henry, was named governor of that province.

It would be incorrect to assign any special role in the process of Portuguese expansion to the west or down the western coast of Africa to Henry, the "Navigator." Prince Henry never navigated anything, and no one in Portugal ever referred to him by that title. Apparently, it was the British librarian R. H. Major who gave the prince the title of "Navigator" and saw Henry—whose mother was English —as one more proof that the English were genetically destined to rule the seas! Considering that Prince Henry's role in North Africa was disastrous and that he spent much of his life as a recluse, it is one of the paradoxes of history that he was credited with Portugal's drive down the western coast of Africa. Prince Henry died the same year that the Cape Verde Islands were discovered (1460), and those voyages were ordained primarily by João I (Henry's father), Duarte (Henry's brother), and Afonso V (Henry's nephew). At no time did Henry concoct any organized plan of exploration, nor was he part of any scheme to reach the country known today as India.

During the fifteenth century there were *three* Indias: southern China and southeastern Asia; India; and Ethiopia. This last, "third" India was believed to be the land of Prester John (thought to extend across the entire continent). Columbus, as we shall soon see, was attempting to sail to "the Indias"; the anglicized form, "Indies," is misleading, for it now has a specialized (insular) meaning. Columbus may have been heading for the first or second India, but the Portuguese were seeking the third India (which was supposedly Christian) to help them conquer the Muslims. After Bartolomeu Dias reached the Cape of Good Hope (1487) and Ptolemy's idea of a landlocked Indian Ocean was discredited, Portugal began to alter its strategy. The same year that Dias was sent to the cape, an overland expedition was sent to Ethiopia and India. Prester John was nowhere to be found, but part of the expedition reached Gôa (in India) and later returned to Cairo. From there a report of the journey was sent to João II, thus paving the way for Vasco da Gama's 1497–98 crossing of the Indian Ocean. But this is getting ahead of the story.

We have seen that the Portuguese used most of the fifteenth century—1415 to 1487—to reach the southernmost tip of Africa. Of their original objectives in Africa, only one was accomplished: a major source of gold was located at what is now El Mina, Ghana, and by 1482 the huge fort of São Jorge da Mina had been constructed at the site. During this period of exploration and conquest along the western coast of Africa, sailing westward on the Ocean Sea was accorded a very low priority. Nevertheless, as mentioned, a few discoveries (actually rediscoveries) were made by ships returning to Portugal. By accident, then, Madeira, Porto Santo, and the Azores were acquired. There were also a few occasions when Portugal became involved with voyages west of the Azores. Perhaps the most fascinating of these voyages—certainly the most controversial—was the westward sojourn of João Vaz Côrte-Real.

In 1470, Afonso V of Portugal proposed to Christian I of Denmark that there be a joint Dano-Norwegian/Portuguese voyage of exploration. This suggestion was a result of the fact that the two royal families were related by marriage, but it was also a way for the Portuguese to repay the Danes for helping in Morocco and for sending observers with them to the Cape Verde Islands. Prince Pedro (Henry's brother and regent until Afonso V was old enough to rule) visited Erik II of Denmark in the 1420s and may then have sown the seeds of this joint voyage. The Danish captains with the expedition were Diderik Pining and Hans Pothorst, two privateers who had fought the English in the 1467 war over Icelandic fishing rights. The Portuguese sent several participants, including Côrte-Real. The voyage lasted for about a year, from 1472 until 1473, and probably followed the old Viking route to Labrador and Newfoundland. In fact, the Portuguese name "Labrador" may have been a result of this voyage, and Newfoundland was afterward called Terra do Bacalhau (Land of the Codfish) for many years. The name "Terra Côrte-Real" was likewise used for both Greenland and Newfoundland at different times on almost all charts and maps that originated in the Mediterranean region during the sixteenth century.

By 1473 Côrte-Real had returned to the Azores and was given the governorship of the most prosperous island as a reward for his northern exploits. These events are well documented and are fully accepted by scholars in Portugal and Scandinavia.[29] On the other hand, the Côrte-Real voyage is denounced as a sham by intellectuals of equal reputation in Spain and Italy. It is interesting to note that earlier voyages with little or no substantiation are taken at face value as long as they are not too close in time to the Columbus voyages. And the English ignore the Côrte-Real voyage because they credit Bristol sailors with the discovery of Newfoundland in the 1480s.

Two years after Côrte-Real returned from the Dano-Norwegian/Portuguese odyssey to the west, a charter was given to Fernão Teles by Afonso V of Portugal to make voyages of discovery and possibly to find the Island of the Seven Cities. Since this was the first known reference to the Seven Cities, and since the Seven Cities legend was well-known in northern Europe, it is possible that the grant to Teles was made because of certain information brought back by Côrte-Real. Let us linger for a brief moment on this critical year, 1475. Not only did Afonso V grant a charter to Teles to explore to the west, but the king also had a plan to move to the east: Portugal invaded Castile and occupied most of the province of León. The invasion eventually ground to a halt, and Afonso failed to win assistance from the French on the east. In 1476 Afonso went to France to make a direct appeal for support and found himself in the middle of a struggle between Louis XI and Charles the Bold (the Duke of Burgundy). His attempts to mediate the dispute failed completely: both sides were alienated. Totally depressed by his lack of success both on the battlefield and in the diplomatic arena, Afonso V renounced the Portuguese throne and departed for the Holy Land. Before he could leave France, however, Louis XI detained him and sent the disillusioned king home to Lisbon, where he arrived in November 1477.

Prince João, heir to the throne, was actually proclaimed King João II when his father gave up the throne in 1477, but when Afonso V returned, João pleaded with his father to once again become king. Technically, Afonso V reassumed power, but in reality he and João functioned as co-rulers until Afonso's death in 1481. João had been in complete charge of all overseas exploration and colonial policy since 1474; he was king in 1477, "co-king" from 1477 until 1481, and king from 1481 until 1495. Thus anyone who wanted to sail the Ocean Sea after 1474 petitioned Prince João and, after 1481, King João II. Such a petitioner arrived in the person of Christopher

Columbus; the war that Afonso V had started with Castile was the main reason Columbus came to Portugal.

The "Grand Design": The Plan to Reach the Indias

On 13 August 1476, Christopher Columbus was on board the *Bechalla*, a Flemish vessel commanded by Cristoforo Salvago and included as part of a little fleet of five ships bound from Genoa to Bristol, England. There were approximately four hundred crew members and passengers in the convoy, including a number of people who had been, and were to be, closely associated with Columbus. Among them were shipowners and captains Nicolò Spinola, Gioffredo Spinola, and Gian Antonio Di Negro. The fifth captain, Teramo Squarciafico, was a member of an important shipping family. Columbus had probably been in their employ on an earlier voyage to Chios (then a Genoese colony, now in Greece) in 1474 or 1475.

The 1476 voyage marked the first time that Columbus saw the Ocean Sea, probably on 10 or 11 August when the fleet passed through the Strait of Gibraltar. Near Cape Saint Vincent—only a stone's throw from where Prince Henry had built his villa on the wind-swept promontory at Sagres— the tiny convoy was attacked by a French squadron of fifteen vessels. Though this was a case of mistaken identity on the part of Portugal's French ally (Genoa was neutral), it did not prevent the total destruction of all five ships. Tradition has it that Columbus, with the aid of an oar, managed to swim ashore; a few years later he referred to this incident as a "miracle." It marked the beginning of Columbus's Portuguese residency, which may have been as short as six years or as long as nine. There simply is no reliable evidence to establish the precise length of time.

The twenty-five-year-old sailor went to Lisbon; indemnities had to be paid for the unprovoked attack, a new Genoese fleet had to be assembled, survivors had to be provided for, and a number of diplomatic problems had to be addressed. The voyage probably commenced anew in 1477, but there is nothing to indicate whether or not Columbus remained with the convoy. History often guards its secrets with great jealousy; this was certainly the case with Columbus in Portugal. More likely than not he continued to work for one of the Genoese shipping concerns that had employed him previously; there was a large contingent of Genoese merchants and mariners in Lisbon, thus making that a pleasant environment in which to live.

Columbus was engaged in hauling sugar from Madeira to Lisbon in 1478, and he seems to have lived on Madeira and neighboring Porto Santo for a few years. The gap between the possible Madeira residency and his original arrival in 1476 has been used to place Columbus wherever one scholar or another wished to situate him. Most scholars imagined that he visited Bristol; some accepted the myth that he was in Iceland in February 1477.[30] There, of course, Columbus might have heard of the Vikings' exploits. Yet there is not one hint of truth to this tale of a voyage to Iceland, even though Ferdinand mentions it.[31] One may rest assured that Columbus—who was never burdened with modesty—would not have failed to write and talk about such an adventure. Even when listing his blue-water accomplishments, Columbus cited only his sailing experiences in the Mediterranean and to the Guinea coast of Africa. He most surely would have added such a voyage to his résumé when he was attempting to sell himself, first to the Portuguese and later to the Castilians.

Other than the commercial voyages to Madeira/Porto Santo, the only other travels by Columbus were to Genoa, in the late summer of 1479 (to give testimony in a legal proceeding), and to São Jorge da Mina (in 1482), on the Guinea coast. This latter voyage is referred to a number of times in the log of the "First Voyage of Discovery." When Columbus returned from Genoa in 1479, he brought with him his brother Bartholomew, who at that time was about eighteen years old. Very shortly after arriving in Lisbon, Columbus had married Felipa Monis. A great deal of haze surrounds the Monis family, but Felipa was *not* the daughter of Porto Santo's first governor, as some historians have claimed.[32] Her family was of the minor nobility, however, and Columbus attached a great deal of importance to this fact. Sometime in 1480 a son, Diego, was born, probably on the island of Porto Santo.

Many scholars associate Columbus's idea to sail to the east by way of the west with his tenure on Porto Santo or its close-by neighbor, Madeira. Historians seem to perceive an aura surrounding those islands, some invisible force that singled out Columbus and pointed him toward the west. There is the story Ferdinand tells of a mysterious chest full of old maps and charts— did it contain charts for a passage to the New World?—given to Columbus by his mother-in-law when he went to live at Porto Santo after marrying Felipa. The only problem with this story is that Ferdinand did not know who Felipa's parents were and thus he assigned ownership of the sea chest to the wrong person![33] There are also descriptions of exotic ocean-borne debris that washed onto Portuguese shores and gave Columbus all sorts of ideas. However, probably the most exciting event, one that may or may not have occurred, was recorded by a number of sixteenth-century chroniclers, including Las Casas, Gonzalo Fernández de Oviedo, Francisco López de Gómara, and Garcilaso de la Vega.[34] The most complete account is the one in the *Historia* of Las Casas.[35]

The tale is a simple one: a ship was blown off course and carried westward across the Ocean Sea, in the year 1483 or 1484. In time it was driven to an island—presumably Hispaniola, in the Caribbean Sea—where the natives went without clothes. After many days of hardship and suffering, three to five surviving crew members (of the original seventeen men) managed to reach Madeira. At that time Columbus was a resident of the island and took care of the pitiful survivors as best he could. Unfortunately, all died within a few days, but before the pilot died, he gave his log and charts to Christopher Columbus. Las Casas said that the story was true and that all of his friends on Hispaniola in 1502 believed it. On the other hand, Oviedo questioned the story and thought it to be false. Ferdinand Columbus completely rearranged the account, saying that it was a corrupt version of a known trip by Vicente Dias from Guinea to the Azores.

If the "Story of the Lost Pilot" (as it has come to be called) is true, it may have meant one of two things: (1) the event not only gave Columbus the idea to sail west but also provided the charts for the voyage; or (2) Columbus already had the idea and viewed this as an act of Divine Providence that sustained him during the many years he struggled to win approval. There is, of course, virtually no chance that we shall ever know what actually happened. One of the oddities about this rumor of a lost pilot is that more than ten years elapsed before anyone mentioned it. Madeira had a bustling maritime trade in 1483–84, and it would seem that the return of a Portuguese vessel after such a harrowing voyage would have caught the attention of everyone on the island. But the story did not surface until *after* the "First Voyage of Discovery" by Columbus. When the tale of the lost pilot did begin to make the rounds, it mattered not whether the circulating rumor was true or false. What mattered was that practically everyone believed it and that, as a result, Columbus appeared to be a maritime plagiarist. Thus, to offset the story, an incredible hoax was perpetrated, one that was purported to demonstrate the origins of Columbus's "Grand Design" to look for the Indias and one that was so well conceived and so cleverly executed that most students of the Columbian voyages have been taken in by it.[36]

This hoax was built on an imaginary exchange of letters and charts, first between the great Florentine physician-cosmographer Paolo Toscanelli dal Pozzo and a Portuguese cleric named Fernão Martins and later between Toscanelli and Columbus. The time frame is exact: all of the correspondence had to have occurred between 25 June 1474 (the date that appears on the first letter) and 10 May 1482 (the date that Toscanelli died). If Columbus had really been in contact with Toscanelli, it had to have been after he went to Portugal (1476), for it was there that he learned (by some means not disclosed) that Toscanelli had written a letter on 25 June 1474, in Florence, Italy, and had sent it to Fernão Martins of Lisbon. Martins, according to the story, had been asked by King Afonso V of Portugal to obtain information regarding a western route to the Indies. On hearing of Toscanelli's correspondence with Martins, Columbus immediately wrote to the learned Florentine, asking to be made privy to the earlier letter. When Toscanelli received Columbus's inquiry—so the story goes—he quickly responded. That is, he responded to a total stranger with an undated letter (but not later than 1482) and sent a copy of the 1474 letter, one originally intended for the king of Portugal, via Martins. And for good measure—keep in mind that Toscanelli had no idea who Columbus was or what he was up to—a copy of the map that had been sent to Martins in 1474 was included. Yet another letter followed.

Altogether there were three letters and one map: (1) a copy of Toscanelli's letter to Martins (dated 1474); (2) a short cover letter to Columbus from Toscanelli (undated), explaining the above letter; (3) a second letter to Columbus from Toscanelli (undated); and (4) a map of the route to the Indies.[37] Not one original letter of this so-called letter-exchange exists, and of course the map has disappeared. There are three versions of the Toscanelli-to-Martins letter: in Latin, Italian, and Spanish (all copies or translations). Versions of the short cover letter and the second letter to Columbus are found in Italian and Spanish. The Latin "originals," like the map, are lost. Because all of the correspondence is available in many places (Benjamin Keen's translation in Ferdinand's *Historie* is excellent), only the important Toscanelli-to-Martins letter is reproduced here:

Paolo the physician, to Fernão Martins, canon of Lisbon, Greetings.

I was glad to hear of your intimacy and friendship with your most serene and magnificent King. I have often before spoken of a sea route from here to the Indies, where the spices grow; a route shorter than the one which you are pursuing by way of Guinea. You tell me that His Highness desires from me some statement or demonstration that would make it easier to understand and take that route. I could do this by using a sphere shaped like the earth, but I decided that it would be easier and make the point clearer if I showed that route by means of a sea-chart. I therefore send His Majesty a chart drawn by my own hand, upon which is laid out the western coast from Ireland on the north to the end of Guinea, and the islands which lie on that route, in front of which, directly to the west, is shown the beginning of the Indies, with the islands and places at which you are bound to arrive, and how far from the Arctic Pole or the Equator you ought to keep away, and how much space or how many leagues intervene before you reach those places most fertile in all sorts of spices, jewels, and precious stones. And do not marvel at my calling "west" the regions where the spices grow, although they are commonly called "east"; because whoever sails westward will always find those lands in the west, while one who goes overland to the east will always find the same lands in the east.

The straight lines drawn lengthwise on this map show the distance from east to west; the traverse lines indicate distance from north to south. I have also drawn on the map various places in India to which one could go in case of a storm or contrary winds, or some other mishap.

And that you may be as well informed about all those regions as you desire to be, you must know that none but merchants live and trade in all those islands. This is as great a number of ships and mariners with their merchandise here as in all the rest of the world, especially in a very noble port called Zaiton, where every year they load and unload a hundred large ships laden with pepper, besides many other ships loaded with other spices. This country is very populous, with a multitude of provinces and kingdoms and cities without number, under the rule of a prince who is called the Great Khan, which name in our speech signifies King of Kings, who resides most of the time in the province of Cathay. His predecessors greatly desired to have friendship and dealings with the Christians, and about two hundred years ago they sent ambassadors to the Pope, asking for many learned men and teachers to instruct them in our faith; but these ambassadors, encountering obstacles on the way, turned back without reaching Rome. In the time of Pope Eugenius there came to him an ambassador who told of their great feeling of friendship for the Christians, and I had a long talk with him about many things: about the great size of their royal palaces and the marvelous length and breadth of their rivers, and the multitude of cities in their lands, so that on one river alone there are two hundred cities, with marble bridges very long and wide, adorned with many columns. This country is as rich as any that has ever been found; not only could it yield great gain and many costly things, but from it may also be had gold and silver and precious stones and all sorts of spices in great quantity, which at present are not carried to our countries. And it is true that many learned men, philosophers and astronomers, and many other men skilled in all the arts, govern this great province and conduct its wars.

From the city of Lisbon due west there are twenty-six spaces marked on the map, each of which contains two hundred and fifty miles, as far as the very great and noble city of Quinsay. This city is about one hundred miles in circumference, which is equal to thirty-five leagues, and has ten marble bridges. Marvelous things are told about its great buildings, its arts, and its revenues. That city lies in the province of Mangi, near the province of Cathay, in which the king resides the greater part of the time. And from this island of Antillia [*sic*], which you call the Island of the Seven Cities, to the very noble island of Cipango [i.e., Japan], there are ten spaces, which make 2,500 miles, that is two hundred and twenty-five leagues. This land is most rich in gold, pearls, and precious stones, and the temples and royal palaces are covered with solid gold. But because the way is not known, all these things are hidden and covered, though one can travel thither with all security.

Many other things could I say, but since I have already told them to you by word of mouth, and you are a man of good judgment, I know there remains nothing for me to explain. I have tried to satisfy your demands as well as the pressure of time and my work has permitted, and I remain ready to serve His Highness and answer his questions at greater length if he should order me to do so.

Done in the city of Florence, June 25, 1474.[38]

Anyone who knows anything about the state of knowledge in fifteenth-century Florence will readily see that this letter is apocryphal. It was created by someone who relied on three primary sources: (1) the *Geographia* of Ptolemy, first printed in 1475; (2) Marco Polo's *Il milione*, first printed in 1477; and (3) Columbus's log of the "First Voyage of Discovery." The map described is a virtual duplicate of Behaim's 1492 globe, which includes a note about the golden buildings of Japan. Basically, though, the letter is a minuscule abstract of a portion of Marco Polo's writings.

Marco Polo had returned from China in 1295 and died in Venice in 1324. Forty-four years later (1368) the Ming Dynasty arose in China, replacing the Mongol Dynasty known to Polo. By the time of the alleged Toscanelli letter to Martins, *every Mongol name*—Cathay, Great Khan, Mangi, Quinsay, Zaiton—*had been replaced*. If Toscanelli had written this letter, he would have known this and would have relied on information from more recent travelers to the Orient. And there were many such travelers. Furthermore, Toscanelli states in the letter that he had a long talk with the Chinese ambassador to Pope Eugenius IV (reigned 1431–47). This is an out-and-out fabrication, for surely the Chinese ambassador would have known that the Ming Dynasty had replaced the Mongol many years before.

The letters are forgeries, written to provide a scientific basis for the first voyage and to offset the "Story of the Lost Pilot." The forger could have been any of several people loyal to Columbus, but his brother Bartholomew is the logical candidate. The letters are too full of Italianisms to have been the work of Ferdinand or Diego (Columbus's sons); their first language was Spanish. Also, Ferdinand's Latin was vastly superior to that found in the correspondence. The purpose of the forgeries was to enhance the prestige of Columbus *after his death* (1506), at a time when legal proceedings were contesting the titles and properties of the Admiral. The letters were written by someone who knew very little about the East, except that which was gleaned from Ptolemy, Marco Polo, and Columbus himself. The letters were written to conform to the geography of the first voyage, not the other way around. Further, there never was a map. Not only are all of the original documents conveniently missing, but there are no Portuguese records of anyone named Fernão Martins, no one in Italy had ever heard of Toscanelli's plan, nothing among Toscanelli's papers even remotely hinted of a connection with Christopher Columbus, and no one knew anything about the correspondence until Ferdinand Columbus revealed it in 1517. Christopher Columbus was unaware of the alleged exchange between Toscanelli and Martins or else he would have used the information when he so desperately needed support, first in Portugal and later in Spain.

The foremost spokesman for the nonbelievers of the Toscanelli-Columbus correspondence was Henry Vignaud, who devoted an entire book to the subject.[39] Others who side with Vignaud include Simon Wiesenthal, Dr. Consuelo Varela (Spain's leading authority on the texts, documents, and handwriting of Columbus), the late Dr. Armando Cortesão (for many years Portugal's premier expert on medieval charts), and this author. The majority of Columbus scholars, however, accept the correspondence as authentic, believing that Columbus's contact with Toscanelli was a fundamental part of the scientific research that led to the discovery of the New World. They argue that the validity of that research was proven by the discovery.

There is no reliable way to ascertain what information Columbus was privy to during his stay in Portugal and/or the Portuguese islands of Porto Santo and Madeira. There is a possibility that he was acquainted with Martin Behaim, whose 1492 globe not only is the oldest one extant but also was the last to depict the world before the Columbus discoveries. Behaim was a German-born cosmographer, longtime resident of the Azores, adviser to João II on navigational and cartographical matters, and for a time, keeper of the royal map room. If there was a map or chart in Portugal, Behaim knew about it. And through Behaim, perhaps, Columbus also knew. If Christopher Columbus put together a plan to sail to "the Indias" by way of the west while he was in Portugal, it had to have been between the years 1476 and 1485. But the evidence already discussed concerning the dates of the marginal notes in his books suggests that serious planning occurred only after he departed Portugal for Spain, probably in 1487 or 1488. In other words, there was no "Grand Design" based on elaborate scientific research during his stay in Portugal.

If Columbus had petitioned João II for a charter to sail west and discover new lands, he would have learned very quickly that such a charter had already been made to Fernão Teles in 1475. The next year, 1476, when Columbus arrived in Portugal, Castile and Portugal went to war, and exploration was not even feasible until 1479, when the war ended. Columbus was in Genoa part of that year and also was married in Lisbon late in 1479. By 1480 he must have been in Porto Santo or Madeira, where Diego was born, and in 1482 or 1483 he made at least one voyage to the Guinea coast of Africa. A close examination of Columbus's will suggests that he had no knowledge of Lisbon after 1482, and it appears as though he ended his Portuguese residency in Madeira or Porto Santo, going directly to Castile from there. Nevertheless, we cannot be certain of the year, nor do we know the route taken. It may have been via Lisbon, but if so, Columbus could have stayed there only briefly.

Any plan Columbus may have had before 1485 for sailing west to the east was a far cry from a "Grand Design." Portugal was clearly the most advanced maritime state in the world in the late fifteenth century, with an abundance of superior pilots and navigators. Also, it must be remembered that Portugal was not trying to reach southeastern Asia or China. As late as 1485, the Portuguese were still seeking the "Third India"—Ethiopia, or the kingdom of the fabled Prester John. Those who honestly believe that there was a "Grand Design" for the voyage west also accept the Toscanelli correspondence. In fact, that is why the correspondence was created. On the other hand, the "Story of the Lost Pilot" smacks of a coincidence beyond credulity, though it could be true. The most probable basis for the "Grand Design" or scheme to sail west would seem to be an idea taken from the Portuguese—either formally or informally—and, during Columbus's sojourn in Spain, blended and modified with the tenets of Ptolemaic geography, which Columbus is known to have accepted. Indeed, the "Grand Design" may have started as something no more complicated than an idea born in a Portuguese waterfront tavern, on some night when the tales being told by sailors were as deep as the Ocean Sea itself.

The Four Voyages

Tradition has it that Columbus came to Castile in 1485 after finding no interest for his plan in Portugal. Others say that he was merely running from his creditors. History also tells us that his wife, Felipa, had died in Lisbon, leaving Columbus with a young son, Diego, who was about five years old in 1485. Very little has been said about the fact that not one word was mentioned about Felipa before Diego refers to her in his will in 1509, three years after Christopher's death. Among the mysterious questions left unanswered—and generally ignored—are those that ask if Felipa was really dead before Columbus went to Spain and if there were other children at the time. The term "your other lawful sons" is used in the agreement that was drawn up to authorize Columbus's will (23 April 1497). And Columbus biographer Martín Fernández de Navarrete quotes a letter of 1500, written by Columbus, that says, in reference to leaving Portugal, "I left wife and sons that I never saw again."[40] Whatever the motives were for leaving Portugal, Columbus did enter Castile at Palos, Huelva, or La Rábida, all within a mile or so of each other. Why there? Probably because Columbus had a sister-in-law living in Huelva. Felipa's only sister, Violante, was married to Miguel Muliarte of Huelva, who later was a member of the crew of Columbus's second voyage.[41]

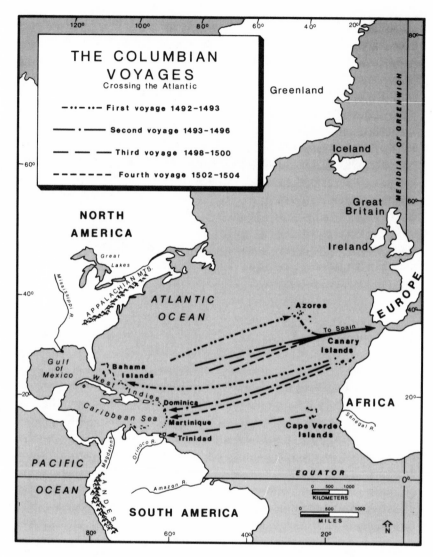

Map 3.1 The Columbian Voyages: Crossing the Atlantic.

The pre-voyage years in Spain, which were years of petitioning and waiting, were also years of reading and planning. Most of Columbus's library was assembled during this period, and evidence seems to have been gathered that would support whatever scheme he brought to Spain. There is no indication that Columbus modified his Ptolemaic concepts in any way. Anything that seriously contradicted that view was discarded, not

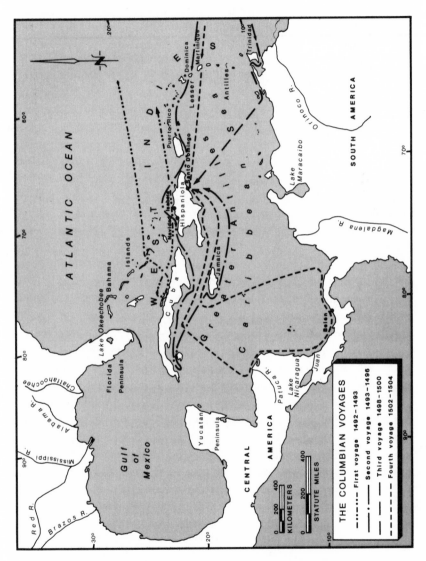

Map 3.2 *The Columbian Voyages.*

weighed and debated. It was also during these years that Columbus became enamored of Beatriz Enríquez de Arana, and Ferdinand was born of
this union, in 1488.

When authorization for the first voyage was granted (on 17 and 30 April
1492), the town of Palos was selected as the port of departure. It is possible
that Columbus chose Palos as his departure port for three reasons: relatives
in the area, friends at the monastery of La Rábida, and the immediate availability of two caravels that Palos had been ordered to supply. If there were
ships at his disposal in other ports, the factors of family and friends in the
vicinity of Palos would have probably given that town the edge. But, in all
probability, it was the availability of ships that provided the deciding factor. These two caravels that Palos owed the Crown were partial payment of
a penalty for not reporting taxes during the Peninsula War of 1475–79. Sailors from Palos were the greatest offenders, and it is known that nine voyages were made without royal authorization.[42] Queen Isabella made repeated demands that mariners from Palos obey her command and carry a
royal secretary on any ship sailing near the African coast. The secretary was to
see to it that the Crown received its share of profits (legal or illegal). If Palos
was the only port city guilty of tax evasion during the war, then perhaps
that was the only place for Columbus to get ships. Whatever the reasons
for the selection of Palos, however, it was the site destined to go down in
history as the departure point of the first voyage. In the small Spanish sea-
port town, Columbus made his preparations in May, June, and July of 1492.

The caravels supplied by Palos (by royal edict) were the *Pinta* and the
Santa Clara. The latter, named for the patron saint of Moguer—a town close
to Palos—was commonly called the *Niña*, the feminine form of its owner's
surname, Niño. The *Santa María* was chartered from its owner, Juan de la
Cosa, who sailed on the first voyage as the ship's master. Before Columbus
leased la Cosa's ship, it was known as *La Gallega*. The *Santa María* was approximately 77 feet long and 26 feet wide, with a draft of about 7 feet. She
carried a crew of no less than thirty-nine and no more than forty-two men
on the first crossing. The smaller *Pinta* (70 feet long, 22 feet wide, draft of 7
feet) was manned by twenty-six men; the *Niña* (67 feet by 21 feet, draft of
just under 7 feet) had a ship's company of twenty-four men.[43] The total cost
of the expedition, in terms of today's money, was about $750,000. That in-
cluded the money spent to lease the *Santa María*, pay all wages, and buy all
supplies. Not only were the expenditures low, even by fifteenth-century
standards, but for *every cent* invested in the enterprise, Spain received
$17,330 during the sixteenth century.

The First Voyage: 3 August 1492–15 March 1493

On Friday, 3 August 1492, Christopher Columbus made this entry in his journal of the first voyage: "We set sail on this third day of August, 1492, at 8 o'clock in the morning, from the bar of Saltes.[44] The wind is strong and variable, and we had gone 45 [nautical] miles to the south by sunset. After dark I altered course for the Canary Islands, to the southwest and south by west."[45] The *Pinta*, under the command of Martín Alonso Pinzón, was forced to put in at Grand Canary on 9 August to repair a broken rudder. On 12 August, Columbus in the *Santa María* and Vicente Yáñez Pinzón in the *Niña* reached the island of Gomera. When the *Pinta* failed to appear after a few days, Columbus and the younger Pinzón returned to Grand Canary. While repairs on the *Pinta*'s rudder were being completed, the *Niña* was re-rigged from lateen to square sails. By 2 September all three vessels were back at Gomera, and on 6 September the little flotilla departed for the westward voyage over the uncharted Ocean Sea. Only one serious obstacle confronted the fleet at the outset: there was no wind. Finally, on Saturday, 8 September, at three o'clock in the morning, the northeast tradewind began to blow. A line in Columbus's journal for that day says it all: "I set my course to the west."[46]

The island of Hierro faded from sight the next day (9 September), and no land was to be seen until 12 October, thirty-three days later. On that day, Rodrigo de Triana, a sailor aboard the *Pinta*, sighted an island in the moonlight, at about 2:00 A.m. Discovery Day—12 October 1492—was reckoned by the Julian calendar; our present-day Gregorian date is 21 October. Christopher Columbus and his men had come upon a small island in the Bahamas, known to the native Taino (Arawak) Indians as Guanahaní.[47] Almost immediately Columbus renamed the island San Salvador (Holy Savior). Though a debate still continues over the precise identity of San Salvador—some ten of the more than seven hundred islands and cays in the Bahamas have been suggested as the landfall island—only two islands are serious contenders for this singular honor: Watlings Island and Samana Cay.

Were it not for tradition and the slavish adherence to the discredited ideas of Samuel Eliot Morison, Watlings Island would also be out of the running. Of the significant geographical features cited in the Columbus journal as lying between San Salvador and Cuba, twenty-eight of thirty occur on the Samana track and only fourteen of thirty on the Watlings route.[48] In other words, the probability is above 90 percent for a Samana Cay landfall; it is less than 50 percent for Watlings. For a Watlings landfall, the geography of the journal must undergo a substantial revision, and Christopher Columbus must be accepted as a bumbling, incompetent navigator.

The solution to the landfall riddle is really very simple. Take any good version of the journal and follow the Bahamian sojourn day by day and mile by mile on an up-to-date nautical chart.[49] If Samana Cay is the starting point (San Salvador), the route will take you to Columbus's second island of Santa María de la Concepción (Acklins-Crooked), the third island of Fernadina (Long Island), and the fourth island of Isabela (Fortune Island). From there the route goes to the Islas de Arena (Ragged Islands) and thence to Cuba. Assuming that Watlings is San Salvador, the route runs to Rum Cay, Long Island, Crooked–Fortune Island, and then to the Ragged Islands and Cuba.

The reader is challenged to follow both routes and then reach an independent decision. A shortcut method for finding the real San Salvador is to believe what Columbus wrote on 20 November: that he was seventy-five nautical miles northeast of Puerto del Príncipe (modern-day Bahía Tánamo), Cuba, and that Isabela (the fourth island of discovery) lay thirty-six miles away (to the north), and that San Salvador lay twenty-four miles from Isabela. If Samana Cay is San Salvador and if Fortune Island is Isabela, then Columbus was exactly correct. If Watlings is San Salvador, Columbus made a serious mistake: Watlings is eighty miles from the Isabela (Crooked-Fortune) Island required by that route.

Since the 1981–86 investigation by the National Geographic Society concluded, beyond any reasonable doubt, that Samana Cay was the Guanahaní of the Indians and the San Salvador of Columbus, it behooves this student of Columbus to accept the same position. Careful analysis of the National Geographic Society's research methodology indicates a total commitment to objectivity and the scientific method. This investigation, published in 1986, establishes the journal of the first voyage as an exceedingly accurate document.[50] If the fortnight's sail through the Bahamas (12–26 October) commences at Samana Cay, all of the geography of Columbus's journal is found in its proper place and in the correct sequence. The Samana Cay track is described by Columbus in his journal; the Watlings track was invented many years later.

On his arrival at San Salvador (Guanahaní), Columbus took possession, noting this historic event in his journal:

> At dawn we saw naked people, and I went ashore in the ship's boat, armed, followed by Martín Alonso Pinzón, captain of the *Pinta*, and his brother, Vicente Yáñez Pinzón, captain of the *Niña*. I unfurled the

royal banner and the captains brought the flags which displayed a large green cross with the letters F and Y at the left and right side of the cross. Over each letter was the appropriate crown of that Sovereign. These flags were carried as a standard on all of the ships. After a prayer of thanksgiving I ordered the captains of the *Pinta* and *Niña*, together with Rodrigo de Escobedo [secretary of the fleet], and Rodrigo Sánchez of Segovia [comptroller of the fleet] to bear faith and witness that I was taking possession of this island for the King and Queen. I made all the necessary declarations and had these testimonies carefully written down by the secretary. In addition to those named above, the entire company of the fleet bore witness to this act. To this island I gave the name *San Salvador*,[51] in honor of our Blessed Lord.[52]

The island was "big enough" *("bien grande")*, flat, green, with many lakes and a large lagoon in the middle of the coast. A reef encircled the island, but there were breaks in it; one such opening served as an entrance to the inner harbor. The latter was described by Columbus as "quiet as a well" and "large enough for all the ships of Christendom." There was a peninsula that could be cut through in a couple of days, thereby creating a small island suitable for a fort. The people were shy and, later, friendly. Columbus saw mostly young men on San Salvador, and he found no large settlements. The most populous place had only six houses. The people brought cotton and parrots to the Spaniards and, in exchange, received tiny glass beads, red caps, and pieces of broken crockery. Seen for the first time by Europeans were hammocks, tobacco, manioc (cassava), and canoe paddles. Probably seen for the first time were sweet potatoes, corn, and several kinds of American beans. There was no reason to linger on San Salvador: there was no gold of any quantity. But some gold was seen to adorn the natives, and this was sufficient cause to shove off in search of the mother lode. Columbus was directed to the south or southwest, and he stated that he intended to sail that way on 14 October.

It is at this point in the story of the first voyage that a question or two must be asked. First, where did Columbus actually think he had landed? If he really believed that he was on one of the many islands depicted on the *mappaemundi* of the times or on the globe of Martin Behaim, islands fronting the coast of China, why would he take formal possession of territory that he believed to be under the suzerainty of the Great Khan? It would seem to have been an act of abject madness to land on an island within the Khan's domain and lay claim to it.[53] Second, why did Columbus load up on glass beads and other trinkets when setting off to see the Great Khan? If he had had the good (?) fortune to run into the Khan, what would he have presented to the Chinese ruler? Glass beads? Hawks' bells? Broken crockery, perhaps? A little red cap? It would have seemed more prudent to carry along at least a fine sword of Toledo steel with an emerald-studded hilt—or maybe exquisite pieces of Venetian glass. The evidence seems clear: Columbus fully expected to encounter natives who would trade gold for trinkets. Perhaps he expected to find a people comparable to those he had seen in western Africa. It is possible that he never really intended to meet the Great Khan face to face. He was probably lucky that he did not!

On 6 October, Columbus noted in his journal that Japan lay southwest by west of his course. This is the correct course for Japan as it is charted on Behaim's globe and numerous contemporary *mappaemundi*. And its misplacement southward by 20° (or more) not only justifies the course change on 7 October but also explains why Columbus thought that Cuba was Japan. Cuba is in the approximate latitude of the mischarted Japan, and Japan on the old charts was not even Japan! It was Taiwan.[54]

The journal entry for 21 October reads, in part: "Then I should sail for another great island which I strongly believe should be Japan . . . where they say there are many great ships and navigators. And from that island I intend to go to another that they call Bohío [Hispaniola]. . . . As to any others that lie in between, I shall see them in passing, and according to what gold or spices I find, I will determine what I must do. But I have already decided to go to the mainland and to the city of Quinsay [Hangzhou, China], and give Your Highnesses' letters to the Great Khan and ask for a reply and return with it."[55] And, on 23 October: "I want to leave today for the island of Cuba, which I believe to be Japan."[56]

Columbus was on Isabela (Fortune Island) from 19 October until 24 October. From the Indians he began to derive a geography that conformed to everything he had previously learned. This is demonstrated by the journal entry for 24 October: "The Indians indicated that I should sail to the southwest to get to Cuba, and I believe them because all my globes and world maps seem to indicate that the island of Japan is in this vicinity and I am sure that Cuba and Japan are one and the same."[57]

By 30 October, Columbus had heard that the "king of Cuba" (who he assumes is the emperor of Japan) is at war with the Great Khan of China.[58] And by 28 October, the day Columbus landed in Cuba, he was convinced that the Chinese mainland was a ten-day journey. At his transatlantic speed of about four knots—or one hundred miles—a day, this would place China one thousand miles farther to the west.[59] But by 1 November he had reduced the distance to three hundred miles, more or less, and made a remarkable statement: "I am certain now that this [Cuba] is the mainland."[60] This belief is reiterated on the next day.[61] Ten days later (12 December), Columbus has returned to his earlier conception and calls Cuba an island.[62] After being in the New World for two months, Columbus understood just enough of the Indians' language and signs to misunderstand them much of the time. He also was having a great deal of trouble reconciling his actual route with the wildly inaccurate charts he had with him or had seen. By Christmas Eve the Admiral had heard of a new region, Cibao. This was—and still is—the interior valley of the Dominican Republic, but Columbus thought Cibao was Japan.[63] The geographical conceptions of Columbus are most logical. He sailed to a position near the island of Japan (Cipango), as indicated by virtually every *mappamundi* of the late fifteenth century. After weaving in and around a number of small islands—four of which he stopped at—he came to an immense island. The measured latitude and the carefully assumed longitude gave a positive fix on this location: Japan, the island the inhabitants called Cuba. There was one thing wrong with this, however. The northern coast of this island called Cuba was much too long to be the island of Japan. Because of this, Columbus could not decide whether or not this was really an island. Perhaps it was the mainland. This notion was reinforced after Hispaniola was discovered to the *east* of Cuba. Hispaniola must be Japan, or it must lie very close to Japan. Then Cuba, to the west, must be the mainland!

The loss of the *Santa María* on Christmas Eve and the mutinous behavior of Martín Alonso Pinzón and his men—the *Pinta* sailed on its own from 21 November to 6 January—did not afford Columbus the time to sift and sort all of this information; therefore, the first voyage was somewhat lacking as a voyage of discovery. But it laid the foundation for the voyages to come, and it influenced and confused European cartography for half a century. But the first voyage was not intended to be a voyage of discovery per se. It was certainly not likely that Columbus, if asked why he had sailed west, would have anticipated Sir Edmund Hillary's comment about climbing Mount Everest and said, "I sailed the Ocean Sea because it was there."

Christopher Columbus sailed for many reasons, but God, glory, and gold were the top three. We cannot be certain of their order, that is, of the priorities set by the Admiral. In many ways the three are inseparable. To do God's work costs money; clearly God and gold go hand in hand. It even costs money to achieve glory, for ships and crews were not free in 1492. Perhaps one could seek gold as a solitary activity and enjoy its fruits in anonymity. Based on everything we know of Columbus, however, this seems an utter impossibility. Columbus was not destined to remain anonymous. The well-known Columbus student John Boyd Thacher believed that the "Admiral of the Ocean Sea" revealed his primary exploratory objective or "Ultimate Design" (not the "Grand Design") in his journal entry for 26 December 1492. After lamenting the loss of the *Santa María* two nights before, faulting the town of Palos for the sorry condition of the ship, and placing the blame for the vessel's loss on Juan de la Cosa and his crew from northern Spain, Columbus suddenly sees all of this as an act of Divine Providence. "All this was the will of God," said the Admiral. Columbus ended the entry for that day with the following:

> I hope to God that when I come back here from Castile, which I intend on doing, that I will find a barrel of gold, for which these people I am leaving will have traded, and that they will have found the gold mine, and the spices, and in such quantities that within three years the Sovereigns will prepare for and undertake the conquest of the Holy Sepulchre. I have already petitioned Your Highnesses to see that all the profits of this, my enterprise, should be spent on the conquest of Jerusalem, and Your Highnesses smiled and said that the idea pleased them, and that even without this expedition they had the inclination to do it.[64]

For Thacher, the "Ultimate Design" (and, therefore, the motivation for the discovery of the New World) was an elaborate plan that would culminate in the conquest of the Holy Land—the ultimate Crusade. It was not merely a scheme for sailing westward across the Ocean Sea to Asia. Apparently that was only Phase One. The next step, Phase Two, was to obtain the wealth to finance the operation, to repay loans for Phase One and to cover the necessary expenses accrued in gathering the wealth (gold, silver, spices, etc.). Phase Three was the liberation of Palestine and, coincidentally, the destruction of the heathen Moors. All of these were interwoven, and they were interdependent. According to Thacher, that is what Columbus was attempting to sell. If this was true, it is no wonder the Portuguese rejected the idea. They were already going about the business of destroying the Moors' base in northern Africa; they were about to link up with an important ally in the struggle (the illusive Prester John); and they had found the gold of La Mina (in Ghana). Their plan seemed to be in place.

Castile and Aragon (embryonic Spain) could not even dream of the Ultimate Conquest until they completed the Reconquest. Once this was done, it would take a bold and dramatic event to catch up with the Portuguese.

Columbus understood more than navigation, or at least it seemed so in the beginning. He understood profit and loss. Columbus offered Spain that bold and dramatic event. A little bit of this economic side of Columbus is seen in the journal entry for 14 January, two days before he departed the New World for home:

> His Divine Majesty well knows how much controversy I had before starting from Castile, and no one else was supportive of me except God, because He knew my heart; and, after God, Your Highnesses supported me, but everyone else opposed me without any reason whatsoever. And they have been the reason why the Royal Crown of Your Highnesses does not have a hundred million more in revenue than it has, because I came to serve you seven years ago, on the 20th of January, this very month. In addition, there would have been the natural increase from that time on. But Almighty God will take care of everything.[65]

The concept of profitable trade was mentioned a number of times during the first voyage. Various suggestions were put forth for seizing the opportunities that had emerged. In fact, the last journal entry written in Hispaniola before the departure for Spain discusses the profit to be made from New World cotton, mastic, gold, copper, and chili pepper.

The discovery portion of the first voyage ended on 16 January 1493, when the *Niña* and the *Pinta* sailed from what is now Puerto Rincón in the Dominican Republic. They left behind a small garrison in Navidad, representing the first Spanish settlement in the New World and named after the Christmas Eve on which the *Santa María* had been lost. In one of the true ironies of the first voyage, the last bit of land to fade from view was modern-day Cape Samaná. Other than the accent, the modern names of the first landfall and the last cape are identical.[66]

Whereas the voyage to the New World was essentially uneventful, the homeward leg was exactly the opposite. It was filled with danger and adventure. The two little caravels were separated in one of the most furious storms ever documented by a fifteenth-century crew. The *Pinta* missed the Azores altogether; despite an incredible example of dead-reckoning navigation, Columbus, in the *Niña*, barely made it to the Azorean island of Santa Maria. Once there, half of the crew were imprisoned for no reason, and Columbus came very close to retaking his men by force of arms. After departing the Azores, the *Niña* once again was set on by the full fury of a raging Ocean Sea. With great trepidation, the *Niña* was steered into the harbor at Lisbon by the Admiral in March 1493.

João II questioned Columbus at length about the voyage and was not at all certain that the Admiral spoke the truth when he avowed that Portuguese sovereignty had not been violated. Columbus had not spoken the truth, for he knew full well that he had been south of the line established by the Treaty of Alcáçovas (1479), separating Castilian and Portuguese claims in the Ocean Sea. With the exception of the Canary Islands, the Ocean Sea south of approximately 27° north was the exclusive domain of Portugal. In the presence of João II, Columbus must have said or done something that implied there had been an infringement of Portuguese territorial rights. The king told Columbus, during their conversation of 9 March 1493, that he "was greatly pleased that the voyage had been accomplished successfully, although he understood that in the capitulation between the [Spanish] sovereigns and himself the conquest belonged to him."[67] Additional support for believing that João II thought that Columbus was withholding the truth is demonstrated by the fact that João II sent a representative to the Spanish monarchs the next day for further clarification, ordered Francisco de Almeida to assemble a fleet and seize the newly discovered lands, and gave serious thought to placing Columbus under arrest.

Columbus was, of course, aware that he had entered Portuguese waters when he had altered course to the west-southwest on 7 October. And this illegal entry into Portuguese territorial waters explains several things. First, to keep the voyage perfectly legal, Columbus was careful to avoid any reference to a latitude south of 27° north. On the very first day at San Salvador, Columbus wrote, "We are on an east-west line with Hierro in the Canaries."[68] This is completely ridiculous, for even if drift and leeway are disregarded, Columbus was well aware of the fact that he had sailed for five days west-southwest of the due-west course. Second, Columbus *never* reported a correct latitude reading during the West Indian portion of the trip. He hid his readings by using one of the several trigonometric scales that were on the quadrants of that time; they only appeared to be correct. By this method of taking a reading on one scale and recording it from another the positions were secure even if the log fell into unfriendly hands. The recorded latitudes (all 34° or higher) preserved the myth that the discovery by Columbus occurred on the Spanish (north) side of the treaty line. Third, the northward displacement of the newly discovered islands on all early charts (beginning with the famous Juan de la Cosa chart of 1500) was probably a result of the initial deception by Columbus.

It becomes apparent from the foregoing that the Papal Demarcation Line of 1493—hastily drawn by the Spanish pope, Alexander VI—was an immediate consequence of the first voyage and King João's suspicions. Unlike the 1479 line, the new one was a meridian, 300 miles west of the Azores and Cape Verdes. These island clusters are not on the same meridian but are 300 miles from a common one, and the line was redrawn in 1494 (Treaty of Tordesillas). The 1494 meridian was 1,110 miles west of the Cape Verde Islands. By accepting a meridian, Portugal at first (1493) thought it had made a very good deal: all of the East Indies were on the Portuguese side. But its future Asiatic interests also lay south of the 1479 line, as did all of modern-day Latin America, except for a small portion of northern Mexico. As defined by the Treaty of Alcáçovas, *every* discovery made by Columbus over the course of his *four* voyages was in Portuguese territory. By accepting the 1493 meridian, Portugal surrendered the entire New World to Spain. The only possible explanation for the Portuguese acceptance of the 1493 meridian would have been King João's belief that the Columbus discoveries were in Asia, that the Admiral had, indeed, found the (East) Indies. Why, on the other hand, would the Spanish accept the 1493 meridian? Under Columbus's Ptolemaic conception of the world, the (East) Indies lay on the Spanish side. In a sense, the Spanish were right: the Indies were in their exclusive zone. It would be several years before it was learned that these were the *West*, not East, Indies.

The 1494 line did give Portugal a claim to Brazil before it was discovered, though secret, pre-1494 knowledge of that land may have been the reason the Portuguese negotiated the Treaty of Tordesillas. The line also located (a few years later) a misplaced Newfoundland on the Portuguese side of the boundary. On the negative side, by pushing the 1493 meridian some seven or eight hundred miles farther west, Portugal lost the Philippines to Spain. Finally, Columbus's attempt to hide his entry into Portuguese territory south of the Alcáçovas line has led astray a number of people seeking the true landfall of Columbus.[69] It must be remembered that he had a very good geopolitical reason for keeping his discoveries north of 27°. As covert operations go, this was a good one, fooling not only the king of Portugal but also several students of the Columbus voyages.

Christopher Columbus departed Portugal on the morning of 13 March 1493 and arrived at the bar of Saltes at sunrise on 15 March. An hour later, the *Pinta*, which had not been seen since that night in the tempest, 14 February, sailed into view. Immediately on his arrival, Columbus dispatched a letter to his friend and sponsor Luis de Santangel. This famous letter *(La Carta de Colón)* had with it a letter for the Catholic sovereigns, who were in Barcelona at the time. Within a few days Columbus was summoned to Barcelona and to the court. Almost by the time the Admiral reached the court, the letter to Santangel had been published, no later than in early April 1493. This was the first printed notice of the discovery of America.[70] By May the letter had been translated into Latin and published in Rome. At least ten other editions were printed before 1493 came to an end. The rapid diffusion of the *Letter of Columbus* offers an excellent and dramatic example of the importance of the newly introduced printing technology. Without printing, it might have been months—even years—before the first voyage had an effect on Europe.

The impact on the Catholic sovereigns was immediate. Here was the way to finance the liberation of the Holy Land—perhaps this was part of the "Ultimate Design," as suggested by Thacher. Not only were gold and silver, and spices and pearls, to be found in the Indies, but the East Indian spice trade itself could be wrested from Arabic-Turkish domination. The holy fathers now had an unlimited supply of souls to save, and there might even be a tidy profit on the side. The cosmographers and the intellectuals, on the other hand, must have been devastated by the news of a successful first voyage to the East. Had Columbus actually been correct about the size of the earth? Was it only a thousand leagues across the Ocean Sea? Did the Admiral really reach Cipango and Cathay? If so, where was the evidence of great cities and imperial wealth? Clearly, the retinue of ten Indians and their crude artifacts were not what Marco Polo had described. But never mind the discrepancies, the contradictions, or the unanswered questions. The Admiral of the Ocean Sea had discovered a land never seen before by a European. And he did bring some gold with him. For these and the reasons already stated, authorization for a second voyage was granted without delay. And it was to be a trifle more ambitious.

The Second Voyage: 25 September 1493–11 June 1496

Sometime between the middle of April and the second week of May 1493, Christopher Columbus wrote a letter to King Ferdinand and Queen Isabella, apparently in response to a request from them to prepare for a second voyage and to outline his ideas about settlement and development in the islands he had found on the first voyage. Nowhere in the literature of the Columbian voyages is there to be found a more succinct and introspective commentary on this letter than the one made by John Boyd Thacher:

When we consider this document, it discloses a vast scheme of colonisation. There is no proposition to equip a fleet to go in quest of the Great Khan and to conquer his dominions. Armies are not to be gathered. Soldiers are not to be conscripted. The regions sought have been found. And these regions were not the lands of Asia. If Columbus believed he was on the eastern coast of Asia, where were the people of the Great Khan? Where were the shores alive with commerce? Where were the countless cities with marble temples and roofs of gold? If the lands discovered by Columbus belonged to the Great Khan, why were his subjects not there in vast numbers digging gold and picking pearls? Whatever Columbus may have thought, or pretended he thought, as to the contiguity of the newly found lands to Asia, he knew at least that no Asiatic potentate claimed authority over them or ever had knowledge of the least of the islands.

The question now with Columbus is one of settling the new lands with two thousand Spaniards, of building domiciles, of erecting churches, of establishing towns, of tilling the soil, of searching for gold during certain appointed seasons when the ordinary avocations may for a time be neglected. A permanent occupation is contemplated. The new lands are to be enduring homes for the Spaniards of the Old World. There is to be a new Castile with softer skies. There is to be another Andalusia with more fertile fields.

We can imagine the pictures drawn by Columbus himself, and the still more fanciful and hopeful descriptions given by the officers and men of the *Pinta* and *Niña*. Whereas on the first voyage the ships bore unwilling sailors, now, wherever the Admiral went, the adventurous Spaniards begged of him the privilege of going to the New World. The Admiral recommended that the first settlers be two thousand in number. Accommodations were found for only twelve hundred, and we know not how many were disappointed.

This letter reveals Columbus in a new light. Suddenly, without preparation, without having handled in all of his life either golden ducats or silver castellanos, this sailor-man—this visionary, this man with a strange geographical theory—developed into a trained financier, equipped with plans for conducting large operations in gathering, smelting, coining gold and silver into money of the realm and for peopling a new land with a safe yeomanry and with skilled mechanics. And further, this letter presents to us the generous soul of the Admiral. He welcomes the proscribed Jew to the New World.

He saw the people of Israel driven from Spain, going out in sorrow, beating their breasts in woe and agony, and he saw this as he was unfurling his sails in the great adventure of his life. He was a man of vows. Perhaps he silently registered a promise that if ever there was vouchsafed him an answer to his prayers and the sought-for lands were given him, he would share their peaceful shores with this homeless and persecuted people. And this generosity of soul extended to permitting all men—all adventurers who desired—to embark on the discovery and exploring of new lands. The New World was to be free. It was a privilege which might be abused. Its acceptance, indeed, led in an indirect way to robbing him of the great glory attaching his name for ever to the New World. But no man and no circumstance could rob him of his generous impulses or cheapen his liberality.[71]

Written in the hand of Columbus, the letter to the sovereigns is, like virtually everything else connected with the Admiral, a subject for debate. There are those (including this writer) who accept the date of 1493 for its composition. On the other hand, there are authorities who assign the letter to 1498, on the eve of the third voyage.[72] Such assignation is based on the form of the signature, not on the content of the letter. If 1493 is the correct date, then this is the only letter written by Columbus before 1498 that employs both his cryptic anagram and his Greco-Roman signature (:Xpo. Ferens ./).[73] But if it was not written in 1493, immediately before the second voyage, its content makes no sense, and the recommendations Columbus is making to the sovereigns have become moot.[74]

Columbus did not get the two thousand settlers he asked for; the total number sailing on the second voyage was somewhere between twelve hundred and fifteen hundred. The lower number is probably closer to the actual figure. Seventeen vessels were dedicated to this voyage—more than would sail on the other three voyages combined. Fourteen of the ships were the trusty little caravels, including the *Niña*, refitted and ready to become the first vessel in history to make a second journey from Europe to the Caribbean. The other three vessels were larger carracks, similar in most respects to the *Santa María*. In fact, Columbus's flagship on the second voyage was also named *Santa María*, and this has led to some confusion. The first *Santa María* had been lost on the sandbar near modern-day Cap Haitien, Haiti. To add a little more to the confusion of names, the crew called the second *Santa María* "Santa María la Galante"—Saint Mary the Gallant, to be literal. Usually this was shortened to "Maríagalante."

The original plan called for the ships to depart Cádiz on 15 July, but bureaucratic bungling and out-and-out fraud vied with administrative incompetence to delay departure until 25 September. Without a doubt, the single biggest mistake made by the Catholic sovereigns was to entrust the outfitting of the fleet to Juan Rodríguez de Fonseca, archdeacon of Sevilla, later bishop of Palencia, and still later bishop of Burgos. Bishop Fonseca was the epitome of evil incarnate. He was a self-serving, ruthless, immoral tyrant. To a very large degree, he was responsible for undermining Columbus at every turn and bringing chaos to the lands of the New World. In 1493 Fonseca was the king's choice to organize the second voyage. Within a few months he was Minister of the Indies; he later became President of the Council of the Indies. Fonseca's role in the second voyage should not be understated. His operation was awash in graft and corruption. Much of the funding came from extortion, sequestering the property of banished Jews, and payments (bribes) made to secure certain rights of passage.[75] The vessels were overloaded, with an extremely poor assortment of people, chosen largely by what they were willing to pay or to whom they were related. This, of course, caused a serious gap in necessary skills. While Fonseca denied hundreds of skilled people the permission to sail, two hundred "gentlemen volunteers" were permitted to crowd the ships.

Defective stores and provisions were loaded; good meat and biscuits were somehow exchanged for bad; armor and weapons were sold; twenty-five fine Arabian horses were spirited away, only to be replaced by twenty nags ready for the glue factory. And this was all done under the watchful eyes of Fonseca's clerks, inspectors, and notaries, who recorded every item placed on board the vessels. This was the same Bishop Fonseca who sent Pedro Árias (Pedrarias) de Ávila to Panama in 1514; Pedrarias executed Vasco Núñez de Balboa and was directly or indirectly responsible for the deaths of over a million Indians. But when Bishop Las Casas petitioned Fonseca in 1515 for better treatment of the Indians, Las Casas was told that "the death of the Indians meant nothing to the king or himself." Fonseca scolded Las Casas as a fool, in front of Oviedo.[76] In 1518, Fonseca virtually doomed the voyage of Ferdinand Magellan before it sailed. Three of Magellan's five captains were chosen by Fonseca, four of the five pilots, and more than half of the officers and senior noncommissioned officers. The second-in-command of the Magellan voyage was Juan de Cartagena, the son of the bishop (but always referred to as his "nephew"). While still along the coast of Africa on the outward voyage, Cartagena attempted mutiny and was placed in chains. In addition to having problems with Fonseca's hand-picked crew, Magellan, before reaching Tierra del Fuego, discovered that half of his supplies had not been loaded. Officially, Portuguese spies in Sevilla were blamed; unofficially, Fonseca stole the provisions.

Thus the second voyage to the New World was organized and ready to sail. Taking the well-traveled route to the Canary Islands, the fleet reached Grand Canary on 2 October and three days later put in at Gomera. The latter island, it will be recalled, had been the takeoff point for the first voyage and was governed by Doña Inés Peraza de García.[77] Some have suggested that Columbus favored Gomera because Doña Inés was there; others think it was because Gomera was the last place with European inhabitants in the Canaries and the last place to pick up additional provisions or effect necessary repairs.

Since no log for this journey has survived, we must trust other sources, such as letters written by participants, verbal accounts given to others who wrote the accounts down, and secondhand written histories (such as that of Ferdinand Columbus) whose authors may have had access to the official records. None of these sources, however, tells us the exact date of the departure from Gomera. It was on about 10 October, and Hierro faded from view on 12 or 13 October. The crossing took only twenty-two days, and landfall was made in the Lesser Antilles on 3 November, a Sunday. The day of arrival gave the name to the island: Dominica.[78]

Other than the captain-general, Christopher Columbus, there were a number of notables on the voyage, men who were destined to become famous or infamous, depending on your point of view. There were no women on the journey. There were also no Pinzóns on this trip. A few of the interesting participants are listed here, in order of the alphabet and not in order of importance: Diego de Alvarado, who was many years later to sail from Guatemala to Peru to challenge Francisco Pizarro for control of that land; Friar Bernardo Buil, a Benedictine monk and apostolic delegate, who headed the entourage of a dozen clerics and who was to say the first Mass in the New World; Dr. Diego Alvarez Chanca, the queen's physician and medical head on the voyage, whose detailed written account of the journey has survived; Diego Colón, Columbus's younger brother; another Diego Colón, a Taino Indian who was a baptized Christian and had served the Admiral as his chief interpreter since the first landfall at San Salvador in 1492; Guillermo Coma, whose letter about the voyage, written to Nicolò Syllacio of Italy, was printed in 1494 or 1495 and was the next imprint, after Columbus's famous letter of 1493, to discuss the New World; Juan de la

Cosa, one of the finest pilots of his time and the owner of the *Santa María* on the first voyage, who was destined to make the first known map of the New World in 1500; Michele de Cuneo, a "gentleman volunteer" from Savona, Italy, who may have known Columbus as a boy and whose 1495 letter concerning the voyage is a primary source; Francisco de Garay, later the governor of Jamaica and an opponent of Hernán Cortés; Pedro de Las Casas, the father of Bishop Bartolomé de Las Casas; Friar Antonio de Marchena, who had befriended Columbus at the monastery of La Rábida in 1485; Alonso de Ojeda, the first governor of what is now Venezuela and Colombia and a protégé of the duke of Medina-Celi; Francisco, Diego, and Gabriel de Peñalosa, all uncles of Bartolomé de Las Casas; and Juan Ponce de León, later the governor of Puerto Rico and the discoverer of Florida.

The vessels of the second voyage carried more than notable people. They carried horses and pigs—and probably cattle and goats—and it was this voyage that introduced sugarcane, oranges, and lemons to the New World. It is possible that bananas also entered at this time, but they are not positively documented until 1516.

Let us return to the itinerary of the fleet. As the flotilla approached the Carib isle of Caire, which the Admiral renamed Dominica, three other islands could also be observed: Martinique (Matinino) to the south; the smaller Ayay (Maríagalante, Marie Galante) to the northeast; and the very large Turuqueira or Kerkeria (Santa María de Guadelupe, Guadeloupe) to the northwest. A suitable anchorage could not be found at Dominica, so the fleet moved to the island that Columbus named for his flagship, Maríagalante. On 4 November, the ships moved on to the island of Guadeloupe. What was to have been a brief stop lasted six days when Diego Márquez, the royal inspector and a caravel captain, took an unauthorized shore leave and got lost in the forests of Guadeloupe. If only Márquez had disappeared, Columbus might have sailed on, but he took two of the pilots and eight men with him. Ojeda, with a search party of forty men, could not locate the eleven missing men. They were eventually spotted when Márquez built a large signal fire. After being rescued, the captain was slapped into chains. And the fleet moved north, on 10 November.

Columbus named the next island Monserrate (Montserrat) and learned that the Caribs had depopulated that island by eating all of the inhabitants. A small round island rising from the sea, which Columbus said one needed a ladder to climb, was called Ocamaniro by the Caribs and Santa María la Redonda by the Admiral. A few more miles and the ships were at the Carib island of Yaramaqui; Columbus renamed it Santa María la Antigua. Both of these last two islands still use part of the names chosen by Columbus: Redonda and Antigua. After departing Antigua, the fleet sailed northwestward, and Ferdinand, in his *Historie*, said: "They sighted many other islands to the north that extended in a northwesterly direction; they were all very high and densely wooded. The Admiral anchored at one of these islands and named it *San Martín*." Columbus then moved on to an island he named Santa Cruz, arriving there on 14 November.[79] It is along this path in the Leeward Islands that many so-called authorities on the voyages of Columbus have twisted fact to create fiction. In today's parlance, one might term this portion of the sail a "docu-drama." Columbus did not name every island in the Caribbean!

Ferdinand Columbus and Bartolomé de Las Casas had access to the Admiral's journal, and Ferdinand talked about this voyage many times with his father. With specific reference to the events of the week of 14 November, Ferdinand said: "Nor did I ever hear the Admiral mention it. And since it was his daily custom to write down all that happened or was told to him, he would have certainly noted down anything . . . etc."[80] This statement referred to a shipwreck, not to islands, but it indicates that Ferdinand (and Las Casas) would have had firsthand information about the islands visited and named north of Antigua. Further, Dr. Chanca, Coma, and Cuneo—all of whom were present—do not contradict Ferdinand or Las Casas. In spite of this, Columbus has been credited with things he never did.[81] Part of the problem lies in the fact that several of the Columbus "scholars" have freely quoted from the historical fiction of Washington Irving and others. Second, they never felt burdened by precise documentation, and it is virtually impossible to tie down any one claim to a general list of "works cited" that is given, without page numbers, at the end of a book. And last, there has been a tendency to place great faith in wildly inaccurate maps, such as the Juan de la Cosa chart.

According to Morison, Paolo Emilio Taviani, and others, Columbus named most, if not all, of the islands between Dominica and Puerto Rico. The sequence of names suggests (and it is only a suggestion, since documentation is lacking) that the written material has been made to conform to the arrangement of islands on the Juan de la Cosa chart.[82] Unfortunately, the copies of the chart are incorrect, and the chart was wrong in the first place.[83] If la Cosa is followed, San Martín is the next middle-sized island north of Montserrat, with an unnamed little island between. If the unnamed island was Redonda, then the next would have been modern-day

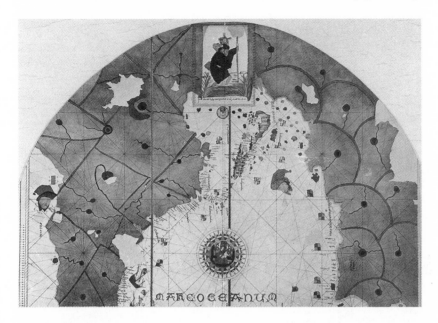

3.2 *The New World portion of the world map by Juan de la Cosa (1500). This was the first map to show the Columbian discoveries in the western Atlantic and Caribbean. The small inset in the west of the map (at the top) is of Saint Christopher. The flags along the coastline north of the Greater Antilles probably were intended to designate Cabot's discovery of North America in the final years of the fifteenth century. Courtesy Museo Naval, Madrid, Spain.*

Nevis (Nuestra Señora de las Nieves).[84] And if Columbus named this San Martín, then both modern-day Nevis and modern-day Saint Martin have had their names switched about, and their history books are all wrong!

Columbus, however, named no islands between Antigua and Santa Cruz; the latter is the modern-day Saint Croix in the American Virgin Islands. Those islands were named *after* the second voyage, most probably by a variety of different explorers. La Cosa did not even depict the island of Martinique (Matinino) on his map, and he was on the first voyage when it was discussed at length and on the second voyage when it was visible on landfall day. And why does he use the Indian name for Puerto Rico when all of his other names in the Lesser Antilles are in Spanish?

At Santa Cruz (Saint Croix) the Spaniards experienced their first serious encounter with the Caribs and the first death of a European at the hands of an Indian—in this case, a Carib woman—since the time of the Vikings.

3.3 *The Western Hemisphere portion of the world map by Alberto Cantino (1502), showing the introduction of geographical knowledge from the Columbian voyages into European lore. The peninsula of land northwest of Cuba is probably intended to be the Mangi province of China rather than a depiction of the Florida peninsula, which was not discovered until after the map was drawn. Courtesy Biblioteca Estense e Universitaria, Modena, Italy.*

From all accounts, only one Carib died in this first skirmish. Sailing northward from Saint Croix, the fleet came to a large cluster ("more than fifty," said Ferdinand) of islands that Columbus named Las Once Mil Vírgenes (The Eleven Thousand Virgins). The largest—possibly modern-day Saint Thomas—he called Santa Ursula.

By 18 November the fleet was in sight of Puerto Rico, which the Indians knew as Boriquén and Columbus named San Juan Bautista (Saint John the Baptist). Later the name given by Columbus was to become the name of the city founded by Ponce de León, first governor of that island. The first anchorage in Puerto Rico is still debated, but it was probably at the Rio Añasco in the northwestern portion of the island. Finally, on 22 November, the squadron reached the northeastern coast of Hispaniola. At Samaná Bay one of the Indians who had made the trip to Spain was released. Now the land was familiar to the Admiral and a few others from the first voyage.

The fleet anchored at Monte Cristi on 25 November and were off the reefs of Navidad by the twenty-seventh. But no response came from shore when the cannons were fired. All of the garrison left by Columbus—thirty-nine to forty-two men—were dead. Some had died of disease, some in battle with the cacique Caonabó in the interior after they deserted the fortress, some in battle with Caonabó when he attacked the fortress, and some in battle with each other for gold and women. The fortress had been burned to the ground, and Columbus's friend Cacique Guacanagarí had been severely wounded, fighting to defend the Europeans.

On 7 December, the Admiral abandoned the ill-fated colony at Navidad and took the fleet eastward to Monte Cristi. From here Columbus continued to follow the coast to the east, mainly because the source of gold appeared to lie in that direction. A site for a permanent settlement—Isabela—was selected at the northernmost part of the present-day Dominican Republic, on the western side of modern-day Cape Isabela. The date of the establishment of Isabela is, naturally, disputed. Morison and Taviani (among many others) give 2 January 1494. Coma, who was there, says it was "the week before Christmas," or 18 December 1493.[85] For a while, then, the second voyage took a long pause: to build a town and to send twelve ships home (2 February 1494) with several hundred ill and/or unhappy colonists, some Indians (mostly Caribs), a little gold, and a long report (the "Torres Memorandum") to the sovereigns.[86] Columbus also wanted to survey the island, punish Caonabó, and engage in additional exploration from a fixed base.

Between 11 December 1493 and 12 March 1494, the Admiral was too ill to maintain his daily journal. The nature of this illness (and more illnesses in the future) is just one additional mystery. Ferdinand mentioned gout, but diabetes, syphilis, and a liver disorder are also possibilities. Columbus was well enough to be able to explore inland between 12 March and 29 March, and on 24 April he left in three caravels to determine if Cuba was or was not an island. His "flagship" for this expedition was the sturdy little *Niña*. While away from Isabela, Columbus appointed a council to rule the island. His younger brother, Diego, was named president of that body.

The three caravels reached the western end of Hispaniola on 29 April, and on the thirtieth he entered and named Puerto Grande (Guantánamo Bay). For three days Columbus sailed along the southern coast of Cuba, to the cape he named Cabo Cruz. On 3 May the vessels turned southward for Jamaica, which the Admiral had heard of on the first voyage. The first landing on Jamaica was made at modern-day Saint Ann's Bay (Santa Gloria). Sailing westward, they had a brief skirmish with the Indians at Puerto Bueno (Dry Harbour). On 14 May the fleet returned to Cabo Cruz. Following the Cuban coast, the fleet entered a maze of islands the Admiral named Las Jardines de la Reina (The Queen's Gardens), a name retained to this day. Also, it was here that the Spaniards saw their first flamingos. During this passage Columbus was feeling exhausted; he noted in his log (according to Ferdinand) that he had not had a full night's sleep since September.

On 10 June the Admiral had a conversation, through his Taino interpreter Diego Colón, and was told that Cuba was definitely an island. This encounter probably occurred on the shores of Cienfuegos Bay. Nevertheless, a very strange thing happened on board the *Niña* on 12 June, one of those events that history has mistreated. Columbus asked his notary, Fernando Pérez de Luna, to take some witnesses and go to each ship and interview each person—officer, seaman, or ship's boy. The notary was to ascertain if there was anyone on the expedition who had any doubt that Cuba was the mainland. If there were any who doubted this, the notary was to beg them to say so, for the Admiral wanted to prove to them that Cuba was continental land.

But Pérez de Luna made this event not only important but very complex. The notary drew up a formal statement and went to each man and forced him to sign it, under the threat of paying a fine of ten thousand *maravedíes* and having his tongue cut out. Columbus did not see the document until after Pérez de Luna had died. There was never a forced oath or any sort of penalty authorized by Columbus. In fact, the document itself states that these were Pérez de Luna's own ideas.[87]

The day after everyone swore that Cuba was the mainland—13 June—Columbus decided to turn about. Provisions were low, and the caravels were in bad shape. As much he wanted to, this was not the time to sail on across the Indian Ocean and go back to Spain by way of the Red Sea with, perhaps, a stopover in Jerusalem. The ships stopped at the Isle of Pines (San Juan Evangelista) for water and wood, made an attempt to get out of the Gulf of Batabanó by heading south, and were then forced to return by the way they had come. They did not actually depart the Isle of Pines until 25 June. And Cabo Cruz was not reached until 18 July. Both ships and men were suffering greatly.

Since the wind was unfavorable for a direct sail to Hispaniola, Columbus decided to return via Jamaica and on 22 July departed Cabo Cruz for that island.[88] Columbus probably landed at Montego Bay (Golfo de Buen Tiempo), from which he had departed for Cuba on 14 May. The fleet then coasted along the western and southern sides of the island up to modern-day Portland Bight (Boca de las Vacas). On 19 August the fleet lost sight of Morant Point (which Columbus named El Cabo del Farol), and on 20 August the western end of Hispaniola (Cabo de San Miguel) was sighted.

Near the end of August the *Niña* arrived at a small island south of modern-day Cabo Beata. The caravels *San Juan* and *Cardera* had strayed from the little flotilla, and the Admiral sent some men to climb the mountain on the tiny isle he called Alta Vela. The large island next to Alta Vela may have been named Santa Catarina at this same time; today it is known as Isla Beata. It was hoped that the men would be able to see the missing ships from the top of Alta Vela, but the ships did not arrive for six days. Once reunited, the vessels sailed to Isla Beata and from there northeastward to either Bahía de Neiba or Bahía de Ocoa. Nine men were landed, with orders to cross Hispaniola on foot, by way of the then-established forts of Santo Tomás and Magdalena, to Isabela.

Columbus and his men did not reach the eastern end of Hispaniola until 15 September, when they anchored at an island the Indians called Adamaney, which the Admiral renamed La Bella Sãonese, for Savona, a city near Genoa and the home of Cuneo. Columbus gave the island to Cuneo, and the latter was apparently overjoyed.[89] A storm kept the boats bottled up for almost a week and a half, giving Cuneo time to tidy up his island, weather permitting. On 24 September the ships sailed to Puerto Rico by way of an island the Indians called Mona, a name that has survived. During this voyage the Admiral fell gravely ill, with a high fever, drowsiness, and a complete loss of sight and memory. Because of this, the plan to explore more of the Lesser Antilles (Carib Islands) was abandoned, and the fleet made directly for Isabela, arriving on 29 September. Though Columbus improved, he lay ill for five months.

When Columbus and his expeditionary force of three caravels returned to Isabela they found that Antonio de Torres, who had taken the twelve ships to Spain in February, had returned. Accompanying him was Bartholomew Columbus, the Admiral's closest brother. Christopher immediately appointed Bartholomew to be *adelantado* (governor) of the Indies.

The early part of 1495 was one of turmoil in Hispaniola. The Spaniards— and there were now only 630, many of whom were women and children— committed an untold number of outrages against the Indians. And the Indians, led by four strong caciques, were in a virtual state of revolt. There were numerous skirmishes and a great loss of Indian lives. Many prisoners were taken, some to be sent to Spain. A tribute system was established for every Indian over fourteen years of age. Every three months Indians in the gold-producing region of Cibao had to each fill a large hawk's bell with gold dust; others paid in cotton. Each Indian had to wear a token around his neck as a receipt; failure to have the token meant instant punishment.[90]

This vicious system, coupled with imported diseases (mostly measles and smallpox), destroyed two-thirds of the Taino population in less than five years. Columbus believed that the demise of the Indian population was punishment by God for their sins. God, then, had assisted in the pacification of Hispaniola. But even with Divine help, word was reaching the sovereigns that all was not well in the New World. Columbus decided to return home to squelch these rumors, and on 10 March 1496, he departed Hispaniola with 225 Spaniards and 30 Indians. His flagship was none other than the *Niña*. He sailed for Maríagalante, a journey that took until 9 April. On the tenth he moved over to Guadeloupe in search of food. Eventually a conflict arose, and the Spaniards looted a village and made their own cassava bread. Women ruled this part of Guadeloupe, thus supporting the story, which Columbus had heard during the first voyage, of an island of amazons. Columbus not only made peace with these Carib women warriors but actually persuaded the female cacique and her daughter to accompany them to Spain. On that same vessel was Cacique Caonabó, the Indian who had slain many of the Navidad colonists. The Spaniards finally learned why Caonabó was feared so greatly on the island of Hispaniola: he was a Carib from the Lesser Antilles.

Departure for Spain was on 20 April; the Portuguese coast was sighted on 8 June. Food ran low during this lengthy voyage, and two solutions to the problem were submitted to the Admiral: the Europeans wanted to throw the Indians overboard; the Caribs wanted to eat a few of the Tainos. Columbus rejected both plans and, with God's help, navigated to within a few miles of Cape Saint Vincent. When *India*, the first ship constructed in the New World, and *Niña*, the veteran of the first voyage, entered the harbor of Cádiz on 11 June 1496, the second voyage was over.

The Third Voyage: 30 May 1498–20 November 1500

The third voyage of Christopher Columbus to the New World was filled with both victory and defeat, both elation and despair. Columbus, now called "The Admiral of the Ocean Sea and Viceroy and Governor General of the Islands and Mainland of Asia and the Indies," discovered a continent, an event that has occurred very infrequently in the course of history. And this same Christopher Columbus ended the momentous voyage in chains and disgrace, an event that has occurred all too frequently in the lives of history's heroes.

Although Columbus considered the second voyage to have been a successful one, he knew in his heart that all was not right in the Indies. The children of God, living in their own Eden and innocence, had been brutalized by men whom the Admiral could not control. The colonists' numbers had declined, and there were now food shortages in what had been a land of plenty. The mutual affection between Indian and European in 1492 had evolved into a state of mutual fear. The Spaniards would not work, and the Tainos were not able to. Though temporarily pacified by the harshest of means, the Spanish Island—Hispaniola—was close to anarchy. These details had been reported to the sovereigns, and one can only suspect that the people opposed to the Admiral had the loudest voices. They certainly had Fonseca, who had been Columbus's enemy since the beginning. It is not surprising, then, that it took so long to assemble men, ships, and supplies for the third voyage.

Although Columbus was well received by the sovereigns at Burgos on his return, it was almost a year before even two relief ships were sent to the colonists. After all, ships were in short supply. Spain and France were at war, and things were so bad that only 130 vessels could be sent as an escort when Princess Juana went to Flanders to marry Philip of Hapsburg and when Philip's sister, Margarita, was brought to Spain to marry Prince Juan.

The Admiral spent half of 1497 in Burgos and the first part of 1498 in Medina del Campo, following the court. The departure of the fleet for the third voyage was delayed time and again. This was largely due to the deliberate mismanagement of Bishop Fonseca. Columbus had asked for eight ships. He received six, but three were supply ships that were to proceed directly to Hispaniola. The three vessels of the exploratory fleet consisted of one carrack and two caravels. The carrack was named *Santa María de Guía*, making three *Santa Marías* in as many voyages.

A primary goal of this voyage was to ascertain if there was a continental landmass south of the Indies. There were many rumors and some circumstantial evidence that the Portuguese had discovered a continent. If this was true, which side of the Treaty of Tordesillas line was it on? As noted earlier, the Portuguese must have had some motive for renegotiating the 1493 Demarcation Line and moving it much farther west with the Treaty of Tordesillas (1494). The latter meridian was about eight hundred miles west of the former one, and it sliced through the then-undiscovered eastern bulge of Brazil. Added to this fact was a total blackout of information from Portugal concerning maritime activity between 1488 (when Bartolomeu Dias returned to Lisbon after reaching and rounding the Cape of Good Hope) and 1497 (when Vasco da Gama sailed for Calicut, India). Did the Portuguese actually suspend ocean voyaging for nine years after struggling for seventy-five years to reach the tip of Africa?

It has been argued that the Columbus discovery prompted political debate, papal action, treaty negotiations, and—at the Portuguese court—a great deal of confusion. While all of these things may have been true, they do not explain why Portugal called to a halt its southern African maritime activity for a full four years before the first voyage of Columbus. The death of João II in 1495 may have been a further disruption, but such a long hiatus is illogical and not easily explained. Another puzzle is this: how was it possible for Vasco da Gama to sail from the Cape Verde Islands to southern Africa on an arcing course that kept him from sighting land for three months (3 August to 4 November 1497)? Had the trail already been blazed? And finally, João II believed there was a continent to balance Africa, a rejuvenated bit of Stoic philosophy and the birth of a rumor that the Portuguese had already discovered a continent south of the island archipelago explored by Columbus on his first and second voyages.

The Columbus fleet departed Sanlúcar de Barrameda on 30 May 1498. For the first time a stopover was made in Porto Santo (7 June) and Madeira (10 June). This shift in course may have been due to the possibility of a French squadron lying in wait along the traditional route to the Canary Islands. After receiving a thunderous reception in the Portuguese islands (where the Admiral had once resided), and after taking on additional water, wood, and supplies, the six ships sailed for Gomera in the Canaries. Near Gomera the Spanish fleet did have a run-in with the French and rescued two Spanish vessels that had been captured. Gomera was reached on 16 June, three days after sailing from Madeira. On 21 June the course was set for Hierro, the westernmost of the Canaries. At this point the three supply ships sailed directly for Hispaniola, via Dominica.[91] Columbus set his course for the Cape Verde Islands, in order to launch his voyage to the west from a more southern latitude and possibly find the "Portuguese continent."

Columbus was in the Cape Verdes from 27 June until 7 July, his first voyage to what he found to be a miserable and melancholy place. The islands were populated by goats, turtles, and lepers. The Admiral said that 75 percent of the people were sick, and the rest had a sickly color.[92] Although Columbus tried to depart on 5 July, with the intention of sailing south of the Equator, the currents delayed him, and the island of Fogo was in view until the seventh. The island was well named—"Smoke"—for it was belching both fire and smoke at the time.

Columbus sailed to within five degrees of the Equator, but the ships were becalmed for eight days and the heat was unbearable, so he altered course to the northwest and climbed to 7° north. He sailed west along this latitude and, on 31 July, concluded that the Lesser Antilles were to his north. Since all of his provisions were spoiling and there was a critical shortage of water, a course was set for Hispaniola, giving up the search for a southern continent. The next day—1 August—Alonso Pérez Nizardo, a sailor from Huelva, sighted three mountains to the west. This island was Trinidad (Trinity). The southeastern tip was named Cabo de la Galera (Galeota Point); Erin Point on the southern coast was called Punta de la Playa. While sailing between these two locations, the sailors sighted land—South America—to the south. Not realizing that this was the continent he had been looking for, Columbus named it Isla Santa (Holy Island). This was the first documented sighting of the South American continent, and that part seen by Columbus is known today as Punta Bombeador, part of the Orinoco Delta in Venezuela.

The fleet entered the Gulf of Paria (Golfo de la Ballena) through a strait still called by the name given by Columbus: Boca de la Sierpe (Serpent's Mouth). He spent the next two weeks exploring the gulf, finally departing on 13 August through the strait called Boca del Dragón (Dragon's Mouth). Many features within the Gulf of Paria were named, but the names of only a few, such as Punta del Arenal (the southwestern point of Trinidad), have survived. The name "Paria" was used by the natives for their land, but Columbus did not apply it to any feature.

On Sunday, 5 August 1498, Columbus sent several small boats to the land he called Isla de Gracia (the Paria Peninsula of Venezuela). This was the first recorded landing of Europeans on the South American mainland. The site of the event was about fifteen miles west of modern-day Punta Penas, on the southern side of the Paria Peninsula. Another significant date is 10 August 1498. Quoting Columbus directly, Las Casas wrote, "Y vuestras Altezas ganaron estas tierras, tantas, que son otro mundo [And your Highnesses will acquire these lands, so vast, which are another world]."[93] Another world—in the Admiral's famous letter to Doña Juana de Torres (October 1500) he said, "I have placed under the dominion of the king and queen, our sovereigns, a second world."[94] Unless one is hung up on semantics, "another world" and "a second world" sound a lot like "a new world." The Admiral was no longer thinking about Asia.

On 14 August 1498, Columbus wrote in his journal, "I believe that this is a very great continental land, that until today has not been known." Again, it was illogical that the Admiral was associating this land with that of Marco Polo. Christopher Columbus fully realized that he had discovered something never reported before by another European. In fact, he thought he had discovered the Terrestrial Paradise of medieval geographical lore, and in the Admiral's report to the sovereigns, on 18 October 1498, he cites some of his "proofs" for this belief.[95] This report ends with, "Your Highnesses have another world [un otro mundo] here."

On departing through Dragon's Mouth, Columbus reported two islands in the distance to the northeast: Asunción and Concepción. Despite the great distance—about seventy-five miles—some scholars believe these to be Grenada and Tobago. And some also believe that Tobago was sighted on 4 August and named Belaforma. After leaving the Gulf of Paria, Columbus sailed westward along the Pearl Coast, at least close enough to see Margarita, which he named. Although few of the many names chosen by Columbus remain unadulterated, Los Testigos (The Witnesses), a cluster of small islands north of Venezuela, kept its original designation. The pearl fisheries of Margarita were not seen during this voyage, but pearls from here were in the possession of Indians on the shore of the Gulf of Paria. Information about the abundance of pearls in the region led to their exploitation as early as the summer of 1499, by Alonso de Ojeda.

The fleet reached Isla Beata, at the extreme southern tip of Hispaniola, on 20 August. Columbus was upset with himself for falling to the leeward of Santo Domingo (Hispaniola) by some seventy-five miles. This was the only navigational error after sailing over uncharted waters for over two months—from Africa to South America to the West Indies. It was an incredible bit of dead-reckoning navigation that could not be duplicated today by one navigator out of a hundred thousand, using the same instruments and after stowing away the charts.

On 30 August the Admiral sailed into the harbor of Santo Domingo, the Nueva Isabela that his brother Bartholomew had built in his two-and-a-half-year absence. But the new city was overshadowed by old problems—old problems that had become worse. Many people had died, and most of the survivors had syphilis. Many had joined in a rebellion led by the alcalde, Francisco Roldán.[96]

The Roldán rebellion was later complicated by the arrival of Ojeda on 5 September 1499. In effect there was now a three-way struggle for leadership of the fledgling colony. Although Columbus made concessions, there was no hope of satisfying all of the rebels or even the nonrebels who did not like the Columbus brothers. Eventually word of this chaos reached Spain, and the sovereigns sent Knight Commander Francisco de Bobadilla to Hispaniola to investigate and solve the colony's problems. Bobadilla arrived at the end of August 1500. Christopher and Bartholomew were out of town, trying to pacify the countryside. Bobadilla simply moved into Columbus's home and seized his property. The commander also took depositions from everyone that hated Columbus—and their numbers were legion. He then declared himself governor.

Bobadilla summoned Columbus with a letter from the sovereigns. Without taking any evidence or holding a hearing, Bobadilla clamped chains on both Christopher and his brother Diego and placed them aboard ship under a heavy guard. When Bartholomew returned, he too was imprisoned. Bobadilla ordered the ship's captain, Andrés Martín, to keep the Columbus brothers in chains and turn them over to Bishop Fonseca in that condition. As soon as they put to sea Martín wanted to release the prisoners, but Christopher refused, preferring to let the sovereigns see what his enemies had done to him.

Columbus reached Cádiz no later than 20 November 1500. He may have arrived a few days earlier, but on that date he wrote the sovereigns about his situation, and it is unlikely that he would have postponed that for even an hour. The third voyage ended thus, on or about 20 November, with the sovereigns promising to make amends, restore the Admiral's property, punish the rebels, and remove Bobadilla. In general, these things were done.

The Fourth Voyage: 9 May 1502–7 November 1504

The goal of the third voyage had been to find the great southern continent, already rumored to have been discovered by the Portuguese. This was accomplished, but there is every reason to believe that the significance of this momentous event was not fully appreciated or even understood at court. And there were many who were willing to profit by the discoveries of Columbus while, at the same time, they undermined his position. Almost two years passed after the Admiral's return before he was able to sail again, and this time there were numerous conditions set forth by the sovereigns. Among them, Columbus was forbidden to go to Hispaniola on the outward voyage; there would have been a conflict of authority with the new governor, Nicolás de Ovando. Permission was granted for a stop there on the return, if absolutely necessary. Also, fourteen-year-old Ferdinand was allowed to accompany his father.

The fleet of four caravels—all rather old and worn—departed Cádiz on 9 May 1502. Bartholomew Columbus was captain of one of the vessels, and another was commanded by Pedro de Terreros, the only man known to sail on all four voyages with the Admiral. The ships stopped in Morocco to assist the Portuguese at Arcila and may have caused the Moors to lift their siege of that fort. From there it took four days to reach Grand Canary, where they arrived on 20 May. The westward sail began on 25 May and reached Martinique on 15 June, a total of twenty-one days and the fastest crossing of the four voyages. Puerto Rico was coasted on the twenty-fourth, and the Admiral went directly for the forbidden island, Hispaniola. Here he hoped to replace one of his caravels but was denied permission to dock at Santo Domingo.

When Columbus sent Terreros ashore to request permission to enter the harbor—on 29 June—he also sent a message to the governor telling him that a storm was brewing and that no ships should depart for eight days. There were twenty-eight ships ready to leave for Spain. They carried the deposed governor Bobadilla, the rebel Roldán and his troops, and even some gold that belonged to the Admiral. The storm—obviously a hurricane—struck the next day, 30 June. Columbus managed to find a safe harbor, but as the storm gained in intensity on 1 July, three of the vessels were torn from their anchorage and had to ride out the tempest in the open sea. When the weather cleared, all of Columbus's ships were safe. Of the twenty-eight homeward-bound vessels, only one—the one carrying the Admiral's gold—later made it to Spain. Twenty-four were washed off the face of the earth, with a loss of all hands, the despised Bobadilla, and Roldán and his gang. Everything considered, it does indeed look as though Divine Providence was at Columbus's side this time.

The fleet of the fourth voyage had rendezvoused at Azua (south of modern-day Azua, now Puerto Viejo). From there it sailed to Puerto Brasil (Jacmel, Haiti). The vessels departed Haiti on 14 July, were becalmed for a spell, and were carried by the current to Jamaica, where they spent at least a day at the Morant Cays east of that island. The fleet sailed (or drifted) to the northwest, passing Jamaica on the north and reaching Cuba during the last week of July. The exact location in Cuba is not known. It could have been anywhere between Cienfuegos and the Isle of Pines. From here the course was set to the southwest and the ultimate goal of the fourth voyage.

Columbus had, in his mind, constructed the following geography: Cuba was a part, a peninsula, of the Asian mainland; Paria, a land running east and west like Cuba, was another peninsula, this one on the great southern continent. Somewhere between these two mainlands—between Asia (Cuba) in the north and the Other World in the south—there *must* be a passage to the Indian Ocean. Surely, by sailing southwest from Asia (Cuba), he would come to the end of the Malay Peninsula and be able to pass on to the lands (India) already reached by the Portuguese. In fact, Columbus carried with him credentials to show the Portuguese, if he should by chance encounter them. And, he carried Arabic interpreters just in case he sailed on to the Arabian Sea. Once the strait was found, Columbus would determine whether to sail on around the world, reversing Vasco da Gama's route, or return by the familiar route to the east. This voyage, then, was to search for water, not land. He missed his goal by fifty miles—the distance across the Isthmus of Panama.

On 31 July the fleet reached the Bay Islands of Honduras. They landed on one he called Guanaja. Modern-day Cape Honduras was named Punta Caxinas. It was here that the Spaniards saw their first Mayas: a merchant canoe with forty or fifty men, women, and children. It carried a variety of products, including the first cacao beans ever seen by a European. Some have said that this was the first big mistake the Admiral made on this voyage; he should have turned around and discovered the Maya civilization. On the other hand, he knew that these people lived only a short distance to the west of where he had explored in Cuba. They could be visited another day. It was reassuring, however, to know that there were people who made fine cloth, wore elaborate clothing, and fashioned magnificent boats.

It took seventy days to sail the two hundred miles from Punta Caxinas to the cape we still call Gracias a Dios. The coast drops south at that point, and it was no longer necessary to tack against a strong headwind. When conditions suddenly improved, where today Honduras and Nicaragua meet on the Caribbean Sea, Columbus said, "Thanks to God." Thus the cape was named, on 14 September 1502. During the long ordeal of trying to sail into the trades, the fleet stopped many times. On 14 August they held a Mass on the beach. This was probably the first Mass ever said on the mainland of the New World. And on 17 August, the day on which boats were sent ashore to take formal possession of Central America, the Spaniards may have eaten their first turkey dinner. The first deaths during this voyage occurred on 16 September, when two men drowned as a boat was swamped while they attempted to get water at the mouth of the Rio Grande de Matagalpa, in Nicaragua. Columbus named the river, quite appropriately, Rio de Desastres.

From 25 September until 5 October the fleet was anchored off the Indian village of Cariay, which Columbus called La Huerta and which is known today as Limón, Costa Rica. Here the ships were careened and the Spaniards were well received by the local inhabitants. By 5 October the ships were at the bay named for the Admiral, Almirante Bay (Panama), and they entered the neighboring bay, now called Chiriquí Lagoon. The Spaniards were in the vicinity of Chiriquí Lagoon until 17 October, then sailed leisurely down the coast of Panama, trading with the Indians, observing their customs, learning about the environment, and keeping on the lookout for gold. In the present-day Panamanian province of Veragua they saw a great deal of gold. On 2 November, Columbus entered and named the harbor Portobelo. And beautiful it is. The original name has been kept, and Portobelo later became a key city on the Spanish main. Columbus tarried for a week because of foul weather; little did he know that, on average, Portobelo is the wettest town in Panama and has the shortest dry season, if any at all.

Departing Portobelo on 9 November, the vessels sailed eastward for about twenty-five miles but because of contrary winds were forced to put in to a harbor, probably at present-day Nombre de Dios. The Admiral called this Puerto de Bastimentos (Harbor of Provisions) because of all the maize fields in the area. The Admiral and his men remained there until 23 November, repairing the ships, which were in terrible condition. They sailed eastward again for a few miles, stopping at a little harbor Columbus called Retrete (Puerto de los Escribános). They were there nine days because of miserable weather. During this time there was one major confrontation with the Indians (and several minor ones), resulting in the death of a few natives. These were the Cunas (San Blas), with whom Núñez de Balboa later had excellent relations.

After deciding that the northeast tradewinds were not going to weaken, Columbus turned back toward Veragua on 5 December, stopping for one more night at Portobelo. The variable winds—first east, then west—made sailing almost impossible.[97] After twelve days of storms and even waterspouts, the fleet anchored at a place the Indians called Huiva, near the Caribbean entrance to the Panama Canal. Departure was on 20 December, but again refuge had to be sought in an unnamed harbor. On the twenty-third Columbus tried once more to put to sea but was blown back to Huiva, where he remained until 3 January 1503. The variable winds and currents caused the Admiral to name this coast La Costa de los Contrastes.

On 6 January 1503, the fleet anchored at a river that Columbus named Belén (Bethlehem) and the Indians called Yebra. This was probably the Rio Concepción and not the modern-day Rio Belén.[98] The mountains that Columbus named San Cristóbal are the Serranía de Tabasará in Panama; the great summit he saw in the clouds is Cerro Baltazar (6,400 feet), the highest mountain in Veraguas. The Spaniards were at Belén until 16 April 1503, during which time they attempted to establish the first settlement on the mainland of North America.[99] Though they did build a dozen cane-and-thatch houses, at the end of more than three months they had little to show for their labors. They lost all of their huts, most of their supplies, the caravel *La Gallega*, and some fourteen or fifteen men. The Admiral was ill much of the time, and Bartholomew played the more important role. Perhaps the gold extracted from the Guaymi Indians made it all worthwhile.

They sailed back to Portobelo, and here the caravel *Vizcaína* was abandoned, having been almost devoured by shipworms. The two surviving ships sailed past the San Blas Islands (Las Barbas) to a point now called Punta Mosquito. Columbus named it Marmóreo (Marble). On 1 May 1503, the two caravels sailed northward from Panama, passing Little Cayman and Cayman Brac (Las Tortugas) on 10 May. On 12 May Columbus arrived at Las Jardines de la Reina in Cuba. They almost lost the *Santiago* (also called the *Bermuda*) in a storm and barely made it to the Cuban mainland for food. Since the winds were not favorable for going to Hispaniola and the ships were leaking badly, the Admiral set a course for Jamaica, landing at Puerto Bueno (Dry Harbour). There was no water there—hence the modern-day name—so Columbus moved eastward to present-day Saint Ann's Bay (Santa Gloria). The two remaining caravels (the *Santiago* and the *Capitana*) were in such poor shape that Columbus ran both of them into the beach.[100] They shored up the beached ships and built cabañas on the decks. In effect the Spaniards constructed a fortified encampment on the shore.

After almost two months on the beach at Saint Ann's Bay, it was obvious that no ship was going to pass their way. Columbus then decided to send Bartolomeo Fieschi, captain of the *Vizcaína*, and Diego Méndez de Segura, a squire, to Hispaniola for help. Each had an Indian canoe with ten Indians and six Spaniards. The object was to paddle night and day over 108 nautical miles of open ocean. On arrival at the western tip of Hispaniola, Fieschi was to return with the news that the canoes had made it (if they had!) and Méndez was to travel another 300 miles to Santo Domingo. The crossing was made, but two or three Indians died along the way. No one would return with Fieschi, so Columbus was not to learn of the successful voyage for months.

Back at the site of the marooning, the brothers Francisco and Diego de Porras, with forty-eight followers, staged a mutiny, claiming that the Admiral had sent false information to Santo Domingo (via Méndez) and was only trying to save himself and regain his authority. Columbus was too ill—Ferdinand said he suffered from gout—to make a strong stand, and Bartholomew Columbus became the effective leader. The mutiny occurred on 2 January 1504, and the mutineers took the Spaniards' ten canoes and headed for Hispaniola on the first calm day, taking with them a number of Indians to paddle. After the mutiny, Columbus lost a great deal of power over the local Indians, and they would no longer trade food for trinkets. The Admiral reestablished his dominance by correctly predicting the full lunar eclipse of 29 February 1504. After that feat the Indians treated him as though he were supernatural. Shortly thereafter, the mutineers returned. Unfavorable weather had caused panic, and eighteen Indians had been thrown overboard to lighten the canoes, without success. When the mutineers came back, they occupied an Indian village.

In March 1504, a caravel arrived with some supplies, but no one was taken aboard. A message was brought to the Admiral from Méndez—the first word since he had departed in the canoe the previous July. Columbus now knew that Méndez would come back. Attempts to negotiate with the mutineers were unsuccessful; eventually Bartholomew took them by force, killing several and capturing Francisco de Porras. The ship that Méndez had arranged for arrived on 28 June 1504. Everyone departed—friends and enemies alike, according to Ferdinand—and reached Santo Domingo on 13 August 1504. Governor Ovando promptly released Porras and the other rebels.

Christopher Columbus, his brother Bartholomew, and his son Ferdinand sailed from Santo Domingo on 12 September 1504. The "Fourth Voyage of Discovery" ended on 7 November 1504, when the ship entered the harbor of Sanlúcar de Barrameda. Within three weeks (on 26 November) Queen Isabella died. The Admiral, now tired and old for his years, would live only another eighteen months. There would be no more voyages for the first Admiral of the Ocean Sea.

Christopher Columbus died in Valladolid, Spain, on the Feast of the Ascension, 20 May 1506. According to John Boyd Thacher, the first notice of the Discoverer's passing was made on the back of the Royal Cédula addressed by King Ferdinand to Nicolás de Ovando. Dated 2 June 1506 and written in the hand of some nameless clerk, the note said, "E agora el dicho Almirante es fallecido [The said Admiral is now dead]."[101]

In the first chapter of Peter Martyr's *Second Decade*, published in 1516, we read: "In the declaration of my decade of the ocean . . . I described how Christopher Columbus found those islands whereof we have spoken, and that turning from thence toward the left hand southward, he chanced upon great regions of lands and large seas distant from the equinoctial line as much as from five to ten degrees; where he found wide rivers and very high mountains close to the shore and covered with snow, and harbors most quiet. Columbus, already having departed out of this life, the King began to take care how that these lands might by colonized with Christians for the increase of our Faith."[102] And as Thacher observed, "It is a strange commentary on man's forgetfulness of his fellow that Christopher Columbus, who had filled so large a place in the world at the close of the fifteenth century, should die and be buried without any unusual expression of public sorrow and with no mention of his end by historian or chronologer."[103]

Thus, almost in anonymity, the Admiral of the Ocean Sea died at the age of fifty-five. During four voyages for Spain, covering a brief span of twelve years, Christopher Columbus did what no one had ever done before: he discovered one continent, opened the gates to another, discovered countless islands in a sea he found, and was for a time governor of more territory than even the Great Khan whom he had sought so futilely.

Although Columbus was born in the Middle Ages, he matured in the Renaissance. It might even be correct to say that without Columbus (or someone like him), there would have been no Renaissance. He was objective, methodical, shrewd, and always ready to learn. He could be compassionate, and at times he was as hard as nails. Although Columbus had no peer as a navigator, he was unable to sail the ship of state or tame the political seas.

When Columbus and his men reached Guanahaní on that twelfth day of October 1492, the history and the geography of the world were altered—instantly, completely, and irrevocably. Never had such an event happened before in all of human time; never will it happen again.

4 / Early Spanish Exploration: The Caribbean, Central America, and the Gulf of Mexico

ROBERT S. WEDDLE

Columbus in 1492 opened the door to a labyrinthine new world, any one of whose myriad passages would disclose previously unknown vistas. He could not begin to fathom its complexities. In three succeeding voyages, 1493–1504, he established on Hispaniola a permanent base for the continuing discovery; he also discovered the Lesser Antilles, Puerto Rico, and Jamaica, as well as the mainland of Central and South America. Yet his discoveries were limited by natural phenomena he did not understand. The Caribbean Current, coursing westward along Cuba's southern shore toward the Yucatán Channel, figured in his decision on the second voyage to turn back from the Ensenada de Cortés rather than risk, with short provisions and tattered rigging, a difficult or impossible return against the stream. Thus, he failed to recognize that Cuba was an island and not an Asian peninsula. The current also influenced his decision, after reaching Honduras on the fourth voyage, to turn east instead of west. He thus failed to discover the Yucatán Peninsula and the impressive Mayan ruins along its Caribbean coast. Instead, he ran the isthmian shore in a fruitless search for a strait to the Indian Ocean so that he might sail home to Spain by going around the world.[1]

It was the third voyage, reaching the Paria Peninsula of Venezuela, that shifted the focus of Spanish interest from Cuba and Jamaica south across the Caribbean Sea. The Admiral's reports of friendly natives wearing pearl necklaces and ornaments of alloyed copper and gold stirred the sanguine souls of would-be usurpers. This eager bunch, mindless of the injustice being done to Columbus by his imprisonment and the Crown's breach of contract, suffered no compunction over pirating his maps and reports so as to exploit this *otro mundo* ("other world") while its discoverer languished in jail. Indeed, each extension of the discovery had seemed to emphasize that it was too vast and too complex for one man to hold sway over or even to understand. The Crown, ever more eager to make sweeping concessions before a discovery than to honor its commitments afterward, opened the door in 1495 for opportunistic adventurers to explore the Indies. The third-voyage disclosures provided the incentive for them to do so.

Columbus died in 1506 without knowing the great extent of the southern continent he had found. In Central America he had discovered only the southern tip of the continent that extended northward; he had no inkling of its vastness. The Admiral had only heard of the other ocean beyond the Isthmus of Darién (Isthmus of Panama), which he coasted on the fourth voyage with expectations of finding a strait. He never reached the end of his "peninsula" of Cuba to glimpse the Gulf of Mexico. Yet he had introduced to "the Indies" the hardy band of adventurers who would carry forth the discovery to yet undreamed-of ends of the earth. The second voyage especially featured a roster of names to be heard again in connection with discovery voyages, names of settlers and governors-to-be of the Greater Antilles and "the Spanish Main," of participants in conquests across the Caribbean and the Gulf of Mexico: Alonso de Ojeda, Juan de la Cosa, Juan Ponce de León, Francisco de Garay, Diego Velázquez de Cuéllar, and Sebastián de Ocampo. Not all were men of exemplary character; some even schemed to strip Columbus of his discovery rights, to usurp the wealth and glory that the Crown had promised him. Yet they held one admirable trait in common: they dared to face the unknown. In extending the conquest to the various Caribbean islands and onto the mainland, they often subsisted on moldy biscuit and tainted meat, drank fetid water, and ran the risk of leaky ships and uncharted shoals; of corsairs, scurvy, and hurricane; of cannibalism, poison arrows, and mutiny by sailors disinclined to long suffering. They bore the brunt of the navigation explosion brought on by the discovery, with its concomitant shortages of skilled seamen and trained pilots, shortages that often put ships and men in jeopardy. They devised the means of circumventing the outmoded navigation and shipbuilding technology that was designed for coastal sailing rather than ocean travel. They charted the unknown seas, marking the hidden shoals and probing the mysteries of wind and current. It was on them that the onus fell for proving or disproving Columbus's geographical conception.

Columbus continued to believe, until his death, that he had found islands off the eastern coast of Asia. His opinions were not always shared by his shipmates or by European cosmographers. His detractors maintained that the islands he had found were those of the legendary Antilla, the Isle of the Seven Cities shown on fifteenth-century maps midway between Iberia and Asia. Yet Columbus's idea was by no means totally rejected; maps that seem to show a Gulf of Mexico or a Florida peninsula before their actual discovery may indeed have been intended to depict Asia. New World explorers were divided on the question. Although some suspected, as the fifteenth century drew to a close, that Cuba was an island rather than the Chinese province of Mangi or the Malay Peninsula, as the Admiral supposed, no one had yet determined where it ended or what lay beyond.[2]

As evidence accrued that the unbroken coast of South and Central America represented a new continent, completely unknown to Europeans, there arose a concern for proving its limits. If this was not Asia, where was the strait that led through it? How great was the landmass that separated the Ocean Sea from another that must lie beyond, and how far across that sea to Asia? (The idea of another ocean in itself was a startling concept, for to this point a single body of water was thought to encompass all the world's landmasses.) Of greater importance still, how big was the earth? (There was a growing suspicion that it was bigger than Columbus claimed.) And how long was a degree of its 360° arc? There were to be no quick and easy answers. Yet the key to at least some of the riddles might lie in the shadow of one of the islands that Columbus had discovered or within any of a number of bays and inlets along the extended coast. Such was the magnet that drew ungovernable Spanish adventurers into Columbus's wake. Some sought, for personal gain, peoples to exploit or gems and precious metals. Others searched for a strait that would lead to Asia, to wealth and glory for themselves and to material advantage for all Spain. All of them contributed to expanding geographical awareness.

Bishop Juan Rodríguez de Fonseca, the queen's chaplain and archdeacon of the Cathedral of Seville, was chosen by Queen Isabella in 1493 to take charge of matters relating to the newly discovered lands. It was he who oversaw preparations for Columbus's second voyage. Thenceforth, he stood solidly between the Admiral and the Crown and was responsible for disavowing the perquisites promised Columbus before the discovery of the New World became a reality. The Casa de Contratación was created in 1503 to manage Spain's overseas commerce and serve as a center for collecting and interpreting geographical information. Still Fonseca, while advancing through a succession of bishoprics with scant concern for his ecclesiastical duties, retained his iron-fisted control over Indies affairs at least until 1522. He held the power of life or death over the aspirations of New World explorers and conquerors.[3] In a conscious effort to curtail Columbus's rights, he encouraged trespassers on the legitimate Columbian realm.

Among the beneficiaries of such a policy was the rapacious Alonso de Ojeda, who with Juan de la Cosa and Amerigo Vespucci made the first voyage into territory that, strictly speaking, belonged exclusively to Columbus. There followed in quick succession the Caribbean voyages of, among others, Pedro Alonso (Peralonso) Niño and Cristóbal Guerra, Rodrigo de Bastidas, and Vicente Yáñez Pinzón, who entered the Caribbean via his discovery of Brazil.[4] All of these received the same consideration accorded Ojeda: a glimpse of Columbus's charts and reports of his third voyage, when he had visited the Pearl Coast of Venezuela. They all responded to the Admiral's glowing report of the riches he had discovered just as the venal bishop had hoped they would. Each was granted authority for voyages to the same region, couched in terms designed to obscure Fonseca's malevolent intent of curbing the discoverer's privileges. This first wave of explorers, concentrating their efforts on the southern Caribbean, all sailed from Spain: from Cádiz–Santa María, Palos, or Seville. The second wave, beginning about 1508, was launched first from Hispaniola (comprising present-day Haiti and the Dominican Republic) to explore the other islands of the Greater Antilles and then from Puerto Rico, Cuba, and Jamaica to extend the discovery into the Gulf of Mexico.

Across the Caribbean

Alonso de Ojeda, because of his father's loyal service, enjoyed the monarchs' special favor. He was drawn to Fonseca's notice through a cousin and namesake, a Dominican friar, and became the bishop's favorite as well. This jolly rogue may be considered the prototype of the New World conquistador-explorer. Schooled in the wars of the Reconquest, by which Spain terminated almost eight centuries of Moorish occupation, he distinguished himself on Columbus's second voyage as the twenty-one-year-old captain of a caravel.[5] A daring and brutal fighter, he held to a religious belief that, to his mind, protected him from his enemies without censuring his misdeeds.

With Fonseca's license, Ojeda obtained financial backing from Seville merchants eager for a share of New World wealth. He sailed from Puerto de Santa María on 20 May 1499 with three caravels, two of which were outfitted by Amerigo Vespucci, the Florentine ship chandler for whom Amer-

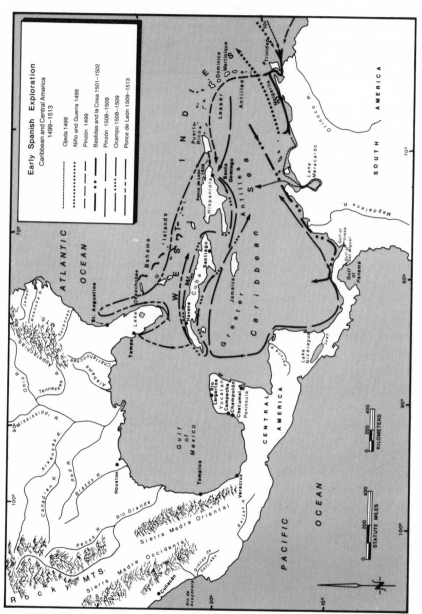

Map 4.1 Early Spanish Exploration: Caribbean and Central America, 1499–1513.

ica is named, at his own expense. The crews included several sailors who had visited the Venezuelan coast with Columbus. More noteworthy, however, was the chief pilot, Juan de la Cosa, owner and master of the *Santa María* on the first Columbian voyage and mapmaker on the second.

On the series of ventures to the Spanish Main that Martín Fernández de Navarrete termed "minor voyages"—more recently studied and more aptly titled by Louis-André Vigneras[6]—la Cosa was the pilot of discovery. He stands vis-à-vis Antón de Alaminos, the pilot of discovery for the Bahama Channel and the Gulf of Mexico. As Alaminos conducted the first four voyages to enter the Gulf of Mexico, la Cosa, having sailed twice with Columbus, conducted four voyages to the Caribbean coast of South and Central America before dying during the last one. La Cosa, like Alaminos, is an enigmatic character. Faulted by Columbus for his seamanship, if not his personal fortitude, in the loss of the *Santa María*, he nevertheless sailed with the Admiral a second time. Afterward, he remained in Spain for almost five years, using the royal trade concession granted him in compensation for the loss of his ship to recoup his fortunes.[7] Then came his first venture with Ojeda, as an investor and partner. Various writers have been so taken with la Cosa's abilities as a navigator that they have excused his part in Ojeda's piracies, slave raiding, and generally bad treatment of the Indians. Yet la Cosa's independent exploits give him a record no less blemished than that of his rowdy comrade.

The little fleet, having committed along the way piracies by which Ojeda picked up another caravel, made its first American landfall in the Guianas. Vespucci, who identified South America with Asia and was eager to find the continent's southeastern point, split off to sail down the coast. It was of this voyage that Vespucci wrote to friends in Italy, with results that seem to have escaped his control. Following his southeasterly course, his two caravels passed the Amazon River, described as sixteen miles wide and sending a stream of freshwater more than twenty-five miles into the ocean. After passing the equator, they turned about to rejoin Ojeda. Vespucci went ashore at Trinidad among naked Indian archers, of yellowish-brown color, who from all appearances practiced cannibalism. Yet the voyagers were received amicably, were well fed, and departed in peace after one day. Proceeding thence to Paria, they were again accorded hospitality and gifts of pearls.

From the landfall, Ojeda and la Cosa had sailed northwestward toward Trinidad. Passing through the Gulf of Paria and out the Boca del Dragón (Dragon's Mouth), they gave a group of small islands, Los Frailes (The

Friars), their lasting name and went ashore on Margarita, the Venezuelan island that became known for its pearl fishery. High-handed treatment of the natives there and elsewhere along the "Pearl Coast" evidently prevented their gathering any significant quantity of the gems. At a place called Maracapana, they paused to careen the ships and joined the local Indians in raiding a tribe of cannibals among the Caribs. One Spaniard was killed and a score of others were wounded—just enough to get Ojeda's blood stirring. With considerable plunder, they sailed on west along islands and mainland hitherto unglimpsed by Europeans. Vigneras thinks that Vespucci, returning from his jaunt southeast, overtook them at Cape Cordero, slightly west of the midpoint of the Venezuelan coast. Reaching Curaçao, they named it Isla de los Gigantes (Island of the Giants) for the size of its warriors. Probably at the island of Aruba, the natives' houses built on stilts inspired the name given the region: Venezuela (Little Venice). Here the seemingly friendly natives swarmed aboard the vessels, then became alarmed and dived overboard to swim away while those in canoes loosed a flight of arrows at the Spaniards. Ojeda, in character, responded with gunfire, killing numerous Indians.[8]

After entering the Gulf of Venezuela, the ships sailed around Colombia's Guajira Peninsula to Cabo de la Vela before loading up with dyewood and hauling off for Santo Domingo (Hispaniola). Ojeda, after making himself unwelcome by stirring up trouble between Francisco Roldán and Columbus, sailed off to neighboring islands to seize more than two hundred slaves to be sold in Cádiz. Reaching Spain before Ojeda and la Cosa was Pedro Alonso (Peralonso) Niño of Moguer, who had sailed for the Pearl Coast in a single caravel about two weeks later, with a similar license from Fonseca. But before taking up that voyage, let us dispense with the matter of Amerigo Vespucci: his descriptive pen and its lasting effect on history and historiography and the implications of Vespucci's distorted account for the famed Juan de la Cosa map, drafted at Puerto de Santa María soon after the Ojeda voyage ended.

Amerigo wrote, under the date of 18 July 1500, what is taken as a reasonably accurate account of this voyage and addressed it to his former employer in Florence, Lorenzo de Medici. Later, there appeared in print in Italy an embellished and distorted version of this and his other writings, purported to be a letter to an old schoolmate, Pier Soderini. The "Soderini letter," while bringing Vespucci the honor of having the Western Hemisphere named for him, has besmirched his memory by causing him to be branded a liar and a usurper who claimed for himself a 1497 voyage that he never made. Frederick J. Pohl makes a strong case for exonerating Vespucci in the matter, arguing that his letters were pirated following Medici's death in 1503, then sensationalized with pornographic detail to make a best-seller.[9] The spurious Vespucci account was translated into Latin and appended to a new edition of Ptolemy, in which the translator, Martin Wald-seemüller of Saint-Die, Loraine, suggested the naming of America for the Florentine. In 1507 Waldseemüller used the name "America" on his own world map, with Vespucci's portrait as an inset. The name took hold and by midcentury was generally accepted outside Spain.[10] Vespucci is not known to have protested. The hoax apparently created little stir in Spain and Portugal, where the facts were known and Vespucci had a solid reputation.

The dust has not settled after five centuries; the Vespuccian myth refuses to die. In one of its various forms, it has Vespucci participating in a voyage by Pinzón and Juan Diaz de Solís between May 1497 and October 1498. This imaginary expedition is supposed to have touched first at Honduras's Cape Gracias á Dios and proceeded thence around the Yucatán Peninsula into the Gulf of Mexico and on up the Atlantic coast as far as Chesapeake Bay. This version, by the nineteenth-century New England historian John Fiske, following the Brazilian Adolpho Varnhagen, suggests that Vespucci's "Little Venice," where people lived in houses built over the water, indicates not the place so named by Ojeda in 1499 but Tabasco, at the bottom of the Gulf of Mexico. Fiske claims Vespucci's "Parias" was an editorial substitution for "Lariab," which to his mind had "a Huastec ring," and he therefore identifies it with the Tampico area. In reality, it was quite the opposite; "Parias" in an early manuscript was misprinted as "Lariab" in the published version.[11]

In summation, it seems clear that the voyage of which Vespucci wrote to friends in Italy was the one he made with Ojeda and la Cosa in 1499 and that he never entered the Gulf of Mexico or glimpsed Chesapeake Bay. The naming of the American continents for him, with or without his sanction, represents a disservice to the true discoverer, Christopher Columbus; and Vespucci himself was ill-served by those who perverted his honest writings for motives of profit. Among other misconceptions that have arisen from the Vespucci distortions is that Amerigo's imagined thrust into the Gulf of Mexico accounts for the form of Juan de la Cosa's map, which according to the document's inscription was made in Puerto de Santa María, across the bay from Cádiz, in 1500. How else, it has been asked, could la Cosa have known that Cuba was an island, when it was not otherwise proved so until 1508? The Argentine writer Roberto Levillier, for example, contends that all the pre-1508 maps that indicate an insular Cuba or depict the Gulf of Mexico—maps such as those of la Cosa, Alberto Cantino, Nicolo Canerio, and Waldseemüller—derive from the pretended 1497 Vespucci voyage. Close study of la Cosa's map, as well as knowledge of the whereabouts of la Cosa himself during this period, indicates otherwise.[12]

What might be taken as the Gulf of Mexico on the la Cosa map is obscured by a vignette of Saint Christopher. There is no representation of either Yucatán or Florida. The extent of actual discoveries is indicated with flags—Spanish, English, and Portuguese. The westernmost banner on the southern coast designates Colombia's Cabo de la Vela, where la Cosa and Ojeda terminated their exploration. No Portuguese flag appears west of the Azores and the Cape Verde Islands. The British flags mark the territory discovered for England by John and Sebastian Cabot: northern New England and Newfoundland. The unmarked portion of the map, indicating unexplored territory, was given a configuration based on information from the natives or on the author's guesswork.

Arguments that the map was made at some later date or that it stemmed from some unknown voyage are denied by the map itself. La Cosa was at Puerto de Santa María from the time he returned with Ojeda, in about June 1500, until the following February, when he sailed with Rodrigo de Bastidas. Had the map been made after the Bastidas voyage, it would have reflected subsequent discoveries. La Cosa could not have completed it, as some have suggested, after Cuba was proved an island, in 1508–9, for he sailed again for South America before that time and never returned. The suggestion that he left his sketch map with a draftsman, who altered it after learning that Cuba had been circumnavigated, is well taken; yet the discoveries shown are those of 1500, not 1509.[13]

If la Cosa learned, before leaving Santo Domingo on his final voyage, that Cuba had been circumnavigated and proved an island, he had no opportunity to update his map, which was back in Spain. Evidently hidden away in the royal archives, the map exerted little influence on other mapmakers. Of greater influence was an anonymous Portuguese cartographer's work that emerged two years later: the so-called Cantino map, which depicts not only an insular Cuba ("Ysabella") but also a peninsula that is alternately taken to be Cuba, Yucatán, and Asia. Alberto Cantino was a secret agent in Lisbon for the Italian Ercole d'Este, Duke of Ferrara, who was concerned about the effect that Portuguese discoveries were having on traditional Far Eastern trade routes. Obtaining the map from an anonymous mapmaker, he delivered it to his employer in 1502.[14] The Cantino map is clearly oriented by the meridional line separating Spanish and Portuguese territories, a line established by the 1494 Treaty of Tordesillas. The Tropic of Cancer and a compass rose confirm the orientation. The captions "Ilhas Antilhas del rey de Castella" and "Oceanus Occiditales" clearly show that the Greater Antilles is meant. Yet, considering that Columbus's geographical notions were still widely accepted, one cannot rule out the possibility that the peninsula so often taken for Florida was drawn under the misapprehension that it was the mainland of Asia.[15]

The case for identifying Yucatán as the peninsula jutting southeastward toward "Ysabella," though interesting, is still less plausible. This hypothesis comes from a Netherlands geographer, E. Roukema, who attempts to reconcile the difference in orientation necessary to support it with the suggestion that directional indicators might have been added to the original sketch by a draftsman.[16] Theorizing that the map derives from an unknown voyage—perhaps Portuguese—that entered the Gulf through the Straits of Florida in the spring of 1502, Roukema fixes its first Yucatán landfall at Punta Arenas, the northwestern promontory. He supports his supposed eastern course of the voyage by identifying place-names on the Cantino map with present-day toponymy of the Yucatán coast. By striking coincidence, the Río Lagartos, on the northern end of the peninsula and supposedly named by Francisco Hernández de Cordoba in 1517, corresponds with the Río de los Lagartos on the reoriented Cantino map. This is a captivating idea, yet the author's assertion that "there can be no reasonable doubt" goes a bit far.[17] Other attempts to explain the Cantino map cover a variety of possibilities: the portrayal of Florida derives from the Cabots' or Vespucci's voyages (none of which reached the Florida peninsula), from unreported forays of Spanish slave-hunters in the Bahamas and along the mainland coast, from the natives' reports, or from the mapmaker's lucky guess.[18]

La Cosa's influence on others' work was limited, although some of his features, including the Cuba configuration, appear on an anonymous world map, c. 1509–19, in an Italian archive.[19] Even though the Cantino map itself remained hidden away in Italy for almost a century, its coastal configurations and toponyms soon appeared on other maps—as many as fourteen, representing various countries and dated to 1520, by one count.[20] It has been surmised, therefore, that the prototype remained in Portugal, where it was repeatedly used to shape Europe's ideas of the New World. The Genoese chartmaker Nicolo Canerio's 1504 map bears an undeniable resemblance to Cantino's, extending the North American mainland beyond "Florida" to show an island-studded bay or gulf, but there is no Yucatán Peninsula on the southeast. Engraved in Florence in 1506, Giovanni Matteo Contarini's world map—the first printed map to show any part of the New World—gives the Cantino configuration to "Tierra de Cuba." Some of Cantino's coastlines, including Cuba, came via Canerio to Martin Waldseemüller's 1507 world map and his 1513 *Tabula Terre Nove*, the first printed atlas page with major emphasis on the New World.[21]

The record fails to show whether or not la Cosa, while drafting his map in the summer or fall of 1500, compared notes with Peralonso Niño and Cristóbal Guerra, who had returned from the Pearl Coast more promptly— and more successfully. Shortly after Ojeda and la Cosa's departure on the 1499 voyage, the conniving Bishop Fonseca had permitted Niño a look at Columbus's map from his ill-starred third voyage. Although the map has not survived, it is presumed to have shown the northern coast of South America explicitly; Columbus is said to have entered on his charts every new island and coastline as he sailed along, and the single sketch that survives bears this out. Niño, no less impressed than Ojeda with the Admiral's report and map, obtained from Fonseca a similar license. He recruited a crew from family and friends in the Niebla-Moguer area of southwestern Spain and cast about for a financial backer on the basis of his experience as a pilot on two Columbian voyages. To obtain the backing of the Triana merchant Luis Guerra, Niño had to give up the captaincy of the single caravel to Guerra's younger brother Cristóbal.[22] With thirty-three men, Niño and Guerra sailed from Palos in June 1499, about two weeks after Ojeda's sailing. Piloted by Andrés de Morales, who became known for his studies of the Caribbean Current, they sighted Trinidad while Ojeda was still down the coast, and they proceeded to the Gulf of Paria to cut dyewood. In the Boca del Dragón they encountered a canoe fleet of head-hunting Caribs, whom they put to flight with cannon fire. They traded for a quantity of pearls at Margarita Island and then on the mainland coast of Cumaná (Venezuela), where luxuriant tropical forests towered above the sea. They also obtained specimens of a copper-gold alloy called *guanín*. For three months they bartered with friendly, naked natives adorned with necklaces and bracelets of pearls, which were given freely or exchanged for trinkets.

Coasting westward, the caravel reached the Guajira Peninsula, the northernmost promontory of Colombia. In the Gulf of Venezuela, where Ojeda had preceded them, the voyagers were met by "a thousand" canoes of native archers, made wary of foreign intruders by their previous visitors. Niño and Guerra, preferring profit to war, turned back to Curiana (on the northern Venezuela coast) to resume their peaceful pearl trade until February 1500. On their return to Bayona, Galicia, in mid-April, Niño and some of his associates were jailed on Guerra's charge that they had evaded taxes on their share of the loot. Freed for want of evidence, Niño resumed his profession of pilot and captain on voyages to Hispaniola.[23]

The success of this expedition to the Pearl Coast, having yielded the best return of all New World voyages to that date, was not soon to be repeated. Vicente Yáñez Pinzón, captain of the *Niña* on Columbus's first voyage, sailed from his native Palos on about 1 December 1499. He reached the Gulf of Paria via Brazil in the spring of 1500 and, after loading up with dyewood, sailed along the Lesser Antilles for Santo Domingo. Thence, his caravels visited the Bahama Islands, where two of the four ships were lost, with all hands, in a hurricane. Pinzón returned to Palos the following September with his cargo of dyewood and twenty Indian slaves.[24] Diego de Lepe, his kinsman and fellow townsman, sailed from Palos the same month and almost duplicated the Pinzón voyage.

Cristóbal Guerra, chosen to head an official undertaking for the Crown, returned to Paria in the latter part of 1500 with Diego de Grajeda. Unable to obtain significant quantities of pearls, he turned to slave raiding, thus bringing on himself the wrath of the queen. It was slave raiding, on the Colombian coast in 1504, that finally cost Cristóbal his life. His brother Luis was lost with his ship on the same voyage.[25]

While the Guerras went about their sorry business, Ojeda and la Cosa followed separate paths for a while. La Cosa, after completing his famous map, sailed from Seville early in 1501, as chief pilot with Rodrigo de Bastidas of Triana. Another noted pilot, Andrés de Morales, who had sailed with Niño and Guerra, was part of the crew, as was Vasco Núñez de Balboa. With two caravels outfitted by a company of investors that Bastidas had organized in Seville, they proceeded via the Canaries to Cabo de la Vela, on the Guajira Peninsula. Following the Colombian coast, they discovered the Santa Marta site and named Cartagena Bay. They acquired both gold and pearls before reaching the Gulf of Urabá at the base of the Isthmus of Darién and proceeded some distance along the isthmus—a region with which Núñez de Balboa would have much to do in the future. As they returned to Hispaniola, both vessels wrecked at Cape Tiburón. The men walked to Santo Domingo, where Bastidas was jailed and his goods were confiscated by the royal commissioner, Francisco de Bobadilla. The matter was rectified shortly, when Nicolás de Ovando took over as the island governor. Bastidas and la Cosa returned to Spain in the fleet that carried the retiring Bobadilla, with Bastidas and la Cosa sailing on the one ship that survived the crossing. The *capitana* (flagship), in which Bobadilla sailed, was lost, with all hands. Years later, in 1526, Bastidas founded Santa Marta (Colombia) on the site he had discovered, but he died at sea soon afterward while returning to Santo Domingo.[26]

La Cosa, after a spying mission to Portugal in 1503, received royal permission in February 1504 to undertake, at his own expense, a voyage to the Gulf of Urabá. The queen had mitigated her earlier stance to allow cannibals and rebellious Indians to be sold into slavery. A 1503 royal *cédula* permitted the taking of the natives of Cartagena and Urabá. The new voyage, therefore, offered improved prospects for profit without penalty. La Cosa and his partner, Pedro de Ledesma, proceeded via the Canaries to enter the Caribbean through the Dominica Passage and sailed west along the Venezuelan and Colombian coasts. At Cartagena Bay they encountered the Guerra expedition in time to share its miseries following Cristóbal's death and joined Luis Guerra's scurvy crew in a slave raid. Of six hundred Indians captured, only the aged and otherwise unfit were released.

La Cosa's ships left Guerra's to plunder along the Gulf of Urubá, which he and Bastidas had discovered in 1501–2. On a foray through the woods, they came on a secluded native hut containing gold artifacts weighing seventy-two marks. Across the bay in Darién province, they seized another forty marks. The gold, as in Hernán Cortés's *noche triste* (the sorrowful night when he was forced to flee the Aztec capital), was to become an onerous burden. With the ships still harbored in a Darién river mouth, la Cosa received word of the Guerra expedition's further disaster. Luis, sailing for Spain with his cargo of brazilwood and slaves, had struck a reef; his ship had sunk with most of its crew, including Luis himself. The remaining caravel, trying to rejoin la Cosa, was so badly riddled by *teredos* (shipworms) that it had to be beached. La Cosa's attempted rescue was foiled by his own misfortune; his ships too were leaking badly and had to be beached. Stranded at Urubá for a year, the Spaniards lost half their number to disease. The survivors at last decided to make a try for Hispaniola in a boat and two brigantines. The boat reached Cuba; the other vessels reached Jamaica, where one was wrecked by storm. The gold, transported around Cuba by Indian porters, led to a death plot against the Spaniards; the plot was discovered just in time. About sixty men reached Hispaniola, fifteen via Cuba, to return to Spain by March 1506, with their precious gold.[27]

Ojeda, meanwhile, received through Fonseca the Crown's authorization to return to Venezuela as governor of the Coquivacoa province. To provide the wherewithal, he took Juan de Vergara and García de Campos as partners, each to captain a caravel. The fleet of four ships sailed from Cádiz in January 1502, on an ill wind. When it reached the Gulf of Paria in mid-March, there was trouble with the Indians, and sixteen men were killed in a single battle. One ship wrecked near Margarita. The men were soon near starvation. Ojeda sent a vessel for provisions and, when it failed to return, another to search for it. With the remaining ship, he himself sailed west to found his abortive Fort Santa Cruz at Bahía Honda on the Guajira Peninsula to guard against English poachers. The natives proved surly, and trading efforts failed. The men, led by Ojeda's partners, mutinied and bore the captain-general off to Santo Domingo in irons to stand trial. Rescued from his plight by Fonseca, Ojeda returned to Spain before the end of the year. Under the influential bishop's aegis, he was favored in 1504 with a new contract for establishing a fort on the Gulf of Urubá. Little is known of the voyage; apparently only a feeble effort was made before Ojeda returned to Hispaniola to take up land.[28] He was soon called to a new venture, which brought him together again with la Cosa.

Following Queen Isabella's death in 1504, Ferdinand was forced to yield Castilian rule to his daughter, Juana, and her husband, Philip, and was relegated to his own kingdom of Aragón. In this period of uncertainty, the spirit of discovery flagged. After Philip's death in 1506—arranged by Ferdinand, some believe—Juana was removed because of her mental instability. Ferdinand, returning to the Castilian throne, summoned to court at Burgos in 1508 a panel of navigators, including Díaz de Solís, Pinzón, la Cosa, and Vespucci, to consider means of renewing the discovery effort. Out of the conference came three concrete steps: (1) the appointment of Vespucci as pilot-major with responsibilities for training navigators and keeping, in the Casa de Contratación, the official master chart of all discoveries; (2) a voyage to seek a route through the so-called Indies to the Far Eastern Spice Islands; and (3) an attempt at colonizing the South American mainland now popularly called Tierra Firme. The second step was to be carried out by Díaz de Solís, the third by la Cosa and Ojeda.[29]

The participants in this conference were considered the most knowledgeable to be found. Their voyages, coupled with those of Columbus, had explored not only the Greater and Lesser Antilles but also the mainland coast from Honduras to the Brazilian Elbow. From native contacts, they doubtless knew that the land narrowed beyond the Gulf of Urubá and that there was another ocean on the other side. It is also likely that they had seen Waldseemüller's 1507 world map, based partly on their reconnaissance, partly on "an inspired guess," and to a large degree on the mapmaker's interpretation of the Cantino-Canerio configuration.[30] The German geography teacher Waldseemüller, joining the fragmented discoveries into an uninterrupted coastline from latitude 50° north to 40° south, expressed the prevailing uncertainty as to the western limits by drawing them in straight lines. Thus, mainland North America terminated along his 280th meridian, with "Zipangi" (Japan) ten degrees farther west. South America's proportions were given with remarkable accuracy.[31] If this hypothetical rendering was consulted at all in planning the search for a strait, the thin sliver of land extending from Darién to northern Mexico must surely have drawn the focus, and Pinzón and Díaz de Solís sailed from Cádiz in the summer of 1508, proceeding first to Santo Domingo and then west. More of this voyage will be discussed later, in connection with the discovery of the Gulf of Mexico.

La Cosa, in the meantime, had sailed again with Ojeda, who with la Cosa's backing had received joint Crown appointment with Diego de Nicuesa to govern the coast from Cabo de la Vela to Cape Gracias á Dios (Honduras). Considering their natural antipathy for each other, Ojeda and Nicuesa divided the territory at the Gulf of Urubá (near Panama at Colombia's northwestern corner). Nicuesa took the western side, Ojeda the eastern. Arriving at Santo Domingo early in 1509, Nicuesa and Ojeda acquired as a third partner Martin Fernández de Enciso, who remained on the island to recruit colonists and gather supplies.

Ojeda, with three hundred colonists from Santo Domingo, chose the site of Cartagena (Colombia) for his settlement. He and his followers, raiding Indian tribes for slaves, suffered severe retribution in February 1510, when sixty-nine Spaniards were slain by poison arrows. Among them was one of the most skilled navigators and mapmakers of the discovery period: Juan de la Cosa. Ojeda saved himself from a like fate by cauterizing his wound with hot steel.

Following the poison-arrow episode, Ojeda moved his Tierra Firme colony from Cartagena Bay to the Gulf of Urubá, where his starving men soon threatened mutiny. Ojeda left Francisco Pizarro in charge and caught a passing pirate ship for Santo Domingo for supplies, only to be shipwrecked in western Cuba. Fernández de Enciso, arriving with supplies just in time to turn back Pizarro's retreating colonists, brought Núñez de Balboa, who had stowed away on the ship to escape his Hispaniola creditors. Enciso, having finally mitigated his anger and backed off on his threat to put his unwelcome passenger ashore on a desolate island, would find Núñez de Balboa to be a mixed blessing. It was Núñez de Balboa who saved the colony by moving it to the western side of the Gulf of Urubá, which was away from the poison-arrow attacks and which was where he had been with Bastidas and la Cosa. There Santa María la Antigua del Darién was founded on Colombia's western edge, not far from the Panamanian border. It was the first European town on the mainland of greater North America.[32]

As Bartolomé de Las Casas tells it, Núñez de Balboa then "acquired a bloated sense of pride."[33] First, he deposed Enciso—claiming the latter lacked jurisdiction because the colony now was in Nicuesa's territory—and then he deposed Nicuesa, who was sent away on 1 March 1511 in a leaky brigantine that was never heard of again.[34] Enciso was sent to Spain, and the Spaniards of Santa María were split into bitter factions.

Núñez de Balboa, exploring the territory, made alliances with important caciques. From a native chieftain he heard of the other ocean—and gold—that lay to the south, and he received an awesome account of the impediments to reaching it. The path, he was told, lay over rugged mountains inhabited by cannibals; to reach this southern sea, he would need a thousand well-armed men.[35] Returning to Santa María, Núñez de Balboa sent Juan de Valdivia, who had recently escorted Enciso as far as Santo Domingo, back to Hispaniola. Valdivia, taking gold to lubricate official wheels, was to seek Diego Columbus's help in obtaining the needed men and supplies from the king. With Valdivia went fifteen men and two women, including the cleric Gerónimo de Aguilar of Ecija, in Andalucía. Aguilar also had a message for Don Diego: the colony was being defeated by the division within it.[36]

Valdivia failed to return. Rodrigo de Colmenares and Juan de Caezedo, sent after him, were shipwrecked near Cuba's western cape. They and their crew traveled east along the route already taken by Ojeda and his pirates and finally reached Hispaniola. Valdivia and his company were not so fortunate. Blown by hurricane upon Las Víboras shoals southwest of Jamaica, they boarded the ship's boat only to find it unmanageable in the strong current. For thirteen days they drifted westward. Seven men died of dehydration. The rest were tossed ashore near Yucatán's Cabo Catoche. Several, including Valdivia, were sacrificed to the Mayas' pagan idols. Aguilar and half a dozen others, including the two women, were spared to become slaves, for most of them just a slower means of death. Only Aguilar, the first European to land on Yucatán and survive to tell about it, was to live again among his countrymen. Valdivia's shipwreck, with its visible impact on history, destroyed the purposes of Núñez de Balboa while advancing those of Hernán Cortés. Had Valdivia reached Hispaniola to send on to Spain the gold and the news of the other ocean that lay south of the isthmus, King Ferdinand would probably have provided the support Núñez de Balboa requested. Núñez de Balboa might have proceeded not only to discover the Pacific Ocean but also to conquer the Inca empire. Pedro Arias (Pedrarias) Dávila, who became the scourge of Central America and Núñez de Balboa's executioner, would have been left out of the picture.[37] As it was, Núñez de Balboa, crossing the isthmus in Panama about fifty miles west of Santa María la Antigua, succeeded in reaching the South Sea, or Pacific Ocean, without the help he had sought. He sighted it from a mountain peak on 25 September 1513 and four days later reached the Gulf of San Miguel on the Pacific shore. The feat came too late to forestall his fate, however.

Enciso, after arriving in Spain, had made the most of his friends at court, including Fonseca, to obtain Pedrarias's appointment as governor of Castilla del Oro (Golden Castile), embracing the prior concessions of both Ojeda and Nicuesa. With twenty ships and fifteen hundred men, Pedrarias arrived off Santa María la Antigua on 29 June 1514 to take charge, to undo Núñez de Balboa's efforts, and last, out of jealousy, to try to execute Núñez de Balboa on trumped-up charges of treason.[38] With priestly counsel, Pedrarias put aside his jealousy for a time, cementing a friendship with Núñez de Balboa by pledging the troth of one of his daughters. Núñez de Balboa built brigantines at the new town of Acla (Careta) and transported them across the isthmus to explore the Pacific coast and islands. But at this point he was betrayed by a trusted subordinate with whom he had once had words over his Indian mistress. Pedrarias, his natural jealousy aroused by falsehoods or half-truths, summoned the unsuspecting Núñez de Balboa and had him arrested. He was tried and, with four companions, beheaded in 1517.[39]

Pedrarias seems to have set the tone for the region. Jealously guarding his claims against all comers, he blocked the advances of Gil Gonzáles de Avila, exploring from Panama to the Nicaraguan lakes in 1522. Pedro de Alvarado, moving south from Mexico a year later, was contained in Guatemala by Pedrarias's agent, Francisco Hernández de Córdoba (not to be confused with the 1517 discoverer of Yucatán). Hernández de Córdoba, after founding towns in Nicaragua, was beheaded by Pedrarias for suspected involvement with Hernán Cortés.[40] Pedrarias himself, having moved his capital to Panama in 1519, went to Nicaragua as governor in 1526. All the conquistadors in Central America, it has been noted, founded towns and disputed the claims of the others.[41] Pedrarias Dávila held forth in Panama until his death in the late 1520s. His son-in-law Rodrigo de Contreras succeeded him as governor.

The so-called minor voyages, which had carried New World exploration forward from Columbus's initial efforts, had proved to be anything but minor. In the beginning the voyagers from Andalucía had rested upon Columbus's misconception that the new lands were the eastward extension of Asia. Gradually, through continued probing, that idea melted away in the realization that the coastline was continuous, from the Brazilian Elbow at least to Honduras. Columbus had heard of the other ocean beyond the Isthmus of Darién. He himself had searched for a strait that would lead to it, expecting that it would prove to be the Indian Ocean, the key to his passage around the world. Yet all the succeeding voyages to the southern Caribbean found only an unbroken coast. The strait had to be sought either to the north or to the south.

With two voyages begun in 1508, the existence of the long-surmised Gulf of Mexico became a proven fact. Yet, by the time Núñez de Balboa found his way across the isthmus to the South Sea in 1513, there was no knowledge of what lay inside the Gulf; no report of the Yucatán Peninsula had yet reached Spain. Núñez de Balboa's discovery of the Pacific Ocean paved the way for determining the southern and western limits of the territory so far seen in a single dimension. But the land seemed to have no beginning or ending and no break in the middle—unless it lay within the yet-unknown Gulf of Mexico.

The Greater Antilles

Peter Martyr wrote in 1510 that Cuba, "that land so long believed a continent because of its great extension," had been proved an island. Although the la Cosa and Cantino maps, with their depiction of an insular Cuba and some hint of the Gulf of Mexico, had stirred speculation, the first to provide actual proof, according to Martyr, was Vicente Yáñez Pinzón, who had sailed from Cádiz with Juan Díaz de Solís in 1508.[42] Although preparations for this voyage are well documented, the voyage itself is not. Having

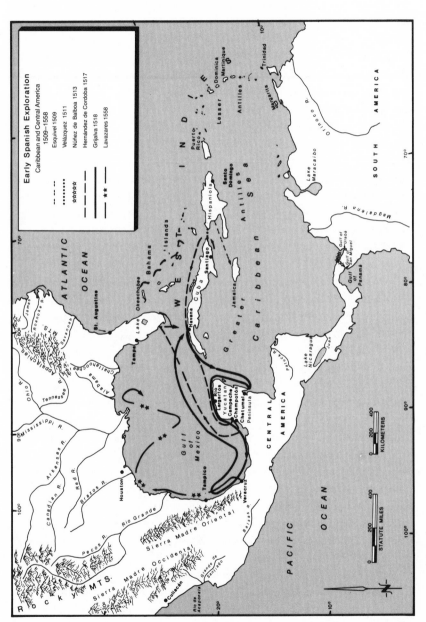

Map 4.2 Early Spanish Exploration: Caribbean and Central America, 1509–1558.

been under consideration for a number of years, it has been dated by some interpreters as 1506, whereas others credit voyages in both 1506 and 1508, both concerned with seeking the strait that Columbus had supposed to link the Caribbean Sea with the unknown southern ocean.[43] The political upheaval following Queen Isabella's death in 1504, however, caused the 1506 voyage to abort. In early summer 1508, Pinzón and Díaz de Solís put to sea with two caravels, the *Isabelita* and the *Margarita*, fifty and sixty tuns burthen, each carrying a crew of fifty-two.[44] Pinzón and Díaz de Solís, according to Martyr, reported on their outbound voyage to Governor Ovando at Santo Domingo, then sailed west along Cuba's southern shore to the island's western promontory, Cabo San Antón (Cape San Antonio). For reasons untold, they did not sail into the unknown Gulf of Mexico beyond the cape but "continued on and encountered other lands west of Cuba . . . already touched by the Admiral." Falling off to the left, the ships "coasted eastward, passing the bays of Veragua [Panama], Urubá, and Cuchibacoa [Venezuela], and approached the land called Paria and Boca del Dragón."[45]

In testimony given in 1513 in litigation contesting hereditary rights of the Columbus descendants, Pinzón himself supported Martyr's version: he had sailed east from Guanaja, in the Honduras Bay Islands, to the "province of Camarón," evidently meaning Cabo Camarón a hundred miles east. Pedro de Ledesma, a pilot on the voyage, claimed, in the same lawsuit, that the ships went north from Guanaja to latitude 23.5°. Ledesma, having participated in the fourth-voyage mutiny in Jamaica, is hardly to be regarded as a credible witness in matters affecting the claims of the Columbus heirs. His testimony is not substantiated by any account of what he might have seen along the claimed route, which would have taken the ships up the Yucatán coast and into the Gulf of Mexico.[46] Pinzón and Díaz de Solís may have been the first to prove that Cuba was an island and to glimpse the Gulf waters, but there is only the word of a prejudiced witness to suggest that they explored beyond Cabo San Antón. By the time they returned to Santo Domingo, about a year after leaving it, Sebastián de Ocampo had circumnavigated Cuba, had proved it to be an island, and had discovered the Gulf of Mexico.

By 1508 Nicolás de Ovando, governor at Hispaniola since 1502, found his island charge facing an exploding Spanish population, a diminishing gold supply, and a severe labor shortage as the natives' mortality rate soared under European abuse.[47] Hence, he dispatched Ocampo to exam-

ine Cuba and assess its settlement potential while Juan Ponce de León began the conquest of Puerto Rico and while Andrés de Morales undertook
the detailed mapping of Hispaniola. Morales, "the first geographer to
make a map and description from field observation of any part of the New
World," had sailed with Columbus on the third voyage, had sailed to ·
South America with Peralonso Niño and Cristóbal Guerra, and had twice
sailed with Juan de la Cosa.[48]

Ocampo's voyage drew scant notice, considering its importance.
Ocampo himself is an obscure figure, posing one of the greatest enigmas of
the discovery period. Las Casas and the Spanish chronicler Antonio de
Herrera y Tordesillas describe him as a Galician hidalgo and former *criado*
(servant or protégé) of Queen Isabella's who had come to Hispaniola with
Columbus on the second voyage and taken up land. Actually, he was a fu-
gitive from a death sentence pronounced in 1501 "for differences he had
with Juan de Velázquez of Jerez." By royal intervention the sentence had
been commuted; Ocampo, sent to perpetual exile in Hispaniola, was forbidden to leave the island colony.[49] Defying that restriction, he carried on
an extensive trade across the Caribbean, ferrying supplies to the colonists
in Tierra Firme and Darién, including Diego de Nicuesa and Vasco Núñez
de Balboa. His connection with high colonial officials, such as a business
partnership with the watchdog royal treasurer Miguel de Pasamonte at
Santo Domingo, apparently enabled him to conceal his activities from the
Crown. Yet, by June 1514 he was in Seville, making out his will and issuing
instructions for his burial, in a manner suggesting that he had been
brought home to face the old death sentence.[50]

Sometime after Pinzón and Díaz de Solís left Hispaniola, late in 1508,
Ocampo embarked with two vessels on the eight-month voyage around
Cuba. Sailing west along the northern shore, he entered the Gulf of Mexico
through the Old Bahama and Nicolás Channels and paused at Havana's
site to careen his ships, from which event the place was called Puerto de
Carenas. Doubling Cabo San Antón, he put into Cienfuegos Bay, called
Jagua by the natives, and feasted on mullet, which the natives provided
from sea corrals of woven reeds. In early spring 1509, he returned to Santo
Domingo to give his report.[51] Cognizant of his lame-duck status, Ovando
made no move to follow up the Ocampo voyage before Diego Columbus—
heir to his father's rights and titles and therefore called the Second Admiral—came to succeed him. Don Diego, though planning to conquer and
settle Cuba eventually, faced more immediate problems in both Jamaica

and Puerto Rico. In Puerto Rico, the problem was Ponce de León, a gentleman volunteer on the second Columbian voyage who had aided the Hispaniola conquest, then settled at Salvaleón de Higüey, the island's easternmost settlement. When an Indian brought him a gold nugget from Boriquén (the Indian name for San Juan, which later became Puerto Rico), Ponce de León's interest shifted across the Mona Passage. In July 1508 he crossed over to begin "pacifying"—often a euphemism for terrorizing and enslaving—the inhabitants. The reigning cacique accorded him a friendly welcome and conducted him on a tour of the island, through deep, rich valleys watered by flowing streams and among fruiting groves and dense woodlands that lay among the wildly beautiful mountains. The chief also revealed to him the gold-bearing rivers. Appointed governor of the island of San Juan by Ovando in 1509, Ponce de León refused to yield the post gracefully when Diego Columbus succeeded Ovando. When the Second Admiral sent replacements for Ponce de León, the latter packed them off to prison in Spain and proceeded with his own exploitation, "a lesser but accelerated version of that of Española (Hispaniola)."[52] The peaceful, friendly Arawaks, forced to produce the Spaniards' food, labor in their gold placers, and bear their burdens, died quickly under the oppression. In desperation, the natives rose in a rebellion, which merely hastened their extinction. Within a decade, San Juan was virtually depopulated.

Don Diego's appointees to govern the island, Juan Cerón and Miguel Díaz de Aux, eventually were restored by the king. But Diego found himself also in danger of losing Jamaica, where his father had been marooned for a year and had withstood the Porras brothers' mutiny. Ojeda and Nicuesa had designs on this Columbus family jewel as a supply base for their Tierra Firme colony. Soon after his arrival, therefore, Diego sent Juan de Esquivel, with Pánfilo de Narváez as his second-in-command, to seize the island, which, lacking gold, had not been subjected to exploitation as had Hispaniola. With but one small mountainous region, the Jamaican soils were fertile and productive. Ever since Columbus first visited the island in 1494, it had from time to time served as a haven for voyagers returning from Tierra Firme. Its native Arawaks were pacific by nature. Of how they fared under Esquivel and Narváez there is little record. Indications are, however, that they were distributed under the Spanish lords for forced labor, building roads and growing food for export to Tierra Firme. They seem to have endured no better than their counterparts on the other islands; when Francisco de Garay came to govern in 1515, he voiced concern over the small number of natives.

With matters stabilized in Jamaica and Puerto Rico, Diego Columbus turned his attention to Cuba. In the interim since Ocampo's reconnaissance of the island, Spaniards from the Tierra Firme colony had been cast upon its shores to become its unwitting explorers. Among them was Ojeda himself, who was shipwrecked at Cuba's Jagua Bay. He and the pirates with whom he had hitched a ride (as mentioned previously, in the account of Ojeda's Urubá colony) walked the length of the island before obtaining a native canoe to take them to Jamaica. Esquivel provided a rescue ship to transport the castaways to Santo Domingo. Fernández de Enciso already having sailed for Urubá with provisions, Ojeda remained in Santo Domingo, dying there in 1515 of natural causes.[53] Others from Tierra Firme, meanwhile, encountered similar experiences on Cuba's shores. Pizarro, left behind at the Urubá settlement of San Sebastián, watched his colonists steadily dying of starvation. At last he boarded the survivors on two brigantines and sailed for Hispaniola. The vessels became separated. Pizarro's ship met Fernández de Enciso and returned with him to San Sebastián. The other ship was carried by the westering current into the Yucatán Channel and ran aground near Cuba's Cabo San Antón. Like Ojeda and the pirates, the castaways walked toward Hispaniola, following the northern coast. While crossing a large bay, twenty-six were killed by Indians, leaving only García Mexía and two women to be rescued during the conquest. From this massacre the bay took its name: Matanzas.[54]

When King Ferdinand, in 1510, authorized Diego Columbus to proceed with Cuba's occupation, the choice of a leader was somewhat narrow. The command fell to Diego Velázquez de Cuéllar, one of those who had come with Christopher Columbus on the second voyage but who had allied himself with the anti-Columbus faction. Velázquez's role in the Hispaniola conquest had been a bloody one. In Ovando's 1503 march on Xaragua, he massacred eighty-four chiefs who had assembled peaceably. While Ponce de León and Esquivel overran Hispaniola's southeastern peninsula in the 1504 Higüey war, Velázquez subdued the western part of the island (present-day Haiti). He founded its towns and enslaved its Indians, causing many to flee across the Windward Passage to Cuba. In November 1511, Velázquez crossed some three hundred men over the Windward Passage from Hispaniola to Cuba's Point Maisi. With Jamaica under control, Narváez left Esquivel to join Velázquez as his field commander and second. Las Casas, on his way to becoming the Indians' champion, came from Hispaniola at Velázquez's urging to serve as chaplain.

It is to Las Casas, who formed, with Gonzalo Fernández de Oviedo and

Peter Martyr, the triad of chroniclers of the early conquest and exploration, that we are indebted for what is known of Cuba as the Spaniards found it. In the level expanses, he says, the woods were so dense that one might walk the length of the island in their shade. Stately cedars, red-hearted and thick as an ox, provided the wood for the natives' dugout canoes, which carried up to seventy men and voyaged on the sea. The standing cedars' heady fragrance was matched by the scent of burning sweet gum, from which the natives made their night fires. There was also the *jagua* tree, producing a honey-filled fruit that was as large as a veal kidney, that ripened after picking, and that was more delicious than candied pears. Throughout the island, huge grape clusters dangled from vines thicker than a man's waist. Casava plantings abounded, providing an ample supply of the native bread. Parrots were so numerous that native boys snared them by the hundreds. Sea turtles weighing up to a hundred pounds, valued for both their meat and their eggs, bred in the islands of Las Jardines de la Reina (The Queen's Gardens) and came on shore to bury their eggs in the sand. They were caught with sucker fish, which were tethered to a fifty-fathom line and which would attach themselves beneath the turtle's shell. The natives had cane weirs between the islands in which they kept a ready supply of both turtles and mullet. Never, says Las Casas, was there a land discovered in the Indies to surpass Cuba in the abundance of food and other necessities.[55]

Just as the conquest of Cuba was getting under way, Sebastián de Ocampo, returning from a voyage to Darién to take supplies to Núñez de Balboa, reached Jagua Bay with his ship disabled by a storm. Before Velázquez was able to send help, a number of Ocampo's sailors began walking toward Velázquez's headquarters at Asunción (present-day Baracoa). Narváez, setting out to look for them, learned that nine had been murdered in the Caonao River town of Zucayo. There followed the Spaniards' brutal retaliation. After his men had been hospitably received by the Zucayans, as Las Casas tells it, a soldier drew his sword and began ripping open bellies and slashing throats of the men, women, and children who had fed them. The others followed on cue while Narváez sat his horse like a block of marble, silently watching the bloody spectacle.[56] Before reaching the northern coast, Narváez's men heard that the three Spanish castaways who had come from San Sebastián on the Gulf of Urubá three years previously were living among the natives of Havana province. In the fall of 1513 the two women, clad in leaves and able to speak only in monosyllables, were brought to them by Indian canoe. The man, García Mexía, was found later and related the sequel to Ojeda's 1510 disaster. As Carl Ortwin Sauer has put it, "There was no conquest of Cuba other than by terrorizing the natives." But this was only the beginning of the Indians' suffering. Francisco López de Gómara wrote some forty years later, "Cuba was densely populated by Indians; today there are only Spaniards."[57]

By 1510 most of the lands washed by the Caribbean had been reached by Europeans. The notable exception was Yucatán, still unreported in Spain; if the peninsula had been reached at all, it was only by a miserable band of castaways facing a grim future. The pacific, agricultural Arawaks of the Greater Antilles bore the brunt of the first confrontation between Europeans and American natives. It was here—first in Hispaniola, then in Puerto Rico and Cuba—that the Spaniards became infected with gold fever. The Arawaks, forced into slavery and with their lands overrun, suffered badly. In enslaving and eventually exterminating the Arawaks, the conquerors nevertheless took from them a cultural legacy. The natives, forced to raise food for their oppressors, grew the crops they were accustomed to growing. Thus, corn and cassava (*casabí*, the tuberous root of the manioc plant) became staples in the Spanish diet and helped to fuel the voyages of discovery and exploration to other regions. The conquerors also acquired the native taste for tobacco. On shipboard they took their rest in *hamacas*, a new word in their vocabulary acquired from the Arawakan Tainos of Hispaniola, who probably fashioned their hammocks from the cotton they grew.[58] The more warlike and less numerous Caribs fared better than the Arawaks. Occupying the less desirable islands of the Lesser Antilles and having a subsistence economy based on hunting and gathering rather than agriculture, they were spared the full force of the Spanish conquest. Although the Caribs were judged cannibals and therefore were subject, under the royal decrees, to being enslaved, their islands remained unoccupied because the Spaniards found little there to covet.[59]

Spain, having claimed in the Greater Antilles more islands than it could reasonably say grace over, laid aside the less desirable ones and thus left them open for seizure by rival European powers. In the conquest of the Greater Antilles, the Spaniards secured the island bases that would serve in extending exploration and conquest to other regions: to Florida and the Gulf coast of the United States, to Mexico and beyond. Whereas the first wave of explorers, focusing on the southern Caribbean, had come directly from Spain, the second sailed mostly from the islands: Hispaniola, Puerto Rico, Cuba, and Jamaica.

The Bahama Channel and the Gulf

Juan Ponce de León was granted, as compensation for his removal as governor of Puerto Rico, a royal concession to discover and settle "the island of Bininy" and distribute its natives in *repartimiento*. With three ships, he took his departure from Aguada, at Puerto Rico's northwestern point, on 4 March 1513, and sailed northwest along the outer edge of the Bahamas. It is doubtful that the voyage had anything to do with the legendary Fountain of Youth, of which Peter Martyr took notice in 1516 and which was later linked to Ponce de León's name by Oviedo. The royal chronicler or *cronista* Herrera perpetuated the alleged connection into the next century.[60] Actually, Ponce de León, not yet forty, should not have needed the fabled fountain's restorative powers.

Whatever his objective at the start, Ponce de León discovered Florida, which he mistook for an island, and ran its coast from just north of Cape Canaveral to a point on the western side of the peninsula a short distance north of the Florida Keys. He also discovered the Bahama Channel and the Gulf Stream, both of which played important roles in navigation between Europe and America throughout the age of sail. Columbus, on his first voyage, had utilized the northeast tradewinds and a westerly current to take him across the Atlantic. On subsequent voyages he refined the course to derive the maximum benefit from prevailing winds and currents on the outbound voyage from Spain, entering the Caribbean by one of the several passages through the Lesser Antilles. The most desirable route for the return voyage, however, proved elusive. Although Ponce de León's discovery of the Bahama Channel was a key, the accretion of knowledge from several voyages was required to ascertain and prove the route. The instrument to that achievement was present on Ponce de León's 1513 voyage: Antón de Alaminos of Palos.

Not quite thirty in 1513, Alaminos had sailed with Columbus on the fourth voyage. With Ponce de León, he was attached to Master Diego Bermúdez's caravel *Santiago* and served as chief pilot, a billet he was to fill on the first four discovery voyages into the Gulf of Mexico. On those exploratory thrusts he observed that the Caribbean Current, entering the Gulf through the Yucatán Channel, made a wide circuit before flowing out through the Straits of Florida as the Gulf Stream. After coursing north through the Bahama Channel, the stream flowed east across the Atlantic. The prevailing winds followed a similar pattern. It was in piloting Hernán Cortés's proctors to Spain in 1519 with the first shipment of Aztec treasure that Alaminos was able to prove that these natural forces could be utilized on the entire round-trip from Spain to the Caribbean and the Gulf of Mexico and back again. Thus, he established the lasting route for sailing to Europe from the Indies. He may justifiably be called the pilot of discovery for the Gulf of Mexico, as Juan de la Cosa was for the Caribbean.[61]

What is known of Ponce de León's voyage comes from the royal *cronista* Herrera, who is supposed to have had access to an original log that has not been seen since. Interpreters of Herrera's account have been inclined to make it say more than it does. Sailing through the Bahamas, the ships passed quite near Columbus's first American landfall. Herrera indicates where that was thought to be: "On the fourteenth they arrived at Guanahaní, in 25°40', where they repaired a ship for crossing the Windward Gulf of the Lucayo Islands. This Guanahaní Island was the first that Admiral Don Christóbal Colón discovered and where, on his first voyage, he went ashore and named it S. Salvador." The latitude, slightly more than 1.5° too far north, indicates the island presently known as San Salvador, or Watlings Island, between 23°57' and 24°07'. That this was the Admiral's first landfall is only Ponce de León's opinion—or Herrera's. But it is consistent with an important fact made evident by other data in the Herrera account: that Alaminos's latitudes throughout the voyage were consistently more than a degree too far north, the error being attributable to out-of-date tables or a faulty astrolabe.[62]

On Easter Sunday—Pascua de Flores, or Pascua Florida—the voyagers passed Great Abaco Island, which was not familiar. The following Saturday, 2 April, they sighted the Florida coast in "30°08'" and named it for the Easter festival. The location was probably near Ponce de León Inlet, in 29°5'. How much farther north they went before turning back south is not known, for Herrera fails to account for five days. Heading back down the coast, they encountered the full force of the Gulf Stream where it escapes the confines of the mainland coast and the Little Bahama Bank to gush forth into open water—"so strong," says Herrera, "that it drove them back, though they had a favorable wind."[63] Alaminos was making mental notes that would serve well on a future occasion.

On 15 May the mariners, having passed Biscayne Bay, sailed along a string of islets that were named the Martyrs, observed at latitude 26°15', possibly 1.5° too far north. Here a hiatus occurs in the account until the twenty-third, when they were sailing north and northeast. Interpreters, tending to ignore the missing link, have jumped the ships over the keys and taken them north as far as present-day Charlotte Harbor, Tampa Bay, and even Pensacola. Given the distance, the capabilities of the ships, and the tedium of navigation through the keys—which Herrera says offered no passage in forty leagues to accommodate even a brigantine—not even Charlotte Harbor looks possible. The conclusion seems warranted that they went north little farther than Cape Romano and that the bay where the Spaniards on two occasions were attacked by Indian canoe fleets lay between Cape Romano and Cape Sable.

On 14 June the ships hauled off the mainland coast and discovered the Dry Tortugas, which their Indian captives had mentioned. Leaving the Tortugas, they sailed southwest by west, seeking Cabo San Antón, so that they might return to Puerto Rico along Cuba's southern shore. Some days later they sighted a shore that no one recognized and followed it for two days, believing they had reached a new land. The claim has arisen that they had crossed the Yucatán Channel to make a previously uncredited discovery of Yucatán. To have done so, they would have had to have sailed farther in those two days, bucking the current coming out of the Gulf of Mexico, than they had in four days of blue-water sailing at the start of the voyage.[64] Alaminos, understanding that the current had set the ships farther south than expected, directed the return to Florida. They picked up the islet called Achecambei (Matecumbe, in the Florida Keys) in two days, much too short a time for returning from Yucatán.

Ponce de León withdrew through the Bahamas to Puerto Rico. Captain Juan Pérez de Ortubia, with Alaminos as his pilot, extended the voyage to discover Bímini but no Fountain of Youth. They returned to Puerto Rico on 20 February 1514, and Ponce de León sailed for Spain with Juan Bono de Quejo, a Basque from San Sebastián who had captained a vessel on the recent voyage. In recompense for Ponce de León's achievement, King Ferdinand made him *adelantado* of Bímini and "the island of Florida," which he was entitled to settle and govern. But before he could return to his discovery, he had to undertake a campaign to free the Lesser Antilles of the cannibalistic Caribs.

For the Carib expedition, Ponce de León and Bono de Quejo bought three caravels in Spain and returned to the Indies. By one account, the expedition began and ended with a disastrous attack on Guadeloupe, where most of Ponce de León's men were killed. Aurelio Tió, on the other hand, offers documents to show that Ponce de León went on to discover both Yucatán and New Spain in 1516. The evidence consists mainly of depositions taken in 1606 by the Audiencia of Guatemala to support a grant petition by Ponce de León's great-grandson Perafán de Ribera. The earliest piece is a 1571 declaration by a former resident of Puerto Rico; eighty-one years old and with a failing memory, he claimed that Ponce de León had sailed to such a discovery in a single caravel with Alaminos as pilot.[65] The total lack of verification raises doubt. In fact, Alaminos has not been solidly connected with the campaign at all. Bono de Quejo did extend the effort well beyond Guadeloupe but, as Las Casas tells it, got diverted from its purpose; in about 1516 "Juan the Bad" made a slave raid on the peaceful Indians of Trinidad, who were the Caribs' enemies.

Neither Alaminos nor Bono de Quejo had a part in Ponce de León's next venture, his second voyage to Florida in 1521, for which he purchased two ships at his own expense. In February, just over two weeks before sailing, Ponce de León announced to Emperor Charles V his plans to return to "that island" with settlers; he intended to explore it further to determine whether it was an island or was joined to the mainland that had recently been discovered on behalf of Diego Velázquez. It has been generally assumed that Ponce de León's second landing was at or near the first, but this is only an assumption. In any event, the company was attacked while erecting buildings, and many were killed. Ponce de León himself was wounded in the thigh, and the lesion became infected. He withdrew to Havana and died there the following July at age forty-seven; like Columbus, he died without knowing the extent of his discovery.[66]

During the period of Ponce de León's discovery of Florida, other explorations were taking place from the Cuban base. Scarcely a year after the Cuban conquest was completed, the native population had been reduced to the extent that Velázquez was sending ships to the Honduras Bay Islands and the Lucayos on slaving expeditions. In 1515 a vessel returned to Puerto de Carenas, the future Havana site, with four hundred natives from the Bay Islands: Guanaja, Roatán, and Barbareta. While most of the ship's crew was ashore the Indians forced the hatch cover, sprang from the hold, and murdered their guards. With seamanship abilities that the Spaniards had not reckoned with, they weighed anchor and sailed for home, six hundred miles away. Velázquez's next slaving expedition found remains of the stolen ship, wrecked and burned, on a reef in the Bay Islands.[67]

By popular assessment, it was such a slaving voyage from Cuba that led to the 1517 discovery of Yucatán. Cuba had had an influx of the disenchanted from Pedrarias Dávila's colony in Castilla del Oro, including the renowned Bernal Díaz del Castillo. With the native population already distributed among the conquerors, the newcomers cast about for an outlet for their energies.[68] At the same time, Francisco Hernández de Córdoba, Lope de Ochoa, and Cristóbal Morantes, some of the island's most substantial citizens, formed a partnership, purchased two caravels and a brigantine, and fitted them out for a slaving voyage to either the Bay Islands or the Lucayos. Hernández de Córdoba, as captain, was the only one of the partners to sail. Velázquez also had a part in the venture, although participants who became followers of Hernán Cortés later alleged that Velázquez got into the act by fraud so as to claim Hernández de Córdoba's discoveries as his own. Whatever the origin of the voyage, a part of its intent was the discovery of "new lands"—lands, it was hoped, that would yield economic advantage for the discoverers, whether in the form of slaves, precious metals, or other resources.[69] With such objectives in mind, the partners sought out Antón de Alaminos and asked him to serve as chief pilot. Alaminos, whose path since his involvement with Ponce de León in 1513 remains obscure, was himself a newcomer to Cuba. But his reputation had preceded him; because of his previous role in voyages of discovery, he was chosen to accompany this fleet to seek new lands. The vaunted pilot told Hernández de Córdoba his feelings concerning the unknown sea west of Cuba. With Columbus in 1502, says Las Casas, Alaminos had observed that the Admiral was "much inclined" to sail in that direction, but for want of better ships he had turned toward Veragua instead. Thus, Hernández de Córdoba was persuaded to alter the plan for his voyage.[70] If Alaminos had previously visited Yucatán with Ponce de León, he kept it a close secret; the various chroniclers of the expedition, in fact, offer testimony to the contrary.

The ships, fitted out at Santiago de Cuba, sailed along Cuba's northern shore to Cabo San Antón. "We sailed west," says Díaz del Castillo, "without knowing of shoals, currents, or winds . . . at that latitude." After weathering a storm that put the ships at risk, they made landfall at Cabo Catoche, the northeastern promontory of Yucatán. Natives who came out in large canoes with both oars and sails invited the Spaniards ashore, leading them into an ambush. The Spaniards' crossbows and muskets soon put the Mayan archers to flight, but the Indians had inflicted grave damage. It was at Gran Cairo, as Hernández named the Maya town, that two cross-eyed Indian boys, Melchior and Julián, were captured. The cleric Alonso González plundered a native temple of idols and pendants of *guanín*, creating the illusion that gold was to be had in Yucatán.[71]

On 19 March 1517, Lazarus Sunday, the explorers anchored before a sizable town whose Indian name, Campeche, has survived to the present. They filled their water casks and puzzled over the natives' repetition of a word that sounded like "Castilan." After viewing the blood-spattered altars of human sacrifice and narrowly averting another set-to like that at Gran Cairo, they resumed the southward voyage. By the time they reached Potonchán (today's Champotón) they were again in dire need of water—the one commodity that the Mayas, in the Yucatán dry season, could ill spare. With the caravels anchored a league from shore, the voyagers set up camp on the beach. The Mayas came during the night to cut off their retreat. In the bloody battle the next day, fifty-odd Spaniards were slain. All the soldiers and most of the sailors were wounded. Regaining the vessels, they lacked able-bodied men to haul the rigging. The brigantine was stripped and burned. Still lacking water, they returned northward. Not daring to stop again at Campeche, they at last put into an inlet, called Estero de los Lagartos for its numerous alligators (today's Río Lagartos), but found only brackish water before a storm arose that nearly cast the ships upon the lee shore.

It was Alaminos who saved the day. With the wind contrary for Cuba, he set course for the Florida bay he had visited with Ponce de León; they arrived four days later. The pilot went ashore with twenty soldiers, including Díaz del Castillo. After filling the water casks, they washed clothing for the more seriously wounded. Then came the Indians, shooting arrows and attempting to seize the boat. In the fight, thirty-five Indians were slain. Half a dozen soldiers were injured, and a Spanish sentry was carried off alive. Alaminos had a painful arrow wound but was able to direct the course back to Puerto de Carenas. Weighing anchor well into the day, they "passed that day and night near some small islands called the Mártires."[72] From Ponce de León Bay, the Florida Keys were reached in less than a day's sail. Hernández de Córdoba's wounds proved fatal, raising the final death toll to fifty-seven. "How difficult it is to go out and discover new lands," wrote Díaz del Castillo. "No one can imagine what we endured who has not experienced such excessive hardships."[73]

The specimens of gold and the declarations by the two Maya boys that plenty of gold was to be had in Yucatán caused a stir of excitement in Cuba. Diego Velázquez, claiming the discovery as his own, organized a new voyage, with his kinsman Juan de Grijalva as its captain. With a license from the friars of San Jerónimo at Santo Domingo, four caravels were fitted out. Graviel Bosque was master and pilot of Grijalva's flagship. The other captains are better known for their later exploits, but it was the Grijalva voyage that shaped their destiny. They were Pedro de Alvarado, Alonso de Avila, and Francisco de Montejo, each to have a key role in the Mexican Conquest. Alaminos, now the unquestioned authority on navigation in the

Gulf of Mexico, again sailed as chief pilot, "as there was no other as skilled as he."[74] Departure was delayed to await the healing of his wounds. Julián, one of the Maya captives, had learned a little Spanish and was taken along as interpreter. Departing Santiago on 25 January 1518, the caravels proceeded slowly along the northern shore, taking on provisions. On 1 May they cleared Cabo San Antón in fair weather and landed in forty-eight hours not at Cabo Catoche but at Cozumel, seventy miles down the Caribbean coast. Before crossing to the "Island of Yucatán," Grijalva laid down strict rules forbidding his men to trade with the Indians; they should not even speak to the Indian women—a rule that occasioned dissatisfaction among his followers.

After visiting three mainland towns, the captain directed the course south to search for a man who had been lost from Hernández de Córdoba's expedition and who the Indian boy Julián claimed was still alive. The ancient ruins of Tulum, "so large that the city of Seville could not look larger or better," were sighted at sunset on 8 May.[75] Holding the course until 13 May, sailing day and night, the voyagers reached a shallow bay, which was named Bahía de la Ascensión for the feast day. The distance and Alaminos's latitude (17°) indicate not the bay presently known by that name, in latitude 19°40', but Chetumal Bay, somewhat farther south. It was, as Oviedo described it, the nearest bay to the Gulf of Higueras.[76] This extensive body of water was judged to mark the end of the land called Yucatán, which was believed to be an island.

Whether or not Alaminos was solely responsible for this judgment, as some have claimed, is not clear. That the pilot was under some pressure from the captain-general is evident from the fact that Alaminos had given Grijalva a written ultimatum during the southward voyage: either allow him to do his job or relieve him of the chief pilot's responsibilities.[77] Relations were not improved as the ships, towed by launches, sought a passage through the bay to the Gulf of Mexico. As soundings revealed rapidly diminishing depth, Alaminos called for withdrawal: they had to return the way they had come and sail around Yucatán on the north to reach the Gulf. Passing Isla Mujeres—inhabited by a race of amazons who lived without men, as the chaplain Juan Díaz tells it[78]—the explorers reached Campeche in desperate need of water. In the face of hostile demonstrations, they spent two days filling their casks from a weak well near the beach, repeatedly drawing it dry, while the native Mayas alternately offered threats and friendly gestures. Following the inevitable battle, the Spaniards had one man killed and several wounded, some of which died later.

On 31 May they found a desired haven—*puerto deseado*—at the Laguna de Términos, where the wounded convalesced while a leaky ship was repaired. Four Indian fishermen were captured, to be schooled as interpreters, and Alaminos brought his computations up to date. Having coasted along three sides of Yucatán and believing he had found the mouth of this same passage on the other side, he now was certain that it was an island; the seemingly endless body of water extending from Puerto Deseado (at the pass later called Puerto Escondido, long since closed) must open into the Bahía de Ascensión, he felt. The two mouths, by his calculations, were in 18.5° and 17° and were twenty leagues (sixty-odd miles) apart.[79] This bay, forever after to be known as Laguna de Términos, marked the end of Hernández de Córdoba's discovery. Whatever was to be discovered thenceforth would be Grijalva's. Until Francisco de Montejo, beginning the Yucatán conquest in 1527, proved that it was joined to the mainland, European mapmakers vacillated, showing it first as an island, then a peninsula, then an island again. It was occasionally shown as an island as late as 1544.[80]

After a five-day interlude, the caravels coasted westward along the "new land." Pausing at the Río de Tabasco—now renamed Río de Grijalva—the captain-general found that the Maya boy Julián from Cabo Catoche could no longer make himself understood by the natives. Thus Pedro, one of those captured at the Laguna de Términos, came into play, for he could converse in both Mayan and Tabascoan languages. He became the medium for arranging a profitable trade among the friendly Tabascoans, whose golden earrings and gold-worked helmets and shields provoked lively interest. It was Pedro too who described the country to the south: there were great mountains, a river with much gold, and another sea that could be reached in fifty or sixty days' travel. Grijalva's orders forbade settlement. Now that there was gold to be found, his strict adherence to these orders caused the men to murmur. The captain-general failed to understand that he was expected to disregard his orders when there was good reason for doing so.

The ships sailed on west along a coast lined with Indians brandishing turtle-shell shields. Past the Río de Coatzacoalcos, the volcanic mountains of San Martín loomed behind the shore, then Orizaba's snow-capped peak rose in the distance. Entering the Río de Papaloapán, Pedro de Alvarado damaged his ship so badly that Grijalva decided some days later to send the vessel back to Cuba with his report to Velázquez and the accumulated gold. The others sailed on; at a small island within sight of present-day Veracruz, the voyagers encountered the grim evidence of pagan worship and human sacrifice, in all its ghastliness. Ascending the stone staircase of a lofty temple, they entered a room with marble statuary and a bloody sacrificial font amid severed heads and putrefying, eviscerated bodies. An Indian demonstrated with gestures how the victims were decapitated and the hearts removed with flint knives to be burned with pine faggots and offered to the plumed idol that stood beside the stone font. The captain-general gave the island its lasting name: Isla de los Sacrificios. On St. John's Day, 24 June, Grijalva went ashore at the present Veracruz site and took formal possession. He named the province for the feast day, joining it with a corrupt form of the native name for Mexico: Colúa. Hence the island rimming Veracruz harbor was called San Juan de Ulúa.

While Alvarado sailed for Cuba, Grijalva proceeded north with the remaining three caravels. Heedless of his company's discontent at not being allowed to settle, he cleaved to his orders, oblivious to the opportunity of a millennium.[81] At the Río de Canoas—its name soon corrupted to Río de Cazones—a shower of arrows from a canoe fleet provoked the Spaniards' response with harquebuses, artillery, and crossbows, killing four natives and sending the others scurrying back to shore. Alaminos, meanwhile, continued to warn of the current that bore them northward; their return against the flow would not be so easy. On 28 June, the voyagers turned about at Cabo Rojo to withdraw to the bottom of the Gulf. It was a mistake not realized till later. The flagship, *San Sebastián*, having sought shelter from a heavy sea in the Río de Tonalá, struck a shoal and had to be careened. The captives Pedro and Julián escaped. When at last the ships regained the open sea to sail homeward, they found wind and current against them. For almost a month they were able to make little progress, beating into the northeasterlies and the steady westward flow of the Caribbean Current. Alaminos took the hard lesson; in the future, he would turn the wind and current to his advantage.

Falling back on the Tabasco coast, Grijalva discovered a more prominent pass into the lagoon south of Puerto Deseado and named it Boca de Términos. Here, where the ferry now crosses between Puerto Real and Isla de Aguada, they saw Indians going from Yucatán to "the other country" every day in canoes under sail.[82] The homeward voyage was resumed toward the end of August. Reaching Potonchán, the scene of Hernández de Córdoba's disaster the previous year, Grijalva landed on the small offshore island in preparation for an attack on the town; he later thought better of it, but his men, bent on vengeance, could not be controlled after they landed.

The voyagers finally arrived at Puerto de Carenas on 30 September to learn that Alvarado had returned safely. Other happenings during their absence became known as they progressed slowly toward Santiago. Before Alvarado's arrival, Velázquez had sent Cristóbal de Olid to look for the overdue expedition. Alvarado's return increased the governor's apprehension, for he learned that Olid had not overtaken Grijalva. The governor was upset also at the news that Grijalva, having found a rich native paradise, was adhering to his orders against forming a settlement. Hastily, he put together a new "trading expedition," attempting to justify himself with the euphemistic wording of his orders. The voyage was necessary, he set forth, to seek Grijalva and Olid, both long overdue, and also to look for the six Spanish castaways in Yucatán of whom the Maya boy Melchior had told him—possibly castaways from Diego de Nicuesa's ship, which had not been heard from since leaving Darién. And, with Alvarado's report of the wealth of Grijalva's discoveries, he was obliged to "explore all the islands and lands to learn their secrets." In this manner Velázquez excused his haste in ordering the new expedition led by Hernán Cortés instead of waiting for Grijalva, who by all means should have been accorded the right of first refusal. Embarrassed when both Grijalva and Olid returned, Velázquez sought to withdraw his authority from Cortés. But Cortés had taken bit in teeth and would not be checked. Truly, Grijalva was, as Oviedo described him, "a luckless man."[83]

Velázquez's orders to Cortés embraced the objectives of advancing Grijalva's discovery and opening new avenues of trade. The pilots were to examine all rivers and ports, take soundings, and chart their observations; to learn "the secrets of said islands and lands," the manners and customs of the people, the flora and fauna, and of course, whether or not there was gold, precious stones, or spices; and to ascertain the truth behind reports of people with enormous ears and others with faces like dogs and the whereabouts of the amazons of whom the Indian captives had spoken.[84]

At this juncture, scarcely more than a quarter century from the initial discovery, the North American continent proper was little known. The peninsulas of both Florida and Yucatán had been determined to be islands flanking a continent whose full proportions could be only a guess. Grijalva, in sailing along more of the mainland coast above Central America than anyone before him, had encountered strange cultures centered on the worship of pagan gods demanding human sacrifice and had glimpsed tokens of their opulence. Yet the nature and extent of those peoples, their wealth, and their territories, as well as the enmities that divided them, remained a mystery. The truth of the Darién natives' tales of another ocean had been proved by Núñez de Balboa. Grijalva had learned that it lay south of Tabasco as well as south of Darién. Still there remained the nagging question of a strait. Surely there was a water passage to the South Sea, but where? The ocean current, always running west through the Caribbean, added to the puzzle for both theorists and practical navigators. Peter Martyr in 1515 discussed the matter with the noted pilot and hydrographer Andrés de Morales and the historian Oviedo. Morales's theory came closest to the truth: striking the continent west of Cuba, the flow turned north, forced by the coastal configuration to take a rotating course back along Cuba's northern shore.[85] Alaminos would provide the proof.

Cortés, anticipating the governor's reaction to Grijalva's return, hastened his departure from Santiago before Velázquez could stop him. Gathering in Grijalva's men as he moved up the island, he was joined by Alaminos as chief pilot, by the pilots Juan Alvarez of Huelva and Pedro Camacho of Triana, who had sailed with both Hernández de Córdoba and Grijalva, and by Pedro Arnés de Sopuesta of Moguer. Captains of the eleven ships included Grijalva's three, Alvarado, Avila, and Montejo, as well as Olid. There was a liberal sprinkling of both Grijalva's men and Hernández de Córdoba's throughout the crew, including Bernal Díaz del Castillo, who would serve as the eyewitness historian of the Mexican Conquest.[86]

At Cozumel, Cortés had the good fortune to receive as his interpreter a castaway from Núñez de Balboa's Darién colony, Gerónimo de Aguilar. His fleet then followed Grijalva's route around Yucatán and Tabasco. At the Río de Grijalva, he fought with the Tabascoans, who had turned hostile since Grijalva's visit; his cavalry mounts became the first Spanish horses landed on the North American continent. Victorious, the Spaniards received the gift of twenty young women, including a Mexican princess by birthright who had been sold into slavery. Christened Doña Marina, she became Cortés's mistress and interpreter and a vital force in the Mexican Conquest. Proceeding to the island of San Juan de Ulúa, Cortés went ashore on Good Friday 1519 and met Moctezuma's emissaries, from whom he received valuable gifts, and began to employ the stratagems by which his meager force would ultimately defeat the powerful Mejican empire.

While Cortés received visitors from the Totonac capital of Cempoala, Alaminos and Montejo sailed north to look for a more promising settlement site. They found a suitable anchorage beneath the mountainside Totonac village of Quiahuitzlan, a keystone of the Conquest. Here was founded Villa Rica de la Vera Cruz, the first mainland settlement north of the isthmus. Cortés now cast off his allegiance to Velázquez, had himself elected governor and captain-general of New Spain of the Ocean Sea, and tapped Alaminos and Montejo for another important mission: taking to Spain the accumulated plunder and a report calculated to win the king.

Alaminos doubtless had his course charted before making sail. The ship, sailing from Villa Rica on 16 July 1519, put into Marién on the northern shore of Cuba to reprovision at Montejo's hacienda. The mission was compromised, and Velázquez dispatched two caravels from Santiago to intercept it.[87] Alaminos, calling on knowledge gained during his 1513 voyage with Ponce de León, eluded the pursuit by sailing north through the Bahama Channel, pushed speedily along by the Gulf Stream. Thus he inaugurated the lasting sailing route to Spain. Cortés, meanwhile, proceeded to the conquest of the Mejican, or Aztec, empire, a feat that he accomplished largely by his wits. Much of the land he marched over remains little changed after four and one-half centuries, but the native civilizations were destroyed before they were adequately recorded. Yet to Cortés belongs one of the most remarkable discovery episodes of the New World.

The victims of the conqueror's stratagems included not only Moctezuma and his minions but also all Spaniards who opposed Cortés. The first of the latter group was Alonso Alvarez de Pineda, whose four ships appeared off Villa Rica just as Cortés was about to begin his march on Mexico. Refusing an invitation to come ashore and parley, Alvarez de Pineda nevertheless left half a dozen of his men in Cortés's clutches. Cortés used gold to seduce Narváez's followers, sent by Velázquez to arrest him, and Francisco de Garay, whose effort to establish his own domain in the Pánuco region threatened to limit Cortés's expansion. Cristóbal de Tapia, sent by Bishop Fonseca to mark the boundary between the territories discovered for Garay and Velázquez, was so frustrated by Cortés's battery of hostile witnesses that he withdrew in confusion, if not in fear for his life.[88]

Cortés recognized that the key to successful occupation of conquered territory lay in "learning its secrets." Between stages of the Conquest, he sent soldiers to seek the mines that were the source of the Aztec treasure and to identify the likely seaports. The men were always instructed to observe the country and its natural resources: mineral wealth, building materials, soil fertility, flora and fauna. Combing the countryside for hundreds of miles around the capital, they found gold in the streambeds of Tututepec (Oaxaca) and both gold and the native Zapotecs' washing troughs in the rivers of Jaltepec province. A map prepared by Moctezuma's artists led the explorers to the Río de Coatzacoalcos, viewed as the only promising harbor in more than two hundred miles south of San Juan de Ulúa. Natives of the region, pledging tribute to the Spaniards, offered gifts of gold, cotton, featherwork, and jaguar skins.[89]

A spur to the conqueror's exploration was the threat to his far-reaching territorial designs by other Spaniards: Pedrarias Dávila and Gil Gonzáles de Avila on the south and Garay on the north. Additionally, Cortés was goaded by necessity born of his difficulty in obtaining munitions from Spain. Seeking metals for making bronze artillery, his men found tin and iron near Taxco. Sulphur for making gunpowder was brought up from the Popocatépetl volcano by an anonymous daredevil who was lowered several hundred feet into the smoking crater. Not satisfied with the port at Villa Rica, Cortés made a personal reconnaissance of the coast and selected a site on the Río Jamapa, which he named for his birthplace in Spain, Medellin.[90] Cortés envisioned making his "Nueva España del Mar Océano" a conduit to the Spice Islands, by either a yet-unknown strait or an overland route from sea to sea. Other explorers had the same idea, resulting in armed conflict pitting Spaniard against Spaniard.

The Search for a Strait

Antón de Alaminos is said to have suggested to Francisco de Garay the voyage that led to Garay's quest for a strait linking the Atlantic and Pacific Oceans. Alaminos, sometime after returning from the Grijalva voyage and before embarking with Cortés, called to Garay's attention the unknown territory between Ponce de León's discovery of Florida on the east and Grijalva's of the Mexican coast on the west—a region ripe for discovery.[91] Garay seems already to have had such a thought. While in Spain in 1514, treating at court for appointment to the lieutenant governorship of Jamaica, he purchased two caravels at Puerto de Santa María and outfitted them in a manner that suggests preparations for a discovery voyage.[92] Problems in his island charge, followed by the voyages of Hernández de Córdoba and Grijalva, appear to have held his plans in abeyance. Moved by Alaminos's suggestion, Garay obtained from the friars of San Jerónimo at Santo Domingo—the Crown administrators for the West Indies since 1517—permission to search the mainland coast for a strait. To command the voyage he chose Alonso Alvarez de Pineda, who sailed from Jamaica with four ships and 270 men, probably in April 1519. What is known of the voyage consists of a few paragraphs in the work by Díaz del Castillo (the only source to mention Alvarez de Pineda by name), passing mentions in Cortés's letters, and a royal patent later issued to Garay granting him authority to settle the region discovered in his name.[93]

Searching for the nonexistent passage, Alvarez de Pineda proved that Florida was a peninsula, not an island as Ponce de León had supposed. He discovered more of the Gulf of Mexico littoral than any other single navigator: from the Florida peninsula to Cabo Rojo on the Veracruz coast, a distance of more than three hundred leagues (almost a thousand miles). Unable to clear the Florida Keys and ascend the eastern coast because of contrary wind and current, the ships turned about and sailed west. They passed close enough to the present-day Mississippi River to perceive its mighty discharge and give it a name, Río del Espíritu Santo, on or about the Festival of the Holy Ghost, or Pentecost, 2 June 1519. They held the westerly course "until they encountered Hernando Cortés and the Spaniards who were with him on the same coast."[94] Alvarez de Pineda sent six men ashore to apprise Cortés of his intent to settle north of Nautla. When they were seized, Alvarez de Pineda sailed for Pánuco, where, according to Díaz del Castillo, he already had begun a settlement.

After leaving Villa Rica, Alvarez de Pineda sailed six leagues up a large river—assuredly the Pánuco and not the Río Grande or the Mississippi, as has so often been stated—to spend six weeks "careening his ships," or beginning a settlement. In late fall, the vessels returned to Jamaica; from there some of the pilots carried to Spain an account of the expedition to support Garay's petition for discovery rights. We can be certain that the verbiage of the report, consisting of somewhat fanciful descriptions of the land and its people, is echoed in the royal patent issued to Garay on 4 June 1521 and naming him *adelantado* and governor. According to this document, the entire coast was pleasant and fruitful and was inhabited by pacific natives of affectionate nature who gave every indication of being suitable subjects for conversion to the Catholic faith. In places, the people were exceptionally tall, standing seven feet; in other places were midgets of no more than three and one-half to four feet. Some of the natives, it is said, wore gold jewelry in their nostrils and earlobes, and there was wide distribution of the precious metal in the territory.[95]

The pilots who took the report to Spain also carried a map sketch of the voyage, the first to describe the Gulf of Mexico from actual observation. The map showed the coast to be contiguous mainland, with both Yucatán and Florida joined to it; there was no strait to the South Sea. The source for the portrayal of the southern Gulf and of Yucatán, in its proper peninsular

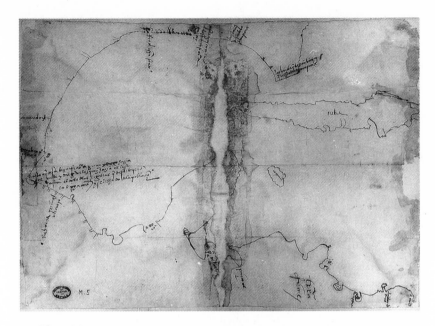

4.1 Map of the Gulf of Mexico by Alvarez de Pineda (1519). This is the first map to depict accurately the American coast of the Gulf of Mexico and the first to locate the mouth of the Mississippi River ("Espíritu Santo"). Courtesy Archivo Generale de Indias, Sevilla, Spain.

form, is not known but could not have been Alaminos, who thought Yucatán was an island. In this respect the map was years ahead of its time. Although European geographers and mapmakers seem to have acknowledged the peninsular form given to Florida, they clung doggedly to the idea of an insular Yucatán. Yet certain features of the sketch found their way onto the standard maps almost immediately and endured for well over a century, for example, the Río del Espíritu Santo, generally conceded to represent the Mississippi, with a large enclosed bay at its mouth. Although there are few place-names, the Río Pánuco appears in its proper place. The Río de las Palmas, which by common misconception Alvarez de Pineda is said to have named, is not shown, for good reason; it was not so named until 1523, and it was Garay who named it, not Alvarez de Pineda. The map credits Ponce de León with reaching a point west of the Florida peninsula, the basis for the occasional judgment that he reached Pensacola Bay in 1513. Whereas Ponce de León's voyage is expanded, Grijalva's is curtailed, the end of "discoveries for Velázquez" indicated between Tamiahua and Villa Rica.

The Alvarez de Pineda sketch makes for interesting comparisons with the map published with the August 1524 Nuremberg edition of Cortés's second letter. Authorship of this map, the first specifically of the Gulf of Mexico to be printed, is generally attributed to Cortés but is much in question. Cortés himself makes no mention of it in his reports to the Crown. The map uses most of the toponyms from the Alvarez sketch, including the Río del Espíritu Santo and the Río Pánuco. It also has the Río de las Palmas, not shown by Alvarez de Pineda. Florida is joined to the mainland, but Yucatán is shown as an island, reflecting Alaminos's error. Seemingly in refutation of Cortés's authorship, the map shows Sevilla (the name Cortés gave to the Totonac capital of Cempoala) but not Villa Rica, the town he founded; and Provincia Amichel, the name given to the territory explored for Garay and a name not used on the Alvarez sketch, appears south of the Río Pánuco.[96] As determined as Cortés was to negate Garay's claim, it hardly seems plausible that he would have recognized it on his map.

The royal patent issued at Burgos granted Garay authority to settle the "Provincia de Amichel" that Alvarez de Pineda had discovered. Actually, the permission had been anticipated by more than a year. Soon after the expedition returned, says Díaz del Castillo, Garay "sent back to Pánuco three ships . . . with up to 240 soldiers and many horses, and Alonso Alvarez de Pineda as captain."[97] Indeed, it seems likely that Alvarez had never left the Pánuco but remained with part of his force to begin the settlement while sending the ships home to report.

In about January 1520, Diego de Camargo, bringing supplies and reinforcements, arrived at the site six leagues up the Pánuco. Shortly afterward, the Huastec Indians turned hostile. Alvarez de Pineda and many of his men were slain. Camargo undertook the evacuation of sixty survivors, most of them wounded, to Villa Rica, where they joined Cortés's army of conquest as soon as they were able.[98] Two more supply ships sent by Garay later reached Pánuco and, finding the settlement abandoned, sailed south to join Cortés. In June 1523, Garay embarked to occupy Pánuco himself. He landed instead at the Río de las Palmas (the present-day Río de Soto la Marina). After a nightmarish march to Pánuco, he found that Cortés—with royal authority that superseded his own—had conquered the province and founded the village of Santiesteban del Puerto (present-day

Pánuco, Veracruz). Checkmated, Garay went to Mexico to treat with the governor; he died there shortly after Christmas 1523 of pneumonia.

Cortés also viewed as rivals Pedrarias Dávila, who was advancing northward from Castillo del Oro, and Gil González de Avila, who had transported ships over the isthmus to explore the Pacific coast. Both were seeking the sea-to-sea passage. Cortés countered by sending Pedro de Alvarado in December 1523 to subdue Tututepec on the South Sea (Pacific) coast of Oaxaca and to march from there to Guatemala. Cristóbal de Olid built ships at Colima to explore the Pacific shore.[99] The conqueror also wanted "to know the secrets of the coast . . . between the Río Pánuco and Florida, the discovery of Juan Ponce de León, and beyond that region north as far as Bacalaos [the land of the codfish, discovered by John Cabot in 1497–98, in the New England–Canadian area] because in that coast it is certain there is a strait to the South Sea." The degree to which his projections were carried out remains in doubt. Francisco López de Gómara, however, relates that in January 1524, two ships went "to explore the coast between Pánuco and Florida [an indefinite use of the term] to look for a strait."[100]

About that time Olid sailed for Havana with six vessels to buy horses and supplies for establishing a colony at Cape Higueras, Honduras. From there he was to send Diego de Hurtado to explore the coast southward. At this point, however, Olid—allegedly persuaded by Velázquez—decided to cut free of Cortés and set himself up independently.[101] In Honduras, he expelled the forces of González de Avila and arrested their leader. He did the same with Francisco de las Casas, sent by Cortés to bring him to heel. Cortés himself, in the absence of news from that quarter, decided to go and straighten out the mess. His march, along the most difficult route possible, revealed much concerning the lowlands of Tabasco, Chiapas, and Guatemala. From the Río de Coatzacoalcos, his troop followed a map drawn, on henequen cloth, by native traders whom he employed as guides. The traders, who usually traveled by canoe, had no concept of the needs of a land march driving herds of horses and swine. Swimming the Tonalá and Agualulco Rivers, the pigs were lost to sharks and alligators. In the next fifty miles the Indian workmen built as many bridges, some of them almost half a mile long. To reach the Maya Chontal province of Acalán, the march led across the central lowlands of Chiapas, through forests so dense that only the sky immediately overhead and the ground underfoot could be seen. At Acalán, Cortés hoped to meet supply ships coming through Bahía de Ascensión to the estuary believed to connect with the Laguna de Términos. Not only was it an impossible plan, but the ships and crews were lost before it could be tested. The expedition very nearly cost Cortés his life, threatened to undo the Conquest, and marked the beginning of the end of his dominance in the land he had conquered.[102]

The search for a strait through North America went on in one quarter or another for many years. In 1519 Ferdinand Magellan had discovered the passage at the southern tip of South America (Strait of Magellan). With him at the time was the pilot Esteban Gómez, a Portuguese like Magellan. Gómez viewed the tempestuous strait as being too far south to be useful; he seized the ship he was piloting and sailed for Spain, where he was jailed for mutiny. His insistence that he could find a better strait through North America went unheeded until 1522, when Emperor Charles V freed him from jail. Spurred by reports of an impending voyage for France by Giovanni da Verrazzano, the emperor had a ship built and outfitted at La Coruña. Verrazzano, however, had completed his voyage before the ship was ready for sea. Gómez sailed in September 1524 and reached the American coast the following February, near Cape Breton, Nova Scotia. From there he ran the Atlantic coast south to Florida, exploring the larger rivers and bays, and touched at Santiago de Cuba before sailing for home. In the main, he succeeded only in casting a pall over the image of the northern continent, which seemed to offer little produce not readily available in Europe.[103] Gómez's negative portrayal of the Atlantic coast was intensified by the 1525 colonizing expedition of Lucas Vázquez de Ayllón, a judge of the Audiencia of Santo Domingo and an honorable man. An expedition he had sent out in 1521 turned into a slave raid, stirring up the Indians where he hoped to settle later. With 500 men, women, and children, Vázquez de Ayllón set out in 1525 to establish his colony of Chicora on the South Carolina coast. Undisciplined settlers, uncooperative natives, disease, and shipwreck compounded the colony's woes. Vázquez de Ayllón himself died of a fever in October 1526, and the colony disbanded. Only 150 of the original 500 returned to Santo Domingo.[104]

The efforts of Gómez and Vázquez de Ayllón are recorded by Diogo Ribeiro, the Portuguese cosmographer employed by Charles V in 1526 to make an official general map. Ribeiro sought to record the latest discoveries. His 1529 world map shows both "Tiera de Ayllón" and "Tiera de Estebā Gómez" on the Atlantic coast, below "Tiera Nova de Cortereal," with historical notes concerning the voyages. The map has "Tiera de Garay" on the North American mainland, and a channel across the base of the Yucatán Peninsula connects the Gulf of Mexico and the Caribbean.[105]

Interest in the Atlantic coast was revived by a combination of factors:

foreign encroachment and the need to guard the shipping lane through the Bahama Channel. Yet the idea of a strait linking the two great oceans died slowly. Pedro Menéndez de Avilés, after founding Saint Augustine, Florida, in 1565, contemplated exploring Chesapeake Bay for such a passage. In Havana, he discussed with Fray Andrés de Urdaneta—who had recently discovered the eastward sailing route across the Pacific—"the strait, which it is believed certainly exists in Florida, where goes the return from China . . . and the means that can be had for knowing its secret." Menéndez's Chesapeake Bay reconnaissance appears to have been quite limited, but a Jesuit mission, established on the York River in 1570, lasted only a few months before it was terminated by an Indian massacre.[106]

The Coast of "Florida"

The declining fortunes of Cortés put a new face on exploration in the Gulf of Mexico. His unfortunate Honduras expedition, lasting until May 1526, was followed closely by his *residencia* (the review of a colonial official's conduct in office) and the curbing of his authority as governor. While his ships explored the Pacific coast as far north as the Gulf of California, the territories he claimed fell away in chunks. Nuño Beltrán de Guzmán, Cortés's dedicated enemy, was sent in 1526 to govern Pánuco. In the same year, Alonso de Cáceres conquered Honduras for Pedro de Alvarado, who asserted his independence from Cortés. In the following year another of the conqueror's former captains, Francisco de Montejo, was granted independent rights to Yucatán. Sailing from Sanlúcar de Barrameda in Spain at or about the same time as Montejo was Pánfilo de Narváez, to explore and conquer between the Río de las Palmas and "the island of Florida."

The last effort launched a series of disasters that characterized early attempts to conquer the northern Gulf shore and gave rise to the amazing adventures of Alvar Núñez Cabeza de Vaca. Landing at Tampa Bay in the spring of 1528, Narváez sent his ships to explore the coast while he took an expedition to march on land. He never saw the ships again. He and his men, threatened with annihilation by Indians and the wilderness, killed their horses for meat and used the hides to cover the crude boats they were able to build with tools fashioned from the iron of stirrups and crossbows. From near Saint George Sound they embarked in the shaky craft for Pánuco. The boats and their crews, in separate disasters, were tossed upon the Texas shore from Galveston Bay to the Río Grande. The boat of Peñalosa and Telles progressed the farthest, crashing on the Tamaulipas shore. The Camones Indians killed the boat crew and stripped them of their clothing. Narváez himself drifted out to sea while sleeping on his boat at Texas's Matagorda Bay. Two boats, including that of Cabeza de Vaca, were cast ashore near Galveston Island. Ultimately, the entire expedition perished, except for Cabeza de Vaca and three companions, who escaped their Indian captors to begin their march across the continent in August 1535. After crossing the Río Grande, they were warned of the coastal Indians' extreme hostility; they were approaching the region in which Guzmán had made brutal slave raids, creating lasting enmities. The four castaways turned westward across northern Mexico. After traversing the Texas Big Bend region and the Sierra Madre Occidental, they were rescued in the spring of 1536 by Guzmán's slave raiders on the Río Yaqui in the present-day Mexican state of Sonora.[107]

The survivors' reports of what they had seen and heard gave rise to the expedition of Francisco Vázquez de Coronado, searching for Gran Quivira. By the time Cabeza de Vaca returned to Spain, Hernando de Soto, formerly associated with Pedrarias Dávila in Castillo del Oro and with Francisco Pizarro in Peru, had been designated governor of Cuba and *adelantado* of Florida. He was organizing a new expedition to conquer "La Florida," which in sixteenth-century context embraced the region from the Río de las Palmas to peninsular Florida. Cabeza de Vaca declined to join it.

Soto landed at a bay on the western side of the Florida peninsula on 30 May 1539. Like Narváez, he left his ships and marched inland, eventually losing contact with them. After setting foot in nine present-day U.S. states (from South Carolina to Texas), Soto's men, led by Luis de Moscoso Alvarado after Soto's death on the Mississippi, built crude boats to reach the Gulf. They left the river via Southwest Pass and ran the coast to Pánuco, where they arrived fifty-three days later, on 10 September 1543. Of almost six hundred soldiers and servants who had left Havana four years previously, hardly more than half had come out of La Florida alive.[108]

From this expedition came most of the information for the so-called Soto map, drawn by Alonso de Santa Cruz, the cosmographer in the Casa de Contratación. The map did not surface until Santa Cruz's death in 1572, when it was found among his papers. When Juan López de Velasco began his landmark assessment of Spain's overseas possessions the following year, he judged Santa Cruz's map the best-available portrayal of the northern Gulf shore.[109] The Soto *entrada*'s influence on the map is manifest from the fact that fourteen of its sixty-odd names for Indian towns correspond to

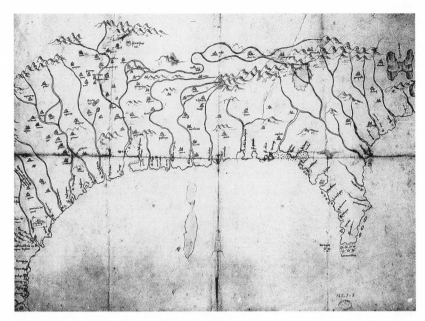

4.2 "Mapa de Golfo y Costa de Nueva España" (Alonso de Santa Cruz, c. 1572). *The date of the map is uncertain, and the 1572 identification signifies only that the map was found among Santa Cruz's papers after he died in that year. Although no one knows with any certainty when it was drawn, the map was obviously created after the Soto and the Coronado explorations. Courtesy Barker Texas History Center, The University of Texas at Austin (JPB 66–1572).*

those given in the three primary accounts of the expedition. To call it the Soto map, however, is to limit its context. The map evidently represents Santa Cruz's running record of discoveries. Beginning in the region explored by Vázquez de Ayllón, it traces the shoreline from Punta de Santa Elena (South Carolina) around the Florida peninsula and the northern Gulf coast to Pánuco. Use of the name "Quivira" suggests information from the Coronado expedition. The mountains with silver mines, south of the Río Grande, probably bespeak Cabeza de Vaca's contribution. All in all, the map accurately reflects the state of knowledge of the northern Gulf coast and adjacent lands in the mid–sixteenth century.

Whereas the earliest explorer maps, such as that of Alvarez de Pineda, showed only the mouths of rivers, Santa Cruz was able to represent their inland courses. Some of the drainage systems were shown quite accurately. The map reflects knowledge of the Appalachian Mountain range.

There are mountains farther west also, situated about right for the Ozarks. Like all maps of the period, it shows the Río del Espíritu Santo (Mississippi) flowing straight south into a sizable bay rather than angling southeast, as the Mississippi does in its lower reaches. Nor is there any hint of the Mississippi delta. The river seems to rise in two forks, one meandering from east to west for a great distance before turning south to join the other, which rises in the mountains to the north and west. Although some features of the map are more or less accurately presented, it was not to be taken as gospel. For example, both the map and the written accounts of the Soto expedition had an undue influence on the next European explorer to descend the Mississippi to its mouth: the Frenchman La Salle, 140 years later. La Salle's attempt to make more of the Soto chronicles than was warranted contributed to his utter confusion when he sought the river mouth from the Gulf of Mexico and landed instead at Matagorda Bay.[110]

Ten years after the Soto *entrada* came Fray Luis Cáncer de Barbastro, a Dominican friar backed by the Indians' champion, Bartolomé de Las Casas, with the conviction that a spiritual conquest might succeed where the military approach had failed. With a single ship he landed near Tampa Bay in May 1549. After leaving three companions who were captured by the natives, he withdrew to the Charlotte Harbor area and there, in a final attempt to win the Indians, was himself killed.[111] The Florida natives' "bad press" resulting from the Cáncer affair intensified five years later when storms wrecked three Spanish merchant ships on Padre Island, some distance north of the Río Grande mouth. While a boat crew set off to Veracruz with news of the disaster, some 250 castaways walked south toward Pánuco. Only one arrived. The others, including four Dominican friars, died in the wilderness, most of them at Indians' hands. It mattered not that the people responsible were an entirely different group from those involved in the Cáncer episode or that the two disasters were hundreds of miles apart. Both occurred on "the coast of Florida," in sixteenth-century parlance.[112]

One of the more reasoned voices advocating action to stem the growing chain of disasters was Fray Andrés de Olmos, who had just founded a mission at the Tampico site and had journeyed among the natives as far as Las Palmas. His appeal would have been ineffective, however, without the support of an important participant in the Soto fiasco: Roderigo Ranjel, Soto's secretary, author of a firsthand account of the expedition, and lately the *alcalde mayor* of Pánuco. The Olmos plan, advocated by Ranjel and the Pánuco vicar, called for settlements at three locations: the Río de las Palmas, the Río Bravo (Río Grande), and Ochuse (Pensacola Bay).[113]

Viceroy Luis de Velasco, favoring the plan, ordered explorations to determine the most suitable site for what was to become the colony of Tristán de Luna y Arellano. The first voyage, and the best known, was that of Guido de Lavazares (or Las Bazares), a veteran of the 1542 expedition of Ruy López de Villalobos to the Spice Islands. Lavazares, piloted by Bernaldo Peloso, late of the Soto *entrada*, sailed from San Juan de Ulúa on 3 September 1558 with three of the smallest ships yet to take part in an extensive exploration of Gulf waters. Ascending the western side of the Gulf, he came in 28°30′ to a large but shallow bay, which he named San Francisco—evidently Matagorda Bay. Contrary winds forced him to fall off to the south. He regained the coast ten leagues west of Mobile Bay, which he later explored and named Bahía Filipina. Foul weather forestalled his efforts to enter Pensacola Bay.[114] What appears to have been a follow-up effort sailed from San Juan de Ulúa shortly after Lavazares's return. A single ship piloted by Gonzalo Gayón and captained by Juan de Rentería proceeded to Havana and from there sailed counterclockwise around the Gulf. It "discovered the port of Polonza [Pensacola Bay], the port of Filipina, and the Costa de Médanos [Médanos de Magdalena of Padre Island, site of the 1554 shipwrecks] in the land of Florida and the coast of New Spain."[115] It evidently was this voyage that caused the Luna colony to be placed at Pensacola Bay rather than at Mobile Bay, the location that Lavazares had favored.

The Luna *entrada*, 1559–61, was managed from Mexico. Viceroy Velasco kept such a stranglehold on the operation that Luna had no room for independent action, even had his physical and mental condition permitted. Velasco strained to make the venture succeed, giving it every possible advantage. Yet it seems to have been doomed from the start, by the vagaries of the weather, Luna's illness, and mutiny. Its significance lies not in what it did but in what it sought to do. Velasco's great plans—of exploring all the rivers and bays from the Mississippi to the Florida Keys; of linking the Florida colony with Mexico by means of an overland route from Zacatecas and extending the route eastward to the Atlantic; and of finding the gold that Narváez and Soto had overlooked—all died aborning. In the end the viceroy was forced to admit that the project under Luna's disabled leadership could not be salvaged; he sent Angel de Villafañe to remove the colony by sea to Santa Elena on the Atlantic coast. But even that venture was thwarted: a hurricane—the third to afflict the enterprise—scattered Villafañe's force on 14 June 1561 before he could find a harbor.[116] The idea of bridging the wilderness with a Florida-Mexico road arose again in the early years of Pedro Menéndez de Avilés's Saint Augustine colony. In 1566 and 1567 Juan Pardo, under Menéndez's orders, led expeditions from Santa Elena with expectations of approaching Mexico through country previously traversed by Soto. Five days short of Coosa, which had been visited by both Soto's men and Luna's, Pardo's force turned back under threat of Indian ambush.[117]

Menéndez's dream of exploring and "pacifying" all of greater Florida, from the Pánuco to the Atlantic, had little basis in reality. As he and his heirs defaulted, Luis de Carvajal y de la Cueva moved into the breach from the other end of the spectrum. As *alcalde ordinario* at Tampico, Carvajal capitalized on his seizure of a band of helpless Englishmen put ashore just north of the Pánuco in October 1568 by Master John Hawkins following his loss of ships in a shoot-out with the Spanish fleet at Veracruz. Other deeds that Carvajal claimed for himself were carefully designed to beef up his credits. On the basis of his inflated record, he returned to Spain early in 1579 to win a royal *capitulación* as governor and captain-general of an ill-defined territory extending two hundred leagues north and west of Tampico. The contract committed him to explore across Mexico from sea to sea and to occupy all the ports from Tampico to Saint Joseph's Bay (present-day Florida) within five years. It seems unlikely that he had any real intention of carrying out the coastal settlement. His efforts were pointed largely at acquiring mines—by discovery or usurpation—and slave raiding. Finally arrested and threatened with exile, he died in prison in Mexico City in 1590.[118]

Fruits of Discovery

Thus, the sixteenth century, which had seen such great strides in exploration across the Caribbean Sea, the Gulf of Mexico, and the adjacent mainland territories, came to a close with much remaining to be done. The Caribbean still had scores of islands that Spain had been unable to occupy or had seen no reason for doing so. The door was left open for foreign encroachment, by the British, the French, and the Dutch. A heavy penalty would be exacted for the neglect. Foreign rivals, ever covetous of the wealth of Spain's possessions, moved in to establish bases from which to harass Spanish shipping and coastal settlements. Taking up the vacant islands, they sought to divest the discovering nation of as many of the rewards as possible. Such were the fruits of Spain's efforts. At the end of the century there was no road connecting Spanish Saint Augustine with Mexico, and there would be none. The entire Gulf coast from the Florida Keys to Tampico was empty wilderness, with the feeble penetrations by Narváez, Soto, Cáncer, and Luna soon to be forgotten. Few of the bays and river mouths were known, and the maps still showed such erroneous features as a large enclosed bay, called Espíritu Santo, at the mouth of the Mississippi. Despite Soto's discovery of that great river, no idea of its importance had dawned and no further exploration had been made.

Indeed, Spain regarded the region north of Mexico with ambivalence, typified, it seems, by the survivors of the Soto expedition returning to Pánuco in 1543. Regarding the mean circumstances of the Pánuco settlers, the Soto men viewed this area as "inferior to the one they themselves had forsaken. . . . The glory of the many fine provinces they had discovered increased." La Florida now seemed a land of fertility and abundance, offering soil suitable for all kinds of crops, with pasturelands, woods, and rivers for raising any kind of livestock. The pearls they had scorned now seemed a great wealth. "And as they compared those riches and noble estates with the present miseries and paucities," they were moved to melancholy thoughts: "Were not the lands we left better than these where we at present are? Where, if we should attempt now to stop and settle, might we become richer than these people who are our hosts? Do they by chance have more gold? Or even the riches that we scorned?" Whereas Soto's men might have become feudal lords, they had been reduced to begging.[119]

Yet no one stepped forward to lead a new *entrada*. Instead of returning to La Florida, some of Soto's men settled in Mexico, but most went to Peru. A few took part in later explorations that, like Soto's, went down in failure. A meager settlement was maintained at Saint Augustine to offer a refuge for storm-tossed or pirate-plagued ships sailing the Bahama Channel. But there remained a great void in geographical knowledge of the Gulf littoral that spread toward Pánuco and to the adjacent inland territory. The void would remain until that region was threatened by foreign invaders.

Had this northern sector proved to be "another Mexico," with abundant mineral wealth, the early failures doubtless would have been followed by a more determined effort. Yet its abandonment should not be laid so much to a dearth of gold as to the tragedy attending all efforts to explore it. More to the point, Spain simply lacked the resources, both material and human, to occupy all the territories it had discovered. That Spain was interested only in the regions that offered gold is a myth that is easily disproved; priorities had to be set, and it would have required great vision indeed to turn away from the obvious riches of the Aztec empire to colonize a savage wilderness whose only wealth lay in its soil. Neither France nor England, nor any other nation, would have done so. Whatever motives have been ascribed to the three major colonial rivals for North America, their objectives were essentially the same: economic opportunity and extension of empire. Each sought these goals in its own way, under the influence of homeland conditioning, the nature of the New World segment to which fortune assigned it, and the character of the natives it found there. If greed was a factor in Spain's misjudgments, this was not a peculiarly Spanish failing but a human one. Although civilizations were destroyed in the Mexican Conquest and the natives generally fared badly under Spanish abuse, they did not do so well under the English either. Each of the colonizing powers in North America stands guilty of making the natives into pawns in its rivalry with the others.

The feats of Spanish exploration in the century following the discovery of the New World are as astounding today as they were at the time. Even though educated Europeans in 1492 generally acknowledged that the world was round, there certainly were sailors in Columbus's crew who held a genuine fear of being lost in the vastness of the Ocean Sea. From that point in darkness, Spanish explorers of the Caribbean and the Gulf opened the way for a vital commerce, the likes of which the world had never seen. The ships of this trade left Spain on the course Columbus had established. Following the prevailing wind and current, they usually sailed in convoy to enter the Caribbean through the Dominica or Martinique passage. The fleet then split. Vessels bound for Tierra Firme sailed southwest to sight the South American coast just west of Trinidad and from there west to the ports of Cartagena, Santa Marta, and Portobelo. Those bound for New Spain sailed west along the Greater Antilles to the Yucatán Channel and from there into the Gulf of Mexico with the Caribbean Current. On the return, the separate fleets rendezvoused at Havana. From here they sailed north together through the Bahama Channel with the Gulf Stream, the route Alaminos had pioneered in 1519 on the basis of his observations with Ponce de León in 1513. Under normal circumstances, they were able to utilize the prevailing wind and current on the entire round-trip voyage.[120] The early explorers had done their work well.

Spanish explorers had first accepted, then questioned, Columbus's belief that his island discoveries were the fringes of Asia. Through constant probing, they established that a new continent barred the way to the Asiatic mainland and that another ocean lay beyond this continental barrier.

From these discoveries sprang the search for a sea-level passage connecting the North Sea with the South (the Atlantic with the Pacific). The quest, begun with firm conviction, wavered as the possibilities waned, then ended with the certainty that no such passage existed south of Florida.

Almost from the moment of the discovery of the New World, Hispaniola was the focus of Spanish activity in the so-called Indies—the supply base, the way-port for fleets sailing for more distant destinations, the springboard for voyages to the unknown. That it did not remain so was due to the continuing discoveries that advanced the frontiers of geographical knowledge and created new demands. Cuba, after its conquest, came to the fore as the staging area for explorations into the Gulf of Mexico. With the Mexican Conquest and the establishment of the new sailing route to Spain, Havana's importance mounted as the gathering place and provisioning point for the homeward-bound fleets from Mexico and Tierra Firme. The Cuban capital, though regarded as the key to the New World and the bulwark of the West Indies, basked in a reflected glory cast by the greater discoveries across the Caribbean Sea, the Gulf of Mexico, and the Straits of Florida.

In the continuing exploration of the New World, the Spaniards had four basic motivations: scientific, military, economic, and religious. All operated to greater or lesser degree from the first discovery, often in combination. Not until the Enlightenment of the late eighteenth century did purely scientific expeditions come to prominence. Yet hardly any exploratory endeavor was devoid of scientific concerns, for science figured in both economic and defensive (or military) considerations and often in religious *entradas* as well. The key to conquest and settlement of a given territory was the goal expressed in the phrase that appears so often in the *capitulaciónes* and *informes* that passed between the Crown and the explorer: "To know its secrets."

5 / *Hacia el Norte!* The Spanish *Entrada* into North America, 1513–1549

DENNIS REINHARTZ AND OAKAH L. JONES

Herbert Eugene Bolton once wrote, "Exploration was a necessary antecedent to the colonization, exploitation, and social development of any part of the New World."[1] Thus, Columbus and the explorers who followed opened an entire "New World" with its geographical features, climates, and diversified peoples. America was the "gift of Spain" largely because the initial discovery was followed by a "brilliant era of exploration on sea and land" that led to colonization and permanent settlement.[2] This presentation of Spain's "gift" of America to the world was initiated with the Columbian voyages of discovery and exploration between 1492 and 1504. Although Columbus, on his four voyages of discovery, failed to make a North American landfall, his explorations of the Caribbean and Middle American regions led to the establishment of the India House of Trade (Casa de Contratación), centered in Seville and Cádiz, which together with the Council of the Indies, created in 1511, was in charge of Spanish America. The Casa and the Council not only directed Spanish exploration and settlement in the New World but also functioned as a collation center and clearinghouse for information about the Americas and the "Indies."[3] As Charles F. Lummis observed, "The honor of giving America to the world belongs to Spain—the credit not only of discovery, but centuries of such pioneering as no other nation ever paralleled in any land."[4]

Motives and capacities for exploration and settlement came together in this age of exploration, which began in the fifteenth and sixteenth centuries and continued for nearly 350 years. There were many motives for individual explorations and the establishment of the first European colonies in the Americas: missionary zeal; the expansion of national power and prestige; searches for mythical kingdoms, advanced Native American civilizations, and the secret Straits of Anián or some other geographical feature that would provide a shorter and easier route from Europe to Asia; individual and national drives for economic gain and control of trade; curiosity and adventure; the search for slave labor; acquisitiveness; and defense against other rival nations as well as hostile native peoples of America.[5] Yet, motives alone do not explain the age of exploration, since by themselves they could not have been effective unless the individuals and nations conducting the explorations had the capacities to carry out the expeditions.

Developments and conditions in the late Middle Ages enabled Spain and Portugal to take the lead. Both nations had achieved degrees of national, monarchical unity earlier than the rest of Europe. Both embraced the theory of mercantilism in which trade was emphasized and colonies were believed important for the benefit of the mother country. Although neither Spain nor Portugal could financially support proposed explorations at the beginning of the Age of Discovery, money was available in private hands, and a new middle class arose to provide such necessary assistance. Still the monarchs maintained control of these expeditions by approving and authorizing each one while regulating the conditions of settlement and jurisdictions. Also, improvements in navigation and in the construction of oceangoing vessels had occurred by the fifteenth century. The compass, the lateen-rigging of sails enabling ships to sail into the wind, and changes in ship design were only a few of the major developments, along with the preparation of the first simplistic charts and maps.[6] An expanded interest and knowledge in the world outside of Europe, made possible partly by the first printing presses and the reawakening of ideas from classical times, likewise contributed to the burst of exploratory activity. Finally, the geographical location of Spain and Portugal, accompanied by the end of internal strife within the Iberian Peninsula, aided the exploration. Thus the final defeat of the Moslems at Granada, in January 1492, enabled King Ferdinand and Queen Isabella to concentrate on America, which became a logical extension of the seven-century Reconquista in Spain.

All of these motives and capacities were present, singularly and collectively, in Spanish expansion northward after the initial explorations and settlements of the Greater Antilles (Española [Hispaniola], Cuba, Puerto Rico, and Jamaica) and the conquest of the Aztec confederation by Hernán Cortés in the period from 1492 to 1522. Franciscan and Jesuit missionaries accompanied explorers on expeditions from Florida to California. In the sixteenth century, Spaniards sought such mythical kingdoms and indigenous civilizations as Biminí, Apalache, Chicora, the Seven Cities of Cíbola, Gran Quivira, and later the "Great Kingdom of the Tejas,"[7] among others. They also sought the mythical short route to the Orient and the riches of Cathay and Cipango, perpetuated in early European cartography of North America; indeed, one legendary or theoretical geographical feature, the "Straits of Anián" connecting the Atlantic and the Pacific through the midsection of the continent, persisted as a goal of explorers well into the eighteenth century. Defensive exploration and expansion occurred against the threats of American Indian groups—and French, Russian, and British threats from La Florida (the present-day southeastern United States) to Alta California (today's California), as well as the northwestern coast of North America. In fact, the areas of modern-day Texas and California, explored early but not occupied until the eighteenth century, were largely annexed to the Spanish Empire for defensive reasons.

Furthermore, the explorations and eventual settlements of northern New Spain and La Florida occurred because capacities coincided with motivations. Spanish authorities—the Hapsburg kings, viceroys of New Spain after 1535, and governors and captains-general in the Caribbean Islands—provided permission and outlined privileges and conditions to individual explorers through licenses known as *capitulaciónes*. Explorers, almost universally known in the sixteenth century as *adelantados* (literally, "those who went before"), undertook exploration and sometimes settlement of their assigned regions largely through private funding, with finances raised by themselves or with funds supplied by backers. The king and his royal treasury contributed little or nothing financially except in two expeditions to La Florida (Tristán de Luna y Arellano and Pedro Menéndez de Avilés). In fact, the king or his designated representative in the Americas could deny permission for exploration and settlement. Furthermore, an explorer's *capitulación* specifically stated that the expeditions would be made at limited or no cost to the Crown, a provision well understood by *adelantados*. They were responsible not only for financial backing but also for recruitment of the companies composing the expedition, for supplies, for provisions, and for weapons and munitions. Early Spanish exploratory expeditions in North America abided by these terms as explorers raised funds privately and secured the necessary royal permission to undertake their voyages and overland expeditions. Not until the time of the eighteenth-century Spanish Bourbon kings did the monarchs supply considerable financial and provisioning assistance to explorers and colonizers.

Ships for seafaring expeditions came largely from the Caribbean Islands, Spain, or, for Pacific explorations, the western coast of New Spain. Vessels from Spain were used for the early maritime ventures to and along the Atlantic coast. Land expeditions in northern New Spain were equipped with men and provisions largely obtained in Mexico City or from local resources in places already occupied by Spain in its expansion northward. By modern standards Spanish expeditions were small and carried limited amounts of provisions. Usually the entire complement amounted to one hundred to three hundred men, with horses, cattle, sheep, goats, and foodstuffs provided for only a limited duration; these ventures often had to live off the land and its Native American inhabitants before they returned to their points of origin. Obtaining food from the Indians, sometimes by force, often exacerbated unfriendly relations or caused them from the outset. Although some of these explorations were intended for both discovery and settlement, generally they were temporary in nature, and exploration was to be followed by colonization enterprises. In the southeastern part of the present-day United States, for example, at least five exploratory expeditions and temporary settlements were attempted before permanent occupation occurred in Florida in 1565. Similarly, Francisco Vázquez de Coronado and other explorers preceded by more than a half century the colonization of New Mexico in 1598, the first occupation of the northernmost frontier of New Spain.

The Initial Period of Spanish Exploration in North America

Spanish exploration of the Americas, beginning with the first voyage of Columbus, was continuous over the course of three centuries, and North American exploration, beginning in 1513 for La Florida and in the 1520s for northern New Spain, was an important component of Spain's reaching out to the world. As the historian J. H. Parry has pointed out, the main interest of discoverers was not discovery for its own sake but a European link with other areas known or believed to be of economic importance.[8] Whereas the discoveries of Columbus caused a "reorientation of world knowledge" that accelerated in the subsequent centuries of exploration,[9] Ralph H. Vigil has explained that Spanish exploration and conquest should be considered as the "dramatic prologue to the more prosaic work of settlement and possession." Indeed, according to Vigil, bands of "conquistador-explorers" soon advanced northward from the islands of the Caribbean and Mexico City. They were led by their curiosity for the "northern mystery," tall tales, the

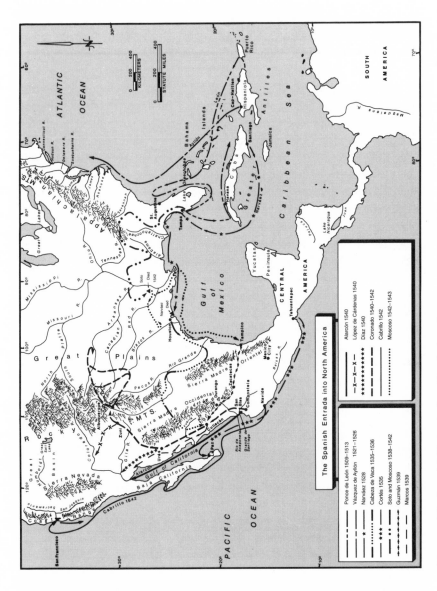

Map 5.1 The Spanish Entrada into North America.

search for rich and exotic civilizations, and a quest to find the mythical Straits of Anián.[10] This interest in and preoccupation with exploration and with expansion of Spain's sovereignty in the Americas ultimately led Spain into the Florida peninsula first, then to the remaining portions of La Florida, and finally to the northern extremities of New Spain. The "European presence in the United States," wrote Vigil, "thus begins in the Spanish Borderlands."[11]

Spanish exploration and eventual settlement of North America followed two distinct geographical routes: the expansion from the Caribbean Islands to the Florida peninsula, Guale (Georgia), the Carolina coast, and briefly to Chesapeake Bay; and the advance of the frontier northward from Mexico City into the northern kingdoms and provinces of New Spain. These two thrusts, though often considered separately, in reality sometimes overlapped, causing jurisdictional disputes and individual rivalries. Furthermore, any study of the expeditions of explorers such as Alonso Alvarez de Pineda, Alvar Núñez Cabeza de Vaca, Hernando de Soto, and Coronado reveals that they encompassed vast areas, sometimes including the Southeast with northern New Spain and the Southwest. Yet, in spite of all Spanish efforts, the gap between the Southeast and the Southwest was never effectively closed, and the Gulf coastal region remained a target for other Europeans to intervene and to challenge Spain.

Chronological examination of Spanish penetration of North America necessarily begins with expeditions to the Florida peninsula, the Gulf coast, and the Atlantic coast, along with advances into the interior of the present-day southeastern United States. While some of these ventures originated in Spain, others sailed from the Caribbean islands of Española, Cuba, Puerto Rico, and Jamaica. All had licenses from the king or other royal authorities. Most of them were largely privately financed, and their forces penetrated into initially uncharted seas and unmapped land areas. With each succeeding expedition, knowledge of geographical features and indigenous cultures expanded in this first region of the Spanish Borderlands.

Whether one stands at the monastery of La Rábida near the mouth of the Río Tinto in Spain, where Columbus first developed his plan to sail westward in search of the Indies, or faces northward from San Juan, Puerto Rico, where Juan Ponce de León set sail for unknown lands twenty-one years later, the enormity and uncertainty faced with courage by early explorers may well be visualized. As D. W. Meinig has observed: "Geography and history are not only analogous, but complementary and interdependent."[12] An appreciation of geography enables historians to understand better the conditions under which exploration occurred. Meinig also noted that we must begin a study of exploration in Europe "because it was Europeans who reached across the Atlantic and initiated the radical reshaping of America."[13] The historical process of exploration, conquest, and settlement of the Americas that Columbus unknowingly initiated on that August day of 1492 brought two civilizations—European and Native American—into close contact and conflict, changing both cultures forever. Thus exploration should not be viewed in an abstract way but in human terms involving both the explorers and those whom they encountered.

Spanish explorers of the present-day southeastern United States were motivated largely by the search for mythical kingdoms and rich civilizations, as well as the quest to find a strait through the North American continent. In the early years of the sixteenth century, geographical knowledge of North America was so incomplete as to allow Spanish explorers to imagine almost any kind of geographical configuration that would allow the fulfillment of the European objective of a short route to the Orient; this was, after all, the primary motivating factor behind the voyages of Columbus and most other early explorers. Religious objectives to convert the Native Americans to Christianity and to westernize them were added later, as was the motive of territorial defense—a major factor after the permanent colonization of Florida later in the sixteenth century.

Between 1513 and 1549, more than half a dozen individual exploratory expeditions and attempts to settle were made in this vast region between the Mississippi River and the Atlantic coast, concentrating on the coast of the present-day state of South Carolina and the peninsula of Florida. While a few of these expeditions originated in Spain, most of them began in the islands of the Greater Antilles. Even those begun in Spain usually made intermediate stops at Española, Cuba, or Puerto Rico en route to their final exploratory destinations. Thus the Gulf of Mexico, known in the early sixteenth century as "The Spanish Sea," became what Robert Weddle has called "the theater for the earliest and most determined efforts to conquer the natives and explore and settle the interior."[14]

Juan Ponce de León formally opened the history of the Spanish Borderlands frontier.[15] As Columbus was to the discovery of America, Ponce de León was to the discovery of North America. Both initiated a period of exploration that ranged far beyond the original regions of their voyages and extended over many years following their initial voyages. Born in Valladolid, Spain, in 1460, of noble parents, Ponce de León sailed with Columbus on the second voyage in 1493 to Española. There he settled ultimately at the village of Higüey on the island's eastern end. In 1509, with the permission of royal authorities and at his own expense, he departed with an expedition to Boriquén (Puerto Rico) to conquer and settle that island. He was attracted by rumors of gold and did succeed in finding placers (surface deposits) in sufficient quantity to become the basis for his wealth. Appointed governor of Puerto Rico, he was subsequently removed from that office in 1512 but had already heard from an Indian about a legendary river, called Biminí, whose waters would restore one's youth. He then sought and obtained a royal license or contract on 23 February 1512, giving him the right to equip ships at his own cost and to discover and settle the "island of Biminy." Nothing was said in the contract or thereafter during and after the voyage of a "Fountain of Youth," but that term has been deeply implanted and forever associated with Ponce de León.[16] Although his goal seems to have been to find a river of this description and to make new discoveries, Ponce de León's primary goal, according to Bartolomé de Las Casas (the sixteenth-century "Protector of the American Indians"), was to obtain slaves.[17]

Ponce de León's expedition sailed from Puerto Rico on 4 March 1513, with three ships. Headed by chief pilot Antón de Alaminos, a native of Palos in Spain, the vessels proceeded northward through the Mona Passage to the Bahama Islands, landing at San Salvador and the Great Abaco Islands. Then the thirty-nine-year-old Ponce de León and his followers departed from the Bahamas, sailing westward. On 2 April the expedition sighted the Florida coast near the later establishment of San Agustín. Here Ponce de León named the new land "La Florida" (a term that would shortly be attached to the entire southeastern portion of the landmass north of the Caribbean and the Gulf), commemorating the Easter festival Pascua Florida or Pascua de Flores, which had occurred on 27 March. He also observed that Florida was an island, like those of the Bahamas he had already visited.[18]

The expedition then turned southward along the Atlantic coast of Florida and rounded the tip of the peninsula on 8 May, thereafter proceeding through the Florida Keys (which he called "Los Martires") and then northward up the western coast of Florida. The explorers landed again, probably at modern-day Ponce de León Bay south of Charlotte Harbor, and then returned to Puerto Rico on 21 August via the tip of the peninsula, the eastern coast of Florida, and the Bahama Islands.[19]

Ponce de León's voyage of five and one-half months failed to achieve its principal objective, but it succeeded in finding new lands and encountering the first American Indians north of the Greater Antilles. The expedition's leader seems to have made no attempt to settle either the Bahama Islands or La Florida. Yet, he was a pathfinder, and the geographical knowledge he gained was valuable to future explorers. However, his erroneous belief that Florida was an island persisted for several years.

This geographical misconception was exploded six years later with the exploratory voyage of Alonso Alvarez de Pineda. His expedition was organized, financed, and dispatched by Francisco de Garay of Jamaica. Garay, like Ponce de León, arrived in Española on Columbus's second voyage of 1493. As a settler there, he favored the interests of Columbus's son Diego Colón, became involved in stock raising and gold mining at Minas Nuevas outside the city of Santo Domingo, and held various public offices until he was appointed governor of Jamaica in 1514. Three years later he obtained permission to provision ships to search for a strait that the Spaniards felt would, in foreign control, be a threat to their domains elsewhere in North America. However, there is no account of a voyage sent out for this purpose by Garay thereafter.[20]

Still interested in a voyage of discovery in 1519, Garay instead sent out an expedition of four ships commanded by Alvarez de Pineda. It sailed by the end of March 1519, probably from the port of Sevilla on the northern coast of Jamaica. It proceeded through the Yucatán Channel to the western end of the tip of Florida, then continued eastward to the tip of the peninsula before doubling back to follow the Gulf coastline of Florida. Alvarez de Pineda and his ships explored westward and reached the mouth of what is today known as the Mississippi River on 2 June 1519, the feast of Espíritu Santo. He named the river that he had discovered the "Río del Espíritu Santo." The expedition continued westward along the Texas coast, sailed past the mouth of the Rio Grande, and then turned southward to the Río Pánuco in New Spain. After an encounter with the expedition of Hernán Cortés near Veracruz, Alvarez de Pineda returned to the Río Pánuco in late July or early August. The ships remained there for forty days before returning to Jamaica, but Alvarez de Pineda evidently chose to stay in the settlement at Pánuco, remaining there until his death during an attack by Huastecan Indians.[21]

Alvarez de Pineda's explorations and discoveries have often been overlooked by historians, some of whom claim that Hernando de Soto discovered the Mississippi River. It is clearly evident that Alvarez de Pineda discovered the river near its mouth and gave it the first name of Río del Espíritu Santo. Furthermore, from present-day Ponce de León Bay in Florida to Cabo Rojo in the modern-day Mexican state of Veracruz, he was the first European to see the entire shoreline of the Gulf of Mexico. His expedition also proved that the Florida peninsula (which he called "Amichel") was not an island as Ponce de León claimed. Finally, Alvarez de Pineda and his pilots produced reports and the first known map of the Gulf of Mexico, showing in a rudimentary but recognizable fashion the shoreline from the peninsula of Florida to the northeastern part of New Spain.[22] Both the reports and the map were transmitted back to Spain, and the level of Spanish geographical understanding of North America was increased enormously by Alvarez de Pineda's voyage.

Two years later Ponce de León embarked on his second voyage to Florida. Having obtained a contract in 1514, soon after his return from his first expedition, to occupy and govern the islands of Biminí and Florida,[23] he was delayed until 1521, when the venture finally got under way. Records of this second voyage are scanty, but it is apparent that its two ships sailed from Puerto Rico on 26 February. They carried some two hundred men, including friars and a priest, fifty horses, cattle, and other livestock; evidently the intention was to settle somewhere in Florida. This the men did in the Everglades region, where they were soon engaged in warfare with the American Indians. With many of his followers killed and himself wounded, Ponce de León decided to give up his colonization effort. The ships and remaining men sailed to Havana, Cuba, arriving in July after five months in Florida. There Ponce de León died at the age of forty-seven.[24]

After the return of Alvarez de Pineda's ships to Jamaica, Governor Garay sent out a follow-up fleet of three ships and 240 men, commanded by Diego de Camargo, to evacuate survivors from the settlement at Pánuco, but instead of returning to Jamaica, this force sailed on to Veracruz, where they joined the army of Garay's hated rival Hernán Cortés. Determined to challenge Cortés for the control of New Spain, Garay himself as "adelantado of Amichel" sailed from Jamaica on 14 June 1523. His destination was not Florida but Pánuco. His formidable fleet consisted of eleven ships carrying 600 men (including 150 horsemen), among whom were Juan de Grijalva as captain of the fleet and nineteen-year-old Angel de Villafañe, who later replaced Tristán de Luna y Arellano as governor of La Florida. Stopping en route at the Cuban port of Jagua (today Cienfuegos), Garay refitted the expedition and decided to name his new colony in New Spain "Victoria Garayana." On 24 June this force sailed from Cuba, crossed the Gulf of Mexico, and landed on 25 July not at Pánuco but near a river Garay named the "Río de las Palmas," probably the Río Soto la Marina in the present-day state of Tamaulipas. He thought the region was too inhospitable for a settlement, but during his stay one of his exploratory parties succeeded in capturing and describing an armadillo. This creature, which subsequently died when taken aboard one of the ships, was described as "a quadruped a little larger than a cat, with the face of a wolf, silver colored, scaly, and caparisoned as the armed cuirasser going into battle caparisons his horse. A sluggish creature, it folded itself up like a hedgehog or a tortoise on seeing a man at a distance and allowed itself to be caught."[25] Garay then made a grueling march overland to Pánuco while Grijalva took the ships along the coast. Finding that Cortés had already conquered the region and established a settlement at Santiesteban del Puerto before returning to Mexico City, Garay, who had been ordered not to interfere with Cortés's territory, now went to Mexico City to negotiate with the conquistador for colonization rights on the Río de las Palmas. While there, he was taken ill and died three days later. His Río de las Palmas became the commonly accepted boundary between Amichel (Florida) and New Spain during the sixteenth century.[26]

Thus ended Garay's involvement with exploration and attempted colonization, but not long afterward renewed efforts to explore and settle La Florida and the Atlantic coast of North America would be made. In 1524 Esteban Gómez, the Portuguese pilot from the voyage of Ferdinand Magellan, offered King Charles I of Spain the opportunity to find a better route to the Indies by searching for a strait through the North American continent. His ten-month voyage departed from La Coruña, Spain, in the early part of the year, reached the shores of North America north of La Florida, and then proceeded northward along the Atlantic coast past Cape May, the lower bay of New York, the mouth of the Hudson River, and Narragansett Bay before reaching Cape Cod. Having found neither the desired strait nor any prospect of wealth, Gómez sailed back to La Coruña, taking with him some Algonquin Indians of both sexes, presumably to sell as slaves. King Charles ordered the release of the Indians, but not before their presence in Spain caused the rumor that Gómez had discovered the Spice Islands. Apparently word had spread that Gómez had returned with a cargo of precious stones and *clavos* (cloves). Someone, in reading or hearing of the Gómez voyage, had missed the first syllable of *esclavos* (slaves). Reports of a possible contact with the Spice Islands notwithstanding, the Gómez voyage, the only such exploration paid for by the Spanish Crown, did not result in follow-up expeditions.[27] It did, however, provide European cartographers with additional information on the Atlantic coast of North America.

The early practice of searching the Bahama Islands and La Florida for Native American slaves undoubtedly contributed to the first hostilities between Europeans and indigenous peoples. It also hindered rather than helped the permanent Spanish settlement of the Southeast for decades to come. With the rapid decline of the native population (mostly Arawaks and Caribs) of Española, Cuba, Puerto Rico, and Jamaica, a critical shortage of labor developed. Spaniards resorted to two solutions to this problem: the legal importation of black slaves from Africa; and the illegal taking of Native American slaves from the islands of the Lesser Antilles and the Bahamas, the northern coast of South America and the eastern one of Central America, and the mainland of North America. Indeed, Bartolomé de las Casas may have been accurate in his observation that Ponce de León sought slaves on his expedition of 1513. This may have been the reason for the explorer's clash with the Timucuas soon after his initial landing in Florida.

The most prominent slave hunter by the early 1520s was Lucas Vázquez de Ayllón. An *oidor* (hearer or judge) of the Audiencia of Santo Domingo, Vázquez de Ayllón became the owner of a prosperous sugar operation at Puerto Plata on the northern shore of Española. This town was the center of slave-hunting enterprises to the Bahama Islands. Probably because of the labor shortage on the island and especially the demand for workers in his sugar business, Vázquez de Ayllón became a partner in the dispatch of a small ship under the command of Francisco Gordillo in 1521 to explore the islands and mainland and to search for slaves.[28] The expedition landed on the mainland at about 32° north and named the district "Chicora." Successful in taking American Indians captive, the sailors then returned to Puerto Plata.[29]

Among the captives was a young Native American to whom Vázquez de Ayllón was especially attracted. Apparently a member of the Spaniard's household (perhaps as a personal servant), he learned Spanish, was baptized, and became known as Francisco Chicora. Vázquez de Ayllón was captivated by the tall tales related by Francisco about giant kings and queens, wealth, and hospitable conditions in Chicora. Seeing a golden opportunity to carve out a territory for himself on the mainland of North America and probably at the same time ensure a constant supply of cheap labor for his interests at Puerto Plata, Vázquez de Ayllón departed for

Spain. He took Francisco with him so that they both might convince the king that this discovery of a fertile land with amicable indigenous peoples would be suitable for settlement. In Spain, Francisco fascinated many of his listeners—among whom was the influential Peter Martyr—with his tales of tribes ruled by peaceful giant kings and queens, the report of one tribe of native people with tails as thick as an arm and as long as a palm's span, and stories indicating the potential for wealth and profit.[30] In Martyr's account of Vázquez de Ayllón's speculations, the land of Chicora lay in the same latitudes as the province of Andalucia in Spain and was, therefore, quite probably a rich and fertile region. It also was, in Martyr's view, connected with the cod fisheries to the north (Newfoundland and Labrador), first discovered by John Cabot in 1497 and appearing on contemporary maps since that time.[31]

As a result of these accounts, the king issued a royal contract in June 1523, granting Vázquez de Ayllón permission to explore and settle Chicora while providing religious instruction in the Christian doctrine to the natives there. As usual, the venture was to be undertaken at his own expense. Both Vázquez de Ayllón and Francisco returned thereafter to organize, recruit, and provision an exploratory and colonization effort in the assigned territory on the mainland.[32] As a first step, Vázquez de Ayllón dispatched an expedition from Española in 1525, commanded by Captain Pedro de Quejo, who had been with the Gordillo expedition in 1521. Quejo undertook a rapid but nonetheless careful coastal reconnaissance of the area between Florida and Delaware Bay, the first such by the Spanish. Taking bearings and soundings along the coast, he also erected crosses periodically, claiming the area for Holy Roman Emperor Charles V and Spain. Quejo's accounts were not enthusiastic, reporting the discovery of little more than "barrier islands with sand dunes and pine barrens along a sparsely settled coast [that] failed to suggest a Mediterranean-like new Andalucia."[33] They were enough, however, to prompt Vázquez de Ayllón to recruit and supply his own expedition of exploration and, hopefully, colonization. The Quejo accounts also worked their way into European cartography via the 1526 map of Juan Vespucci, along with the reports of Vázquez de Ayllón's expedition and others.

The major expedition of this period, commanded by Vázquez de Ayllón and with Francisco accompanying, sailed from Puerto Plata in mid-July 1526. It consisted of six ships, five hundred to six hundred men including three Dominican friars, eighty-nine horses, and provisions for the initial settlement.[34] This force landed below the mouth of a river that the men called the "Jordan," on the coast of today's South Carolina, but Vázquez de Ayllón's flagship ran aground and was lost with most of the food supply and equipment.[35] Francisco deserted soon after landing, and Vázquez de Ayllón found the site to be too sandy and swampy for a suitable settlement.[36] Reembarking his men on the remaining ships, a disappointed Vázquez de Ayllón departed from this site and sailed southward to the Río Gualdape in the province of Guale, named for the Muskogean Indian word meaning "southern," in present-day Georgia. There he planted his settlement of San Miguel de Gualdape on or south of the site of today's city of Savannah. However, from its beginnings until abandonment, the community was strife-torn, disease-ridden, and short of food and provisions. Dissensions among the men, hostility toward Vázquez de Ayllón for his weak leadership and lack of resolve, and distrust led to murders and the flight of some of the expedition's members from the colony. Although Vázquez de Ayllón did provide knowledge of the South Carolina and Georgia coasts, along with descriptions of the flora, fauna, and American Indians of the region for the information of later Spanish explorers and colonizers, he proved to be a poor leader of an exploratory-colonizing expedition. He was essentially a bureaucrat and an entrepreneur, not an effective explorer and colonizer. On 18 October 1526, Vázquez de Ayllón died of a fever, and soon afterward the 150 or so remaining sick and starving colonists abandoned Gualdape, returning to Santo Domingo.[37]

By the time of his death, Spanish knowledge of the lands and peoples of North America was still in an unformed state, although the results of the voyages of both Gómez and Vázquez de Ayllón quickly appeared in various European sources of geographical information on the New World. Peter Martyr included extensive data on Spanish activities (particularly those of Vázquez de Ayllón) in the posthumously published edition of his *Decades of the New World* (1516). The results of Vázquez de Ayllón's cycle of explorations also appeared on many European maps, particularly those derived from the work of Diogo Ribeiro, the Portuguese cartographer employed by the House of Trade in Seville to produce the Spanish standard map of North America.[38] Ribeiro's work became the basis for contemporary Spanish cartography of the Atlantic coast of North America, and even the noted 1534 map of the Italian cartographer Giovanni Battista Ramusio contained a province of "Ailon," just north of Florida, and the name "Gomez," inserted near what was probably an early representation of the Penobscot River in present-day Maine. Still, this cartography was crude

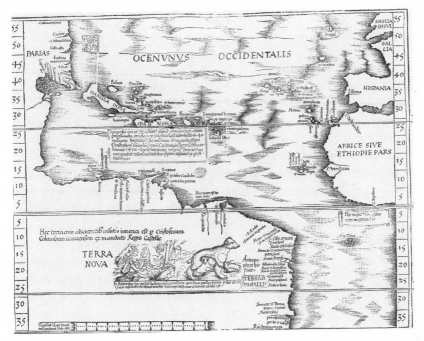

5.1 "Tabula Terra Nova" (Martin Waldseemüller, 1525). This map illustrates the European view of North America before the entradas of the 1540s. On this edition of the map, the bear vignette covers up some of the empty space of the unknown. Courtesy Special Collections Division, The University of Texas at Arlington Libraries, Arlington TX.

and inconclusive, and Alvarez de Pineda's accounts of the Gulf of Mexico region remained the most reliable Spanish geographical data available on North America. Within a period of less than twenty years, however, this situation would change dramatically.

The Prelude to the Great *Entradas*

In the same year as Alvarez de Pineda's epochal voyage from Florida to northeastern Mexico, one of Spain's greatest conquistadores began to establish control over another major part of the periphery of North America. Although Spanish control over Mexico was not consolidated until the 1540s, Hernán Cortés's amazing conquest of the Aztec Empire in 1519–21 and the founding of Mexico City at the heart of what he named New Spain soon provided Spain with a major staging point for the exploration of North America. Born in Medellín, in the harsh and barren Estremadura province of Spain, which was the homeland of so many of Spain's New World adventurers, Cortés was one of Spain's most ambitious, courageous, and flamboyant conquistadores. Perhaps better than any other single man in the New World, he embodied the motivations that initiated the exploration of the north in the two decades following his triumphs in Mexico and Central America in 1524–26. Cortés's ambition and curiosity brought him to the Americas to find fortune and glory for himself, his king, and his God. In addition to appropriating a substantial part of the wealth of the Aztecs, Cortés sought to establish a proprietary empire for himself in Mexico and to evangelize its native peoples.

But soon after the subjugation of these new lands and peoples, Cortés's powerful and equally ambitious rivals began to severely undermine his authority. While Cortés perhaps dreamed of becoming emperor of Mexico, he realistically settled for an appointment as governor and captain-general of New Spain in 1522. Yet, by 1526 his enemies succeeded in having him ousted from the governorship. Oddly enough, it was the conflict between Cortés and his rivals that, at least in part, stimulated one of the greatest of the sixteenth-century Spanish explorations as Spanish interest shifted from the Atlantic coast to the previously explored Gulf coast, nearer the contested territory of Cortés and his competitors.

The initial task of continuing exploration of the Gulf coast was assigned to Pánfilo de Narváez, who was no newcomer to the New World. In 1519, he had been sent by Governor Diego Velázquez de Cuéllar from Cuba with eight hundred men to arrest Cortés, but he was instead defeated by Cortés near Veracruz. Narváez lost an eye and was arrested, and his force was co-opted for the conquest of Mexico by Cortés. In 1527, however, Narváez rebounded from this defeat and was appointed the *adelantado* (governor) of Florida, Río de las Palmas, and Río del Espíritu Santo. His commission was to explore and colonize these new domains. Spanning the years 1527–36, the expedition of Pánfilo de Narváez and its continuation by four of its survivors—Alvar Núñez Cabeza de Vaca, Captain Andrés Dorantes de Carranza, Captain Alonso del Castillo Maldonado, and the blackamoor servant Estebanico—covered a vast area from the Gulf coast of La Florida to Sinaloa in New Spain. Cabeza de Vaca's later publication of his account of both the voyage of Narváez and his own later experiences in present-day Texas and northern New Spain provided perhaps the fullest details available on any Spanish exploration of North America before 1540. Although it is the report of only one participant, its value as a primary source is unparalleled for the study of Spain's early explorations in North America. Historian Frederick W. Hodge has pointed out, "In some respects the journey of Alvar Núñez Cabeza de Vaca and his three companions overland from coast to coast during the eight years from 1528 to 1536 is the most remarkable in the record of American exploration."[39]

The Incredible Journey of Cabeza de Vaca

Cabeza de Vaca was born in 1490 in Jérez de la Frontera near Cádiz; in 1527 he was appointed the royal treasurer to the Narváez expedition and was named second-in-command.[40] Given the lack of abundant and precise records, the exact routes of the Narváez expedition (as well as of the *entradas* of Coronado and Soto) and its survivors are not known. North America was slowly revealing itself to be unimaginably vast, alien, and hostile, even more so than the Indies, Central America, or Mexico, and the conquistadores were, after all, soldiers more interested in fortune and glory than geography. What is known is that the Narváez expedition sailed from Sanlúcar de Barrameda at the mouth of the Río Guadalquivir in Spain, on 17 June 1527, "to conquer and govern the provinces of the main[land], extending from the River Palmas to the Cape of Florida."[41] Putting together the expedition was probably particularly time-consuming because of the law of 17 November 1526 enacted by the Spanish Crown. To prevent the further depopulation of Cuba, Hispaniola, Jamaica, and Puerto Rico, it forbade the Spanish residents of these islands to participate directly in the conquest and colonization of the American continents, under penalty of death and confiscation of property. Hence, Narváez and others were required to recruit their colonists in Spain and elsewhere.[42]

After a forty-five-day passage across the Atlantic, the fleet arrived at Santo Domingo on the southern shore of Española. There 140 men elected to remain when Narváez sailed for Cuba. At Santiago de Cuba and later at Jagua (Cienfuegos) in February 1528, Narváez succeeded in recruiting some additional adventurers (including the pilot, Diego de Miruelo) and replenishments of food and equipment.[43] With four hundred people (including ten women) and eighty horses, Narváez sailed from Jagua on 22 February 1528.[44] After crossing the Gulf of Mexico in rough weather and having difficulty with shoals along the coastline, the expedition sighted

Florida on 7 April and landed in a shallow bay north of present-day Tampa Bay two days later. Two of the ships were wrecked during the landing, and sixty men lost their lives, but there remained a fleet of five ships, carrying the surviving colonists, their supplies, and horses.[45] A day after landing, Narváez and Cabeza de Vaca, leading six men, discovered Tampa Bay, having dispatched the ships along the coast to meet them there.[46]

Narváez was motivated primarily by the search for gold and for a passage to the Pacific Ocean. Having discovered some traces of the precious metal and learning from native peoples that it did not come from this region but from a distant northern place called "Apalachen" (Apalache),[47] he injudiciously split his forces, sending his ships north to find a bay allegedly known to his pilot, Diego de Miruelo; there Miruelo was to rendezvous with Narváez and the rest of the force (260 infantry and 40 horsemen), which would be traveling overland.[48] Narváez would never see Miruelo and the ships again, but the commander did lead his force, including two friars and three other clergymen, northward in anticipation of a meeting. Traveling through marshes, quicksand, and sloughs and in almost constant contact with the Indians, the army slogged forward, crossing the Suwannee River after forty-five days and reaching Apalache one week later, on 24 June. On this march north Narváez skirmished with the Indians and raided their villages for gold (which he did not find) and for food, guides, bearers, and hostages. Indian resistance increased, as did casualties among the expedition members and their horses; malaria broke out, later claiming Narváez himself; and the supplies to be found became more meager. After exploring inland until about 20 July, the expedition reversed its direction and sought the sea and the ships, finally reaching the upper part of Apalachee Bay near the Río de Magdalena (Ochlockonee River) in early August.[49]

But Narváez did not find ships, laden with much-needed supplies and waiting as he had expected. His fleet had sailed north as ordered, but after not finding Miruelo's bay, the ships again sailed south as far as Tampa Bay in search of signs of Narváez and his people. With still no report of Narváez, for a year the fleet searched the eastern coast of the Gulf of Mexico before finally giving up and sailing on to Pánuco in New Spain, also as ordered.[50] Meanwhile, Narváez's situation became desperate. His food supplies continued to diminish; his group was under regular attack from the Indians; more men became ill; and the possible desertion of the remaining horsemen became a real problem. The surrounding terrain and the presence of hostile natives made an overland exit all but impossible. So, the officers decided that what was left of the expedition should put to sea to search for their ships or to sail to New Spain if need be. Primitive open boats were constructed by forging armor, crossbow iron, spurs, and the like into tools and nails, which in turn were used to form and hold together an assortment of native materials. Gradually, the horses were killed for food, and their hair and hides, along with pieces of clothing, were used to make sails. For this reason the Spanish called the place Bahia de Caballos (Bay of Horses). Work on the ships commenced on 4 August and concluded on 20 September. The rest of the horses were then killed, and the neighboring Indian fields were raided one last time for food. With horsehide bags filled with water, five precariously crowded craft, carrying about 250 survivors, set sail for New Spain.[51]

The makeshift fleet sailed west along the coast, at first sheltered by barrier islands but constantly harassed by Indians. As the boats passed the Mississippi Delta, the discharge from the great river and a stiff north wind pushed them far out to sea and out of sight of land. By the time they reached land again a few days later, the boats were scattered some distance west of the Mississippi River, sighting each other only periodically. On 6 November, Cabeza de Vaca's boat wrecked on the beach of what the Spanish called Isla de Malhado (Island of Misfortune, probably either present-day Galveston Island or present-day Follet's Island west of Galveston Bay), where they were cautiously received by Indians. The next day Cabeza de Vaca and his followers were joined by the crew of the boat of Andrés Dorantes de Carranza and Alonso del Castillo Maldonado; their boat had washed ashore a day earlier on another part of the island. Among the crew was Dorantes's slave, Estebanico, a black from North Africa. Four men and an Indian companion then set out on foot toward the west in search of Pánuco, which they somehow believed not to be too distant. These survivors originally numbered about eighty, but by the following April only fourteen remained, the rest having fallen prey to starvation and disease. It was probably during this time that Cabeza de Vaca and others, due to their ministering to the sick and praying over the dying in Latin, began to establish reputations as medicine men among the Indians.[52]

While Cabeza de Vaca was away with some Indians foraging for oysters, twelve of the survivors left the island and began to march west along the coast toward Pánuco. On Matagorda Island they met the lone survivor of the four who had left to find Pánuco the previous November, and he told them of the fate of two more of Narváez's boats and of Narváez himself. According to survivors, the two boats had reached the Matagorda Bay area

probably in early November 1528, and Narváez, having decided to spend a
night on one of the boats with only two of his men while the rest slept
ashore, drifted out to sea in the boat and was never seen again. The rest
had died in the winter of 1528–29, often turning on each other and being reduced to cannibalism or being taken by Indians as slaves.[53]

The few others that now remained with Dorantes and Castillo soon
found themselves separated and enslaved. In this greatly reduced condition they were constantly taunted, tortured, and otherwise brutalized by
their Indian captors, who also often gave them only minimum amounts
of food. Eventually, Dorantes, Estebanico, and a few others escaped the
Karankawas on Matagorda, only to be reenslaved by other groups on the
mainland. Meanwhile, Cabeza de Vaca, who had been desperately ill, recovered; he escaped from a group of Indians who had taken him captive,
only to end up among the Charruco Indians in the Big Thicket area of
Texas. But he improved his lot by becoming a medicine man and a trader
for them. He had a good deal of freedom of movement, and for over three
years he bartered local goods such as shell knives and trinkets among distant tribes for flint arrowheads, arrowshafts, and skins. On his travels he
observed much, all the time yearning to escape to Pánuco, but he could not
persuade Lope de Oviedo, the one remaining Spanish captive on the Island of Misfortune, to go with him. Finally, however, Oviedo agreed to escape with Cabeza de Vaca, and they fled to another, crueler group of Indians, the Guevenes, who informed them of the sad fates that had befallen
several of their former cohorts. Some had died, some had simply been put
to death, and others had received brutal beatings, the nature of which the
Guevenes then demonstrated on Cabeza de Vaca and Oviedo. Oviedo escaped, deserted Cabeza de Vaca to head back to the island, and was never
heard of again.[54]

Now alone in his slavery, Cabeza de Vaca was reunited temporarily with
Dorantes in the fall of 1532 when several Indian bands came together to
gather pecans. The two men exchanged stories, Cabeza de Vaca for the first
time hearing of his commander's fate, and talked of escape. Eventually,
Castillo and Estebanico also were contacted and joined in the planning. In
1534 the four met again and made final plans when the Indians came together to harvest the tuna fruit of the prickly pear cactus. At this time,
Cabeza de Vaca also learned the fate of Narváez's fifth boat. It had wrecked
on the coast of one of the barrier islands south of the Río Grande, and its
crew had quickly been killed and stripped of their clothes and other possessions by Indians who displayed some of these trophies at the tuna gath-

ering. It was during this period that Cabeza de Vaca recorded the first European sighting of the North American bison or buffalo:

Cattle come as far as here. Three times I have seen them and eaten of their meat. I think they are about the size of those in Spain. They have small horns like the cows of Morocco; the hair is very long and flocky like the merino's. Some are tawny, others black. To my judgment the flesh is finer and fatter than that of this country [Spain]. Of the skins of those not full grown the Indians make blankets, and of the larger they make shoes and bucklers. They come as far as the seacoast of Florida, from a northerly direction, ranging through a tract of more than four hundred leagues; and throughout the whole region over which they run, the people who inhabit near, descend and live upon them, distributing a vast amount of hides into the interior country.[55]

Along with a few emeralds and some turquoise, one of the gifts Cabeza de Vaca brought from his adventures across North America to his king in Spain was a buffalo robe.[56]

In September 1534 Cabeza de Vaca, Castillo, Dorantes, and Estebanico finally escaped from their Indian captors to begin their long journey to New Spain. For the best part of the next two years they moved southwest along the coastal plains of Texas from encampment to encampment and tribe to tribe in the general direction of Mexico. They functioned principally as shamans, healers, and traders, living like their Indian companions. As Cabeza de Vaca related, they were often naked and had only the sometimes very meager Indian fare to sustain them. Even their native tongue grew unfamiliar to them. And on occasion they were again reduced to states of semi-slavery. Yet, despite the adverse conditions often suffered by Cabeza de Vaca and his companions during this leg of their odyssey, he continued to take note of and marvel at his surroundings along the way. Of special interest were the Indians and their unusual customs.

Their method of cooking is so new, that for its strangeness I desire to speak of it; thus it may be seen and remarked how curious and diversified are the contrivances and ingenuity of the human family. Not having discovered the use of pigskins, to boil what they would eat, they fill the half of a large calabash with water, and throw on the fire many stones of such as are most convenient and readily take the heat. When hot, they are taken up with tongs of sticks and dropped into the calabash until the water in it boils from the fervor of the stones. Then whatever is to be cooked is put in, and until it is done they continue taking out cooled stones and throwing in hot ones. Thus they boil their food.[57]

This and the numerous other descriptions of Indian ways by Cabeza de Vaca demonstrated that he developed a realistic attitude toward the possibility of more cordial and cooperative European-Indian relations. He came to believe that the two peoples could work and live together if both were adaptable and if the Europeans took the time to understand Indian values. To him, the Indians were not inferior or childlike; rather, they were human beings who had followed a different course of development. They had intelligence, aspirations, motivations, and emotions similar to those of the Spaniards. Cabeza de Vaca clearly reflected this belief, for example, in his account of life and death among the Indians he met on the island of Malhado:

Those people love their offspring the most of any in the world, and treat them with the greatest mildness. When it occurs that a son dies, the parents and kindred weep as does every body; the wailing continuing for him a whole year. They begin before dawn every day, the parents first and after them the whole town. They do the same at noon and at sunset. After a year of mourning has passed, the rites of the dead are performed; then they wash and purify themselves from the stain of smoke. They lament all the deceased in this manner, except the aged, for whom they show no regret, as they say that their season has passed, they having no enjoyment, and that living they would occupy the earth and take ailment from the young. Their custom is to bury the dead, unless it be those among them who have been physicians. These they burn. While the fire kindles they are all dancing and making high festivity, until the bones become powder. After the lapse of a year the funeral honors are celebrated, every one taking part in them, when the dust is presented in water for relatives to drink.[58]

Cabeza de Vaca's attitude toward the Indians was similar to that of Las Casas; it was a minority point of view, opposed to that of Narváez, Soto, and others throughout the early history of European-Indian contact.

Eventually, to avoid more hostile Indians, the four travelers decided to leave the coastal plains behind and turn inland. They also hoped to find better support in the more heavily populated interior and to formulate a better conception of the land in its totality. After traversing what is now southern Texas, they crossed the Río Grande and then the Sierra Madre Occidental. Emaciated, burned by the sun, and hardly recognizable in their looks or their language as Spanish, in April 1536 the four castaways were finally rescued when they were picked up by one of Governor Nuño Beltrán de Guzmán's slaving parties near the Río Yaqui to the north of Culiacán.[59]

After eight years of wandering and then being entertained in San Miguel by its mayor, Melchior Díaz, and in Compostela by Governor Guzmán, the four finally reached Mexico City, Viceroy Antonio de Mendoza, and Cortés on 24 July 1536. There Cabeza de Vaca and Dorantes jointly recorded an account, with maps, of the Narváez expedition and its survivors, but it was subsequently lost. Cabeza de Vaca returned to Spain and was welcomed at the court of Emperor Charles V in the autumn of 1537. Thereafter, Cabeza de Vaca wrote his own *relación* of his wondrous journey; addressed to Charles V, it was first published at Zamora in 1542.[60] In this document, Cabeza de Vaca presented an accurate picture of the vast barrenness of the lands he crossed, and he was perhaps the first to gain some appreciation of the continent's true size. These were lands devoid of the wealth of the Aztecs and Incas and populated by often savage Indians. Although he may not always have understood what he observed of these peoples, he recorded his encounters accurately and dispassionately. According to Woodbury Lowery, the historian of the American Southeast, Cabeza de Vaca's narrative lacks the "marvelous stories of giants, pygmies, troglodytes, cynocephali, and other monsters, the common stock of all travellers' tales" at that time. His descriptions of the Indians were especially informative and fair, and he was the first real European source on the native peoples of the North American interior.[61] Stuart Udall perhaps best summarized Cabeza de Vaca's contribution: "No sixteenth-century Spaniard gave more of himself to his king—or to humanity—than Alvar Núñez. As an explorer of undiscovered country, he stands on a pinnacle alone. He gave 'two lives' to the New World: he is unforgettable as an Indian man— and his prodigious walks on two continents [across the American Southwest and southern Brazil] will never be surpassed."[62] Although some might feel that Cabeza de Vaca and his three companions were not technically explorers but adventurers, it should be remembered that the three Spaniards and the blackamoor from Europe and Morocco were the first to traverse what is today Texas and northern Mexico, encountering various native peoples, describing flora and fauna, and noting the geographical features of the terrain. Indeed, they were explorers or, perhaps better, "pathfinders." What they learned and later related would give impetus to others who would follow—explorers as well as colonizers—many years afterward.

Their exact route from Matagorda Bay to Sinaloa can never be reconstructed precisely, although it has been the subject of much investigation, conjecture, interpretation, and sometimes national and state boasting. Historians and anthropologists have arrived at different conclusions concerning the route, but the most probable one is that depicted in Donald E. Chipman's recent study.[63] Based on intensive analysis of Cabeza de Vaca's narrative, with its references to rivers, mountains, and the prickly pear region west of the Nueces River, and supported by the detailed tracing of the route by three anthropologists in 1940, along with Chipman's own knowledge of southern Texas, this study clearly shows that the expedition did not wander northward and westward into the trans-Pecos area of western Texas and southern New Mexico, nor did it reach the vicinity of present-day El Paso. Instead the travelers turned southward a bit west of Corpus Christi Bay and crossed over what they described as a river as large as the one at Sevilla (the Guadalquivir). Another pertinent observation by Cabeza de Vaca is that the party saw mountains near their river crossing, rising fifteen leagues (about forty-five miles) from the sea and running in a north-south direction. The Sierra de Cerralvo in the northern part of Nuevo León runs in that direction and is almost exactly forty-five miles inland from the sea.[64] Turning westward after crossing the Río Grande instead of proceeding southward because of reports of hostile Indians along the coast, they skirted south of the Sierra de Cerralvo and continued through what is today northern Coahuila and the Big Bend country of western Texas to the vicinity of La Junta de los Ríos, where the Río Conchos joins the Río Grande in the Ojinaga-Presidio vicinity of eastern Chihuahua. There they were received amicably by village-dwelling Native Americans from whom they heard of a fertile valley and similar village natives (later called Pueblos) farther northward in the Río Grande valley of New Mexico. That Cabeza de Vaca and his companions were there was corroborated by an observation of António de Espejo while he was at La Junta de los Ríos in 1582. The Indians told him that "three Christians and a Negro had passed through here."[65] Proceeding westward along the Río Conchos and across the present-day Mexican state of Chihuahua, the party crossed the Sierra Madre Occidental, encountered Opata and other Indian groups, and finally met twenty Christians on the Río Sinaloa. These were slave hunters sent out from the Spanish community of San Miguel de Culiacán in Sinaloa, where the four survivors of the four hundred men originally in the Narváez expedition arrived on 1 April 1536, eight years and thirty-seven days since their departure from Cuba.[66]

Although the appearance of Cabeza de Vaca in Spain and the publication of his *relación* helped lift the veil of mystery about the North American interior, these events may not have done much toward dispelling the disappointment of Spain and its conquistadores over not finding a Northwest Passage or new riches like those of Mexico and Peru. True, Cabeza de Vaca made little mention of a shortcut to the Orient, but he did repeat whispers heard among the Indians along the Río Grande about the pueblos of New Mexico (although never referring to them as Cíbola). Could these be the fabled Seven Cities? The Spanish yearned for more fortune and glory and fervently wanted to put the failures of Ponce de León, Vázquez de Ayllón, and Narváez behind them. The arrival of Cabeza de Vaca in Seville "brought matters to a head" and set in motion a chain of explorations that culminated in Francisco Vázquez de Coronado's and Hernando de Soto's explorations, the major Spanish *entradas* of the sixteenth century.[67]

Cortés and Guzmán in Northern Mexico

Within a decade following the final entrance of Hernán Cortés into Tenochtitlán and the defeat of the Aztec confederation, Spaniards began looking outward from their center in Mexico City. Explorers and conquistadores advanced southward into Oaxaca, Chiapas, Yucatán, Guatemala, El Salvador, and Honduras while others moved westward into Michoacán. Most important, they began their three-century quest into the vast, unknown northern reaches of New Spain (present-day northern Mexico and the southwestern United States from Texas to California). Always they were accompanied by Native American auxiliaries, who served as troopers, informants, spies, scouts, burden-bearers, and suppliers of provisions. The advance of the *frontera septentrional* (northernmost frontier) of New Spain became a continuous characteristic of the Viceroyalty of New Spain (begun in 1535), with its resulting problems as well as achievements. The northern frontier became a dynamic region of great change, constantly opening new areas discovered by explorers, and faced with almost continuous adaptation to newly encountered native peoples who understandably resisted the advance of Spaniards into their domains. As in the southeastern part of the modern-day United States, various motives encouraged Spanish explorers and colonizers in the vast northern region. Of primary importance was the desire to find mineral deposits that offered wealth for both the discoverers and the king. As D. W. Meinig has observed, "The Spanish intensively probed that north in search of precious minerals, making a series of discoveries of rich silver deposits, and establishing a number of great mining camps."[68] Silver became the great incentive for Spanish exploration, but not all Spaniards explored and colonized for the purpose of discovering silver. Simultaneously and independently they also sought to establish the sovereignty of Spain over the native peoples they encountered,[69] undertook to discover possibilities for settlement and to search for basic information,[70] sought mythical kingdoms—the "Río de las mujeres," the Seven Cities of Cíbola, and Gran Quivira—to conquer and enslave, pursued the long and fruitless quest for the Straits of Anián, and, finally, undertook to spread Christianity and Westernize the indigenous peoples by establishing missions.

The first Spanish explorers and conquistadores in the northern frontier regions of New Spain had focused their efforts on the region of the Río Pánuco. Cortés himself both explored and settled Pánuco before 1523, establishing the town of Santiesteban on the southern bank of the river. There he was challenged unsuccessfully by Francisco de Garay, the governor of Jamaica, who had earlier dispatched Alvarez de Pineda on his voyage of exploration.[71] Although Cortés succeeded in maintaining his control over the Pánuco region temporarily, he was precluded from exploring the northern Mexican interior by a hated rival and formidable foe: Nuño Beltrán de Guzmán. Trained as a lawyer, Guzmán was appointed governor of Pánuco in 1526 to replace Cortés. On his arrival over a year later, having just missed Cortés, Guzmán initiated a severe persecution of those of Cortés's followers who remained, forcing many of them to flee and abandon their properties. By the time Cortés returned with his new title of *marqués*, Guzmán had fully diluted his power in Pánuco and tried futilely to thwart his efforts to explore Baja and the Gulf of California. Guzmán also found that what had been explored of his new domain was bereft of tangible wealth, especially gold and silver. To offset this shortage, he began raiding Indian villages ever deeper into the interior for slaves. These slaves were sent to the Antilles as labor to replace the native Arawaks decimated by European diseases; in return for these slaves, the governor of Pánuco received the needed supplies for his province. Guzmán's brutal disregard for the Indians was typical of many of the early Spanish conquistadores. It is evident that he not only engaged in slaving himself but also planned the slaving ventures of others and personally supplied them with horses and provisions at his own expense.[72] Such behavior engendered a growing fear of the Spanish among the Indians and gradually led to more violent resistance. Over the course of the sixteenth century, this type of treatment and resistance made the exploration and settlement of the Americas vastly more difficult than it might otherwise have been.

Dreams of finding another Mexico also pushed Guzmán to further exploration. There were rumors of pearl-ringed islands to the northwest, populated only by women, amazons who wore pearls and gold. And in 1530, a Teya Indian from the valleys of Oxitipar related to Guzmán a story that he had heard from his father, a traveling trader, about seven Indian towns, larger than Mexico City (the population of which, according to some nineteenth-century historians, numbered only about one thousand but which was, more probably, one of the largest cities in the Americas with a population nearing one million).[73] These seven reported Indian towns were supposedly located far to the north and were abundant in gold and silver. The report was probably an account of the pueblos of the American Southwest, one of the first such accounts picked up by the Spanish. But it was also related to the native tradition of which the Spanish were probably aware: that the Nahuatl ancestors of the once-mighty Aztecs originally came from seven caves in northern Mexico, the mystical "Aztlan." And here too the Indian tradition dovetailed with the European legend that, well before Columbus's first voyage, Portuguese Christians led by the archbishop of Oporto and six other bishops, fleeing the Moors, had founded seven cities on the fabled island of Antilla somewhere to the west of the Azores and Canaries.[74] The legend of Antilla was powerful enough that the islands in the Caribbean discovered by Columbus and his contemporaries were named "the Antilles," a name they bear to this day. Over the intervening period between Columbus's initial discovery and the report presented to Guzmán, the Seven Cities had moved from ocean to desert. But they still existed in the Spanish imagination.

Whether lured by tales of the amazons and the Seven Cities, by the idea of a Northwest Passage connecting the Atlantic and the South Sea (or the Pacific), or by the prospect of more slaves to supply the growing Spanish plantation system of the Antilles, Guzmán , after having served as the first president of the Audiencia of México (the viceroy's administrative and judicial council) in Mexico City, was ready in 1530 for a new adventure. His grand design was to link Sinaloa with Pánuco in a giant kingdom of "Mayor España" (Greater Spain).[75] In his enterprises to search for precious metals, slaves, and a kingdom of his own to rival that of the hated Cortés, Guzmán became both a discoverer of new routes to the interior and a conqueror. In the spring of 1530 he took two hundred horsemen and three hundred foot soldiers and began the exploration and conquest of Jalisco and Sinaloa in northwestern Mexico. Along the way he also drafted many thousands of Indians into service. After a year's march of some six hundred miles, Guzmán had explored as far northward as the Río Fuerte and had crossed the Sierra Madre Occidental into the present-day state of Durango. He had not found gold, silver, or pearls, but at the end of his march he reached the fabled "land of the amazons." These were nothing more than villages of women and children deserted by their men for fear of being enslaved by the Spanish; no gold and pearls were discovered here either. Despite his failure to locate riches, along the route of his expedition into the northwest Guzmán founded the towns of Guadalajara, Compostela, and Culiacán, among others. Culiacán, with one hundred soldiers as *vecinos* (householders or settlers) and a parish priest, became the northern outpost of the new province of Nueva Galicia, and Guzmán was named its first governor in 1531. In 1533 he opened up a major road through the Sierra Madre Occidental to connect Nueva Galicia and Pánuco. This overland journey took him over an unexplored terrain, and after an arduous march in which he lost soldiers, horses, and some slaves, he arrived at Santiesteban in July 1533.[76] But in less than five years, Guzmán lost both his governorships and returned to Spain.[77] Aside from his slaving raids and his unsuccessful effort to carve out his kingdom of Greater Spain, Guzmán contributed notably to the geographical knowledge of today's northern Mexico, especially in Sinaloa and at Pánuco. Furthermore, he was a pathfinder in crossing the previously unknown interior of the north from west to east, thereby proving that the Gulf of Mexico and the Pacific Ocean regions might be linked. What Guzmán had set in motion was followed by one of the greatest of all Spanish explorations—that of the Coronado *entrada*.

During the years of Guzmán's northern activities, his rival Cortés made a visit to Spain in 1528–30 to plead his case to the king; he was honored and rewarded but failed to have his governorship restored. Instead, Cortés was made the Marqués del Valle de Oaxaca by Emperor Charles V, and Antonio de Mendoza subsequently was named the first viceroy of New Spain.[78] On his return to Mexico, however, Cortés's ambition and inquisitiveness remained undaunted. His new title did bring with it the privilege to explore the Pacific coast of New Spain in the hope of finding further sources of readily available wealth and a Northwest Passage to the Orient, which had been the Spanish dream ever since Vasco Núñez de Balboa had crossed the Isthmus of Darién (Isthmus of Panama) and first sighted the Pacific Ocean in September 1513. Like so many others at this time, Cortés believed that Asia was much closer to North America than it actually was and that the distance across the continent was far shorter than it actually was, about the same distance as it was across Mexico at the latitude of Mexico City. This misconception of the real size of North America did not even begin to be rectified until the accounts of the odyssey of Alvar Núñez Cabeza de Vaca and the *entradas* of Francisco Vázquez de Coronado and Hernando de Soto were made public.[79]

In 1535 an expedition sent by Cortés discovered and planted a settlement on the tip of present-day Baja California. And in 1539, responding to the tale of Cabeza de Vaca's journey, he sent three ships, under Francisco de Ulloa, from Acapulco to explore still farther north along the coast. Ulloa sailed the full extent of the Gulf of California (to which he gave the name "the Sea of Cortés") and more, exploring a total of two thousand miles of coastline and proving that California was not an island.[80] In June 1541, after returning finally to Spain, Cortés filed in Madrid a map of Baja, the first of the great cartographic productions of the western parts of New Spain.[81] But his efforts, as significant as they were, were only preparatory to those of his successors.

Fray Marcos Prepares the Way for Coronado

The first half of the fifth decade of the sixteenth century was an important period in the Spanish exploration of the Americas. In 1540, as the *entradas* into North America began, Pedro de Valdivia, a veteran of Peru, carried out the conquest of Chile, and in 1541–42 Francisco de Orellana descended the Amazon from Peru to its mouth into the Atlantic Ocean. At the same time, Viceroy Mendoza of New Spain, believing that the fabled Straits of Anián, which separated California from Asia and linked Atlantic to Pacific, were farther up the coast than previously explored (where the two landmasses allegedly came closer together), began sending out expeditions to verify his belief. In 1542, Ruy López de Villalobos, Mendoza's brother-in-law, sought to cross the Pacific after proceeding north along the Mexican coast. After possibly discovering Hawaii along the way and pioneering the future route of the famous Manila galleons, this expedition vanished in Asia around Cochin in 1547. Also in 1542–43, an expedition under the command of Juan Rodríguez Cabrillo, a veteran of Mexico and Guatemala, and Barné Ferrelo explored a thousand miles of the Pacific coast of North

America from La Navidad as far north as Cape Mendocino and Oregon. They discovered San Diego Bay but missed San Francisco Bay, and they picked up reports of Melchior Díaz and Coronado from the Indians along the way.[82] The major Spanish efforts of the 1540s, however, were the North American *entradas*.

It would seem logical that Cabeza de Vaca, the Spanish traveler with the greatest experience and the best understanding of the Indians and their languages, would have played a major role in those *entradas*. However, after failing to secure the governorship of Florida, which went instead to Soto, Cabeza de Vaca declined to join either the Coronado or the Soto *entrada*. In 1540, he was made *adelantado* of Paraguay and led an expedition across southern Brazil, but eventually he was returned to Spain in chains, dying destitute in 1557. His companion Dorantes also rejected offers to return to the north, and he and Castillo eventually were lost to history. Of the party that first traversed the North American continent, only the Moorish slave Estebanico returned northward. Viceroy Antonio de Mendoza was determined to follow up on Cabeza de Vaca's reports concerning the rumored wealth and native civilizations of seven cities to the north of Cabeza de Vaca's route. Before dispatching a major expedition northward, Mendoza selected Fray Marcos de Niza to lead a reconnoitering venture into the *tierra desconocida* (unknown land). Estebanico was assigned by Dorantes to Mendoza to guide and translate for this expedition in 1539.[83]

The Father Provincial of the Franciscan Order in New Spain and a veteran of the conquest of Peru, Fray Marcos was also vice-commissioner general of northern New Spain. Allegedly on the advice of Governor Mendoza's friend Bartolomé de Las Casas, who wanted to initiate a new and more humane Indian policy in the northwestern region, Fray Marcos was selected to travel into the areas already explored by Cabeza de Vaca, to undo some of Guzmán's terror and find sites for new monasteries among the Indians.[84] Accordingly, Marcos departed from Culiacán on 7 March 1539, taking the Indian trails northward; he was accompanied by one lay brother (Fray Onorato), Estebanico, and some of the Pima Indians who had accompanied Cabeza de Vaca on the last part of his journey and had since been Christianized. Shortly after the beginning of the journey, as the party reached the Río Sinaloa, Fray Onorato fell ill and had to be returned to Culiacán on a litter; Marcos, now the sole Spaniard in the party, continued without him, northward to the Río Fuerte and the Río Mayo.

Almost from the beginning the Indians whom Fray Marcos and his party encountered told them stories of wealthier tribes farther to the north.

Many of these stories probably contained grains of truth, but by this time the Indians, especially those of northern Mexico, had learned to tell the Spanish invaders whatever they wanted to hear. Sometimes, while so doing, the Indians could extract a profit from the Spanish by acting as guides or bartering supplies. More often, their motives were to get the Spanish to move on to the lands of other Indians, perhaps even an enemy tribe. And so Fray Marcos and his group went northeastward from Indian camp to Indian camp. Like other Spanish explorers who came after him, Fray Marcos followed established Indian trade-trail networks that connected northern Mexico and the interior of the American Southwest; he did not have to waste time blazing trails or seeking "watering holes and hidden mountain passes." Finally arriving at a place he called "Vacapa" in Sonora, Marcos rested to await and celebrate Easter. He sent messengers to the sea, approximately 100 miles distant, and perhaps having heard of Cíbola for the first time, Fray Marcos decided to send Estebanico and an Indian youth, Bartolomé, to reconnoiter to the northeast for about 150 miles "to see whether it was possible to learn of something grand," such as the rumored natives living in settlements and wearing gold ornaments.[85] If a discovery should be made, Estebanico was instructed to send a courier back to the main party, with a white cross one palm long if the discovery was moderately important, two palms long if it was of great importance, and a large cross if it was "something greater and better than New Spain."[86] After the departure of Estebanico on 23 March 1539, the two were never to see each other again.[87]

The mischievous Estebanico was finally in his element—on his own, in charge, and probably as free as he had ever been during his adult life. Playing the shaman and shaking the medicine rattle that he had brought back from his journey with Cabeza de Vaca, he led his Indian companions northward, evidently as far as the Zuni pueblos of western New Mexico. He soon began to send back messengers to Marcos, bearing crosses as high as a man, recounting his progress, and, for the first time, attaching the name "Cíbola" to the marvelous stories of the seven cities. Two days after celebrating his Easter Mass, Marcos, after hearing some confirmation of Estebanico's tales from other messengers he had sent to the coast, followed Estebanico to the northeast along the Río Mayo, taking a route that led him up the Río Sonora, over the continental divide near the present international boundary, and then north to the Gila River and supposedly northeast to the Zuni pueblos. As he took possession of the land, Marcos marked his passing with the erection of great crosses. As he proceeded northward trying to overtake his messenger, he continued to receive messages from Estebanico, and he heard stories of Indians who dressed in clothing of fine cotton, who wore turquoise and decorated their houses with it, and who sailed interior lakes in eagle-prowed ships. He also saw the hide of a buffalo or a mountain sheep, which he took to be that of a unicorn.[88] But Estebanico did not wait for Marcos, as he had originally been instructed, and instead maintained his lead.

In May 1539 Marcos, still following Indian trails, was crossing the wilderness of what is today Arizona and New Mexico, apparently only three days from Zuni, when one of Estebanico's companions arrived in camp with news of a disaster at Cíbola. Two days later other fugitives arrived, "all bloody and with many wounds," reciting the events of a clash at Hawikuh Pueblo, the principal village of the Zunis, during which Estebanico and his party had died.[89] The news was received with bitterness and fear, and thereafter only a small number of Marcos's Indian entourage could be placated with gifts and persuaded to go on with him toward Cíbola. He allegedly went to within sight of the first of the Seven Cities of Cíbola, the Zuni pueblo of Hawikuh, which he reported as being the best he had seen in the north—with its many-storied, flat-roofed houses of stone. According to his fanciful descriptions, it was larger than the city of Mexico. He decided not to enter it, however; rather than risking death at the hands of the inhabitants of Cíbola, he would return to New Spain so that an account of the discovery could be made to authorities. Taking possession of Cíbola in the name of the viceroy and the king by erecting a pile of stones with a small cross at the top, Fray Marcos began his return journey over the same route to the Sonora Valley, Río Mayo, and finally Culiacán and Compostela, arriving there by the end of June. His vague and often exaggerated account was authenticated in Mexico City on 2 September 1539 in the presence of Viceroy Mendoza and Coronado.[90] Marcos's account was controversial from the very beginning; he drew no map but described the events and encounters of his travels in rich, vivid colors, being the first to refer to the "Seven Cities of Cíbola" and to designate the adobe Indian villages of the American Southwest as "pueblos."[91] He might have imagined Cíbolan walls studded with turquoise, but he did not talk excessively of gold and silver. At best, he was guilty of gross misinterpretation and, at worst, of outright lying to vindicate himself and his failed efforts. Whereas Hawikuh may have been as large in population as Mexico City after a generation of European disease and slavery had decimated the original population of the latter, and whereas mountain sheep could be romantically misjudged as unicorns, some historians, such as the Coronado expedition chronicler A. Grove Day, believe that Marcos never saw Cíbola and made up the story, based on Indian accounts, to justify his retreat after the death of the intrepid Estebanico.[92] Whatever the case, word of Marcos's discoveries spread rapidly across Spanish America and to Europe and stimulated Mendoza and Coronado to further action. The serious search for the continental counterpart of mythical Antilla was about to begin.

The Coronado *Entrada*

Francisco Vázquez de Coronado was born in Salamanca in 1510 and came to the New World in 1535 as Mendoza's secretary. Coronado's brother Juan became the first governor of Costa Rica, and another brother, Pedro, served King Philip II of Spain and Don Juan of Austria. Francisco married Beatriz de Estrada, daughter of Alonso de Estrada, who was the illegitimate son of King Ferdinand of Spain and who served as treasurer of New Spain until his death in 1530; Beatriz was also the cousin of the emperor. Possessing these impressive family connections, and being a close friend of the first viceroy of New Spain, Coronado was poised for greatness when he arrived in the New World. In 1536–37, his first assignment was to put down a series of black slave revolts in Mexico. On the heels of this success, Mendoza appointed him to a one-year term on the town council of Mexico City and to the governorship of Nueva Galicia to replace Cristóbal de Oñate (who had in turn eventually replaced Guzmán) in 1538. And in 1539 Coronado was appointed captain-general of "Spain's grandest *entrada* in the New World": to seek out Fray Marcos's Seven Cities of Cíbola, to find a Northwest Passage, and to explore the American Southwest.[93]

In 1540, even with the reports of Cabeza de Vaca and others, the Spanish really knew very little about the North American interior. They still underestimated the width of the continent by almost ninefold and thought it to be much smaller north to south and much closer to Asia than it actually was. They also believed that north of the latitudes traversed by Cabeza de Vaca there existed a water connection between the Atlantic and the Pacific Oceans. This belief was reinforced by the French discovery of the Saint Lawrence River in 1535, thought by Jacques Cartier, its discoverer, to be the eastern entrance to the Northwest Passage.[94] The Spanish referred to the passage as the Straits of Anián, and their goal was to find the western terminus of the fabled waterway across North America, thus forestalling any attempts on the part of France or England to control the waterway by entering it from the Atlantic side of the continent. Although the search for Cíbola was of paramount importance in mounting the Coronado expedition, of nearly equal importance was the determination of the existence of the Straits of Anián, a mythical geographical feature of enormous potential in terms of both imperialistic strategic concerns and economic advantages to its discoverers.

After hearing Fray Marcos's report, Mendoza and Coronado, in November 1539, dispatched Melchior Díaz, *alcalde* (mayor) of Culiacán, and his lieutenant, Juan de Saldívar, a kinsman of the Oñate family, with fifteen horsemen to the north on a reconnaissance to verify the monk's story. Returning in March 1540, Díaz met Coronado on his march north and joined him, sending Saldívar to report to Mendoza. Having journeyed into eastern Arizona, Díaz essentially confirmed Fray Marcos's account but also did not report the presence of gold and silver. Fearing that rivals like Cortés or Soto might hear the full story of Marcos's journey, Mendoza and Coronado had hurriedly prepared the expedition. With much fanfare Coronado had departed Compostela on 23 February 1540, with over 300 men (225 of them mounted) and as many as 800 Indian allies and their equipment and baggage. Part of this equipment consisted of some small pieces of artillery, which would later prove inadequate during various pueblo sieges. Mendoza accompanied the army for the first few days and then turned back. Fray Marcos went with the expedition to show the way and to help set up missions; he eventually became more and more despised by many of the others as the disappointment of not finding a new Mexico or Peru grew. The principal chroniclers of the *entrada* were Coronado himself, in a series of reports to Mendoza, and two soldiers, Pedro de Castañeda de Nacera and Juan Jaramillo.[95]

On 9 March, to parallel Coronado's route and to maintain contact with him and carry some of his excess supplies, Mendoza sent three ships under Hernando de Alarcón up the western coast of New Spain to the mouth of the present-day Colorado River. On this journey up the Gulf of California (Sea of Cortés) to its northern terminus, Alarcón again proved California to be part of the North American mainland rather than an island; but old myths die hard, and the "pearl-ringed island" of California would remain a fixture on many Spanish maps for another century and more. On 26 September, having long since lost all contact with Coronado, Alarcón decided to ascend the Colorado River to find him. Alarcón and some of his men, taking two ship's boats, became the first Europeans to enter the Colorado.

On the way up the river, they often met with stiff resistance from Indians who came to see Alarcón as a sorcerer because he claimed to have been sent by the Sun and because of his demonstrations of the use of gunpowder. Alarcón's party also heard the story of the death of Estebanico and, finally, accounts of the passage of Coronado to the east of the river. Alarcón's first penetration of the Colorado was relatively short, but on his second ascent he traveled well over two hundred miles up the river, halting near present-day Yuma, Arizona, where he erected a large cross and left letters for Coronado before returning to Mexico.[96]

Meanwhile, Coronado followed many of the Indian trails traveled by Cabeza de Vaca, Fray Marcos, and Díaz before him. He and his men saw for themselves many of the sights described by their predecessors—like the great spring floods of the Acaponeta River near the village of Aztatlán. Being overburdened with baggage contributed to their mounting hardships, and the excess was gradually jettisoned; their progress increased, but so did attacks from hostile Indians. At Chiametla, upstream on the Río Presidio from present-day Mazatlán, Coronado was joined by Díaz and Saldívar and heard their report. Given the absence of sufficient sustenance ahead, Coronado decided to push on to Cíbola with a smaller force of about one hundred men, most of them mounted and including Díaz, Marcos and all the other religious, plus some blacks and Indians, along with some of the artillery.

On 8 July 1540, Coronado and his men sighted the first of the Seven Cities of Cíbola (of which, as Jaramillo truthfully admitted, there were only six): the Zuni pueblo of Hawikuh. It was located on the upper Zuni River in present-day New Mexico near the Arizona border.[97] After a fierce hour-long battle, in which Coronado, marked as the leader by the Indian defenders, sustained several wounds, the pueblo and its valuable food stores fell to the Spanish. Thereafter, the rest of the province came quickly into Coronado's hands. Although he was the first European to provide detailed descriptions of the Indian pueblos, Coronado did not find gold or silver or even large quantities of turquoise in the land of Cíbola. Castañeda offered the following account:

> When they saw the first village, which was Cíbola, such were the curses some hurled at Friar Marcos that I pray God may protect him from them. . . . It is a little, unattractive village, looking as if it had been crumpled all up together. There are mansions in New Spain which make a better appearance at a distance. It is a village of about 200 warriors, is three or four stories high, with the houses small and

having only a few rooms, and without a courtyard. One yard serves
for each section. The people of the whole district had collected here,
for there are seven villages in the province, and some of the others
are even larger and stronger than Cíbola. These folks waited for the
army, drawn up by divisions in front of the village. When they refused to have peace on the terms the interpreters extended to them,
but appeared defiant, the Santiago [the traditional Spanish battle cry,
invoking Saint James] was given, and they were at once put to flight.
The Spaniards then attacked the village, which was taken with not a
little difficulty, since they held the narrow and crooked entrance.
During the attack they knocked the general down with a large stone,
and would have killed him but for Don García López de Cárdenas
and Hernando de Alvarado, who threw themselves above him and
drew him away, receiving the blows of the stones, which were not
few. But the first fury of the Spaniards could not be resisted, and in
less than an hour they entered the village and captured it. They discovered food there, which was the thing they were most in need of.
After this the whole province was at peace.[98]

In August, Coronado sent Díaz back to Sonora with a letter for Mendoza,
along with gifts of local flora, fauna, and minerals and pictures of Cíbola,
painted on skins by Indian artists; the letter also instructed the balance of
the expedition to come to Cíbola. Sending the letter and gifts on to Mexico
City in October, Díaz remained in Sonora as ordered to take command of
the garrison there. Díaz then, seemingly on his own initiative, set out with
a party of twenty-five men to the coast to find Alarcón. He heard stories
about Alarcón from the Yuma Indians and found the cross and letters Alarcón had left behind. Along the way, Díaz was severely wounded by accidentally falling from his horse onto his own lance. The expedition quickly
returned to Sonora, but Díaz died on the journey and was buried in the
desert.

In late July, Coronado sent out an expedition under Pedro de Tovar and
Fray Juan de Padilla to the northwest across the Painted Desert to the land
of the Hopis, of which stories even more glorious than those of Cíbola had
been heard. They returned in August with reports of a great river farther to
the west (the Colorado), which Coronado rightly suspected might lead to
the Sea of Cortés and thus to Alarcón. Consequently, Coronado sent a
dozen riders under Don García López de Cárdenas to find and descend the
Colorado (Firebrand) River. Cárdenas initially retraced Tovar's route and
eventually reached the Grand Canyon. Sadly, the original report of the first

sighting of this natural wonder does not survive, but the experience was later recorded by Castañeda:

They came to the banks of the river, which seemed to be more than 3 or 4 leagues above the stream which flowed between them. This country was elevated and full of low twisted pines, very cold, and lying open to the north, so that, this being the warm season, no one could live there on account of the cold. They spent three days on this bank looking for a passage down to the river, which looked from above as if the waters was 6 feet across, although the Indians [Hopi guides] said it was half a league wide. It was impossible to descend, for after these three days Captain Melgosa and one Juan Galeras and another companion, who were the three lightest and most agile men, made an attempt to go down at the least difficult place, and went down until those who were above were unable to keep sight of them. They returned about 4 o'clock in the afternoon, not having succeeded in reaching the bottom on account of the great difficulties which they found, because what seemed easy from above was not so, but instead very hard and difficult. They said they had been down a third of the way and that the river seemed very large from the place they reached, and from what they saw they thought the Indians had given the width correctly. Those who stayed above had estimated that some huge rocks on the sides of the cliffs seemed to be about as tall as a man, but those who went down swore that when they reached these rocks they were bigger than the great tower of Seville. They did not go farther up the river, because they could not get water.[99]

With a chronic water shortage up on the rim and with the Grand Canyon barring his path, Cárdenas wisely, but reluctantly, decided to return to Coronado at Hawikuh.[100]

Following up reports from some of his new allies, the Jémez Indians, in late August, Coronado sent out twenty men under Hernando de Alvarado and Fray Juan de Padilla to the east, where they first came upon the impressive "sky city" pueblo of Acoma and then the Tigua pueblos of the Río Grande valley at the base of the Sandia Mountains near what is today the city of Bernalillo, New Mexico. The better living conditions at Tiguex reported by Alvarado convinced Coronado to move his expedition from Cíbola to seek winter quarters among the Río Grande pueblos; the bulk of the Coronado *entrada* spent the next two winters there. Alvarado meanwhile explored north along the Sandias to the large pueblo of Cicuye (Pecos), where he encountered a strange Indian captive who was from the Great

Plains and whom the Spanish (some of whom were veterans of recent Habsburg-Turkish wars) nicknamed "the Turk" because of his strange turban-like Pawnee headgear. To gain his freedom and fortune, he spun tales of the gold of his homeland—Quivira—far to the northeast. In initially pursuing these stories to the east of the Sandias, Alvarado and his men encountered great herds of buffalo before returning to report to Coronado. After hearing what the Turk had to say, and desperate for gold, Coronado made plans to conquer the new Eldorado of Quivira.[101]

The winter of 1540–41 in Tiguex was a severe one for its inhabitants and for Coronado and his men. As the weather deteriorated, so did relations between the Spanish and their Indian hosts. The Spanish treatment of the Indians became more and more harsh as the Europeans attempted to extract greater comforts from the Indians; such treatment finally precipitated a major pueblo revolt and a winter of war. It took almost two months of siege at Tiguex, but eventually the Spanish under Cárdenas very cruelly suppressed the uprisings. Thus, in the spring, Coronado, still anxious to make his *entrada* a financial success, was at last ready to follow the conniving Turk to Quivira and, on 23 April 1541, departed to cross the Great Plains to the fabled city. He was guided by the Turk and two other Indians from Quivira who had been enslaved by the Tiguas. One, named Sopete, who was not a Pawnee like the Turk but a Wichita, proclaimed the Turk a liar from the outset. But Coronado, blinded by visions of gold and silver, would not listen.

On the plains, Coronado also encountered herds of buffalo and their Indian hunters. He and his men experienced a tornado, and they met an old blind Indian who remembered meeting the Spanish before. Jaramillo assumed this meeting to have been with the party of Cabeza de Vaca: "I believe we had been traveling twenty days or more in this direction [northeast, toward Quivira], at the end of which we found another settlement of Indians of the same sort and way of living as those behind, among whom there was an old blind man with a beard, who gave us to understand, by signs which he made, that he had seen four others like us many days before, whom he had seen near there and rather more toward New Spain, and we so understood him, and presumed that it was Dorantes and Cabeza de Vaca."[102]

By the first week in June, Coronado and his men had traveled well over six hundred miles; lacking any real verification of the golden city of Quivira, they finally came to seriously doubt the Turk's stories. It was then decided that Coronado and thirty-six men should push on to Quivira while the bulk of the force returned to Tiguex. Some thirty days later Coronado crossed the Arkansas River and a week thereafter reached Quivira, villages of grass huts in which lived the Wichita Indians, in present-day Kansas at the Great Bend of the Arkansas River. Castañeda gave the following brief description of Quivira: "The people are of almost the same sort and appearance as the Teyas. They have villages like those in New Spain. The houses are round, without a wall, and they have one story like a loft, under the roof, where they sleep and keep there belongings. The roofs are of straw. There are other thickly settled provinces around it containing large numbers of men."[103]

At first, since it was certainly not as the Turk had promised, Coronado thought the village might be a colony set up by some of the survivors of Narváez's expedition. But here too he was to be disappointed. After he found no gold, his disappointment turned to rage, and he had the Turk tortured and executed. Castañeda recounted:

They asked the Turk why he had lied and had guided them so far out of their way. He said that his country was in that direction and that, besides this, the people of Cicuye had asked him to lead them off on to the plains and lose them, so that the horses would die when the provisions gave out, and they would be so weak if they ever returned that they could be killed without any trouble, and thus they could take revenge for what had been done to them. This was the reason why he had led them astray, supposing they did not know how to hunt or live without corn, while as for gold, he did not know where there was any of it. He said this like one who had given up hope and who had found that he was being persecuted. . . . They garroted him. . . . Neither gold nor silver nor any trace of either was found among these people. Their lord wore a copper plate on his neck and prized it highly.[104]

After spending a month in the Quivira region, hoping—but failing—to discern information about perhaps still more distant Mexicos and Perus, Coronado returned to Tiguex by what would later be known as the Santa Fe Trail, arriving in September.[105]

Coronado gathered supplies for the winter and sent parties to explore the Río Grande valley to the north and south. His men spent a restless second winter in Tiguex. In the spring, Coronado fell from his horse and suffered a severe head wound. This wound, his longing for his wife, the worsening demeanor of his men, and the apparent failure of his *entrada* all finally contributed to Coronado's decision to return to Mexico. He and his men released their Indian slaves and began the journey homeward in April 1542. Fray Juan de Padilla and others stayed behind to seek conversions, though they were eventually martyred. Coronado and his command retraced their steps back through Hawikuh; dejected, disgraced, and impoverished, Coronado returned to Mexico City in September.

Even though Coronado had returned essentially empty-handed and his expedition had been a financial failure, he had much to report. He and his men had been among the Yumas and Wichitas and had lived in the pueblos of the Zunis, Hopis, Acomas, and Tiguas. They had crossed the Colorado, Gila, Canadian, Arkansas, Pecos, and Cimarron Rivers and the Río Grande, as well as the continental divide. They also brought back knowledge (as related by Indians) of the Missouri River system, which they mistakenly thought to be the Mississippi; but in their mistake, they rightly hypothesized the two rivers as one network.[106] They had seen the Grand Canyon and Palo Duro Canyon, the Sangre de Cristo Mountains, and the Great Plains filled with buffalo. And although the map drawn by the Alarcón expedition and that drawn by Coronado of the route to Tiguex in 1540, "the very first map of any part of what is now the American West by one who had been there,"[107] have long since been lost, Coronado did contribute the place-names of Quivira, Tiguex, and many others, along with their general locations, to the future cartography of North America. In all, Coronado and his men had traversed parts of present-day northern Mexico, Arizona, New Mexico, Texas, Oklahoma, and Kansas. Perhaps Castañeda best summed up the true nature of this achievement: "Granted that they [Coronado and his men] did not find the riches of which they had been told, they found a place in which to search for them and a good country to settle in, so as to go farther from there."[108] But it was not "a good country to settle in" that had motivated Coronado; it was the prospect of wealth, of another Mexico or Peru if not the fabled Antilla. And so too did this prospect stimulate the other great and the longest *entrada* of the sixteenth century, that of Hernando de Soto in the land called "Terra Florida."

The Soto *Entrada*

Born in Villa Nueva de Barcarrota, Spain, around 1500, Hernando de Soto brought two decades of New World experience and several veterans of American expeditions to his Terra Florida adventure. He had first served with Pedro Arias (Pedrarias) Dávila in Darién in 1514, then in Nicaragua,

Guatemala, and Yucatán, and finally in Peru with Francisco Pizarro. These episodes won Soto fame, wealth, and family connections. He married the daughter of his first commander, Pedrarias, and thereby became the brother-in-law of Núñez de Balboa (who also married one of Pedrarias's daughters but who was later killed by Pedrarias). It was his fame, fortune, and cunning that greatly facilitated Soto's securing the titles of Governor of Cuba and Captain-General of Florida and the rights thereto in 1537, three months before Cabeza de Vaca returned to Spain.[109]

Unlike the Coronado expedition, about which relatively few primary sources remain, five types of sources on the Soto *entrada* have survived. The first type encompasses the four original narratives of the expedition. Roderigo Ranjel, Soto's secretary, left a daily account, except for the last year. There is another daily account written by an anonymous Portuguese, identified only as a "Gentleman of Elvas"; this is not as detailed as that of Ranjel but is more so than the brief account-recollection of Luis Hernández de Biedma. And last there is the work of "the Inca," Garcilaso de la Vega; this secondary source was conceived and written in 1567–99 and published in 1605 but was based on the now lost accounts of Alonso de Carmona and Juan Coles and interviews with other survivors.[110]

The second type of source consists of the surviving reports of the later expeditions led by Tristán de Luna y Arellano and Juan Pardo, who retraced some of Soto's steps. Third, there are the early maps depicting Soto and Coronado information. These include the 1545 "De Soto Map" of Alonso de Santa Cruz and the maps of Sebastian Cabot (1544), Giacomo Gastaldi (1546, 1556), Battista Agnese (1556), Gerardus Mercator (1569, 1587), Abraham Ortelius (1570, 1589), and Richard Hakluyt (1587), among others.[111] The last two types of evidence are the archaeological remains left behind by the passing of the Spanish, and by the Indians they contacted, and the information to be gleaned from an examination of the historical geography of Terra Florida.[112] All combined, these sources allow for a reasonably accurate reconstruction of Soto's *entrada*.

At the time of the Soto *entrada*, as little was known about the interior of La Florida as about the interior of the American Southwest. The Spaniards thought that it was a vast land, stretching to New Spain, and that its vastness must contain untold riches and other wonders, including the great river hinted at by Alvarez de Pineda and Cabeza de Vaca. But few even began to understand its true vastness or the real nature of its riches and wonders. The state of Spanish, French, and English cartography was such that North America was shown as a separate continent on some maps and as an

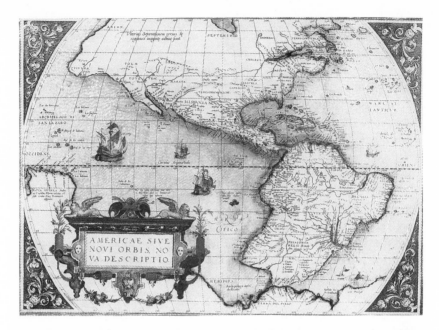

5.2 "Americae Sive Novi Orbis, Nova Descriptio" (Abraham Ortelius, 1570). This Ortelius map (one of many by the famed cartographer) provides an early cartographic record of the geographical knowledge contributed by the entradas. *Courtesy Special Collections Division, The University of Texas at Arlington Libraries, Arlington* TX.

eastern appendage to Asia on others. Some maps, particularly those derived from the early Spanish explorations of the Atlantic coastal region by Vázquez de Ayllón and others and from Giovanni da Verrazzano's coastal voyaging, showed a great extension of the Pacific Ocean thrusting into the North American continent from the west, with a narrow isthmus separating the Atlantic and the Pacific in what is now the coastal area of North Carolina. This great western arm of the Pacific was an analogue of the Gulf of Mexico, with the imagined isthmus being similar to that crossed by Núñez de Balboa in 1513.[113] In addition to the hypothetical riches of the as-yet-undiscovered kingdoms in the interior, Spanish exploratory objectives could have included the discovery of the "Sea of Verrazzano" and the still-hoped-for route to the Orient.

Soto's expedition is equal, in significance, to that of Coronado and, in his cruelty to the native peoples, to the Mexican Conquest of Cortés and the conquest of Peru by Pizarro. With ten ships and almost six hundred men, Soto finally reached Florida and, on 25 May 1539, put into present-day Tampa Bay near the site of Narváez's landing years earlier. At the same time, far to the west, Fray Marcos was descending through Sonora on his way to Mexico City. Although comparatively well supplied, Soto had no reliable maps or guides. But in the first weeks he did rescue from Indian captivity one Juan Ortiz, a Narváez survivor of eleven years, who then served as the expedition's chief translator until he died in the winter of 1541–42. Initially, Soto generally tried to retrace Narváez's route and looked for the places and landmarks mentioned by Cabeza de Vaca and Dorantes in their report. But Soto was reckless and greedy and from the beginning used poor judgment, especially in his treatment of the Indians.[114]

In October, one of Soto's patrols to the sea found Narváez's "Bay of Horses," and he ordered that some of his ships be brought up to anchorage there. In the following March, Soto, having heard stories from the Indians of a rich land to the east, moved on toward the northeast. On this leg of his journey, he unknowingly crossed the future goldfields of southern Georgia.[115] At Cofitachequi, an Indian town ruled by a female chief, on the Savannah River near present-day Augusta, Soto found large quantities of mussel pearls, but many of them had been damaged by the heat applied by the Indians to free them from their shells. Describing the pearls that Soto and his men found in an Indian burial temple in Cofitachequi, the Inca, perhaps with exaggeration, said:

All the chests, both great and small, were filled with pearls and seed pearls. And these gems were separated and arranged according to size that the largest were on the bottom in the first chests, and those not so large were in the second, those still smaller were in the third, and so on gradually to the seed pearls which were in the little chests highest up. In this collection of chests, there was such a great quantity of pearls and seed pearls that on seeing them the Spaniards confessed that what the Señora [female chief] had said of the temple and burial place was neither presumption nor exaggeration but the truth, and that even though all might load both themselves and their horses (there being more than nine hundred men and upwards of three hundred beasts), they would never be able to remove from the temple all the pearls it contained. But the sight of such quantities of these gems should not produce much amazement if one considers that the Indians never sold any of these that they found but brought them all to their burial places, and that they must have been doing so for many centuries. And in comparison, we might say (since it is seen each year) that if all the gold and silver that has been brought and is being brought to Spain from Peru were not removed from that land, the people there would be able to cover many temples with roofs of such metals.[116]

Eventually, Soto witnessed how the pearls became discolored:

And on the ensuing day before the canoes arrived, he [a chief] had a great amount of firewood piled up on some level ground alongside the river and lit so many embers might be available. When the canoes returned, these embers were spread out and the oysters cast upon them. Thus the shells opened with the heat of the fire and one could search within their flesh for pearls. From among the first that opened, the Indians removed ten or twelve gems as thick as medium sized chick-peas. These were taken to Curaca [the chief] and the Governor [Soto], who had been watching together, and they observed that they were perfect in all respects except for the fact that the heat of the fire and the smoke had damaged their fine natural color.[117]

Soto also found artifacts of Vázquez de Ayllón's failed colony. On this part of their journey, he and his men became the first Europeans to cross the Appalachian Mountains, already having pioneered a route from the Gulf of Mexico almost to the Atlantic Ocean.[118]

From Cofitachequi, Soto proceeded first to the northwest through the Carolinas across the Appalachians and then south, descending the Tennessee and Coosa Rivers and reaching the fortified Indian town of Mobila between the Alabama and Tombigbee Rivers on 18 October 1540. In the Spanish effort to secure lodging in the town, there ensued the *entrada's* largest battle with the Indians. When it was over, Soto had gained the town, but he had also lost twenty of his men, and most of his baggage, including a large cache of pearls for the king of Spain, had been destroyed in a fire. The Spaniards now found themselves in a desperate situation,

without doctors, medicines, bandages or lints, without food and without clothing, with which to cover themselves, or houses or even huts in which to take refuge from the cold and the night air, for the evil fortune of the day had deprived them of all help. And even though they might have wished to go in search of some remedy for their situation, the obscurity of the night, their ignorance as to where they might find assistance, and the very sight of themselves wounded and deprived of so much blood that most of them were unable to stand—all of these things hampered them. There remained to them now only an abundance of sighs and groans, which the pains from their injuries and the inadequate treatment of the same drew from the very depths of their being. Therefore from the bottom of their hearts and in loud voices they called upon God to shelter and assist them in their affliction, and Our Lord as a compassionate Father did come to their aid by bestowing upon them in that hardship, an invincible spirit, the spirit which has always enabled the Spanish nation above every other nation of this world to succour itself in its greatest necessities, just as these Spaniards did in their present want.[119]

In total, Soto had so far lost 102 men to the Indians and to disease since landing in Florida.

A month later, still in search of profit in the form of another Mexico or Peru, Soto set out again to the northwest, eventually to find winter quarters and also hunger and privation among the Chickasaws in mid-December. During his stay, he cut off the hands of those of his unwilling hosts who stole from the Spanish. Soto departed again to the northwest in March 1541, reaching and crossing the mighty Mississippi, reported by Ranjel to be a larger river than the Danube, in rapidly constructed boats on 8 June. Almost aimlessly, Soto and his force now moved west across the Arkansas River and into present-day Oklahoma, noting the declining sophistication of the Indians along the way and therewith losing all hope of finding gold and silver. Finally giving up, they began their return by descending the Ouachita River to spend their third winter near present-day Camden, Arkansas, at the village of Utianque. At their farthest penetration toward the northwest, they came within about three hundred miles of Coronado's thrust into the central Great Plains, nearly linking the two great Spanish *entradas* of the sixteenth century.

Soto returned to the east again in March 1542, intending to reach the sea and his ships. Proceeding down the Arkansas River, he reached the Mississippi in mid-April in the chiefdom of Guachoya, but the Indians there professed no knowledge of the sea. Here Soto became ill of a fever, and after turning over command to his adjutant, Luis de Moscoso Alvarado, a fellow veteran of Peru, he died on 21 May 1542. To prevent the mutilation of his body by the Indians whom he had so ruthlessly exploited and who consequently so hated and feared him, his men at first secretly buried Soto in the Spanish compound. According to the Inca:

For they feared that those people might commit upon his body such outrages and dishonors as they had inflicted upon other Spaniards. Disinterring and dismembering their victims, they had placed them in trees, each joint upon a separate limb; and it was easy to believe that these Indians, in order to insult the Spaniards further, would offer to the Governor, as their commander in chief, even greater and more abusive affronts. And our men declared that since their commander had not received such treatment in life, it would not be right that through their negligence he receive it in death. . . . For this reason, therefore, they agreed to bury him at night with sentinels so placed that the Indians would not see him or know where he was.[120] But then, to be sure to prevent desecration, the men weighted the body with sand and deposited it in the Mississippi River.[121]

On 5 June, hoping to retrace the steps of Cabeza de Vaca, Moscoso led the expedition to the west to find Mexico. They traveled almost four hundred miles, reaching through present-day East Texas and across the Trinity River before turning back and retracing their steps to the Mississippi a third time to spend their fourth winter at Aminoya, south of present-day Natchez, near where Soto had died. In Texas, near the Brazos River, Moscoso had encountered an Indian woman who had run away from Saldívar after he had rejoined Coronado the previous July, thereby establishing the only link between the two great Spanish *entradas* of the sixteenth century and briefly offering Moscoso the false hope of finding and following Coronado's route back to Mexico. But at no time had the two expeditions actually been closer than three or four hundred miles to each other.[122]

At Aminoya, Moscoso and his men constructed seven boats, and on 2 July 1543, the 322 Spaniards and their Indian servants set sail down the Mississippi for New Spain. It took seventeen days to reach the Gulf of Mexico, with much of the time spent under attack from Indians along the way. They exited the Mississippi to the southwest and fifty-three days later, on 10 September, reached Pánuco. In the Gulf, they were again often harassed by Indians, but they also found pitch in the oil seeps of East Texas; utilized by the Indians for medicinal purposes, the pitch was used by the Spaniards to waterproof their boats. In October 1543, Soto's ships under the command of Francisco Maldonado, having long searched the Gulf coast for the expedition, sailed into Veracruz.[123]

The return of the surviving members of the Soto-Moscoso *entrada* to New Spain reawakened Spanish interest in the dormant legend of a new Andalucia or the land of Chicora in the coastal regions north of Florida. Although the survivors' reports of the southeastern coast were far from favorable, the apparent presence of sophisticated native peoples in the interior suggested that the old Chicoran tales may have been true after all.

Although no permission was granted for further exploration or attempted colonization along the coast, the last of the cycle of explorations into La Florida, a cycle that had reached its pinnacle in the Soto-Moscoso journey, occurred six years after the return of Moscoso's party. This final expedition, in 1549, was led by Fray Luis Cáncer de Barbastro, a Dominican priest, who went forth with the charge to undertake missionary work in the Florida peninsula.[124]

Fray Luis, a native of Zaragoza in Aragón, had come to Española before 1530 and later founded a monastery in Puerto Rico before joining Bartolomé de Las Casas in the kingdom of Verapaz (Guatemala) in the late 1530s. There he became devoted to Las Casas's efforts to civilize and convert the Indians by kindness and good example instead of force. Fray Luis made two trips to Spain with Las Casas, the second in 1547, when he presented his plan for a missionary *entrada* to La Florida in which he intended to use the missionary methods employed by Las Casas. With Las Casas's approbation of the project, he received a royal *cedula* (order) on 28 December 1547, granting him permission for this venture and instructing Viceroy Mendoza to supply Fray Luis at royal expense for everything needed on the enterprise.[125] After numerous lengthy delays in Spain, mostly caused by bureaucratic foot-dragging, Fray Luis sailed alone to Veracruz, arriving in late summer of 1548. In New Spain he enlisted two priests, Fray Gregorio de Beteta and Fray Juan Garcia, along with Fray Diego de Tolosa and a lay-brother named Fuentes, to accompany him. Viceroy Mendoza supplied him with one ship and a pilot, Juan de Arana. The company sailed in early 1549, stopping at Havana, where it enlisted an American Indian woman named Magdalena as an interpreter. Departing from Havana, this missionary expedition sailed northward and sighted the coast of La Florida on 29 May. It landed near present-day Tampa Bay, where unfriendly Indians seized three of the party—a sailor named Juan Diego, Fuentes the lay-brother, and Magdalena—and disappeared into the interior. Determined to rescue the captives and proceed with his missionary enterprise in spite of the opposition of Fray Gregorio, who wanted to leave, Fray Luis succeeded in persuading the rest of the party to sail to Charlotte Harbor, where he landed with two priests and went to a nearby Indian village to seek information on the captives. There, on 21 June, the priests saw Magdalena but did not succeed in rescuing her. Instead, they rescued a Spaniard named Juan Múñoz, who had been captured ten years earlier from Soto's force. Múñoz told the priests that the Indians had killed the other captives, but Fray Luis persisted in his goal to save the souls of the natives.

Against Fray Gregorio's entreaty not to land again, Fray Luis did so on 25 June. He waded ashore alone and was greeted on the beach by Indians who snatched his hat and felled him with a blow to the head before killing him.[126] The ship departed three days later for New Spain, leaving Fray Luis a martyr to his cause and a victim of Indians whose hostility had been incited by earlier expeditions to La Florida.

The Post-*Entrada* Image of the Continent

Like Coronado's expedition, Soto's was a geographic success and a financial disaster. But it also succeeded in accomplishing more than "mainly . . . covering distance and demonstrating fortitude," as has been charged, and had important ramifications for the future of North American discovery, exploration, and settlement.[127] The travels of Soto and Moscoso, along with those of Coronado and Cabeza de Vaca, offered the first composite image of the vastness and diversity of the North American continent. If there existed a passage to the South Sea and the Orient, it must be far to the north of the routes of the *entradas*, for neither Coronado nor Soto had found it or heard of it; much of the continental penetration of North America in search of the passage over the next 250 years was to be predicated on that assumption.

The Spanish imagery of North America emerging from the Narváez–Cabeza de Vaca, Coronado, and Soto-Moscoso *entradas* is therefore both interesting and significant not only because of its geographic detail and misconceptions but also because of its influence on further exploration and discovery. To the north of the Spanish traverses, the continent was seen as opening up like a fan, the central ribs of which were formed by the estuaries of the great Missouri-Mississippi system. The principal source of this river network was believed to be in a range of high mountains (the Rockies?), described by various Indian attestants to be somewhere to the northwest of Quivira, near the Pacific shores and not distant from Asia. The Cíbolan domains in turn were held to be a possible offshoot of India. Another mountain chain (the Appalachians?) was seen as coming in from the east in a latitude north of Quivira. Based on this continental view, cartographers for many years wrongly portrayed the Appalachian Mountains running more east to west than north to south. At its widest, the continent stretched for over one thousand miles (still only approximately one-third of its actual size) from the Atlantic near Iceland to the Pacific near China, with a passage connecting the two oceans somewhere to the north. The northwestern coast of America was separated from China by the fabled Straits of Anián. Eventually, cartographers placed Quivira, the Tontonteac of the Hopis, and other lands discovered by Coronado on the western shore of these straits and even made the straits themselves a Northwest Passage.[128] And though this land had many wonders, it did not seem to contain Aztec and Inca-like Indian civilizations and their readily appropriated wealth.

The impact of the *entradas* on Native American populations and culture is more difficult to interpret. Certainly it is true that for years, the stories and legends of Cabeza de Vaca's "medicine man" journey westward were told among the southwestern and Texan tribes. Coronado's entry into the plains left little lasting cultural impact, but periodically an artifactual remnant of that journey appeared in the form of a Comanche, an Apache, or another Indian clad in cast-off Spanish armor or helmets. The Soto *entrada*'s impact on the Indians it contacted, on the other hand, seems to have been particularly profound. Soto was the first "to encounter the large Indian chiefdoms in the interior" of the American Southeast. At the time of his coming, they were at their peak of development, and his brutal passing among them helped to initiate their decline. It has been estimated that the Soto *entrada* killed outright some four thousand Indians, approximately ten for every one of its eventual survivors.[129]

And more important, as part of the biological consequence of the "Columbian exchange,"[130] the rapidly increasing interchange between the Old World and the New, these Spaniards introduced European germs among the Indians they met, an event that for at least two decades thereafter had a devastating effect. Thus the failed colonizing expedition of Tristán de Luna y Arellano sent by Viceroy Velasco in 1559–61 to this area found, among Indians such as the Coosas, a far different situation from what had existed at the time of first contact. Soto's cruelty and germs had brought about a severe decline in population and a corresponding decline in the complex social system of the Coosas. In return for food, Luna even had to send some of his men under Captain Mateo del Sauz to help the once great Coosas resubjugate their vassals, the troublesome Napochi Indians.[131] European diseases also seem to have had a similar, but somewhat less deleterious, effect among Pueblos after the passing of Coronado and his men among them.

Perhaps better than any other contemporary Spanish exploratory efforts, the ineffective *entradas* of Coronado and Soto exemplify the Spaniards' initial failure in the first half of the sixteenth century to colonize

North America. Woodbury Lowery eloquently captured the situation after the return of Luna's relief, Angel de Villafañe, to Hispanola on 9 July 1561: "Almost half a century had now elapsed since the Spaniard had first set foot upon our soil. Vigorously and boldly he had explored the Atlantic and Pacific coasts, had pierced the forests of the east, had crossed the boundless plains of the west, had threaded the valleys . . . to the mountain chains, but 'the god of his idolatry,' the Eldorado of his dreams, had not disclosed to him his secret abode, and he concluded that the region lay too far from the Tropic of Cancer to be gold producing; so the search for the precious metal was now abandoned in sheer desperation."[132]

Thus far, North America—with its vast size, harsh extremes of climate, rugged terrain, hostile people, and absence of wealth—had proven resistant to conquest and colonization. But some of the resistance had been of the Spaniards' own making. In large part due to gross geographic misperceptions regarding size, climate, landscape, and native inhabitants, but also due to breakdowns in command and organization, the *entradas* had failed in establishing even the minimum of coordination, between their inland thrusts and their naval support, necessary for some hope of real success. The conquistadores were, after all, soldier-colonists who cared more and knew more about gold than geography or agriculture. With their greed and cruelty, they helped to engender an often extreme alienation of the Native Americans from the Spanish. The European terrorizing of the Indians by killing or maiming them, pressing them into servitude and slavery, stealing their food and other goods, and often arrogantly proselytizing among them was in large part responsible for stimulating the often fierce Indian resistance. Although the treatment of the Indians by some like Guzmán, Narváez, and Soto was most extreme, the conquistadores generally did not follow Bartolomé de Las Casas's more humane and wise council found in his various writings, which inspired the later New Laws of 1542 on Indian treatment. Consequently, but largely as a result of the failure of the various *entradas* to find sources of ready wealth, to find a passage to Asia, or to leave behind permanent settlements, on 23 September 1561 King Philip II temporarily declared an end to the Spanish attempt to colonize the Atlantic coast of Terra Florida.[133]

With the founding of San Agustín, the first permanent settlement in North America, in Florida by Pedro Menéndez de Avilés in 1565 and the establishment of the capital of Nuevo Mexico at Santa Fe by Pedro de Peralta in 1610, the century of the great *entradas* drew to a close, and at least the outline of the Spanish "gift" of North America was relatively complete. Although the parameters and details established by Ponce de León, Cortés, Cabeza de Vaca, Coronado, Soto, and the others in the first century of exploration defined the scope of Spanish North America, its substance would take another two centuries to develop fully. The conquistadores had discovered the new continent and searched its southern reaches. They traveled many of the great trails of North America and blazed others across it for those who would follow; they beheld some of its natural wonders, experienced its flora and fauna, and began to sample its riches; they found shelter for their frail ships in some of its fine harbors; and they encountered its diverse native peoples, guardedly gaining respect for the natives' humanity. But at the beginning of the new century, most of them still failed to comprehend the true nature and value of what they had discovered. The Old World notions they brought with them were hard to apply to New World geography and produced false expectations and misunderstandings. Although clarification would come slowly, the Spanish presence had been established. Thus Europe came to know America, and the character of the New World took shape.

6 / The Northwest Passage in Theory and Practice

DAVID BEERS QUINN

One of the obsessions of sixteenth-century geographers and cartographers, a debate that was carried over into later centuries, was whether or not there was a water channel between Europe and Asia in northern latitudes. After the discovery of the Americas, this question had practical implications for the English and, later, the Dutch and to some extent the Norwegians. A passage in high latitudes, but one not too firmly impeded by ice, opened the possibility of rapid and short access to Asia, which could undercut the long-route access established by the Portuguese round the Cape of Good Hope and by the Spanish through the Strait of Magellan (or more effectively through contacts between Mexico and the Far East). In the projects of the period through the sixteenth and early seventeenth centuries, the Northeast Passage was almost as frequently discussed and attempted as the Northwest Passage, and thinking and acting about both were intertwined, but it is the search for the Northwest Passage that primarily concerns the exploration of North America.

It is not possible here to separate theory, cartography, and exploration into sharply separate spheres. Each was involved with the other, but it was theory, and the maps emerging from it, that kept exploration going in its early stages especially, just as it was theory that revived the attempts at exploration in the later eighteenth century.[1] For medieval cartographers, in both the pre-Ptolemaic and the pre-portolan maps, there was no problem. For Christians the unity of the earth's surface was assumed; its central point was Jerusalem, and the medieval world map was a demonstration not so much of cartography as of the sacred character of the earth's surface revealed by Scripture and predestined to be encompassed as a whole, in the near or distant future, by Christian Europe. The medieval maps might show a "world island" surrounded by water, but the character of the oceanic part was rarely a matter for discussion or of relevance to those who compiled the maps. When, from the later thirteenth century, Mediterranean seamen were compiling the early portolan charts from their on-shore observations, the rapid emergence of the Mediterranean tended to shift Western cartography from a religious to a secular and temporal basis. The gradual addition of the shores of western Europe and of Atlantic islands to the Mediterranean on these charts began to raise questions about the character of the landmass as a whole. Could it be represented in a way that would enable the reports of travelers outside Europe to contribute factual, or supposedly factual, information to maps that were beginning to be made showing the known world as a whole? The concept of the earth as a globe on which the limit of the landmass was unknown but was not believed to extend much beyond somewhat more than half the earth's circumference was a result of the reemergence of ancient Greek views of the circumference of the globe. However, the characteristic method of showing the known world in the first two-thirds of the fifteenth century was by a circular world map in two dimensions. In such maps the circumambient water, or the Ocean Sea, surrounding the landmass, or the World Island, was taken for granted and was shown on all of them. The gradual addition of Atlantic islands indicated, however, that there was much more to be known even about the West, let alone the East, than had been suspected.

The breakthrough in such concepts was the translation of Ptolemy's *Geographia* into Latin and its circulation in manuscript in the early fifteenth century. This gradually affected the portolan charts, but very slowly, before printed maps and globes appeared. By showing so much of the Eastern lands as were known to the Romans (and probably the Byzantines), Ptolemy enlarged the scope of knowledge of the World Island. By confining it between parallels of latitude and longitude, he was able to give a reference grid, however imperfect, which had previously been developed only empirically for the Mediterranean and its adjacent coastlines. Moreover, Ptolemy was able to confirm what earlier Greek writers were by now known to have maintained: that half the globe's surface, or thereabouts, was water. The Ptolemaic text was not dogmatic about the precise proportions of land and water, and the maps that accompanied his text and that showed the earth's surface as far as it was known to him (or to the Byzantine cartographers who supplied his maps) did not show a final terminus to land in the farthest east, leaving it to be assumed that there was more than what had yet been discovered or written about. Marco Polo's account of his Far Eastern journeys was also circulating in manuscript and may well have reinforced the view that Asia extended much farther to the east than had been believed. Knowledge of the known world was gradually reinforced in the fifteenth century by discoveries of islands farther and farther out in the Atlantic. The western Azores, a thousand miles from Portugal, had been reached by midcentury; Portuguese voyages down the western African coast were adding new land and new theories about sea contacts with Asia while Arab knowledge of eastern Africa was also seeping into Europe. The culmination of this increase in knowledge came in the late 1450s with Fra Mauro's world maps showing a much more refined picture of the landmass and, most interesting for the future of discussion about the Arctic, showing indications of fur traders working along the northern rim of the Eurasian continent, opening up the prospect of access by the northeast to Cathay and China. The concept of a Northeast Passage thus gave a specific spur to exploration, though it is not known to have been followed up. But there could be no question of any real discussion of a Northwest Passage, since there existed quite insufficient knowledge, or even theory, about the western Atlantic, and what did exist was concentrated in low latitudes.

It was only in the last quarter of the fifteenth century that men like Columbus and the Cabots and the Côrte-Reals began to postulate the existence of further lands to the West, lands beyond those real and mythical islands that appeared on the medieval maps. The revolutionary concepts of Paolo Toscanelli dal Pozzo and others convinced Christopher Columbus that direct access to Asia might very well not involve sailing halfway round a globe whose circumference was some twenty-five thousand miles but might involve something very much less—perhaps as little as nineteen thousand miles. This conceptual shortening of the earth's circumference made the discovery of what lay across the Atlantic appear possible. Columbus may have believed, in a quasi-religious fashion, that what lay within reach of the Canaries was Cipango (Japan) and that the Asiatic mainland was accessible from there, but Bristol merchants and the Azorean Portuguese may well have found land some two thousand miles to the west in the 1480s. This land they may not have regarded as Asia at all but just as some more islands useful for fishing, as the Azores had proved to be. These discoveries, however, might have brought both the Bristol men and the Portuguese fishermen to a more realistic appreciation of the continental landmass to the west than Columbus was to gain in over twenty years of voyaging and theorizing. Only when it could be maintained that a substantial block of land lay in the west in higher latitudes could any such concept as a Northwest Passage be born, and both the Portuguese and the

English were in a better position to recognize this sooner than the Castilians, whose presence can be traced only from the 1540s. Consequently, if Columbus discovered what turned out to be continental land (even if he did not understand that it could not be Asia), it was the pioneers in northern waters, the English and the Portuguese, who developed the concept of North America and who consequently could think of a possible way round it to reach Asia by the northwest.

The Early Discoveries in the Northwestern Atlantic

There seems little doubt that whatever may have been discovered before the 1490s by the English or the Azorean Portuguese, in the years after Columbus's initial discoveries the activities of both rapidly established that the lands to the west were no mere isolated islands but, rather, a substantial landmass. Moreover, it was quickly determined that this landmass was not Asia, since it did not have any of the characteristic features of Asia as recorded by Marco Polo and Sir John Mandeville, namely high culture and precious commodities.[2] Gaspar Côrte-Real's contact with the mainland in 1500, if he sailed due westward from Cape Farewell, where it is agreed his first landfall took place, would have brought him to the cold barren northern tip of Labrador or even into the eastward current and floating ice of Hudson Strait—certainly a land with different characteristics from those of the Asia of Polo and Mandeville. That Gaspar Côrte-Real was lost in this region is probable; but one of his vessels did return to Portugal to report the discovery, perhaps having turned south in time to avoid Côrte-Real's fate. His brother Miguel, in 1501, may or may not have persevered with exploration of the same area, but his turn southward brought him down past Newfoundland, most probably to the Maritimes or farther south. When he too failed to return—though one of his ships, bearing Indians as slaves, did so—there can have been little doubt in Portugal that a continental landmass had been discovered. The further search for the lost brothers by Eanes or another Côrte-Real can only have confirmed this view. The origin of the opinion, not documented until the 1530s, that the Côrte-Reals, or unknown followers in their tracks, had discovered a passage all around this landmass and leading westward to a presumed exit into the sea that washed Asia's shores is unknown. It is not inconsistent, however, with the hazily known activities of the descendants of the Côrte-Real brothers later in the century. The question of whether a Portuguese discovery of Hudson

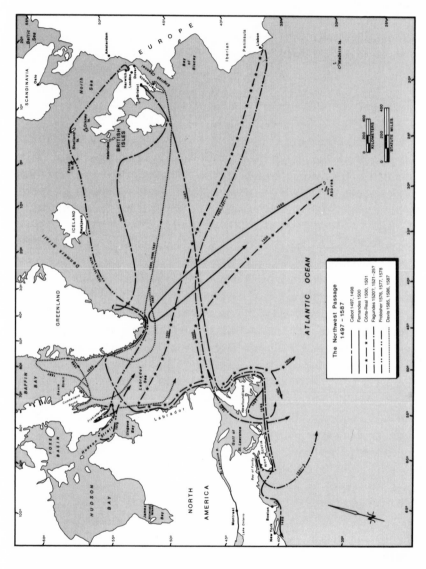

Map 6.1 *The Northwest Passage, 1497–1587.*

Strait, or even Hudson Bay, took place must remain an insoluble mystery, except that belief in it by later cartographers helped to put the strait, and keep it, on the maps as "The Strait of the Three Brethren."

Meanwhile, the English were also engaged in pursuing the exploration of the rumored lands to the northwest. That a possible voyage of Bristol men in 1481 disclosed Newfoundland as only a landmark for a fishery is still uncertain,[3] but the stated objective of John Cabot and his sons, when they set out across the Atlantic with Bristol and royal support in 1497, was to find an outshoot or peninsula of Asia, called the Horn of Asia on several pre-Columbian maps, which in higher latitudes would be easier to access than the supposed Asia of the Columbian discovery. Cabot did succeed in reaching Newfoundland, the first European to land on North American shores since the Norse nearly four centuries earlier. His first voyage returned successfully to Bristol but with relatively limited geographical information—other than that the lands to the west were more probably continent than island. The subsequent voyages of Sebastian Cabot and other Bristol men in the years 1501 to 1505 achieved primarily the discovery and exploitation of the Newfoundland fishery; from what we know of these men, however, they explored a substantial part of the mainland as well. It now seems likely that Sebastian, most probably in 1504, explored part of the coast of Labrador and may have reached Hamilton Inlet, which appeared as if it might prove to lead farther west. But there was not enough solid information upon which to base further exploration, and the Bristol voyages ended in 1505. However, the absence from England of Sebastian Cabot between Easter 1507 and May 1509 provides space for his famous, if obscure, voyage for the discovery of a Northwest Passage in 1508–9.[4]

At some time immediately after Cabot's September 1512 discharge from English service to enter the employ of Ferdinand II of Aragon, he made the acquaintance of the Hispaniolized Italian Peter Martyr (Pietro Martire d'Anghiera), one of the most significant chroniclers of the early New World voyages, and the two men became friends. At some point during the period between 1513 and 1515, Sebastian gave Martyr an account of a voyage to the north. In his *Third Decade of the New World (De orbe novo decades)*, published in 1516, Martyr gave the first and probably most authentic report of this voyage.[5] Sebastian maintained that at his own cost he equipped two ships with two hundred men (Martyr may well have got the number wrong) and sailed northwest along the North American coast until in July he found great icebergs floating but the land free by the melting of the ice.

He was forced by his crews to turn back, and he made his way southward along the mainland shore. In the Italian translation of Martyr's later chronicles (1534), Cabot was said to have reached 55° only, which would have brought him to Hamilton Inlet at the farthest.[6] But later (how much later it is not clear), Cabot wrote to Giovanni Battista Ramusio that he had reached 67°30', which would have brought him well up the eastern shore of Baffin Island, beyond the Arctic Circle.[7] Since he stated that, this far north, the sea was still open and ice free, a claim for such a northerly extent seems most improbable. Cabot did not make a personal contribution on the northern lands to the 1544 world map that goes under his name, but according to Richard Willes, in the "Cabot" map's revised edition of 1549 for which Willes was responsible (no copy has survived), Cabot claimed that a passage opened near the 318th (65° west) meridian between 61° and 64° north and continued at the same breadth some 10° west before trending southward.[8] He did not claim to have traversed this passage, and he may have given some of his data on the basis of other maps and globes showing the strait. From these conflicting reports it may be deduced that Cabot did succeed in entering Hudson Strait, from which in July many icebergs were flowing east and south, but did not penetrate it. Nevertheless, he certainly told lies. To Peter Martyr, Sebastian said the ships were his own and equipped by him; he told Ramusio that they were Henry VII's. Searches in English records have so far failed to find any royal ships being released at this period. If he himself equipped two vessels, it must have been with the financial assistance of English merchants, since it would almost certainly have been beyond his means to have done so. Could his ships have been hired on the Continent? If so, France is the only possible place from which they could have come, but no hint of sponsorship by Louis XII has emerged. In view of the supposed priority of Cabot's voyage, it appears worth giving any evidence we have in detail, but it must be admitted that the claims made for one or the other of the Côrte-Real brothers—as the first to have entered Hudson Strait—cannot be eliminated.

Apart from his varying tales about his exploit, what makes Cabot's voyage significant in a negative way is that after he entered the Spanish service he never proposed, insofar as is known, that Spain should make an attempt to follow his route as described to Martyr. It is possible he refrained from doing so because he felt his experience showed that the passage, if he continued to believe in its existence, was too far north to prove a commercial success. Moreover, after his return to England in 1547, when he was discussing with London merchants the desirability of making a northern voyage to Asia, the debate centred on a transpolar route, a northwesterly versus a northeasterly one; he finally endorsed the latter of these and did not insist that his experience in 1508 should be repeated. It may never be known whether the voyage of Sebastian Cabot as set down in Peter Martyr's chronicles ever took place. In the final analysis, perhaps, it makes little difference, for the geographical knowledge of this possibly apocryphal voyage became an important feature of maps of North America from the early 1500s onward.

Early Theory and Cartography of the Passage

Maps were crucial in the creation of discussions of an open northern sea and a potential sea passage to the Orient by the northwest. The Contarini-Rosselli map of 1506, accepting that the new lands in the west were peninsulas of Asia, presented an open sea around the North American landmass, following the style of the late medieval maps of the World Island with its all-encircling Ocean Sea.[9] But the map and globe of Martin Waldseemüller in 1507 showed two new continental landmasses, the northern one terminating abruptly at about 50° north, with open water to the north of it.[10] This formed a basis on which other cartographers built when this northern landmass became, in about 1520, to be linked by name with the new southern continent as America.

Peter Martyr in 1516 felt he should preface his first account of Sebastian Cabot's "Northwest Voyage" with some cosmographical explanation. He said it was generally accepted that a great current of water flowed from east to west and continued round the globe. This view was founded on the Northeast Trade Winds (Canaries Current), which dominated the passage of the Atlantic in the Iberian mind. But Martyr was perplexed by where it went after it reached the West Indies. Was there a passage through the land to the north of Cuba? Was there no passage at all, and the current was turned back toward the east (and was therefore *not* continuous round the globe)? Or, finally, was there not a passage by which the current was diverted into the Arctic and from there flowed westward to continue in this irregular way round the earth? This, he said, had been demonstrated by Cabot, since that explorer had established that "those waters flow likewise to the west, not swiftly, however, but gently with a continual passage."[11] Some such theory continued to appear in cosmographical and geographical works for the next two generations at least. Martyr's second proposi-

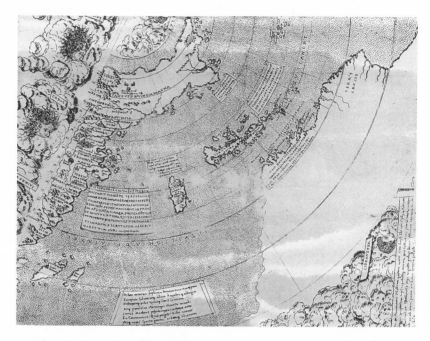

6.1 New World portion of the world map by G. M. Contarini (1506). This first published map to show any part of the New World depicts the area discovered by John Cabot and the Côrte-Reals as a peninsula of Asia, a geographical conception that lasted for several decades after initial discovery. The Asian mainland west of Cuba contains information from Marco Polo. Also from Polo is the island of Cipangu, or Japan, lying between Cuba and the Asian coast. By permission of The British Library.

tion, that there was a passage through the northern landmass, dominated the attempts to discover a passage—by Giovanni da Verrazzano on behalf of the French (1524), by Esteban Gómez on behalf of the Spanish (1524–25), and by Jacques Cartier on behalf of the French (1534–42)—and was not dead even in the 1580s in England.

It was maps and globes and the explanations of them in the geographical literature of the succeeding fifty years after Martyr's discussion that kept alive the concept of the open-sea passage to the Orient. Generally this was in the form of a sea-level strait around or through North America, but it also took the form of a claim that there was an open passage across the North Pole. This was put forward by Robert Thorne in 1527, in his letters to

King Henry VIII and to the merchant Edward Lee. Thorne's general proposition was that there was "no lande inhabitable, nor Sea innavigable," consequently he could advocate that it was worthwhile "to attempt if our Seas northward be Navigable to the Pole."[12] This open polar sea thesis was to lie behind many of the English attempts later in the century, that of John Davis in 1585–87 for example and those of William Baffin and others later, as an alternative to seeking a passage westward somewhere between the sixtieth and seventieth parallels of latitude, a route that Cabot had pioneered.

We may well ask who, after Cabot had gone to Spain, aroused English interest in the cartography of North America in relation to Asia. Some authorities would probably put the cartographer Simon Grynaeus first, since he visited Sir Thomas More and More's brother-in-law John Rastell and since the latter was the first, in 1517, to attempt an Atlantic passage—even if his ships got no farther than Ireland.[13] A printed voyage collection by Johann Huttich, with maps by Grynaeus (*Novus orbis regionum*, 1532), included a world map that kept to the Waldseemüller profile of North America, though with a few variations.[14] Grynaeus did show a few islands to the north of the continental mainland and an island and a narrow southwesterly strait at the Asiatic end and may, thus, have been an important influence on the growing English interest in the passage. The famous cosmographer Gemma (Reinerus) Frisius (1508–51) was a much more long-standing influence than Grynaeus, however, largely stemming from his tenure as a professor at Louvain University, where his most famous pupil was Gerardus Mercator. His maps and globes, several in collaboration with Mercator, were to prove very influential, as were the additions he made to works by Peter Apian. Apian's world map of 1520[15] and a repetition of it in 1530 merely followed Waldseemüller, but his later works, under the influence of Gemma, showed more originality. The major work of Gemma, *De principis astronomiae . . . Item de orbis diuisione, & insulis. rebusque nuper inventis*, published in Antwerp in 1530, went into many editions,[16] the world maps varying from time to time in successive editions. His collaboration with Mercator, however, produced in 1537 what was perhaps the most influential depiction of a Northwest Passage in the sixteenth century.[17] The map showed, between North America and an Arctic landmass, a widening strait labeled "Fretum arcticum siue trium fratrum quod lusitania orientem ex ad Indos moluccas nauigare conati sunt." This "strait of the three brethren of Portugal who sought to navigate to the Indies" (a probable reference to Gaspar, Miguel, and Eanes Côrte-Real) had a southward-turning passage at its western end, which later became the Straits of Anían, a Spanish

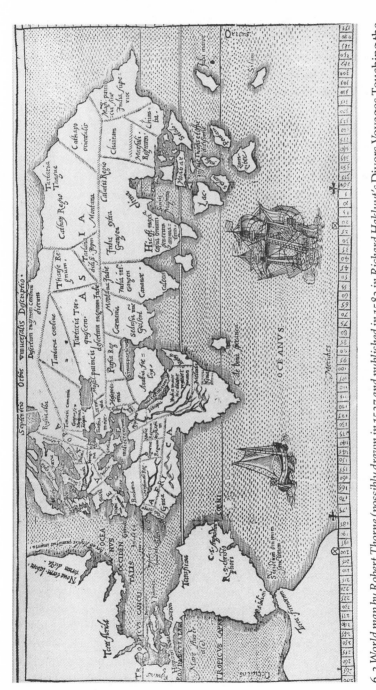

6.2 *World map by Robert Thorne (possibly drawn in 1527 and published in 1582 in Richard Hakluyt's* Divers Voyages Touching the Discouerie of America*). Thorne's map, possibly the earliest postmedieval map by an English cartographer, was intended to show the route to "the most richest londes and ilondes in the worlde" and was used as a propaganda map late into the sixteenth century. Courtesy The Newberry Library.*

version of the Northwest Passage; the map acted as a lasting inspiration to later generations of navigators, merchants, and cartographers. Mercator's own double-condiform world map showed between the North Atlantic and the Pacific a narrower passage, which was inscribed as a potential passage.[18] Peter Apian's *Cosmographica*, published in Antwerp in 1545, was improved and amended by Gemma, and its map showed a clearly defined passage with a broad exit to the Pacific around an island (intended to be Japan?). Then too Sebastian Münster's edition of Ptolemy, *Geographia Universalis*, published in Basel in 1540, contained in its "tabula novarum insularum" the first independent map of the Americas, which showed a clear passage around North America. This map was reprinted many times later in the century and, with other works of Münster's, was widely circulated for many years.

Cumulatively, the concept of a passage, usually between a complete or a divided Arctic landmass, was firmly established by these works. So far as England was concerned, the greatest influence the works had was on John Dee, who studied at Louvain under Gemma between 1547 and 1550 and brought back with him, among other cartographical materials, terrestrial and celestial globes made by Frisius-Mercator.[19] From this time onward, though not overtly until much later, Dee was to be the major theoretical influence on this subject in England. Richard Eden too was aware by 1550 of the famous globe of 1537 and of the writings of Peter Apian and Gemma Frisius. At the same time, no serious attempt was made to organize an English venture in search of a passage. Roger Barlow, it is true, did present to Henry VIII in 1541 "A Brief Summe of Geographie,"[20] which did advocate such a venture, but no notice was taken of it, and in the aforementioned critical discussions of 1547–53, after Sebastian Cabot's return to England, no detailed argument for an attempt to locate the Northwest Passage has been found, although documentation is lacking for almost all the discussions of these years.

During the time that the Northwest Passage concept was taking firm root in England, cartographers and geographers on the Continent were having a similar impact on the geographical thinking of the European nations, particularly the French. The 1540s were a great period for the cartographers of France, notably of the Dieppe School, whose maps survive mostly in manuscripts of great beauty and complexity, many presented to members of the royalty or nobility. The maps of America usually depict Labrador in some detail, though in varying form, suggesting French familiarity with at least parts of its shores though not indicating any attempts to penetrate into subarctic regions. On some of these maps, Labrador is shown disproportionately large and placed in latitudes lower than those it actually occupies. The most extraordinary depiction of Labrador is in the 1542 *Boke of Ideography* by Jean Rotz, which shows Labrador as a great peninsula, elongated and projected toward the east.[21] On the northeastern side of the peninsula there are a few names inscribed, possibly of Portuguese origin, although not found elsewhere. There are even two names inscribed on the northern side of the peninsula, the land ending there in a profusion of vegetation and giving no indication of any passage farther to the west. The enlargement and eastward orientation of Labrador may be explained by confusions about latitudes in western waters, but it remains puzzling. It may point indirectly to Portuguese exploration of the coast and, also indirectly, to French fishing activities along its shore. Rotz presents evidence of knowledge, in his detailed map, of Cartier's first voyage into the Gulf of Saint Lawrence (knowledge gained when he made the map in about 1540). He also indicates possession of some information on the second Cartier voyage—evidenced on a hemisphere map that he produced for Henry VIII in 1542, this map also indicating a much-reduced Labrador. A map by Pierre Desceliers at about the same time is very specific about the entry to the Strait of Belle Isle and an area a little to the north of it, but the greatest novelty of this map is in showing French or Spanish Basques whaling from a boat some way from the mouth of the strait.[22] Scholars have uncovered from documents in Spain a mass of information about the creation of a Basque whaling industry on the strait, centering on Red Bay,[23] but no clear evidence has been found that whaling was pursued up the Labrador shore or that any attempt was made by these Basque whalers to reconnoiter a Northwest Passage. There are some indications, probably correct ones, that French cod fishing was, by the 1540s, taking place off the shores of Labrador, but again (as indicated in the Dieppe School maps), there is no indication that this activity extended anywhere as far north as Cape Chidley at the northeastern tip of Labrador. French official concerns, from 1535 to 1543, were concentrated on the Saint Lawrence River and the promise it gave of a water passage through North America or at least of a divide from which access to the Pacific ought not to be difficult. With the failure of the Roberval colony in 1543, this preoccupation lapsed, not to be revived for more than a generation, and the cod fishery proceeded without official intervention.

Back in England, the matter of a Northwest Passage was to lie dormant for some time after 1553. The success of the Muscovy Company in trading with Russia through the White Sea and, from 1558, through the Baltic as well, together with the expeditions of Anthony Jenkinson to the Caspian and beyond, stimulated the notion of a passage eastward rather than westward, in spite of the failure of William Borough's attempt in 1556 to press his way through the ice south of Novaya Zemlya in an attempt to find a Northeast Passage. Borough's efforts did give Englishmen some experience with navigating in Arctic conditions, however, and in the 1560s the issue of a Northwest Passage again became part of official discussions in England. Humphrey Gilbert (born about 1537) was, for example, busily reading the continental geographers and examining their maps as the decade of the 1560s opened, and in 1565 he began an argument by letter with Anthony Jenkinson on the respective merits of a Northeast and a Northwest Passage, Jenkinson taking the side of the Muscovy Company (which claimed, by rather dubious arguments, rights over the northwest route as well).[24] Gilbert seemed to have converted Jenkinson to his views, and he wrote the first version of a tract attempting to prove that the Northwest Passage existed. But Jenkinson went on an expedition to Persia, and Gilbert went off to fight in the Irish wars, so the question of the passage lay in suspense until after Gilbert was free.

In the meantime, in 1558 at Venice, an engraved map in Nicolo Zeno's *Commentarri* purported to illustrate a fabricated fourteenth-century voyage by the Zeno brothers, Nicolo and Antonio, into the northwestern Atlantic.[25] This map showed an enormous Greenland, trending northwest-southeast but still attached to the old World Island landmass (as a peninsula of Europe), to the south of which various islands were added by invention. The largest of these islands, southeast of Greenland and south of a much enlarged Iceland, was called "Friesland." A passage was shown northwest of Friesland and trending along a mainland first northward and then west. To the south of the passage, landmasses emerged at the western margin of the map, captioned "Estotiland" and "Drogeo," and beyond the northward trend of the passage the open sea continued to the west. The Zeno map was taken as gospel, more or less, for a generation after 1558. It survived into the 1570s and the period of renewed Northwest Passage activity largely through Mercator. He accepted most of its features in his great world map of 1569, which very soon came to be regarded as the authentic view of the world, with copies taken by explorers on such significant voyages as that of Martin Frobisher in 1576.[26] It is true that Mercator detached Greenland from the Old World landmass and showed it as an island—but he retained the Zeno orientation. Friesland appeared southeast of Greenland only slightly reduced; Drogeo was relegated to an island off Labrador, but the northern part of a much-distorted Labrador was named "Estotiland." Mercator also added, from the Zeno text, a great island west of Greenland, marking the turning of the passage from north to west. This misleading picture led even as experienced a navigator as John Davis to retain Friesland on his charts, and Friesland was shown on the "English Globe" of 1592 and was retained in the 1603 revision. It was thus a mirage that continued to haunt explorers of the passage route for nearly half a century.

Frobisher Takes Up the Search for the Passage

There is some obscurity about how the Northwest Passage question was revived in England. Certainly Michael Lok, a London merchant who for long had traded in the Mediterranean and elsewhere, became convinced of the need to explore the route to the northwest. In 1578, a contemporary English author tried to make out that Martin Frobisher had for a long time been a protagonist of such a venture, but this lacks confirmation. What is certain is that John Dee came forward as the learned adviser of Lok and other London merchants in their discussions about an attempt to find the passage, for which Dee had become and was to remain, until 1583, a vigorous protagonist and would-be participant. Indeed, by 1576, preparations had begun for an expedition to seek the passage when Gilbert's tract, which he had revised in the early 1570s, was put into print by the poet George Gascoigne as *A Discourse of a Discoverie for a New Passage to Cataia*.[27] Gilbert cited many of the geographers and cartographers already mentioned, from Peter Martyr, through Gemma and Münster, down to Abraham Ortelius, whose *Typus Orbis Terrarum* in his *Theatrum Orbis Terrarum*[28] of 1570 had added, since Gilbert's first draft of his *Discourse*, a very clear and colorful depiction of an open passage to the north of North America, although Gilbert did not mention the most famous of Mercator's world maps, that of 1569, which also showed an open passage through Arctic waters. In his tract, Gilbert also knew of the 1537 globe with its Strait of the Three Brethren and argued strongly for the existence of a circumpolar current that appeared to provide empirical proof of the cartographers' assumptions. Others of his arguments might seem trivial, but together they presented a good case, based on what was known and had been surmised about the northern waters. The Gilbert tract thus provided ammunition for

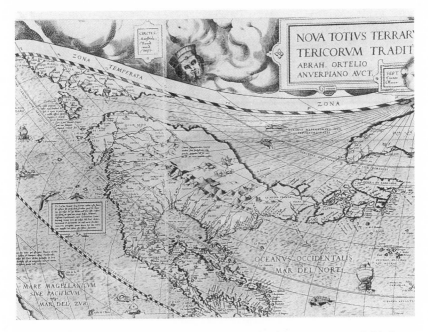

6.3 Detail from the North American portion of "Nova Totius Terrarum Orbis Lusta Neotericorum Traditiones Descriptio," the world map by Abraham Ortelius (1564). After Gerhardus Mercator, Ortelius was the most famous European geographer-cartographer of the sixteenth century. He compiled this section of the map from several different sources (including the explorations of Coronado, Soto, and Cartier) in an attempt to show the Northwest Passage via an open sea north of North America, connecting with the Straits of Anían and the Pacific Ocean to the west. By permission of The British Library.

Lok, Dee, and their chosen instrument, Martin Frobisher, to launch the first serious expedition in 1576.

Attention would soon be centred on English experiments regarding the passage; it would be valuable to have evidence of attempts of rival European powers, but such evidence is very thin. For example, the Côrte-Real family bequeathed to their descendants a belief that the original "Three Brothers" had, indeed, found indications at least of a passage to the west, but we have no information on how systematically their heirs and successors tried to exploit this belief before the 1570s. A report of a voyage by Vasques Eanes Côrte-Real in or about 1574 came into the hands of Richard Hakluyt when he was collecting voyage information for Gilbert early in

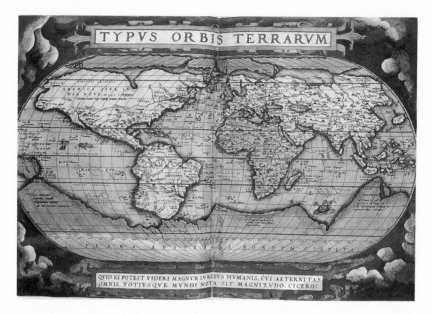

6.4 "Typus Orbis Terrarum" (Abraham Ortelius, 1570). This map, part of Ortelius's great atlas Theatrum Orbis Terrarum (Antwerp, 1570), clearly shows an open sea route between the northern portions of North America and a polar landmass. Courtesy National Maritime Museum, London.

1582. This report indicated that Côrte-Real, "arriving on the coast of the saide America, in fiftye eyghte degrees of latitude, founde a great entrance exceeding deepe and broade, without all impediment of ice, into which they passed above twentie leagues, and found it alwaies to trende towardes the South, the land lying lowe and plaine on eyther side. And that they perswaded themselves verely, there was a way open to the south sea."[29] According to the report, Côrte-Real's ship turned back only because it did not have enough provisions to go farther. This might well suggest, though the latitude was at least two degrees too low, that this vessel entered Hudson Strait. But there was to be little further indication as to the nature of the voyage and its apparent results.

The preparations for the first English voyage under Frobisher were carefully made, and two vessels were constructed.[30] The vessel intended for Frobisher himself was the *Michael*, designed by the famous shipwright Matthew Baker with the assistance of Joseph Addye. It was of only thirty tons burden, together with a pinnace of seven tons, and its master was to be Owine Griffyne. We fortunately have all the details of the ship construction and furnishing. The latest navigation instruments were provided for the use of the crew, and the large Mercator map of 1569, the Ortelius map of 1570, and three other manuscript maps, no doubt all showing a passage, were carried. The other vessel, the *Gabriel*, was also small (twenty-five tons); its master was the experienced Christopher Hall, who was to leave a detailed account of the voyage. Frobisher himself had little previous nautical experience, being primarily a soldier. His judgment on maritime matters was uneven, and his dependence on experienced ship's masters, like Christopher Hall, was almost absolute.

The vessels left Gravesend on 12 June 1576. The ships proved only moderately seaworthy, and it was 27 July before they cleared the Shetlands. They found land on 12 August, taking the latitude as 61° north. This was southern Greenland, but on their maps it was the independent island of Friesland, derived from the Zeno map of 1558, still incorporated (as has been shown) in Mercator's map. Hall described the land as "rising like pinnacles of steeples, and all covered with snow," the ice offshore being such that Frobisher could not make a landing.[31] Crossing the mouth of Davis Strait, the expedition nearly came to an end in a fierce gale. The *Michael* was damaged and barely survived, its pinnace lost; the *Gabriel* was affected less. The *Michael* was repaired at sea sufficiently to proceed as the storm died down. The land sighted on 30 July was taken to be Labrador, but attempts to approach it were unsuccessful. It was in fact Resolution Island (named Queen Elizabeth's Foreland), at the mouth of Hudson Strait. They were soon off the southeastern tip of Baffin Island, and working their way north, they found a series of small islands and then a sound and sandy bay (Priors Bay they called it) on 13–15 August. Icebergs were now moving south and cleared sufficiently to enable Frobisher to enter the sound (present-day Frobisher Bay). After some exploration he found that land was to be seen on either side, and he sailed into the sound; he claimed to have followed the passage for 150 miles, assuming the land to the north to be Asia and that on the south America. He named the sound Frobisher's Straits and assured himself that it was indeed the passage.

Contact by boat with an Inuit group brought the first descriptions of this people. A man taken on board was understood to indicate that the sound continued indefinitely to the west. However, the boat that took the Inuit back to land passed out of sight and was captured by the Inuits, along with five of the crew, who were never seen again. At a later contact, by a trick, the English hoisted an Inuit man in his kayak into the ship to take to En-

6.5 The North Atlantic from Gerardus Mercator's 1569 world map. This map, depicting much information obtained from the Zeno brothers' map of "Frisland," "Estotiland," and "Drogeo," attempted to fit the imaginary cartography of the Zeno brothers into what was taking shape as more accurate information on the northwestern Atlantic. The map was carried by Frobisher on his first voyage. Courtesy Maritiem Museum "Prins Hendrik," Rotterdam, the Netherlands.

gland. A number of small islands were named and specimens collected from them after a formal ceremony of taking possession in the queen's name. On 26 August the men concluded that they could do no more and turned for home, picking up "the Cape Labradore" (Cape Chidley?) on the twenty-seventh and Greenland (as Friesland) on 1 September. They made the run to Orkney by 25 September, after surviving another storm, entered

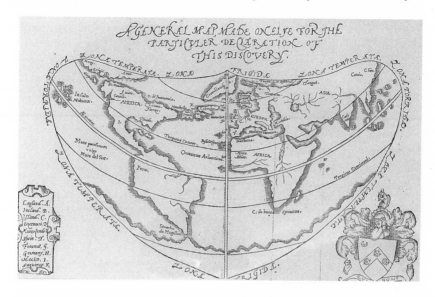

6.6 Copy of the Ortelius world map of 1564. This map was drawn by Sir Humphrey Gilbert to illustrate his Discourse of a Discoverie for a New Passage to Cataia *(London, 1576) and was clearly designed to provide "proof" of the existence of a Northwest Passage to the Moluccas (shown off the North American coast to the west). Courtesy The Newberry Library.*

Harwich Harbour on 2 October, and were well received at Blackwall on 9 October. Frobisher, at least, was convinced the passage had been found and soon communicated this to the sponsors of the voyage. The Inuit man who was brought to England by Frobisher created a great deal of interest not only in the city but also at court. His clothing, his appearance—particularly the somewhat Oriental cast of his features ("like unto a Tartar")— and his kayak, together with the stories that the explorers told about his people, not only generated interest but also furthered the belief in the proximity of Frobisher's discovery to Asia. Several portraits were made of this Inuit man, and information on him was conveyed to the Netherlands quite rapidly. Unfortunately he did not survive his intensive scrutiny for long, dying either of an unfamiliar diet or, it was thought, of pneumonia.[32]

Frobisher had brought back not only the Inuit man but also samples of whatever the crew could find to indicate that they had actually been on land: "floures, some greene grasse, and one . . . peece of a blacke stone, much like to seacole in colour, whiche by the weighte seemed to be some kinde of mettal or Mynerall."[33] The stone was the only tangible thing (other than the passage itself) that might be of interest for future exploration. It was brought to the attention of "certain Goldfinders" in London, who found, to their satisfaction, that it contained a substantial quantity of gold. This caused much excitement and many offers to go to find more or to finance further exploration, and "Frobisher's gold" was even brought to Queen Elizabeth I's attention when she was lodging with the Earl of Warwick in Essex. Lok's investment appeared to have been worthwhile, and shortly after Frobisher's return a charter was granted to "The Company of Cathay" to pursue the matter further.

For this voyage, the queen herself adventured the *Aide*, a ship of two hundred tons, and the *Michael* and the *Gabriel* were fitted out again. Frobisher, on the *Aide*, had with him as his lieutenant George Best, who was later to write the most substantial tract on the series of voyages; Christopher Hall was master. Edward Fenton commanded the *Gabriel*, with William Smyth as master, while the *Michael* had Gilbert Yorke as captain and James Beare as master. The expedition left the Thames on 27 May 1577[34] but put into Harwich to discharge some men (including convicts for mining), since Frobisher's expedition was believed to be overmanned. This was now an official voyage, and the orders to do this came from the Privy Council. The ships touched at Orkney on 7 June and from there reached southern Greenland ("Freeseland" to them) on 4 July. Frobisher made several landings as they sailed north but soon set course for "Frobishers Strait" and, after surviving a storm, reached the islands that lay at its mouth on 17 July, locating the northern side and "Halls Island," where the ore had been found. None was discovered this time, though many specimens were found on other islands searched, which indicated to the "goldfinders" that the same mineral was widespread. One island, the Countess of Warwick's (Kodlunarn) Island, was even selected for mining, and twenty tons of ore were extracted and loaded on the three vessels. Before any mining was attempted, however, Frobisher went ashore on Baffin Island and set up a cairn on the highest point in honour of the Earl of Warwick, now one of their principal sponsors. It was some days before contact was made with the Inuits, and though discussions with the native people started well, they soon turned to hostility. The Englishmen came under arrow-fire, although they contrived to capture another man to take home to England. Frobisher's party eventually found a secure anchorage inside the "strait" and visited the southern shore, which they thought to be the American mainland. Frobisher, on the *Aide*, explored into the "strait," but it was still blocked at its head with ice; at this point, Frobisher appeared to be convinced by his men that it was not a passage but only a deep inlet—a fact not stressed in subsequent reports of the voyage.

The ships set out on their return voyage to England on 24 August; the return was uneventful, although the vessels were separated on the way home, with the *Gabriel* coming to Bristol and the *Michael* round the north of Scotland to Great Yarmouth while the *Aide* put in at Milford Haven and lay there until orders came for it to deposit the ore (and presumably the *Gabriel's* also) at the Castle of Bristol. At Windsor, Frobisher reported on the voyage to the queen, who was pleased to name the land newly discovered "Meta Incognita." The "goldfinders" on the expedition had brought to London numerous samples to be tested, which were, to almost all the experts' satisfaction, said to contain sufficient ore to make further venturing worthwhile, even if the stone was so hard that pulverizing it and washing it were beyond existing facilities; preparations had to be made to set up a blast furnace at Deptford.

Much had been learned on this voyage about the Inuit people and was published in Dionese Settle's *A True Reporte of the Last Voyage into the West and Northwest Regions*, which came out very rapidly (Settle had been a gentleman adventurer on board the *Aide*). Moreover, to add to the initial capture of an Inuit man, a woman and her year-old child had been seized later. At Bristol these people were visited by artists (they had already been drawn on board ship by John White), and the man was to give displays with his kayak. He soon fell ill and died, largely from injuries sustained when he was captured, and the woman followed him soon after, but the child was taken to London and lived for a time there before she too died. A little book with engravings of these people was published early in 1578, and although no copy has survived, it was one of the sources for the intense publicity about these people. The publicity spread over much of Europe in the next few years,[35] since the semi-Asiatic appearance of the Inuits—linking them with Samoyeds in northern Russia—seemed to confirm that the peoples of northern America and of Asia were of the same stock, therefore indicating a close conjunction of the two continents.

The result of England's interest in both the "gold" and the seemingly Asiatic natives was a rush to subscribe to a bigger and better venture. Lok, as the business head of the new enterprise, poured his own fortune, all that came in by subscriptions, and all he could borrow into preparing a fleet of fifteen vessels.[36] There was even a subscription of one thousand pounds from the queen to turn it into a national enterprise. The *Aide* was again the flagship, with the experienced *Gabriel* and *Michael*, but the miscellany of other vessels making up the rest of the fleet was assembled from various ports. Frobisher went ahead with the ships first ready and waited at Harwich for the remainder to come from the Thames.[37] They were duly united and sailed from Harwich on 31 May, but this time they sailed into the English Channel (picking up Cornish miners on the way) and past Ireland, leaving the coast on 5 June. It took them only to 20 June to reach Greenland, which they formally annexed as West England (still thinking it to be Friesland, though some had begun to have doubts of its separateness from Greenland). This time the passage of Davis Strait was much less straightforward than it had been before. Storms and fog scattered the ships, with only a few making it directly to Frobisher's "straits," where they found much greater concentrations of ice than previously; indeed one of the vessels (the *Bark Dennis*) was crushed and sank, though its complement was saved by boats from its consorts.

Initially, a number of smaller ships made their way into the "strait," though not without difficulty; only gradually did the rest find their way to "the Queenes Forland" (or Lok's Land), Frobisher's *Aide* being among the last. Frobisher, with several vessels, found himself swept southward, first thinking he was in his "strait," then eventually realising he was not; yet he followed the new opening. Best says: "The rest of the Fleete following the course of the Generall whyche ledde them the way, passed vp above 60 Leagues within the seyd doubtfull and supposed straytes, having always a fayre continente uppon their starreboorde syde and a continuance still of an open Sea before them." Best tells us that Frobisher tried to convince the seamen that he was on his own "strait" (even though he knew he was not) in order to get the other ships to follow him. "Howbeit I suppose he rather dissembled hys opinion therein, than otherwyse. . . . And as some of the company reported, be hath since confessed, that if it had not bin for the charge and care he had of ye Fleete, and fraughted Shippes, he both would and could have gone through to the South Sea, called Mare del Sur, and dissolved the long doubt of the passage which we seeke to find in the ritch Countrery of Cataya."[38]

It seems clear that Frobisher did put into Hudson Strait; indeed, if he had proceeded 180 miles along it he would almost have passed through it into Hudson Bay. This was indeed the first known passage by any ships on the way westward from Davis Strait, and some of the seamen even claimed to have seen land to the south and to have observed the passage widening as they went.

On their way out, the fleet of Frobisher's third voyage had called at Cornish ports and there collected 120 miners who were to mine as much rock on the chosen island as they could while three ships, the *Judith*, the *Gabriel*, and the *Michael*, were to remain on the island over the winter, with one hundred men in all, in a house specially prepared for them, under Geoffrey Fenton's command. The miners among them were to work when possible to prepare material for the following season. Unfortunately, some sections of the house and the provisions designed for the party had gone down with the *Bark Dennis*. Nonetheless, Fenton offered to stay over with a smaller number of men (sixty instead of one hundred), and indeed a small stone house and other accommodations were built so that a holding party might stay, even though Frobisher forbade any such attempt. From 30 July onward, the miners were at work on Kodlunarn Island; "the Goldfinders made tryall of the Ore," and after the *Gabriel* arrived on 2 August (it had been far up the "strait"), Frobisher gave them only until 28 August to complete the task of raising and stowing two thousand tons of stone. Meanwhile, in a pinnace hastily constructed on land, George Best explored inland in the "strait," which he found to narrow as he progressed, and later Frobisher retraced his route and went still farther, to find that the "strait" petered out into a tangle of small islands. The ore was stowed by 30 August, and the fleet set out over the next few days; they were scattered by storms and landed in England in several ports, but, as Best claims, all survived. Frobisher got to London to report his success but there was met with bitter disappointment. The blast furnace at Deptford had been put into action and the various methods of extracting precious metal from the pulverised rock tried, but no gold could be found. The hard stone of the Canadian Shield yielded nothing more than iron pyrites and mica (to which a modern-day expedition adds feldspar, quartz, and quartzite, all of them sparkling stones).[39]

In the 1850s Charles Francis Hall found Frobisher relics at Kodlunarn and brought back many items, which were once in the collections of the Royal Geographical Society and the Smithsonian.[40] These items, except for one piece of iron bloom recovered in the 1970s in the Smithsonian, have been lost. The next visit to the Frobisher site came with the Rawson-Macmillan subarctic expedition of the Field Museum of Chicago in 1927, when photographs of the ruins of the small stone house and of the mining trenches were brought back, along with a few European artifacts.[41] In 1974, W. A. Kenyon, of the Royal Ontario Museum, made a further search and clarified some aspects of the site.[42] Finally, in 1981, a full-scale expedition was mounted by the Smithsonian Institution; a full report of this expedition has not yet been published. The work done in 1981 was concerned with making a detailed topographic map and with laying out the plans of the surviving traces of buildings and mining excavations while collecting all the evidence that could be found about the island. The preliminary report states that "the major features at Kodlunarn Island include a 'ships-way' (dry dock), a probable smithy, assay office, water reservoir (or mine), a 'sentry house,' a possible long shed or barracks, two large caches, pits, and two other designated structures." Finds included "fragments of building-brick, firebrick, roofing-tile, ceramic vessels (including crucibles), iron nails, slag, mortar, charcoal, wood (much of it apparently oak) . . . [and] three new complete iron blooms."[43]

The Frobisher ventures were the largest made overseas by the English in the sixteenth century—the third voyage alone costing more than twenty thousand pounds. Their failure destroyed the confidence of London merchants in overseas speculative voyaging and slowed up attempts to colonize North America. Lok, financially ruined, retired badly hurt; the investors lost all they had subscribed. It was not until 1612 that a venture comparable to that of Frobisher's was again mounted. Small and tentative voyages, involving relatively limited financial outlay, did follow between 1585 and 1611, and the geographical results they brought were very substantial and kept alive the belief in the feasibility of making further discoveries and, finally, discovering the passage itself. In the meantime, new theoretical approaches to the passage were developed.

Theory and the Passage after the Frobisher Voyages

Although the bulk of geographical theory regarding the passage still focused on the northwestern Atlantic, where Frobisher had explored, the possibility of an approach to the Northwest Passage from the Pacific side of North America was not ruled out by the cartographers. Ortelius added to his 1575 edition of *Theatrum Orbus Terrarum* a map of the Straits of Anían, showing a ship sailing smoothly southward through a wide inlet between Asia and America.[44] This is not known to have aroused any interest in Spain, which had turned a blind eye to the possibilities of exploring the western coast of North America since the 1540s. But it could well have been influential in England. During the 1576–77 discussions that preceded the launching of Francis Drake's expedition, the possibility that he should explore the prospects of the Pacific end of the Northwest Passage was raised and was included in the preliminary list of objectives that he might aim for, though in fact this list was ultimately modified to limit his official duty in the Pacific to determining how far down the western coast of South America the Spanish had penetrated.[45] Nonetheless, when Drake was faced in 1579 with the almost certain possibility that the *Golden Hind* would be intercepted if it attempted to return to England by way of the Strait of Magellan, the possibility of making a voyage homeward by the mythical strait (and the equally unknown passage) presented itself to him as an idea worth investigating. He had learned in Mexico that to make his way north, he would have to sail far out into the ocean to obtain a wind that would carry him in that direction. This he did, although there has been controversy over how high a latitude he reached. John Davis, who would have ascertained the facts from Drake's men after the return of the *Golden Hind*, stated firmly in *The Worlde's Hydrographical Discription* (1595) that Drake "coasted all the westerne shores of America untill he came into the Septenrionall latitude of forty eight degrees [48° north] being on the backe syde of [the] new found land."[46] This appears to be virtually conclusive: Drake turned eastward in the cold Japan Current toward the North American shore, thereby abandoning any further search for the Straits of Anían toward the north. The points at which he attempted to land and eventually did land on the Pacific coast have formed a topic of controversy for years. They are irrelevant here, but the naming of Nova Albion and its formal annexation to the English Crown was not a mere gesture but the very real staking of England's claim to the Pacific shore. If, as Drake appears to have believed, there actually was a Northwest Passage with an exit to the Pacific at the Straits of Anían, then an English claim, even a paper one that appeared on subsequent maps, to a "discovery" on the western coast of North America might conceivably assist those who eventually achieved the breakthrough from the Atlantic to the Pacific.

If English interest in the Pacific was aroused by Drake's voyage, the real theoretical basis for the passage continued to be the explorations—from Cabot to Frobisher—in eastern Canada. Gilbert's map of 1576 owed most to Mercator and Ortelius (who had derived their data from the Cabot and Côrte-Real voyages) in the depiction of the supposed passage, and the two maps in George Best's *True Discourse* (1578) were the result of specific explorations during the three previous years. The general map in Best's work was again influenced by Ortelius in what it showed of the "Terra Septentrionalis" or "Northern Lands," but it was able to depict islands in the

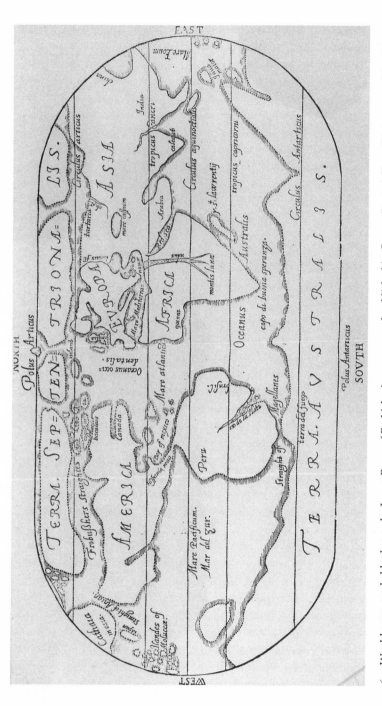

6.7 World map, probably drawn by James Beare of Frobisher's voyages and published in George Best, A True Discourse of the Late Voyages of Discoverie (London, 1578). The map illustrates a continuous navigable passageway of "Frobishers Straightes" and the "Straight of Anian" between the Atlantic and the Pacific and was intended to serve as further incentive for British exploration in North American waters. Courtesy John Carter Brown Library at Brown University.

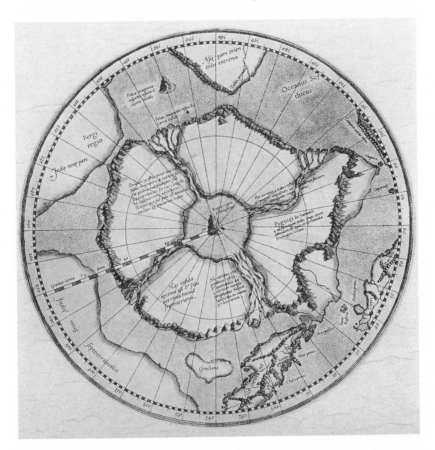

6.8 The Arctic, inset from Mercator's world map (1569), depicts a conception of polar geography borrowed by Mercator from a fourteenth-century tract, Inventio fortunatae, *describing the "indrawing seas" derived from medieval Norse geographical lore. Courtesy Maritiem Museum "Prins Hendrik," Rotterdam, the Netherlands.*

wide strait that, west of the region actually explored, was boldly labeled "Frobisher's Straighte." Best's more specific map concentrated on the areas explored. "East England," it is true, remained an anomalous island, but north of "The Mistaken Straightes," which ran right through to "the way trending to Cathaiai," was one group of islands, each named, that formed both the northern limit of the Mistaken Straits and the southern shore of "Frobisher's Straighte," with Frobisher Bay still assumed to be a strait. On the north side, six islands explored were named and seven more un-

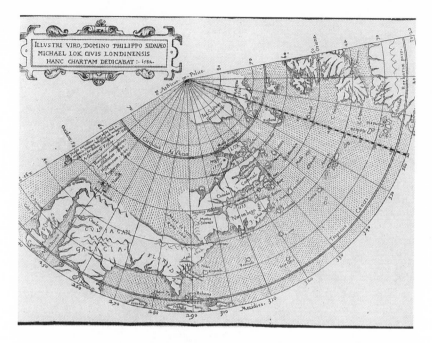

ILLVSTRI VIRO, DOMINO PHILIPPO SIDNÆO
MICHAEL LOK CIVIS LONDINENSIS
HANC CHARTAM DEDICABAT : 1582.

6.9 Map of the Northern Hemisphere by Michael Lok (?), probably drawn in 1581 and published in Hakluyt's Divers Voyages Touching the Discouerie of America *(1582). Compiled on this map are sources from Saint Brendan to Frobisher, including many mythical geographical features. The map was intended to bolster English claims to North America and to serve as propaganda for further exploration in search of a Northwest Passage. Courtesy The Newberry Library.*

named, all enclosing the main strait, which trended southeastward, though not so far as to show a western opening. However crude this might appear to our eyes, it was a revelation to contemporaries, but in the short term, after the collapse of the Company of Cathay, there were few to take in what was represented.

One who did not lose faith was John Dee. In 1580 he did two things: first, he presented to the queen a great map (still extant), which showed a clear passage,[47] and second, he acquired from Sir Humphrey Gilbert—whose patent of June 1578 was assumed to give Gilbert preemptive rights over North America wherever it was not already occupied by Europeans—all lands north of 50° north. During the years 1580 and 1583, Dee consulted spirits through his medium, Edward Kelley, and convinced himself that they promised success in this area. He formed a partnership to exploit his grant with Adrian Gilbert, Sir Humphrey's younger brother, and with John Davis, who had been in service with the Gilberts as a boy and was, by this time, an accomplished seaman and navigator. However, Dee was distracted by the prospect of a visit to Poland and Bohemia in order to follow his spiritualist and alchemist bent, and so he left Northwest Passage business entirely in September 1583. Nonetheless, Adrian Gilbert, in 1584, received a patent entitling him to exclusive exploitation of the supposed passage.[48] Gilbert, in turn, is not known to have done anything more positive about the project except to turn it over to Walter Raleigh and his business partner, the London merchant William Sanderson, who raised enough money to launch John Davis on an exploring voyage in 1585.[49] They had the goodwill of Sir Francis Walsingham, the queen's secretary of state, who had discussed the Northwest Passage question with Dee before he left England. Richard Hakluyt too, in 1584 when he wrote his long confidential brief for the queen ("A Particular Discourse," generally known as *Discourse of Western Planting*), included a substantial section on "the northwest passage to Cathaia and China," using many of the arguments of the continental geographers and cartographers of the time.[50]

The Northwest Passage Voyages of John Davis

John Davis set out on his first voyage in command of the *Sunshine* (fifty tons), accompanied by the *Moonshine* (thirty-five tons) with William Bruton as captain.[51] The vessels left on 7 June 1585 and, in fog, rounded southern Greenland (still regarded as Friesland on the charts) and made harbor at Godthaab Fjord on 29 July. Davis identified the landfall as Greenland and thought this marked the southern limit of the island (naming it "Gilbert Sound"). Proceeding some way up the coast, he then crossed what was to become known as Davis Strait to Baffin Island, inside the Arctic circle, naming the large promontory Mount Raleigh, discovering the entry to Cumberland Sound (which he named), and penetrating it some little way in the hope that this might be *the* passage. He worked southward to mark an eastern point (Cape Walsingham) and then decided to return to England, which he did (with his consort vessel), reaching Dartmouth on 30 September. On 3 October he wrote to Walsingham in most optimistic terms, going so far as

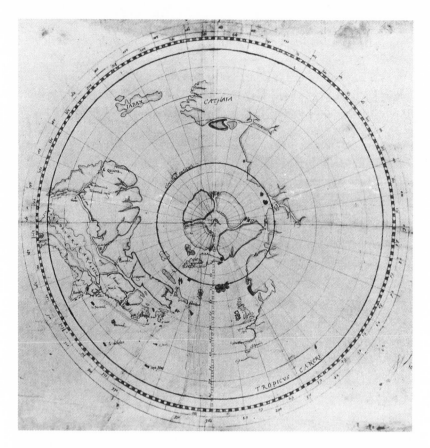

6.10 *Chart of the Northern Hemisphere by John Dee (c. 1582). Dee, the noted Elizabethan scholar, drew this map for Sir Humphrey Gilbert. The map shows several alternate routes to the Orient from the Atlantic, including several through the North American continent. Courtesy Rare Book Department, Free Library of Philadelphia.*

to say, "The northwest passage is a matter nothing doubtfull but at any tyme almost to be passed the sea navigable, voyd of ice [he had sailed in a very favorable season], the ayre tollerable and the water very depe."[52]

The result of Davis's first voyage raised the hopes of western merchants already hampered in their trade with the Iberian peninsula by Spanish intransigence. Several merchant towns in the southwest of England—Exeter, Totnes, and Dartmouth—were willing to support a new voyage. Now that Greenland had been identified, there was a chance that a route to Asia might be found by sailing northward through Arctic waters east of Greenland, where fishing voyages were already under way a considerable distance up the coast. Vessels were sent to make this attempt, but they failed to press it home. It was left to Davis to do so in his second voyage of 1586 in which he, in the *Moonshine*, would continue his exploration of the western coast of Greenland and further his knowledge of what we know as Baffin Island.[53] His contacts with the Inuits, whom he encountered on the first voyage, were developed further during the second voyage, but Davis's exploration absorbed most of his interest; he did note, however, the possibility of getting sealskins and walrus leather from the Inuits for trade. He crossed safely to Baffin Island, evidently just north of the Middle Pack (the ice island that dominates the Davis Strait toward the north), and worked into Cumberland Sound, about which his experience of 1585 had centred. Alas for him, he was to find that this too was an inlet, as he believed Frobisher Bay to be. Sailing down the coast, he eventually came to a channel from which there was a "furious outfall" against which the *Moonshine* could not make its way. This was clearly Hudson Strait, the same "Mistaken Straits" of 1578. He noted fine cod fishing (the French had already done so) off the Labrador coast and arrived home at the end of September. This time he was more cautiously optimistic about the passage; writing to William Sanderson on 4 October, he said that he was "sure it must be in one of four places or not at all," though he does not give any clue as to the four places.[54] The southwestern towns that had given him cloth and other merchandise to sell in China were now disillusioned, and no further help was forthcoming even though he was set on making another voyage in 1587.[55] For this voyage, thanks to Richard Hakluyt, we have his log, and the "occurrences" on it fill out his brief narrative. But his log also reveals his careful navigation and his charting of his discoveries as he went, even though the charts have not survived.

This time, again in the *Moonshine*, though arranging for two ships to fish off Labrador, he recovered the Greenland coast and made his way northward, making occasional contacts with the Inuits and doing a little trading. However his main objective was to sail as far north as seemed reasonable, given the size of his ship and the stores he had. We might think that the attempt to search the eastern Greenland coast in 1586, which had come to nothing, and his new determination to sail north arose from the revival of an old English theory, first put forward by Robert Thorne the Younger in 1527, that there was an open Polar Sea and that it was possible to sail across the Arctic Ocean. Certainly, Davis had no difficulty in reaching 72°12' north to a point he named "Sanderson his hope," also naming a Hakluyt Island on his way. He did not know that he had entered the North Water, a zone that remains mysteriously free of ice (the precise reason for which has eluded modern scientists) before the solid ice of the northern waters again takes hold a few degrees farther north. He was sure he could have gone on indefinitely, eventually either crossing the Pole or turning south to Asia by a voyage at about 75° northwestward and then southward. But he was not foolhardy, and so he turned back, again bypassing the Middle Pack at about 69° north. Sailing southwest, he picked up his old landmark, Mount Raleigh on Baffin Island, and continued on down the coast. Once again he noted Hudson Strait as an "inlet or gulfe . . . the sea falling down into the gulf with a mighty overfall, and with such sort as forcible motions like whirlepooles,"[56] but once again he lacked the capacity to enter it, though he made his mark by naming Cape Chidley at its southern point of entry (the name has remained). His careful charting of his route was his great achievement, and he was able to return satisfied that he had done his best and had placed the great entry, shortly to be known as Davis Strait, indelibly on the maps (even if he still believed that southern Greenland was a separate island).

Davis's determination to find the passage is seen in his desperate plan to sail into the Pacific and find the passage's eastern end, which some cartographers had placed as low as 40° north. Accordingly, he sailed with Thomas Cavendish in 1591, who was bound for the Philippines and China, expecting that, when this expedition sailed westward to Asia, he could continue northward until he encountered the eastern end of the passage. His heroic attempts to get through the Strait of Magellan and into the Pacific against the full force of the westerlies brought him twice free of the land to be twice beaten back into the strait and forced to turn back. His voyage home was a nightmare in which most of his men died after his store of barreled seabirds went bad, but he survived to return to England in 1593, where he discovered that Cavendish, before dying in the Atlantic after Davis turned back, had blamed him for desertion. He was able to disprove these charges but was destined to give up the search for the passage, except in writing, for the rest of his seagoing life, which ended in the Straits of Malacca in 1605. However, his two small books, *The World's Hydrographical Description* (1595) and *The Seaman's Secrets* (1599), valuable as they were for showing his navigational expertise, reiterated his view that the passage should still be sought. In 1595 he was pressing the Privy Council to renew the venture, and in 1599 he stressed the relatively kindly climate and conditions in the short Arctic summer. But his efforts were to no avail: he entered the service of the East India Company and gave up his vision. The Wright-Molyneux globe of 1592 (reissued in 1603) put "Fretum Davis" on the map but showed the entries from Hudson Strait to Cumberland Sound as mere inlets, whereas the real passage was indicated far to the north.[57] This picture was broadly repeated in Edward Wright's American map he made in 1599 for Hakluyt, which became the standard for some years.[58]

Early-Seventeenth-Century Attempts to Find the Passage

Between 1587 and 1602 there is no clear indication of any further moves in England or other European countries to renew the search for the passage, though the possibility of a revived interest in the subject remained. Some of this interest was stimulated by the word that had reached England of Portuguese attempts to discover the passage. During the same time that Frobisher and Davis had been seeking the passage, the Portuguese continued to maintain their own interest in the Northwest Passage. The fact that the exiled Portuguese government, established in France in 1584–85, displayed continuing interest in and knowledge of the Northwest Passage idea strongly suggests that Portuguese concern with the passage and its possibilities for Portuguese Asiatic trade, in the course of which so many vessels were being lost, was much greater than surviving documents reveal. Richard Hakluyt's information, gained in 1582, of a voyage by Vasques Eanes Côrte-Real in about 1574 (noted above) was extremely sketchy. Later, as chaplain to the English embassy in Paris in 1583–84, Hakluyt had several opportunities to discuss with Dom António (the leader of the expatriate Portuguese government) and his entourage matters of mutual interest, including the question of the Northwest Passage. Hakluyt found the Portuguese willing to talk, and Dom António showed him a map, presumably based on Portuguese discoveries or theories, that delineated a passage from the Atlantic to the Pacific at 57° north. Hakluyt did not report extensively on these conversations and expanded only slightly the data on the 1574 voyage from what he had already written in 1582. As brief as Hakluyt's comments were, they were significant. He stated that, at 57° north, the explorer (Côrte-Real) had found "a great entraunce very deep and broad . . . unto which they passed xx^ti [twenty] leagues and found it alwayes trended toward the south."[59] Hakluyt had been told by the Portuguese that Côrte-Real's vessel would have continued its voyage through

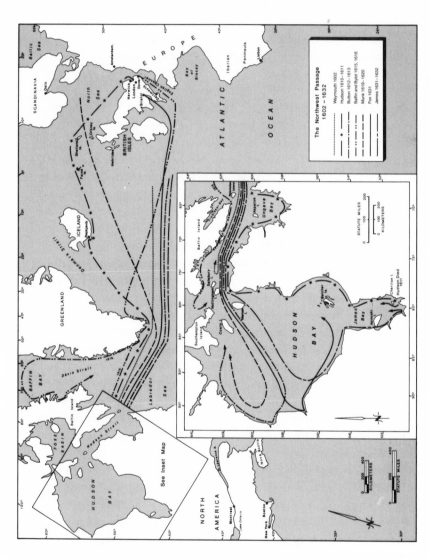

Map 6.2 The Northwest Passage, 1602–1632.

the passage if it had had sufficient supplies to enable him to do so and had there been more than a single vessel available to negotiate the passage. Why the latitude should have been given as 57° rather than the 60° at which Cape Chidley (the starting point for the entry to Hudson Strait) stands is not clear. The Portuguese were very skilled at taking latitudes, and an error of two or three degrees appears improbable. Perhaps the commander of the ship wanted to indicate a passage in lower latitudes than he actually established in order not to discourage those who followed him. An alternate suggestion is that he discovered only Hamilton Inlet at about 55° and wanted to exaggerate his northing. Hakluyt was told that the Portuguese had intended to follow up the discoveries that had been made by this expedition, but nothing appears to have been done. Portugal fell into turmoil in the late 1570s, and it seems unlikely that the Spanish, when they took over Portugal in 1580, would have known about these voyages and projects or, indeed, that they would have been seriously interested in following up on these explorations. In considering what has been said about Portuguese enterprises in search of the Northwest Passage, it should be remembered that the evidence we have comes to us verbally, second- or thirdhand. The sole exception is the map that Hakluyt saw; this map was clearly (in part, at least) a theoretical construction rather than a chart of an actual voyage, but it did contain material that had not otherwise been published.

English interest in the passage was rekindled by the publication, in volume 3 of Hakluyt's *Principal Navigations* (1600), of the accounts of the Frobisher and Davis voyages, along with some of the Portuguese information.[60] On 31 December 1600, the charter of what came to be known as the East India Company was granted to a group of members of the Muscovy and Levant Companies and some others, and preparations were made to send an expedition to the East Indies. However, the realization of the long voyage by way of the Cape of Good Hope and of the chances of obstruction by the Portuguese and the Dutch led to alternative plans for an expedition to find the Northwest Passage. Captain George Waymouth was chosen to lead an expedition with two flyboats (cargo carriers of the smaller sort), *Discovery* (seventy tons) and *Godspeed* (sixty tons). They were to go to China and present letters to the Great Khan as well as gifts and some cargo. They set out on 2 May 1602 and sighted the southern part of Greenland (now released from the mythical Friesland) on 18 June.[61] They sailed westward to find, unlike Davis's experience in 1587, that ice and storms were to be their lot. They identified Warwick's Foreland at 62°30′ north on 29 June and ascertained that they were at Frobisher Bay. Standing to the south, it seems they identified Resolution Island at the mouth of Hudson Strait, "which if it be so [i.e., an island] then Lumley's Inlet, and the next Southerly Inlet, where the great Current setteth to the West, must of necessities be one sea, which will be the greatest hope of the passage that way." If the observation was correct, then the opening of Hudson Strait had been more sharply discerned by Frobisher in 1578. However, they were met with storms and ice floes and were forced back until 17 June and could not recover the strait but sailed northward to what is given as 68°53', far up the eastern coast of Baffin Island. Some commentators have taken this to mean that Waymouth had passed the strait and had gone northwest into Foxe Channel. This is not credible in view of what follows in the narrative because, having come south again, they attempted, apparently unsuccessfully, to enter an inlet at 61°40', Hudson Strait again it might seem. However, the crucial dates are 28 to 30 July. Waymouth declared that the new entry being 40 leagues broad (120 nautical miles), he had "sayled an hundred leagues west and by South, within this inlet," and that this was "a passage of more possibilitie." However, his men refused to go farther, seeing that they had not the means to winter in the north, and he gave way to them and turned homeward, arriving at Dartmouth on 5 September. If what he says is true, Waymouth must be credited with having traversed the greater part of Hudson Strait for the first time. There must be some slight reservation, however, for on another voyage, Waymouth is known to have given distances and locations that were much exaggerated.[62]

Despite the doubt that Waymouth, on his journey of 1602, sailed so far to the west as his narrative asserts, the optimism that he expressed on his return impressed the court of the East India Company, even though he had not succeeded in finding a passage. He was ready and willing to try again in 1603, hoping to set out earlier to make better use of the short summer season in the northwest; but after approving the idea in principle, the court retracted its permission and decided to abstain from further experiments in this direction. In 1606, however, the project of a northwest voyage was again brought up. Though the eastern trade was now established, it was expensive in lives and ships as well as in time. Waymouth was not available, since he was then planning a second North American voyage to follow up the exploration of part of Maine in 1605 (he never made the 1606 expedition and is untraced for several years, though it is known that he turned his hand to shipbuilding before 1610). Given Waymouth's unavailability, the company this time chose John Knight, who had been with a pioneer Danish exploration of Greenland in 1605. The voyage was a fiasco.[63] It got no farther than the Labrador coast, and Knight was killed on land by Indians after the *Hopewell* went aground and could not be brought off. The crew rigged the shallop from the wreck, and Oliver Browne and the rest of the crew brought it to Newfoundland, from which they found passage to England. The voyage is scarcely worth recording except perhaps to underline the seamanship of men like Davis and Waymouth who had done so much before. The East India Company did not follow up this unfortunate episode.

It spite of all that the English had done in the search for the passage, it was Dutch enterprise in northern waters that led to the first major breakthrough on the Northwest Passage route. Henry Hudson in an English ship did attempt in 1607 the East Greenland coasting to follow up the notion of a passage in high latitudes or over the North Pole; it was a good-weather year, and he reached an unprecedented latitude of 80° north before being barred by ice. He was then taken into the Dutch service to attempt a Northeast Passage search. In 1609, finding himself blocked by ice south of Novaya Zemlya, he boldly turned westward to Greenland but resisted the temptation to attempt the Northwest Passage. Instead he sailed south to explore the as-yet-unexplored region between Delaware Bay and southern New England, finding and ascending the Hudson River and making a claim for the Hudson basin for the United Netherlands. On his return he put into an English port and was held there, though his ship, the *Halve Maen (Half Moon)*, bore the news of his discovery to the Dutch.

Hudson's charts and his enterprise led him to obtain backing from an English syndicate for an expedition to the Northwest Passage, which Waymouth claimed to have clearly defined. The *Discovery* and its shallop set out on 22 April 1610 and were in the vicinity of Frobisher Bay on 9 June.[64] Between 5 July and 2 August they worked through, with difficulty, what was to be called Hudson Strait, and on the latter date Hudson sighted to the north, as they entered open sea, a headland he named Salisbury's Foreland, 250 leagues (750 miles) from the eastern part of Davis Strait. As the ships emerged into what was to be named Hudson Bay, he called the capes north and south, respectively, Cape Digges and Cape Wolstenholme. From there they worked their way slowly and perilously down the eastern shore of Hudson Bay until they came "to the bottom of the bay," as it was called by Abacuk Prickett, the on-board representative of the subscribers. They had reached the southern tip of James Bay at 53° north. Realising they were in a cul-de-sac, Hudson and his men tried to get out into open water and succeeded in making a little way westward, but with the need to find a place to spend the winter (since a two-season voyage had been prepared for), they returned to James Bay, where there was timber and perhaps fish and fowl, laying themselves in at the beginning of November and becoming frozen in on 10 November.

There had been quarrels with the crew, and Hudson replaced Robert Juet, his master, who had been the recorder of his 1609 voyage, with Robert Bylot and made some other changes as well. It was evidently a weary winter, and food ran short. Most significant, it was alleged that as food diminished for the crew, Hudson diverted the reduced stores to his own cabin, where he and a few favorite companions (such as the surgeon Edward Wilson) fed themselves better than the remainder of the crew. Clear evidence of this is not forthcoming, but the story was believed by a growing number of the company. However, during much of the winter there were birds to be killed (mostly ptarmigan or milk-white partridges) and in the spring fish to be caught, so the food situation was scarcely desperate. Hudson encountered a single Indian, with whom he traded for a few beaver and deer skins, but when he took the shallop westward out of James Bay to try to make contact with an Indian group and get meat from them, he returned empty-handed. He nonetheless appears to have expected the crew to follow him in further explorations westward. This brought all their discontents to a boiling point, since the food stock was much too low. A conspiracy was hatched, which led on 22 or 23 June to Hudson and his son John being put into the shallop by force, ostensibly so that the crew could search for the supposed secret supply of food (it was not found). Other men suffering from scurvy and other diseases were put in with the Hudsons, making nine in all, and they were cast off; the shallop and its small party, including the Hudsons, were never seen again. Meanwhile the master, Robert Bylot, took the *Discovery* northward. At Salisbury Island (as Bylot now knew it to be), two men were killed by the Inuits when trying to obtain food. Several others died on the voyage, but the rest came into Berehaven almost starved. Getting some supplies there, they were able to make Plymouth and, eventually, the Thames. There they reported to Sir Thomas Smith, who was evidently the leading member of the sponsoring syndicate.

The story told by Prickett, the subscribers' representative, led to much investigation. The Trinity House at Deptford examined the survivors between 23 June and 24 October. There was a generally hostile attitude toward the men, and it was expected that they would be charged, but for some reason nothing was done at the time. The question of their responsibility was revived in 1617, when Robert Bylot and Francis Clements were examined in the High Court of Admiralty, but no action was taken against them. Hudson was lost, but had the passage been found? Trinity House could only ask questions after the examination of the evidence put before it: "Whether that great Bay must not be fedd from ye [western] Oceans? Whether the Ocean lye not Norwest of Salisbryes headland and the Straights? Whether that Ocean can bee any other than ye South Sea?"[65] But the general expectation was that at last the Northwest Passage had been found, and Hessel Gerritz was able to publish, in Amsterdam in 1612, a map *(Descristio et delineatio geographica detectionis freti ab H. Hudsono inventi)* obtained through one or another of the survivors, showing the new discoveries and pointing the way to the west.[66] The details of this and a subsequent voyage were conveyed to Spain and caused some apprehension there that the English had indeed discovered a route to the East by a Northwest Passage.[67]

Hudson had been financed by twenty-three adventurers, together with the Muscovy and East India Companies, and had the goodwill of young Prince Henry, who had drawn up instructions for the journey. The same group was now prepared to attempt to follow up on the discovery. Captain Thomas Button was equipped with a fresh expedition over the winter of 1611–12, and he set out from the Thames in April 1612 with the *Resolution* and the *Discovery*.[68] He had with him both Prickett and Bylot. The ships made their way safely through Hudson Strait. At Digges Island, Button put together a pinnace carried on board and sailed westward, expecting to pass indefinitely to the end of the passage, but he came up against an apparently unbroken expanse of land, the western shore of Hudson Bay (he named the point where he realised this "the Checks"). He worked down the shore conscientiously and named the land New Wales (he was from Glamorgan). He reached the wide estuary of the Nelson River and there set up his winter quarters, which he named Port Nelson (not the site of the later Hudson's Bay Company post of the same name). There is a lack of detail about Button's experiences, since his journal has not been found, but it is clear that food ran short, scurvy attacked his men, and his ship *Resolution* was crushed by ice and sank, but evidently in the spring they were able to get enough food from bird and beast to rehabilitate themselves. They set out northward in the *Discovery*, penetrating into Roes Welcome, a possible opening to the north, but at 65° north turned back, thinking that it was only a bay after all. Though this was on 29 July 1613, Button may have met un-melted ice. He came south again and coasted part of Southampton Island on his way eastward. The *Discovery* made its way back safely, Button having done an extensive piece of exploration. He had determined that Hudson Bay did not offer a passage to the west, but his venture into Roes Welcome had shown that to the northwest of the bay there were still possible channels that could lead further.

The excitement slowly but surely engendered by the discovery of Hudson Bay emerged while Button was still at sea. On 26 July 1612 a charter granting exclusive rights to the exploitation for six years of the supposed passage was issued by James I to the "Governor and Company of the Merchants of London, Discoverers of the Northwest Passage," with a list of no less than 388 grantees, headed by Henry Prince of Wales (who was soon to die).[69] This was comparable only to the second Virginia Company charter of 1609 and showed that English concern with, and willingness to invest in, western ventures had reached a peak not previously attained. Achievement, however, was not to match expectations. William Gibbons set out in the spring of 1613 in the *Discovery* once again. This time the vessel did not even get into Hudson Strait. It had sailed in March and probably reached the mouth of the strait too early, since it was a cold year and the passage was blocked with ice. Gibbons sailed the ship southward along the coast of Labrador, evidently hoping that the ice would clear and they could proceed, but instead they were icebound for some ten weeks in "Gibbons His Hole," variously stated to be at 57° or 58° north. When the ship came free, it could only sail for home. This was a considerable disappointment to investors.

Robert Bylot had been with Hudson, Button, and Gibbons before he was elected to command the *Discovery* in 1615. His mate and pilot was the meticulous William Baffin, whose skill as a pilot was well known to the Muscovy Company but who had not previously been on a Northwest Passage venture except to accompany James Hall on a journey up the eastern coast of Greenland. For this voyage of 1615 we have Baffin's meticulous log, in which much of the layout of the Hudson Bay region is recorded.[70] Baffin later described how he calculated longitude (correctly) by lunar distances, a complex mathematical and observational feat not equaled until the eighteenth century. Leaving on 16 March, Bylot and Baffin entered Hudson Strait on 27 May. This year, even though the ship was caught for a time by ice, was a good year for sailing, and Baffin carefully charted the shores of Hudson Strait. Button had brought news of a tidal flow from east to west, but Bylot and Baffin could not identify it; instead, the water movement appeared to be into or out of Davis Strait. By the end of June they were able to explore the shores of Salisbury Island and Nottingham Island in detail. The entrance to Foxe Channel was observed but not penetrated (so it should really be named Bylot or Baffin Channel). They next proceeded to Bell Island and then to Southampton Island and for the first time worked round its northeastern shore and, near its northern tip, discovered an entry trending northwest, but since it was blocked by ice, they could only name it Frozen Strait and leave it. They made no attempt to round the southern shore of Salisbury Island into Roes Welcome, deciding instead to turn back, which they did safely, arriving in England on 8 September. Once again no passage had been found, and even Button's discoveries had not been fully followed up, but the adventurers now had an accurate chart (which has survived) and a log that precisely located much of the Hudson and Button discoveries.

Baffin returned disillusioned about the chances of getting farther west from Hudson Bay. Episodes like the discovery of the Frozen Strait in mid-July influenced him in his view. He turned back to the record of the Davis voyage of 1587. It is desirable to quote him at this point: "And now it may be that some expect I should give my opinion concerning the passadge. To those my answer must be, that doubtless there is a passadge. But within this strayte whome [which] is called Hudsons Straytes, I am doubtfull, supposinge the contrarye. But whether there be or no, I will not affirm . . . but the mayne will be up Fretum Davis."[71] Baffin's instructions for the voyage of 1616, in which he was again to be mate and pilot (under Bylot), were to go up Davis Strait and continue westward, from where he could turn until he came to Japan—such was the confidence of the promoters, not eroded it seems from the lack of success in 1612–15. The indestructible *Discovery* was to be used again. Setting out on 26 March, Baffin and his men sailed down the English Channel in bad weather but were in Davis Strait before the middle of May, when they had already reached as far north as 65°20′ north.[72] They anchored at 70° north at a place Davis had named "London Coast"; by the thirtieth they passed Davis's farthest north, Cape Sanderson (72°12′ north). Running among many small islands, they reached open sea (the north water) at 75°40′ north on 1 July. They named one cape at 76°40′ after Sir Dudley Digges, an island at about 77° north after Hakluyt, and a sound after Sir Thomas Smith. The weather turned foul, and they took shelter in what they named the Cary Islands (at this point Hakluyt's successor in chronicling English exploration, Samuel Purchas,

confessed that their detailed map was too costly to print, and it is, regret-
fully, lost). They could continue no further in a northerly direction but, as
required by instructions, turned westward and came first to what they
called Jones Sound and then to "another great Sound, lying in the latitude
of 74 degrees 20' and . . . called . . . Sir James Lankasters Sound." For
some unstated reason, no attempt was made to enter either sound, but the
discovery of Lancaster Sound was to prove in the end a passage to the Far
West. As they went south their hope of finding a passage lessened daily.
They found the shore of Baffin Island barred by an ice ledge. They were
gradually pushed eastward by the ice and moved south into the region explored by Frobisher and Davis, where there was no hope of a passage.
They sailed over to Greenland in hope of getting provisions, since scurvy
was rampant; here they got some scurvy grass and, from the Inuits, some
salmon. On 6 August they turned for home and were able to anchor at
Dover on the thirtieth of that month.

In many ways the exploration of the northern waters of Davis Strait and
what soon became known as Baffin Strait represented a geographical addition as valuable as that of Hudson Bay, even if, in the longer run, it was less
profitable. But in many ways, the venture was a conclusive one, and the
cartographers of the period were inclined to follow Gerritz's maps of the
Bylot-Baffin voyages, with only minor variations. The hopes of 1612 were at
an end: if a pilot as skilled as Baffin could not find a passage, then who
could? It is true that the mathematician Henry Briggs attempted, on Baffin's return, to argue a case for a Northwest Passage, citing all the tales, tall
and not so tall, about a sea to the west of North America, principally urging
that America was shown as much too wide on most maps and that Button's
tales of currents and the stories emanating from the Virginia Colony of the
existence of an ocean to the west could not be false. His map, printed in
1625 by Samuel Purchas, was tentative enough about northern passages
but left a number of channels open and unexplored, whereas California
was shown as a great island, eating into western America.[73] This kind of academic lore was by now, in effect, out-of-date. The experimental voyages
had shown that there was no easy way either out of Hudson Bay or by
Baffin's northern route. The 1612 company had come to the end of its resources as surely as had the Company of Cathay nearly forty years before.
It is consequently not surprising that there was almost nothing to be heard
of the Northwest Passage for some years. And when a revival of interest
did come, it came not from the English but from the Danes.

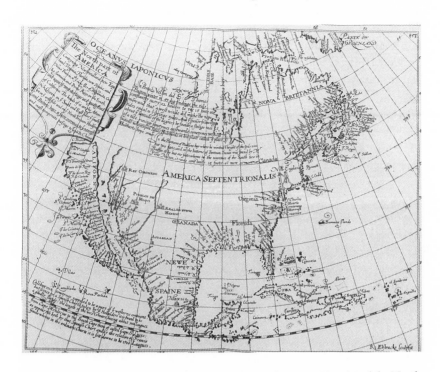

6.11 North America by Henry Briggs (c. 1625), to illustrate "Treatise of the Northwest Passage to the South Sea, through the Continent of Virginia, and by Fretum Hudson," published in Samuel Purchas, Purchas His Pilgrimes (London, 1625). This is the first map to include the name of Hudson's Bay and depicts a connection between the bay and the head of the Gulf of California. Briggs's geographical ideas were part of the Northwest Passage hypothesis tested by Captain Fox. Courtesy John Carter Brown Library at Brown University.

The Final Search for the Northwest Passage in the Seventeenth Century

Voyages early in the century under James Hall had given the Danes some knowledge of Greenland and a claim to revive their old sovereignty, even if no trace had been found of the medieval Norse colonists to whom Danes could claim familial connection. Jens Munk, an experienced seaman, had been to England and Amsterdam and learned much there about the English ventures. Editions of Hessel Gerritz's book on the north had, after

1612, added accounts of what had been done since Hudson's voyage. In 1618 Munk persuaded Christian IV to back an expedition that would press through Hudson Strait and find a passage to the southwest—in Hudson Bay, though why he should have deduced there was one in this direction is unknown. His ships, the *Unicorn [Enhiornin]* and the *Lamprey [Lampreen]*, left Denmark in May 1619.[74] William Gordon, a seaman who had sailed with Bylot and Baffin in 1615, was Munk's pilot. Munk had been given the latitude of 62°30' as that of the entrance to Hudson Bay, and he kept to it, only to find himself in Frobisher Bay by 8 July. Learning he was too far north, he worked round Resolution Island into the strait. His passage through the strait was beset by storms and ice. He was probably the first person to make a fairly detailed examination of Ungava Bay, but he followed instructions and sailed southwest across Hudson Bay to Jenk's "Winterhaffen," as he called what was to be the later Fort Churchill of the Hudson's Bay Company, on 7 September. Munk's River was to prove no passage, and the two ships settled into winter quarters; in spite of being able to catch ptarmigan and other creatures for a time, the expedition gradually fell victim to scurvy. Man after man died through the winter and spring; there were only eleven men alive in May when the geese returned; there were only three by the end of June, but they had recovered, and Munk was one of them. He and his remaining companions abandoned the *Unicorn* and fitted out the *Lamprey* as best they could, making a remarkable return voyage, barely managing to reach home in late September. Even though Munk was willing to try again, the futility of his voyage, in spite of personal courage, made such a project pointless. The Danes retired from the search for the passage, though they took some part in the whaling ventures east of Greenland at Spitsbergen.

There remained in England, however, a few survivors of the Northwest Passage Company (notably Sir John Wolstenholme) who still believed in a passage; their propaganda remained fruitless until a new monarch came to the English throne. Then permission was given for a voyage under Captain William Hawkridge.[75] In the king's pinnace, the *Lion's Whelp*, and another vessel, Hawkridge returned to the area in which he had sailed with Button in 1612. Little is known of his voyage, since no journal has been found, but he sailed rather late, in June 1619, and like Munk, he reached Frobisher Bay rather than Hudson Strait. He eventually explored the western end of Hudson Bay and a number of the islands to the north and northeast already examined by earlier expeditions and came home safely but with nothing new to record. The passage search was taken no further. Later in

1625, it is true, Samuel Purchas came out with his vast voyage collection, *Hakluytus Posthumus or Purchas his Pilgrimes*, in the third volume of which he reprinted in abbreviated form much that had been in Hakluyt's 1600 work on the earlier northwest voyages and added detailed accounts of those made between 1602 and 1616.[76] Although there was in this collection much to ponder over, it produced no further exploits for some years. But around 1630 a revival of interest took place, precisely why is not clear, among both the London merchants and those of Bristol. Perhaps it was because by then wars with France and Spain had come to an end, and the prospects of sharing in some of the great wealth brought home by the East India Company was too tempting not to inspire some rivalry. The voyages of Luke Fox from London and of Thomas James from Bristol in 1631–32 mark both a new beginning and an end. Both were to be extensively documented and were to remain classic narratives of subarctic enterprise for many years.[77]

Luke Fox represented the practical seamen of the English eastern coast and had made his reputation as a seaman at Hull, whereas Thomas James had served on West Country vessels and was intimately linked with Bristol. Their preparations followed parallel lines, but Fox had access to support from King Charles I, whose pinnace the *Charles* was provided for him. He was backed by Sir John Wolstenholme, who had never given up his interest in the passage, and by Trinity House. James's backing came primarily from the Society of Merchant Venturers of Bristol, but he did not sail without royal permission, and his ship was loyally named the *Henrietta Maria*. Charles was willing to see the rivalry of London and the outports in action and hoped that one, if not the other, would bring back fresh information. Their instructions were similar: to round out the land contours of Hudson Bay, to confirm, or disprove, the existence of a passage beyond its northern tip, and to explore farther to the north in the channels that had been observed somewhat to the east, in the hope that there was a promising opening.

Although it is more usual to consider Fox first, it may be worth following James instead.[78] James was well equipped in theory for the work, since he had some sea experience and could use navigational instruments with some mathematical and observational skills; but he was not a very effective commander. It has been suggested that some of the difficulties he had in sailing came from keeping too close to the shore and therefore running into more ice than he would have if he had remained in deeper water. Leaving Bristol on 3 May 1631, he reached Resolution Island on 17 June and pro-

6.12 "Polar Map or Card" by Captain Luke Fox, published in his North-West Fox *(London, 1635). The dotted line shows Fox's voyage of 1631. Although he found no route to the Pacific, he left the possibility of such a route open on his map by showing an open-ended outlet pointing west from Hudson's Bay. By permission of The British Library.*

ceeded into the strait, but on leaving it, he had some difficulty in clearing both Nottingham Island and Digges Island. At his most northerly he was at 63°15', but sailing southward he coasted Mansel Island and Coats Island before swinging southwestward toward Port Nelson, where he landed and rechristened the land New Wales (like Button, he was a member of a Glamorgan gentry family). He then coasted eastward until he came to the cape at the entrance to James Bay, to which he gave the name Cape Henrietta Maria (this name survived). He charted as he moved southward into the bottom of the bay, even though his map of 1633 incorrectly showed a peninsula that divided the bay into two. He encountered Fox on 29 August, and they had a pleasant meeting, even though Fox despised James and considered him an amateur. James picked Charlton Island near the bottom of the bay as his winter quarters. He had lost his shallop and decided to build a new one as well as constructing stout winter quarters and preserving his ship from the ice. The last he did by the expedient of sinking the ship after it was unloaded. The winter houses, made of the plentiful timber on the island, were only moderately protective, but with some hardship, James and his party survived the winter, though before green vegetation began to appear and was boiled to vary their provisions, scurvy was becoming a serious problem. During June they raised the ship and luckily found the rudder that had fallen off. Their provisions, in their icebound storehouse, were fresh, yet the original intention to carry on for another season was not practicable because the ship was in poor shape. In later summer they did their best to explore northward in the passage between Nottingham Island and Bell Island but were checked by an ice barrier at 65°30' when they were in Foxe Channel, already named by James's rival. James turned for home and brought his creaking and barely seaworthy ship to Bristol on 22 October. From that port city he went to London, where he was well received, and rapidly put his book together (with an appendix by the mathematician Henry Gellibrand) in 1633. He could offer no further hope of a passage.

Luke Fox was a better practical sailor with a superior vessel. He learned all he could about previous voyages and consulted Henry Briggs about the theoretical aspects of navigation in northern waters. He left the Thames on 5 May 1631 and followed the east coast route by way of Orkney.[79] Late in June he was off Baffin Island, reviewing the route of Frobisher and pointing to the latter's failing to pass "the Mistaken Straits"; he made his way into Hudson Strait, with some difficulty because of ice, by the beginning of July. He passed the strait and then sailed south toward the western shore of Hudson Bay, entering Port Nelson and putting the land between there and Cape Henrietta Maria (named by James) on his chart. He did examine James Bay in detail but stood northward to Bell Island and then north-northwest into what was to be named Foxe Channel, reaching 66°47' before he turned back (as James was to do at the lower latitude the following year). It was by now mid-September, and though he was victualed for eighteen months, he made for home, reaching the Downs on 31 October after a very efficient piece of navigation, though with no novel achievement beyond the speculation that his "channel" might suggest that further searches should be made to the north (James reached the same conclusion). After delivering his vessel to Wolstenholme, to whom the king presented the ship, Fox retired to Hull and slowly wrote his long disquisition, which was not published until 1635. It contained much valuable observation but was rough in style and uncharitable to his compatriots in the lengthy search for the Northwest Passage. It was, however, very much a seaman's book and, for all its incongruities, became a much reprinted text.

The enterprises of Fox and James brought to an end the long series of expeditions conducted from 1575 to 1632. The search for the passage had added much to the map of the subarctic and opened doors to the Arctic. Davis had made clear the outline of Davis Strait; Hudson had opened the way to the great expanse of Hudson Bay. Hudson, Button, Munk, and James had proved that men might survive over the winter, even if they could do so only at the margins of subsistence. But even if Lancaster Sound and Foxe Channel were to play significant parts in early-nineteenth-century exploration, it would be a long time before major progress was made by sea, and only in the 1850s did English navigators sketch out the way through the islands and the ice to the western Arctic and, ultimately, the Pacific. But Davis had discovered the value of Davis Strait for whaling and of the Labrador shore for cod, whereas Button had indicated that there might be furs to be found in the Hudson Bay region, even though he did not make a point of it. Geographically, the voyages of the passage search were therefore significant in opening up a very large region. Economically, the voyages were to have future significance but little in the short run. The myth (or the hope) of a short passage to Cathay and the Indies was dampened but not extinguished. It resurfaced from time to time in reprints of older voyages and was revived spasmodically in the eighteenth century, until the discovery of such a passage became a major object of British state policy in the early nineteenth century.

The cessation of exploration in search of the Northwest Passage from 1632 onward cannot be easily explained. Probably it was the result of disappointment at the inability of the latest discoveries to get past Hudson Bay. The French were certainly interested in the English discoveries. Through the Montagnais Indians, whom Samuel de Champlain met frequently at Quebec and Tadoussac, it is certain the French learned much about the Hudson Bay area. Champlain included, from English sources, a good depiction of the bay in his famous map of New France in 1632. The Dutch too were interested in the prospects of a passage, but their northern activities were centred on Spitsbergen, and their perspective looked toward a northern route around Greenland rather than an exploration by way of Hudson Bay, though we do not hear of any significant attempts to test this northern route. For the most part the Dutch, like the French, were inclined to follow English versions of what had been found so far, yet through passages con-

6.13 *Map of the Arctic by Henricus Hondius, published in Amsterdam in 1636 and included in the British edition of the* World Atlas *by Hondius and Mercator. This map reflects the cumulative geographical knowledge of the Northwest Passage following the voyages of Fox and James. By permission of The British Library.*

tinued to appear from time to time on later maps and to be mentioned in academic discussions.

There were two separate diversions from the sending of expeditions to the northwest, apart from expense. First, there was the enduring French belief that, provided they managed to impel their explorers ever farther to the west, the Great Lakes system would eventually lead them either to the Pacific or to a divide from which the Pacific would be easily accessible. Some of the Jesuit missionaries were believers in this possibility. The name of the Lachine (China) Rapids near Montreal may have showed that the belief in the accessibility of the Pacific was formal and official, or the name may have been cynically ironic. The former is much more likely. The second obstacle to further Northwest Passage explorations was the belief of some Virginia promoters and colonists that after the mountains in the interior were reached, then the watershed would provide navigable streams flowing down to the Pacific, assuming of course that the width of the continent had been exaggerated by some cartographers. The most notorious map that showed the opposite—that is, a narrow continent—was John Farrer's "A Mapp of Virginia" (1650–51), and its many subsequent editions continued to place the Pacific only a very short distance from the Appalachians.[80] French knowledge of the north was to change rapidly in the 1650s as a result of the fur trade. Through French knowledge, the lore possessed by the English also changed, leading eventually to the exploitation of Hudson Bay by the English fur trade, a process that was to have only a marginal influence on the existence or nonexistence of the Northwest Passage for a considerable period after the foundation of the Hudson's Bay Company in 1670.

In the larger picture of European expansion and the effect on perception of the layout of the land and water and of the resources to be gained from exploration, the Northwest Passage occupies only a small corner of interest. The passage was a toy of cartographers, just as was the supposed great southern continent, and when maps showed the passage in one form or another, it was taken for granted to exist. But it apparently did not offer any major intellectual or economic challenge. There was just the one spurt of major interest when the Frobisher voyages appeared to have resulted in the discovery of gold in the north, and English narratives of exploration were then for the first time widely circulated in Europe. This interest, however, died away rapidly when the ventures failed to produce valuable results. Not until Hudson's discovery of Hudson Bay excited the Dutch for a time did any response to the question of a Northwest Passage arouse widespread intellectual or even cartographic interest.

The early northern voyages in search of a passage had, however, stimulated the public mind. Part of this stimulation was the attractiveness of the unknown and undiscovered. A larger part, however, was human interest: the bringing of Inuit (Eskimo) people to Europe. A recent study has shown how the likenesses of those Inuits brought to Europe—first a man brought by a French vessel in the 1560s and then another man, followed by a man, a woman, and a child by Frobisher in 1576–77—were drawn, painted, and engraved by artists and circulated widely throughout the Continent. This brief human and popular interest was not fed by any further sequence of captures and soon died away.[81] Some intellectuals remained excited because the Inuits had an Oriental look, indicating a link between the lands of the northwestern Atlantic and Asia. This excitement too faded rather quickly. The representations of the Inuit peoples, along with exotic peoples of other of the world's regions, continued to adorn maps as decorative insets and borders into the seventeenth century, and this was perhaps the last evidence for an earlier interest in a Northwest Passage. For most Europeans, there were grander and more world-shaking events to write and think about. The Northwest Passage faded into the icy mists in which it still lay undiscovered.

7 / A Continent Revealed: Assimilation of the Shape and Possibilities of North America's East Coast, 1524–1610

KAREN ORDAHL KUPPERMAN

North America was little known in the early sixteenth century. Geographers did not even agree on whether it was a continent or merely a series of islands. Explorations in the Southeast by Spanish venturers such as Hernando de Soto, along with regular traffic to the Newfoundland Banks in the early sixteenth century, gave important points of reference for the vast extent of North America but little knowledge of the land between the northern and the southern landfalls. First interpretations, derived from analogies with South and Central America, hoped for a limited east-west expanse or at least for a narrow waist somewhere that could be easily traversed by water. Fishermen appreciated the rich banks off Newfoundland, but for most promoters North America was seen as a potential barrier in the quest for new routes to the East rather than as a new and interesting site for development in its own right. Initial explorations of the coast were all in search of a passage through this mass.

Early Voyages

Spain and France both sent out voyages in 1524, each with the goal of finding the elusive passage to the South Sea and the riches of Asia.[1] Esteban Gómez, a Portuguese pilot who had sailed with Ferdinand Magellan, was hired to conduct such an expedition for Spain. His commission, signed by the Emperor Charles V, was for the exploration of "Eastern Cathay."[2] Contemporary comments on his voyage, which apparently traversed the coast between Newfoundland and Florida, are confusing, but all agree that it

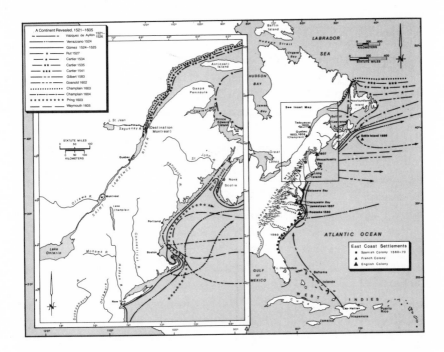

Map 7.1 A Continent Revealed, 1521–1605.

was a disappointment. Commentators gleefully told of the misunderstanding when the ship returned with its cargo of fifty-eight Indians, "all innocent and half-naked people." Those on shore at La Coruña on the northwestern coast of Spain misunderstood the shouted news that the expedition had brought slaves (*esclavos*) and excitedly spread word in the capital that Gómez had returned with a valuable cargo of cloves (*clavos*). Though the Spanish historian Gonzalo Fernández de Oviedo pointed to "rich furs" and the possibility of silver and copper from northern lands, most followed Peter Martyr, an Italian churchman in the service of Spain, in dismissing ventures northward: "But what need have we of what is found everywhere in Europe? It is towards the south, not towards the frozen north, that those who seek fortune should bend their way; for everything at the equator is rich."[3]

Giovanni da Verrazzano's contemporaneous voyage for France produced much more hopeful results and contributed to a more sophisticated understanding of the shape of North America's coastline. The central purpose of his voyage was to find a route to "Cathay and the extreme east of

Asia."[4] This objective notwithstanding, it is clear that Verrazzano—at least after his voyage—had other purposes in mind. On his return to France, he wrote a long letter to King Francis I, describing the new lands; his underlying assumption was that the French would want to develop the region for its own sake, and his account abounded with favorable descriptions of its people, who were full of intelligence, beauty, and skill, and of the plants and animals that grew there. Verrazzano presented a remarkably detailed ethnographic record, stressing the receptivity of the people to European culture and describing fully realized Indian societies with established gender and class roles, similar in many ways to Europe's own ancient ancestors. In this account the land welcomed Europeans as much as the people, offering newcomers a good life and investors rich returns.[5]

Verrazzano kept careful records of his travels, with consistently taken position readings and soundings and notations of tides and currents, but his report included misleading hopes. The expedition's first landfall was on the coast near Cape Fear; Verrazzano's notes said 34°. Even in the early sixteenth century, experienced navigators such as Verrazzano were capable of calculating latitude with a high degree of certainty; longitude involved much more guesswork.[6] From this landfall, he traveled south for "fifty leagues" but then turned north again "so as not to meet with the Spaniards," and traveled up the coast as far as Newfoundland. In his early landfalls, he encountered what he thought were sure signs of Oriental traces in both the Indians and the vegetation, and he mistook the sounds beyond the Carolina Outer Banks for the South Sea (the Pacific), a mistake that was to be enshrined in geographical lore for much of the sixteenth century.[7]

Verrazzano commented on the possibilities of the land as he moved up the coast. Though he apparently missed Chesapeake Bay, Verrazzano described New York harbor and the narrows that today bear his name. He and his men enjoyed a long, happy fortnight's rest in Narragansett Bay and Newport Harbor, which they called "'Refugio' on account of its beauty." As their voyage progressed northward, they came finally to the well-known territory of Newfoundland ("Bacalaia, so called after a fish") and from there headed homeward. His voyage had produced a remarkable picture of North America's east coast; his narrative called on promoters to focus attention on this land and its resources, seeing it as an opportunity rather than a barrier.[8]

Perhaps the most significant impact of the Verrazzano voyage was on European cartography of North America in the years before 1550.[9] Although it is possible that Verrazzano himself drew a map depicting his discoveries, such a map has not survived. However, his brother Gerolamo produced a number of maps that could have provided the model for what became the standard European image of North America for at least a quarter of a century. In both the widely circulated manuscript maps of Battista Agnese and the popular printed maps of Sebastian Münster, for example, there appears a great eastward arm of the Pacific Ocean (Sea of the South) extending into the North American continent toward the Atlantic. This "Sea of Verrazzano" is separated from the Atlantic only by a narrow isthmus at around the fortieth parallel of north latitude. Other maps and globes between 1527 and 1551 show this false sea as far south as $34°$ north and as far north as the fiftieth parallel. Such a geographical configuration held out great hopes for Europeans interested in a route to the Orient shorter than that available around the Cape of Good Hope or the soon-to-be-revealed route through the Strait of Magellan. In particular, the Sea of Verrazzano offered a solution to the puzzle of the sea route to Cathay now being sought by the French. The voyages of Jacques Cartier were, at least in part, a response to what was emerging as the French view of North America.

In the meantime, English geographers were also interested in the shape of North America. In 1517 the lawyer and writer John Rastell, brother-in-law of Sir Thomas More, set off on a voyage to America, which ended in frustration when the crew refused to travel beyond Ireland. His description of the voyage, written as a drama, *A New Interlude and a Mery of the Nature of the iiii Elements*, was published sometime between 1623 and 1628.[10] Rastell's failure notwithstanding, another English effort was soon in the field. John Rut, captain in King Henry VIII's service, made an exploration of the North American coast for England in 1527. He made landfall in regions north of Newfoundland and traveled down the coast. Rut's letter of 3 August 1527, sent home by a fishing ship from Newfoundland, offered the king "a plaine Mariners Letter endorsed in homely phrase." He reported the loss of one of his two ships as they entered a region filled with "Ilands of Ice."[11] As with the Gómez voyage, no written account of Rut's exploration of the coast survives, but clearly France, Spain, and England were all made aware, by the three expeditions of Gómez, Verrazzano, and Rut, of the nature of the North American continent as it faced Europe. In a period of three short years, the continent had been revealed to European eyes. The coast apparently had no major breaks, and no sea-level strait to the Pacific or the Sea of the South existed. The continent was a solid landmass but possibly with an isthmus—somewhere around latitude 40° north—that resembled the Panamanian isthmus much farther south. This much was clear. What remained to be seen was whether the land itself offered good inducements to further exploration.

Francis I of France, building on extensive European knowledge of the Newfoundland region gained through fishing voyages, decided to follow up Verrazzano's explorations with a new venture designed both to investigate the land's resources and to probe once again for a decisive break or narrowing in the continental outline. This expedition, led by an experienced mariner named Jacques Cartier, was to begin with the area known so well. Cartier left France on 20 April 1534 and, after a remarkably brief voyage of twenty days, landed in eastern Newfoundland, recording the latitude as 48°30'. The two ships traveled north around Newfoundland and entered the Strait of Belle Isle, between the Long Range Mountains and the southeastern coast of Labrador, in June when the danger of floating ice was sufficiently cleared, keeping careful accounts of their soundings and impressions as they traveled. Good harbors and channels were plentiful, as were birds for food, but Cartier found the mainland so repellent, "being composed of stones and horrible rugged rocks," that he concluded: "In fine I am rather inclined to believe that this is the land God gave to Cain."[12]

Cartier missed the entrance to the Saint Lawrence River on this voyage but made a thorough exploration of the shores of the Gulf of Saint Lawrence. The islands and mainland on the south and east of the gulf impressed Cartier as "the finest land one can see, and full of beautiful trees and meadows," complementing the abundance of animals and birds they encountered everywhere. The gulf itself was broad and deep enough that Cartier hoped it would provide a passage to the Pacific. In Chaleur Bay, which flows into the Gulf of Saint Lawrence between the Gaspé Peninsula and New Brunswick, the expedition encountered a party of Micmac Indians, who beckoned to the Europeans to come ashore, "holding up . . . some furs on sticks," a sure sign that they had encountered Europeans before and knew exactly what the strangers wanted. Such encounters brought the Indians the metal tools, cloth, and other useful goods they could not manufacture for themselves, so they were eager to establish trade. Cartier had demonstrated his understanding of the Indians' desires some days before when he had tried to attract the attention of a lone Indian man he had seen by leaving a knife and a length of wool cloth for him.

After some false starts, the Indians convinced Cartier of their true friendliness, and trade commenced; sometimes the Indians sold even the furs they wore. The French believed that these Indians would always welcome Europeans and would be easy to convert.[13] As the ships moved up the coast to the Gaspé Peninsula, the men met with Iroquoians who had come to the coast to fish for mackerel but who lived inland along the Saint Lawrence near the present-day site of the city of Quebec. These Indians, who had not come equipped for trade, looked mean and savage to Cartier. After several encounters in which the Indians showed signs of joy at the presence of the French, their chief, Donnacona, was kidnapped. He ultimately agreed that two young men, one of whom was his son, would accompany the mariners back to Europe.[14]

Cartier was misled by Anticosti Island, bounded on the north by what is known today as Jacques Cartier Passage and on the south by Honguedo Strait, and so he missed the entrance to the Saint Lawrence River as he moved away from the Gaspé Peninsula back toward the Straits of Belle Isle and home. The return trip from Newfoundland to France was as efficient as the first, and the ships arrived back at Saint-Malo on the northern coast of Brittany on 5 September. Though he had not found the channel through the continent, Cartier could report, on the basis of summer experience, a fruitful land "more temperate than Spain and the finest it is possible to see." Moreover, the two Indians who accompanied him soon learned sufficient French to assure the court that the mighty river on which they lived did flow from far in the interior and that the nation of Hochelaga, rich in the goods prized by the French, lived along it. Sufficient hope to justify a second venture certainly existed.[15]

In 1535 a second expedition under Cartier's command, this time with three ships, set out to plant a colony that would remain in the land through the winter. The report on this venture, probably written by purser Jean Poulet, presented a much more mixed picture. Much of it was extremely promising. Cartier and his men, with the direction of their now French-speaking Indian guides, quickly located and explored the mouth of the Saint Lawrence River after their arrival in Newfoundland on 7 July. They followed the river west, noting where the Saguenay flowed into it from the north, and soon entered the native territory of their two guides, an area that the explorers thought was called Canada, and the guides' village, Stadacona.[16] The two young Indian men had a joyful reunion with Donnacona and all their people, but the Iroquoians' attitude toward the French seemed to have changed. They were now unwilling to guide Cartier and his men to Hochelaga; the Indians were generally disturbed by the hostile appearance of the Europeans and their constantly carried weapons.

Though the exchange of friendly gestures continued, with the Indians even offering gifts of children as evidence of their goodwill, Donnacona strongly tried to persuade Cartier to give up his plan of exploring farther along the river, possibly hoping to protect the Stadaconans' centrality in access to European goods. Donnacona and the French-speaking Indians, dressed in ceremonial garb, conveyed divine warnings of the danger should Cartier persist and said "that there would be so much ice and snow that all would perish." The mariners laughed and told the Indians "that their god Cuduoagny was a mere fool who did not know what he was saying . . . and that Jesus would keep them safe from the cold if they would trust in him."[17]

As the exploring party of fifty sailors and Cartier and all the gentlemen set out in the small bark brought for this purpose and in two longboats on 19 September, the men were entranced by all the trees, grapevines, and birds that they saw. The river teemed with fish and the land with huge animals. The Indians they encountered were friendly, warning the mariners of rapids along the river and again offering Cartier a young child, this time a girl of eight or nine. The bark was left at Lake Saint Peter because the water was so shallow, and Cartier forged ahead in the longboats. Finally they arrived at Hochelaga, near modern-day Montreal, estimated by Cartier to be at least three hundred leagues from the mouth of the Saint Lawrence; they were greeted by a thousand men, women, and children, who treated the French as honored guests. The expedition recorded every aspect of life in this large Indian city, from foods and household economy to political life. The fortified city was described in detail, as was the Indians' most valuable article: wampum, beads made from shells with ceremonial and spiritual power. The Iroquoians of Hochelaga were described as overlords over the Iroquoians of Canada, as well as eight or nine other nations. The explorers climbed Mount Royal, the great mountain of Hochelaga, and saw the river extending yet farther into the interior, though with terrible rapids. The Indians assured them that one could travel on the river for three months more and that there was another great river (the Ottawa) that flowed from the west, offering the continued hope of a water route through the continent to the Pacific. The land they saw "was the finest and most excellent one could find anywhere."[18]

Some of the lore the French picked up was extremely confusing; the explorers struggled to understand it because it was always presented in the context of discussions of precious metals. The kingdom of Saguenay was said to have gold, silver, and copper and to be peopled by men and women who wore European clothes, but its location was mysterious: far to the west or the north. Though confusing, the lore seemed to offer hope.[19] Word of the rich kingdom of Saguenay, whose citizens wore European-style clothes, soon spread throughout Europe; the Portuguese diplomat João Fernando Lagarto reported to King John III of Portugal on his conversations with Francis I of France about the rich possibilities.[20]

Cartier and his men, returning triumphantly, were soon to see the great difficulties that stood in the way of anyone who tried to exploit the newfound lands for European gain. Having made their reconnaissance, including a remarkable ethnographic report, Cartier and his men returned on 11 October to find that the men left behind had built a fort at Sainte Croix, near modern-day Quebec, close to Stadacona. The Indians of Canada now seemed much less admirable by comparison with those of Hochelaga; Cartier had the fortifications greatly strengthened, and a period of strained relations ensued.[21]

In December, word came that a terrible "pestilence" had broken out among the Indians. Though the explorers cut off contact, they soon found themselves attacked by a disease "accompanied by most marvellous and extraordinary symptoms." This sickness, which modern-day researchers have identified as severe scurvy, caused the men to lose strength in their arms and legs, which swelled and turned black; their gums became so rotted that they lost their teeth. By February, of the 110 men in the company, "there were not ten in good health so that no one could aid the other." They now saw nothing of the Indians. Cartier, fearing that half the men would not survive, ordered prayers and extraordinary religious services. An autopsy revealed extensive damage to a victim's heart and lungs, but no one could understand the "strange" disease. As he watched his able-bodied force drop to three men, Cartier adopted ruses to make the Indians think the men were well but working below decks. The French experienced the full force of the Canadian winter. Their ships were frozen in ice "which was more than two fathoms in thickness," while the snow on land was four feet deep from mid-November 1535 to mid-April 1536. Even below the hatches of the ships, "there was ice to the depth of four finger breadths." Twenty-five men had died.

Cartier learned of a way to cure the strange disease from one of the Indians who had been taken to France, Dom Agaya. He came to the fort and showed the captain how to gather and prepare the leaves and bark of a tree the Indians called the "annedda," probably the eastern white cedar, *Thuja occidentalis*. The cure, from the vitamin C in the preparation, was miraculous; Cartier said those who had suffered from syphilis were also cured of that disease.[22] Now Indians came again freely to the fort, bringing provisions, though they too were on short rations. Donnacona was away hunting, and Cartier feared he was attempting to gather support for a concerted attack on the French. After the hunters returned, Cartier's suspicions grew, so the Frenchman seized Donnacona and decided to take him back to France, promising to return him in a year. The Canada Indians were greatly distressed. Their presentiments were correct: Donnacona, along with the eight adults who accompanied him, was to die later in France. The ships began the return journey down the river, leaving Newfoundland on 19 June and arriving at Saint-Malo on 16 July 1536.[23]

At about the same time an English adventurer, Captain Richard Hore, embarked with two ships for an ill-fated voyage to Newfoundland, possibly hoping to follow up Cartier's exploration of the Gulf of Saint Lawrence in 1534. Hore, described by Richard Hakluyt as "a man of goodly stature and of great courage and given to the studie of Cosmographie," assembled a group of gentlemen "desirous to see the strange things of the world" for his "voyage of discoverie upon the Northwest partes of America." The venture, which embarked in April 1536, was poorly planned, with unclear goals. The two ships were separated near the Strait of Belle Isle. Hore's, the *William*, took up the role of a normal fishing vessel and returned safely home. The *Minion*, on which most of the gentlemen sailed, was stranded on the coast of Labrador, where their distress caused some men allegedly to kill and eat others. Finally the men were able to capture a French ship, whose crew they forced to transfer to their own disabled ship. They then returned home through "Mightie Islands of yce in the sommer season," arriving at Cornwall at the end of October 1536 to tell their story.[24] Publication of the accounts of the Hore voyage, however, did not take place until nearly fifty years later when Richard Hakluyt interviewed the last living survivor, Thomas Butts, for his *Principall Navigations*.

France continued to plan for further exploration along the Saint Lawrence River. In 1541, Jacques Cartier, who had been hoping to return since 1538, once again embarked for America, though this time the overall commander of the expedition was to be a Protestant nobleman, Jean François de La Rocque, sieur de Roberval. Cartier set out with five ships on 23 May 1541, carrying food for two years and livestock to found farms; Roberval was to come later. Arriving after a frustrating three-month journey, Cartier began a settlement, Charlesbourg Royal, on Cape Diamond nine miles upstream from the former fort, and ordered the men to plant turnips and other vegetables, which he joyfully reported "sprong up out of the ground in eight dayes." This success encouraged him to think that the land could easily be tilled and planted with European crops; he may also have been trying to store up vegetables to prevent a recurrence of scurvy. He also saw tokens of gold, diamonds, and other minerals.[25]

Cartier set out on 7 September to find the kingdom of Saguenay, renewing his acquaintances as he went and leaving two boys with the "Lord of Hochelay" between Canada and Hochelaga to learn the language. His determination to follow the river was thwarted by the *saults* (rapids) they encountered, and his party continued on foot, acquiring four young men as guides. By interrogating Indians met along the way, the explorers were finally convinced that "the River was not navigable to goe to Saguenay," though they were convinced, by a diagram of sticks and branches the informants arranged on the ground, that the land journey around the *saults* was only six leagues. At the same time, Cartier, worried about his own vulnerability, became convinced that the Indians were conspiring to attack him, and he returned to his fort.[26]

When Roberval arrived at Newfoundland on 8 June 1542 with three ships and two hundred men and women colonists, he encountered Cartier, who was preparing to return to France and who ignored Roberval's commands to return with him up the river to Canada. Cartier explained "that hee could not with his small company withstand the Savages, which went about dayly to annoy him." Roberval, thinking that Cartier sought the glory of finding gold and diamonds solely for himself, ignored the warnings of an experienced seaman, Martin de Actalecu, and decided to forge ahead to Cartier's abandoned fort. The cryptic account of Roberval's experiment in colonization, translated and published by Richard Hakluyt in the second edition of his *Principal Navigations* (1600), described in some detail how the fort was enlarged and made grander for Roberval's two hundred settlers, the first French North American colony to include women. The report became briefer as it recorded their realization that their food supplies were inadequate for the winter. Finally the scurvy once again set in, "and there dyed thereof about fiftie." This grim fact is followed by a one-sentence paragraph that must have carried a tremendous weight of emotion despite its brevity: "Note that the yce began to breake up in April." The colonists were prisoners of the weather in their fort, and Roberval used various punishments—some colonists were put in irons, "and divers were whipped, as well men as women"—to keep the little settlement going under those terrible conditions.[27]

Roberval set out on 5 June 1543 to discover the kingdom of Saguenay. No account of that expedition survives, but he returned by the end of the month. When supply ships came from home, he and his remaining settlers returned to France, arriving in September. No further attempt to settle in these regions would be made for decades. The news of the vast lands explored by Cartier—their intractability, especially the severity of the winters, and the elusiveness of the riches promised somewhere in the interior—quickly spread over Europe, being published in French in 1545, in Italian in Giovanni Battista Ramusio's *Navigationi et viaggi* in 1556, and in English in Richard Eden's *Decades of the Newe World or West India* in 1555.[28] Equally important were the conclusions drawn from Cartier's accounts: that North America was relatively close to Asia on the west and that a water passage still existed. For example, a Portuguese report describing the Cartier-Roberval expedition stated that the river entered by the French was "very long . . . and that on the other side it empties itself into a great sea."[29] The rutter or sailing and navigational aid of Jean Allfonce, pilot on Roberval's vessel during the 1541–42 voyage, also demonstrated a belief in the passage to the Pacific; the Saguenay River, according to Allfonce, widened above its confluence with the Saint Lawrence and began "to take on the character of an arm of the sea." He added, "For which reason I estimate that this sea leads to the Pacific Ocean or even to *la mer du Cattay*."[30]

By the middle of the 1540s, much was known about the eastern coastal region of the North American continent. Those interested in overseas ventures knew that between Newfoundland and Florida it appeared to be a solid landmass, with possible straits penetrating it. Cartier's explorations toward the interior gave geographers a sense of the east-west expanse of the continent and may have spelled the beginning of the end of the Sea of Verrazzano myth (although the French would later replace the Sea of Verrazzano with their own mythical Sea of the West).[31] Whether the land was worth the enormous expense of life and treasure that would be needed to develop it for European investors was much less clear. Furs could be had in abundance, but precious minerals remained to be proven. More important, the difficulties of establishing the kind of presence that regular trade would necessitate were glimpsed in the experiences of Cartier's, Roberval's, and Hore's expeditions. Their stories demonstrated that the fishermen's reports of the North American summer had not prepared Europeans for the Canadian winter; both seasons involved extremes of temperatures unknown to the moderate maritime climate of western Europe.[32]

7.1 Western Hemisphere on the planisphere made by Juan Vespucci (1526). This is the first known map to show the early Spanish discoveries along the Atlantic coast, as well as those of Verrazzano. The open nature of the coast above the Florida peninsula suggests an early version of the "Sea of Verrazzano." Courtesy The Hispanic Society of America, New York. [412–413]

7.2 *Western Hemisphere portion of the world map by Diogo Ribeiro (1529). On this beautiful map are shown the results of the explorations of Vázquez de Allyón, the Côrte-Reals, Gómez, and Cabot. Ribeiro's map demonstrates the rapid increase in geographical knowledge within forty years of the first Columbian voyage in 1492. Courtesy of the Biblioteca Apostolica Vaticana, Vatican City.*

Northern Fisheries

Fish differed from all other commodities in that it could be produced entirely by European efforts. Cartier's voyages had revealed to thoughtful prospective adventurers the profound reliance on the American natives that all other enterprises involved. The explorers were dependent on the Indians for food, despite the rich resources they themselves described; in addition, much of their geographical information came not from the instruments and expertise of which they were so proud but from their Indian informants. The crippling of Cartier's colony by scurvy and the fear of conspiracy that drove them away in 1536 conclusively demonstrated that Europeans would be forced to form partnerships with Indians if they were to achieve any of their goals within North America.

Meanwhile the fishing industry grew independently. The annual visits of the fishing fleets to the rich Newfoundland Banks and Gulf of Saint Lawrence were already well established in the 1540s and continued to grow as Europe's dramatic population increase expanded the demand for new and inexpensive sources of protein.[33] A fishing voyage to Newfoundland could be undertaken by anyone owning a small ship, without any extraordinary preparation or expense. Portuguese and French fishermen were already well established in the trade during the first decade of the sixteenth century. Both groups had access to good supplies of salt and could therefore stay at sea on the Newfoundland Banks, laying down a heavy coating of salt between each layer of fish.

English participation in the industry grew more slowly, especially after 1570. English fishermen pushed the French out of the areas best suited to their own needs, particularly the Avalon Peninsula on the southeastern tip of Newfoundland. Since they had poor sources of salt, English mariners stayed closer to shore, laying out the catch to dry in the sun and wind, thus requiring much less salt to preserve it. The Portuguese fisheries declined as the English expanded, particularly after Portugal came under Spanish control in 1580. The English merchant Anthony Parkhurst estimated in 1578, on the basis of his own eyewitness investigations, that 350 ships came to Newfoundland each year, of which 50 were English, 100 were Spanish, 50 Portuguese, and 150 French, including Bretons.[34] Modern-day estimates put the number higher, around 500 ships overall, with the French figure set much higher than in Parkhurst's estimate.[35] By the end of the century, the English share was much larger. Important though they undoubtedly were, these summer-only visits did not require colonies, since the stages or platforms on which fish were dried and the accommodations for the men could be rehabilitated or reconstructed every spring; salt-rich fishermen spent little time on shore. Fish, the established gold of the northern lands, already came to Europe in abundance. Was it worthwhile to try to extend the search for commodities?

After the well-publicized failures of the 1530s and 1540s, plans for colonization in the northern region, or for extensive operations in the interior, were given up. The fishing went on, however, and though it seemed to prove that colonies not only involved great difficulty but were unnecessary, regular visits by the fishing fleets created the preconditions for the future planting of settlers in North America. The experience garnered from the fishing industry helped create a cadre of skilled mariners, pilots, and captains who would lead later expeditions. Merchants developed sophisticated understandings of the finance, insurance, and logistics necessary to colonial success, and the capital that flowed from the cargoes made financing other, more risky ventures possible. In addition, the returning ships added incrementally to geographical knowledge and understanding.[36]

The international community of fishermen formed a self-regulating group, with a representative of a different nation elected as admiral each year. Rough territorial assignments had been worked out over the years and were usually honored as the fishing fleets returned each spring. At times various European powers sought to take over the Newfoundland fisheries. Little-documented Portuguese colonization attempts in the 1560s and 1570s may have left some permanent settlers, or at least cattle and pigs, on Sable Island as their legacy.[37] In 1583 Sir Humphrey Gilbert, a favorite of Queen Elizabeth's, traveled to Newfoundland with the aim of claiming the island under his royal patent and setting up a semifeudal plantation, probably in New England. He had been urged on by the observations of Anthony Parkhurst.[38] Accounts of Gilbert's expedition claimed that his authority had been accepted by the fishermen in the harbor of Saint John's. Stephen Parmenius, a young Hungarian poet and scholar who traveled with Gilbert, wrote a long letter to Richard Hakluyt describing the company's adventures. He wrote that Gilbert "tooke possession of the Country, for himselfe and the kingdome of England." The twenty or so Spanish and Portuguese ships, not being able to resist, submitted to this claim of authority, and the English, "although they were of them selves strong ynough, and safe from our force, yet seeing our aucthoritie, by the Queenes letters patentes, they shewed us all manner of dutie and humanitie."[39] The profundity of this acceptance was never tested, since Gilbert did not follow up his claims with the establishment of any administrative machinery.

Gilbert and Parmenius both died in shipwrecks on the voyage home, and English interest in northern colonization lay dormant for some time. Sir Humphrey had conducted investigations of the mineral resources of the island and had departed with high hopes. Edward Hayes, the chronicler of the voyage, wrote of Gilbert: "For where as the Generall had never before good conceit of these North parts of the world: now his mind was wholly fixed upon the New found land." He resolved to return to Newfoundland the next year, "affirming that this voyage had wonne his heart from the South, and that he was now become a Northerne man altogether."[40] His opinion was not, apparently, generally shared. Parmenius, like many others of Gilbert's company, had found Newfoundland depressing: "But what shall I say, my good Hakluyt, when I see nothing but a very wildernesse?" He admitted that "of fishe here is incredible abundance," but the perpetual mist and rain and the floating "mountaines of yce" made him yearn "by the helpe of God to passe towards the south, with so much the more hope every day, by how much greater the thinges are, that are reported of those Countries."[41] The coastal nature of the fishing industry had demonstrated that no major break in the continental outline existed in the region of the fisheries, and English efforts to secure the passage to the Pacific shifted farther to the north, to Arctic water. The focus of European colonization also shifted and was now firmly on the areas to the south; Newfoundland continued to be the province of the fishermen.

Southern Settlements

France had been interested in permanent settlements in the southern regions from the 1560s, with three goals in mind: forestalling continued Spanish expansion into North America from the Caribbean; locating the resource-rich areas described in early Spanish accounts of the Southeast; and finding the still-elusive passage to the Pacific. French ships had been patrolling West Indian waters since the 1520s looking for opportunities to prey on the Spanish fleet carrying treasure from Havana to Seville. These ventures had built a fairly sophisticated French understanding of the geography of the southern coast of North America, all of which was then called La Florida. The French knowledge of La Florida that derived from privateers was probably less significant, however, than that obtained from the Verrazzano voyage and from the efforts of the Spanish, whose explorations of the 1520s had contributed significantly to European geographical conceptions of the American Southeast. French cartography of the mid-1550s, particularly that of the Dieppe School (a center of French cartography in the sixteenth and seventeenth centuries), was based on both the Verrazzano maps and the maps of Agnese and Münster, which in turn showed the heavy influence of Diogo Ribeiro, the "official" Spanish cartographer of the Seville House of Trade. Many of the most striking Dieppe maps and globes of the period showed (or at least hinted at) a continental narrowing somewhere between the thirty-fifth and fortieth parallels of latitude. The location of such a narrowing may have provided some of the incentive for the period of French colonization in the southern regions. In addition, the publication in 1552 of Francisco López de Gómara's *Historia general de las Indias* and, in 1557, of the "Gentleman of Elvas" account of Hernando de Soto's explorations renewed interest in the legends of "Chicora," a land located north of the Florida peninsula and described by early Spanish explorers as fabulously rich.[42] Three other works published in the 1550s—Eden's *Decades of the Newe World*, Ramusio's *Navigationi et viaggi*, and Andre Thevet's *Les singularitez de la France Antarctique*—reinforced Gómara and the Gentleman of Elvas.[43] On the other hand, Gaspard de Coligny, the Hugenot admiral of France to whom fell the task of implementing French policy in La Florida, apparently had access to Guillaume Le Testu's beautiful 1555 Dieppe atlas, *Cosmographie universalle*. On Le Testu's map of Florida, there was no hint of the Sea of Verrazzano or even of rivers connecting the Atlantic and the Pacific. But the folio page of description opposite the map in Le Testu's atlas carried the words "In this region gold is abundant, with emeralds and pearls."[44] The American Southeast, or "La Florida," was apparently a land well worth the effort of attempting colonization.

In 1562 Jean Ribault, of Dieppe, responding to these incentives in an effort sponsored by French Huguenots, explored the southeastern coast from a point near present-day Saint Augustine northeastward to Port Royal Island, charting inlets, rivers, and harbors as he went. Ribault left a tiny colony of only twenty-six men at Charlesfort on Port Royal Sound on the coast of South Carolina between Hunting Island and Hilton Head Island. When the renewal of religious conflict in France thwarted his efforts to amass new shipments for the settlers, Ribault persuaded an English adventurer, Thomas Stukely, to set out a fleet to relieve them in 1563, but the

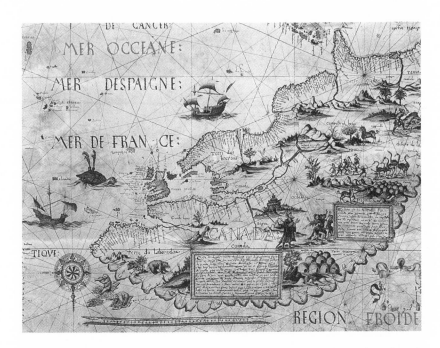

7.3 East coast of North America from the world map by Pierre Desceliers (1550). Placing south at the top rather than the bottom, this example of the great Dieppe (France) school of cartography was one of the first to show the full scope of geographical knowledge added by Cartier in the Saint Lawrence region. By permission of The British Library.

ships went privateering instead.[45] When relief failed to return on schedule, the settlers fell into disarray and sailed for home on a ship they had built.[46]

A second settlement, La Caroline, was erected on the Saint Johns River, along the eastern coast of Florida, in 1564 under the command of René Goulaine de Laudonnière, who had been part of the 1562 group. This settlement did some exploring, led on by hopes of riches, but it, like its predecessor, was rent by hostility. Some of the men, seduced by thoughts of "the great wealth that they should gaine," mutinied and went on a privateering expedition in the Caribbean, which helped seal the colony's fate.[47] Spain, determined not to allow a base from which their fleets could be assaulted, attacked the settlement in 1565. Despite the reinforcement of the colony by a shipment under Ribault, La Caroline succumbed to the Spanish under Pedro Menéndez de Avilés, partly because of divided command between

7.4 Atlantic coast of North America from the Cosmographie universalle *by Guillaume Le Testu (1555). This map of Florida, Canada, and Labrador (west is at the top of the map) is from one of the fine decorative atlases of the sixteenth century. Courtesy The Newberry Library.*

Laudonnière and Ribault.[48] French reports spoke of a "terrible slaughter," which saw the deaths of women and children along with the men, "insuch a way that it is impossible to conceive of a massacre which could be equal to this one in cruelty and barbarity."[49] About one hundred French escaped the attack, and some of them were ultimately rescued and returned to France, among them Laudonnière and the painter Jacques Le Moyne de Morgues, whose striking pictures of La Florida were presented in Part II of Theodor de Bry's *America* (1591) and still form one of the best visual records of North America's Atlantic region during the period of exploration and discovery.[50]

Despite these failures in the field, the reports generated by the French attempts at colonization still held out rich hopes. Laudonnière, for example, believed the land was rich in minerals; he repeated what the Indians had told him: "In the Mountaines of Appalatcy there are Mines of Copper, which I thinke to be Golde." He also thought valuable dyes could be exported from Florida, and he reported "great store of Mulberrie trees white

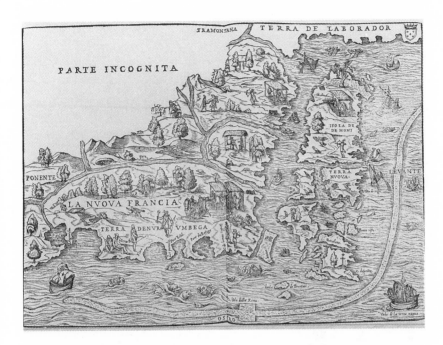

7.5 "La Nueva Franca," published in Giovanni Battista Ramusio, Navigationi et viaggi *(Venice, 1556). This map, although more primitive in design than many of its contemporaries, influenced much later cartography. Despite the fact that the map was drawn well after the Cartier explorations, the geographical knowledge presented is drawn almost entirely from Verrazzano. Courtesy The Newberry Library.*

and red, on the toppes whereon there was an infinite number of silke-wormes."[51] It is apparent from the tone of this report that the old Spanish legend of Chicora, derived from the explorations of Lucas Vázquez de Ayllón in the 1520s, was still a part of the European image of North America. Ribault explained the first venture's failure to explore inland in search of "Chicuola" by describing the extreme difficulty of navigating American rivers with large ships and the danger of leaving the ships unattended. Laudonnière also attributed La Caroline's lack of exploration in part to the unruliness of his own men.[52] Such investigation of the land that did take place was motivated largely by the search for precious minerals or great walled towns rich in gold, silver, and pearls, rather than by the search for a passage through the continent. The lesson of these ventures again stressed the difficulties involved in American colonization, the extreme dependence of settlers on Indian aid for both sustenance and guidance in devel-

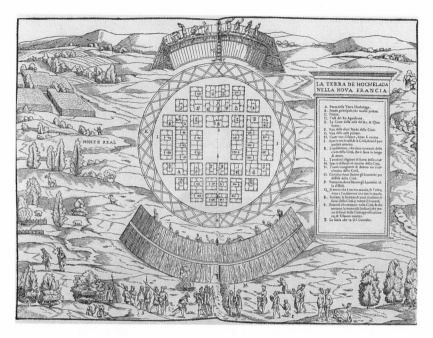

7.6 Plan of the city of Hochelaga from Ramusio, Navigationi et viaggi *(Venice, 1556). This "city plan" was based on a description of a Native American town near what became Montreal. The description itself came from Cartier's accounts. Courtesy The Newberry Library.*

oping commodities, and the dangers from hostile forces. In the final analysis, the favorable tone of Laudonnière's reports notwithstanding, to the French the southern region looked no more welcoming to permanent settlement than the northern areas.

On the strength of the same incentives that the French possessed and with the added imperative of preventing the establishment of a French base near their Caribbean empire, the Spanish also sought to extend their holdings into the North American continent from the Caribbean, a move for which the attack on La Caroline had set the stage.[53] Pedro Menéndez de Avilés, in his agreement, or *asiento*, with King Philip II, undertook to explore the entire east coast of North America from

> Los Ancones and the Bay of San Josepe, which is one league from Florida toward the west, as far as the Cape of Los Mártires, in twenty-five degrees; and thence as far as Terranova, which lies between fifty and sixty degrees [north latitude], east or west and north and south:

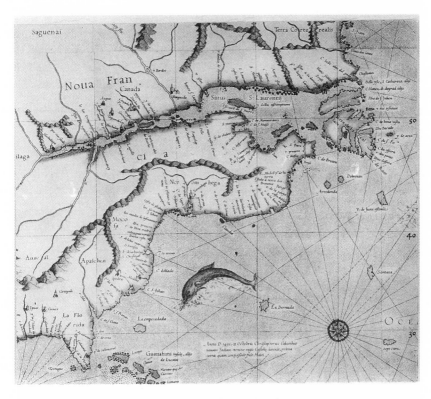

7.7 Detail from Mercator's world map (1569). Mercator's map was one of the most influential ever produced. This detail of eastern North America is remarkably accurate for the time, being the first to show the Appalachians in their alignment parallel to the coast. Courtesy Maritiem Museum "Prins Henrik," Rotterdam, the Netherlands.

the whole coast, in order to reconnoitre and test the harbors and currents, rocks and shoals and inlets there may be on the aforesaid coast; having them marked and indicated as accurately as you can by their latitudes and ships' courses, so that the secret of the said coast and the harbors which may be thereon, shall be known and understood.[54]

Menéndez landed his colonists from a small harbor that he estimated to be at 29.5°, which they named for the day, San Agustin. Having rid himself of the civilians, he prepared to attack La Caroline.[55] He reported the slaughter of the French, members of "the wicked Lutheran sect," and justified putting to the sword even those who had surrendered on his promise of

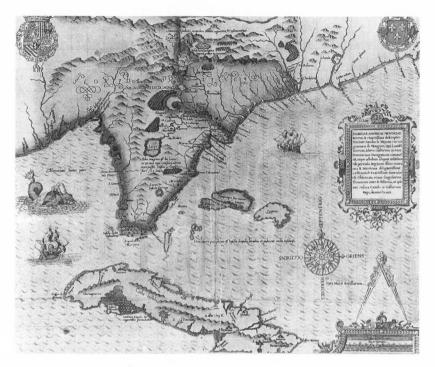

7.8 "Floridae America Provinciae" (A. J. Le Moyne, [1590]). This map, drawn by the artist who accompanied Laudonnière's expedition of 1564–65, served as a model for maps of the American Southeast for the next century. At the top of the map can be seen the coast of the Sea of Verrazzano. Published in Theodor de Bry, America (Frankfurt, 1591). Courtesy Rare Books and Manuscripts Division, The New York Public Library, Astor, Lenox, and Tilden Foundations.

mercy. He built a new fort, San Mateo, on the site of La Caroline, and in his reports he corrected the French calculation of its position, saying it was at 30.25° north latitude.[56]

The correspondence between Menéndez de Avilés and Philip II reveals some of the geographical misinformation that drove the Spanish to exterminate the French colonies. Because longitude could not be calculated accurately and the explorations of Hernando de Soto, Alvar Núñez Cabeza de Vaca, Francisco Vázquez de Coronado, and other Spanish explorers had been inconclusive on this point, no one understood the east-west extent of the North American continent in the south. Menéndez was convinced that Mexico was a short overland journey from the coast where the French had been established; in 1566 he sent out an expedition under Juan Pardo to establish this overland route. Thus, in Menéndez's opinion, the French settlers represented not only a base from which the treasure fleets could be attacked but also a threat to the heart of New Spain. He argued that control of this coast was essential to the protection of the Spanish American empire.[57]

Menéndez's endeavor, consisting of over one thousand people, overcame one of the deficiencies that had plagued earlier operations. He established a third fort at Port Royal on present-day Parris Island, South Carolina, which he named Santa Elena, but his real objective was Chesapeake Bay, known to the Spanish as the Bahía de Santa María de Ajácan, which is at 37° north latitude. Menéndez had visited this great bay in 1561 and had been intrigued by its reach into the interior.[58] The result was that the Spanish presence in North America, already seen as peripheral in old and New Spain, was stretched too thin, and the forts were constantly subject to discontent, shortages, and Indian hostility.[59] These problems were interrelated, since shortages led to pressure on the natives for supplies, and resulting Indian hostilities led to a sense of imprisonment in the forts, breeding discontent.[60]

In addition to the presumed proximity of the Florida coast to Mexico, Menéndez also believed in the presence of an inland passage to Canada or a sea-level passage to the Pacific via the "Salado River," or Chesapeake Bay, which he was convinced extended west to the Pacific. In 1566, the same year in which the Pardo expedition set out to discover the overland route to Mexico, an expedition of soldiers and Dominican priests, accompanied by Don Luis, an Indian captured in Menéndez's 1561 expedition, set out to explore the North Carolina and Virginia coast, to establish a Spanish presence in Chesapeake Bay, and to attempt to locate the passage to the Pacific. Despite earlier Spanish success, however, the mariners were unable to enter the bay because of a great storm. The ship then turned south and entered an inlet of the Carolina Outer Banks, which were claimed for Spain.[61] In 1570 a new venture was sent to Chesapeake Bay. The mission was composed entirely of Jesuits, except for one Spanish boy and Don Luis. No soldiers accompanied the priests, who were led by Juan Baptista de Segura; they believed that Don Luis would build a bridge between them and the Indians. Wishful thinking misled them, and Don Luis quickly returned to his own people. During the winter all the priests were killed; only the boy, Alonso de Olmos, was spared. The message was clear: the priests, who represented an assault on the Indians' own culture and religion, were destroyed.[62] This failure marked the end of expansive efforts from Spanish

Florida; Menéndez spent the rest of his life in Spain, his hopes for riches and the supposed way to the Pacific destroyed, and the outposts in Florida took on the character of a holding operation.[63] Pedro Menéndez Marques, Menéndez's nephew and successor in Florida, made one last voyage to Chesapeake Bay but found nothing on which to build hope for further ventures there.[64]

Early English Endeavors

International politics, which always at least partially reflected religious conflict in the sixteenth century, dramatically affected the growth of knowledge about North America. French Protestants tried to found colonies on the southern coast partly as a refuge from conflict at home but partly also to forestall the expansion of Spain, the leader of the Roman Catholic powers, into that continent. As the French temporarily faded from the scene after the middle of the century, England slowly began to emerge as the Protestant nation leading the fight to stop the aggrandizement of Spain in America. None of this would have happened without the Reformation, which split Europe into two camps. One result of the Reformation and especially of Roman Catholic efforts to root out pockets of heresy was the spread of knowledge over Europe as skilled artisans and mariners fled to safer havens. Geographical knowledge and navigational skills also spread. England benefited greatly from this diaspora, as mapmakers and pilots formerly in the service of Catholic countries now came to London as well as to the tolerant Netherlands. At his London residence, Durham House, Sir Walter Raleigh—in a forerunner of the modern-day "think tank"—brought together English scholars and navigators, such as Thomas Hariot and Thomas Cavendish, with these foreigners whose skills were so advanced. The captains of Raleigh's fleet were trained in basic trigonometry by Hariot and were exposed to the latest in cartographical thinking. Richard Hakluyt the Younger learned all he could of continental advances in geographical understanding while he was chaplain to the English ambassador to France between 1583 and 1588.[65]

Simão Fernandes, a Portuguese from the Azores known in the English documents as Simon Ferdinando, offers a case in point. He was an experienced pilot in the Spanish service who claimed to have been in Chesapeake Bay in the 1560s. He came to England in the 1570s and joined the international community of pirates who operated in the English Channel and along the European coast. When captured by the English authorities, he saved himself by offering them his expertise. Fernandes had special reasons to serve his new country. He is variously described as a Lutheran ("Lutheran" was a blanket term for Protestant among the Spanish) or a Jew. He apparently came to England with a hatred of Spain, an enmity that was cemented when the union of the Portuguese and the Spanish Crowns in 1580 meant the extension of the Inquisition to Portugal and the Azores. He was fully prepared to put his knowledge at the disposal of his new employer.[66]

Fernandes became "Master Secretary Walsingham's man." Sir Francis Walsingham, secretary of state to Queen Elizabeth, sought to use his position to further England's entry into the race to establish international trade and settlements to further that trade. His patronage was essential in bringing together men capable of supplying the elements necessary to success and placing them in positions where they could pool and make use of their knowledge and skills. Fernandes first played the role designed for him in the voyages of Sir Humphrey Gilbert between 1578 and 1580. At the same time he was conferring with Dr. John Dee, who sought to produce an accurate map of the eastern shores of the Atlantic for Gilbert; Fernandes gave Dee a Spanish "Sea Carte" of the Atlantic. Fernandes also served Edward Fenton as pilot on a projected voyage around Africa to the East Indies and China in 1582.

Many of the expeditions on which Fernandes served broke down because of his propensity (and that of many other mariners) to interpret English defiance of Spain broadly. This often led to an undisciplined piracy that sank the more sober objectives of the voyages. Englishmen frequently found themselves uncomfortably yoked with foreigners like Fernandes. Rev. John Walker, who was on the Fenton voyage, considered Fernandes a bad influence on the English crews, "for that he rejoyced in thinges starke naughtey, bragginge in his sundrye pyracyes."[67] When Richard Madox, another minister on the voyage, pointed out that England and Spain were officially at peace, Fernandes, whom Madox called "a ravenous thief," replied that he had "a free pardon from five Privy Councilors for carrying on war with Spain."[68]

Whether English planners liked it or not, though, foreign experts were absolutely necessary to English transatlantic voyages. English mariners lacked the skill to navigate in Caribbean and North American coastal waters; sixteenth-century voyages typically relied on Spanish and Portuguese pilots. It was only through participation in the sea war between England

and Spain from 1585 to 1603 and through the privateering made possible by this war that English mariners learned the navigational skills to make them surefooted participants in the colonization of the seventeenth century.[69] This prolonged sea war, itself a product of the religious tensions of post-Reformation Europe, was the final ingredient in the catapulting of England into the race to explore and colonize North America. English adventurers had long been interested in American ventures. Thomas Stukely had laid plans to inject an English element into the first French colony of the 1500s, and John Hawkins, returning from a West Indian voyage, had visited and aided Laudonnière and his struggling La Caroline in 1565.[70] All such efforts would remain small-scale, however, until Queen Elizabeth, goaded by Spanish threats, allowed conflict to erupt into open war at sea after 1585. War opened the door to privateering and the wealth that would reward the outlay necessary to sponsor colonies and exploration.

Fernandes first became associated with Raleigh through their participation in Sir Humphrey Gilbert's schemes. The Portuguese sailor served as pilot for Raleigh's ship on an ill-fated venture in 1578. He was to play a crucial role in efforts to establish a permanent English presence within the Carolina Outer Banks in the 1580s. Raleigh planned an American settlement that would provide a base from which ships of the Spanish treasure fleet could be attacked, thus crippling the enemy and bringing capital into England. Raleigh's plans involved long-term thinking as well. He sought economic independence for England, whose ailing textile industry, the backbone of the nation's economy, could be revived and put on a surer footing if sources of dyes, fibers, and fixatives could be found and developed in English-owned territories. Such sources would free England of dependence on Mediterranean products. The infusion of capital from privateering would help pay for the long-term development of settlements and the steady income they would produce. Finally, Raleigh was thinking—as were many of his countrymen—of the location of a route to the Pacific.

By the 1580s, as a result of seven decades of exploration along America's Atlantic coast, the choices for a western route from Europe to the Orient had narrowed to three possibilities: a northern route above the sixtieth parallel of latitude, such as the one pursued by Martin Frobisher between Newfoundland and Greenland in 1576–78; a middle route near the fiftieth parallel via the Saint Lawrence and its tributaries, hypothesized by Cartier on the basis of his explorations of the 1530s; and a southern route through the midlatitudes of North America utilizing one of the rivers or bays between 35° and 40° north that French maps of the mid–sixteenth century, following the tradition of Verrazzano-based cartography, persisted in showing. Sir Humphrey Gilbert had evinced an interest in this southern route as well as in the middle route. After his death, Raleigh's attention was also drawn to the southern region and its potential for a route through the continent.

The First Roanoke Colony

Both short-term and long-term goals necessitated a southern location for the settlement. Raleigh inherited his half-brother Sir Humphrey Gilbert's patent for colonization of North America's east coast, but whereas Gilbert had looked to the north, Sir Walter focused on the Carolina Outer Banks. Such a situation was necessary to catch the Spanish ships, which had to exit the Caribbean through either the Florida Channel or the Old Channel; either course brought the treasure fleet close to the Outer Banks. Fibers and dyes essential to the cloth industry were thought to come only from hot regions, thus necessitating a southern settlement. Gold and other precious minerals, always a hope in any exploration venture, were also—so the scientists said—possible only where the sun shone hottest.[71] And there still remained the unanswered questions regarding a passage to the Pacific. In his *Divers Voyages* of 1582, Richard Hakluyt the Younger listed the evidence in support of such a passage and reproduced a map by Michael Lok showing the Sea of Verrazzano with an isthmus between the Atlantic and the Pacific at around 40° north latitude.[72]

A reconnaissance voyage sent out by Raleigh in 1584 under the command of Philip Amadas and Arthur Barlowe reported finding the perfect location for the base: Roanoke Island, sheltered between the mainland of North Carolina and the sandbars that make up the Outer Banks. Though it was farther from the treasure fleet's course than Florida, the gain in defensive capability was seen as substantial. The reports generated by this voyage, on the basis of which Raleigh gambled heavily, demonstrate the difficulty of obtaining truly accurate information about American geography, climate, and settlement possibilities. Amadas and Barlowe were guided to the Outer Banks by the ubiquitous Fernandes, who claimed to have personal knowledge of the area. Barlowe's report was circulated and then published by Hakluyt in *Principal Navigations*; it described an idyllic setting of plenty and peace. Barlowe said the "soile is the most plentifull, sweete, fruitfull, and wholsome of all the world." In this land of abundance, the Indians, whom Barlowe described as "most gentle, loving, and faithfull, void of all guile, and treson, and such as lived after the manner of the golden age," were able to live "without toile or labour."[73] Barlowe made the site sound ideal; though he admitted they had entered through one of the inlets in the Outer Banks "not without some difficultie," he assured readers that from within "the Haven" they saw "another mightie long Sea" between the Outer Banks and the continent, a statement that could have been a direct derivation from Verrazzano's original letter to Francis I.[74] The Barlowe account did not speak of the shallowness of these waters on both sides of the Outer Banks, a feature that made it impossible for large ocean-going ships to approach closely. This silence had profound implications for the effort to found a settlement at Roanoke; Barlowe's desire to please Raleigh with a favorable report in many ways doomed the larger effort.[75]

Raleigh enlisted the support of Richard Hakluyt, home on leave from the Paris embassy. Hakluyt gathered information wherever he went; Paris was a particularly good place for such activities in the 1580s because the court of the pretender to the Portuguese throne, Dom António, had sought refuge in France. The pretender himself discussed geography and cartography with Hakluyt and allowed Hakluyt access to the maps, navigators, and cartographers he had brought with him. English planners thus had access to the most sophisticated knowledge available. When back in England, Hakluyt wrote "A particular discourse concerninge the greate necessitie and manifolde commodyties that are like to growe to this Realme of Englande by the Westerne discoveries lately attempted," which is known as *Discourse of Western Planting*. This document brought together all the arguments for English colonies and voyages of exploration, with extensive quotations from authorities, emphasizing the benefits of colonization—from the propagation of the true Christian faith to the revitalization of English trade and the diminution of Spain's power. The *Discourse* was meant for the eyes of the queen and a few potential backers; it was not published until modern times. "Its purpose was to gain over the Queen, and to provide a textbook on colonisation for Sir Francis Walsingham." Hakluyt's older cousin, the lawyer Richard Hakluyt, also wrote a promotional tract, *Inducements to the Liking of the Voyage Intended towards Virginia in 40, and 42, Degrees of Latitude*. This took a practical approach, arguing that colonization was essential to the English economy for the effect it would have on trade and industry: "Traffique [trade] followeth conquest."[76]

Everything began to come together in the fall of 1585. Amadas and Barlowe returned to London at the end of September, and Hakluyt presented his *Discourse* to the queen on 5 October. The reconnaissance voyage had brought back two Indians, Manteo and Wanchese. Wanchese was apparently a Roanoke native, and Manteo was of the Croatoans, who lived on an island farther south in the Outer Banks. Thomas Hariot set about learning Carolina Algonquian from them and began to teach them English; together, they were to be a major source of information about the challenges and possibilities of the land. Their presence in London created a great stir. All this activity was apparently convincing, since the government now gave the enterprise many signs of favor; Queen Elizabeth conferred a knighthood on Raleigh, who had become a royal favorite, and allowed the lands claimed by him to bear the name "Virginia" in her honor. The new Sir Walter circulated Barlowe's report and prepared for a full settlement. The model chosen for this colony bespoke its military and exploratory goals: it was composed of just over a hundred soldiers. Sir Richard Grenville, Raleigh's fellow West Countryman, was to be general and admiral of the fleet. He would be in command as long as he remained in the colony. His flagship, the queen's galleass *Tiger*, sailed with Simão Fernandes as master and chief pilot of the expedition. Second-in-command was Thomas Cavendish, who would later repeat Francis Drake's feat of circumnavigating the globe, as high marshall. Captain Ralph Lane, released by the queen from service in Ireland, was governor-designate of the settlement.

The voyage, which began in April 1585, followed the usual route of English expeditions to the southern mainland: down the Old World coast to catch the trade winds, across to the West Indies, and then up the American coast on the powerful Gulf Stream Current. Here the incompatibility between the goals of exploration, settlement, and privateering began to plague the venture, and a bitter feud erupted between Grenville on the one side and Cavendish and Lane on the other. Delays in the West Indies shortened the time for erection of a settlement at Roanoke.

The first experience of the Outer Banks at the end of June was a discouraging one. The *Tiger* ran aground on the dangerous sandbars, and though the ship was saved, most of the food supplies, "corne, salt, meale, rice, bisket, & other provisions that he should have left with them that remained behind him in the countrie was spoiled."[77] A journal kept by an anonymous member of the *Tiger* company laid the blame on the unpopular foreigner who had piloted the Amadas-Barlowe voyage that had praised the site as well as this venture: "The 29. wee waighed anker to bring the Tyger into the harbour, where through the unskilfulnesse of the Master whose name was Fernando, the Admirall [flagship] strooke on grounde, and sunke."[78]

On 11 July Grenville took the expedition's pinnace and three boats across Pamlico Sound to explore the mainland. The group of about sixty men explored the rivers flowing into the sound and visited several Indian villages in an attempt to discover the trade possibilities of the region. One of the villages, Aquascogoc, accused of having stolen a silver cup from the English, received a vivid foretaste of what having Europeans in their midst would mean. "We burnt, and spoyled their corne, and towne, all the people beeing fledde."[79] Knowing that the men he left in America would be dependent on Indian aid through the coming winter, because of the accident to the *Tiger*, Grenville believed that vengeance for all slights, not conciliation, was the key to success. If the Indians believed they could get away with challenging the English, then, the English thought, no settler would be safe.[80]

Because Roanoke was clearly unsuitable for a settlement such as that planned by Raleigh, a great deal of exploring was done by these colonists. Captain Amadas explored Albemarle Sound during the month of August. As the ships left for home and more privateering on the way, the tone was hopeful. Ralph Lane wrote to Richard Hakluyt of the many commodities he hoped the land would provide: "It is the goodliest and most pleasing territorie of the world (for the soile is of an huge unknowen greatnesse, and very well peopled and towned, though savagelie) and the climate so wholesome, that we have not had one sicke, since we touched land here." If horses and cattle were brought over, "I dare assure my selfe being inhabited with English no realme in Christendome were comparable to it."[81]

One party traveled north to Chesapeake Bay and probably spent the winter there; Manteo and Wanchese as well as Fernandes may have convinced Lane that this site offered better opportunities than Roanoke. The explorers apparently knew that they would meet powerful and highly organized Indian polities on their travels. The venture, under the command of one of Lane's captains, traveled up Currituck Sound as far as possible and then exited through an Outer Banks inlet to move along the coast and into Chesapeake Bay. They apparently traveled partway up the Elizabeth and Nansemond Rivers and across Hampton Roads to the James-York peninsula. They appear to have established friendly relations with the Chesapeake Indians. The records of this exploration are vague, probably to fool rival colonial powers. The party returned full of enthusiasm for the area, and Raleigh was to plan his final colony for Chesapeake Bay.[82]

In contrast to the comparative silence on the northward exploration, Ralph Lane presented a full description of his own expedition up the Chowan and Roanoke Rivers in March 1586. Like Cartier's trip on the Saint Lawrence, this venture was driven by rumors of a great tribe, far into the interior, that possessed rich mineral resources. Wingina, chief of the Roanokes, encouraged Lane to make this journey, telling him of a powerful tribe, the Chowans on the Chowan River, and of the Mangoaks, with stores of copper or gold inland. Lane's first act at Chowanoac, seat of the Chowans, was to seize their chief, Menatonon, "a man impotent in his lims, but otherwise for a Savage, a very grave and wise man," intending to hold him hostage for the good behavior of the tribe. In their two days of discussion, probably through the translation of Manteo, Menatonon "gave mee more understanding and light of the Countrey then I had received by all the searches and salvages that before I or any of my companie had had conference with." Menatonon described a great king with huge stocks of fine pearls on a great sea, probably Chesapeake Bay, three days' journey up the Chowan River and four days' trek overland to the northeast, but warned "that king would be loth to suffer any strangers to enter into his Countrey, and especially to meddle with the fishing for any Pearle there, and that hee was able to make a great many of men into the fielde, which he sayd would fight very well."[83]

Menatonon also reinforced Lane's desire to see the Mangoaks, an Algonquian name for the Iroquoian Tuscarora tribe in the west. To get to their territory, Lane would have to travel against the "violent . . . currant from the West and Southwest" and through "many creeks and turnings" on the Morotico (Roanoke) River to the seat of the Morotucs. Beyond them were the Mangoaks. Thirty or forty days' travel beyond Morotico would take the explorers to the head of the river, standing near a great salt sea. Judging by the description, Thomas Hariot thought this river "either riseth from the bay of Mexico, or els from very neere unto the same, that openeth out into the South Sea," by which he meant the Pacific Ocean. This was the land of Chaunis Temoatan, from which the Mangoaks obtained their precious metals. These Indians were described as panning for alluvial copper, in exceptionally pure form: "two parts of metall for three partes of oare." From the descriptions of this copper's softness and color, Lane dared to hope that it was really gold, since, as he said, "they call by the name of Wassador every mettall whatsoever."[84]

Chaunis Temoatan was the equivalent of Cartier's Saguenay. Both stories involved sophisticated natives with great riches far in the interior; both seemed to promise access to the great western ocean. In fact, both stories of rich metals inland may have been describing copper from the Lake Superior region, copper that was traded all over eastern North America. Both also diverted attention from the problems of settlement to the dream of riches and access to the South Sea and further confused sixteenth-century European attempts to come to terms with North America. The vague promise of riches at Chaunis Temoatan and the sight of a great salt sea seemed more important to Lane than following up the leads on Chesapeake Bay.

Lane released Menatonon but sent his son Skiko to be held as a hostage at Roanoke Island. Lane then pressed forward toward Chaunis Temoatan with about thirty men. The venture, begun with such high hopes, soon degenerated into a terror-filled rout. The villages of the Morotucs, where Lane had hoped to acquire food and guides, were deserted: "Having passed three dayes voyage up the River, we could not meete a man, nor finde a graine of corne in any their Townes." With two days' supply of food left, Lane thought they should return home immediately; he thought they had come 100 miles up the Roanoke River, which would have put them 160 miles from Roanoke Island. He presented the case to his men and asked them to consider the situation overnight. Next day all but a few affirmed "that whiles there was left one halfe pinte of corne for a man, that we should not leave the search of that River, and that there were in the companie two mastives [dogs], upon the pottage of which with sassafras leaves (if the worst fell out) the companie would make shift to live two dayes" during which they could travel back down the river on the current.[85]

After further travel (Lane is unclear about the chronology), they heard some Indians calling to Manteo from the shore. "Whereof we [were] all verie glad, hoping of some friendly conference with them, and making him to answere them, they presently began a song, as we thought in token of our welcome to them; but Manteo presently betooke him to his peece and tolde mee that they ment to fight with us." The boats were soon fired on, after which the Indians fled; their pursuers were stymied by the natives' superior knowledge of the environment. As Lane said, "They had wooded themselves we know not where." The men realized that even if they could exact retribution on a few Indians, they "should bee assured to meete with none of their victuall." The "whole companie" was now ready to return to Roanoke with all speed, "for they were nowe come to their dogs porredge, that they had bespoken for themselves." On the return voyage, the current carried them as far in one day as they had gone in four days against it. The men were now reduced to eating sassafras leaves, even their dog meat being gone. Heavy winds delayed them from entering Albemarle Sound for one day. On Easter, 3 April, they traveled in the sound to a formerly friendly village, Chepanum, and found it also deserted, though the men, some of whom were "far spent," were able to take fish from the village's weirs. The next day, they were back in Roanoke.[86]

Governor Lane, reflecting on his experiences and piecing together what he had learned on his travels as well as from his prisoner, Skiko, believed that Wingina, chief of the Roanokes, had betrayed him. Wingina had changed his name to Pemisapan, possibly a war name, and Lane believed that he had encouraged the English to travel up the river while secretly arranging with the tribes along the way to sabotage the venture. What Lane did not realize was that the presence of the English had dramatically changed Wingina's position. The Roanokes, as suppliers of corn to the colonists, received English trade goods and in turn became the source of these highly prized items for other Indians. Therefore, Wingina, over the course of the winter, had become a much more important leader, able to build a consensus over what to do about the English intrusion. Wingina clearly demonstrated to the ill-prepared settlers that he had the upper hand. Lane wrote that Wingina had considered leaving Roanoke without planting crops in the spring of 1586: "If he had done [so], there had bene no possibilitie in common reason, (but by the immediate hand of God) that we could have bene preserved from starving out of hand. For at that time wee had no weares for fishe, neither could our men skill of the making of them, neither had wee one grayne of corne for seede to put into the ground." Wingina relented, Lane said, because he was so amazed to see that the exploring party had survived—but the seeds of conflict remained.[87]

Lane expected the balance of power soon to be righted because he believed that a new supply from England had been promised for Easter. All colonial ventures depended on a slender thread of help from home; in this case, help came too late. Wingina did withdraw onto the mainland, and Lane heard rumors that he was planning a huge meeting of tribes to attack the colony. The governor had been forced to disperse his company along the Outer Banks and on the mainland to live off the land, leaving the settlement weak. Thus, Lane decided on a preemptive attack on Wingina's new mainland base. The attack, on 1 June, ended with the death of Wingina.[88]

Lane had been expecting the new supply for almost six weeks. One week after Wingina's death, an English fleet was finally sighted off the

Outer Banks. This was not the expected supply, however, but the ships of
Sir Francis Drake, who had been careering through the Spanish colonies
for almost the same period of time that the colonists had been in Roanoke.
Drake's large fleet was to have been the first to make use of the facilities
that the base would make available to privateers. Sir Francis Drake had
capped his venture in the Caribbean by attacking the Spanish bases in Florida. The garrison at San Agustín eluded him, but Drake destroyed the
town, carrying away equipment that he thought would be useful to the
Roanoke settlers. He also attacked Santa Elena. In addition to supplies, he
may also have brought several hundred former slaves whom he had freed
from captivity by the Spanish.[89]

Governor Lane told Drake that he had a plan to send expeditions both
by land and by sea to Chesapeake Bay and, finally, when a suitable location
had been determined, to move the entire settlement there away from
Roanoke and its harbor, "(which by proofe is very naught)."[90] Drake offered to help the colony by replacing some of the unfit men with men of his
own and by giving them a bark, two pinnaces, and some boats, together
with equipment and weapons. Just as the bargain was concluded, a storm
of unprecedented ferocity scattered Drake's fleet, sending the *Francis*, the
promised bark, far out to sea. When the *Francis* failed to return, the discour-
aged colonists embarked with Drake for home, just weeks or days before
the new supply arrived.[91]

The information brought home by this Roanoke colony was enticing but
inconclusive. Roanoke was clearly a disastrously poor site for a base such
as Raleigh planned, but Chesapeake Bay seemed to offer a good deepwater
port, though with possibly more threatening Indian confederations. The
promise of precious metals and access to the Pacific through the land of
Chaunis Temoatan was tantalizing but unproven. Expedition cartographer
and draftsman John White's map showing the initial series of explorations
by Lane and others, for example, carried in its manuscript form an inset depicting a river route from the Atlantic to a large body of water—either the
Sea of Verrazzano or a large lake that some other English maps of the period showed as lying between the Atlantic and Verrazzano's sea. But the
published version of White's map, remarkable in its accuracy for the Outer
Banks area, did not contain this depiction of theoretical-but-unproven geography.[92] Ralph Lane no longer believed the land was promising enough
in itself. He urged Raleigh to follow up his Chowan River exploration, "for
that the discovery of a good mine, by the goodnesse of God, or a passage to
the Southsea, or someway to it, and nothing els can bring this country in

request to be inhabited by our nation." Lane also argued that the exploration must be supported by a settlement on a deepwater port such as was apparently offered by Chesapeake Bay.[93]

Scientific Reporting from the Roanoke Venture

Raleigh listened to other voices. This was the first American settlement supported by a scientific team: Thomas Hariot, Raleigh's mathematical and scientific expert, and the painter John White had accompanied the 1585 colony. Their charge was to create a full natural history of coastal Carolina, including the people and the flora and fauna. Together, these men produced the most remarkable American report of the sixteenth century; their meticulousness would be matched by few others in any century.

Hariot had prepared for the task by learning to speak Carolina Algonquian from Manteo and Wanchese between the 1584 reconnaissance voyage and the sailing of the 1585 colony expedition. He and White apparently achieved and maintained a close relationship with the Indians both on the Outer Banks and the near mainland; their portraits of individuals—men, women, and children—indicated a high degree of trust. They portrayed Indian life in all its homely aspects, conclusively demonstrating, by their portrayals of Indian villages surrounded by cornfields, that the Carolina Algonquians were a people who lived a civilized life, with religious rituals at the center of their communal life. John White's paintings of American life were influenced by his association with Jacques Le Moyne de Morgues, who had accompanied Laudonnière to Florida in 1564–65. Le Moyne, a technically more accomplished artist than White, fled religious persecution in France after the Saint Bartholomew's Day Massacre and spent the last years of his life, 1572–88, in England. Only one of Le Moyne's paintings of Timucua Indian life in Florida survives, but the engravings made from them by Theodor de Bry of Frankfort show the range and power of his work.[94] John White was clearly influenced by the techniques and models that Le Moyne was able to put before him.

Thomas Hariot wrote a brief description of the region, its people, and its possibilities for colonization. He intended this work to be no more than a prospectus for a full natural history that he and White were to produce, but nothing more was ever published, partly because much of their work was lost in the confusion as they hurriedly left Roanoke. Lane wrote, "Most of all wee had, with all our Cardes, Bookes and writings, were by the Saylers cast over boord, the greater number of the Fleete being much agrieved with their long and daungerous abode in that miserable road."[95] His book, circulated in manuscript to interest investors in continuing with the effort despite the mixed results of the 1585–86 venture, was published in 1588 with the title *A Briefe and True Report of the New Found Land of Virginia.* Hariot, with his command of the language, gave a fully rounded picture of Indian life, religion, government, and social structure. He was sensitive to the changes being wrought in that life by the coming of Europeans; he reported the Indians' agonized bewilderment over the diseases that killed so many of them. Hariot's report also gave a sober assessment of the commodities that investors might expect to reap from the land. He played down precious metals and instead wrote of silk grass, medicines, furs and skins, and wood products. He repeatedly emphasized that any return would come only after investment of time and energy; in short, until English men and women were prepared to invest themselves in a long-term commitment to building a new society in America, no wealth would be forthcoming. With such a commitment, Hariot stressed, there was plenty of food and materials for building. Hariot's intent was to pull Raleigh away from Lane's emphasis on searching for the elusive mine or privateering base and toward genuine colony building.[96]

Thomas Hariot and John White carried out their assignment to chart the region so successfully that they produced a map unequaled for North America in the sixteenth century. White and Hariot worked as a team, with White making concrete Hariot's measurements. The two men traveled constantly during their year on the Outer Banks, making sketches, taking measurements, and collecting samples. Their instructions have not survived, but those drawn up for a similar project for a voyage under Sir Humphrey Gilbert's patent would have been comparable. After elaborate lists of all the plants, animals, minerals, and features that were to be noted, the instructions, which were for a surveyor-artist named Thomas Bavin, ordered the captain to see that he be equipped and attended as follows:

[19] Another to attend always, Baven with penne onck paper & pensill with black leade and Ephimerides or with somme other Calculated Tables to observe the latitude./

Another to attend him alweis with an uneversall Dyall a Crosse staffe and A Sayling Compasse.

[20] Another to attend him alweis with an Instrument for the varyation of The Compasse and with the Instrument for the Declynation of

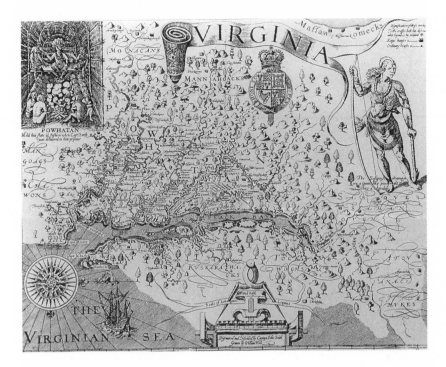

7.9 "A Map of Virginia," by Captain John Smith, engraved by William Hole, published at Oxford in 1612. Smith's map is the first to depict the Chesapeake Bay area with any degree of accuracy. The artwork was based on Theodor de Bry's engravings of John White's illustrations. By permission of The British Library.

the nedle. Another to attend him alweis when he draweth with all his marckes written in parchment to oversee him that he mistakes not any of the sayd marckes in his plottes which are sett down as followeth./

All the equipment would enable the surveyor to take accurate readings. Bavin's own instructions were even more elaborate, requiring him to carry accurate clocks and giving him minute directions for how to survey and to make sketches on cards that would later be fitted together to make maps, as well as to draw sketches of all the flora and fauna.[97] Assuming Hariot and White's instructions were similar, the two men carried them out extremely well.

Theodor de Bry, a Protestant of Liège who had fled to Frankfort to escape persecution, set up his printing works there. He planned to publish a

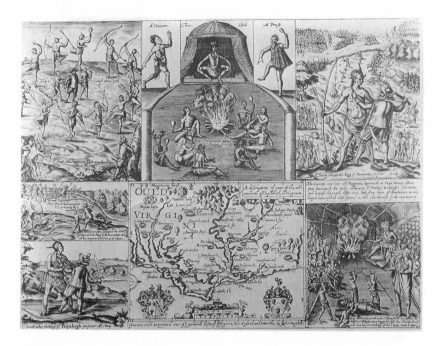

7.10 Map of Virginia by John Smith. Engraved by Robert Vaughn for John Smith's Generall Historie of Virginia *(London, 1624). Perhaps more important than the map itself (which was not followed by later cartographers) are the illustrations, drawn from Smith's account of his explorations. Courtesy John Carter Brown Library at Brown University.*

comprehensive history of Protestant efforts to colonize in territories formerly exclusively under the control of Roman Catholic monarchs. De Bry was in England in 1587 and again in 1588; he was interested in the work of Le Moyne as well as White and Hariot, and he acquired the drawings of both artists in 1588. Hariot's *Briefe and True Report* was republished in 1590 with woodcuts done in de Bry's studio from White's drawings and with notes to the paintings written by Hariot. It was published in four languages—Latin, French, German, and English—as Part I of de Bry's great work *America*; woodcuts of Le Moyne's paintings were in Part II. The woodcuts, though faithful in many respects to the originals, Europeanized the faces, bodies, and postures of American native peoples. In this form the Indian life portrayed by Hariot and White became known all over Europe; de Bry's versions of White's Indians were reproduced again and again to illustrate Indians all over North America.[98] De Bry's reproduction of Hariot and White's map visibly reinforced the impression gained from reading the documents; the wrecks of oceangoing ships litter the Outer Banks and their treacherous shallows.

Roanoke: The Lost Colony

Sir Walter Raleigh digested all this information and prepared to try again with a different design and a new location for a settlement. The final Roanoke colony, sent in 1587, had all the features of a successful plantation. It was sponsored by a small corporation, a joint-stock company known as The Governor and Assistants of the City of Raleigh in Virginia, which apparently promised continued support. The passengers of the first ships were families; later experience would prove that no colony lacking women would long survive. The governor was to be John White, one of the few 1585 colonists who was enthusiastic enough to return to the colony; his pregnant daughter, Eleanor Dare, and her husband accompanied him. The settlers expected to support themselves by farming, and carefully chosen craftsmen were included. Finally, the site was to be Chesapeake Bay. Richard Hakluyt had agreed with Hariot that this location was the best yet found.[99]

The company of 114 colonists was deposited not on Chesapeake Bay but back at Roanoke, where they arrived on 22 July 1587. During the voyage, grating tension had developed between Simão Fernandes, who again was pilot and master, and John White; Fernandes had risked the settlers' lives and shortened their supplies by undertaking an extended privateering sweep before sailing to Roanoke. Fernandes, according to White, said the colonists must accept being left at the old location because the "Summer was far spent." White, enraged because precious time had been spent privateering, accused Fernandes, to Raleigh, of endangering the entire enterprise. On the other hand Fernandes, who was a member of the corporation and who had been in Chesapeake Bay, may have felt that this location was too risky for the little band. The Roanoke houses and fort still stood, and Manteo's Croatoans were still friendly to the English. Fernandes's ships stayed with the settlers for over a month, till the end of August. When they left, John White sailed with them to put the planters' plight before Raleigh personally. Meanwhile, the colonists agreed that they would endeavor to make their way to Chesapeake Bay and would wait there for White and supplies in the spring.[100]

The final Roanoke colonists, including Virginia Dare, White's newborn granddaughter, were never seen again by Europeans. The association of privateering and colonization forced by the need to make each venture self-supporting killed the colony. Raleigh, with the backing of his freshly reorganized corporation, prepared a fleet to send new colonists and supplies early in 1588, but this fleet, like all other seaworthy ships, was pressed into action to meet the threat of the Spanish Armada.[101] No voyage was planned for 1589, for reasons that remain unclear, and when White did reach the island in a small ship in 1590, the site had been deserted, though apparently by an orderly departure, and the cryptic message "CROATOAN" was the only indication of where the settlers may have gone. Attempts to follow up this clue were thwarted by a hurricane. No further voyages went in search of the colonists until those of Samuel Mace in 1602 and 1603.[102]

Colonization as a support for privateering did not make sense. This became clear during the 1590s as privateering thrived without any colonies or bases. As English mariners became more adept at navigation and more knowledgeable about American waters, their ability to spend long periods in the West Indies grew. Increasingly large amounts of money came into England from privateering during this decade, as much as 10 to 15 percent of total imports in some years, and the thought of colonies receded.[103] Settlements were sponges that soaked up capital; privateering could reward investors with handsome returns. While privateering flourished, there would be little investment in colonization. English mariners joined French and Dutch seamen in the all-out war on Spanish shipping in the West Indies and the Atlantic.

By the beginning of the seventeenth century, then, North American realities were clearly conceived in the minds of European promoters. Settlements were extremely difficult to maintain there, requiring large amounts of support over long periods of time. Colonies composed of soldiers were almost impossible to control and motivate during long winters in isolated forts. Colonies of families seemed too fragile for the hardships and uncertainties of the colonial lifeline to Europe. More important, there was yet no real reason to establish colonies. No precious metals had been seen; and no sure passageway to the Pacific had been found. North America did offer products of value, but the fish and furs of the north and the privateering booty of the south did not require colonies to acquire them. Colonies were, simply, an expensive irrelevance.

Northern Ventures

While the energies of British and French promoters went into the privateer-ing frenzy of the 1590s and therefore focused on the southern region, other, less grandiose projects continued to experiment with northern settlement. Newfoundland attracted fishing voyages from all over western Europe, and the summer population continued to grow. It remained an interna-tional community, despite the conflicting paper claims to sovereignty by Portugal, England, and France. At the same time, some expeditions—Spanish Basque, French Basque, and later French and English—ventured farther into the Gulf of Saint Lawrence in search of whales, walrus, and seals. Furs, initially acquired as novelties by fishermen, began to occupy a major role in the trade. Even in the 1580s, voyages had been sent out from France specifically to trade for furs. Richard Hakluyt alerted his country-men to this valuable commerce, from which he feared the English might be excluded. While in France, he had seen the cargo returned by his "frende Stephen Bellinger of Roan" with "divers beastes skynnes, as bevers, ot-ters, marternes, lucernes, seales, buffes, dere skynnes all dressed and painted on the innerside with divers excellent colors, as redd, tawnye, yel-low, and vermillyon." Bellenger's cargo was worth just over four hundred crowns, but Hakluyt said the "kinges skynners" in Paris had received furs worth twenty thousand crowns in 1583. He argued that England's eco-nomic problems could be solved by American trade "if by our slackness wee suffer not the frenche or others to prevente us."[104]

Involvement in the fur trade dramatically altered the European relation-ship with North America and irrevocably changed Indian life. Fishing had allowed Europeans to remain temporarily on the fringe of the continent, facing east. The fur trade forced its participants to face west and to estab-lish relationships with American natives. Venturers found themselves ex-ploring both the intricacies of the land and the complexities of Indian politi-cal relationships in order to keep the flow of furs coming. Hakluyt reported that Bellenger explored two hundred miles along the coast of Nova Scotia as far as the Bay of Fundy. He traded with the Indians at ten or twelve places and discovered a "Towne of fourscore houses covered with the barkes of trees upon a ryvers side about C [one hundred] leagues from the aforesaid Cape Briton."[105]

Though explorers did not realize it at the time, Indian life was trans-formed by the fur trade. Indians who had found their principal livelihood at the coast now found themselves turning and forming relationships with tribes to the west who had access to the furs. Formerly complex economies with a high degree of self-sufficiency now became specialized and therefore dependent on outside sources for necessities. Increasingly, items of native manufacture were replaced by European trade goods, especially in the substitution of metal utensils for those made of pottery and stone. Initially the trade goods simply enhanced native life, but as the old skills were lost in the new economic specialization, the trade ultimately spelled dependency.[106]

Massive political changes due at least in part to competition in the fur trade for European goods were evident even in the reports of Samuel de Champlain early in the seventeenth century. When Cartier and Roberval explored the Saint Lawrence, the river was controlled by a confederation of Iroquois villages. By 1603, everything was different. Few Indian villages were located along the riverbanks. Most of the Indians encountered by the explorers were Algonquian rather than Iroquoian and were nomadic rather than town-dwellers. The fur trade favored movement, not a sedentary life. The Saint Lawrence Iroquois of Hochelaga and Stadacona had disappeared.[107]

Modern-day reconstructions of events in the Saint Lawrence Valley during the second half of the sixteenth century place the fur trade firmly at the center of the mystery generated by that disappearance. The fur trade gave Indians along the river unique access to the European trade goods so much desired by inland tribes. Scholars postulate that a series of attacks by members of the Five Nations Iroquois League to the south, particularly the Mohawks, in search of access to trade goods led to the dispersion of the Saint Lawrence Iroquois. Though the river Indians were dispersed, the Mohawks never gained control of Tadoussac, where allied Montagnais and Algonquins traded with French mariners, and their attacks were still going on as the seventeenth century opened.[108]

Interest in furs and other commodities and the continuing hope for a passage through the continent led to new plans for colonies. Many of these plans were based on the growing body of promotional literature centered on the area between the Saint Lawrence and Penobscot Bay ("Norumbega"). A series of books published in the 1580s in both France and England supported colonization as a means of exploiting resources and searching for the route to the Pacific. In 1580, Giovanni Florio's English translation of Cartier's narrative of his first two voyages appeared, presenting the best and most accurate information on the Saint Lawrence area and also offering the hope in that great river as a route to the Pacific. In 1582 *Les trois mondes*, by Lancelot Voisin, Sieur de La Popelinière, was published in Paris; Books Two and Three of this work contained information on English, Spanish, and French voyages along the Atlantic and repeated the legends of Chicora and the Sea of Verrazzano. Also in 1582, Richard Hakluyt the Younger's *Divers Voyages Touching the Discouerie of America* was published in London; Hakluyt covered everything from the evidence supporting belief in a passage to the Pacific to a catalogue of resources of the North American coastal area, and he provided what was, for the time, the best practical guide to colonization.[109]

While Sir Humphrey Gilbert, on the strength of such information as that contained in the works by Hakluyt and others, had been planning his fiefdom in Newfoundland, Troilus Mesgouëz, Seigneur de La Roche, won a patent for a New France in America. Like Gilbert, La Roche favored the hypothetical middle route between the Atlantic and the Pacific and focused his attention on the Saint Lawrence–Norumbega area. The patent, written in 1577 and augmented in 1578, gave La Roche the grandiose powers of viceroy over all the new lands. In 1584, when the returns of the fur trade were proven, La Roche went out with three hundred colonists for Newfoundland, but the "voyadge was overthrowen by occasion that his greatest shippe of CCC [three hundred] tonnes was caste away . . . and so the enterprize for this yere ceseth."[110]

For over a decade, conflicting claims and ventures by French and English competed unsuccessfully in the north. Jacques Noël, nephew of Jacques Cartier, possessed a "sea chart" done by his uncle; he had repeated Cartier's voyage to Mount Royal and now tried to revive Cartier's claims with his partner, Etienne Chaton de La Jannaye. Though King Henry III granted him a twelve-year monopoly for Canada and its environs in 1588, it was revoked when French merchants involved in the Canada trade raised an outcry. Meanwhile English adventurers became increasingly aware of the rich resources of the Saint Lawrence and sought a role in the reopening trade in the 1590s. A Protestant French Basque pilot, Stephen Bocall, was recruited in 1593 to guide English ships into the gulf. English investors believed that a permanent base would give them security in the competition with the many and varied voyages participating in the fishing and trading each year. A small group of separatist Protestants who had been imprisoned in England for their beliefs were attracted to the idea of a refuge in America and signed on with the project. The ships, carrying just four of the separatist leaders who were to winter over in America, embarked in 1597.

7.11 Map of New France by Samuel de Champlain (1613). Published in an early edition of his Voyages *(Paris, 1613). Champlain was one of the very few early explorers who was also a talented cartographer, and his map is a model of accuracy, given the extent of his geographical knowledge. Courtesy The Newberry Library.*

The base was to be on the Magdalen Islands at the mouth of the Gulf of Saint Lawrence. This venture was a predictable failure. One of the two ships ran aground on Cape Breton Island; by sheer luck its crew was picked up on the return voyage by the other. The vessel that got through was driven from the proposed site by a combined force of Basques, Bretons, and Indians; in any case, four men weakened by prison could not have survived the winter unaided. Planning for this colony shows how little the difficulties of settlement were understood despite much previous experience.[111]

In 1596, La Roche revived his efforts to found a New France; Henry IV, after his conversion to Roman Catholicism, was restoring peace to the nation, and such projects were once again feasible. Sable Island, where the wreck of Portuguese settlements of more than two decades earlier could be seen, was the chosen location. This island, located ninety miles east of Nova Scotia, "is the sole point rising above sea level from the sub-oceanic plateau long known to navigators as . . . the Banks."[112] A reconnaissance venture disguised as a fishing voyage embarked in 1597. The main colony sailed in 1598; it was composed of two hundred men and fifty women recruited from among more than eight hundred "strong tramps and beggars" rounded up in Rouen.[113] La Roche, having seen his colony established, returned to France with his ships at the end of the summer and prepared for the next supply. The colonists were supplied by ships under the command of Thomas Chefdhostel in 1599, 1600, and 1601, and each time the settlers had furs and oils ready for transport back to France. It is not known why no ship sailed in 1602. When Chefdhostel arrived in 1603, he found the little plantation in a state of mutiny. The governor and the storekeeper had been killed, and many of the others had fled; only eleven colonists remained. These eleven were returned to France and given royal pardons, much to La Roche's chagrin. The dispersed settlers formed another "Lost Colony" in America.[114]

A similar attempt at fur trade colonization was undertaken by the Protestant entrepreneur Pierre Chauvin de Tonnetuit in 1599. Religious peace in France and the Treaty of Vervins between France and Spain allowed Henry IV to give favors to Protestants as well as Roman Catholics. Chauvin's patent allowed him to trade and colonize along the Saint Lawrence. In 1600 he set out with the largest fleet sent to those parts since the days of Cartier. His assistant was François Gravé du Pont, described by Champlain as "very skilled in sea voyages from having made many." The announced plan was to carry "five hundred men to build forts and defend the country."[115] Chauvin determined to build his first post ninety miles upriver at Tadoussac, since he judged that to be the best place for trade. Gravé argued for traveling farther upstream. Champlain later criticized the choice among "these very forbidding localities." It was, he said, "a place the most disagreeable and barren in the whole country. There are nothing but pines, firs, birches, mountains and almost inaccessible rocks, and the soil very ill-adapted for any good tillage, and where the cold is so great that if there is an ounce of cold forty leagues up the river, there will be a pound of it here." The sixteen men left to winter over soon realized "thoroughly the difference between France and Tadoussac." They were ravaged by disease and were forced to throw themselves on the mercy of the Indians, "who charitably took them in." Champlain noted, "Some died miserably; the others in great distress awaited the return of the ships."[116] Chauvin did return in the spring and made several more voyages before his death in

1603, but Tadoussac was henceforth nothing more than a summer-only trading post. It remained, however, the most important port on the Saint Lawrence for the next three decades.

The Voyages of Samuel de Champlain

Samuel de Champlain's first voyage to Canada was in 1603, when he sailed as an observer with a fleet sent out by Chauvin's successor as monopoly holder, Aymar de Chaste, under the command of François Gravé. This expedition happened on a great Algonquin feast near Tadoussac celebrating a victory over Iroquois enemies; the Indians were welcoming and well-organized for trade.[117] Champlain explored "twelve or fifteen leagues" up the Saguenay River and, largely through interviews with Indian informants, finally understood the trade routes of Cartier's "Kingdom of Saguenay." He thought the Saguenay "a fine river." The Indians told him of crossing nine great waterfalls and then an intricate series of lakes and rivers, to the head of the river, "from which headwaters to the said harbour of Tadoussac is a journey of ten days in their canoes." Champlain recorded the far-reaching effects of the fur trade. He said that tribes came from the north with "beaver and marten skins" to trade with Montagnais Indians along the river "for other merchandise, which the French ships bring to the said Montagnais."[118] These northern Indians were reported to live "in sight of a sea which is salt." Rather than jump to the conclusion that he had discovered the elusive route to the Pacific, Champlain correctly concluded that the salt sea, later labeled as the James Bay section of Hudson's Bay, was "some gulf of this our sea, which overflows in the north into the midst of the continent; and indeed it can be nothing else." He added, "This is what I have learned of the river Saguenay."[119]

The entire expedition embarked on an exploring voyage down the Riviere de Canada, the Saint Lawrence, on 18 June. Champlain identified Trois Rivieres as an ideal site for a trading post. The explorers were stopped, as Cartier had been, by the Saint Louis rapids. The difference this time was that they now had the facility to communicate with the Indians. Through Indian informants, the party came to understand the intricacies of the river and lake system beyond the falls. They learned of the Hudson River, the Ottawa, and the Great Lakes. They also learned of the Indian trade routes beyond the falls.[120] Ambiguous information about the quality of the water in Lake Huron led Champlain to conclude that it might be salt and therefore the long-sought "South Sea" (the Pacific), "the sun setting where they say it does." Champlain began to speculate about easier ways to reach this sea. The expedition spent a few days in Gaspé, where he obtained information about Acadia from Jean Sarcel de Prévert, who had explored the region in search of a copper mine. Champlain praised the land: "All this country is very beautiful and flat, and in it are all kinds of trees." He and Prévert were convinced it held rich minerals. He believed this area would escape the harsh winters experienced by Cartier's and Chauvin's men on the Saint Lawrence. He also hoped that it might offer an easier route into the great lake system and the hoped-for South Sea. Such a passage, if it could be found, would do "as well for navigation of ships, which would not be subject to so many perils as they are in Canada, as for the shortening of the way more than three hundred leagues."[121]

In 1603 Pierre du Gua de Monts, who had sailed as an observer with Chauvin to Tadoussac in 1600, was granted a monopoly of trade and colonization between the fortieth and forty-sixth parallels by Henry IV of France. Armed with this patent, he was able to attract sizable investments and in 1604 set out to find a suitable location in the Acadia by which Champlain set such store. The three ships carried François Gravé as lieutenant, Champlain as geographer, and Jean de Biencourt de Poutrincourt, with de Monts in overall command. This expedition landed at Port au Mouton on the coast of Nova Scotia and then proceeded to search for an ideal location for settlement. The explorers rounded the southern coast of Nova Scotia and traveled up the eastern coast, where they discovered "one of the finest harbors in all these coasts where a great number of ships can ride in safety." Champlain thought this place was "most suitable and pleasant for a settlement," and he named it Port Royal.[122]

De Monts decided to press on to the top of the Bay of Fundy, which he called the Baie Française, in search of the copper mines Prévert believed were there; though Prévert's description was found to be inaccurate, Champlain was sure the explorers had seen good copper and iron sources.[123] The voyagers then traveled south along the coast of New Brunswick. In Passamaquoddy Bay they thought they had found an ideal site for a post on Saint Croix Island. This island location, well up the Saint Croix River, offered access to Indian trade with good defense capabilities against both Indian and European attackers; Champlain noted, "Vessels could only pass along the river at the mercy of the cannon on the island."[124] At the end of the summer, the ships returned to France carrying Poutrincourt and Gravé; de Monts, Marc Lescarbot, and Champlain remained at Saint Croix with

about eighty settlers. On 2 September, Champlain set out to explore southward in Norumbega, the area later named "New England" by Captain John
Smith. Champlain described Mount Desert and explored Passamaquoddy
Bay, traveling up the Penobscot River as far as the site of modern-day Ban-
gor. Here his party was welcomed by Bashabes (called "Bessabez" in the
French documents), the sagamore of the eastern Abenaki Indians, whose
territory included much of the present-day state of Maine. Bashabes, who
looked forward to French partnership in the fur trade, provided Champlain with guides. The voyage south, whose goal was the Kennebec River,
was cut short as the party ran into foul weather, and Champlain was back
in Saint Croix by early October.[125]

Winter in Saint Croix was unbearable. Scurvy set in and killed thirty-five
or thirty-six men; forty more were "stricken." The southern location had
lulled the men into a false sense of security, and they suffered in their
inadequate houses without sufficient firewood. The planters looked for
"annedda," which had cured Cartier's men, but as Marc Lescarbot, who arrived in 1606, was told, "The savages of these regions know it not." Lescarbot, a young Parisian lawyer and poet who had come to America with a
"desire to flee a corrupt Europe and to examine the new world with his
own eyes," wrote *The History of New France*, published in 1609 and partially
available in an English translation in the same year. He reported earnest
discussions about what might cause this strange condition; an autopsy
conducted on the body of a black colonist who had died of the disease
revealed that his stomach "had wrinkles resembling ulcers." Lescarbot
thought scurvy was caused by eating "meats which are cold, dry, coarse
and rotten" and by drinking corrupt water. He thought cutting down trees
and opening the land to the cleansing wind and sun would prevent it altogether.[126]

Now the colonists began to understand the problems created by focusing too much on defense in siting a colony. The island lacked wood and water. When either was required through the merciless winter, "they were
constrained to cross the river, which on either side is more than three times
as broad as the Seine at Paris."[127] The water that protected them also isolated the little company. Their sense of isolation increased with winter conditions: "The cold was severe and more extreme than in France, and lasted
much longer." Champlain recorded that the snow lay "to a depth of three
or four feet up to the end of the month of April." He also warned against
judging these northern sites on the basis of summer-only experience: "It is

difficult to know this country without having wintered there; for on arriving in summer everything is very pleasant on account of the woods, the beautiful landscapes, and the fine fishing for the many kinds of fish we found there. There are six months of winter in that country."[128]

In the spring, reinforced by Gravé and fresh supplies, de Monts decided to rectify the colonists' situation by once again looking for a good location farther south. The party, including Champlain, made its way along the coast, missing the entrances to the Piscataqua and Merrimack Rivers. On Cape Ann, Champlain drew a map of the cape, after which the Indians with whom he parleyed sketched for him "with the same charcoal another bay which they represented as very large (Cape Cod)." They also placed six pebbles to illustrate the territories of the "chiefs and tribes."[129] The expedition continued on to Cape Cod, which de Monts named Cap Blanc, where they were pleased to see corn cultivated in fields.[130] They traveled in Boston Harbor and Plymouth Harbor, the latter named Saint Louis by the explorers. After rounding the tip of Cape Cod, they arrived at Nauset Harbor, called "Mallebarre" by de Monts.

Nauset Harbor was deemed too treacherous, "a very dangerous port on account of the shoals and sandbars, where [the men] saw breakers on every side." The explorers liked the land and thought "the place would be very fine if only the harbour were good." Then a band of Indians attempted to take a kettle from sailors who were filling them with fresh water in the sandhills. In the ensuing fight, one of the sailors was killed. The party was later approached by other Indians "making excuses by signs and outward show that it was not they who had done this evil deed but others farther off in the interior." After these events, and facing unfavorable weather and the end of their supplies, the party decided to turn back and look elsewhere for a settlement site. "We had been unable to find such a place on any of the coasts we had explored on this voyage."[131]

De Monts now decided to move his colonists and their dismantled houses across the Bay of Fundy to Port Royal, where colonists enjoyed the protection of the neighboring Micmac Indians (the "Souriquois" in the French documents) and their chief, Membertou. Lescarbot reported that Membertou was "already a man of great age, and saw Captain Jacques Cartier in that country" six decades before. His position was enhanced by his friendship with the French and by access to their goods, and he understood well the opportunities and dangers of such an alliance. Lescarbot noted, "Being himself a Sagamos, he considers himself the equal of the

King . . . and often said to M. de Poutrincourt that he was his great friend, brother, companion, and equal, showing his equality by joining together the fingers of each hand which we call the index or pointing finger."[132]

The winter at Port Royal was less difficult than that at Saint Croix, though ten or twelve settlers succumbed to scurvy, including both the priest and the Protestant minister, who were buried in a common grave. Gravé's efforts to begin yet another southern voyage were cut short by accident and his own ill health. Only on 24 July, as all of the settlers except for a small holding party were abandoning the colony, did reinforcements and supplies arrive with Poutrincourt, the new governor of Acadia.

Another expedition set out on 5 September, repeating the exploration of the coast, which Champlain felt "was not a wise decision." He noted, "We lost much time in going over again the discoveries that the Sieur de Monts had made as far as Port Mallebarre." They arrived at Nauset Harbor only on 2 October.[133] The explorers rounded Cape Cod but met with disaster in Stage Harbor. A party of mariners, refusing to return to the ship after the French had bought grain from the Nauset Indians, were attacked and four were killed, with another wounded. The expedition was forced to leave the harbor, which they named Fortune, and attempted to cross Nantucket Sound but turned back because of unfavorable weather. After further misfortunes, they returned to Port Royal on 14 November. No more ventures attempted the southern coast, and no good prospect had been found. In the spring, after a much less severe winter, word came that de Monts had lost his patent, and the settlement was withdrawn. Though the contribution to an understanding of the geography of North America was substantial, the 1604–7 voyages left a negative impression in the minds of French investors.[134]

Champlain's contribution to geographical understanding was extensive. "His maps . . . marked the beginning of the modern mapping of Canada."[135] Champlain made remarkable charts of the harbors that he and his parties explored on the Saint Lawrence as well as in Acadia and Norumbega. He produced several maps, which are quite accurate for the areas he had personally surveyed. He was known to be exceptionally skilled with the astrolabe, and his latitude readings are excellent. The sketches, maps, and charts, combined with the journals, constitute an unparalleled record and dramatically enhanced the understanding of the coast and the interior drainage systems of the region.[136] Perhaps most important, Champlain reported faithfully on what he had observed, and he eliminated speculation on what he had not. The mythical Sea of Verrazzano, which had been a fixture on French, English, Spanish, and Italian maps since the 1520s, was absent from Champlain's cartography, as was the theoretical "Mer d'la Ouest" (Sea of the West), which dominated so much of French cartography later in the seventeenth century.

Renewed English Efforts

Meanwhile English expeditions also explored Norumbega (sometimes called the "North Part of Virginia" in English documents) in a series of voyages whose aim was the establishment of a trade in furs to be sustained by settlements and was only peripherally the reconnaissance of the land area or an attempt to locate a passage to the Pacific.[137] In March 1602 a small expedition under the command of Bartholomew Gosnold sailed to "North Virginia," apparently hoping to set up a fur-trading post on the site of Verrazzano's 1524 "Refugio" in Narragansett Bay.[138] The party, whose first landfall was in southern Maine, explored Cape Cod Bay and Nantucket Sound, naming Martha's Vineyard and establishing a fort on Elizabeth's Isle (the Cuttyhunk Island of today). When the twenty men who were to remain over the winter realized they were to be left with only a six-week supply of food, they refused to stay, and the entire company returned home in July.[139]

Gosnold's voyage, as related in John Brereton's account, which went through two editions in 1602, reawakened English interest in American trade. Brereton vividly told of their first encounter with American natives—a party of Micmac Indians who were several hundred miles south of their home territory, were partly dressed in European clothes, and were sailing a Basque ship. Gabriel Archer recorded that the Indians drew a map of the coast with a piece of chalk and "seemed to understand much more than we, for want of Language, could comprehend." This exchange demonstrated both the sophistication of the Indians and the highly organized nature of the European-American trade. Brereton's tract stressed the variety and plenty of flora, fauna, and resources of the region and, after reporting trials of English seeds, judged that in comparison, "the most fertil part of al England is (of it selfe) but barren." All in all, it was a fit place for English endeavors.[140]

In 1603, at the same time that Champlain was exploring the Saint Lawrence, a second English voyage set forth to follow up the achievements of Gosnold's company. Martin Pring's 1603 expedition was sent out by a Bristol company for the purpose of trade; no plans to leave men in America over the winter accompanied it. Though the intended location for a summer trading station was Cape Cod Bay, the venture made landfall on the coast of Maine at about 43°30′. The explorers then worked their way down the coast to Cape Cod, where they built a fort near the site of modern-day Provincetown. The fur trade was disappointing, but the men loaded their two ships with sassafras, considered a cure for syphilis, taking an amount "sufficient to glut the market for several years." The narrative of this voyage, not published until 1625, stressed, as Brereton had done, the plenty and fruitfulness of North Virginia and especially the great return from fishing.[141]

In 1605 George Waymouth was selected to lead another expedition to North Virginia; Waymouth was the author of a tract on navigation and exploration, "The Jewel of Artes," which he had presented to King James I in 1604. His venture was partly supported by a combine of Roman Catholics who sought to create a refuge in America; further support came from merchants who wanted bases from which to exploit the rich fishing. Though the voyage had aimed at resuming the search for Verrazzano's "Refugio" south of Cape Cod, the mariners turned north from the cape and made landfall at Monhegan Island. From there, they performed limited explorations of the mainland and the Saint George's River, concluding that it was an excellent area for settlement. The company returned after a month in America, once again praising the rich fishing of the New England coast. Though a glowing (and misleading) account of the "most prosperous" voyage was written by James Rosier and was published immediately, its promise was not followed up. The idea of a Roman Catholic refuge was shelved later in the year after the exposure of the Gunpowder Plot conspiracy to blow up the Houses of Parliament and the king, resulting in hostility toward Catholics.[142]

Various groups had made plans to exploit the possibilities pointed out by the Gosnold, Pring, and Waymouth voyages. These became melded with the larger plans for two great Virginia Companies in 1606, which were to found a northern and a southern Virginia colony. The New England colony was sponsored by a company whose headquarters was Plymouth; it included Bristol and Exeter backing as well. This Western Merchants' Company sent out a voyage under Richard Challons in late summer 1606, but the ship was captured by Spaniards before it reached New England. In the fall and winter of 1606 an expedition under the command of Thomas Hanham and Martin Pring explored "Mawooshen," as they called the area of modern-day Maine. Hanham and Pring determined that the Sagadahoc

River (the Kennebec) was an admirable place to found a colony.[143] Accordingly, the Plymouth company's Sagadahoc colony set out at the end of May 1607 with about a hundred settlers and planted Fort Saint George on a small peninsula a short way upriver. The winter was an ordeal; 1607–8 was one of the most notable cold winters of the Little Ice Age: the Thames River froze solid in London. Samuel Purchas, successor to Richard Hakluyt as collector and publisher of chronicles of exploration, bemoaned "that unseasonable Winter (fit to freeze the heart of a plantation)," and backer Sir Ferdinando Gorges later recalled how "all our hopes were frozen to death."[144] Scurvy took its toll, as in the French colonies, and the plantation's governor, Captain George Popham, was among the dead.

Nor did there seem to be any reason to support the colony. Few furs or other products of value were acquired. When relief ships brought the news that one of the scheme's chief backers, Lord Justice Sir John Popham, had died in England, the colonists decided to return home. New England was considered a poor risk for a colony.[145] In fact, as John Smith wrote as part of his later campaign to rehabilitate the region in English eyes, "This plantation was begunne and ended in one yeere, and the Country esteemed as a cold, barren, mountainous, rocky desart."[146] North Virginia was written off by promoters for more than a decade.

The other Virginia colony, Jamestown, founded by the London Virginia Company, faced the rockiest first year of almost all the European settlements in North America, and yet it survived to become the first permanent English settlement in the New World. Jamestown's planners had the benefit of thorough surveys of the southern coast done by mariners from many nations. Thanks to the efforts of the Roanoke colonists, they knew where the plantation should be set. The problems of shallow and dangerous waters that had plagued Roanoke would be overcome as the ships venturing in the deep waters of Chesapeake Bay and the James River could tie up to the shore by a tree branch. The preceding decade of privateering had provided English mariners with an education in seamanship; the voyagers were freed of reliance on foreigners.

Permanent European Presence

Much remained to be learned. Jamestown's immediate site, chosen for its defensibility, proved extremely unhealthy; the initial contingent of over one hundred men was reduced to thirty-eight by the first winter, terrible even as far south as Virginia. Despite this inauspicious start, Jamestown had what all previous English enterprise had lacked: massive backing from home. James I had brought the privateering war to a halt after his accession to the throne at the death of Queen Elizabeth, and all the anti-Spanish energies generated by that conflict went into blocking further Spanish colonization of North America by a permanent English establishment in Chesapeake Bay. This venture could not be allowed to fail. Although Virginia continued to be unhealthy for new planters, posing a major problem for promoters and settlers alike, the colony succeeded where others had not. Largely responsible for the success was the resolution of the great question facing the colony: how to provide commodities that would repay investors in England and keep the flow of supplies and settlers coming. Though many plans were laid, it would be a decade before the unexpected answer, tobacco, would emerge and the future of Virginia would be secure.[147]

At the same time, events went forward to the north. Champlain returned to France after his three-year stay "in the country of New France" and urged de Monts to try for a new royal patent. Failure in Acadia should not doom further attempts. Champlain was convinced that Acadia had been a poor choice for settlement, and he argued strongly for a permanent habitation on "the great St. Lawrence river," which he "knew well." Champlain argued that Acadia would require a massive force for defense "because of the infinite number of its harbours" and that the fur trade would be superior on the Saint Lawrence because of the highly organized Indian trade. The king was apparently convinced by Champlain's report laying out the alluring possibility of finding, beyond the Saint Lawrence, the "passage to China without the inconvenience of the northern icebergs, or the heat of the torrid zone." De Monts, armed with a one-year trade monopoly, gave Champlain his first command. Champlain sailed with a new expedition in April 1608.[148]

After a clash with Basque traders who had taken over the fur trade at Tadoussac, and another voyage up the Saguenay River, Champlain determined to found his colony at the site of Quebec. "I could not find any more suitable or better situated [place] than the point of Quebec," in "the fine, good country of the great river," where the "land is level and pleasant to see." After putting down a mutiny among some of his men who were unhappy at the prospect of spending a winter on the river where so many Frenchmen had died, Champlain put his men to work building a habitation that demonstrated how much he had learned from previous experience. The buildings were snug, built in a square with a gallery running around the outside, "which was a very convenient thing." He emphasized the need for a strong storehouse with a vast cellar and provided both for defense and for adjoining gardens, each necessary to the settlers' health. The colonists found nearby the ruins of Jacques Cartier's fort, a reminder of the stakes involved. Partly through Champlain's leadership and experience and partly through luck, this was to become the first permanent French settlement in North America, to succeed where so many others had failed.[149]

By 1608 permanent colonies, French and English, joined the Spanish Florida settlements in establishing continuous European presence along the east coast of North America. Why were Europeans finally able to establish successful plantations where so many had failed before them? The answer must lie in the steady accumulation of knowledge of the preceding century. Not only was much of the basic climate, drainage, and productivity of the continent understood, but fishing and its spin-off, fur trading, and privateering had taught mariners the skills to handle problems of navigation, exploration, and supply. This knowledge came to explorers partly through their own experience and judgment, particularly where surveys of the coast were undertaken; growing sophistication in the use of instruments was crucial. But the documents clearly indicate that knowledge of the interior and of river and lake systems came almost entirely through the Indian tutelage of explorers. Further, the Indians controlled the flow of such knowledge. Cartier and later explorers were prevented from going farther up the Saint Lawrence than the Saint Lawrence Iroquoians, who sought to protect their position in the fur trade, were willing to allow.[150] Not only did the Indians contribute sophisticated knowledge of the regions in which they lived and the territories beyond, but they also clearly understood the possibilities presented by Europeans and the desire for trade and they attempted to control these possibilities in their own favor.

Knowledge was important, but so was ignorance. Perusal of the documents shows that no amount of adverse experience could entirely kill the dreams of wealth: rich mines of gold and silver, tropical plants, mild climates, and a route to the South Sea. Ignorance was crucial because, had promoters fully understood the hardships and the waste of lives and money that lay ahead, along with the humble nature of the commodities that North America would eventually produce, they would probably have put their money into enterprises more apt to produce guaranteed returns. As it was, despite the fact that many adventurers lost their entire investments, the hopes lived on to fuel additional ventures.

8 / The Early Exploration of the Pacific Coast

W. MICHAEL MATHES

By the beginning of the sixteenth century, the increasingly evident failure of Christopher Columbus to discover a western maritime route to Asia gave rise to intensified activity within the Caribbean basin by Spanish navigators and explorers searching for local sources of wealth, as well as for a way to the Indies. With the immensity of the latitude of the American landmass and of the longitude of the Pacific Ocean, explorations continued for three-fourths of a century following the first Columbian voyage before its initiator's dream was realized and trade was established with Asia. The discovery and occupation of the Philippine Islands and the establishment of a return route from the western Pacific to New Spain were the beginning, and searches for a safe midway port on the California coast for the ships plying this route, as well as for a direct course to Spain via the much-desired Straits of Anián, would occupy yet another century.

This process began in 1508 when Diego de Nicuesa received a concession for the colonization of the isthmus of Panamá, a region reputedly rich in gold. Nevertheless, climate, the lack of provisions, and yellow fever caused such discontent among Nicuesa's colonists that they rose in revolt, led by Vasco Núñez de Balboa, who assured his followers that he would conduct an active search for wealth. To comply with his promise, Núñez de Balboa initiated exploration toward the interior, and on encountering a group of Indians with ornaments containing pearls, he was informed that these gems were to be found along the coast of the great sea that was a short distance to the south. Following these indications, in September 1513 Núñez de Balboa became the first European to view the Pacific Ocean from its eastern shore. Named the "South Sea" by Núñez de Balboa due to its location relative to the isthmus, this body of water, because of its heavy tides and surf, was recognized as a great ocean by the Spaniards, who were experienced in maritime matters; what was not realized at the time was that they had discovered the area of the shortest distance between the Atlantic and the Pacific.[1] Within two decades, due to internal political considerations, problems of supply and personnel, and the failure to discover attractive sources of wealth, Spain had acquired direct knowledge only of the islands of the Caribbean, the northern coast of South America, part of Central America, and Florida and indirect knowledge of Brazil, the Indian Ocean, and the Molucca Islands as a result of Portuguese discoveries made since the opening of the century. This knowledge was, nevertheless, sufficient to make it evident that Columbian calculations of the distance between Spain and Asia on a westerly course were grossly deficient and that great expanses of land and sea remained to be crossed.

The Opening of the Pacific Coast of North America and Transpacific Navigation

News of the discovery of the South Sea gave greater impetus to the search for a maritime passage to it from the Atlantic, as well as to terrestrial expansion to secure possession by Castile of appropriate ports from which to initiate the voyage westward. As a small part of this expansion, in February 1517, searching for Indian slaves, Francisco Fernández de Córdoba sailed westward from Cuba and reached the peninsula of Yucatán. Recognizing the presence of a civilization far more advanced than any known to date in the New World, Fernández de Córdoba landed, and he and his men attempted the pillage of the settlement. Repulsed by the people known as the Mayas, and with their captain mortally wounded, the Spaniards returned to Cuba, where they recounted their discoveries. In April of the following year, the governor of Cuba, Diego Velázquez de Cuéllar, sent his nephew, Juan de Grijalva, to explore Yucatán; the latter also failed to establish peaceful relations with the inhabitants, and Velázquez was forced to plan a third expedition, for though the eastern and part of the northern coasts of the Yucatán peninsula were known, these areas evidently formed only a part of a larger landmass.[2]

To lead this new enterprise, Velázquez named Hernán Cortés, his secretary and companion at arms in the conquest of Cuba. Tiring of the delays in mounting the expedition, in November 1518 Cortés took over Velázquez's ships and, with six hundred followers, sailed for Yucatán, where he landed in February of the following year. Aided by the linguistic and geographic knowledge of Gerónimo de Aguilar, a prisoner of the Mayas for several years, who knew of population centers, routes between them, and the nature of their inhabitants and their wealth, Cortés continued exploration of the coast of Yucatán, entering the Gulf of Campeche and coasting the area of Tabasco. There he received, as a gift of the Mayas, a slave girl of Mexica origin, Malintzin, known to the Spaniards as Marina, who told him, through Aguilar, of the existence of a yet greater civilization to the interior.

Following this information, Cortés disembarked in May 1519 at the site that he named Villa Rica de la Vera Cruz, taking possession of the region in the name of the king of Spain, Charles I (Emperor Charles V). To avoid possible desertions, Cortés ordered the destruction of his ships, thus committing himself to the enterprise, and began his march to the interior in August, in search of the great city of Tenochtitlan, the modern-day Mexico City, and its ruler, Moctezuma. In the highlands to the west of Veracruz, Cortés defeated the Tlaxcaltecans, who, as enemies of Moctezuma, allied themselves with the Spaniards, thus increasing not only the number of their troops but also their confidence in the superiority of their cannons, harquebuses, and horses in combat with the Indians.

Moctezuma, apprised that his attempts to halt the advance of the strangers through the sending of gifts were futile, launched an attack by his army against that of Cortés at Cholula, but again Spanish arms triumphed, and the route to Tenochtitlan remained open. After crossing the mountains surrounding the city, Cortés was received by Moctezuma in November 1519 and was conducted, with his officers, to the ruler's palace as Moctezuma's guests. Finding himself surrounded by forces superior to his own, Cortés took Moctezuma hostage as a means of ensuring the Spaniards' safety, as well as obtaining the payment of an immense ransom in gold. Nevertheless, this security was short-lived, for in May 1520 Cortés received word of the arrival at Veracruz of an expedition sent by Velázquez to take him and his followers prisoner and return them to Cuba in chains. Leaving the command to his lieutenant, Pedro de Alvarado, Cortés marched to the coast, where he forced the retreat of Pánfilo de Narváez and the remaining loyal soldiers and incorporated a large part of Velázquez's troops into his own force. On returning to Tenochtitlan, Cortés found the situation greatly changed, for during his absence Alvarado and his soldiers had fired on the Mexicas, and they had rebelled against the intruders. As this resistance grew, on 30 June the Spaniards were forced to flee the city and seek refuge in Tlaxcala. Due to the strategic location of Tenochtitlan, built on an island in the center of a lake and accessible only by causeways from the shore, a direct invasion of the city would be virtually impossible. Nevertheless, Cortés, determined to conquer it, began the construction of brigantines to enable him to beseige the city from the water. By May 1521 preparations for the assault were complete, and four boats, with cannon mounted in the prow, were launched in the waters of the Lake of Mexico. Cortés's strategy succeeded, and after a lengthy siege, the cutting of the aqueduct that supplied the city with drinking water, and the spread of epidemics among the people, the Spaniards victoriously entered Tenochtitlan on 13 August 1521.[3]

The fall of Tenochtitlan merely initiated Spanish expansion throughout the region to become known as New Spain. Stories of the existence of gold mines to the west, sources of the wealth of Moctezuma, and rumors that, as stated by Cortés in the third *Carta de relación* to Emperor Charles V of 15 May 1522, "exploring these regions of the South Sea, there will be found many islands rich in gold and pearls and precious stones and spices,"[4] led to expeditions to the regions of Michoacán, Jalisco, Colima, Guerrero, and Oaxaca by Cristóbal de Olid, Gonzalo de Sandoval, Pedro de Alvarado, Rodrigo Alvarez Chico, and Francisco Cortés. This exploration, though disappointing from the standpoint of discovering great wealth and finding a water passage through the region from the Atlantic to the Pacific, did establish knowledge of numerous protected anchorages between Cabo Corrientes, near modern-day Puerto Vallarta, and Tehuantepec, south of present-day Acapulco, as well as the presence of adequate timber and naval stores in the adjacent mountains to permit the opening of shipyards on the Pacific coast.[5] These discoveries were of particular importance in light of the many disasters that occurred during the first circumnavigation of Ferdinand Magellan and Juan Sebastián de Elcano in the very years of Cortés's conquest of Tenochtitlan. Sailing from Spain in 1519, Magellan's expedition had discovered and traversed the straits that now bear the commander's name and had proceeded across the Pacific to the Philippine Islands. There, Magellan was killed, and Elcano, succeeding to the command, was able to navigate the surviving ship, *Victoria*, through the Indian Ocean, around the Cape of Good Hope, and back to Spain in 1522.[6]

Cortésian Expeditions and the Origins of California

Although the problem of maritime contact with Asia would appear to have been resolved with this epic voyage, the passage through the Strait of Magellan was so extraordinarily dangerous under the best of circumstances, and the long transit from north to south across the Atlantic and then the diagonal track across the Pacific was of such high risk and expense, that it was evident that it would be much more practical to initiate transpacific navigation from the western coast of New Spain. Already, in 1523, Cortés had established his first shipyard in Guatulco, on the Oaxaca coast, transporting cable, nails, tools, and other materials from Veracruz across the Isthmus of Tehuantepec via the Río Coatzacoalcos, with the intent of constructing vessels for exploration to the Molucca or Spice Islands.[7] In his fourth *Carta de relación* to Charles V on 15 October 1524, Cortés reported his progress and plans: "I was brought a report from the lords of the province of Ciguatán which greatly affirms that there is an island entirely populated by women, without any men at all . . . and that this island is ten days travel from this province [Colima]. . . . They also tell me that it is very rich in pearls and gold; as soon as I have the equipment, I will work to find out the truth and will make a lengthy report to Your Majesty relative to it."[8]

Concurrent with the European discovery of the New World was the expansion of the greatest technological advancement of mankind, printing with movable metallic type, which permitted the production of books in editions of several hundreds of copies at relatively low cost. As literacy grew through the availability of books, so also did the demand for popular literature, and by the end of the fifteenth century, several of the great medieval romances of chivalry, such as *Amadís de Gaula*, had appeared in print. These works were particularly popular among the men who formed part of the first Spanish settlers in the Western Hemisphere, for the stories not only entertained them during the long voyage across the Atlantic but also suggested the possibility that these men could lead lives equally adventurous as those of their heroes. This popularity resulted in the publication of sequels and continuations of the traditional romances, and such a new rendition came from the press of Jacob Cromberger in Seville on 12 July 1510 under the title *Las sergas de muy esforzado caballero Esplandián*, produced by the councilman of Medina del Campo, Garcí Ordóñez de Montalvo. Widely read by the mariners and soldiers who conquered New Spain, the work went through four editions by 1540. Esplandián, the son of Amadís, enjoyed many heroic adventures, the most transcendental of which occurred in Chapter CLVII: "Be it known that to the right hand of the Indies there was an island, called California, very near to the region of Earthly Paradise, which was populated by black women, without a single man to be found among them, so that their style of life was almost that of Amazons. . . . The island itself was the most covered with cliffs and rugged crags to be found in the world; their armament was all of gold, and also were the adornments of the wild beasts, . . . on all of the island there was no other metal at all." Closing with the fervent hope for the conversion of the queen, Calafia, and all of her subjects to Christianity, this adventure also echoed the policy of the Spanish monarchy and its colonizers.[9] If this great island was the same as the one described to Cortés, it certainly required verification.

Cortés's opportunity came with the loss in the Moluccas in 1524–25 of the expedition of García Jofré de Loaysa, who had been sent to follow the course of Magellan-Elcano.[10] Royal authorization was granted not only to search for Loaysa but also to outfit and conduct voyages to the Moluccas and other areas of the East Indies. In accordance with these orders, in July 1527 Cortés dispatched his relative, Alvaro Saavedra Cerón, from Tehuantepec to the Moluccas.[11] The expedition was lost in the East Indies, but in the interim, in 1528, Cortés received, together with the captaincy-general of New Spain and the title of Marquis of the Valley of Oaxaca, a monopoly for exploration of the South Sea with rights of occupation, governing, and exploitation of its undiscovered lands, and he commenced the construction of new ships with which to exercise his privilege.[12]

In June 1532, the well-outfitted *San Marcos* and *San Miguel*, under the command of Diego Hurtado de Mendoza, sailed from Tehuantepec in a northwesterly course, bound for the Moluccas. Because of summer storms, the ships were separated, and the *San Marcos*, with Hurtado de Mendoza aboard, disappeared, while the *San Miguel*, having sighted the Islas Tres Marías, was able to reach the coast of Nayarit in Nueva Galicia, where it was confiscated by Cortés's rival, the conqueror and governor Nuño Beltrán de Guzmán.[13] Incensed by this action, Cortés ordered the construction of new vessels and the outfitting of a new expedition to establish his rights to the Pacific coast and recover the *San Miguel*.

The third Cortés expedition was composed of the *San Lázaro* under the command of Hernando de Grijalva and the *Concepción* under Diego de Becerra. In October 1533, the ships sailed from Tehuantepec and, the first night at sea, were separated in a storm, the former forced to the west, discovering the island named Santo Tome in the Revillagigedo group, and the latter continuing its course to the north. Led by the pilot Fortún Jiménez, a part of the crew of the *Concepción* mutinied, killed Becerra, and, anchoring on the coast of Michoacan (later named Los Motines for this event), put ashore the loyal crew along with the Franciscan missionaries who were aboard. Jiménez continued sailing northward and, after several days, reached land in the area south of the present-day bay of La Paz, thus by

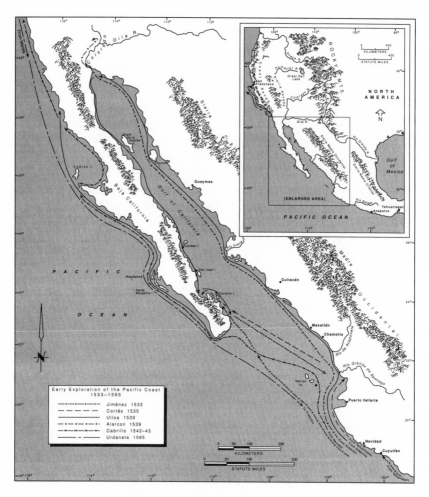

Map 8.1 Early Exploration of the Pacific Coast, 1533–1565.

pure accident becoming the discoverer of the Californias. Going ashore, Jiménez and his followers attempted to take some pearls from the Pericú Indians who had come out to meet them, and in so doing, they were killed. Only the few who remained on board the ship survived and were able to reach the Nayarit coast, where, after their arrest and the confiscation of the ship by Guzmán, they told of the new land they had sighted and the presence there of pearls.[14]

During the absence of the Grijalva-Becerra expedition, Cortés had begun recruiting a force to march against Guzmán, and hearing of this additional insult, as well as the discovery of new land over which he had legitimate domain, he determined personally to lead the new contingency. At the head of a land party supported by three ships—the *San Lázaro*, the *Santo Tomás*, and the *Santa Agueda*—Cortés reached an agreement with Guzmán in Compostela and in April 1535 sailed from the Sinaloa coast to explore the land now known as Baja California, accidentally discovered by Jiménez. Crossing the gulf, the expedition passed two islands and entered a great bay, where, on 3 May, Cortés took formal possession of it and all of the adjacent lands and seas in the name of Emperor Charles V, naming the area Santa Cruz in accordance with the liturgical calendar. On the inner shore of the bay a small colony was established; nevertheless, isolation, the arid, hot climate and surrounding countryside, the lack of effort on the part of colonists, and, particularly, the uncertainty of supply mitigated against its success. Although some exploration of the surrounding coast southward to the cape and up the Pacific coast some 150 miles was achieved, doubt remained as to whether Santa Cruz was an island or a peninsula, and these problems, together with reports of legal and administrative difficulties in Mexico City and the establishment of a viceroyalty under Antonio de Mendoza, news brought by Francisco de Ulloa in 1537, led to Cortés's abandonment of Santa Cruz, leaving Ulloa in command to return remaining colonists to New Spain a few months later.[15]

Although continuing his shipbuilding enterprise, Cortés was removed from the main thrust of exploration by Mendoza. As reports were received of great, rich cities to the north—first in 1536 from Alvar Núñez Cabeza de Vaca and the other survivors of the Pánfilo de Narváez expedition to Florida, lost in 1527, and second from Fray Marcos de Niza who, in 1538, had penetrated present-day Arizona under orders from the viceroy—Mendoza took full control of the licensing of new expeditions. Relying on his titles relative to the South Sea, however, Cortés prepared a maritime reconnaissance under Ulloa, who sailed from Acapulco with the *Santa Agueda*, the *Trinidad*, and the *Santo Tomás* on 8 July 1539. The last vessel was lost off the coast of Sinaloa, but the other two continued northward along the eastern coast of the Gulf of California and reached a point that was named Ancón de San Andrés, near the mouth of the Colorado River, on 28 September. After taking formal possession, Ulloa returned southward along the Baja California coast to Santa Cruz, where he anchored on 18 October, and then proceeded to round Cabo San Lucas and proceed northward to Isla de Cedros, about midpeninsula, which was reached on 20 January 1540. The

Santa Agueda was then sent back to New Spain, and Ulloa continued northward with the *Trinidad*, returning later to the coast of Nayarit, where he
was killed.[16] This final Cortésian expedition clearly established the peninsularity of Santa Cruz—which in common usage was becoming known as
California, the island described in the *Sergas de Esplandián*—and marked
the end of privately organized and sponsored exploration in New Spain.

Mendocine Expeditions

Mendoza, far more interested in pursuing the reports of Niza, had organized a massive land expedition to the north under the governor of Nueva
Galicia, Francisco Vázquez de Coronado. As a means of reprovisioning the
overland contingency, a maritime element comprising the *San Pedro* and
the *Santa Catalina*, under the command of Hernando de Alarcón, sailed
northward from Acapulco on 9 May 1540 bound for the region of the Ancón
de San Andrés. Reaching the mouth of the Colorado River, which he
named Río de la Buena Guía, Alarcón anchored his ships and proceeded
upstream to its confluence with the Gila. Far distant from the Coronado
party, Alarcón did not make the desired contact; marking a large tree
where he buried a pottery jug with a message, he returned southward,
reaching Acapulco in November. Several months later, Melchior Díaz,
with a detachment from the land expedition, found the Alarcón message,
thus confirming by land the peninsularity of California as established by
Ulloa and Alarcón by sea and so depicted by European cartographers.[17]

The depopulation of Nueva Galicia (the modern-day states of Jalisco,
Nayarit, Zacatecas, and Aguascalientes), resulting from the large number
of Spaniards and Indian allies enlisted in the Coronado expedition, gave
occasion to an uprising of the Cazcanes in the highlands of the Mixtón. To
restore order, Mendoza marched from Mexico City at the head of a number
of troops and, reaching Nueva Galicia, was reinforced by others brought
by sea from Guatemala by Pedro de Alvarado. The death of Alvarado in
combat at Nochistlán in 1541 left the ships and crews at Navidad under the
control of the viceroy, and the pacification of the Cazcanes in the same year
freed them for his service. Desirous of finally achieving the maritime contact with Asia sought during the preceding fifty years, Mendoza dispatched Ruy López de Villalobos to the East Indies, where, after taking
possession and naming the Philippines in honor of Philip, Prince of As-
turias, and noting the active trade between the islands and China, he died

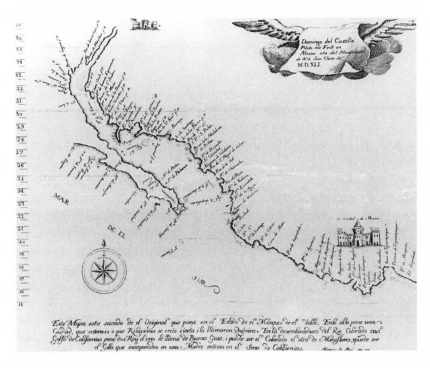

8.1 *Western coast of Mexico by Domingo del Castillo. Published in Francisco Antonio Lorenzana,* Historia de Nueva Espagna *(Mexico City, 1770). The cartographer was a pilot with Alarcón, who explored to the head of the Gulf of California in 1540–42 and entered the mouth of the Colorado River. The original of this published map has never been found, and the printed version shown here may contain information added as late as the eighteenth century. Courtesy The Newberry Library.*

from fever on the island of Java. The survivors, unable to proceed with exploration, were subsequently rescued by the Portuguese and taken to Lisbon.[18] A second expedition, to proceed northward beyond Isla de Cedros in search of great settlements and a rumored northern water passage between the Pacific and the Atlantic, was placed under the command of Alvarado's lieutenant, Juan Rodríguez Cabrillo.

Sailing from Navidad on 27 June 1542 with the *San Salvador* and *Victoria*, Rodríguez Cabrillo reached Cabo San Lucas on 3 July and proceeded northward along the Pacific Coast to San Pedro (Bahía Magdalena) on 12 July. By 25 July, Santiago (Laguna San Ignacio) was sighted and Punta Abreojos was passed, and on 5 August anchorage was made at Isla de Cedros. Formal possession was taken on 22 August at Puerto de la Posesión (Bahía San Quintín) and at San Mateo (Ensenada de Todos Santos) on 17 September, and the expedition continued to San Miguel (San Diego) on 28 September. After a five-day respite, Rodríguez Cabrillo proceeded north to the Santa Barbara Channel Islands, passed numerous Canalino, Ventureño, and Chumash villages, again took possession, and reached Cabo de Galera (Point Conception) on 18 October, when contrary winds forced an erratic course, delayed advancement, and caused the expedition to anchor at Isla Posesión (San Miguel).

While there, Rodríguez Cabrillo fell and fractured his shoulder; despite the severe pain, he continued northward on 25 October, unable to clear Point Conception until 11 November. Five days later, Bahía de los Pinos (Monterey) was reached, and because of severe weather, cold, and the infection of his injury, Rodríguez Cabrillo turned southward, anchoring again at San Miguel on 23 November. Awaiting better weather, on 3 January 1543 Rodríguez Cabrillo died from gangrene, and his pilot, Bartolomé Ferrelo, assumed command. At the dying request of his captain, Ferrelo sailed on 19 January, attempting to reach a more northerly latitude; he arrived off Monterey on 25 February, but faced with winter weather and a sick, disheartened crew, on 3 March he could go no farther than the earlier attempt and returned southward. On 24 March Ferrelo halted at Cedros and on 2 April continued to Navidad, anchoring there in mid-April.[19]

By the end of 1542 the first great phase of exploration northward from New Spain had terminated, with generally negative results. No detailed diaries, logs, rutters, or navigational charts of the region had been prepared, and those that survived the tragic Rodríguez Cabrillo expedition were unclear. None of the areas visited had shown evidence of civilization approaching that of the Mexicas, nor had any similar sources of precious metals been located. Rather, increasingly hostile inhabitants, climate, and terrain appeared to be the rule as expeditions went farther northward. The isolation of California, the contrary winds and currents along its Pacific coast, and the evident poverty of its natives made it a particularly difficult area to explore and settle, and thus, within a decade of its discovery, it was relegated to a position of geographical, political, and economic unimportance in the scheme of Spanish imperial design. More specifically, European wars, the succession of Philip II, and the development of mines in Aguascalientes and Zacatecas diverted royal interest from the Pacific; nevertheless, the promise of trade with Asia, elusive even after a half-century, remained a high priority as a known source of wealth.

The Opening of Asian Commerce and Foreign Threats to Spanish Hegemony

Following the establishment of Philip II on the throne, in 1559 the monarch revived interest in colonization of the Philippines, the islands that bore his name. Command was given to Miguel López de Legaspi, who was to employ all the men, equipment, and provisions necessary to make his enterprise definitive. Appointed as chief pilot and navigator was the former pilot of the Loaysa expedition, Andrés de Urdaneta, who had become an Augustinian friar. Called out of his religious life as the most experienced and knowledgeable veteran of transpacific navigation, Urdaneta was to prepare a detailed memorandum of the material needs of the expedition and the methods to be followed to ensure its success. In 1561, the navigator presented his document, which, in addition to listing supplies, equipment, and personnel and describing the route to be followed, also expressed geopolitical concepts that would establish future patterns of maritime exploration in the eastern Pacific basin.

As early as the sixth century B.C., Anaximander, the Greek founder of scientific geography, had proposed the symmetry of the terrestrial globe, dividing it into four hemispheres surrounded by water. This concept was perpetuated by the Roman geographer Aurelius Macrobius in the late fourth century A.D. and by the English cartographer Johannes de Sacrobosco (John of Hollywood) in the early fourteenth century; by the late fifteenth and early sixteenth century, virtually all European cartographers ascribed to it. In keeping with this concept, world maps reflecting the great discoveries of the period depicted each of the four known continents as being separated from the poles by open sea; in the northern hemisphere this was the *fretum arcticum,* or arctic strait. This hypothetical strait extending over North America from the Atlantic to the Pacific attracted even more interest after the publication in Basel in 1540 of the *Typus Orbis Universalis Terrarum* of Claudius Ptolemaeus (Ptolemy), which depicted the strait with the legend "Per hoc fretum inter patet ad Moluccas" (Through this strait there is access to the Moluccas).[20]

These geographical concepts were placed in political perspective by Urdaneta, who recommended to the Royal Council that the expedition depart New Spain in March and proceed northward along the Pacific coast beyond the point reached by Rodríguez Cabrillo as far as would be necessary to allow discovery of the strait. He gave a justification for this added time and expense:

In this New Spain there have been reports that the French have discovered a passage to the sea to the west of this New Spain between the land of Bacallaos [Labrador] and that which is further to the north, and that having entered heading to the west in seventy degrees and more North Latitude, and sailing to the west heading southwest, they went so far that they came down to less than fifty degrees North Latitude, and found open sea that enabled sailing across it to China, the Spice Islands, Peru and New Spain, easily to all areas which can be reached by ship in this Western Sea. Upon their return to France they continued to the coast of Florida, which is in the north, and they found an outlet to the sea of Spain and France in less latitude than that where they first entered, for it was not more than forty some degrees where they came out, and it was not as much as fifty.

Since such a strait would permit access to the Pacific basin, and therefore to the western coast of America, China, and the East Indies, Urdaneta continued, it would be of greatest importance to Spain to verify its existence and, if it did exist, to settle its narrows or some other strategic point to control the passage of foreigners.[21] Although based on hearsay, the long-standing cartographic description of the strait and Urdaneta's recognized competence as a navigator gave credence to the memorandum and led to a general acceptance of his concepts in the Spanish court and among his colleagues. Coincidentally, also in 1561, the strait was named by the Venetian cartographer Giacomo Gastaldi, who engraved the legend "Ania Pro.[vincia]" on the extreme northwestern edge of America on his *Il disegno della terza parte dell'Asia*, thus establishing "Streto de Anian" as the common nomenclature used by Italian and Dutch cartographers for many decades.[22]

As a result of many delays in outfitting, the additional exploration recommended by Urdaneta was eliminated, and in November 1564 Legaspi sailed from Navidad directly to the Philippines, which he reached in February 1565. By mid-1565, the expedition had gained control of the island of Cebú, and thus a base was established in the islands. The outbound voyage had followed prevailing winds and currents westward, as had earlier explorers. However, there remained the problem of the return to New Spain; if attempted in the same latitude, this return would be going against the same winds and currents. Such a return voyage was of both immediate and long-range necessity, for the Legaspi force needed supplies, and if the long-sought commerce between Spain and Asia was to be achieved, merchandise would have to flow through New Spain to avoid conflict with Portugal and other European powers in the Indian Ocean and along the western African coast. Under the command of Esteban Rodríguez, with Urdaneta charged with navigation of the return route, the *San Pablo* sailed from Cebú on 1 June bound for the western coast of New Spain. Aware of the change of direction of prevailing winds in different latitudes, Urdaneta set a northern course toward the coast of Japan, and there, as calculated, he encountered winds out of the west and, unexpectedly, a strong current, the Kuro Sivo or Japan Current, which carried the ship northeast in an arc to 39°30′ north and then southward, across the Pacific, to the coast of California. Making landfall recorded in 27°12′ north latitude, the *San Pablo* followed prevailing winds and currents southward, reaching Acapulco on 8 October.[23]

The discovery of the return route, or "vuelta de poniente," established the Philippines as Spain's gateway to Asia and the long desired commerce with China and Japan, for it provided a lengthy but fixed and secure route for the transportation of goods to New Spain and a way westward for the colonization of the islands that would be used by annual trade ships. Beginning in 1566, the Manila galleon or China ship, as it was known, would leave Cavite, the port of Manila, in July, laden to maximum capacity with silks, spices, porcelain, lacquerware, and gold and silver, commodities that were relatively inexpensive in Asia and could be sold at four or five times their cost in Mexico City. Following the course northeast to the coast of Japan, the galleon proceeded across the vast Pacific to the California coast between 45° and 35° north and from there continued southward to Acapulco, arriving in late January or early February of the following year. The return voyage to Cavite, carrying supplies, colonists, missionaries, and investors, generally departed Acapulco in March, reaching its destination in late May or early June. The hardships of this voyage, aboard overladen ships that maneuvered badly in high seas and frequently suffered severe damage during storms, were many, and the lack of fresh water and nutritious foods contributed to a high rate of illness and mortality among the crew and passengers; only the great profits to be gained in this trade mitigated its risks. Due to these factors, it was evident that a port midway in the voyage between Manila and Acapulco was desirable as a place of rest and reprovisioning, but the navigators, exhausted from the long trip, were not interested in searching for it either on the high seas or along the California coast, and the route was merely shortened by dropping landfall southward to Isla de Cedros in 28° north.

Although the galleons of 1568 and 1578 had been lost off Guam, and those of 1572 and 1574 were forced to return to Cavite, all due to storms, the

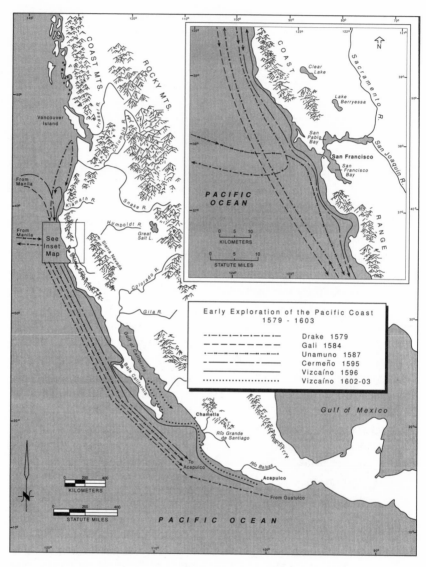

Map 8.2 Early Exploration of the Pacific Coast, 1579–1603.

Pacific Ocean had been under the total dominion of Spain since its discovery in 1513, and only nature threatened the Spanish mariners.[24] Navigation routes and geographical aspects of the coasts and islands had been jealously guarded, with security based on the theory that if the enemy was unable to reach them, they could not be attacked, rather than on the arming of ships and the fortification of ports. This absolute dominion ended, however, on 16 September 1578 when the English corsair Francis Drake, guided by pilots captured on the coast of South America, entered the Pacific with a fleet of five ships. Proceeding northward along the Chilean and Peruvian coasts, Drake sacked Spanish towns, and off Guayaquil, in Ecuador, he succeeded in capturing the galleon *Nuestra Señora de la Concepción* (alias *Cacafuego*), from which he took a great booty of silver bars. Continuing his pillage along the coasts of Central America, Drake ended his raiding at the port of Guatulco on the coast of Oaxaca in April 1579 and then disappeared from view.

Drake's ship, the *Golden Hind*, laden with silver and after two years at sea, was badly in need of repair before being able to attempt the return voyage to England; hoping to escape the danger of Spanish ships that were searching for him and hoping to find refuge in northern latitudes outside of settled areas, where he could careen his ship, Drake directed his course northwest out to sea. Sailing some 120 miles off the coast, Drake turned eastward to the north of Cape Mendocino, made landfall, and then coasted southward, anchoring in the lee of Point Reyes in June 1579. There he carried out the necessary repairs and took possession of the region for Queen Elizabeth of England, naming it New Albion. From there, he sailed across the Pacific, through the Moluccas, across the Indian Ocean, and around the Cape of Good Hope in June 1580, anchoring in Plymouth on 26 September, without having been observed by Europeans since departing Oaxaca more than a year earlier.[25]

The presence of Drake in the Pacific, and his unknown return route to England, produced great concern in the court of Philip II. Spain could no longer enjoy the absolute security of dominion in the Pacific; moreover, stimulated by the voyages of the Englishman Martin Frobisher of 1576–78 in search of a strait on the northern Atlantic coast of America, opinion was widespread that Drake had discovered the Straits of Anián, which would permit England unobstructed access to the great ocean. These factors gave new dimensions to the need for a midway port for supply and for rehabilitation of the crews of the Manila galleon, who now might be called on to defend their vessel and its cargo against attack, and to the need for the exploration and fortification of the Pacific coast, as proposed by Urdaneta two decades earlier. The least expensive and most direct method for achieving these objectives was the employment of the galleons themselves as exploring ships during their voyage from Manila to Acapulco; however, because the crews would be suffering from the very deprivations they were seeking to halt and because the possibility of other enemy ships in the Pacific remained, reconnaissance was delayed until adequate data could be collected, and no further unidentified ships were sighted.[26]

Francisco Gali, an experienced transpacific navigator, initiated the search for a midway port, and sailing from Acapulco on 10 March 1583, he reached Cavite in June. Outfitting for almost a year, Gali departed for Macao on the southern coast of China in June 1584 and, commanding the *San Juan Bautista* laden with merchandise, sailed for Acapulco on 29 July, following a northeastern course to a point some nine hundred miles east of Japan, where he experienced a strong current out of the north until he was some six hundred miles off the California coast, where he made landfall in 37°50' north latitude. Coasting southward, Gali reached Acapulco in January 1585 and submitted to Viceroy-Archbishop Pedro Moya de Contreras a report in which he suggested that the current he had experienced was the outfall of the Straits of Anián; he described an abundance of timber, seals, rivers, coves, and bays along the temperate California coast.[27] This reconnaissance was not sufficiently detailed, however, and on 25 March Gali sailed for Manila to await viceregal orders relative to a second exploration.

The return voyage was delayed, initially because of the unseaworthiness of Gali's ships and subsequently because of his sudden death in early 1586.[28] By June 1587, the Audiencia of Manila had appointed Pedro de Unamuno, an experienced galleon pilot, to succeed Gali; however, he had been arrested while trading in Macao, and a ship had to be sent to secure his release. On 12 July 1587, Unamuno sailed from Macao in command of the *Nuestra Señora de Esperanza*, and after a month spent unsuccessfully searching for the mythical Islas Rica de Oro and Rica de Plata that had been reported to the east of Japan by Augustinian Fray Andrés de Aguirre,[29] he proceeded to the California coast, where he made landfall in 37°30' north latitude. Coasting southward, on 18 October Unamuno anchored in a large bay that, in accordance with the liturgical calendar, he named San Lucas, today Santa Cruz Bay. Going ashore with Father Martín Ignacio de Loyola, twelve soldiers, and some Filipinos, Unamuno explored the surrounding region for two days, and although the Costanoan Indians evaded them at that time, the party was ambushed on the beach as it disembarked for the ship. As Unamuno proceeded southward, he entered a heavy fog bank that forced the suspension of exploration on 28 October, and a direct course was set for Acapulco. Off Cabo Corrientes, Unamuno was intercepted by a small boat and advised of the presence of an English corsair along the coast; however, he was able to continue his voyage without incident, making port in Acapulco on 22 November.[30]

The same fog that had prevented coastal exploration by Unamuno also saved him from attack, for two days after his arrival at Cabo Corrientes, the galleon *Santa Ana*, which had left Manila on 2 July, fell prey to the English at Cabo San Lucas. Following the track of Drake, and probably using his diaries and rutters, Thomas Cavendish had sailed from Plymouth on 31 July 1586 and reached the Pacific Ocean on 6 March 1587. Proceeding northward, as had Drake, Cavendish sacked towns along the coast of South America and burned Guatulco on 3 August; after raids on the coast of Nueva Galicia at Navidad, Acatlán, Chacala, and Mazatlán in September and October, he rested his crews and repaired his remaining ships, the *Desire* and the *Content*, at the Islas de Mazatlán preparatory to waylaying the Manila galleon. On 24 October he reached Cabo San Lucas, and on 14 November the *Santa Ana* was sighted. Poorly armed, the galleon surrendered after a few hours of fighting and was boarded by the English, who sacked it, hung the canon of Manila, Father Juan de Almendrales, put its crew and passengers ashore, and on 29 November, after setting the ship ablaze, sailed westward into the Pacific. After burning for four days, the galleon drifted ashore, where the survivors quelled the flames and repaired the keel, in which they left Cabo San Lucas on 22 December, reaching Santiago in Colima on 2 January 1588.[31]

The disaster of the *Santa Ana* further emphasized the need for Spanish security in the Pacific. Cavendish had comfortably rested his men in Spanish territory, had easily taken the poorly armed galleon manned by a weakened and undernourished crew, and although the *Content* was lost, had returned, unopposed, to Plymouth on 19 September 1588.[32] Furthermore, since many months passed before the receipt of the dispatches reporting Cavendish's course through the Philippines, the possibility of his having used the Straits of Anián for his return was considered by the Spanish court. Thus, not only was the discovery of a midway port and the Straits of Anián of great strategic importance, but so also was the settlement of California to prevent its becoming a refuge for the enemy. After waiting long enough to ensure the absence of foreign vessels, on 17 January 1593 a royal order was issued to resume exploration of the coast by the Manila galleons, and in early 1594 Viceroy Luis de Velasco appointed Sebastián Rodríguez Cermeño, a Portuguese navigator in the service of Spain who had been the pilot of the ill-fated *Santa Ana*, to outfit an expedition in Manila.

On 21 March 1594, Cermeño left Acapulco for Manila, where he arrived in June. Finding that his ship was not in condition to make the return voyage, he was able to contract the loan of the *San Agustín*, whose owner, Pedro Sarmiento, desired to send it to Acapulco laden with merchandise. In addition to the necessary provisions, a Philippine longboat for shallow-water exploration was lashed to the deck, and on 5 July 1595 Cermeño sailed from Cavite. Following the established track, the *San Agustín* made landfall in California in 42° north latitude near Trinidad Bay in November and proceeded southward. On 6 November, heavy winds arose, and sighting a high point of land running northeast-southwest, Cermeño brought the ship to anchor under its lee. The Spaniards were peacefully received by the Coast Miwok Indians and launched the longboat to explore the bay, which Cermeño named San Francisco, modern-day Drake's Bay. After three weeks at anchor, a storm arose on 30 November, and the *San Agustín* was battered against the shore and destroyed. Unable to save most of the supplies, Cermeño ordered the gathering of edible plants, and after increasing the draft of the longboat with planking from the wreck, he and the crew headed southward in the newly christened *San Buenaventura* on 8 December. Obtaining food and water from friendly Chumash Indians and finding edible plants and a beached whale on Isla San Martín off the northern coast of Baja California, the survivors reached the coast of Nayarit on 7 January 1596.[33]

As reports of the disaster of the *San Agustín* were being transmitted to Spain, a strange event that would have a major effect on future voyages to the Pacific coast of North America was taking place in Venice. There, one Apostolos Valerianos, alias Juan de Fuca, a native of the Greek island of Cephalonia, in the summer of 1596 met with two English entrepreneurs, Michael Lok and John Dowlass. He told them that, in 1587, he had gone to New Spain aboard the *Santa Ana* and had lost most of his personal fortune to Cavendish. On his arrival in Mexico, because of his forty years of meritorious service to Spain, he had been appointed by the viceroy to lead an expedition of three ships and one hundred men to fortify the Straits of Anián. Although this first voyage had ended in mutiny, Fuca continued, in 1592 the viceroy had again sent him northward in command of one ship and one longboat, and reaching a point on the California coast between 47° and 48° north latitude, he had entered the strait. Sailing through a land rich in gold and pearls, after twenty days he entered the Atlantic and returned to Spain. Because his efforts had not been rewarded, Fuca concluded, he had come to Venice in the hope of interesting the state of Venice in financing a return voyage. Lok, fascinated by the story, wrote to Fuca on 1 July 1596 requesting further details on the planned voyage. Fuca answered from Cephalonia on 24 September that he required only twenty men and the necessary funding to make the voyage and that he was prepared to leave as soon as the money was received. Although nothing came of Fuca's scheme, his story was widely disseminated and taken as true in many circles.[34]

Shortly afterward, and supporting this tale by Fuca, on 27 June 1597 in Manila an important mathematician and navigator, Fernando de los Ríos Coronel, sent a memorandum to the governor of the Philippines in which he recounted a report given him by Augustinian Fray Martín de Rada, a companion of Urdaneta's on the Legaspi expedition. According to Rada, a Basque from San Sebastián, Juanes de Rivas, had participated in a voyage to Newfoundland and during the trip had been told that, in 1545, some Bretons had entered a strait between 52° and 62° north latitude that had previously been used by the Portuguese to sail from Lisbon to China and India and that the return trip from Asia had required only forty-five days.[35] Such unsubstantiated tales abounded, but taken together with the known explorations by the English in search of the Northwest Passage from the Atlantic, they could not be totally discounted and were a prime factor motivating Spanish interest in occupying the northern Pacific coast of America.

Exploration through Private Enterprise

The second factor in achieving security in the Pacific, the settlement of California, also met with failure during the same period. Reputedly rich in pearls, the peninsula had stirred imaginations since its discovery; however, its harsh climate, its isolation, and the withdrawal of Cortés's colony in 1537 deterred further interest until, in 1585, Hernando de Santotis and his partners petitioned the king for a license to exploit pearl beds in the Gulf of California. Setting a pattern for future attempts at settlement, the license allowed exclusive rights for pearling, exploration, and settlement for a period of ten years, at the full expense of the grantee, and required one-twentieth of the value of pearls taken to be paid to the royal treasury.

With many delays, including the burning of his ships at Navidad by Cavendish and the death of a principal partner, seven years later Santotis had not exercised the privileges of the license, and on 29 July 1592 a former investor-merchant in Manila, Sebastián Vizcaíno, and his partners petitioned Viceroy Luis de Velasco for the transference of the license to their enterprise. After lengthy hearings, the transfer was made, and beginning on 1 March 1594 Vizcaíno and his partners would have full rights in the Gulf of California.

Preparations for a voyage of exploration and settlement were begun, but continuous problems of finance, fraud, and criminal action on the part of several of the partners caused numerous delays. Finally, in March 1595 Vizcaíno began the outfitting of the *San Francisco*, the *San Joseph*, and the *Tres Reyes* and on 15 June sailed from Acapulco. At Mazatlán, reached on 13 August, some fifty crewmen and one of the five Franciscans aboard deserted the expedition, and on 24 August the voyage across the gulf was begun. Landfall was made at Cabo San Lucas on 3 September, and an encampment was set up; Vizcaíno sailed northward on 10 September, landing two days later in the bay of Santa Cruz, which, as a result of his peaceful reception by the Pericú Indians, he named Nuestra Señora de La Paz. The remainder of the colonists were brought up to La Paz, and a small settlement and stockade was begun at a site where several artifacts remaining from the Cortés colony had been found.

Exploration for pearl oyster beds was begun by Vizcaíno with the *Tres Reyes* and the *San Joseph* on 3 October; the two ships were separated by a storm, but Vizcaíno continued alone, northward along the coast, for ten days. Going ashore near modern Loreto, Vizcaíno's men were attacked by the Guaycura Indians, and nineteen drowned in their attempt to return to the ship. With this loss, the expedition returned to La Paz on 18 October, where the next day a soldier was mortally wounded by the accidental discharge of his harquebus, and two days later, a wind arose, carrying sparks from a cooking fire to the thatched roof of one of the huts and starting a conflagration that consumed over half the settlement before being extinguished. Faced with this great loss of equipment and supplies, as well as the general depression of the colonists, Vizcaíno ordered their return to New Spain on 28 October, and with the *San Joseph* and a crew of thirty-six, he resumed exploration northward along the coast. Severe weather caused slow headway, and after making anchorage on 9 November near Loreto, the expedition proceeded five days later, although continued storms and sabotage to the ship soon halted this enterprise; on 16 November Vizcaíno turned southward, reaching Salagua on the coast of Colima on 7 December.[36] As had been the case with Cortés six decades earlier, this second attempt at settlement collapsed, again because of isolation and a lack of supplies.

Royal Intervention

The failure of voyages of exploration by Gali, Unamuno, and Cermeño clearly demonstrated the error of using heavy, merchandise-laden ships, manned by mariners who were tired and ill after several months at sea, to carry out detailed reconnaissance of shallow, unknown waters. Thus, as one of his final acts, on 27 September 1598 Philip II issued a royal order authorizing the outfitting of an expedition to the Pacific coast of California and specifically directing it toward maritime coastal exploration, using light draft vessels and commencing in the port of Acapulco.[37] Appointed general of the expedition by Viceroy Gaspar de Zúñiga y Acevedo, Count of Monterrey, Sebastián Vizcaíno selected Toribio Gómez de Corbán, a veteran of the Spanish Armada, as admiral and second-in-command. Two cosmographers, Gerónimo Martín Palacios and the Discalced Carmelite Fray Antonio de la Ascensión, were charged with the scientific tasks of astronomical, cartographic, and hydrographic observation and the preparation of rutters and charts, with Francisco de Bolaños, a Manila galleon pilot and survivor of the *San Agustín*, named as first pilot of the expedition.

Every facility was provided to ensure the total success of the expedition. Although the recruitment of officers was relatively easy, and several of Vizcaíno's friends and former crew from the 1596 voyage enlisted, a full complement was not achieved because of the high risks involved, and in 1601 the viceroy authorized an increase in pay as well as the inclusion of soldiers who had prior sea duty. In addition to Fray Antonio de la Ascensión, who had formal training as a cosmographer in Seville, two other Discalced Carmelites from the province of San Alberto were named to serve as chaplains and missionaries on the voyage. Three vessels, the flagship *San Diego*, the *Santo Tomás*, an ex-Peruvian galleon, and the frigate *Tres Reyes*, were fully outfitted in Acapulco, and on 18 March 1602 Vizcaíno received detailed orders from the Count of Monterrey. Officers' councils were to be held and complete minutes kept of each stage of the expedition, which was to proceed from Acapulco directly to Cabo San Lucas and from that point northward to one hundred leagues beyond Cape Mendocino. The expedition was to enter all bays and river mouths to determine depth, bottom, anchorages, and resources; take daily solar readings and nightly stellar readings, entering them in a log with all data including direction, time, wind, and landmarks; chart the coast in detail, noting winds, bottom, pearl oyster beds, direction, and resources; mark the entry and direction of ports and name them according to the liturgical calendar; and delineate all islands, reefs, and bars in relation to the coastline.

The expedition sailed from Acapulco on 5 May 1602, proceeded to Mazatlán, and crossed the gulf to Cabo San Lucas, anchoring on 11 June. Contrary winds delayed departure until 5 July, when Vizcaíno cleared the cape and proceeded northward charting, sounding, and naming landmarks, bays, islands, and other topographic features. Among others, along the Baja California coast on 21 July Bahía Magdalena was named and charted; on 8 August, Punta Abreojos; on 15 August, Bahía San Hipólito; and on 27 August, Isla Natividad. On 5 September the expedition anchored at Isla de Cedros and charted the island. Continuing the voyage on 10 September, the expedition named and charted, between 12 and 20 October, Bahía San Quintín, and on 5 November, Ensenada de Todos Santos, named San Mateo by Rodríguez Cabrillo, was explored. Five days later, the Bahía de San Miguel of Rodríguez Cabrillo was reached and renamed San Diego, and since it was considered an excellent anchorage with abundant resources of wood, water, and game, ten days were spent in its sounding and charting. Between 24 November and 3 December the Santa Barbara Channel and its islands were charted and named. North of Point Conception, named on 4 December, heavy fog set in, increasing the risk of detailed inshore charting; nevertheless, the Santa Lucía range was named and noted, and on 14 December, anchorage was made in a bay that, the following day, Vizcaíno named Monterey in honor of the viceroy.

The entire expedition disembarked at Monterey, and an encampment was established; extensive exploration of the surrounding countryside found it to abound in game, fresh water, and oak and pine forest. Since over forty of the crew were suffering from illnesses, including scurvy, Vizcaíno ordered their return to Acapulco aboard the *Santo Tomás* under Gómez de Corbán and prepared brief communiqués for the viceroy and the Audiencia, with general descriptions of the value of Monterey as a wayport due to its more northerly latitude, protected anchorage, pine and oak, and plentiful game, fish, and water; he also requested that supplies be sent to La Paz to enable exploration of the Gulf of California on his return southward. The *Santo Tomás* sailed on 29 December, and noting the increasing cold and inclement weather, Vizcaíno proceeded northward on 4 January 1603, naming and charting Point Pinos, Point Año Nuevo, and on the following day, Point Reyes. Rather than risk exploration of Cermeño's Bahía de San Francisco in bad weather, the expedition continued, although the *San Diego* and the *Tres Reyes* were separated in a storm north of Point Reyes late on 5 January. Seven days later, after reaching Cape Mendocino, with an outbreak of scurvy so severe that only two of the crew were able to climb the mast, Vizcaíno ordered the *San Diego* turned southward. The storm intensified, however, and driven northward, Vizcaíno sighted Cabo Blanco in modern-day southern Oregon on 21 January, and he again headed southward. Passing Monterey on 25 January and Santa Catalina Island three days later, and anchoring at Isla de Cedros to take on water on 6 February, Vizcaíno, concerned for the health of his men, made the greatest headway possible, bypassing Cabo San Lucas on 11 February and anchoring at Mazatlán seven days later. After resting and rehabilitating the crew, on 9 March Vizcaíno sailed for Acapulco, anchoring at the port on 21 March.[38]

The *Tres Reyes* had preceded Vizcaíno and reached Navidad on 29 February. After separating from the *San Diego*, it had been forced by storms to a point north of Cabo Blanco; both the commander, pilot Antón Flores, and Corporal Martín de Aguilar, as well as two crew members, had died, and the pilot's aide, Esteban López, had brought the frigate back to New Spain. In heavy seas, with no professional cosmographers aboard, the six survivors aboard the *Tres Reyes* had sighted, to the north of Point Reyes, "a very large river which had seven fathoms of depth at its mouth and which ran inland from the southeast one quarter to the east, and the force of the current did not permit them to enter it"; they named this Santa Inés, probably the modern-day Russian River. Near Cape Mendocino "a very large bay into which a heavily flowing river enters from the north shore; it flows with such a great force of current that, although for an entire day they were forcing with full sail and wind astern, they could not enter it for a distance greater than two leagues"; this was the present-day Rogue River, which they believed to be the Straits of Anián.[39]

Despite the many hardships and problems confronted by the expedition, the viceroy, Count of Monterrey, considered it to have been a success. On 26 March he wrote to Philip III to this effect, stating that two fine ports for the protection of the Manila galleon had been found: San Diego and Monterey. On 28 May, Vizcaíno's log was remitted to the Crown, with viceregal recommendations for the settlement of Monterey Bay, and on 22 November, the remaining logs, reports, rutters, and charts, the last redrawn in final form by the famed cosmographer Enrico Martínez, were sent to Spain.[40] Although the goals of the expedition had been achieved—through the affixing of what would become permanent place-names and the preparation of precise descriptions and detailed charts of the California coast from Cabo San Lucas to Cabo Blanco, charts that would be the basis for the cartography of the region until the late eighteenth century—various factors intervened to halt plans for the settlement of the Pacific coast of North America in the seventeenth century.

Although the colonization of Monterey was strongly sought by the viceroy for whom it was named, succession to the office by Juan de Mendoza y Luna, Marquis of Montesclaros, in 1604 delayed action along these lines, and further opinions on a midway port were heard. Viceregal opposition was primarily founded on the fact that the California coast was so close, relatively, to Acapulco that by the time the galleons made landfall, their captains preferred to make home port, and that the principal dangers of the voyage were over at that point. Although this argument ignored the matter of an unsettled coast becoming a haven for the enemy, Montesclaros concluded that the ideal port would be in the central Pacific, and he suggested the revival of a search for the Islas Rica de Oro and Rica de Plata, reported by Urdaneta to be centers of great wealth and civilization to the east of Japan.[41] Concurring with the opinion of the viceroy, the Crown issued a royal order on 27 September 1607 to Montesclaros's successor, Luis de Velasco, Marquis of Salinas, suspending any plans for the settlement of Monterey and mandating that Vizcaíno should command two ships out of Manila to search for the fabled islands. Velasco then ordered hearings in Manila, and in July 1609, following extensive discussion about the point of departure and the time of exploration, planning of the expedition was begun.[42]

The Islas Rica de Oro and Rica de Plata were not the only suggested alternatives to the settlement of Monterey Bay. Fray Antonio de la Ascensión, Discalced Carmelite, graduate of the Academy of San Telmo (Spain's primary center for the training of pilots and navigators), and second cosmographer of the Vizcaíno expedition of 1602–3, on 18 June 1608 remitted to the Crown the first of many memoranda that would radically alter the geographic concepts of California. Fray Antonio recommended the establishment of a midway port at Cabo San Lucas:

This is the place where the English took the ship Santa Ana which years past came from China, and this was the port where the English-

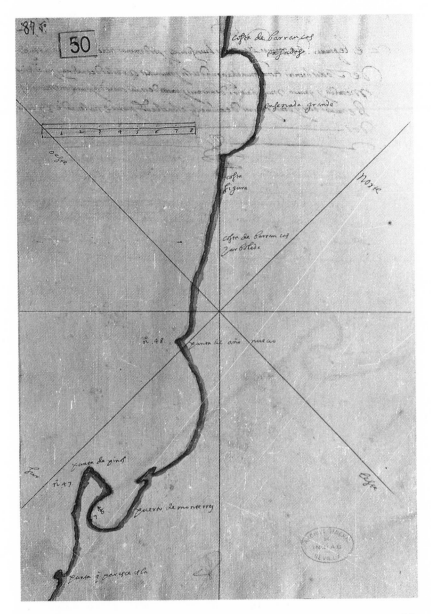

8.2 *Monterey Bay by Enrico Martínez (1603). This is the first detailed map of the California coastal area. The geographical features are extraordinarily accurately placed. Courtesy The Bancroft Library, University of California, Berkeley.*

man was waiting for her. With a fort and settlement of Spaniards there, for Your Highness it will prevent the enemy from taking captives, for here the ships make landfall to head for the port of Acapulco. With this settlement it will be easy to explore to the point reached by the gulf which the sea forms here, because it is a presumption that it crosses through to the North Sea [Atlantic], and if this is found to be the case, and that it is possible for the ships from Peru and all of the South Sea to sail through the strait, they can go this way with greater ease to Spain than by going through Havana, and through here Your Highness can receive all the wealth from Peru and China and this land with much less expense and greater ease, and it will not be necessary for Your Highness to make new expenditures each year to hold this land.

Very succinctly, the Carmelite conceived the Gulf of California as a strait that lay between California and the continent and that reentered the Pacific at its northern extremity at the mouth of the Straits of Anián and the end of the island of California.[43]

Notwithstanding the discoveries of Ulloa and Alarcón, Fray Antonio's veracity was unquestionable, since he was a professional cosmographer, a veteran of the Vizcaíno expedition, and a priest; furthermore, his opinions, which established California as an island for over a century, reflected the most ideal geographic concept, supported by early images of California as an island and reports of navigation of the strait. One such report, perhaps in part derived from that of Juan de Fuca, appeared in the late summer of 1609 in the form of a memorandum to the Crown. Lorenzo Ferrer Maldonado affirmed, through a lengthy description of the Straits of Anián and suggestions for its occupation, that in 1588 he had sailed northwestward from Spain and, passing Greenland, had entered the Straits of Labrador, proceeding inland for some 1,800 miles to a point in 75° north latitude, where there were very high mountains. From there he continued to the southwest for some 450 miles until he entered the Pacific Ocean through the mouth of the Straits of Anián in 60° north. He claimed that although in the shadow of the mountains there was much ice, at Anián the temperature was mild and often hot, since the sun shone for almost twenty-four hours, and that there were fruit trees that bore all year, as well as abundant game, shellfish, and whales. Ferrer further stated that during his sojourn at the strait from April to mid-June, he met some Hanseatic Lutherans who, speaking Latin, told him that they used the passage to trade with China. In view of the fact that the strait was believed to be used by other nations, and with the recent explorations of the English and the French, Spanish control of the passage not only would signify great monetary savings by permitting direct communication with China, the Philippines, and California but also would allow its fortification, he concluded, and this he could accomplish with three ships with metal-clad keels, two longboats, two hundred mariners, arms, munitions, and supplies for two years.[44] Although Ferrer's outlandish proposal was not acted on, clearly the strait had become a matter of increasing concern, particularly in view of the English expeditions in search of the Northwest Passage under George Waymouth in 1602, James Hall in 1605, John Knight in 1606, and Henry Hudson in 1610.

Anxiety over the discovery of the Straits of Anián notwithstanding, the Islas Rica de Oro and Rica de Plata, by pure accident, took priority in the planning of Pacific exploration. On his return to Acapulco in 1609, the governor of the Philippines, Rodrigo de Vivero, had been shipwrecked on the Japanese coast and, during his sojourn, had initiated talks with the Japanese shogunate about the establishment of commerce between Japan and New Spain. Desirous of opening trade, and in need of mining technicians to improve silver extraction, Japan was eager to reach an accord, and Vivero, after his arrival in New Spain in 1610, proposed a formal embassy to the Japanese court. Considered the person most versed in transpacific navigation, Sebastián Vizcaíno was appointed to head the embassy and, at the same time, search for the islands. Sailing from Acapulco in March 1611, Vizcaíno reached Japan in June and presented his embassy before the shogun, Tokugawa Ieyasu, who granted him permission to chart the coasts and conduct his exploration. Because of numerous misunderstandings and conflicts of interest with the Japanese, however, Vizcaíno was not able to carry out his search until 16 September 1612, when he sailed from the port of Uraga on Honshu. Following a zigzag course to the east, he sought the islands until 29 October, when a storm forced the return of the ship to port. On his arrival at Uraga on 7 November, Vizcaíno found his ship to be unseaworthy for the return to New Spain, and after over a year of conflicts, intrigues, and delays, a new ship was acquired, and he returned to Acapulco in January 1614.[45] Almost as quickly as it arose, serious interest in the islands subsided, for two experienced navigators, Unamuno and Vizcaíno, had searched for them in vain; the risk and the expense were great, and with the rising persecution of Christians in Japan, any hopes for relations with that nation rapidly disappeared. These factors notwithstanding, Spain's requirements for security in the Pacific remained, and California again became of strategic importance.

In conformity with the concepts of Fray Antonio de la Ascensión, Spanish policy toward the exploration and colonization of California was radically altered in the early seventeenth century. The failure of the Vizcaíno venture of 1596, and his subsequent appointments to the expedition of 1602–3, the administration of Tehuantepec in 1604, and the embassy to Japan in 1611, had prevented the further exercise of the privileges of his exclusive license to explore, colonize, and exploit the Gulf of California. Envisioned as a strait separating the "island" of California from the mainland and leading to the Straits of Anián, the gulf achieved new importance, and inactivity in its exploration and settlement was detrimental to ensuring rapid control by Spain of the passage. Furthermore, unlike the Pacific coast, the gulf was known to have pearl oyster beds, the exploitation of which would hopefully produce great wealth for the fortunate entrepreneur as well as the royal treasury, and under such circumstances, the Crown could rely on private financing of ships, personnel, supplies, and colonization, thus eliminating a major expenditure.

The Return to Private Enterprise

In 1611, in Seville, a group of investors—Tomás de Cardona, Sancho de Merás, and Francisco de la Paraya—petitioned the transfer of Vizcaíno's rights and license to their enterprise, and on 13 August a royal order granted the petition. Preparations for the expedition to the New World were placed under the command of Cardona's nephew Nicolás de Cardona, who had previously served as a captain in the fleet of General Juan Gutiérrez de Garibay to New Spain in 1610. Six vessels were outfitted in Spain and, under Cardona as admiral and Francisco de Basilio as captain, were incorporated into the fleet of General Antonio de Oquendo, sailing from Cádiz in 1614. Very shortly, the first of many incidents of misfortune that were to plague the enterprise occurred; following a storm that separated him from the fleet, Cardona, left with only three surviving ships, reached Barbados. Proceeding to Puerto Rico via Guadeloupe, Cardona was drafted to hunt sea turtle to supply the island's garrison and was then sent to Grenada, Saint Lucia, and Saint Vincent to aid in the recovery of twenty-eight Christian Europeans, Indians, and Caribbean blacks held captive by the Caribs. Prohibited by law from using Indians as divers, Cardona then sailed to Isla Margarita, a pearl-fishing center off the coast of Venezuela, where he contracted Caribbean black divers for the expedition.

Sailing for New Spain via Santo Domingo (Hispaniola), Cuba, and Jamaica, Cardona reached Veracruz late in the year and proceeded to Mexico City. While there, Basilio, who had fallen ill during the journey, died, and Cardona enlisted Juan de Iturbe as his replacement and Pedro Alvarez de Rosales as military commander of the expedition.

Cardona and his men, after securing the necessary supplies and equipment, then proceeded to Acapulco to outfit three frigates, the *San Antonio*, the *San Francisco*, and the *San Diego*. Although the expedition was prepared to sail in January 1615, news reached the viceroy that a Dutch fleet had entered the Pacific and presented a threat to Acapulco. Thus, further delay occurred when Cardona and his men were ordered to aid in the construction of defensive revetments and form a part of the defense force under Lieutenant Captain General Melchor Fernández de Córdoba. With no further reports of the enemy, and the apparent threat over, on 21 March Cardona and his expedition, with two Franciscans as chaplains and missionaries, sailed for the Gulf of California. Anchoring at La Paz, he took possession for the Crown and, after several days, continued northward along the peninsular coast. Some diving was carried out, and anchorages were made at Bahía San Carlos, Isla Tiburón, and the mouth of the Colorado River, which Cardona considered to be merely a narrow channel that would reenter the open sea a short distance to the north, because he had "passed thirty-four degrees north latitude."

> The early and modern authors who have written about this gulf of California have considered it, and continue to consider it, as enclosed at twenty-eight degrees north latitude as is also shown on the general maps and sailing charts of the South Sea coast. This seems to be in error because that gulf or arm of the sea continues on toward the north, and from thirty-four degrees north latitude there remains more sea to sail and land over which to walk. This gulf is so deep that a sounding lead does not reach bottom, and having passed twenty-eight degrees north latitude and reaching thirty-four degrees north latitude I did not find bottom, and having explored the sea extensively, my opinion is well supported. . . . According to this report and that which I explored and saw up to thirty-four degrees north latitude, this land did not join, and thus California is a very large island.

Nevertheless, little of value was recovered through trade or diving, and after several months of exploration, Cardona turned southward along the Sonora coast, anchored at the mouth of the Río Mayo, where he aided Jesuit Father Pedro Méndez in the pacification of the Mayo Indians, and con-

8.3 *The Gulf of California by Nicolás de Cardona (1632). The Cardona map is one of the most detailed of the Gulf region until late in the eighteenth century. Courtesy The Bancroft Library, University of California, Berkeley.*

tinued to Mazatlán. Remaining with the *San Francisco*, Cardona dispatched the *San Diego* and the *San Antonio* under Iturbe to Acapulco to obtain supplies.[46]

Disaster more severe than that met so far awaited Cardona, for on 8 August 1614, Joris van Spilbergen, with a fleet of six ships, had sailed from Holland with orders from the Dutch East India Company to raid Spanish shipping on the Pacific coast of the Americas. Since the Dutch fleet did not complete its passage through the Strait of Magellan until 28 March 1615, by that date officials in New Spain assumed that any threat to their jurisdiction had passed; nevertheless, in August, reports from Peru indicated that the Dutch menace still existed. Adrian Boot, a leading military engineer, was ordered to design and build formal fortifications at Acapulco, but before these could be begun, on 11 October, Spilbergen entered the port under a flag of truce and exchanged prisoners for provisions. Proceeding northward on 18 October, eight days later Spilbergen found the *San Francisco* at anchor at Zacatula on the Colima coast. The ship was surrounded, and a boarding party sent, but Cardona and twelve others, including one of the Franciscans, jumped overboard and swam to shore. Sergeant Major Pedro Alvarez de Rosales, the pilot Martín de Aguirre, eight crewmembers, and one of the priests were taken as hostages; Spilbergen commandeered the ship, renaming it *Perel*, and sailed northward the following day for Salagua, where fresh water and fruit were available.[47]

Cardona and his men, after reaching the shore, proceeded inland toward Sayula and, en route, encountered a force of two hundred men under the command of Sebastián Vizcaíno, who, as the principal landholder of the region, had been asked to patrol the coast to repel the Dutch. Joining Vizcaíno, Cardona directed the troops to Salagua, and there, on 11 November, the Spanish successfully ambushed the Dutch, preventing them from taking on supplies; Alvarez de Rosales, Aguirre, and other captives from Cardona's ship were recovered. After taking testimony from the Dutch prisoners, Vizcaíno proceeded along the coast to prevent further landings by Spilbergen, and Cardona and his men marched overland to Acapulco with the reports of the skirmish.[48]

On arrival at Acapulco, Cardona was ordered to participate in the fortification project while Iturbe, who had evaded the Dutch, was permitted to return to the Gulf of California with one ship; the remaining vessel was ordered to Isla de Cedros under Bartolomé Juárez de Villalba to warn the Manila galleons of the Dutch presence. After three months at sea, this ship was no longer seaworthy, and Cardona was given viceregal permission to transport merchandise to Callao, the port of Lima, in Peru, and to fish for pearls en route as a means of raising new capital for his venture in California. While Cardona was preparing for departure, in November 1616, Iturbe returned to Acapulco with fourteen to fifteen ounces of pearls, an insufficient amount to cover even the expenses of their acquisition, and Cardona was yet further dependent on the Peruvian enterprise. Nevertheless, before sailing, Cardona was again ordered to relinquish his ship to convoy the Manila galleon of 1617; unable to continue, he disbanded his crew and returned to Spain for financial assistance.

Still considering the potential profit to be great, Tomás de Cardona refinanced the pearl-fishing venture, and on 14 May 1618 a royal order authorized a new expedition. In 1619, Nicolás de Cardona returned to America with the fleet of the Marquis de Cadereita to the port of Cartagena and from there proceeded to Portobello. In July, Cardona crossed the isthmus by mule and at the city of Panamá purchased two frigates and a longboat and recruited over one hundred men. Delayed by pirates blockading the Río Chagres, and being pressed into service for the defense of the city, Cardona and his crew were unable to leave Panamá until the summer of 1620. Proceeding northward, they encountered heavy storms and contrary winds, and at Chiriquí the longboat foundered and one of the frigates caught fire and sank. With his one remaining ship, Cardona continued to Sonsonate, where he went ashore to go overland to Mexico City and present his orders to the viceroy. While in Mexico, Cardona received the report that his ship had been wrecked on the coast of Tehuantepec, and he left the city for Acapulco to contract the construction of two new frigates.

While outfitting and construction was under way in Acapulco in 1621 and 1622, the viceroy, Marquis de Gelves, ordered Cardona and his fourteen divers to Havana to participate in the recovery of treasure from silver galleons sunk in the Caribbean. In Cuba, Cardona served under the Marquis of Cadereita in the recovery of several cargos lost in the Florida Keys and subsequently in salvage operations in the Cayos de Matacumbé off Cuba. These services, together with eight years of misfortune, again prevented Cardona from pursuing his navigation of the Gulf of California, and in late 1623 he returned to Spain in the fleet of General Carlos de Ibarra.[49]

Cardona's statement that the Colorado River was a short narrows exiting into open sea to the north added further evidence to the belief in the island of California. The influence of Fray Antonio de la Ascensión was demonstrated in 1615 with the publication in Seville by Matías Clavijo of the three-volume *Monarquía* Indiana of Franciscan Fray Juan de Torquemada, a friend and colleague of Fray Antonio's. His diary of the Vizcaíno expedition appeared almost verbatim in Book Five, chapters XLV–LVIII, thus promoting his authority over matters relating to the geography of California and the Straits of Anián. The failure of the Cardona enterprise and the general inactivity by the Crown for further development in California also reawakened Fray Antonio's concern over its security.

Writing from the convent of San Sebastián in Mexico City, on 12 October 1620, the Carmelite cosmographer presented a detailed memorandum to the Crown, clearly expressing his geographical concepts and, based on these, the urgency for the strategic occupation of California. The gulf was described as a sea some 150 miles in width between California and Nueva Galicia, extending northward to Nuevo Mexico, Quivira, and ending at the Straits of Anián. Two settlements, one in Nuevo Mexico and one in California, were proposed, to be directly across the sea from one another to facilitate mutual aid and commerce between them and to stimulate the development of pearl fisheries and the extraction of precious metals to be found in the hills of both provinces. Furthermore, the memorandum concluded, the Straits of Anián should be explored to permit direct passage to Spain from the Pacific, as well as the discovery of the great city of Quivira and the kingdom of Anián adjacent to China. Ultimately unheeded was Fray Antonio's prophetic recommendation that all exploration and settlement be undertaken at royal expense to avoid problems arising from conflicts between parties and from personal ambition.[50]

Additional evidence for his geography was given by Fray Antonio to another Franciscan colleague of the convent of San Francisco in Mexico City. Fray Gerónimo de Zárate y Salmerón reported the matter in his account of the exploration and settlement of New Mexico from the time of Fray Marcos de Niza, "Relaciones de todas las cosas que en el Nuevo México se han visto y sabido, así por mar como por tierra, desde el año de 1538 hasta el de 1626." Fray Antonio had told him of a foreign pilot, one N. de Morera, who had accompanied Francis Drake and who, because he appeared to be mortally ill, was put ashore in the Straits of Anián by the Englishman. Morera allegedly told Governor Rodrigo del Río at Sombrerete, Zacatecas, that for four years he had walked through New Mexico for some fifteen hundred miles, that there was a nation of white people who rode horses and possessed lances and daggers on the shore of the sea that divides New Mexico from the land to the west (California), and that Spain could be reached by boat in forty days from where he had been landed. Fray Antonio also told Zárate that Morera had offered to take the governor there and that Fray Antonio thought the white people mentioned by Morera were Muscovites.[51]

After several years of inactivity on the part of members of the Cardona enterprise, in 1627 Pedro Bastán de Santiago requested cancellation of their license and the granting to him of rights for the development of California. This petition was countered in the same year by the royal accountant Martín de Lezama, who stated that his father-in-law, Sebastián Vizcaíno, had never relinquished his right to settle and exploit California, nor had it been formally revoked, and that as his successor, Lezama was entitled to exercise the terms of the license. To avoid conflict that could delay activity and increase expenditures, a royal order of 2 August 1628, directed to the Audiencia of Mexico, decreed the taking of testimony from people who had voyaged to California, or had been directly involved in its development, to determine the practicality of continued efforts to colonize, the value and importance of the area, and its geography. If the evidence was positive, then the respondent was also to provide an opinion as to the best location and means to achieve settlement and exploitation.

Presented to Licenciate Juan de Alvarez Serrano, the testimony began in Mexico City on 9 May 1629. Captain Juan López de Vicuña presented a description of Cabo San Lucas, La Paz, and the peninsula northward, according to information received from reports of Vizcaíno and Cardona, and expressed his belief in the insularity of California and the Straits of Anián. He also rightly underscored the primary deterrent to colonization in California—the shortage of supplies, which diminished substantially due to the long voyage from Acapulco or Colima—and recommended the development of the fertile river valleys of Sinaloa on the coast opposite the peninsula of Baja California as a source of provisions, an enterprise made more attractive by the known presence of pearl oyster beds on the Culiacán coast. The second deposition was given on 27 May by Gonzalo de Francia, who had served as boatswain aboard the San Joseph under Sebastián Vizcaíno in 1596 and who considered his former commander a poor soldier because he had not taken artillery to control the Indians encountered during the voyage. Because of its dry, healthy climate, its potential great wealth in pearls, and its ease of supply from Sinaloa and Nayarit, Francia considered the region of La Paz as ideal for settlement. Two days later, in the Carmelite monastery of Valladolid (Morelia), Michoacán, Fray Antonio de la Ascensión presented his deposition, which closely followed the tenor of his memorandum of 1620, reiterating his proposals for settlement of the gulf coast and the discovery of Anián.[52]

The nature of testimony presented before Alvarez Serrano by the royal accountant Martín de Lezama, son-in-law of Vizcaíno, on 15 June, was substantially different from the foregoing. Stating that his knowledge was based on information acquired from his father-in-law and through Vizcaíno's papers, which he had in his possession, Lezama favored the settlement of Monterey, while concurring in the concept of great wealth in precious metals and pearls on the gulf coast. He further declared that, on behalf of his son, Nicolás Vizcaíno de Lezama, he had begun construction of a ship on the Río Baluarte near Acaponeta on the Nayarit coast to continue the work of Vizcaíno. This project, he stated, was necessarily abandoned, for he had hired a shipwright and carpenter, Francisco de Ortega, who with his brother, Hernando, and Domingo de Zavala had attempted to rob him and had stabbed him the preceding November. Although these men were sentenced by the magistrate to jail in Guadalajara, they were allowed to escape while being taken there and were at large. Nevertheless, Lezama enthusiastically endorsed settlement of the gulf coast, which he held would be easily accomplished due to the promise of great wealth, could be readily supplied from Sinaloa and Nayarit, and, fully in accord with the concepts of Fray Antonio, would facilitate the discovery of the Straits of Anián. Fourteen days later, Captain Lope de Argüelles Quiñones, who had been with Vizcaíno in 1596, echoed the opinions of his companion Gonzalo de Francia, relative to settlement and supply.

A totally contrary opinion was presented on 30 July by the royal cosmographer Enrico Martínez from Huehuetoca, north of Mexico City, where he was directing the initiation of the great drainage system of the valley of Mexico. A scientist, engineer, linguist, and printer, in addition to being a cosmographer and cartographer, Martínez gave a coolly academic deposition, first defining the known perimeters of California, none of which gave proof of its insularity, and then discussing the prior failures of private ventures to exploit the reputed wealth in pearls, the need for the Crown to finance any colonization if it was to succeed, and the lack of any resources of the land. Furthermore, Martínez affirmed, the Manila galleons were too close to port in Acapulco to warrant the establishment of a settlement in Monterey, the great cities and sources of wealth claimed to exist by Fray Antonio to the north had not been confirmed by any evidence, and if the enemy attempted settlement of such distant areas, he would suffer the same hardships, isolation, and shortage of supply as had the Spaniards in their voyages there. This early phase of the hearings in 1629 ended on an optimistic note, however, for Captain Alonso Ortiz de Sandoval, who had also been with Vizcaíno in 1596, enthusiastically testified in favor of the settlement of La Paz, which had an excellent climate and anchorage and was situated amid extensive pearl oyster beds extending from Cabo San Lucas northward. To facilitate supply, he recommended the settlement of Val de Banderas, modern-day Puerto Vallarta, in Jalisco, and he ended his deposition with a petition to the Crown to be allowed to participate, in the capacity that his seniority and service merited, in any enterprise involving the colonization of California.[53]

As the hearings progressed, what threatened to be the loss of valuable territory and resources in California through the inactivity by Cardona and Lezama, as successor to Vizcaíno, led to renewed petitions for transfer of the exclusive viceregal license to a new and promising entrepreneur. The petition of Francisco de Ortega claimed that he would carry out an extensive reconnaissance and return with direct information to present to the hearings, and appearing on his behalf, Juan García de Mercado, a respected and successful merchant in Mexico City, succeeded in bypassing Ortega's alleged attempts against Lezama, and as an investor and guarantor, gained him the license on 22 November 1631 from Viceroy Rodrigo Pacheco y Osorio, Marquis of Cerralvo. In keeping with the concepts of the deponents, Ortega had prepared his base for departure as near as possible to the gulf to facilitate supply and had finished the frigate *Madre Luisa de la Ascención*, begun by Lezama at Acaponeta.[54]

While Ortega was obtaining the license, further testimony was taken. On 22 December, at his sugar mill in Orizaba, Rodrigo de Vivero, Count of the Valley of Orizaba and former governor of the Philippines, testified that on his return to New Spain after being wrecked in Japan, the pilot had been Francisco de Bolaños of the Vizcaíno expedition of 1602–3, who had provided him with extensive information. This knowledge, combined with that of the expedition of Juan de Oñate from New Mexico to the Gulf of California in 1604, led Vivero to testify in full support of the geographical concepts and plans for colonization and development proposed by Fray Antonio de la Ascensión in his memoranda and to reiterate the need for nearby bases of supply in Colima, Jalisco, Nayarit, and Sinaloa. Less complex was the deposition of the merchant Sebastián Gutiérrez of Mexico City, who had accompanied Vizcaíno in 1596 and who saw all of California as rich in pearls and precious metals as well as of strategic importance to Spain.[55]

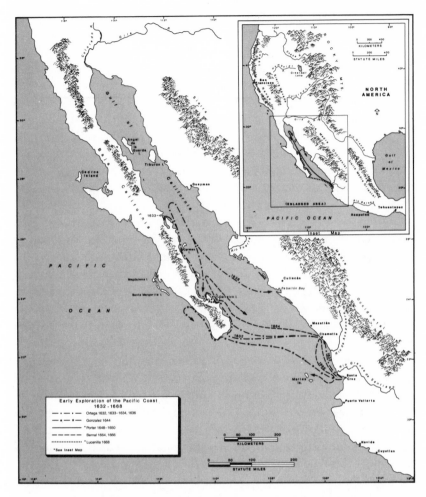

Map 8.3 Early Exploration of the Pacific Coast, 1632–1668.

Ortega continued his preparations, and in February 1632 Ortega moved his ship to the mouth of the Río Santiago near Sentispac, Nayarit, for final rigging and provisioning. He carried, in addition to supplies, arms, and trade goods, a wooden-and-lead two-man diving bell, which he had designed and from which pearl oysters could be raked from the bottom of the gulf. With Licenciate Diego de la Nava, a secular priest from the diocese of Guadalajara as chaplain, Esteban Carbonel de Valenzuela as pilot, and a crew of twenty, Ortega sailed on 27 February and proceeded to Mazatlán, where almost two months passed in provisioning and final preparations; on 1 May he began his crossing of the Gulf of California. On 3 May a large island, which Ortega named Cerralvo in honor of the viceroy, was reached, and the expedition continued to Cabo San Lucas, where it was received in peace by the Pericú Indians. After almost three weeks, on 24 May, Ortega returned northward, spent two days exploring Cerralvo, and proceeded to the next island to the north, which he named Espíritu Santo. After a brief survey of the island, the expedition then entered the Bay of La Paz, on 9 June continued into the Ensenada de los Aripes, where camp was established, and carried out a full reconnaissance. After ten days, Ortega returned to Espíritu Santo, fully surveyed the island, and continued to the coast of Sinaloa, where he anchored on 3 July.[56]

During Ortega's absence, hearings continued, and on 22 March, from the Carmelite monastery in Puebla, where he had retired, Fray Antonio de la Ascensión reiterated his deposition of 1620 and continued to urge settlement of the peninsula. In keeping with the terms of the petition for the license, the pilot Esteban Carbonel de Valenzuela presented a sworn report of the events of the voyage, during which he had used charts given him by Fray Antonio, and of his later trip to the Pacific coast. Chaplain Diego de la Nava also presented testimony of the expedition before Judge Juan de Alvarez Serrano on 19 November and, in addition to providing a brief but detailed description of the voyage, recommended continued effort to settle the areas explored because of the friendly and receptive nature of the Indians and the evidence of extensive pearl oyster beds there.[57] This testimony, Ortega's success in the recovery of a worthwhile quantity of pearls, possibly through the use of his diving bell, and the fact that, on his return to Sinaloa, Carbonel de Valenzuela had been sent to the Pacific coast with his ship to warn the Manila galleon of potential danger from pirates, enabled Ortega to proceed with the exercise of the terms of the license and prepare a second voyage after the return of his ship in May 1633.

Repairing and reprovisioning the *Madre Luisa de la Ascención* and reloading his diving bell at Mazatlán, Ortega sailed for La Paz on 8 September with Nava and an aide, Father Juan de Zúñiga, the pilot Bartolomé Terrazas, and a complement of forty. After further survey of Espíritu Santo and the bay, the expedition landed on 7 October and was happily recognized and received by the Pericúes. After establishing a base at La Paz, Ortega, with a small crew, began exploration of the gulf on 22 October, carefully noting pearl oyster beds and circumnavigating each island. On 25 October, San José was reached and named and, three days later, Las Animas; subsequently, San Diego, Santa Cruz, San Carlos, Monserrate, Danzantes, and Carmen were named, explored, and their oyster beds noted. Proceeding northward, the expedition named Los Coronados, which was found to be devoid of pearl oyster beds, as were San Ildefonso, from which the Sinaloa coast could be seen, San Marcos, and Tortugas. After naming Bahía Concepción, Ortega returned southward to La Paz in late November. In January and February 1634, exploration to the south by land resulted in the naming of Bahía de las Palmas and the recognition of Cerralvo off the coast; having established friendly relations with the Pericúes, many of whom were baptized by Nava, Ortega returned to Sinaloa on 8 April.[58]

Ortega had enjoyed greater success than his predecessors, for he succeeded in recovering a sufficient number of pearls to amortize his voyage, as well as in establishing permanent coastal and insular place-names in the southern Gulf of California. Nevertheless, Nicolás de Cardona had not abandoned his claims to rights in California, and after presenting his "Descripciones Geographicas, e Hydrographicas" describing his earlier voyages and services in 1632, on 9 October 1634 he petitioned the Crown for the continued exercise of his license.[59] A more lengthy report followed from Madrid on 6 November, and Cardona's papers were remitted to Viceroy Lope Díaz de Armendáriz, Marquis of Cadreita, for consideration on 25 April 1635.[60] Matters were further complicated in 1634 by a petition in Madrid of Pedro Porter y Casanate, a graduate of the university in Zaragoza and an experienced navigator and author of treatises on the subject, and of Pedro Botello Serrano for a license to explore the Gulf of California to the Straits of Anián with rights of colonization and exploitation. This license was granted on 26 August 1635, and on 3 November, Esteban Carbonel de Valenzuela presented a petition for the license to the viceroy, citing his experience as a pilot with Francisco de Ortega.[61]

Rather than rely on a monopoly, evidently the Marquis of Cadreita considered the privileges for exploration and colonization in California as competitive and, distinguishing between the latitudes set as goals, on 1 December granted Carbonel de Valenzuela's request and issued a license to him.[62] A few weeks later, on 29 December, Francisco de Vergara, a resident of Puebla, petitioned a license and offered to build a ship in Salagua for exploration and supply. Since Vergara's offer was to settle and exploit an area south of that described by Porter and Carbonel de Valenzuela, on 16 January 1636 he was also licensed by the viceroy to voyage to California under his specifically expressed terms.[63]

Coinciding with this intensification of interest in the Gulf of California

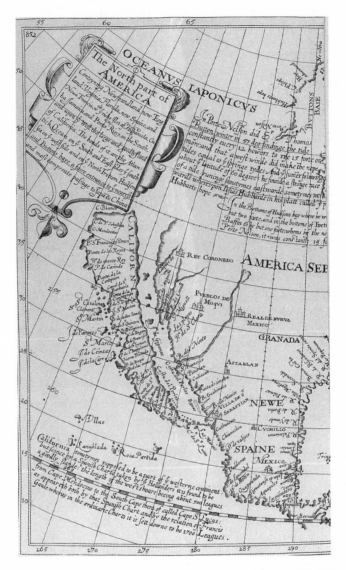

8.4 Western portion of the map of North America by Henry Briggs, published in Samuel Purchas, Hakluytus Posthumus or Purchas his Pilgrimes *(London, 1625). This detail shows the "island" of California, a geographical misconception that Briggs did much to perpetuate because of the popularity of his map. It was not until 1747 that, by royal decree of Ferdinand VI of Spain, California was declared not to be an island. Photo courtesy Edward E. Ayer Collection, The Newberry Library.*

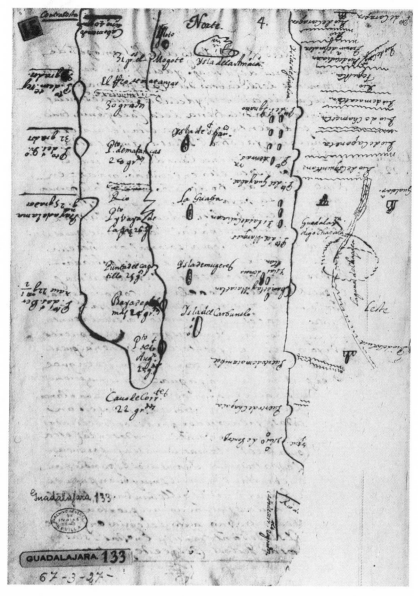

8.5 California in 1632. Manuscript map accompanying hearings held from 1628 to 1632, probably drawn by Fray Antonio de la Ascensión. Courtesy The Bancroft Library, University of California, Berkeley.

and its exploration, colonization, and development was the ultimate triumph of the geographical concepts of Fray Antonio de la Ascensión. In 1624, a curious small book entitled *West Indische Spieghel*, attributed to one Athanasium Inga, appeared from the presses of B. Janszoon and J. P. Wachter in Amsterdam. Included in the work was a map engraved by the cartographer Abraham Goos and titled "t'Norder deel van West-Indien"; this map initiated the reversal of the sixteenth-century cartographical depictions of California as a peninsula and began a century-long practice of showing it as a great offshore island extending from Cabo San Lucas to Cape Mendocino. The map incorporated names established by Vizcaíno as well as the ideas of Fray Antonio, probably taken from charts acquired by Joris van Spilbergen on the captured *San Francisco* of Nicolás de Cardona on the coast of Colima in 1615. Of far greater impact was the insular map published the following year in London by W. Stansby in the three-volume continuation of the work of Richard Hakluyt by Samuel Purchas, *Purchas his Pilgrimes*. Drawn by Henry Briggs and engraved by R. Elstrake, "A Treatise of the Northwest Passage to the South Sea through the Continent of Virginia and by Fretum Hudson" became the model for the great Dutch and French cartographers. It is not known if Fray Antonio was apprised of this immortalization of his geography, for shortly after requesting copies of the Ortega logs and diaries on 24 November 1635, he died at the Carmelite monastery in Puebla.[64]

In the interim, Ortega proceeded with the outfitting of a third voyage to California under the provisions of the license granted by the Marquis of Cerralvo. With his diving bell, Father Roque de Vega of the diocese of Guadalajara as chaplain, Cosme Lorenzo as pilot, and a crew of eighteen, Ortega sailed from Sinaloa on 11 January 1636, reaching the California coast south of La Paz three days later. Anchored outside the entrance to the Bahía de La Paz, the *Madre Luisa de la Ascención* was struck by a storm, which battered the ship for two nights and a day and drove it against the shore. Applying his skills as a professional shipbuilder, Ortega employed planking salvaged from the wreck and, working for forty-six days, succeeded in constructing a small sailing vessel in which to continue his voyage. On 10 March he sailed from La Paz to Cerralvo, then northward to San Jose and, anchoring and going ashore each night, reached San Lorenzo on 20 March. Pearl oyster beds were found, and the expedition proceeded to Tortugas, then along the peninsular coast to San Sebastián, which was considered cold in late April, and northward until 4 May, when Ortega turned southeastward toward the Sinaloa coast, where he arrived on 15 May.[65]

The loss of the *Madre Luisa de la Ascención* and his diving bell left Ortega unable to continue and, with three additional claimants to rights of exploration, colonization, and exploitation in California, virtually eliminated him from further operations. In light of these developments, Porter and Botello reiterated their petition and their offer to explore northward to the end of the gulf or to Anián, on 10 and 18 June and 17 September, in the last document citing extensive scholarly treatises on geography, diaries, reports, and cartographic evidence, such as the writings of José de Acosta, Bernabé Cobos, Alarcón, Francisco de Ibarra, Drake, Cavendish, Oliver van Noort, Jacob Lemaire, Vizcaíno, Ascensión, Juan de Oñate, Cardona, and Jodocus Hondius, demonstrating Porter's excellent knowledge of cosmography and navigation. On 23 September the license was granted; nevertheless, it, along with the others, was to be of little value.[66]

Failures and Decline

Competition for primacy in the California enterprise—for the imagined great fortunes in pearls, for the royal favor that led to successful colonization, and for the glory of becoming the discoverer and conqueror of Anián—was intensified by reports of the relative success of Ortega and led to unethical and illegal practices. Francisco de Vergara, unable to proceed with his project, transferred his license to one Francisco Esteban Carbonel without viceregal consent and, establishing a shipyard in Sentispac on the Río Santiago, began building a vessel for an expedition to California. If this unauthorized transfer was not sufficient cause to halt the project, several of the shipyard workers who had been dismissed reported that Carbonel and various others at the site were allegedly French; because foreigners had been expressly prohibited from participation in voyages of discovery and colonization, Carbonel, Vergara, and others in the company were arrested on 14 May and taken under guard to the jail of the Audiencia in Guadalajara.[67] Concerned with the possibility of more severe occurrences, on 11 November 1636 the Marquis of Cadreita decreed that all licenses for exploration in California, including that of Ortega, be revoked, that they be recovered by viceregal officials, and that anyone making a voyage to California would be subject to the death penalty and confiscation of property.[68]

On 30 April, in Guadalajara, the trial of Francisco Esteban Carbonel, Vergara, and their associates opened. Although several of the accused confessed to being multilingual in Mallorquín, Italian, and Valencian, the last being the language spoken at the times that they were reputedly speaking French, none admitted foreign nationality, and for three years the trial continued through lengthy testimony that, finally, after obtaining a baptismal certificate from Valencia, exonerated Carbonel.[69] Vergara, José Martín, and Carbonel were released from prison on 6 October 1640 by Viceroy Diego López Pacheco, Duke of Escalona, but Carbonel's long incarceration had left him bankrupt.[70] During the Carbonel trial, a petition for reconsideration of licensing was submitted by Porter and Botello but to no avail, and in 1636 Porter returned to Spain.[71]

En route to Europe, Porter's ship was captured by Dutch corsairs, and he was held hostage until 1637, when he was released in Cartagena. On his arrival in Spain, Porter rejoined the Spanish Armada and from 1638 to 1640 served against France. In the latter year, he revived his petitions for the license to California, and on 28 March the council of state recommended to the Crown that the license be granted.[72] Also in 1640, Nicolás de Cardona renewed his petition,[73] but it was overruled by a royal order of 8 August that granted Porter the traditional monopoly of discovery, colonization, and exploitation, without territorial limit to the north and with the title of admiral, to commence immediately.[74] Porter was called back into service, and from 1641 to 1643 he again served against France in the Mediterranean, having been knighted in the Order of Santiago in 1642.[75] With no reports of activity in California, Cardona filed a last petition for restoration of his rights in California in early 1643 but on 4 March was informed by the royal council in Madrid that the license had been granted to Pedro Porter y Casanate.[76]

On 12 March 1643 a royal order relieved Porter of duty in Europe and directed him to go to New Spain as quickly as possible to carry out the terms of his orders relative to California. Embarking at Cádiz with the fleet of general Francisco Díaz Pimienta on 2 June, Porter reached Cartagena in July and his final sailing destination of Veracruz on 22 August. Proceeding to Mexico City, he presented his royal orders to Viceroy García Sarmiento de Sotomayor, Count of Salvatierra, on 25 September and began the recruitment of men and the purchase of supplies. Arrangements were made to carry two Jesuits as chaplains and missionaries, command was given to Alonso González Barriga, who had accompanied him from Spain, and Porter proceeded to Guadalajara, where the Audiencia, on 13 November, gave him the use of a frigate for two years, along with the unfinished ships of the Vergara-Carbonel enterprise. Reports of a Dutch fleet off the coast of Chile altered the plans, however, and Porter offered to warn the Manila galleon off Cabo San Lucas using the frigate *Nuestra Señora del Rosario*. Remaining at Sentispac at the mouth of the Santiago River to oversee shipbuilding operations, Porter dispatched González on 9 January 1644. Sailing northward along the coast, González reached Mazatlán and from there proceeded to Cabo San Lucas, where he anchored on 27 January. Going ashore, he established twenty-four-hour sentinels on the highest hill of the cape, and on 31 January, González rounded San Lucas and sailed up the Pacific coast toward Isla de Cedros in search of the galleon. After three days of sailing against heavy northwest winds and currents, the frigate turned south and reached Cabo San Lucas on 4 February, where González was greeted by friendly Pericú Indians. After no sightings of ships during the following weeks, the expedition sailed for Santiago on 21 February and arrived four days later.[77]

Meanwhile, after assigning tasks and supervising the construction of housing at the shipyard, Porter had left on 15 January for Guadalajara and Mexico to continue the sending of supplies to the coast. In Mexico, on 5 March, Porter received the report of the safe return of his frigate, and on 1 April he left for Veracruz to obtain rigging, sailcloth, and anchors. Returning to Mexico on 28 April he was notified that, on 20 March, some of the crew had fled the shipyard with a boat and supplies; considering this of little consequence, Porter did not leave for Sentispac, and on 10 May the arrival of the post brought news of disaster. On 24 April the two ships under construction, one almost completed, as well as all of the storehouses, had been set ablaze by arsonists and entirely consumed. Led by Antonio González, who confessed that by destroying the enterprise, he hoped to be able to continue pearling without a license, the criminals were brought to trial in Guadalajara, but Porter was ruined. During 1645 and 1646, Porter sought funds in New Spain under authorization of a royal order of 11 October 1645, and in early 1647 he proceeded to the mouth of the Río Fuerte in Sinaloa to begin construction of two new frigates, the *Nuestra Señora del Pilar* and the *San Lorenzo*. Further aid came with a decree of 11 March 1647 naming Porter as governor of Sinaloa, a post that would provide him with a salary for underwriting his enterprise.[78]

With his two ships completed, on 23 October 1648 Porter and González, with Jesuit Fathers Jacinto Cortés and Andrés Báez as chaplain-missionaries, sailed from the Río Sinaloa, crossed the Gulf of California, and began charting and sounding northward along the coast and islands. The voyage continued until heavy currents threatened to force the ship aground in the Canal Salsipuedes in the northern gulf on 4 January 1649, and three days later the expedition returned to Sinaloa. Later in 1649 Porter sailed up the gulf to 31° north latitude, and on 19 November he was again ordered to the Pacific coast to warn the Manila galleon of a reported enemy fleet. Although he was able to carry out some exploration in 1650, his duties as governor of Sinaloa occupied most of Porter's time, and in 1652 he requested permission from Viceroy Luis Enríquez de Guzmán, Count of Alva de Aliste, to resign his post for reasons of health. On 8 November, Porter vacated his post, ceded his two frigates to the Crown, and traveled to Mexico to rest and regain his health. After three years, Porter had recovered; however, he did not return to the California venture, and on 30 October 1655 he was named captain-general of Chile, a post that he held until his death in Concepción on 27 February 1662.[79]

The lack of success in the California enterprise by a person as qualified as Pedro Porter y Casanate, who, although he recovered a few pearls, was far more oriented toward scientific observation, geographic discovery, and colonization, was at best disappointing and had a widespread negative effect. None of the investors in the pearl-fishing monopoly had profited or even succeeded in recovering their costs; none had established a long-term, much less permanent, settlement, notwithstanding the advances and development up the Nayarit-Sinaloa coast; and none had achieved any precise geographic knowledge that would absolutely confirm or deny the existence of the island of California or the Straits of Anián. Thus, despite the intense competition for rights in California during the period 1630–40, the decade following the resignation of Porter saw no activity until 12 February 1661. Basing his petition on his successes in 1632 and 1633–34 and on his failed efforts in 1636, Francisco de Ortega requested the reinstatement of the privileges of his license, reporting that he had six divers available. On 19 February, Viceroy Juan de Leyva, Count of Baños, favored him and on 16 March issued an order permitting Ortega to construct small boats and to hire paid Indian labor at any point along the western coast.[80]

The new attempt by Ortega did not come to fruition, although it did renew, albeit slightly, interest in California. On 22 August 1663, Bernardo Bernal de Piñadero, a mariner with twenty years of service in the West Indies and Venezuela, petitioned the viceroy for the rights and privileges extended to Porter relative to California and Sinaloa. A royal provision on 6 October, confirmed by the Count of Baños, provided Bernal with the title of admiral of the Californias and gave him the rights of exploration, colonization, and exploitation previously granted to Porter; however the provision specifically stated that it did not apply to the governorship of Sinaloa or provide for any salary of any kind.[81] Inflated with self-importance and armed with a staff of authority to emphasize his titles, Bernal began to recruit a crew under promises of great wealth to be obtained, and he prepared a small ship at Sentispac in Nayarit for a voyage into the gulf. Sailing in 1664, Bernal met with almost instant failure; having overworked his men, whose pay was dependent on a share of the pearls recovered, and having failed to discover productive oyster beds near Cerralvo and Espíritu Santo, he caused a mutiny. Although the mutiny was quelled, with Pedro de Escandón and Luis de Segura, two of the principals, cast ashore near Cerralvo, Bernal was confronted with such discontent that he was forced to return to Nayarit without any accomplishment whatsoever.[82]

Claiming that his lack of success was due to lawlessness and disrespect on the part of his crew, and emphasizing his intent to colonize California and bring its natives into Christianity, Bernal requested further powers on 26 April 1665. On 18 May a royal provision issued by Viceroy Antonio Sebastián de Toledo, Marquis of Mancera, granted him the title of lieutenant captain-general of California, without salary, and with it the right to recruit military personnel for service there, wherever he wished and under whatever terms he set forth.[83] Again with a sense of importance and power, Bernal sailed from the coast of Nayarit and returned after fifteen days, bringing a few small nuggets of gold and a few seed pearls. On this occasion, however, his errors were more severe than on his first voyage, for he had sailed without his chaplain, Father Juan Bautista Fernández of the diocese of Guadalajara, who had been left in Sentispac with orders to augment his supplies for Mass, thereby depriving his crew of the required spiritual care and administration of the sacraments. Furthermore, he falsely claimed to have reached the islands of the Gulf of California, when in reality he had gone only to the Tres Marías off the coast of Nayarit and up the coast to Mazatlán. As a result of these reports, and others relating to his abuse of Indian labor in Nayarit and the theft of produce and animals from Indian villages, as well as demands by his crew for payment for their services, Bernal's license was suspended, and he became involved in extensive litigation.[84]

With Bernal removed from the California enterprise, Francisco de Lucenilla, who had arrived in Mexico in September 1665 as a merchant, was encouraged by friends to petition for a viceregal license to replace Bernal, since the friends convinced Lucenilla that great wealth in pearls was to be obtained. Together with Alonso Mateos, Lucenilla presented his request, which, following the litigation with Bernal, was granted in January 1667. A shipyard was established at Chacala on the coast of Nayarit in February, and the construction of two small vessels was begun. By early 1668 the ships were completed, as was provisioning by 1 May, and on that morning, with a crew of fifty-one and Franciscan chaplain-missionaries Fathers Juan Cavallero Carranco and Juan Bautista Ramírez, Lucenilla and Mateos sailed for Mazatlán. After a difficult six-day crossing of the gulf, the expedition reached Bahía de las Palmas north of Cabo San Lucas on 20 May and from there proceeded northward toward La Paz. Bartering knives and trinkets with the Pericúes for pearls, they learned that Escandón and Segura had been killed by the Guaycura Indians. Passing Cerralvo, the expedition reached La Paz on 24 May. Due to the many bars and low tides in the bay, Lucenilla's ship went aground three days later, and when it was refloated, course was set for Isla Espíritu Santo, which was found to be unpopulated. Thus, unable to trade, the expedition proceeded to Cabo San Lucas, but again finding no worthwhile pearls, they followed a return course northward along the coast back to Espíritu Santo, where the crew began to demand to return to Sinaloa. Hoping to discover the promised wealth in pearls, Lucenilla continued heading north to Bahía Concepción; however, by 2 July, with no economic compensation and faced with mutiny, he sailed due eastward through heavy weather, making landfall near Guaymas in Sonora.[85]

The failure of Lucenilla gave new hope to Bernal, who, despite ongoing legal complications and accusations of fraud and abuse, petitioned for the right to make a third voyage, citing that he had three frigates under construction. His request was based on a royal order of 2 June 1668, which, due to a complete ignorance of events in distant Sinaloa, had specified full viceregal support of his endeavors, and on an attempt to ingratiate himself with the Society of Jesus, which maintained the missions of Nayarit, Sinaloa, and Sonora, by requesting Jesuit chaplain-missionaries for his expedition.[86] The tactics succeeded, and on 27 May 1669 the Marquis of Mancera granted the petition with a license to incorporate Jesuits into the expedition.[87] Nevertheless, Bernal was unable to proceed, and on 30 December 1671 he wrote to the Crown complaining of legal entanglements brought about by envy and greed, which had caused the loss of his frigates, and of great delays in aiding to bring missionaries to the Indians of California; he stated that he had made detailed rutters in the event of his death, and he requested appointment as governor of Sinaloa or any other assistance possible.[88]

Advised to proceed with caution by the Council of the Indies, on 29 June

1672 the regent, Mariana of Austria, requested further information from the viceroyalty of New Spain in order to verify Bernal's claims.[89] The Marquis of Mancera answered on 17 June 1673: Bernal was a greedy and not very bright subject who supposedly had made three voyages to the Gulf of California in ships that had been financed by people he had seduced into believing that great wealth would be obtained; he had even been so persuasive that he had obtained eight thousand pesos from the Society of Jesus, but he had returned with only a few seed pearls.[90] Bernal fully confirmed the viceroy's opinion of him by renewing his request for aid from the Crown on 12 July, thus raising greater suspicion, and by royal order of 11 November 1674, hearings were to be held to determine what had occurred in relation to the settlement of California, as well as to set future policy.[91]

Opening on 9 February 1676, this new series of hearings not only condemned the actions of Bernal but also, despite petitions by Nicolás Vizcaíno de Lezama and Juan Vizcaíno Urrutia de Contreras to continue the work of their grandfather, effectively terminated the policies that had been initiated through Sebastián Vizcaíno eight decades earlier. As evidence and accusations against Bernal increased, the hearings were extended to the Audiencia of Guadalajara, where lengthy investigations confirmed them, and on 3 August 1678 Viceroy Archbishop Fray Payo de Rivera Enríquez remitted the testimony to the Crown.[92] In answer, a royal order of 29 December 1679 relieved Bernal of all of his titles and privileges and authorized the viceroy to punish him as he deserved.[93] The scandal arising out of the California enterprise during the preceding fifteen years also produced a new policy for colonization of the region, and on 29 December 1679 another royal order authorized Isidro de Atondo y Antillón, as admiral of the Californias, to conduct missionaries of the Society of Jesus across the Gulf of California and to support and supply them in their attempt to found a mission, which would be financed from the bequest provided for that purpose by Alonso Fernández de la Torre, a wealthy sugar plantation owner in Nayarit, on his death in 1671.[94]

The royal order of 1679 marked the end of an era. For almost a century and a half California, the westernmost edge of North America from Cabo San Lucas northward, had resisted Spanish settlement, whether financed by the Crown or by private enterprise. The former methods had failed because of the many more pressing financial commitments of the monarchy and the highly varying opinions as to the optimum location of colonies; the latter had failed because of excessive optimism concerning the wealth of

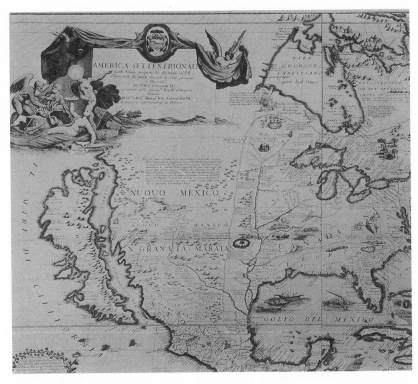

8.6 "America Septentrionale" (detail), by Vincenzo M. Coronelli, published in V. M. Coronelli, Atlante veneto *(Venice, 1690). This late-seventeenth-century map shows the consequences of 150 years of Spanish exploration along the western coasts of North America. The slowness with which Spanish information entered the mainstream of geographical knowledge is indicated by the errors still extant on the map. Courtesy The Newberry Library.*

the area and the greed and corruption generated by it. Both systems had failed because of the isolation of California, the problems of provisioning it from distant ports, and misconceptions of geography. During the seventeenth century, the advance northward along the coasts of Sinaloa and Sonora by missionaries of the Society of Jesus brought agriculture and livestock raising to those areas and, subsequently, civilian settlers, the development of anchorages, and a system of communication and transportation by land and sea. With this base of support for supplies and personnel directly across the Gulf of California from the arid peninsula, by 1680 it was highly feasible to take advantage of the final remaining attraction to the area: the conversion of native peoples to Christianity through missions. The success of this policy during the following century and a half extended the Spanish Empire northward along the Pacific coast to Alaska, resolved the question of the insularity of California, and relegated the Straits of Anián and the wealthy amazons of Calafia to mythology.

Notes

Introduction to Volume 1

1. Martyn J. Bowden, "The Invention of American Tradition," *Journal of Historical Geography* 18, 1 (1992): 3–26.

2. James P. Ronda, *The Exploration of North America* (Washington DC, 1992), x.

3. Much of what follows is derived from the author's essay "New World Encounters," *Great Plains Quarterly* 13, 2 (1993): 69–80.

4. Ted C. Hinckley, "Vanishing Truth and Western History," *Journal of the West* 31 (1992): 3.

5. Richard White, *"It's Your Misfortune and None of My Own": A History of the American West* (Norman, 1991), 119.

6. Kirkpatrick Sale, *The Conquest of Paradise: Christopher Columbus and the Columbian Legacy* (New York, 1990).

7. John K. Wright, "Where History and Geography Meet: Recent American Studies in the History of Exploration," *Proceedings of the Eighth Annual American Scientific Congress* 10 (1943): 17–23, reprinted in John K. Wright, *Human Nature in Geography* (Cambridge MA, 1966), 24–32.

8. See, for example, Bernard DeVoto, *The Course of Empire* (Boston, 1952).

9. Edmundo O'Gorman, *The Invention of America* (Bloomington, 1961).

10. John K. Wright, "Terrae Incognitae: The Place of the Imagination in Geography," *Annals of the Association of American Geographers* 37 (1947): 1–15.

11. DeVoto, *Course of Empire*, ix.

1. Pre-Columbian Discoveries and Exploration

1. Cecil Jane, ed., *The Voyages of Christopher Columbus* (London, 1930), 259.

2. The initial date of arrival south of the ice and the primary role of the ice-free corridor continue to be controversial. Recent work in Alberta and British Columbia suggests that there was no human presence between 20,000 and 14,000 years ago; the first evidence of human occupance in the corridor dates to 10,700 before the present. If earlier dates for sites farther south are confirmed, this may invalidate the "ice-free corridor" theory and suggest that the initial Paleo-Indian advance into the continent came down the Pacific coast. See James A. Burns, "Paleontological

Perspectives on the Ice-Free Corridor," and George C. Frison, "Clovis, Goshen, and Folsom: Lifeways and Cultural Relationships," both in Larry D. Agenbroad, Jim I. Mead, and Lisa W. Nelson, eds., *Megafauna and Man: Discovery of America's Heartland* (Hot Springs SD, 1990).

3. Robert McGhee, *The Tuniit: First Explorers of the High Arctic* (Ottawa, 1981).

4. Sources used to describe the historical Saint Brendan are the following: John J. O'Meara's introduction to his translation of *Voyage of Saint Brendan: Journey to the Promised Land (Navigatio Sancti Brendani Abbatis)* (Atlantic Highlands NJ, 1976); Rev. Denis O'Donoghue's hagiographical but comprehensive *Brendaniana: St. Brendan the Voyager in Story and Legend* (Dublin, 1893); Geoffrey Ashe's speculative *Land to the West: St. Brendan's Voyage to America* (New York, 1962); and Carl Selmer's introductory chapter in his edited version of *Navigatio Sancti Brendani Abbatis: From Early Latin Manuscripts* (Dublin, 1989).

5. A. L. Moir, "The World Map in Hereford Cathedral" (paper read to the Woolhope Naturalists' Field Club, Hereford, U.K., November 1954).

6. R. A. Skelton, Thomas E. Marston, and George D. Painter, *The Vinland Map and the Tartar Relation* (New Haven, 1965), 137–38. The controversial "Vinland Map," dated by the authors to 1440, shows the Azores as "Magnae Insulae Beati Brandani Branziliae dictae."

7. Timothy Severin, *The Brendan Voyage* (London, 1978).

8. Selmer, *Navigatio*, xx–xxv.

9. See S. Baring-Gould and John Fisher, *The Lives of the British Saints*, 3 vols. (London, 1907), 1:233–62.

10. For a full discussion of the Madoc legend in America, see Bernard DeVoto, *The Course of Empire* (Boston, 1952), 68–73, 373–79, 470–71, 568–70, nn. 7, 8, 11, 12.

11. Gwyn A. Williams, *Madoc: The Making of a Myth* (London, 1979), 39 and plate 2. The ensuing discussion relies greatly on this critical and authoritative reference.

12. Williams, *Madoc*, 41.

13. J. B. Morris, trans. and ed., *Hernando Cortés: Five Letters, 1519–1526* (London, 1929), 72.

14. Richard Hakluyt, *Discourse of Western Planting* (1584), edited by Charles Deane as vol. 2 of *The Documentary History of the State of Maine* (Cambridge MA, 1877), 118–19.

15. Williams, *Madoc*, 45–46.

16. Richard Hakluyt, *The Principall Navigations, Voiages, and Discoveries of the English Nation* (imprinted at London, 1589) (reprint, London, 1965), 506.

17. Williams, *Madoc*, 49.

18. Williams, *Madoc*, 51–52. Williams goes on to make a connection between the

Madoc romance and an episode in the *Orkneyinga Saga* by equating the island of Ely with Lundy Island in the Bristol Channel, and Madoc with an unnamed "Freeman of Wales," half-Viking, who retreated to Lundy Island after ravaging the Southern Isles, Tyree, and the Isle of Man and suffering retaliation by Icelanders. Reference to Herman Pálsson and Paul Edwards, trans., *Orkneyinga Saga* (London, 1978), chap. 78, reveals that Williams's "Freeman" was "a chieftain of Wales, a man called Robert, of English descent," and that his victims and pursuers were Hebridean and Orcadian Norse. Williams's argument seems both garbled and unwarranted.

19. F. W. Lucas, *The Annals of the Voyages of the Brothers Nicolo and Antonio Zeno in the North Atlantic about the End of the Fourteenth Century and the Claim Founded Thereon to a Venetian Discovery of America: A Criticism and Indictment* [with an English version of that part of the work entitled "Dello scoprimento dell'Isole Frislanda," etc.] (London, 1898).

20. Lucas, *Annals of the Voyages*. See also Skelton, Marston, and Painter, *Vinland Map*, 197 n. C.

21. Skelton, Marston, and Painter, *Vinland Map*, 198 and plates 18 and 19.

22. F. W. Lucas, *Appendiculae Historicae; or, Shreds of History Hung on a Horn* (London, 1891), 8.

23. Personal communication to the author, from Dr. Selma de Lotbinière Barkham.

24. Robert McGhee, *Ancient Canada* (Ottawa, 1989), 168. See also Warren Cook, "Tempest over Ancient America: A Review Article on the Vermont Conference of 1977 on Transoceanic Contacts," *Terrae Incognitae* 10 (1978): 81–85, and Eugene R. Fingerhut, *Who First Discovered America?* (Claremont CA, 1984).

25. Finn Gad, *The History of Greenland*, vol. 1, *Earliest Times to 1700*, translated from the Danish (1967) by Ernst Dupont (London, 1970), 217–37.

26. See the chapter on "Printing in Iceland in the Sixteenth and Seventeenth Centuries" in Finnbogi Gudmundsson, *Icelandic Sagas, Eddas, and Art: Treasures Illustrating the Greatest Mediaeval Literary Heritage of Northern Europe* (New York, 1982).

27. David Macpherson, *Annals of Commerce, Manufactures, Fisheries, and Navigation*, 3 vols. (London, 1805), 1:280 and footnote.

28. *Encyclopedia Britannica* (1969), 16:375. See also Helge Ingstad, *Westward to Vinland* (Toronto, 1969), 90, 100.

29. Magnus Magnusson, *Viking Expansion Westwards* (London, 1973), 141–43; Anne Stine Ingstad, *The Norse Discovery of America*, trans. Elizabeth Seeberg, 2 vols. (Oslo, 1985), 2:432; McGhee, *Ancient Canada*, 168.

30. Magnusson, *Viking Expansion Westwards*, 143; Anne Stine Ingstad, *Norse Discovery of America* 2:430, 432; McGhee, *Ancient Canada*, 168.

31. Magnusson, *Viking Expansion Westwards*, 143, 144; Anne Stine Ingstad, *Norse Discovery of America* 2:428.

32. Helge Ingstad, *Land under the Pole Star* (London, 1966), a translation of the Norwegian original of 1959.

33. Birgitta Linderoth Wallace, "The L'Anse aux Meadows Site," appendix 7 in Gwyn Jones, *The Norse Atlantic Saga, Being the Norse Voyages of Discovery and Settlement to Iceland, Greenland, and North America*, 2d ed. (New York, 1986), 286.

34. Jones, *Norse Atlantic Saga*, 300–302.

35. Anne Stine Ingstad, *Norse Discovery of America* 1:457. The best discussion of the radiocarbon dates is in Reidar Nydal, "Radiocarbon Dating of Material from L'Anse aux Meadows," chap. 12 in Anne Stine Ingstad, *Norse Discovery of America* 2:363–76. See also Wallace, "L'Anse aux Meadows Site," 296–97, and Alan Macpherson in Richard Colebrook Harris, ed., *Historical Atlas of Canada*, vol. 1, *From the Beginning to 1800* (Toronto, 1987), plate 16. The more precise date comes from W. E. Kieser, "Radiocarbon Dating by Accelerator Mass Spectrometry: Principles and Applications," chap. 6 in *Examples and Critiques of Quaternary Dating Methods* (Short Course 3, First Joint Meeting, Canadian Quaternary Association/American Quaternary Association, Quaternary Sciences Institute, University of Waterloo, Waterloo, Ontario, 4–6 June 1990).

36. Gad, *History of Greenland*, 18–19.

37. Gad, *History of Greenland*, 36–39, 74–76, 80–82.

38. Gad, *History of Greenland*, 41–42.

39. Macpherson, plate 16 in Harris, *Historical Atlas of Canada*.

40. Gad, *History of Greenland*, 86, 103, 136–38.

41. Thomas H. McGovern, "The Economics of Extinction in Norse Greenland," chap. 17 in T. M. L. Wigley, M. J. Ingram, and G. Farmer, eds., *Climate and History: Studies in Past Climates and Their Impact on Man* (Cambridge, U.K., 1981).

42. Norse expansion across the Atlantic through the Faeroes and Iceland was preceded by Irish monastic colonies. In the *Islendingabók*, for example, Thórgilsson noted as a matter of some importance: "There were Christian men here then whom the Norsemen called 'papar.' But later they went away because they were not prepared to live here in company with heathen men. They left behind Irish books, bells, and croziers, from which it could be seen that they were Irishmen." See Jones, *Norse Atlantic Saga*, 144.

43. Anne Savage, trans., *The Anglo-Saxon Chronicles* (London, 1983), 73. The references to attacks on Lindisfarne and Jarrow in A.D. 793 and 794 come from the same source.

44. Jones, *Norse Atlantic Saga*, 37.

45. Gudbrandur Vigfússon and F. York Powell, eds., *Origines Islandicae: A Collection of the More Important Sagas and Other Native Writings Relating to the Settlement and Early History of Iceland*, 3 vols. (Oxford, U.K., 1905), 1:16.

46. Vigfússon and Powell, *Origines Islandicae* 1:15–17; Jones, *Norse Atlantic Saga*, 157–59; Hermann Pálsson and Paul Edwards, *The Book of Settlements, Landnámabók* (Winnipeg, Manitoba, 1972), 17. The analysis of the Iceland and Greenland cycles is largely drawn from these references.

47. Jones, *Norse Atlantic Saga*, 188–91; Magnus Magnusson and Hermann Pálsson, trans., *The Vinland Sagas: The Norse Discovery of America* (Hammondsworth, U.K., 1965), 51–54.

48. The dates in the following pages vary from those listed in Alan Cooke and Clive Holland, *The Exploration of Northern Canada: A Chronology* (Toronto, 1978), 13. Critical discussions are in Jones, *Norse Atlantic Saga*, 135 n. 19, and in Vigfússon and Powell, *Origines Islandicae* 2:591–95. See also Olafur Halldórsson, "The Vinland Voyages," in Charles Ryskamp, ed., *Icelandic Sagas, Eddas, and Art* (New York, 1982), 59–60, where it is argued that Thórfinn Karlsefni and Gudrid Thórbjornsdottir could not have been in Vinland before A.D. 1020–25.

49. Magnusson and Pálsson, *Vinland Sagas*, 56; Helge Ingstad, *Westward to Vinland*, 42 and footnote. See also Jones, *Norse Atlantic Saga*, 193 and footnote 4.

50. Magnusson and Pálsson, *Vinland Sagas*, 57–58.

51. Jones, *Norse Atlantic Saga*, 195.

52. Jones, *Norse Atlantic Saga*, 200.

53. Jones, *Norse Atlantic Saga*, 202.

54. Jones, *Norse Atlantic Saga*, 204.

55. Jones, *Norse Atlantic Saga*, 205; Magnusson and Pálsson, *Vinland Sagas*, 70–71.

56. *Landnamabók* lists Snorri Thórbrandsson as one of Eirík Rauda's original Greenland settlers of A.D. 986. *Eyrbyggia Saga*, on the other hand, indicates that Snorri and his brother Thórleif joined the Greenland colonists later in the tenth century (Vigfússon and Powell, *Origines Islandicae* 2:132). In either case, Snorri's partnership with Thórfinn seems unlikely.

57. Magnusson and Pálsson, *Vinland Sagas*, 94–95.

58. Magnusson and Pálsson, *Vinland Sagas*, 98.

59. Magnusson and Pálsson, *Vinland Sagas*, 98, 100.

60. Jones, *Norse Atlantic Saga*, 229.

61. Magnusson and Pálsson, *Vinland Sagas*, 101, 102.

62. Jones, *Norse Atlantic Saga*, 123.

63. Anne Stine Ingstad, *Norse Discovery of America* 1:315, 320–21, 346.

64. Helge Ingstad, *Westward to Vinland*, 70–75; Fridtjof Nansen, *In Northern Mists: Arctic Exploration in Early Times*, 2 vols., trans. Arthur G. Chater (London, 1911), 2:24, 58–59, 64; Jones, *Norse Atlantic Saga*, 283–85. See also Anne Stine Ingstad, *Norse Discovery of America* 2:310–12.

65. Jones, *Norse Atlantic Saga*, 124; Helge Ingstad, *Westward to Vinland*, 74–75.

66. See Jones, *Norse Atlantic Saga*, 122–24 and footnote 6; Helge Ingstad, *Westward to Vinland*, 75–76; and Anne Stine Ingstad, *Norse Discovery of America*, 307–13.

67. Jones, *Norse Atlantic Saga*, 20.

68. Jones, *Norse Atlantic Saga*, 22.

69. Jones, *Norse Atlantic Saga*, 17, 18, and footnote 9.

70. Skelton, Marston, and Painter, *Vinland Map*, 204. See also Skelton in W. P. Cumming, R. A. Skelton, and D. B. Quinn, *The Discovery of North America* (London, 1971), 38.

71. Cumming, Skelton, and Quinn, *Discovery of North America*, 227 and illustration 272 with accompanying text. See also Skelton, Marston, and Painter, *Vinland Map*, Plate XIX.

72. Skelton, Marston, and Painter, *Vinland Map*, 204.

73. Vigfússon and Powell, *Origines Islandicae* 2:640.

74. Vigfússon and Powell, *Origines Islandicae* 1:94 (*Landnamabók* II.19.1).

75. Vigfússon and Powell, *Origines Islandicae* 2:132 (*Eyrbyggia Saga* 47).

76. Vigfússon and Powell, *Origines Islandicae* 2:627–28.

77. Vigfússon and Powell, *Origines Islandicae* 2:136.

78. E. G. R. Taylor, "A Letter Dated 1577 from Mercator to John Dee," *Imago Mundi* 13 (1956): 66.

79. Jones, *Norse Atlantic Saga*, 95.

80. Taylor, "Letter Dated 1577," 66; Jones, *Norse Atlantic Saga*, 101.

81. Taylor, "Letter Dated 1577," 58–59, 66–67. The report is from Professor Taylor's "rather free translation" of John Dee's *Volume of Great and Rich Discoveries*, in Cotton MS Vitellius C. VII: f.264 *et seq.*, British Museum, London.

82. Taylor, "Letter Dated 1577."

83. Hakluyt, *Principall Navigations*, 249. Another translation appears in B. van 'T Hoff's introduction to *Gerard Mercator's Map of the World (1569)*, Publication No. 6, Prins Hendrik Maritime Museum, and *Imago Mundi*, Supplement No. 2 (Rotterdam, 1961).

84. Taylor, "Letter Dated 1577," 59, 67; Skelton, Marston, and Painter, *Vinland Map*, 180. Dee apparently favoured Nicholas of Lynn, an Oxford mathematician but a Carmelite. Taylor suggests either Thomas Kingsbury, another Oxford mathematician and a Minorite friar of the period, or Hugh of Ireland.

85. Mercator's *Map of the World (1569)* could owe nothing to the English Minorite's lost account for the shores of North America between 54° and 70° north. Instead, he drew on the results of Gaspar Côrte-Real's voyage of 1500 and the fictitious "Zeno Narrative and Map of 1558," designating southern and northern Labrador as "Terra Corterealis" and "Estotilant," respectively.

86. Taylor, "Letter Dated 1577," 66–67.

87. The catalogue of Mercator's library was lost in 1915. It is impossible, therefore, to determine whether he used other sources on Greenland from which he might have obtained the term.

88. W. Dansgaard et al., "Climatic Changes, Norsemen, and Modern Man," *Nature* 225 (1975): 24–28.

89. A. Teixeira da Mota, *Portuguese Navigations in the North Atlantic in the Fifteenth and Sixteenth Centuries* (St. John's, Newfoundland, 1965), 2, 6–9, 16. See also Damido Peres, *A History of the Portuguese Discoveries* (Lisbon, 1960), 27–72.

90. Teixeira da Mota, *Navigations in the North Atlantic*, 7, 9; Peres, *Portuguese Discoveries*, 30–31, 34.

91. Peres, *Portuguese Discoveries*, 30–31, 34.

92. Peres, *Portuguese Discoveries*, 52–53. Peres's "reasonable conjecture"—that de Teive's voyage of discovery took him from Flores to Ireland, thence around Iceland, down the East Greenland coast, and across to Newfoundland before making his way back to Terceira—is unreasonable and unfounded.

93. David B. Quinn, ed., *America from Concept to Discovery* (New York, 1979), 75 n. 33.

94. Quinn, *America*, 77.

95. Peres, *Portuguese Discoveries*, 24–25.

96. Henry the Navigator and his brothers, King Duarte and Pedro of Coimbra, as grandsons of John of Gaunt, were full cousins of Philippa, daughter of Henry IV of England and wife of Erik VII of Denmark, Norway, and Sweden.

97. Nansen, *In Northern Mists* 2:125.

98. Nansen, *In Northern Mists* 2:126–27. Grip's letter came to light in 1909. See also Jones, *Norse Atlantic Saga*, 104 n. 29.

99. Nansen, *In Northern Mists* 2:359.

100. Nansen, *In Northern Mists* 2:132 n. 2.

101. Skelton, Marston, and Painter, *Vinland Map*, plate 19. Resen followed Cornelius Wytfliet (1597) in referring to Scolvus, erroneously, as a Pole (*Polonus*). The polar island appears on Mercator's "World Map" of 1569 as "Groclant."

102. James A. Williamson, *The Voyages of the Cabots and the English Discovery of North America under Henry VII and Henry VIII* (London, 1929), 25–26 n. 16. Williamson quoted the date as in the original document: "1496, March 5" (Treaty Roll 178, membre. 81), but this was under the unreformed Julian calendar in which 25 March was the first day of the year "1497." Under the modern Gregorian calendar, the date would have been in March 1497.

103. Williamson, *Voyages of the Cabots*, 18–19. See also Quinn *America*, 94, and E. M. Carus-Wilson, "The Overseas Trade of Bristol in the Middle Ages" *Bristol Record Society Publications* 7 (1937): 157–58, for another translation.

104. Bernard G. Hoffman, *Cabot to Cartier: Sources for a Historical Ethnography of Northeastern North America, 1497–1550* (Toronto, 1961), 8, following Carus-Wilson, "Overseas Trade of Britol," 164. Quinn, *America*, 92, gives a different transliteration.

105. The Andreas Bianca map, 1436, in Williamson, *Voyages of the Cabots*, 126 and opposite page; the Andrea Benincasa map, 1470, and the Alonzo de Santa Cruz map, 1545, in Cumming, Skelton, and Quinn, *Discovery of North America*, 41 nn. 35, 36. The island made its first appearance on Dalorta's map of 1325 and did not finally disappear from hydrographic charts until 1865. See Hoffman, *Cabot to Cartier*, 8.

106. James A. Williamson, *The Cabot Voyages and Bristol Discoveries under Henry VII*, Hakluyt Society, 2d ser., no. 120 (Cambridge, U.K., 1962), Document 25. The John Day letter was discovered in the Archive General del Reino at Simancas in 1956 and was communicated by Dr. L. A. Vigneras in two articles: "New Light on the 1497 Cabot Voyage" (with Spanish text), *Hispanic-American Historical Review* 36 (1956): 507–9, and "The Cape Breton Landfall: 1494 or 1497? Note on a Letter by John Day" (English translation), *Canadian Historical Review* 33 (1957): 226–28.

107. Williamson, *Voyages of the Cabots*, 39 n. 33.

108. Quinn, *America*, 92 (no. 49). See Williamson, *The Cabot Voyages*, 26, for a different transcription. This reveals, in one vital particular, that the original document read "the pylots mynde," leaving it open to the interpretation that there was only one pilot.

109. Williamson, *Voyages of the Cabots*, 130–31.

110. Williamson, *The Cabot Voyages*, 27–28.

111. Williamson, *Voyages of the Cabots*, 165–66.

112. Williamson, *Voyages of the Cabots*, 149–53; Williamson, *The Cabot Voyages*, 19–32; David Beers Quinn, *England and the Discovery of America, 1481–1620, from the Bristol Voyages of the Fifteenth Century to the Pilgrim Settlement at Plymouth: The Exploration, Exploitation, and Trial-by-Error Colonization of North America by the English* (New York, 1974), 5–23; Patrick McGrath, "Bristol and America, 1480–1631," in K. R. Andrews, N. P. Canny, and P. E. H. Hair, eds., *The Westward Enterprise: English Activities in Ireland, the Atlantic, and America, 1480–1650* (Liverpool, 1978), 81–87.

2. Native North Americans' Cosmological Ideas and Geographical Awareness

1. The first, and arguably clearest, modern statement of these and related ideas is in David Lowenthal, "Geography, Experience, and Imagination: Towards a Geographical Epistemology," *Annals of the Association of American Geographers* 51 (1961): 241–60.

2. Cadwallader Colden, "Memorial to the Honourable George Clarke Esq. Lieutenant Governor of the Province of New York Ec., New York, November 3, 1736," *The Letters and Papers of Cadwallader Colden . . . 1711–1775*, 3 vols. (New York, 1918), 2:158.

3. Louis A. de L. d'A. Lahontan, *New Voyages to North America*, 2 vols. (London, 1703), 2:15. More than one hundred years before Lahontan, Thomas Hariot observed that "Mathematicall instruments sea Compasses . . . a perspective glasse . . . spring-clockes that seeme to goe of themselves . . . so farre exceeded" the capacity of the Indians of Virginia "to comprehend . . . [that] they thought they were rather the workes of gods than of men." "A Briefe and True Report of the New Found Land of Virginia," in Richard Hakluyt, *The Principal Navigations, Voiages, Traffiques, and Discoveries . . .* , 3 vols. (London, 1600), 3:277. In 1566 Pedro Menéndez de Avilés "carried with him many written words in the Indian language, which were very polite and friendly, in order that he might speak to" the natives in Florida. When he addressed them in their own language, however, "they thought that the paper spoke." Pedro Menéndez de Avilés, *Memorial by Gonzalo Solis de Meras . . .* , ed. and trans. Jeanette Connor (De Land FL, 1923), 147.

4. Roland Chardon, "The Linear League in North America," *Annals of the Association of American Geographers* 70 (1980): 129–43.

5. "A Letter Written to M. John Growte Student in Paris, by Jaques Noel of S. Malo . . . 19 Day of June, 1587," in Hakluyt, *Principal Navigations* 3:236.

6. James A. Robertson, ed. and trans., *True Relation of the Hardships Suffered by Governor Fernando de Soto . . .* , 2 vols. (De Land FL, 1932), 199. This assumption of eight leagues per day in the lower Mississippi Valley does not agree well with the five leagues per day used at approximately the same date in the Southwest or the three to four leagues per day reported a few years later in relation to a proposed journey from Fort Saint Augustine, Florida. See Pedro de Castañeda in George P. Hammond and Agapito Rey, eds., *Narratives of the Coronado Expedition, 1539–1542* (Albuquerque, 1940), 195, and "October 15, 1565, Pedro Menéndez de Avilés to Philip II," in Henry Ware, "Letters of Pedro Menéndez de Avilés," *Massachusetts Historical Society Proceedings*, 2d ser., 8 (1894): 426.

7. Arthur T. Adams, ed., *The Explorations of Pierre Esprit Radisson . . .* (Minneapolis, 1961), 64.

8. Guillaume de l'Isle, "Tire de la Relation de la N. Ile france en 1657 et 1658," NA 178-1-25, Karpinski Scrapbook, Newberry Library, Chicago. This factor of twice as fast downstream as upstream was probably an average. It does not compare well with a factor of times four instanced as a particular case by Ralph Lane in Virginia in 1586. See "An Account of the Particularities of the Imployments of the English Men Left in Virginia . . . ," in Hakluyt, *Principal Navigations* 3:259.

9. One early exception states that in Virginia a three days' journey for a laden Indian was "twenty-five or thirty leagues," that is, eight to ten leagues per day. See "Vincente González's Recollections of the 1588 Voyage," in David B. Quinn, ed., *The Roanoke Voyages, 1584–1590*, 2 vols. (Cambridge, U.K., 1955), 2:823.

10. Pierre J. de Smet, *Letters and Sketches with a Narrative of a Year's Residence among the Indian Tribes of the Rocky Mountains* (Philadelphia, 1843), 155.

11. William M. Denevan, ed., *The Native Population of the Americas in 1492* (Madison WI, 1976), 291; Ann F. Ramenofsky, *Vectors of Death: The Archaeology of European Contact* (Albuquerque, 1987), 7.

12. Ian Tattersall et al., *Encyclopedia of Human Evolution and Prehistory* (New York, 1988), 26.

13. "The Narrative of Alvar Núñez Cabeza de Vaca," in Frederick W. Hodge and Theodore H. Lewis, eds., *Spanish Explorers of the Southern United States, 1528–1543* (New York, 1907), 22.

14. Willard Walker, "Zuni Semantic Categories," in William C. Sturtevant, gen. ed., *Handbook of North American Indians*, 15 vols. (Washington DC, 1976–88), 9:510.

15. Robert F. Heizer, "Natural Forces and Native World View" and "Mythology: Regional Patterns and History of Research," in Sturtevant, *Handbook of North American Indians* 8:651, 655, derived from Thomas T. Waterman, "Yurok Geography," *University of California Publications in American Archaeology and Ethnology* 16 (1920): 179–314.

16. Hugh Brody, *Maps and Dreams* (London, 1982), 266–69.

17. The limited concern for these closely related topics doubtless reflects a lack of awareness of their importance. Carl Ortwin Sauer, for long the doyen of American historical-cultural geography, provides an interesting example of this lack of awareness. His last major work, *Sixteenth Century North America: The Land and the People as Seen by the Europeans* (Berkeley, 1971), is permeated with environmental insights and repeatedly draws attention to spatial relationships. Notwithstanding the subtitle, however, there is almost nothing about Indian influences on the Europeans' perception of the land. Karen O. Kupperman, *Settling with the Indians: The Meeting of English and Indian Cultures in America, 1580–1640* (Totowa NJ, 1980), is in the tradition of modern thematic history; the second part of her work is titled "English Culture Confronts Indian Culture." Even so, as in Sauer, there is remarkably little on Indian influences on the development of European ideas about the land. Kupperman is not, however, unaware of these: "No secret was made of the fact that the colonists relied almost entirely on Indian information to learn about the geography and natural resources of America" (p. 96). Though the remaining eight pages of the chapter contain examples of information about native resources and native technology,

there is almost nothing concerning native information about place, environment, or spatial relationships.

18. It could, of course, be argued that the European invasion was not the last but that the migration of Chinese labourers to California after the American Civil War was the earliest phase of a fifth invasion that has accelerated in recent decades with the arrival of immigrants from several parts of eastern Asia.

19. "Beringia: The Chronology of the Ice Ages," in Chris. Scarre, ed., *Past Worlds: The Times Atlas of Archaeology* (London, 1988), 71. The first *Homo sapiens* probably entered the Americas during or before the so-called First Mid-Wisconsin emergence of Beringia, which was at its maximum at approximately 43,000 B.P. The next emergence was at its maximum at approximately 30,000 B.P., by which time South America had probably been peopled. The most recent emergence was at its maximum at approximately 18,000 B.P. by which time there were people in most parts of the Americas.

20. Bartolome Barrieritos, "Vida y Hechos de Pedro Menéndez de Avilés . . . ," in Anthony Kerrigan, ed. and trans., *Pedro Menéndez de Avilés, Founder of Florida* (Gainesville, 1965), 26.

21. These ideas concerning the three cultures are derived from Terence Grieder, *Origins of Pre-Columbian Art* (Austin, 1982). His figure 1 shows their distribution in "recent times within Australasia, Polynesia, Indonesia, south and east Asia and the Americas." Paul Shao's book *Asiatic Influences in Pre-Columbian American Art* (Ames IA, 1976), though conceptually weaker than Grieder's, marshals a great deal of evidence linking third-wave art in Central America and Asia. Grieder's hypothesis is beginning to receive independent support from work on the distribution of genetic markers in living Native Americans, although the two bodies of evidence do not match perfectly. See Robert C. Williams et al., "G. M. Allotypes in Native Americans: Evidence for Three Distinct Migrations across the Bering Land Bridge," *American Journal of Physical Anthropology* 66 (1985): 1–19.

22. Chrétien Le Clerq, *New Relation of Gaspesia, with the Customs and Religion of the Gaspesian Indians . . .* , ed. and trans. William F. Ganong (Toronto, 1910), 136.

23. Joseph F. Lafitau, *Customs of the American Indians Compared with Customs of Primitive Times*, eds. and trans. William N. Fenton and Elizabeth L. Moore (Toronto, 1974), 130.

24. John G. E. Heckewelder, "An Account of the History, Manners, and Customs of the Indian Nations Who Once Inhabited Pennsylvania and the Neighbouring States," *Transactions of the Committee of History, Moral Science, and General Literature of the American Philosophical Society* 1 (1819): 306.

25. Hammond and Rey, *Narratives of the Coronado Expedition*, 242.

26. Richard E. Hughes and James A. Bennyhoff, "Early Trade [in the Great Basin]," in Sturtevant, *Handbook of North American Indians* 11:239, 249.

27. James V. Wright, "Prehistory of the Canadian Shield," in Sturtevant, *Handbook of North American Indians* 6:90.

28. James E. Fitting, "Regional Cultural Development [in the Northeast], 300 B.C. to A.D. 1000," in Sturtevant, *Handbook of North American Indians* 15:45.

29. Robert McGhee, "Thule Prehistory of Canada," in Sturtevant, *Handbook of North American Indians* 5:374.

30. Richard I. Ford, "Inter-Indian Exchange in the Southwest," in Sturtevant, *Handbook of North American Indians* 10:712.

31. Grieder, *Origins of Pre-Columbian Art*, 79–80.

32. "The Proceedings of the English Colony in Virginia, Taken Faithfully out of the Writings of Thomas Studley . . . ," in Samuel Purchas, *Purchas His Pilgrimes*, 4 vols. (London, 1625), 4:170.

33. Thomas T. Waterman, "Yurok Geography," *University of California Publications in American Archaeology and Ethnology* 35 (1920): 191.

34. Gonzalo F. de Oviedo y Valdés, *Historia general y natural de las Indias occidentales* (Seville, 1535), book 16, chap. 11, English translation in David Beers Quinn, Alison Quinn, and Susan Hillier, eds., *New American World: A Documentary History of North America to 1612* (hereafter cited as NAW), 5 vols. (London, 1979), 1:234–35.

35. Henry P. Biggar, gen. ed., *The Works of Samuel de Champlain*, 6 vols. (Toronto, 1922–36), 1:186–87.

36. "Fray Francisco de Escobar's Diary of the Oñate Expedition to California," in George P. Hammond and Agapito Rey, eds. and trans., *Don Juan de Oñate: Colonizer of New Mexico, 1595–1628*, 2 vols. (Albuquerque, 1953), 2:1025–26.

37. William Strachey, *The Historie of Travel into Virginia Britania* (1612), ed. Louis B. Wright and Virginia Freud (London, 1953), 42. Forty years before, Father Luis de Quiros had likewise been told by natives of the same part of eastern Virginia, "Another day's journey or two . . . After crossing the mountains . . . one can see another sea." Clifford M. Lewis and Albert J. Loomie, eds., *The Spanish Jesuit Mission in Virginia, 1570–1572* (Chapel Hill, 1953), 91.

38. John Smith, "Virginia: Discovered and Discribed by Captayn John Smith Graven by William Hole," *A Map of Virginia . . . Written by Captaine Smith . . .* (Oxford, England, 1612).

39. Grieder, *Origins of Pre-Columbian Art*, 100–101. Though much geometrical perfection has not been achieved in man-made constructions in post-Columbian times, pre-Columbian earthworks in Licking and Ross Counties, Ohio, incorporate circles and squares, some of which do approach geometrical perfection and have overall dimensions exceeding 300m. See Cyrus Thomas, "Report of the Mound Ex-

plorations of the Bureau of Ethnology," *Twelfth Annual Report of the Bureau of Ethnology . . . 1890–91* (Washington DC, 1894), 458–70, 471–93.

40. Heckewelder, "An Account of the History," 288.

41. For a reconstruction of the map, see G. Malcolm Lewis, "The Indigenous Maps and Mapping of North American Indians," *Map Collector* 9 (1979): fig. 2.

42. Heckewelder, "An Account of the History," 288–90.

43. Much more contentious are the questions of whether and, if so, how and why rock art ever incorporates geographical representations of the terrestrial world. It would be inappropriate to evaluate the evidence here, but it should be noted that the subject index of the most comprehensive review of North American rock art contains five references under "Map (as rock art design)." See Klaus F. Wellmann, *A Survey of North American Indian Rock Art* (Graz, Austria, 1979), 445. The references are to accounts of rock-art sites in regional chapters on the Great Plains (two), Great Basin, Columbia-Fraser River Plateau and Northwest Coast, and Arctic regions. Catherine Delano Smith evaluates the evidence for the Old World in J. B. Harley and D. Woodward, eds., *The History of Cartography*, 2 vols. to date (Chicago, 1987–), 1:45–49, 54–101.

44. John C. Brandt and Ray A. Williamson, "Rock Art Representation of the A.D. Supernova: A Progress Report," and Dorothy Mayer, "An Examination of Miller's Hypothesis," both in Anthony F. Aveni, ed., *Native American Astronomy* (Austin, 1977), 171–77, 179–201.

45. Claude Britt Jr., "Early Navajo Astronomical Pictographs in Canyon de Chelly, Northeastern Arizona, U.S.A.," in Anthony F. Aveni, ed., *Archaeoastronomy in Pre-Columbian America* (Austin, 1975), 89–107.

46. Lincoln La Paz, "Meteorical Pictographs," *Popular Astronomy* 56 (1948): 328–29.

47. John A. Eddy, "Medicine Wheels and Plains Indian Astronomy," in Kenneth Beecher and Michael Feirtag, eds., *Astronomy of the Ancients* (Cambridge MA, 1979), 1–21.

48. "Big Black Meteor," celestial chart painted on oval buckskin, undated but collected at Pawnee, Oklahoma, in 1906 from a member of the Skidi band of Pawnee Indians, 65 x 43cm., Field Museum of Natural History, Chicago, Department of Anthropology, no. 71, 898-10. Described and reproduced in Ralph N. Buckstaff, "Stars and Constellations in a Pawnee Sky Chart," *American Anthropologist*, n.s., 29 (1927): 279–85.

49. Alice C. Fletcher, "Star Cult among the Pawnee: A Preliminary Report," *American Anthropologist*, n.s., 4 (1902): 732–33, 736.

50. Alfred L. Kroeber, "Handbook of Indians of California," *Bureau of American Ethnology Bulletin, No. 78* (Washington DC, 1925), 661–65; Lowell J. Bean and

Florence C. Shipek, "Luiseno," in Sturtevant, *Handbook of North American Indians* 8:556–57.

51. Louise Lamphere, "Southwestern Ceremonialism," in Sturtevant, *Handbook of North American Indians* 10:751–53.

52. Grieder, *Origins of Pre-Columbian Art*, 131–35. The Mississippi temple-mound culture that flourished in parts of the Mississippi and Ohio Valleys about 1100 to 300 B.P. was probably intermediate between the antecedent and Mesoamerican stages, and there seems no doubt that it was linked to the latter.

53. Louis A. Hieb, "Hopi World View," in Sturtevant, *Handbook of North American Indians* 9:577.

54. Dennis Tedlock, "Zuni Religion and World View," in Sturtevant, *Handbook of North American Indians* 9:499.

55. Charles Callendar, "Fox," in Sturtevant, *Handbook of North American Indians* 15:642.

56. Eustace M. W. Tillyard, *The Elizabethan World Picture* (London, 1943), 5.

57. Tillyard, *Elizabethan World Picture*, 6.

58. Paul Hazard, *The European Mind, 1680–1715* (Harmondsworth, U.K., 1964), 504.

59. Philip K. Brock, "Micmac," in Sturtevant, *Handbook of North American Indians* 15:109.

60. Sven Liljeblad, "Oral Tradition: Content and Style of Verbal Acts," in Sturtevant, *Handbook of North American Indians* 11:653.

61. Liljeblad, "Oral Tradition," 655.

62. Liljeblad, "Oral Tradition," 652.

63. The history of European attitudes toward Native Americans is complex, and the literature on them is voluminous though scattered. Aristotelian and opposing ideas in sixteenth-century Spain are covered in Lewis Hanke, *Aristotle and the American: A Study in Race Prejudice in the Modern World* (London, 1959), esp. chaps. 2–6; see also Anthony Pagden, *The Fall of Natural Man: The American Indian and the Origins of Comparative Ethnology* (corrected with additions) (Cambridge, U.K., 1986), esp. chaps. 5 and 6. English attitudes in the late sixteenth and early seventeenth centuries are described in Kupperman, *Settling with the Indians*, esp. chap. 6. The emergence of the relativistic or hierarchical perspective is covered in Pagden, *Fall of Natural Man*, esp. chaps. 6–8. Much of the evidence in these works is drawn from within what is now the United States. This bias has in part recently been redressed by Bruce G. Trigger, *Natives and Newcomers: Canada's "Heroic Age" Reconsidered* (Kingston, Canada, 1985), chap. 1, "The Indian Image in Canadian History," especially 20–29.

64. The word *epistemology* was first used in 1854 to refer to the theory or grounds of knowledge. Its German close equivalent, *erkennntnistheorie*, was first used in

1789. In European philosophy, interest in human knowledge can be traced back to René Descartes (1596–1650), but it was not a focus of concern until the publication of John Locke's *Essay Concerning Human Understanding* in 1690, almost two hundred years after Columbus reached the New World and approximately eighty years after Spain, France, and England began to maintain permanent communities of their own peoples in North America.

65. Father Juan Rogel to Father Francisco Borgia, Jesuit Archives of the Province of Toledo, A.T. 1157(2), fols. 496–7, English translation in Lewis and Loomie, *Spanish Jesuit Mission in Virginia*, 238–43.

66. Arthur H. Thomas and Isobel D. Thornley, eds., *The Great Chronicle of London* [by Robert Fabyan?] (London, 1938), 320.

67. "Instructions for a Voyage of Reconnaissance to North America in 1582 or 1583," British Library, Additional Manuscript 38823, ff.1–8, reprinted in NAW 3:240.

68. "October 13, 1612, Juan Fernández de Olivera to Philip III," Archivo General de las Indias, Seville, Spain, Santo Domingo 232, 54/5/17, no. 73, reprinted in translation in NAW 5:137.

69. The most useful work on Indian sign language remains, after more than one hundred years, Garrick Mallery, "Sign Language among North American Indians Compared with That among Other Peoples and Deaf Mutes," *First Annual Report of the Bureau of Ethnology . . . 1879–1880* (Washington DC, 1881), 263–552.

70. Susan Tarrow, trans., "Translation of the Cèllere Codex," in Lawrence C. Wroth, *The Voyages of Giovanni da Verrazzano, 1524–1528* (New Haven, 1970), 134.

71. Tarrow, "Cèllere Codex," 141.

72. Hodge and Lewis, *Spanish Explorers*, 26.

73. Hammond and Rey, *Narratives of the Coronado Expedition*, 236–37.

74. "Relation or Diary of the Voyage Made by Juan Rodríguez Cabrillo . . . from the Twenty-Seventh of June, 1542 . . . ," in Henry R. Wagner, *Spanish Voyages to the North West Coast of America in the Sixteenth Century* (San Francisco, 1929), 82–83.

75. René Goulaine de Laudonnière, "The First Voyage to Florida," in Hakluyt, *Principal Navigations* 3:311.

76. Hammond and Rey, *Narratives of the Coronado Expedition*, 175.

77. Hammond and Rey, *Narratives of the Coronado Expedition*, 217.

78. Recent years have seen the beginnings of a serious attempt to recognize the characteristics and roles of such maplike artefacts and to establish their significance in relation to the European and Euro-American exploration and settlement processes. See, for example, Lewis, "Indigenous Maps," 25–32; "Indian Maps," in Carol M. Judd and Arthur J. Ray eds., *Old Trails and New Directions: Papers of the Third North American Fur Trade Conference* (Toronto, 1980), 9–23; "Amerindian Antecedents of American Academic Geography," in Brian W. Blouet ed., *The Origins of Academic*

Geography in the United States (Hamden CT, 1981), 19–35; "Indian Maps: Their Place in the History of Plains Cartography," in Frederick C. Luebke et al., eds., *Mapping the North American Plains* (Norman, 1987), 63–80; "Indications of Unacknowledged Assimilations from Amerindian Maps on Euro-American Maps of North America: Some General Principles Arising from a Study of La Vérendrye's Composite Map (1728–29)," *Imago Mundi* 38 (1986): 934; "Misinterpretation of Amerindian Information as a Source of Error on Euro-Americans' Maps," *Annals of the Association of American Geographers* 77 (1987): 542–63; and "Indian Delimitations of Primary Biogeographic Regions," in Thomas E. Ross and Tyrel G. Moore, eds., *A Cultural Geography of North American Indians* (Boulder, 1987), 93–104. Other important contributions include Louis de Vorsey, "Amerindian Contributions to the Mapping of North America: A Preliminary View," *Imago Mundi* 30 (1978): 71–78, and James P. Ronda, "A Chart in His Way: Indian Cartography and the Lewis and Clark Expedition," in Luebke, *Mapping the North American Plains*, 81–91.

79. "The Relation of the Navigation and Discovery Which Captaine Fernando Alarchon Made . . . ," in Hakluyt, *Principal Navigations* 3:438. Interestingly, the account continues: "And then he [the old man who had drawn the map] requested me that I would describe my countrey unto him, as he had done unto me. And for to content him, I caused a draught of certaine things to be made for him."

80. "The Third Voyage of Discovery Made by Captaine Jacques Cartier, 1540 [1541–42] . . . ," in Hakluyt, *Principal Navigations* 3:235.

81. Biggar, *Works of Samuel de Champlain* 1:335–36.

82. Gabriel Archer, "The Relation of Captaine Gosnold's Voyage to the North Part of Virginia . . . ," in David B. Quinn and Alison M. Quinn, eds., *The New England Voyages, 1602–1608* (London, 1983), 117.

83. Ferdinando Gorges, *A Briefe Narration of the Originall Undertakings of the Advancement of Plantations into the Parts of America* (London, 1658), 4.

84. Map by Miguel (an Indian, perhaps from within what is now Texas). The map has proved difficult to interpret but certainly includes San Gabriel in the Rio Grande valley, New Mexico, and possibly Mexico City and probably represents rivers, trails, and settlements within what is now the south-central United States. The map is endorsed "Pintura que por man do de Don Fran co Valverde . . . ," [1602], MS, 31 x 43 cm., Estante 1, Cajon 1, Legajo 3/22, Ramo 4, Archive General de Indias, Seville.

85. "Account of the Journey Which I, Antonio Espejo, Citizen of the City of Mexico, Native of the City of Cibola, Made at the Close of the Year 1582 . . . ," in Herbert E. Bolton, ed., *Spanish Exploration in the Southwest, 1542–1706* (New York, 1908), 191.

86. Biggar, *Works of Samuel de Champlain* 1:124.

87. Biggar, *Works of Samuel de Champlain* 1:143.

88. Biggar, *Works of Samuel de Champlain* 1:152–55.

89. Biggar, *Works of Samuel de Champlain* 1:161.

90. Biggar, *Works of Samuel de Champlain* 1:144.

91. Biggar, *Works of Samuel de Champlain* 1:164.

92. Henry P. Biggar, ed., *The Voyages of Jacques Cartier* (Ottawa, 1924), 63.

93. Hodge and Lewis, *Spanish Explorers*, 21.

94. "A Relation of the Reverend Father Frier Marco de Nica . . . ," in Hakluyt, *Principal Navigations* 3:366–67.

95. "The Relation of . . . Captaine Fernando Alarchon," 3:428.

96. Robertson, *Governor Fernando de Soto* 2:256.

97. The classification and the nomenclature of natural phenomena in England between 1500 and 1800 are examined in Keith Thomas, *Man and the Natural World* (London, 1983), 51–70, 81–87.

98. Edmund Carpenter, *Eskimo Realities* (New York, 1973), 38, 39, 42, 43.

99. Giacomo Gastaldi, "Tierra Nueva," in Ptolemeo, *La Geografia* . . . (Venice, 1547–48).

100. Biggar, *Voyages of Jacques Cartier*, 201.

101. Samuel de Champlain, "Carte geographique de la Nouvelle Franse . . . ," *Les voyages de sieur de Champlain* . . . (Paris, 1613).

102. Bolton, *Spanish Exploration*, 245.

103. Tedlock, "Zuni Religion," 9:499–500.

104. Edward Sapir, "Language and Environment," *American Anthropologist*, n.s., 14 (1912): 228–29.

105. Sapir, "Language and Environment," 230.

106. Hammond and Rey, *Narratives of the Coronado Expedition*, 199–200, 207.

107. Biggar, *Works of Samuel de Champlain* 2:46.

108. Hammond and Rey, *Narratives of the Coronado Expedition*, 221, 301.

109. ["Report on the Fight with the French Ship in the Saint Johns River"], Archivo de Indias, Seville, Santo Domingo 168, 54/3/19, published in Jeanette Connor, trans. and ed., *Colonial Records of Spanish Florida, 1570–1580*, 2 vols. (De Land FL, 1925, 1930), 2:38.

110. Robertson, *Governor Fernando de Soto* 2:247, 250.

111. Edward G. Bourne, ed., *Narratives of the Career of Hernando de Soto*, 2 vols. (London, 1905), 2:60.

112. "The Third Voyage of the Frenchmen Made by Captaine John Ribault unto Florida," in Hakluyt, *Principal Navigations* 3:352.

113. "The Relation of . . . Captaine Fernando Alarchon," 3:429–30.

114. René Goulaine de Laudonnière, "The Second Voyage unto Florida," in Hakluyt, *Principal Navigations* 3:326.

115. Connor, *Memorial*, 219.

116. Laudonnière, "The First Voyage to Florida," 3:317.

117. "After 24 September 1609, with Postscript of 28 November, Report of Francisco Fernández de Ecija," in Philip L. Barbour, ed., *The Jamestown Voyages under the First Charter, 1606–1609*, 2 vols. (Cambridge, U.K., 1969) 2:298.

118. Thomas F. Davis, trans., "History of Juan Ponce de León's Voyages to Florida: Source Records," *Florida Historical Quarterly* 14 (1935): 18, 20–21.

119. Gonzalo Fernández de Oviedo, *Summario de la natural y general istoria de las Indias* (Toledo, 1526), translation in NAW 1:273–74.

120. "Letter of João Fernando Lagarto to John III of Portugal on His Discussions with Francis I Concerning French Activities in the St. Lawrence Valley, 22 January 1539 or 1540," in Henry P. Biggar, ed., and trans., *A Collection of Documents Relating to Jacques Cartier and the Sieur de Roberval* (Ottawa, 1930), 77, 79–80.

121. Biggar, *Jacques Cartier and the Sieur de Roberval*, 221–22.

122. Hammond and Rey, *Don Juan de Oñate* 2:1024–25.

123. Hammond and Rey, *Narratives of the Coronado Expedition*, 157–160.

124. Biggar, *Works of Samuel de Champlain* 1:99–100.

125. Nicolas Le Chelleux, *Discourse de l'histoire de la Floride* (Dieppe, France, 1566), translated in NAW 2:372.

126. *Narratives of Captivity among the Indians of North America: A List of Books and Manuscripts on This Subject in the Edward E. Ayer Collection of the Newberry Library* (Chicago, 1912): *Supplement I*, comp. Clara A. Smith (Chicago, 1928). These two bibliographies to the holdings of only one library list almost five hundred published works and manuscripts on the subject.

127. Gerald Theisen, ed. and trans., *The Narrative of Alvar Nuñez Cabeza de Vaca* (Barre MA, 1972), 172.

128. Biggar, *Works of Samuel de Champlain* 1:340.

129. Biggar, *Works of Samuel de Champlain* 1:267–68.

130. Champlain, "Carte geographique de la Nouvelle Franse. . . ."

131. Hammond and Rey, *Narratives of the Coronado Expedition*, 243.

132. Battista Agnese, untitled manuscript map of the southern part of North America, c. 1557, Chicago, Newberry Library, Ayer Collection, XII (3), fols. 3v and 4r, reproduced in NAW 1: plate 62.

133. Fredi Chiappelli, ed., *First Images of America: The Impact of the New World on the Old*, 2 vols. (Berkeley, 1976), 2:615–704.

134. According to David B. Quinn, the "total number of titles [i.e., publications about South, Central, and North America] for the first thirty years after Columbus's first voyage was limited," and North America was particularly "slow to come into any such printed accounts." Although the publication of Peter Martyr's *De orbe novo*

decades was completed in 1530, "North America was only a marginal interest" to the author. "The real turning point came with the publication of the first volume of Giovanni Battista Ramusio's collection *Navigationi et viaggi* at Venice in 1550 . . . and by 1559, when this publication was complete in its three volumes, much of value on North America had been included. . . . In 1589 Richard Hakluyt published his *Principall navigations, voiages & discoveries of the English nation*, the first edition of a very important work. It was especially significant in the North American field. . . . [The] second edition of his great work began to appear in 1598 . . . each of its three volumes, 1598, 1599, and above all . . . 1600, stressed the North American theme. . . . The year 1600 thus ends with a substantial corpus of North American material on the activities of all the western European powers in print, the largest single collection of it being Hakluyt's." NAW 1:lxv–lxviii.

135. Richard Hartshorne, *The Nature of Geography* (Lancaster PA, 1939), 44–46.

136. John Smith, *A Map of Virginia with a Description of the Countrey* . . . (Oxford, U.K., 1612), 10.

137. "A Relatyon of the Discovery of Our River, from James Forte into the Maine: Made by Captain Christopher Newport . . . ," reprinted in Barbour, *Jamestown Voyages* 1:82–83.

138. The so-called Velasco map, an untitled manuscript map of the eastern coast of North America, c. 1611, Simancas, Archivo General de Simancas, Estado, Leg. 2588, fo. 22, reproduced in colour at one-third size in W. P. Cumming, R. A. Skelton, and D. B. Quinn, *The Discovery of North America* (London, 1971), 266–67.

139. Biggar, *Works of Samuel de Champlain* 1:143.

140. Biggar, *Works of Samuel de Champlain* 1:160.

141. [Untitled] manuscript map by Cornelis Hendricks of the Hudson, Delaware, and Susquehanna Rivers, often referred to as the "Figurative Map of 1616," The Hague, Algemeen Rijksarchief, facsimile drawing in Edmund B. O'Callaghan, *Documents Relative to the Colonial History of New York* . . . (Albany, 1856), facing p. 11; translation of the legend in Isaac N. Stokes, *Iconography of Manhattan Island*, 2 vols. (New York, 1915), 2:73.

142. G. Malcolm Lewis, "Misinterpretation of Amerindian Information as a Source of Error on Euro-American Maps," *Annals of the Association of American Geographers* 77 (1987): 542–63.

143. Biggar, *Works of Samuel de Champlain* 1:143.

144. G. Malcolm Lewis, "Indicators of Unacknowledged Assimilations from Amerindian Maps on Euro-American Maps of North America: Some General Principles Arising from a Study of La Vérendrye's Composite Map, 1728–29," *Imago Mundi* 38 (1986): 22–31.

145. [The so-called Kraus Virginia map: an untitled manuscript map of 1608],

Austin Humanities Research Center Library, University of Texas, Austin, reproduced in NAW 5: plate 138.

146. Jan Jansson, "America septentrionalis," *Des Nieuwen Atlantis* . . . (Amsterdam, 1641), map 104.

147. Samuel de Champlain, "Carte de la Nouvelle France . . . ," in *Les voyages de la Nouvelle France Occidentale* . . . (Paris, 1632).

148. John Foster, "A Map of New-England," in William Hubbard, *The Present State of New-England, Being a Narrative of the Troubles with the Indians* . . . (London, 1677).

149. Jacques Le Moyne de Morgues, "Floridae Americae Provinciae . . . ," in Theodor de Bry, *America*, part 2 (Frankfurt-am-Main, 1591).

150. George R. Stewart, *American Place-Names* (New York, 1970), 418. All the other examples of native names given here are taken from this alphabetically arranged reference work.

151. [Manuscript map showing the discoveries of Hernando de Soto and Luis de Moscoso Alvarado], apparently compiled 1545 by the royal cartographer Alonso de Santa Cruz, probably on the basis of written and oral reports of members of the 1539–43 expedition, Archivo General de Indias, Seville, Mapas y Planos, Mexico 1.

3. The Columbian Voyages

1. Robert H. Fuson, *The Log of Christopher Columbus* (Camden ME, 1987), 25.

2. R. A. Skelton, *The European Image and Mapping of America:* A.D. 1000–1600, James Ford Bell Lectures No. 1 (Minneapolis, 1964), 10.

3. Charles Singer et al., *A History of Technology*, 5 vols. (New York, 1957), 5:377–410.

4. Paolo Emilio Taviani, *Cristoforo Colombo*, rev. ed., 2 vols. (Novara, Italy, 1980), 2:233–36.

5. Fuson, *The Log*, 64, 70–71.

6. Ferdinand Columbus, *The Life of the Admiral Christopher Columbus by His Son, Ferdinand*, ed. and trans. Benjamin Keen (New Brunswick NJ, 1959), 25. This work is usually referred to as *Historie*, from its Italian title. Many details of Columbus's second, third, and fourth voyages are derived from Keen's translation of the 1571 edition and are often given here with no specific citation.

7. Bartolomé de Las Casas, *Historia de las Indias*, ed. Agustin Millares Carlo, 3 vols. (Mexico City, 1951), 1:68.

8. James A. Williamson, *The Cabot Voyages and Bristol Discoveries under Henry VII*, Hakluyt Society, 2d ser., no. 120 (Cambridge, U.K., 1962), 184.

9. Williamson, *Cabot Voyages*, 186.

10. Armando Cortesão, "The North Atlantic Nautical Chart of 1424," *Imago Mundi* 10 (1953): 1–13; Armando Cortesão, *The Nautical Chart of 1424* (Coimbra, 1954); James E. Kelley Jr., "Non-Mediterranean Influences That Shaped the Atlantic in the Early Portolan Charts," *Imago Mundi* 31 (1979): 27–33.

11. Cortesão, "North Atlantic Nautical Chart," 2–4.

12. L. Carrington Goodrich, ed., *Dictionary of Ming Biography*, 2 vols. (New York, 1976).

13. William H. Babcock, *Legendary Islands of the Atlantic*, American Geographical Society, Research Series No. 8 (New York, 1922), 109–13.

14. Kelley, "Non-Mediterranean Influences," 30.

15. Cortesão, "North Atlantic Nautical Chart," 13.

16. Samuel Eliot Morison, *Christopher Columbus, Mariner* (New York, 1956), 20, 24, 33; Samuel Eliot Morison, *Journals and Other Documents on the Life and Voyages of Christopher Columbus* (New York, 1963), 55, 57; Taviani, *Cristoforo Colombo* 1:102.

17. Geoffrey Ashe, *Land to the West* (New York, 1962), 294–96.

18. Williamson, *Cabot Voyages*, 19–32, 188.

19. Williamson, *Cabot Voyages*, 188–189.

20. Williamson, *Cabot Voyages*, 211–214.

21. Williamson, *Cabot Voyages*, 208–209.

22. Anonymous map, MS. 2803, Egerton Collection, British Museum, London.

23. Robert H. Fuson, *A Geography of Geography* (Dubuque IA, 1969), 43.

24. R. E. Dickinson and O. J. R. Howarth, *The Making of Geography* (Oxford, U.K., 1933), 34.

25. A. E. Nordenskiöld, *Facsimile-Atlas to the Early History of Cartography* (Stockholm, 1899; reprint, New York, 1973), 28.

26. R. A. Skelton, Thomas E. Marston, and George D. Painter, *The Vinland Map and the Tartar Relation* (New Haven, 1965).

27. Babcock, *Legendary Islands*, 42.

28. E. H. Bunbury, *A History of Ancient Geography*, 2 vols. (New York, 1959), 2:175.

29. Ian Cameron, *Lodestone and Evening Star* (New York, 1966), 114.

30. Taviani, *Cristoforo Colombo* 2:108–19.

31. Columbus, *Life of the Admiral*, 11.

32. Morison, *Columbus, Mariner*, 15; Taviani, *Cristoforo Colombo* 1:115–18.

33. Columbus, *Life of the Admiral*, 14.

34. John Boyd Thacher, *Christopher Columbus: His Life, His Work, His Remains*, 3 vols. (New York, 1903–4), 1:325–38.

35. Las Casas, *Historia* 1:70–72.

36. Morison, Thacher, and Taviani are among those who succumbed to the Toscanelli hoax. Taviani, *Cristoforo Colombo* 1:171.

37. Henry Vignaud, *Toscanelli and Columbus* (New York, 1902).

38. Columbus, *Life of the Admiral*, 19–23.

39. Vignaud, *Toscanelli and Columbus*.

40. Thacher, *Columbus* 1:406.

41. Thacher, *Columbus* 1:399–404.

42. Florentino Pérez Embid, *Los descubrimientos en el Atlántico y la rivaldad Castellano-Portuguesa hasta el tratado de Tordesillas* (Seville, 1948).

43. Fuson, *The Log*, 37–42.

44. The "bar of Saltes" is at the mouth of the Odiel and Tinto Rivers; it had to be crossed at high tide to enter the Mediterranean Sea from Palos, Huelva, or Moguer.

45. Fuson, *The Log*, 54.

46. Fuson, *The Log*, 62.

47. The first map to depict Guanahaní was Juan de la Cosa's chart of 1500. The chart is so imprecise, however, that it has generated more heat than light. Some students of the problem have used an incorrect copy of this inexact chart in their attempts to identify Guanahaní. Taviani, *Cristoforo Colombo* 2:296; Taviani, "Why We Are Favorable for the Watling–San Salvador Landfall," *Proceedings of the First San Salvador Conference: Columbus and His World* (Fort Lauderdale, 1986), 228. The first citation uses the poor copy located in the British Museum; the latter uses a copy of that copy. Mauricio Obregón has used a simplified copy of the Taviani copy of the British Museum copy to support his Watlings–San Salvador hypothesis. Mauricio Obregón, "Columbus Landfall Hypotheses: A Sailor-Historian's Summary" (paper presented at the annual meeting of the Society for the History of Discoveries and the Hakluyt Society, London, 3 September 1987), map 3.

48. Joseph R. Judge, "The Columbus Landfall at Samana Cay" (paper presented at the Archive of the Indies, Seville, Spain, 19 November 1988), appendix: San Salvador to Cuba.

49. For excellent maps and charts of the Bahamas, contact the Department of Lands and Surveys, P.O. Box N-592, Nassau, Bahamas.

50. Joseph R. Judge, "Where Columbus Found the New World," *National Geographic* 170, no. 5 (November 1986): 562–99, plus Supplement of 70 pp. and a map.

51. This is an interpolation by the author. The name "San Salvador" is not mentioned until 14 October.

52. Fuson, *The Log*, 75–76.

53. One can only imagine how the Great Khan would have reacted if ninety Europeans had staked out a claim on China.

54. Robert H. Fuson: "The Positive Identification of *Antilia* on the Nautical Chart

of 1424" (paper presented to the annual meeting of the Society for the History of Discoveries, Minneapolis, Minnesota, 15 October 1988) and "The Positive Identification of *Satanaze* on the Nautical Chart of 1424" (paper presented to the annual meeting of the Society for the History of Discoveries and the North American Society for Oceanic History, San Francisco, California, 10 June 1989).

55. Fuson, *The Log*, 90.

56. Fuson, *The Log*, 91.

57. Fuson, *The Log*, 92.

58. Fuson, *The Log*, 98.

59. Superimposed on the 1492 globe of Behaim, the first voyage ended at Cipango (Japan). Judge, "Where Columbus Found the New World," 562–65.

60. Fuson, *The Log*, 100.

61. Fuson, *The Log*, 101.

62. Fuson, *The Log*, 133.

63. Fuson, *The Log*, 149.

64. Thacher, *Columbus* 1:628.

65. Fuson, *The Log*, 174.

66. Fuson, *The Log*, 173. Columbus named this cape "St. Elmo." Morison, *Journals*, 155, incorrectly identifies this cape, as do all of those who have copied Morison.

67. Fuson, *The Log*, 195.

68. Fuson, *The Log*, 76.

69. Arne B. Molander, "The Columbus Journal Translations: A Northern Viewpoint," and John H. Winslow, "Columbus Was Right: The First Landfall Was Near 26 Degrees North" (papers presented to the annual meeting of the Society for the History of Discoveries and the North American Society for Oceanic History, San Francisco, California, 9 June 1989).

70. Carlos Sanz, *La carta de Colón* (Madrid, 1961), 15.

71. Thacher, *Columbus* 3:96–97.

72. Consuelo Varela, "Aproximación a los escritos de Cristóbal Colón," *Jornadas de estudios Canarias-América* 3, 4, 5, 6 (1984): 79, 87–88.

73. Varela, "Aproximación."

74. Thacher, *Columbus* 3:98–113.

75. Columbus, *Life of the Admiral*, 174, 215, 223, 228, 269; Simon Wiesenthal, *The Secret Mission of Christopher Columbus*, trans. Richard and Clara Winston (New York, 1973), 193; Ian Cameron, *Magellan: And the First Circumnavigation of the World* (New York, 1973), 65–67.

76. Juan Friede and Benjamin Keen, *Bartolomé de Las Casas in History* (DeKalb IL, 1971), 75.

77. Everyone, including this author, has erred in the identification of Doña Inés.

She was the widow of Diego García de Herrera and the daughter of Hernán Peraza (Hernando Pérez) and Inés de las Casas. Inés de las Casas was the daughter of Guillén de las Casas and the granddaughter of Alfonso de las Casas. Alfonso had been given his original grant in the Canary Islands in 1420. He sold it to his son, Guillén, in 1430. Doña Inés's father, Hernán Peraza (Hernando Pérez), was the youngest son of Gonzalo Pérez Martél. The latter was captain of the first Castilian force sent to the Canaries in 1393 by Henry III, king of Castile. Hernán Peraza died in 1452, and in 1454 his titles passed to his wife, the first Inés; on her death the titles passed to the second Inés, who was married to Diego García de Herrera. His death, at the hands of the native Guanches, did not alter the line of authority. He may have become Lord of the Canaries when he married Inés, but she had been and continued to be Lady (Doña) of the Canaries. In no way was Doña Inés ever connected with anyone named Beatriz or Bobadilla, as some scholars insist.

78. Martín Fernández de Navarrete, *Viajes de Cristóbal Colón* (Madrid, 1934), 225.

79. Columbus, *Life of the Admiral*, 116; Las Casas, *Historia* 1:355.

80. Columbus, *Life of the Admiral*, 112.

81. The letters of Coma and Cuneo are in Morison, *Journals*, 209–45; the letters of Coma and Chanca are in Thacher, *Columbus* 2:243–281. None of the participants mention the naming of *any* islands between Antigua and Saint Martin (San Martín). Despite local tradition, there is no evidence that Columbus named Saint Kitts (Saint Christopher) or Nevis (Nuestra Señora de las Nieves). And there is no evidence that names given by Columbus to one island have migrated to another.

82. It must be acknowledged that the Juan de la Cosa chart cannot be used as a precision tool for reconstructing West Indian nomenclature. The search for the true Guanahaní has been severely hindered because of those who sometimes looked for more in the chart than is actually there.

83. It is unfortunate, but many who use poorly executed copies of maps and charts are not professional geographers and must rely on secondary sources. In the case of the Juan de la Cosa chart, even the original must be used with extreme caution.

84. Some of the Leeward Islands are mislabeled; some of the Windward Islands have names that no one credits to Columbus. Apparently Columbus students have chosen the islands they needed for their research and discarded the others!

85. Morison, *Journals*, 242; Thacher, *Columbus* 2:257, 282.

86. Thacher, *Columbus* 2:297–308.

87. Thacher, *Columbus* 2:321–32.

88. Columbus, *Life of the Admiral*, 142.

89. The island is today called Saona.

90. The political, economic, and social systems applied to the New World were not necessarily created for that region. A fact often overlooked is that Spain and Portugal had a pre-Columbian laboratory for all of these situations—in Madeira, Porto Santo, the Canary Islands, and to a lesser degree, the Azores. Here they not only worked out systems of land distribution but also developed the institution of slavery. The Canaries, Madeira, and Porto Santo are almost environmental duplicates of the Lesser Antilles (and parts of the Greater Antilles). For many years before 1492, sugarcane was grown on volcanic islands in the tropics, with slave labor. In some respects the New World was only a new location; the system was not new.

91. The Canary-Dominica route was to become the preferred route to the New World from Europe.

92. Columbus, *Life of the Admiral*, 178.

93. Las Casas, *Historia* 2:27.

94. Thacher, *Columbus* 2:437. Columbus also said, "I undertook a fresh voyage to the new heaven and (new) earth, which up to that time had remained hidden." Thacher, *Columbus* 2:431.

95. Morison, *Journals*, 284–88; Las Casas, *Historia* 2:43–61.

96. Columbus, *Life of the Admiral*, 191–214.

97. November and December are the worst sailing months near Portobelo. Rainfall *averages* twenty-five inches in November and seventeen inches in December. The "dry season" occurs in February and March, if there is one.

98. The author has conducted fieldwork in the area: the Rio Concepción appears to be the river Columbus called the Rio Belén. Apparently someone applied the original name to the wrong river.

99. There were earlier attempts in South America by Alonso de Ojeda.

100. There may have been a sandbar some distance from the mainland, making it necessary to use canoes to reach the shore. *Capitana* means "Flagship," and this caravel was probably another in the *Santa María* series.

101. Thacher, *Columbus* 3:506.

102. Thacher, *Columbus* 3:505–6.

103. Thacher, *Columbus* 3:503–4.

4. Early Spanish Exploration

1. Roberto Barreiro-Meiro, "Algo sobre la carta de Juan de la Cosa," *Puerto Rico, La Aguada, Ponce de León, etc.* (Madrid, 1977), 21; Samuel Eliot Morison, *The European Discovery of America: The Southern Voyages, 1492–1616* (New York, 1974), 141–42.

2. George E. Nunn, *The Geographical Conceptions of Columbus: A Critical Considera-tion of Four Problems* (New York, 1924), 90; Samuel Eliot Morison, *Admiral of the Ocean Sea: A Life of Christopher Columbus* (Boston, 1942), 581, and *The European Discovery of America: The Northern Voyages, A.D. 500–1600* (New York, 1971), 98–102; J. H. Parry, *The Spanish Seaborne Empire* (New York, 1977), 45.

3. Bruce B. Solnick, "After Columbus: Castile in the Caribbean," *Terrae Incognitae* 4 (1972): 120; Washington Irving, *The Life and Voyages of Christopher Columbus, to Which Are Added Those of His Companions*, 3 vols. (New York, 1849), 3:436; C. H. Haring, *The Spanish Empire in America* (New York, 1947), 94.

4. These voyages were studied in depth by Louis-André Vigneras, *The Discovery of South America and the Andalusian Voyages* (Chicago, 1976).

5. Vigneras, *Discovery*, 47; Bartolomé de Las Casas, *History of the Indies*, trans. and ed. Andrée M. Collard (New York, 1971), 40, 59–55.

6. Martín Fernández de Navarrete, *Colección de los viages y descubrimientos que hicieron por mar los españoles desde fines del siglo XV, con varies documentos inéditos concer-nientes á la historia de la marina castellana y de los establecimientos españoles en Indias*, 5 vols. (Madrid, 1825–37); Vigneras, *Discovery*.

7. John H. Parry, "Navigators of the *Conquista*," *Terrae Incognitae* 10 (1978): 62–65; "Licencia que pueda sacar cc cahizes de trigo," Archive General de Simancas, Real Guardia del Sello, 1493–94.

8. Vigneras, *Discovery*, 49–54; Morison, *Southern Voyages*, 189.

9. Frederick J. Pohl, *Americus Vespucci: Pilot Major* (New York, 1944), 147–67.

10. Charles Bricker, *Landmarks of Mapmaking: An Illustrated Survey of Maps and Mapmakers* (New York, 1976), 197; Justin Winsor, ed., *Narrative and Critical History of America*, 8 vols. (Boston, 1884–89), 2:146–48.

11. John Fiske, *Discovery of America*, 2 vols. (Boston, 1892), 2:2, 73, 56–57; Mor-ison, *Southern Voyages*, 308.

12. Roberto Levillier, *América la bien lamada*, 2 vols. (Buenos Aires, 1948), 1:100; Roberto Barreiro-Meiro, "Vespucio y Levillier," *Revista General de Marina* 195 (Octo-ber 1968): 351–68; la Cosa map, Museo Naval, Madrid (American portion repro-duced in Bricker, *Landmarks*, 199).

13. Robert S. Weddle, *Spanish Sea: The Gulf of Mexico in North American Discovery, 1500–1685* (College Station TX, 1985), 15–17; Barreiro-Meiro, "Algo sobre la carta," 31.

14. Winsor, *Narrative and Critical History* 1:3, 8, 15.

15. Nunn, *Geographical Conceptions*, 141.

16. E. Roukema, "A Discovery of Yucatán prior to 1503," *Imago Mundi* 13 (1956): 34.

17. Roukema, "Discovery of Yucatán," 37.

18. Nunn, *Geographical Conceptions*, 141.

19. Justin Winsor, *Christopher Columbus and How He Received and Imparted the Spirit of Discovery* (Boston, 1892), 387; W. P. Cumming, R. A. Skelton, and D. B. Quinn, *The Discovery of North America* (New York, 1972), 62–63.

20. Henry Harrisse, *The Discovery of North America: A Critical Documentary and Historic Investigation, with an Essay on the Early Cartography of the New World* (Amsterdam, 1961), 93–94.

21. Bricker, *Landmarks*, 195–96; Cumming, Skelton, and Quinn, *Discovery of North America*, 213.

22. Morison, *Admiral*, 193; Morison, *Southern Voyages*, 195; Vigneras, *Discovery*, 64.

23. Irving, *Life and Voyages* 3:32–38; Morison, *Southern Voyages*, 197.

24. Vigneras, *Discovery*, 71, 73–74.

25. Vigneras, *Discovery*, 124, 126.

26. Vigneras, *Discovery*, 102; Morison, *Southern Voyages*, 200.

27. Vigneras, *Discovery*, 119, 124–29.

28. Vigneras, *Discovery*, 133.

29. Carl Ortwin Sauer, *The Early Spanish Main* (Berkeley, 1969), 166–69.

30. Cumming, Skelton, and Quinn, *Discovery of North America*, 213.

31. Cumming, Skelton, and Quinn, *Discovery of North America*, 213.

32. Irving, *Life and Voyages* 3:126–27; Morison, *Southern Voyages*, 200–201.

33. Las Casas, *History*, 176.

34. Irving, *Life and Voyages* 3:127–36.

35. Irving, *Life and Voyages* 3:147.

36. Bernal Díaz del Castillo, *Historia verdadera de la conquista de la Nueva España*, 2 vols. (Mexico City, 1955), 1:103.

37. Weddle, *Spanish Sea*, 85–87.

38. Irving, *Life and Voyages* 3:202; Morison, *Southern Voyages*, 203–4.

39. Irving, *Life and Voyages* 3:234–45.

40. Antonio Vázquez de Espinosa, *Description of the Indies* (c. 1620), trans. Charles Upson Clark (Washington DC, 1968), 225.

41. Bruce B. Solnick, *The West Indies and Central America to 1898* (New York, 1970), 27.

42. Pedro Mártir de Anglería (Peter Martyr), *Décadas del Nuevo Mundo*, trans. D. Joaquín Torres Asensio (Buenos Aires, 1944), 108.

43. See Irving, *Life and Voyages* 3:46; "Capitulación real con Vicente Yáñez Pinzón y Juan Díaz de Solís," 23 March 1508, in José Toribio Medina, *Juan Díaz de Solís: Estudio Histórico* (Santiago de Chili, 1897), 29–30.

44. "Capitulación," 21–22, 26–34.

45. Mártir, *Décadas*, 172.

46. Ledesma's testimony in *Colección de documentos inéditos relativos al descubrimiento, conquista y organización de las antiguas posesiones españoles de ultramar*, 25 vols. (Madrid, 1885–1932), 7:266–70.

47. Las Casas, *History*, 149.

48. Sauer, *Early Spanish Main*, 41–44, 44 n.

49. Las Casas, *History*, 149; Antonio de Herrera y Tordesillas, *Historia general de los hechos de los castellanos en las islas y tierra firme del Mar Océano*, 10 vols. (Buenos Aires, 1944), 2:94; *Colección de documentos inéditos relatives al descubrimiento, conquista y organización de las antiguas posesiones españoles en America y Oceanía* (hereafter cited as *CDI*), 42 vols. (Madrid, 1864–84), 39:13–14 (quotation).

50. Oficio 4, book 2, *escribanía* Manuel Segura, 1514, ff. 693v, 681v, 686, Archivo Protocolos de Sevilla.

51. Las Casas, *History*, 149; José Manuel Pérez Cabrera, *En torno al bojeo de Cuba* (Havana, 1941), 5–11.

52. Gonzalo Fernández de Oviedo y Valdés, *História general y natural de las Indias, islas y Tierra-firme de Mar Océano*, 14 vols. (Asunción del Paraguay, 1945), 3:216.

53. Herrera, *Historia* 2:117.

54. Diego Velázquez to the Crown, 1 April 1514, Archivo General de Indias, Sevilla (hereafter cited as AGI), Patronato 178, no. 1, ramo I (printed, with errors, in *CDI*, 11:412–29).

55. George Sanderlin, ed., *Bartolomé de Las Casas: A Selection of His Writings* (New York, 1971), 116–21.

56. Sanderlin, *Bartolomé de Las Casas*, 64–66; Velázquez to the Crown, AGI.

57. Sauer, *Early Spanish Main*, 183; Francisco López de Gómara, *Historia general de las Indias* (Madrid, 1932), 113.

58. Sauer, *Early Spanish Main*, 8–9.

59. Sauer, *Early Spanish Main*, 6, 77, 192–94; Solnick, *West Indies*, 9.

60. Mártir, *Décades*, 91; Oviedo, *História* 3:216–17, 223; Herrera, *Historia* 2:212.

61. Weddle, *Spanish Sea*, 417–18, and Robert S. Weddle, "History," in J. Barto Arnold and Robert S. Weddle, *The Nautical Archeology of Padre Island: The Spanish Shipwrecks of 1554* (New York, 1978), 95–97; Parry, "Navigators," 63–65; Robert S. Chamberlain, "Discovery of the Bahama Channel," *Tequesta* 8 (1948): 109–15.

62. Weddle, *Spanish Sea*, 41, 51; Morison, *Southern Voyages*, 531; Harrisse, *Discovery*, 147.

63. Herrera, *Historia* 2:208.

64. Compare Clinton R. Edwards, "Discoveries of Mexico and the Meaning of Discovery," *Terrae Incognitae* 17 (1985): 61–67, and Roberto Barreiro-Meiro, "Sobre Ponce de León, Puerto Rico y Mejico: Réplica a Aurelio Tió y Puntualizaciones á Samuel E. Morison," in *Puerto Rico, La Aguada, Ponce de Léon, etc.*, 41–49.

65. Irving, *Life and Voyages* 2:396; Aurelio Tió, *Nuevas fuentes para la historia de Puerto Rico* (San Germán, Puerto Rico, 1961), 114, 361.

66. Vicente Murga Sanz, *Juan Ponce de León: Fundador y primer governador del pueblo Puertorrigueño, descubridor dela Florida y del estrecho de las Bahamas* (San Juan, 1959), 240, 248 n; John Gilmary Shea, "Ancient Florida," in Winsor, *Narrative and Critical History* 2:234–35; Tió, *Nuevas fuentes*, 331, 334.

67. Herrera, *Historia* 2:344–45.

68. Díaz del Castillo, *Historia* 1:43.

69. "Probanza con motive del incidente que provocó la llegada de Cristóbal de Tapia, año de 1522," *Boletín del Archive General de la Nación* 9, 2 (1938): 181–235.

70. "Probanza con motive"; *CDI* 12:161; Henry R. Wagner, *The Discovery of Yucatán by Francisco Hernández de Córdoba* (Berkeley, 1942).

71. Wagner, *Discovery of Yucatán*, 169; Díaz del Castillo, *Historia* 1:47.

72. Díaz del Castillo, *Historia* 1:53, 55.

73. Díaz del Castillo, *Historia* 1:53.

74. Gravier Bosque Bacernada, "Probanza," Antequera, 9 March 1558, AGI, Patronato 61, no. 2, ramo 2; Henry R. Wagner, *The Discovery of New Spain in 1518 by Juan de Grijalva* (Berkeley, 1942), 158.

75. Juan Díaz, "Diario del viaje que hizo la Armada del Rey Catholico del cargo y mando del Capitán D. Juan de Grijalva acia la Isla de Yucatán en el año de 1515," ms. 2861, Biblioteca del Real Palacio, Madrid.

76. Oviedo, *Historia* 5:65.

77. Oviedo, *Historia* 3:262; Parry, "Navigators," 66.

78. Wagner, *Discovery of New Spain*, 72.

79. Oviedo, *Historia* 3:275–77.

80. Weddle, *Spanish Sea*, 181.

81. Oviedo, *Historia* 3:294.

82. Oviedo, *Historia* 3:301.

83. Oviedo, *Historia* 3:294.

84. Diego Velázquez, "Ynstruccion testymoniada," Ysla Fernandina, 13 October 1519, AGI, Patronato 1, no. 1, ramo 1; *Colección de documentos inéditos para la historia de España* (Madrid, 1842–95), 388.

85. Mártir, *Décades*, 251–54, 299–300.

86. C. Harvey Gardener, *Naval Power in the Conquest of Mexico* (Austin, 1956), 7, 20; Wagner, *Discovery of New Spain*, 51–52, and *Discovery of Yucatán*, 27.

87. *CDI* 12:155–60.

88. Francisco López de Gómara, *Cortés: The Life of the Conqueror by His Secretary*, ed. and trans. Lesley B. Simpson (Berkeley, 1964), 304; Díaz del Castillo, *Historia* 2:100, 150, 156; Weddle, *Spanish Sea*, 122–26.

89. Hernan Cortés, *Cartas de relación* (Mexico City, 1973), 57.

90. Cortés, *Cartas*, 198–99.

91. Díaz del Castillo, *Historia* 1:179, 2:104.

92. "Relación del costo de las dos caravelas latinas de su alteza que francisco de garay alguacil mayor de la Ysla española conpro en el puerto de Santa María," February 1514, Manuscript 1764, doc. 21, f. 89, Museo Naval, Madrid.

93. Díaz del Castillo, *Historia* 1:179, 2:104–5; Herrera, *Historia* 3:133; Navarrete, *Colección de los viages* 3:147–53.

94. Navarrete, *Colección de los viages* 3:148.

95. Navarrete, *Colección de los viages* 3:148.

96. Publication history of the map is in Winsor, *Narrative and Critical History* 2:203; Jean Delanglez, *El Río del Espíritu Santo: An Essay on the Cartography of the Gulf Coast and the Adjacent Territory during the Sixteenth and Seventeenth Centuries* (New York, 1945), 14; and Cumming, Skelton, and Quinn, *Discovery of North America*, 67.

97. Díaz del Castillo, *Historia* 2:104.

98. Díaz del Castillo, *Historia* 2:104–5; Herrera, *Historia* 3:372–73; Alonso García Bravo, "Probanza," AGI, Patronato 83, no. 4, ramo 5.

99. Winsor, *Narrative and Critical History* 2:199–200.

100. Cortés, *Cartas*, 199, 200; López de Gómara, *Cortés*, 322.

101. López de Gómara, *Cortés*, 193–95.

102. López de Gómara, *Cortés*, 349; Díaz del Castillo, *Historia* 2:196, 199; Cortés, *Cartas*, 274.

103. Morison, *Southern Voyages*, 336–41; Woodbury Lowery, *The Spanish Settlements within the Present Limits of the United States, 1513–1561*, vol. 1 (New York, 1901), 169.

104. Morison, *Southern Voyages*, 332–34.

105. Weddle, *Spanish Sea*, 181; map in Cumming, Skelton, and Quinn, *Discovery of North America*, 106–7.

106. Eugenio Ruidíaz y Caravia, *La Florida: Su conquista y colonización por Pedro Menéndez de Avilés*, 2 vols. (Madrid, 1893), 2:152–54; Carl Ortwin Sauer, *Sixteenth Century North America: The Land and the People as Seen by the Europeans* (Berkeley, 1971), 221–25; Jeanette Connor, trans. and ed., *Colonial Records of Spanish Florida, 1570–1580*, 2 vols. (De Land FL, 1925, 1930), 1:322–33.

107. Weddle, *Spanish Sea*, 185–207; Morris Bishop, *The Odyssey of Cabeza de Vaca* (New York, 1933).

108. Translated accounts of Roderigo Ranjel, Luis Hernández de Biedma, and the "Gentleman of Elvas" in Edward Gaylord Bourne, ed., *Narratives of Hernando de Soto and the Conquest of Florida*, 2 vols. (New York, 1922); see also Charles Hudson, Chester B. DePratter, and Marvin T. Smith, "Hernando de Soto's Expedition

through the Southern United States," in Jerald T. Milanich and Susan Milbrath, eds., *First Encounters: Spanish Exploration in the Caribbean and the United States, 1492–1570* (Gainesville, 1989), 77–98.

109. Weddle, *Spanish Sea*, 232–33; Juan López de Velasco, *Geographía y descripción universal de las Indias* (Madrid, 1971), 93.

110. Robert S. Weddle, introduction to Weddle, ed., *La Salle, the Mississippi, and the Gulf: Three Primary Documents* (College Station TX, 1985), 7–8; Peter H. Wood, "La Salle: Discovery of a Lost Explorer," *American Historical Review* 89, 2 (April 1984): 294–323.

111. Fray Luis Cáncer, "Relación de la Florida," in Thomas Buckingham Smith, ed., *Colección de varios documentos para la historia de la Florida y tierras adyacentes* (London, 1857), 191–201.

112. Antonio Rodríguez de Quesada to the Crown, Mexico, 15 July 1554, AGI, Mexico 68.

113. Pedro Fernández (?) Canillas and Roderigo Ranjel to the Crown, Pánuco, 25 April 1557, AGI, Mexico 168.

114. Guido de Lavazares, "Declaración," in Herbert Ingram Priestley, trans. and ed., *The Luna Papers: Documents Relating to the Expedition of Don Tristán de Luna y Arellano for the Conquest of La Florida in 1559–1561*, 2 vols. (New York, 1971), 2:332–39.

115. Gonzalo Gayón, "Probanza," Havana, 13 July 1564, AGI, Santo Domingo 11, ramo 3.

116. Priestley, *Luna Papers* 1:72, 94, 102, 114, 121; Charles Hudson, Marvin T. Smith, Chester B. DePratter, and Emilia Kelley, "The Tristán de Luna Expedition, 1559–1561," in Milanich and Milbrath, *First Encounters*, 119–34.

117. Juan Pardo, "Relación," in Ruidíaz, *La Florida* 2:465–73; Juan de la Vandera in Ruidíaz, *La Florida* 2:481–86; Hudson, DePratter, and Smith, "Hernando de Soto's Expedition," 82–84.

118. Weddle, *Spanish Sea*, 333–47; documents in AGI, Mexico 103, 104, 110.

119. Garcilaso de la Vega, *The Florida of the Inca*, trans. and ed. John Grier Varner and Jeannette Johnson Varner (Austin, 1951), 618–19.

120. See note 61 above.

5. *Hacia el Norte!*

1. Herbert E. Bolton, *Coronado: Knight of Pueblos and Plains* (Albuquerque, 1949), 395; John F. Bannon, ed., *Bolton and the Spanish Borderlands* (Norman, 1964), 87.

2. Herbert E. Bolton, "Defensive Spanish Expansion and the Significance of the Borderlands," in Bannon, *Bolton*, 34.

3. Woodbury Lowery, *The Spanish Settlements within the Present Limits of the United States, 1513–1561*, vol. 1 (1901; reprint, New York, 1959), 100–101.

4. Charles F. Lummis, *The Spanish Pioneers and the California Missions* (Chicago, 1929), 2.

5. J. H. Parry, *The Age of Reconnaissance* (New York, 1963), 20, 33–34; Bolton, "Defensive Spanish Expansion," 43; Ralph H. Vigil, "Exploration and Conquest," in Ellwyn R. Stoddard, Richard L. Nostrand, and Jonathan P. West, eds., *Borderlands Sourcebook: A Guide to the Literature on Northern Mexico and the American Southwest* (Norman, 1983), 33.

6. Parry, *Age of Reconnaissance*, 67–78, 96, 107–8.

7. Herbert E. Bolton, "Preliminaries to the Spanish Occupation of Texas, 1519–1690," in Bannon, *Bolton*, 97.

8. Parry, *Age of Reconnaissance*, 20.

9. Charles Gibson, *Spain in America* (New York, 1966), 5, 21–22.

10. Vigil, "Exploration and Conquest," 32, 33.

11. Vigil, "Exploration and Conquest," 35.

12. D. W. Meinig, *The Shaping of America: A Geographical Perspective of Five Hundred Years of History*, vol. 1, *Atlantic America, 1492–1800* (New Haven, 1986), xv.

13. Meinig, *Shaping of America*, 3.

14. Robert S. Weddle, *Spanish Sea: The Gulf of Mexico in North American Discovery, 1500–1685* (College Station TX, 1985), xiii.; Carl Ortwin Sauer, *The Early Spanish Main* (Berkeley, 1969), 2, notes that the Caribbean Sea became the "Mar del Norte."

15. John F. Bannon, *The Spanish Borderlands Frontier, 1513–1821* (New York, 1970), 8.

16. Weddle, *Spanish Sea*, 38–40; Carl Ortwin Sauer, *Sixteenth Century North America: The Land and the People as Seen by the Europeans* (Berkeley, 1971), 26.

17. Weddle, *Spanish Sea*, 39; Sauer, *Sixteenth Century*, 27.

18. Weddle, *Spanish Sea*, 41–42; Sauer, *Sixteenth Century*, 27.

19. Weddle, *Spanish Sea*, 42–46; Sauer, *Sixteenth Century*, 27.

20. Weddle, *Spanish Sea*, 97–99.

21. Weddle, *Spanish Sea*, 100–102.

22. Weddle, *Spanish Sea*, 100–101, 419.

23. Sauer, *Sixteenth Century*, 28.

24. Weddle, *Spanish Sea*, 48; Sauer, *Sixteenth Century*, 35. Edward G. Bourne, *Spain in America, 1450–1580* (New York, 1962), 137–38, says that there were 850 Spaniards and 144 horses in the expedition.

25. Weddle, *Spanish Sea*, 133.

26. Weddle, *Spanish Sea*, 102–5, 130–42.

27. Sauer, *Sixteenth Century*, 63–69.

28. Sauer, *Sixteenth Century*, 69–70: Joseph Judge, "Exploring Our Forgotten Century," *National Geographic* 173 (March 1988): 336. Bourne, *Spain in America*, 138, maintains that there was only one ship in this expedition.

29. Sauer, *Sixteenth Century*, 69–70.

30. Sauer, *Sixteenth Century*, 70–76.

31. For a full account of the creation of the Chicora legend, see chapter 1 of Paul E. Hoffman, *A New Andalucia and a Way to the Orient: The American Southeast during the Sixteenth Century* (Baton Rouge, 1990).

32. Hoffman, *A New Andalucia*, 70–71; Bourne, *Spain in America*, 139–40.

33. David J. Weber, *The Spanish Frontier in North America* (New Haven, 1992), 36; Hoffman, *A New Andalucia*, 21.

34. Sauer, *Sixteenth Century*, 71–72; Bourne, *Spain in America*, 139–40, but note that he states that there were three ships and the expedition sailed in June.

35. Sauer, *Sixteenth Century*, 72; Judge, "Exploring," 337, 339.

36. Sauer, *Sixteenth Century*, 73, 299.

37. Sauer, *Sixteenth Century*, 73–76; Bourne, *Spain in America*, 140; Judge, "Exploring," 339; Meinig, *Shaping of America*, 27.

38. Hoffman, *A New Andalucia*, 85–86.

39. Frederick W. Hodge and Theodore H. Lewis, eds., *Spanish Explorers of the Southern United States, 1528–1543*, Original Narratives of Early American History (1907; reprint, New York, 1965), 3. Núñez Cabeza de Vaca's narrative is published in this work, 12–126.

40. Cabeza de Vaca wrote the account after his return from his eight-year journey, and it was first published in 1542. Today, it exists in several editions in translation: for example, Cleve Hallenbeck, ed., *Alvar Núñez Cabeza de Vaca: The Journey and Route of the First European to Cross the Continent of North America, 1534–1536* (1940; reprint, Port Washington NY, 1971), or Thomas Buckingham Smith, trans., *The Relation of Alvar Núñez Cabeza de Vaca* (Ann Arbor, 1966). Maps made by Cabeza de Vaca and another survivor, Andrés Dorantes de Carranza, showing the routes of their travels, have not survived. See Bolton, *Coronado*, 472–74. The foremost authority on the mapping of the trans-Mississippi West, Carl I. Wheat, does not even recognize that Cabeza de Vaca made a map and says that he gave no place-names to the European cartography of the New World; see Carl I. Wheat, *Mapping the Trans-Mississippi West, 1540–1861*, 5 vols. (San Francisco, 1957), 1:17.

41. "The Narrative of Alvar Núñez Cabeza de Vaca," in Hodge and Lewis, *Spanish Explorers*, 14.

42. Lowery, *Spanish Settlements*, 173.

43. "Narrative of Alvar Núñez Cabeza de Vaca," 14–15, 17; Sauer, *Sixteenth Century*, 37; Weddle, *Spanish Sea*, 187.

44. Weddle, *Spanish Sea*, 187. Sauer, *Sixteenth Century*, 37, states that there were 180 horses.

45. Weddle, *Spanish Sea*, 187; Hodge and Lewis, *Spanish Explorers*, 4.

46. Smith, *Cabeza de Vaca*, 11–28; Weddle, *Spanish Sea*, 187–88.

47. "Narrative of Alvar Núñez Cabeza de Vaca," 21; Sauer, *Sixteenth Century*, 38; Weddle, *Spanish Sea*, 188.

48. "Narrative of Alvar Núñez Cabeza de Vaca," 25; Weddle, *Spanish Sea*, 189. Sauer, *Sixteenth Century*, 39, says that there were two hundred foot soldiers in the expedition.

49. Smith, *Cabeza de Vaca*, 29–50.

50. Lowery, *Spanish Settlements*, 182; Weddle, *Spanish Sea*, 188–90.

51. Smith, *Cabeza de Vaca*, 43–50.

52. Smith, *Cabeza de Vaca*, 51–79; Weddle, *Spanish Sea*, 195.

53. Smith, *Cabeza de Vaca*, 80–110.

54. Smith, *Cabeza de Vaca*, 84–89.

55. Smith, *Cabeza de Vaca*, 106–7.

56. Smith, *Cabeza de Vaca*, x, 90–114; Lowery, *Spanish Settlements*, 197–201; Weddle, *Spanish Sea*, 195–200.

57. Smith, *Cabeza de Vaca*, 161–62.

58. Smith, *Cabeza de Vaca*, 75–76.

59. Smith, *Cabeza de Vaca*, 115–93; Lowery, *Spanish Settlements*, 201–9; David Beers Quinn, *North America from Earliest Discovery to First Settlements: The Norse Voyages to 1612* (New York, 1977), 192–93, 204; Weddle, *Spanish Sea*, 200–207.

60. Smith, *Cabeza de Vaca*, 194–205; Lowery, *Spanish Settlements*, 209–10.

61. Lowery, *Spanish Settlements*, 175, 27–78.

62. Stuart L. Udall, *To the Inland Empire: Coronado and Our Spanish Legacy* (New York, 1987), 61–63.

63. Donald E. Chipman, "In Search of Cabeza de Vaca's Route across Texas: An Historiographical Survey," *Southwestern Historical Quarterly* 91 (October 1987).

64. Chipman, "In Search of Cabeza de Vaca's Route," 137, 142–44; "Narrative of Alvar Núñez Cabeza de Vaca," 90, 92. Weddle, *Spanish Sea*, 202, 421, supports this route as the most accurate.

65. Chipman, "In Search of Cabeza de Vaca's Route," 146; Weddle, *Spanish Sea*, 201, 209; "Narrative of Alvar Núñez Cabeza de Vaca," 102–4.

66. "Narrative of Alvar Núñez Cabeza de Vaca," 106, 113, 119. Weddle, *Spanish Sea*, 201, states that the encounter with slave raiders took place on the Río Yaqui in Sonora.

67. Miguel Albornoz, *Hernando de Soto: Knight of the Americas*, trans. Bruce Boeglin (New York, 1986), 232–33; Quinn, *North America*, 191–94.

68. Meinig, *Shaping of America*, 14.

69. Meinig, *Shaping of America*, 407.

70. Meinig, *Shaping of America*, 65.

71. Herbert E. Bolton and Thomas M. Marshall, *The Colonization of North America, 1492–1783* (New York, 1922), 37; Donald E. Chipman, *Nuño de Guzmán and the Province of Pánuco in New Spain, 1518–1533* (Glendale CA, 1967), 10.

72. Chipman, *Nuño de Guzmán*, 157–59, 162, 164.

73. Adolph F. Bandelier, *Contributions to the History of the Southwestern Portion of the United States: Papers of the Archeological Institute of America*, American Series V (Cambridge MA, 1890), 172.

74. A. Grove Day, *Coronado's Quest: The Discovery of the Southwestern States* (Berkeley, 1964), 9–12; Lowery, *Spanish Settlements*, 254–56.

75. Chipman, *Nuño de Guzmán*, 231; Hubert H. Bancroft, *History of the North Mexican States and Texas*, Works of Hubert Howe Bancroft, 2 vols. (San Francisco, 1886), 1:28–29.

76. Chipman, *Nuño de Guzman*, 243–44.

77. Day, *Coronado's Quest*, 9–14; Lowery, *Spanish Settlements*, 253–58; Weddle, *Spanish Sea*, 158–59.

78. See Eugene Lyon, "Pedro Menendez's Plan for Settling La Florida," in Jerald T. Milanich and Susan Milbrath, eds., *First Encounters: Spanish Exploration in the Caribbean and the United States, 1492–1570* (Gainesville, 1989), 150; Lowery, *Spanish Settlements*, 86–87; Quinn, *North America*, 191; Weddle, *Spanish Sea*, 95–155.

79. Hallenbeck, *Alvar Núñez Cabeza de Vaca*, 13.

80. See Fr. Angelico Chavez, O.F.M., *Coronado's Friars* (Washington DC, 1968), 46–48; Day, *Coronado's Quest*, 7–20; Lummis, *Spanish Pioneers*, 66; and George Parker Winship, *The Coronado Expedition, 1540–1542* (Chicago, 1964), 7. All of the above historians except Chavez state that Cortés was in part motivated to send out Ulloa by stories of the Seven Cities. Chavez believes that Cortés had not yet heard of them specifically by the time he dispatched Ulloa.

81. Wheat, *Mapping the Trans-Mississippi West* 1:18.

82. John Edwin Fagg, *Latin America: A General History*, 3d ed. (New York, 1977), 108–9; Gibson, *Spain in America*, 33; Lowery, *Spanish Settlements*, 339–50; Udall, *Inland Empire*, 38, 71; Winship, *Coronado Expedition*, 106.

83. Smith, *Cabeza de Vaca*, 202–6, 231–32; Lowery, *Spanish Settlements*, 211–12; Udall, *Inland Empire*, 61–63.

84. See Marcos de Niza, *Relación del descubrimiento de las siete ciudades* (1556), in English in Percy M. Baldwin, "Marcos de Niza's Relación," *New Mexico Historical Review* 1 (April 1926): 193–223.

85. Bolton, *Coronado*, 25–27.

86. Bolton, *Coronado*, 27.

87. Day, *Coronado's Quest*, 42–45; Lowery, *Spanish Settlements*, 260–67; Udall, *Inland Empire*, xvii–xviii. Lowery offers that "Cíbola" is a form of "Shi-uo-na," what the Zuni Indians called their own land.

88. See Lowery, *Spanish Settlements*, 271.

89. Bolton, *Coronado*, 27–34.

90. Bolton, *Coronado*, 35–38; Bancroft, *North Mexican States* 1:74–77; Vigil, "Exploration and Conquest," 34; John Bartlett Brebner, *The Explorers of North America* (London, 1933), 69–72; Sauer, *Sixteenth Century*, 127; Weddle, *Spanish Sea*, 209. The standard source for Fray Marcos's journey is Percy M. Baldwin, "Fray Marcos de Niza and His Discovery of the Seven Cities of Cibola," *New Mexico Historical Review* 1 (April 1926): 193–223. Historians debate just where Fray Marcos reached on this expedition, whether it was actually Cíbola (Zuni), northeastern Arizona, the Santa Cruz River valley, or just below the present international boundary between Mexico and the United States.

91. Day, *Coronado's Quest*, 46–47; Wheat, *Mapping the Trans-Mississippi West* 1:17.

92. Day, *Coronado's Quest*, 59–61. On the other hand, Lowery, for example, defends Marcos against charges of being a "lying monk" and portrays him as being guilty only of reasonable misinterpretation and slight exaggeration; see Lowery, *Spanish Settlements*, 277–78. Also see Winship, *Coronado Expedition*, 40–41.

93. Seymor V. Connor, *Texas: A History* (New York, 1971), 12; Day, *Coronado's Quest*, 21–28; Lowery, *Spanish Settlements*, 261, 286.

94. Bernard DeVoto, *The Course of Empire* (Boston, 1952), 54–55.

95. See Pedro de Castañeda, *Relación de la jornada de Cibola conquesta por Pedro de Casteñada . . . ano de 1540*, and Juan Jaramillo, *Relación hecho por el Capitan Juan Jaramillo de la jornada . . . por General Francisco Vázquez Coronado*. These invaluable sources may be found, along with the letters of Coronado, in the original Spanish and in English translation in Winship, *Coronado Expedition*.

96. Day, *Coronado's Quest*, 167–87; Lowery, *Spanish Settlements*, 289–96.

97. Day, *Coronado's Quest*, 81–112; Lowery, *Spanish Settlements*, 296–301.

98. Winship, *Coronado Expedition*, 203.

99. Winship, *Coronado Expedition*, 209.

100. Winship, *Coronado Expedition*, 209–10.

101. Day, *Coronado's Quest*, 147–57; Lowery, *Spanish Settlements*, 312–23.

102. Winship, *Coronado Expedition*, 376–79.

103. Winship, *Coronado Expedition*, 280–83.

104. Winship, *Coronado Expedition*, 241.

105. Day, *Coronado's Quest*, 189–265; Lowery, *Spanish Settlements*, 318–33; Quinn, *North America*, 202–3.

106. DeVoto, *Course of Empire*, 52–53.

107. Wheat, *Mapping the Trans-Mississippi West* 1:1–2. Also see Bolton, *Coronado*, 472–74.

108. Winship, *Coronado Expedition*, 188. Also see Bolton, *Coronado*, viii, 396–98; Day, *Coronado's Quest*, 256–323; Lowery, *Spanish Settlements*, 333–36; and Quinn, *North America*, 203–6.

109. Lowery, *Spanish Settlements*, 213–17; Lummis, *Spanish Pioneers*, 73; Weddle, *Spanish Sea*, 209–11.

110. See Thomas Buckingham Smith, ed. and trans., *Narratives of de Soto in the Conquest of Florida* (1866; reprint, Gainesville, 1968), and Garcilaso de la Vega, *The Florida of the Inca*, trans. John Grier Varner and Jeanette Johnson Varner (Austin, 1951).

111. Wheat, *Mapping the Trans-Mississippi West* 1:19–27; Weddle, *Spanish Sea*, 221.

112. Charles Hudson, Chester B. DePratter, and Marvin T. Smith, "Hernando de Soto's Expedition through the Southern United States," in Milanich and Milbrath, *First Encounters*, 78–84.

113. Hoffman, *A New Andalucia*, gives a recent, excellent account of the cartography of the period (see chap. 5); an earlier but still reliable work on the same topic is William Cumming, *The Southeast in Early Maps* (Princeton, 1958).

114. Theodore Maynard, *De Soto and the Conquistadors* (New York, 1969), 141–253. Also see Hudson, DePratter, and Smith, "Hernando de Soto's Expedition"; Jeffrey M. Mitchum, "Artifacts of Exploration: Archeological Evidence from Florida," and Charles R. Ewen, "Anhaica: Discovery of Hernando de Soto's 1539–1540 Winter Camp," both in Milanich and Milbrath, *First Encounters*, 77–118; Lowery, *Spanish Settlements*, 218–22; and Weddle, *Spanish Sea*, 213–15.

115. Archeological remains point to the fact that some men of an expedition led by Captain Juan Pardo into the Florida interior in September 1567 may have discovered the Georgia gold and mined it but, having been killed by Indians, never were able to spend it or bring it to the attention of the Spanish Crown. See Milanich and Milbrath, *First Encounters*, 150–82.

116. Garcilaso de la Vega, *Florida of the Inca*, 320.

117. Garcilaso de la Vega, *Florida of the Inca*, 338.

118. Lowery, *Spanish Settlements*, 222–30; Quinn, *North America*, 206–12; Weddle, *Spanish Sea*, 217–18.

119. Garcilaso de la Vega, *Florida of the Inca*, 375–76.

120. Garcilaso de la Vega, *Florida of the Inca*, 502.

121. Connor, *Texas*, 13–14; Lowery, *Spanish Settlements*, 230–47; Maynard, *De Soto*, 204–63; Quinn, *North America*, 212–19; Weddle, *Spanish Sea*, 218–20.

122. Day, *Coronado's Quest*, 258–59; Lowery, *Spanish Settlements*, 247–49; Quinn, *North America*, 219–21; Weddle, *Spanish Sea*, 220–22.

123. Connor, *Texas*, 13–14; Lowery, *Spanish Settlements*, 249–52; Quinn, *North America*, 221–22; Weddle, *Spanish Sea*, 222–26.

124. Hoffman, *A New Andalucia*, 96–101.

125. Weddle, *Spanish Sea*, 234–35.

126. Weddle, *Spanish Sea*, 237–45.

127. Gibson, *Spain in America*, 33. Gibson also holds the same view regarding the Coronado and the Orellana expeditions.

128. DeVoto, *Course of Empire*, 52–57, 61–63.

129. Quinn, *North America*, 222.

130. See Alfred W. Crosby Jr., *The Columbian Exchange: Biological and Cultural Consequences of 1492* (Westport CT, 1972), 35–63.

131. Charles Hudson, Marvin T. Smith, Chester B. DePratter, and Emilia Kelley, "The Tristán de Luna Expedition, 1559–1561," and Marvin T. Smith, "Indian Responses to European Contact: The Coosa Example," in Milanich and Milbrath, *First Encounters*, 119–49.

132. Lowery, *Spanish Settlements*, 375–76.

133. Lowery, *Spanish Settlements*, 376–77.

6. The Northwest Passage in Theory and Practice

1. The clearest narrative on the Northwest Passage is Ernest S. Dodge, *Northwest by Sea* (New York, 1961). In this chapter, to ease reference citation, documentary references will first cite David Beers Quinn, Alison Quinn, and Susan Hillier, eds., *New American World: A Documentary History of North America to 1612* (hereafter cited as NAW), 5 vols. (London, 1979). For world maps produced during the period with which this chapter deals, the best reference is Rodney W. Shirley, *The Mapping of the World: Early Printed World Maps, 1472–1700* (London, 1983). The best source on earlier maps is J. Brian Harley and David Woodward, eds., *The History of Cartography* (Chicago, 1987), vol. 1. This last source gives a full account of medieval world maps down to 1500.

2. Documents for the years 1480–1505 are to be found in NAW 1:91–120, 145–55, and James A. Williamson, *The Cabot Voyages and Bristol Discoveries under Henry VII*, Hakluyt Society, 2d ser., no. 120 (Cambridge, U.K., 1962). See also David B. Quinn, *North America from Earliest Discovery to First Settlement: The Norse Voyages to 1612* (New York, 1977), 108–32.

3. Document 1481 in NAW 1:92. The fullest discussion is in David B. Quinn, *En-*

gland and the Discovery of America, 1481–1620 (New York, 1974), 4–23, 40–59. The interpretation that land was seen in 1481 has been contested by Alwyn A. Ruddock, "John Day of Bristol and the English Voyages across the Atlantic before 1497," *Geographical Journal* 122 (1965): 225–33, and by Samuel Eliot Morison, *The European Discovery of America: The Northern Voyages, A.D. 500–1600* (New York, 1971), 208 n.

4. Documents on Sebastian Cabot's voyages of 1508–9 are in NAW 1:121–27, and Williamson, *Cabot Voyages*, 265–82, 321.

5. Pietro Martire d'Anghiera, *De orbe novo decades* (Alcala de Hanarea, 1516), folio 52.

6. *Summario de la generale historia de l'Indie Ocidentali cavato dalibri scritti dal signor Don Pietro Martiro* (Venice, 1534), folio 65.

7. Giovanni Battista Ramusio, *Navigationi et viaggi*, 3 vols (Venice, 1556), folios 4, 417.

8. Richard Willes [or Willys], *The History of Travayle in the West and East Indies* (London, 1549), folios 231–33.

9. Shirley, *Mapping of the World*, 24–25; W. P. Cumming, R. A. Skelton, and D. B. Quinn, *The Discovery of North America* (New York, 1972), 53–55.

10. Shirley, *Mapping of the World*, 30–31; Josef Ischer and Franz von Weiser, *Die alteste karte mit dem Namen Amerika aus dem jahre 1507* (reprint, Amsterdam, 1968).

11. NAW 1:124.

12. NAW 1:179–89.

13. E. G. R. Taylor, *Tudor Geography, 1485–1583* (London, 1930), 8, 21.

14. Simon Grynaeus and Johann Huttich, *Novus orbis regionum* (Basel, 1532); 1535 version in Cumming, Skelton, and Quinn, *Discovery of North America*, 63–65.

15. Shirley, *Mapping of the World*, 51–52; also Petrus Apianus, *Cosmographie introductio* (Ingoldstadt, 1529).

16. Gemma (Reinerus) Frisius, *De principis astronomiae . . . Item de orbis diuisione, & insulis. rebusque nuper inventis* (Antwerp, 1530).

17. Frisius-Mercator globe, 1537, Osterichishe Nationalbibliothek, Vienna. A not very satisfactory reproduction appears in NAW 4: map 115. The relevant section is shown in Helen Wallis, "Globes in England up to 1600," *Geographical Magazine* 35 (1962): 269.

18. A. E. Nordenskiol, *Facsimile-Atlas* (reproduced from the 1889 Swedish edition) (New York, 1973), plate 43. A comparable map, with much less significant detail, was produced by Orronce Finelin in 1531; see plate Nordenskiol, *Facsimile-Atlas*, 41.

19. Taylor, *Tudor Geography*, 20.

20. Roger Barlow, *A Brief Summe of Geographie*, ed. E. G. R. Taylor, Hakluyt Society, 2d ser., no. 69 (London, 1932). For English plans and actions in northern territo-

ries, see NAW 1:215–26. The Muscovy charter of 1555 (p. 221) permitted it to control English enterprise in the north, northeast, and northwest.

21. Jean Rotz, *Boke of Ideography*, ed. Helen Wallis (Oxford, U.K., 1981).

22. The John Rylands University Library, Manchester. See D. B. Quinn, "Artists and Illustrators in the Early Mapping of North America," *Mariner's Mirror* 72 (1986): 253–55, 264. An enlargement of this episode appears in George Bass, ed., *Ships and Shipwrecks of the Americas* (London, 1988), 73.

23. See Selma Barkham, "Documentary Evidence for Sixteenth Century Basque Whaling Ships in the Strait of Belle Isle," in G. M. Story, ed., *Early European Settlement and Exploration in Atlantic Canada* (Saint John's, Newfoundland, 1982), 53–96. There is now a large but scattered literature on this topic.

24. David B. Quinn, ed., *The Voyages and Colonising Enterprises of Sir Humphrey Gilbert*, 2 vols., Hakluyt Society, 2d ser., nos. 83–84 (London, 1940), 1:105–17. Gilbert's plan for a voyage in 1566 and the comments of the Muscovy Company on it are in NAW 4:188–90.

25. Nicolo Zeno, *De i commentarii del viaggio in Persia . . . Et dello scoprimento dell' isole Frislanda, Eslanda, Engrovelanda, Estotilanda & Icaria fatto il polo artica, da due fratelli Zeni* (Venice, 1558). The map, which was so frequently used and mistakenly relied on later in the century, is reproduced in Cumming, Skelton, and Quinn, *Discovery of North America*, 317.

26. See Shirley, *Mapping of the World*, 140–41. The original was published in twenty-one sheets. There is a copy in the Prinz Hendrik Maritien Museum in Rotterdam, Netherlands.

27. George Gascoigne, *A Discourse of a Discoverie for a New Passage to Cataia* (London, 1576), reprinted in Quinn, *Sir Humphrey Gilbert* 1:129.

28. Abraham Ortelius, "Typus Orbis Terrarum," in his *Theatrum Orbis Terrarum* (Antwerp, 1570).

29. Richard Hakluyt, *Divers Voyages Touching the Discouerie of America* (London, 1582), sign. 2 verso; see NAW 1:186–87.

30. From Public Record Office, London, E166/35, folios 9–26. Details of the preparation were printed for the first time in NAW 4:195–200. The major sources for the three voyages are printed in Vilhjalmur Stefansson, *The Three Voyages of Martin Frobisher*, 2 vols. (London, 1938).

31. Narrative of Christopher Hall in NAW 4:291–307; George Best on the voyage in Stefansson, *Voyages of Martin Frobisher* 1:13–51 (Best's generalization on the passage appears in 13–47 and that on the voyage itself in 47–51).

32. The details of the reception given to the earliest Inuit to be brought to Europe are given in William C. Sturtevant and D. B. Quinn, "The New Prey," in Christian F. Feest, ed., *Indians and Europe* (Aachen, France, 1987), 61–140.

33. Best in Stefansson, *Voyages of Martin Frobisher* 1:150.

34. Dionyse Settle, *A True Report of the Last Voyage into the West and Northwest Regions* (London, 1577); NAW 4:207–16; Stefansson, *Voyages of Martin Frobisher* 1:52–73 (Best) and 2:5–25 (Settle). Settle's pamphlet was the first English report of an overseas voyage to receive extensive currency in Europe and to be widely circulated.

35. See Sturtevant and Quinn, "The New Prey," 98, 111.

36. Lok's accounts for the 1578 voyage are in the Henry E. Huntington Library, San Marino, California (formerly Phillips MS 20821), folio 25.

37. Thomas Ellis, *A True Report of the Third and Last Voyage into Meta Incognita* (London, 1578); George Best, *A True Discourse of the Late Voyages of Discoverie* (London, 1578); Stefansson, *Voyages of Martin Frobisher* 1:80–122 (Best), 2:27–51 (Ellis), 2:55–73 (Sellman). Best remains the fullest authority on the three voyages.

38. Stefansson, *Voyages of Martin Frobisher* 1:93.

39. Stefansson, *Voyages of Martin Frobisher* 2:137–51 (1577) and 2:204 (1578), deals with the ore brought from Baffin Island.

40. Charles Francis Hall, *Life with the Eskimos* (London, 1865), 388–91, 503–6. On the loss of the objects brought back by Hall, see Stefansson, *Voyages of Martin Frobisher* 2:242–44.

41. Summary report and photographs in Stefansson, *Voyages of Martin Frobisher* 2:245–47.

42. W. A. Kenyon, *Tokens of Possession: The Northern Voyages of Martin Frobisher* (Toronto, 1975).

43. I am indebted to Dr. William Fitzhugh, Department of Anthropology, Smithsonian Institution, for giving me some account of the expedition and for allowing me to use the Interim Field Report, "Smithsonian Archaeological Surveys at Kodlunarn Island in 1981" (unpublished typescript). Extensive research on the Frobisher voyages has been conducted by the Meta Incognita Project of the Museum of Civilization (Ottawa), with the cooperation of the Smithsonian Institution and an English task force. Numerous studies and documentary collections on the voyages have been made. Work in mining and anthropology on Baffin Island has produced new information. In regard to the Northwest Passage, opinion has hardened that Frobisher's "Mistaken Straits" of 1578 constituted Hudson Strait and that he probably passed through it before turning back.

44. *Theatrum Orbus Terrarum* published in Antwerp by A. Coppens v. Diest.

45. K. R. Andrews, "The Aims of Drake's Expedition of 1577–1580," *American Historical Review* 72 (1968): 724–41. An extract of the preliminary draft of the instructions is in NAW 1:462–65.

46. John Davis, *The Worlde's Hydrographical Discription* (London, 1595), folio 8, lv.

47. Cotton MS Augustus I.i.1, British Library, Department of Manuscripts.

48. Quinn, *Sir Humphrey Gilbert* 2:483–89; see NAW 4:228–30, for Adrian Gilbert's patent of 6 February 1584. In 1582 Dee prepared for Sir Humphrey Gilbert a chart on a polar projection (reproduced in Quinn, *Sir Humphrey Gilbert*) showing not only an open passage around the northern part of North America but also another that linked the Saint Lawrence River with the Gulf of California (although without naming New Albion).

49. Albert H. Markham, ed., *The Voyages and Works of John Davis*, Hakluyt Society, 1st ser., no. 59 (London, 1880), has not been superseded, and Clement R. Markham, *Life of John Davis*, 2d ed. (London, 1891), is a useful narrative. Since the Markhams wrote, copies of Davis's *Worlde's Hydrographical Discription* have been located. One is in the British Library, with another in the Folger Shakespeare Library in Washington DC. An extract from it, giving a brief account of the three voyages, is in NAW 4:231–33.

50. E. G. R. Taylor, ed., *The Original Writings and Correspondence of the Two Richard Hakluyts*, 2 vols., Hakluyt Society, 2d ser., nos. 76–77 (London, 1935), 1:283–89.

51. NAW 4:253–58 (heading misdated 1585).

52. Facsimile in Albert H. Markham, *Works of John Davis*, facing title page.

53. NAW 4:244–45.

54. NAW 4:247–51.

55. Richard Hakluyt, *The Principal Navigations, Voiages, Traffiques, and Discoveries . . .* , 3 vols. (London, 1598–1600), 3:115.

56. NAW 4:262.

57. This is shown as the "Fretum [Strait] Davis" on the Molyneux Globe of 1592 and 1603. An illustration from the 1603 globe in the Middle Temple is in Helen Wallis, "The Molyneux Globe," *British Museum Quarterly* 16 (1951): 69–70.

58. It is only present in a minority of surviving copies but was probably issued separately as well. See D. B. Quinn, ed., *The Hakluyt Handbook*, 2 vols., Hakluyt Society, 2d ser., nos. 144–45 (London, 1974), 1:62–63, 2:495–96.

59. Taylor, *Two Richard Hakluyts* 2:286–87.

60. Hakluyt, *Principal Navigations*, vol. 3.

61. Samuel Purchas, *Hakluytus Posthumus or Purchas his Pilgrimes*, 4 vols. (London, 1625), cited from edition in 20 vols. (Glasgow, 1906–7), 14:306–18.

62. D. B. Quinn and A. M. Quinn, eds., *The English New England Voyages, 1602–1608*, Hakluyt Society, 2d ser., no. 161 (London, 1983), 69.

63. NAW 4:269–76.

64. NAW 4:277–97. Also G. M. Asher, ed., *Henry Hudson the Navigator*, Hakluyt Society, 1st ser., no. 27 (London, 1860); Miller Christy, ed., *The Voyages of Captain Luke Fox and Captain Thomas James of Bristol in Search of a North-West Passage*, 2 vols., Hakluyt Society, 1st ser., nos. 88–89 (London, 1894), 1:631–54; G. G. Harris, ed., "Trinity

House Transactions, 1609–1625," *London Record Society Publications* 19 (1985): 9–10; Linden J. Lindstrom, *The Bay Where Hudson Did Winter* (Minneapolis, 1980).

65. Christy, *Captain Luke Fox and Captain Thomas James* 2:633–34.

66. His map of 1612 is of considerable importance. For his subsequent writings on Hudson and Button, see Asher, *Henry Hudson*, xliii–xlix, 181–94.

67. Estado Inglaterra 841 1/2, Archivo General de Simancas.

68. Purchas, *Pilgrimes* 14:401–11; Christy, *Captain Luke Fox and Captain Thomas James* 1:162–67.

69. Grant and Instructions in Christy, *Captain Luke Fox and Captain Thomas James* 2:642–64.

70. Baffin's log and map are in the Department of Manuscripts, Additional MS 12206, British Library. The map is reproduced in Clement R. Markham, *Voyages of William Baffin, 1612–1622*, Hakluyt Society, 1st ser., no. 63 (London, 1881), 102.

71. Markham, *Voyages of William Baffin*, 137.

72. Purchas, *Pilgrimes* 14:401–11; Markham, *Voyages of William Baffin*, 138.

73. Brigg's tract and map are in Purchas, *Pilgrimes* 14:411–26.

74. Jens Munk, *Navigatio septentrionalis* (Copenhagen, 1624); C. C. A. Gosch, ed., *Danish Arctic Expeditions, 1605 to 1620*, Hakluyt Society, 1st ser., no. 65 (London, 1897); Thorkild Hansen, *Jens Munk* (Copenhagen, 1965), *Northwest to Hudson Bay: The Life and Times of Jens Munk* (New York, 1970), and *Jens Munk* (Ottawa, 1965).

75. Thomas Rundall, ed., *Narratives of Voyages toward the North-West*, Hakluyt Society, 1st ser., no. 5 (London, 1849); Christy, *Captain Luke Fox and Captain Thomas James* 1:248–59.

76. Purchas, *Pilgrimes*.

77. Christy, *Captain Luke Fox and Captain Thomas James* 1:1–259. Fox prefaces his own account with a review of earlier English voyages, mainly (although not wholly) from Hakluyt and Purchas.

78. Thomas James, *The Strange and Dangerous Voyage of Captain Thomas James in His Intended Discovery of the Northwest Passage* (London, 1633), including a map; R. B. Bodilly, *The Voyage of Captain Thomas James for the Discovery of the Northwest Passage* (London, 1929); W. A. Kenyon, *The Strange and Dangerous Voyage of Capt. Thomas James* (Toronto, 1975).

79. Luke Fox, *North-West Fox; or, Fox from the North-West* (London, 1635). Foxe's original journals are now in the Gilcrease Museum for the American Arts, Tulsa, Oklahoma.

80. For the Farrer map, see R. A. Skelton, *Explorers' Maps* (London, 1958), 258, 270; also see W. P. Cumming, S. Hillier, D. B. Quinn, and G. Williams, eds., *The Exploration of North America, 1630–1776* (New York, 1974), 82.

81. See Sturtevant and Quinn, "The New Prey," 61–140.

7. A Continent Revealed

1. Lawrence C. Wroth, *The Voyages of Giovanni da Verrazzano, 1524–1528* (New Haven, 1970), 14–16.

2. "Agreement Made with Esteban Gómez, Pilot, for the Exploration of Eastern Cathay," in David Beers Quinn, Alison Quinn, and Susan Hillier, eds., *New American World: A Documentary History of North America to 1612* (hereafter cited as NAW), 5 vols. (London, 1979), 1:271–72.

3. For the slaves/cloves story, see the following from NAW: Peter Martyr, *De orbe novo decades*, vol. 8 (1530), 1:274–75; Antonio Galvao, *Tratado dos descobrimentos* (1563), 1:275; and Antonio de Herrera, *Historia general de los hechos de los castellanos en las islas y tierre firme del Mar Océano* (1525), 1:276. For conflicting assessments of the continent's possibilities as revealed by the expedition, see Gonzalo Fernández de Oviedo, *Sumario de la natural y general istoria de las Indias* (Toledo, 1526), 1:274, and Martyr, 1:274–75.

4. John L. Allen, "From Cabot to Cartier: The Early Exploration of Eastern North America, 1497–1543," *Annals of the Association of American Geographers* 82 (1992): 513.

5. Verrazzano's letter of 8 July 1524 appears in Wroth, *Verrazzano*, 133–43.

6. Verrazzano to Francis I, 8 July 1524, in Wroth, *Verrazzano*, 134–35, and see 74–78.

7. Verrazzano to Francis I, 8 July 1524, in Wroth, *Verrazzano*, 136–37; David Beers Quinn, *North America from Earliest Discovery to First Settlements: The Norse Voyages to 1612* (New York, 1977), 155.

8. Verrazzano to Francis I, 8 July 1524, in NAW 1:138–43, quotations on 140, 143. See also NAW 1:89–90. On Verrazzano's voyage and its impact, see Marcel Trudel, *The Beginnings of New France, 1524–1663*, trans. Patricia Claxton (Montreal, 1973), 4–9.

9. Paul E. Hoffman, *A New Andalucia and a Way to the Orient: The American Southeast during the Sixteenth Century* (Baton Rouge, 1990), gives an excellent account of Verrazzano's impact on European cartography; see especially chap. 5 for a discussion of geographical misconceptions arising from the Verrazzano voyage.

10. This voyage can be followed in NAW 1:161–71, which includes extracts of the *Interlude of the Four Elements*.

11. John Rut to Henry VIII, 3 August 1527, in NAW 1:189–90.

12. "Jacques Cartier's First Account of the New Land, Called New France, Discovered in the Year 1534," in NAW 1:293–95.

13. NAW 1:296–300.

14. NAW 1:300–302.

15. NAW 1:300–304, and "The Second Voyage Undertaken by the Command and

Wish of the Most Christian King of France, Francis the First of That Name, for the Completion of the Discovery of the Western Lands . . . by Jacques Cartier, 1536," in NAW 1:304, 1:310–11. See also Quinn, *North America*, 169–78.

16. "Canada," by which Cartier designated the Stadaconans' territory, may have meant "village." See Bruce G. Trigger and James F. Pendergast, "Saint Lawrence Iroquoians," in Bruce Trigger, ed. *Handbook of North American Indians*, vol. 15 (Washington DC, 1978), 361.

17. "The Second Voyage," in NAW 1:307–13.

18. "The Second Voyage," in NAW 1:311–17, 1:320–21.

19. "The Second Voyage," in NAW 1:317, 321, 325. David B. Quinn theorizes that the copper may have come from the Huron Indians of the Great Lakes and that the pale people in tailored clothing may have been Eskimos of the Hudson's Bay region; see Quinn, *North America*, 80–81.

20. Lagarto to John III, 22 January 1539–40, in NAW 1:328–30.

21. "The Second Voyage," in NAW 1:317–22.

22. "The Second Voyage," in NAW 1:322–24; Quinn, *North America*, 182.

23. NAW 1:324–28; "The Third Voyage of Discovery Made by Captaine Jacques Cartier, 1540, unto the Countreys of Canada, Hochelaga, and Saguenay," NAW 1:330; Christopher Carleill, "A Briefe and Summary Discourse upon the Intended Voyage to the Hithermost Parts of America," 1583, in David B. Quinn, ed., *The Voyages and Colonising Enterprises of Sir Humphrey Gilbert*, 2 vols., Hakluyt Society, 2d ser., nos. 83–84 (London, 1940), 2:362–63. For discussion of Cartier's first two voyages and their impact on geographical understanding in Europe, see Trudel, *Beginnings of New France*, chap. 2, esp. 29, 33, and see Quinn, *North America*, 169–83.

24. Richard Hakluyt, "The Voyage of Master Hore and Divers Other Gentlemen, to Newfoundland, and Cape Breton, in the Yeere 1536," in NAW 1:206–8. Richard Hakluyt traveled two hundred miles to take down the story of this voyage from the one survivor still alive, Master Thomas Buts, when Hakluyt was compiling the first edition of his *Principall Navigations*, published in 1589 (in NAW 1:208).

25. "Third Voyage of Discovery," 1:330–32. For the contemporary recognition that scurvy could be alleviated by eating fresh vegetables, see Karen Ordahl Kupperman, "Apathy and Death in Early Jamestown," *Journal of American History* 66 (1979): 33–34.

26. NAW 1:333–34.

27. "The Voyage of John Francis de la Roche, Knight, Lord of Roberval, to the Countries of Canada, Saguinai, and Hochelaga, . . . begun in April, 1542," in NAW 1:337–39.

28. Quinn, *North America*, 185–90; Trudel, *Beginnings of New France*, chap. 3.

29. NAW 1:135.

30. Samuel E. Morison, *The European Discovery of America: The Northern Voyages, A.D. 500–1600* (London, 1971), 451.

31. See the report to the king of Portugal, 12 November 1541, which was intercepted and sent to the Spanish court, in NAW 1:334–35.

32. For the problem that the eastern North American climate presented to colonists, and their attempts to explain why the climate deviated so drastically from that of similar latitudes in Europe, see Karen Ordahl Kupperman, "The Puzzle of the American Climate in the Early Colonial Period," *American Historical Review* 87 (1982): 1262–89.

33. For description of the unique conditions that created the Banks and make them and the Gulf so rich in fish, see Carl Ortwin Sauer, *Seventeenth Century North America* (Berkeley, 1980), 69–71.

34. "A Letter Written to M. Richard Hakluyt of the Middle Temple, Conteining a Report of the True State and Commodities of Newfoundland, by M. Anthonie Parkhurst Gentleman, 1578," in NAW 4:7–8.

35. Quinn, *North America*, 528–29. On the organization of the fishing trade, and the participation of various European countries, see Harold A. Innis, *The Cod Fisheries: The History of an International Economy* (New Haven, 1940), chaps. 2 and 3, and Gillian T. Cell, *English Enterprise in Newfoundland, 1577–1660*, (Toronto, 1969), chaps. 1, 2. See also A. R. Michell, "The European Fisheries in Early Modern History," in E. E. Rich and C. H. Wilson, eds., *The Economic Organization of Early Modern Europe*, vol. 5 of *The Cambridge Economic History of Europe* (Cambridge, U.K., 1977), 134–84.

36. John J. McCusker and Russell R. Menard, *The Economy of British America, 1607–1789* (Chapel Hill, 1985), 97–99.

37. See the documents in NAW 4:183–87.

38. All the documents concerning Sir Humphrey Gilbert's expeditions and the planning that went into them are collected in Quinn, *Sir Humphrey Gilbert*. See also Quinn, *North America*, 347–68, and Douglas R. McManis, *European Impressions of the New England Coast, 1497–1620*, University of Chicago Department of Geography Research Paper No. 139 (Chicago, 1972), chap. 2.

39. Stephen Parmenius, "To the Worshipfull, Master Richard Hakluyt at Oxforde in Christchurche Master of Art, and Philosophie, His Friend and Brother," in David B. Quinn and Neil M. Cheshire, eds., *The New Found Land of Stephen Parmenius* (Toronto, 1972), 175. See also Sir Humphrey Gilbert to Sir George Peckham, 8 August 1583, in Quinn, *Sir Humphrey Gilbert* 2:383.

40. Edward Hayes, "A Report of the Voyage and Successe Thereof, Attempted in the Yeere of Our Lord 1583 by Sir Humfrey Gilbert Knight," in Quinn, *Sir Humphrey Gilbert* 2:418.

41. Parmenius to Richard Hakluyt, in Quinn and Cheshire, *New Found Land*, 175–76.

42. Hoffman, *A New Andalucia*, 105–28.

43. Hoffman, *A New Andalucia*, 136–39.

44. W. P. Cumming, R. A. Skelton, and D. B. Quinn, *The Discovery of North America* (New York, 1972), 153. The Le Testu map is reproduced as plate 163.

45. For a full account of these events and the involvement of the English government in them, see J. Leitch Wright Jr., *Anglo-Spanish Rivalry in North America* (Athens GA, 1971), 23–26.

46. The story of this settlement was told by René Goulaine de Laudonnière in his *L'histoire notable de la Floride* (1586), translated and published by Richard Hakluyt in 1587, excerpted in NAW 2:294–307; and in Lancelot Voisin, Seigneur de La Popellinière, *Les trois mondes*, in NAW 2:307–8.

47. Laudonnière, *L'histoire notable*, in NAW 2:335–39.

48. Laudonnière told the story of this venture in "The Second Voyage unto Florida, Made and Written by Captaine Laudonnière, Which Fortified and Inhabited There Two Summers and One Whole Winter," and "The Third Voyage of the Frenchmen Made by Captaine John Ribault unto Florida," in his *L'histoire notable*, in NAW 2:319–61.

49. Nicolas Le Challeux, *Discours de l' histoire de la Floride*, in NAW 2:374. See also "Memorial Written by Doctor Gonzalo Solis de Merás of All the Voyages and Deeds of the Adelantado Pedro Menéndez de Avilés His Brother-in-Law and of the Conquest of Florida and the Justice he Worked on Juan Ribao and the Other Frenchmen," in NAW 2:424–55.

50. Cumming, Skelton, and Quinn, *Discovery of North America*, 169.

51. Laudonnière, *L'histoire notable*, in NAW 2:281–82, 296–97, 339–40, 342.

52. John Ribault, "The True Discoverie of Terra Florida" (1563), in NAW 2:290–94; Laudonnière, *L'histoire notable*, in NAW 2:333–35.

53. A full account of Spanish exploration in the Southeast during this period may be found in chapters 5 (vol. 1) and 9 (vol. 2) of the present work.

54. "Capitulations and Asiento between Philip II and Pedro Menéndez de Avilés Regarding the Conquest of Florida," 20 March 1565, in NAW 2:385.

55. Menéndez de Avilés to Philip II, 11 September 1565, in NAW 2:391–95.

56. Menéndez de Avilés to Philip II, 15 October 1565, in NAW 2:396–400.

57. Menéndez de Avilés to Philip II, 15 October 1565, in NAW 2:399. For the Pardo expedition, see the documents in NAW 2:541–49, and Quinn, *North America*, 271–74. J. H. Parry offers a full description of the reasoning behind Spanish plans here: see

"The Spaniards in Eastern North America," in David B. Quinn, ed., *Early Maryland in a Wider World* (Detroit, 1982), 84–102. See also Wright, *Anglo-Spanish Rivalry*, chap. 1.

58. Menéndez de Avilés to Philip II, 12 December 1565, in NAW 2:414–17.

59. In 1562, King Philip II had briefly declared that no further attempts should be made to colonize the eastern coast of North America, apparently thinking no other European power would do so; Woodbury Lowery, *The Spanish Settlements within the Present Limits of the United States, 1513–1574*, 2 vols. (1901, 1905; reprint, New York, 1959), 1:376.

60. The story of the Spanish presence can be best followed in Quinn, *North America*, 262–88.

61. Diego de Camargo, reports of 14, 24, 25 August 1566, in NAW 2:552–53.

62. All the documents concerning this mission are collected in Clifford M. Lewis and Albert J. Loomie, *The Spanish Jesuit Mission in Virginia, 1570–1572* (Chapel Hill, 1953). Further analysis of the confrontation occurs in Charlotte Gradie, "Spanish Jesuit Missions in Virginia: Cultural Conflict, Politics, and the Mission That Failed," *Virginia Magazine of History and Biography* 96 (1988), and Carl Bridenbaugh, *Jamestown, 1544–1699* (New York, 1980), 10–19.

63. Hoffman, *A New Andalucia*, chap. 10, gives a good account of Spanish geographical theories during the years 1565–72. See also chapter 5 in the present work.

64. See the hostile description from an official in Havana, "An Account of the Population on the Coast of Florida, and Obstacles That Were Encountered for Its Fortification and Defence" (c. 1572), in NAW 2:581–88. See also Quinn, *North America*, 286. For detailed discussion of Spanish settlements in North America, see Woodbury Lowery, *Spanish Settlements*, vol. 2.

65. On the Durham House Set, see Robert Lacey, *Sir Walter Ralegh* (London, 1973), chap. 15.

66. Henry W. Meyers presented evidence that Fernandes may have been a Jew: see "The Jews in Tudor England and Their Presence on the Raleigh Voyages" (paper presented to the Southern Historical Association, 11 November 1983).

67. "Private Diary of John Walker," in E. G. R. Taylor, ed., *The Troublesome Voyage of Captain Edward Fenton, 1582–1583* (Cambridge, U.K., 1959), 202.

68. "Private Diary of Richard Madox," in Taylor, *Troublesome Voyage*, 192–93, 196–97. On the career of Simão Fernandes, see "A Portuguese Pilot in the English Service," in David Beers Quinn, *England and the Discovery of America, 1481–1620* (London, 1974), 246–63.

69. See Kenneth R. Andrews, *Elizabethan Privateering, 1585–1603* (Cambridge, U.K., 1964), chap. 11.

70. John Sparke included a description of the French colony in his report of the Hawkins voyage, a report that was printed by Richard Hakluyt in the *Principall Nav-*

igations; the excerpt dealing with the Laudonnière colony is reprinted in NAW 2:364–70.

71. For the scientific basis of this thinking, see Karen Ordahl Kupperman, "Fear of Hot Climates in the Anglo-American Colonial Experience," *William and Mary Quarterly*, 3d ser., 41 (1984): 213–40, esp. 217–20, and Kupperman, "Puzzle of the American Climate," 1262–89.

72. Hoffman, *A New Andalucia*, 286.

73. All the documents concerning the Roanoke voyages are collected in David Beers Quinn, *The Roanoke Voyages, 1584–1590*, 2 vols. (London, 1955). Arthur Barlowe's "The First Voyage Made to the Coastes of America, with Two Barkes, Wherein Were Captaines Master Philip Amadas, and Master Arthur Barlowe, Who Discovered Part of the Countrey, Now Called Virginia, Anno 1584," is in 1:91–116, quotations on 106, 108.

74. Hoffman, *A New Andalucia*, 294.

75. Barlowe, "The First Voyage," 1:94, 114–15. The story of the Roanoke colonies can be followed in David Beers Quinn, *Set Fair for Roanoke: Voyages and Colonies, 1584–1606* (Chapel Hill, 1985), and Karen Ordahl Kupperman, *Roanoke: The Abandoned Colony* (Totowa NJ, 1984).

76. On the contributions of the two Richard Hakluyts to planning for the first Roanoke colony, see E. G. R. Taylor, ed., *The Original Writings and Correspondence of the Two Richard Hakluyts*, 2 vols., Hakluyt Society, 2d ser., nos. 76–77 (London, 1935), 1:32–39. *Discourse of Western Planting* is printed in 2:211–26, and *Inducements to the Liking of the Voyage Intended towards Virginia* in 2:327–338.

77. Report in Holinshed, *Chronicles*, vol. 3 (1587), reprinted in Quinn, *Roanoke Voyages* 1:177.

78. Anon., "The Voyage Made by Sir Richard Grenvile, for Sir Walter Ralegh, to Virginia, in the Yeere, 1585," in Quinn, *Roanoke Voyages* 1:189.

79. The incident is reported in the *Tiger Journal*, in Quinn, *Roanoke Voyages* 1:191.

80. See Karen Ordahl Kupperman, "English Perceptions of Treachery, 1583–1640: The Case of the American 'Savages,'" *Historical Journal* 20 (1977): 163–87.

81. "An Extract of Master Lanes Letter, to Master Richard Hakluyt Esquire, and Another Gentleman of the Middle Temple, from Virginia," 3 September 1585, in Quinn, *Roanoke Voyages* 1:207–9.

82. Lane mentions this expedition, "An Account of the Particularities of the Imployments of the English Men Left in Virginia by Sir Richard Greenevill under the Charge of Master Ralfe Lane Generall of the Same," in Quinn, *Roanoke Voyages* 1:257–58. Much of the information on their exploration comes from the map jointly done by Thomas Hariot and John White.

83. Ralph Lane described this voyage in Quinn, *Roanoke Voyages* 1:258–73.

84. Lane, in Quinn, *Roanoke Voyages* 1:259–68, 273–74.

85. Lane, in Quinn, *Roanoke Voyages* 1:264–68, 270.

86. Lane, in Quinn, *Roanoke Voyages* 1:268–73.

87. Lane, in Quinn, *Roanoke Voyages* 1:270–77, 280.

88. Lane, "Account," in Quinn, *Roanoke Voyages* 1:277–88, 293.

89. The story of Drake's attacks on the Spanish bases in Florida is told in Walter Bigges, *A Summarie and True Discourse of Sir Francis Drakes West Indian Voyage* (1589), in Mary Frear Keeler, ed., *Sir Francis Drake's West Indian Voyage, 1585–86* (London, 1981), 264–270, and anon., "The Discourse and Description of the Voyage of Sir Francis Drake and Master Frobisher, Set Forward the 14 Daie of September 1585," in Keeler, *Drake's West Indian Voyage*, 205–9.

90. Lane outlined his plans in his "Account," in Quinn, *Roanoke Voyages* 1:260–63.

91. Lane, "Account," in Quinn, *Roanoke Voyages* 2:288–95; Bigges, *Discourse*, 271–75.

92. Hoffman, *A New Andalucia*, 296.

93. Lane, "Account," in Quinn, *Roanoke Voyages* 1:272–74.

94. John White's paintings were reproduced exactly for the first time in Paul Hulton and D. B. Quinn, eds., *The American Drawings of John White, 1577–1590* (London, 1964). The paintings were published in an inexpensive edition for the Roanoke Quadricentenary; Paul Hulton, *America 1585: The Complete Drawings of John White* (Chapel Hill, 1984). The introductions of both of these books discuss White as an artist and his association with Le Moyne. On Le Moyne, see also Paul Hulton, *The Work of Jacques Le Moyne de Morgues, a Hugenot Artist in France, Florida, and England* (London, 1977).

95. Lane, "Account," in Quinn, *Roanoke Voyages* 1:293.

96. Thomas Hariot, *Briefe and True Report*, in Quinn, *Roanoke Voyages* 1:317–87.

97. Anon., "Instructions for a Voyage of Reconnaissance to North America in 1582 or 1583," in *NAW* 3:239–45. See also E. G. R. Taylor, "Instructions to a Colonial Surveyor in 1582," *Mariner's Mirror* 37 (1951): 48–62.

98. White's originals can be compared with de Bry's engravings in Hulton and Quinn, *Drawings of John White* and in Hulton, *America 1585*. Dover has published a facsimile of the 1590 edition of the *Briefe and True Report* with the woodcuts and Hariot's notes.

99. Hakluyt to Sir Walter Raleigh, 30 December 1586, in Quinn, *Roanoke Voyages* 1:493–94. Hakluyt also argued that the western coast of North America was not far from Chesapeake Bay. See his dedication of his translation of Rene de Laudonnière, *A Notable Historie Containing Foure Voyages Made by Certayne French Captaynes unto Florida* (1587), in Quinn, *Roanoke Voyages* 2:551–52.

100. The developing controversy between White and Fernandes can be followed

in White's narrative, "The Fourth Voyage Made to Virginia, with Three Shippes, in the Yeere, 1587, Wherein Was Transported the Second Colonie," in Quinn, *Roanoke Voyages* 2:515–38. Professor Quinn argues that the Lost Colonists did make their way overland to Chesapeake Bay, where they may have settled with the Chesapeake Indians, a tribe remaining independent of Powhatan's clientage system, and that they may have been killed along with many of the Chesapeakes shortly before the founding of Jamestown in 1607; see Quinn, *Set Fair for Roanoke*, chap. 19, "A Colony Is Lost and Found?"

101. See the order of the Privy Council to Sir Richard Grenville, 31 March 1588, in Quinn, *Roanoke Voyages* 2:560–61.

102. "The Fifth Voyage of Master John White into the West Indies and Parts of America called Virginia, in the Yeere 1590," in Quinn, *Roanoke Voyages* 2:598–622.

103. On the privateering war of the 1590s, see Andrews, *Elizabethan Privateering*. J. H. Parry argues that despite the activities of a large international band of privateers, Spain's flow of silver was at its peak during the last decade of the sixteenth century and the first decade of the seventeenth: Parry, "Spaniards in Eastern North America," 96.

104. Richard Hakluyt, *Discourse of Western Planting* (1584), in Taylor, *Two Richard Hakluyts* 2:227, 233.

105. Hakluyt, "Discourse," 2:227, 266. A league was about three miles, thus the distance was about three hundred miles.

106. On the beginnings of the fur trade, see Trudel, *Beginnings of New France*, 56–58.

107. Samuel de Champlain, *Of Savages* (1603), in Henry P. Biggar, gen. ed., *The Works of Samuel de Champlain*, 6 vols. (Toronto, 1922–36), 1:143.

108. For this reconstruction, see Bruce G. Trigger, "Early Iroquoian Contacts with Europeans," in Trigger, *Handbook of North American Indians* 15:346–47. For critical discussion of other theories, see Trigger and Pendergast, "Saint Lawrence Iroquoians," 357–361. For fuller analysis, see James F. Pendergast and Bruce G. Trigger, *Cartier's Hochelaga and the Dawson Site* (Montreal, 1972), 71–93.

109. Hoffman, *A New Andalucia*, 284–86.

110. Trudel, *Beginnings of New France*, 55–58; Hakluyt, "Discourse," 2:227.

111. These expeditions are the subject of chaps. 12 and 13 of Quinn, *England and the Discovery of America*.

112. Trudel, *Beginnings of New France*, 62.

113. Order of the Parlement of Normandy, 20 May 1598, in NAW 4:309; Report of Monsieur Eaufranc, lieutenant general of the police of Rouen, in NAW 4:310.

114. "Document Sent by the Morquis Troillus de Mesgouës de la Roche-Mesgouëz in Brittany to King Henry IV . . . Chiefly on the Subject of the Trouble and

Opposition He Met with in the Isle de Bourbon" (1606), in NAW 4:310–311. For discussion of the background of these events, see Trudel, *Beginnings of New France*, 60–65.

115. Biggar, *Works of Samuel de Champlain* 3:305–6; Trudel, *Beginnings of New France*, 65–70.

116. Biggar, *Works of Samuel de Champlain* 3:308–11.

117. Samuel de Champlain, *Of Savages* (1603), in Biggar, *Works of Samuel de Champlain* 1:98–106.

118. Marcel Trudel estimates that trade goods were already in the hands of Indians who lived fifteen hundred miles from the Atlantic coast: *Beginnings of New France*, 79–80.

119. Champlain, *Of Savages* 1:121–25.

120. Champlain, *Of Savages* 1:125–57.

121. Champlain, *Of Savages* 1:170–72, 184–85. On the 1603 expedition and its accomplishments, see Trudel, *Beginnings of New France*, chap. 5, and C. E. Heidenreich, *Explorations and Mapping of Samuel de Champlain, 1603–1632* (Toronto, 1976), 1–4.

122. Samuel de Champlain, *Voyages*, in Biggar, *Works of Samuel de Champlain* 1:237–59, 3:340–44.

123. Champlain, *Voyages* 1:260–64, 3:344–47.

124. Champlain, *Voyages* 1:271–72, 3:322–23.

125. Champlain, *Voyages* 3:352–76. On Bashabes, see Dean R. Snow, "Eastern Abenaki," in Trigger, *Handbook of North American Indians* 15:137–47. On the agreement between Bashabes and Champlain, see Neal Salisbury, *Manitou and Providence: Indians, Europeans, and the Making of New England, 1500–1643* (New York, 1982), 61–62, 70.

126. Marc Lescarbot, *The History of New France*, ed. W. L. Grant and H. P. Biggar, 3 vols. (Toronto, 1907–14), 2:257–71.

127. Lescarbot, *History of New France* 1:xi, 2:257.

128. Champlain, *Voyages* 1:302–7.

129. Champlain, *Voyages* 1:334–35.

130. Champlain, *Voyages* 1:336, 350–52.

131. Champlain, *Voyages* 1:311–55, 362–66.

132. Lescarbot, *History of New France* 2:354–55. On this relationship, and the effect of European intrusion on the Micmacs, see Salisbury, *Manitou and Providence*, 60–62.

133. Champlain, *Voyages* 1:393–94.

134. Champlain and Lescarbot both wrote extensively on this experience. For Champlain's version, see Champlain, *Voyages* 1:91–469; for Lescarbot, see his *History of New France* 2:209–372. For discussions of the voyages, see Trudel, *Beginnings*

of New France, chap. 6; McManis, *European Impressions*, 68–85; Quinn, *North America*, 395–407.

135. Heidenreich, *Explorations and Mapping*, xi.

136. On Champlain as a geographer, see Heidenreich, *Explorations and Mapping*, chap. 2, and McManis, *European Impressions*, 40–44.

137. David B. Quinn and Alison M. Quinn, *The English New England Voyages, 1602–1608*, Hakluyt Society, 2d ser., no. 161 (London, 1983), 3–5.

138. Quinn and Quinn, *New England Voyages*, 112.

139. Two accounts were written of this voyage: Gabriel Archer, *The Relation of Captaine Gosnols Voyage to the North Part of Virginia* (1625), in Quinn and Quinn, *New England Voyages*, 114–38; and John Brereton, *A Briefe and True Relation of the Discoverie of the North Part of Virginia* (1602), in Quinn and Quinn, *New England Voyages*, 143–65.

140. Quinn and Quinn, *New England Voyages*. For the encounter with the Micmacs, see Brereton, *Briefe and True Relation*, 145, and Archer, *Captaine Gosnols Voyage*, 117. For trials of English seeds and Brereton's judgment of the fertility, see Quinn and Quinn, *New England Voyages*, 148–52.

141. *A Voyage Set Out from the Citie of Bristoll at the Charge of the Chiefest Merchants and Inhabitants of the Said Citie . . . for the Discoverie of the North Part of Virginia, in the Yeere 1603*, in Quinn and Quinn, *New England Voyages*, 214–28. The quotation is from the introduction to the journal, in Quinn and Quinn, *New England Voyages*, 213. On the Gosnold and Pring voyages, see also Quinn, *England and the Discovery of America*, chap. 16, "'Virginians' on the Thames in 1603."

142. James Rosier, *A True Relation of the Most Prosperous Voyage Made This Present Yeere 1605, by Captaine George Waymouth, in the Discovery of the Land of Virginia*, in Quinn and Quinn, *New England Voyages*, 251–311. For discussion of Rosier's exaggerations, see Quinn and Quinn, *New England Voyages*, 64–70. For discussion of the Gosnold, Pring, and Waymouth voyages, see Quinn, *North America*, 391–94, 400–402, and McManis, *European Impressions*, 90–102.

143. Quinn and Quinn, *New England Voyages*, 76.

144. Purchas, *Hakluytus Posthumous: or, Purchas His Pilgrimes* (1625), in Quinn and Quinn, *New England Voyages*, 352; Sir Ferdinando Gorges, *A Briefe Relation of the Discovery and Plantation of New England* (1622), in James Phinney Baxter, ed., *Sir Ferdinando Gorges and His Province of Maine*, 3 vols. (1890), 1:206–7.

145. All the extant documents associated with the Sagadahoc colony are in Quinn and Quinn, *New England Voyages*, 331–468.

146. John Smith, *Generall Historie of Virginia, New-England, and the Summer Isles* (1624), in Philip L. Barbour, ed., *The Complete Works of Captain John Smith (1580–1631)*, 3 vols. (Chapel Hill, 1986), 2:399.

147. All the documents associated with the Jamestown colony are collected in

Philip L. Barbour, ed., *The Jamestown Voyages under the First Charter, 1606–1609*, 2 vols. (Cambridge, U.K., 1969). See also Barbour, *John Smith*.

148. Champlain, *Voyages* 1:231–32, 2:3–8, 4:31–37.

149. Champlain, *Voyages* 2:9–36, 4:37–48.

150. Trigger, "Early Iroquoian Contacts," 15:346–47; Trigger and Pendergast, "Saint Lawrence Iroquoians," 15:361.

8. The Early Exploration of the Pacific Coast

1. Angel Altolaguirre y Duvale, *Vasco Núñez de Balboa* (Madrid, 1914), lxvii–xcix, 47–65.

2. Henry R. Wagner, ed., *The Discovery of New Spain in 1518* by Juan de Grijalva (Berkeley, 1942).

3. For full accounts in English, see the following: Francisco López de Gómara, *Cortés: The Life of the Conqueror by His Secretary*, ed. and trans. Lesley B. Simpson (Berkeley, 1964); Bernal Díaz del Castillo, *True History of the Conquest of New Spain*, trans. and ed. A. P. Maudslay, 3 vols. (London, 1908–16); and Hernán Cortés, *Hernan Cortés: Letters from Mexico*, trans. and ed. A. R. Pagden (New York, 1971).

4. Hernando Cortés, *Cartas y documentos* (Mexico City, 1963), 191.

5. Carl O. Sauer, *Colima of New Spain in the Sixteenth Century*, Ibero-Americana, no. 29 (Berkeley, 1948), 2–86.

6. Martín Fernández de Navarrete, *Obras*, 3 vols. (Madrid, 1955), 2:365–469.

7. Max L. Moorhead, "Hernan Cortés and the Tehuantepec Passage," *Hispanic American Historical Review* 24 (1949): 370–79.

8. Cortés, *Cartas y documentos*, 213.

9. Pascual de Gayangos, ed., *Libros de Caballerías* (Madrid, 1963), 539. See also Irving Leonard, *Books of the Brave* (Cambridge MA, 1949).

10. Navarrete, *Obras* 3:96–226.

11. Navarrete, *Obras* 3:251–272.

12. W. Michael Mathes, ed., *The Conquistador in California, 1535: The Voyage of Fernando Cortés to Baha California in Chronicles and Documents*, Baja California Travels Series, no. 31 (Los Angeles, 1973), 29, 45–46.

13. Mathes, *The Conquistador in California*, 30–31, 46, 58.

14. Mathes, *The Conquistador in California*, 31–33, 47–48, 58–69.

15. Mathes, *The Conquistador in California*, 34–39, 49–54, 70–79, 103–18.

16. Henry R. Wagner, *Spanish Voyages to the North West Coast of America in the Sixteenth Century* (San Francisco, 1929), 11–50.

17. Richard Hakluyt, *The Principal Voyages, Traffiques, and Discoveries of the English Nation*, 20 vols. (reprint, Glasgow, 1904), 9:279–318.

18. Antonio de Herrera, *Historia general de los hechos de los castellanos en las islas y tierra firme del mar océano*, 14 vols. (Madrid, 1934), 14:307–71.

19. Henry R. Wagner, *Juan Rodríguez Cabrillo: Discoverer of the Coast of California* (San Francisco, 1941), 35–94. See also Harry Kelsey, *Juan Rodríguez Cabrillo* (San Marino CA, 1986).

20. W. Michael Mathes, "The Mythological Geography of California: Origins, Development, Confirmation, and Disappearance," *Americas* 45 (1989): 316, 319.

21. Mathes, "Mythological Geography of California," 318–319.

22. Mathes, "Mythological Geography of California," 320.

23. Luis Cebreiro Blanco, ed., *Colección de diarios y relaciones para la historia de los viajes y descubrimientos* (Madrid, 1945), ii.

24. Wagner, *Spanish Voyages*, 131; William Lytle Schurz, "The Manila Galleon and California," *Southwestern Historical Quarterly* 21 (1917): 107–9.

25. Richard Carnac Temple, ed., *The World Encompassed by Sir Francis Drake* (London, 1926).

26. W. Michael Mathes, *Sebastián Vizcaíno and Spanish Expansion in the Pacific Ocean, 1580–1630* (San Francisco, 1968), 11–13.

27. Wagner, *Spanish Voyages*, 132–37; W. Michael Mathes, ed., *Californiana I: Documentos para la historia de la demarcación comercial de California, 1583–1632* (Madrid, 1965), documento 3; Hakluyt, *Principal Navigations*, 9:326–37.

28. Mathes, *Vizcaíno*, 15.

29. Mathes, *Californiana I*, documento 2.

30. Mathes, *Californiana I*, documento 6.

31. W. Michael Mathes, ed., *The Capture of the Santa Ana, Cabo San Lucas, November 1587*, Baja California Travels Series, no. 18 (Los Angeles, 1969).

32. Samuel Purchas, *Hakluytus Posthumus or Purchas his Pilgrimes* (Glasgow, 1905), 2:149–85.

33. Mathes, *Californiana I*, documentos 16, 17, 20, 21, 26.

34. Martín Fernández de Navarrete, "Examen histórico-crítico de los viajes y descubrimientos apócrifos," *Colección de documentos inéditos para la historia de España* (Madrid, 1842–95), 15:102–4, 262–63; Pedro Novo y Colson, *Sobre los viajes apócrifos de Juan de Fuca y Lorenzo Ferrer Maldonado* (Madrid, 1881).

35. Wagner, *Spanish Voyages*, 176–78.

36. Mathes, *Californiana I*, documentos 15, 18, 19, 22, 24, 27–29, 34, 35, 36, 38, 181.

37. Mathes, *Californiana I*, documento 39.

38. Mathes, *Californiana I*, documentos 40–47, 50–59, 183; Mathes, *Vizcaíno*, 54–107.

39. Mathes, *Californiana I*, documentos 52, 57; Mathes, "Mythological Geography," 327.

40. Mathes, *Californiana I*, documentos 50, 52, 55, 57.

41. Mathes, *Californiana I*, documentos 67–74.

42. Mathes, *Californiana I*, documento 89.

43. Mathes, *Californiana I*, documento 80; Mathes, "Mythological Geography," 328.

44. Mathes, *Californiana I*, documento 7; Navarrete, *Examen históricocrítico*, 15:71–101; Novo y Colson, *Viajes apócrifos*.

45. Mathes, *Californiana I*, documentos 105, 109, 110, 112, 113, 118, 120–23, 125, 126; "Autos sobre el conflicto del puerto de Acapulco, 1614," Audiencia de Mexico, 1844, Archivo General de Indias, Sevilla; Mathes, *Vizcaíno*, 121–53.

46. W. Michael Mathes, ed. *Californiana II: Documentos para la historia de las explotación comercial de California, 1611–1679* (Madrid, 1970), documentos 1–8, 32; Nicolas de Cardona, *Geographic and Hydrographic Descriptions of Many Northern and Southern Lands and Seas in the Indies, Specifically of the Discovery of the Kingdom of California (1632)*, ed. and trans. W. Michael Mathes, Baja California Travels Series, no. 35 (Los Angeles, 1974), 93–98.

47. Mathes, *Californiana I*, documentos 151, 153, 154.

48. Mathes, *Californiana I*, documentos 155, 156.

49. Mathes, *Californiana II*, documentos 8–21, 32.

50. Mathes, *Californiana I*, documento 177.

51. *Documentos para servier a la historia de Nuevo México* (Madrid, 1962), 197–99. The fiction of this account is even further confirmed by mismatches of persons and chronology. Mathes, "Mythological Geography," 340–41.

52. Mathes, *Californiana I*, documento 179; Mathes, *Californiana II*, documentos 25–27; W. Michael Mathes, ed. and trans., *Spanish Approaches to the Island of California, 1628–1632* (San Francisco, 1975), 5–6.

53. Mathes, *Californiana I*, documentos 180–86; Mathes, *Californiana II*, documentos 28, 31; Mathes, *Spanish Approaches*, 7–44.

54. Mathes, *Californiana II*, documento 36.

55. Mathes, *Californiana I*, documento 189; Mathes, *Californiana II*, documento 33; Mathes, *Spanish Approaches*, 45–52.

56. Mathes, *Californiana II*, documentos 34–37, 45–48; Miguel Leon-Portilla, *Voyages of Francisco de Ortega*, Baja California Travels Series, no. 30 (Los Angeles, 1973).

57. Mathes, *Californiana II*, documentos 34, 37.

58. Mathes, *Californiana II*, documentos 45–48; Leon-Portilla, *Voyages of Francisco de Ortega*.

59. Mathes, *Californiana II*, documentos 32, 39–40.

60. Mathes, *Californiana II*, documentos 41–44.

61. Mathes, *Californiana II*, documentos 55, 56.

62. Mathes, *Californiana II*, documento 57.

63. Mathes, *Californiana II*, documentos 49–51, 55, 58.

64. Mathes, "Mythological Geography," 331; Mathes, *Californiana II*, documento 45.

65. Mathes, *Californiana II*, documentos 46–48. This voyage was claimed to be invented in Ernest J. Burrus, "Two Fictitious Accounts of Ortega's 'Third Voyage' to California," *Hispanic American Historical Review* 52 (1972): 272–83. However, documents found by the author in General de Parte, Tomo 11, expedientes 63, 64, Archivo General de la Nación, México, and in Protocolo de Andres de Venegas, Tomo 1606–18, 30 de mayo de 1611, Archivo de Instrumentos Públicos, Guadalajara, prove conclusively that this voyage of 1636 was completely factual.

66. Mathes, *Californiana II*, documentos 59–63.

67. Mathes, *Californiana II*, documentos 49–51, 58.

68. Mathes, *Californiana II*, documento 63.

69. Mathes, *Californiana II*, documentos 48–51, 58.

70. General de Parte, Tomo 8, f. 7v, Archivo General de la Nación, México.

71. Mathes, *Californiana II*, documento 75.

72. Mathes, *Californiana II*, documento 76.

73. Mathes, *Californiana II*, documento 77.

74. Mathes, *Californiana II*, documentos 80–83.

75. Mathes, *Californiana II*, documentos 85, 94, 104, 105.

76. Mathes, *Californiana II*, documento 84.

77. Mathes, *Californiana II*, documentos 94, 104, 105.

78. Mathes, *Californiana II*, documentos 96–99, 104, 105.

79. Mathes, *Californiana II*, documentos 101–14; W. Michael Mathes, "Don Pedro Porter y Casanate Admiral of the South Sea, 1611–1662," *Southern California Quarterly* 54 (1972): 1–9.

80. General de Parte, Tomo 11, expedientes 63, 64, Archivo General de la Nación, México.

81. Mathes, *Californiana II*, documentos 115, 116.

82. Mathes, *Californiana II*, documentos 116–18, 127.

83. Mathes, *Californiana II*, documentos 115, 116.

84. Mathes, *Californiana II*, documentos 127, 134, 135.

85. Mathes, *Californiana II*, documento 119; W. Michael Mathes, ed. and trans., *The Pearl Hunters in the Gulf of California, 1668*, Baja California Travels Series, no. 4 (Los Angeles, 1966).

86. Mathes, *Californiana II*, documentos 116–18.

87. Mathes, *Californiana II*, documento 116.

88. Mathes, *Californiana II*, documento 120.

89. Mathes, *Californiana II*, documentos 121, 122.

90. Mathes, *Californiana II*, documento 123.

91. Mathes, *Californiana II*, documentos 124–26.

92. Mathes, *Californiana II*, documentos 127–36.

93. Mathes, *Californiana II*, documento 137.

94. W. Michael Mathes, ed., *Californiana III: Documentos para la historia de las transformación colonizadora de California, 1679–1686* (Madrid, 1974), documentos 1–4, 15.

Selected Bibliography

North American Exploration, Volume I

The literature of the earliest period of North American exploration encompassed by volume 1 is extensive. The following listing, therefore, is necessarily partial and arbitrary but should be taken to be a reasonably complete thematic coverage of the subject. Most of the books below are secondary sources, available in medium-sized public libraries and most college and university libraries. The latter locations, in particular, will have a good selection of primary source materials as well, and although the interpretations of voyagers and discoveries, of travels and travelers, offered by scholars are worthwhile reading—and hence dominate this selected bibliography—even more valuable are the words of the explorers and their contemporaries. Those for whom the story of North American exploration is more than idle curiosity should seek out those primary sources. It is in the words of the participants themselves that the reader captures the feel of salt spray in the face and, every so often, catches a whiff of sandalwood, borne on the breeze blowing from the Spice Islands.

Ashe, Geoffrey. *Land to the West: St. Brendan's Voyage to America*. New York, 1962.

Asher, G. M., ed. *Henry Hudson the Navigator*. Hakluyt Society, 1st ser., no. 27. London, 1860.

Barbour, Philip L., ed. *The Complete Works of Captain John Smith (1580–1631)*. 3 vols. Chapel Hill, 1986.

Biggar, Henry P., ed. *The Voyages of Jacques Cartier*. Ottawa, 1924.

Bishop, Morris. *The Odyssey of Cabeza de Vaca*. New York, 1933.

Bodily, R. B. *The Voyage of Captain Thomas James for the Discovery of the Northwest Passage*. London, 1929.

Bolton, Herbert E. *Coronado: Knight of Pueblos and Plains*. Albuquerque, 1949.

———, ed. *Spanish Exploration in the Southwest, 1542–1706*. New York, 1908.

Bourne, Edward Gaylord, ed. *Narratives of Hernando de Soto and the Conquest of Florida*. 2 vols. New York, 1922.

Chiappelli, Fredi, ed. *First Images of America: The Impact of the New World on the Old*. 2 vols. Berkeley, 1976.

Cooke, Alan, and Clive Holland. *The Exploration of Northern Canada: A Chronology*. Toronto, 1978.

Cumming, W. P., S. Hillier, D. B. Quinn, and G. Williams, eds. *The Exploration of North America, 1630–1776*. New York, 1974.

Cumming, W. P., R. A. Skelton, and D. B. Quinn. *The Discovery of North America.* London, 1971; New York, 1972.

Day, A. Grove. *Coronado's Quest: The Discovery of the Southwestern States.* Berkeley, 1964.

DeVoto, Bernard. *The Course of Empire.* Boston, 1952.

Dodge, Ernest S. *Northwest by Sea.* New York, 1961.

Gibson, Charles. *Spain in America.* New York, 1966.

Goetzmann, William H., and Glyndwr Williams. *The Atlas of North American Exploration: From the Norse Voyages to the Race to the Pole.* New York, 1992.

Hallenbeck, Cleve, ed. *Alvar Núñez Cabeza de Vaca: The Journey and Route of the First European to Cross the Continent of North America, 1534–1536.* 1940. Reprint, Port Washington NY, 1971.

Hammond, George P., and Agapito Rey, eds. and trans. *Don Juan de Oñate: Colonizer of New Mexico, 1595–1628.* 2 vols. Albuquerque, 1953.

————, eds. *Narratives of the Coronado Expedition, 1539–1542.* Albuquerque, 1940.

Harris, Richard Colebrook, ed. *Historical Atlas of Canada.* Vol. 1, *From the Beginning to 1800.* Toronto, 1987.

Harrisse, Henry. *The Discovery of North America: A Critical Documentary and Historic Investigation, with an Essay on the Early Cartography of the New World.* Amsterdam, 1961.

Hodge, Frederick W., and Theodore H. Lewis, eds. *Spanish Explorers of the Southern United States, 1528–1543.* New York, 1907.

Hoffman, Bernard G. *Cabot to Cartier: Sources for a Historical Ethnography of Northeastern North America, 1497–1550.* Toronto, 1961.

Hoffman, Paul E. *A New Andalucia and a Way to the Orient: The American Southeast during the Sixteenth Century.* Baton Rouge, 1990.

Ingstad, Anne Stine. *The Norse Discovery of America.* Trans. Elizabeth Seeberg. 2 vols. Oslo, 1985.

Ingstad, Helge. *Westward to Vinland.* Toronto, 1969.

Jones, Gwyn. *The Norse Atlantic Saga, Being the Norse Voyages of Discovery and Settlement to Iceland, Greenland, and North America.* 2d ed. New York, 1986.

Kelsey, Harry. *Juan Rodríguez Cabrillo.* San Marino CA, 1986.

Kenyon, W. A. *The Strange and Dangerous Voyage of Capt. Thomas James.* Toronto, 1975.

————. *Tokens of Possession: The Northern Voyages of Martin Frobisher.* Toronto, 1975.

Kerrigan, Anthony, ed. and trans. *Pedro Menéndez de Avilés Founder of Florida.* Gainesville, 1965.

Lowery, Woodbury. *The Spanish Settlements within the Present Limits of the United States, 1513–1574.* 2 vols. 1901, 1905. Reprint, New York, 1959.

Lummis, Charles F. *The Spanish Pioneers and the California Missions.* Chicago, 1929.

Magnusson, Magnus. *Viking Expansion Westwards.* London, 1973.

Magnusson, Magnus, and Hermann Pálsson, trans. *The Vinland Sagas, The Norse Discovery of America*. Hammondsworth, U.K., 1965.

Markham, Albert H., ed. *The Voyages and Works of John Davis*. Hakluyt Society, 1st ser., no. 59. London, 1880.

Markham, Clement R. *Voyages of William Baffin, 1612–1622*. Hakluyt Society, 1st ser., no. 63. London, 1881.

Mathes, W. Michael. *Vizcaíno and Spanish Expansion in the Pacific Ocean, 1580–1630*. San Francisco, 1968.

———, ed. and trans. *Spanish Approaches to the Island of California, 1628–1632*. San Francisco, 1975.

Maynard, Theodore. *De Soto and the Conquistadors*. New York, 1969.

McManis, Douglas R. *European Impressions of the New England Coast, 1497–1620*. University of Chicago Department of Geography Research Paper No. 139. Chicago, 1972.

Milanich, Jerald T., and Susan Milbrath, eds. *First Encounters: Spanish Exploration in the Caribbean and the United States, 1492–1570*. Gainesville, 1989.

Morison, Samuel Eliot. *The European Discovery of America: The Northern Voyages, A.D. 500–1600*. New York, 1971.

———. *The European Discovery of America: The Southern Voyages, 1492–1616*. New York, 1974.

O'Meara, John J. *The Voyage of Saint Brendan: Journey to the Promised Land (Navigatio Sancti Brendani Abbatis)*. Atlantic Highlands NJ, 1976.

Quinn, David Beers. *England and the Discovery of America, 1481–1620, from the Bristol Voyages of the Fifteenth Century to the Pilgrim Settlement at Plymouth: The Exploration, Exploitation, and Trial-by-Error Colonization of North America by the English*. New York, 1974.

———. *North America from Earliest Discovery to First Settlements: The Norse Voyages to 1612*. New York, 1977.

Quinn, David Beers, Alison Quinn, and Susan Hillier, eds. *New American World: A Documentary History of North American to 1612*. 5 vols. London, 1979.

Sauer, Carl Ortwin. *The Early Spanish Main*. Berkeley, 1969.

———. *Seventeenth Century North America*. Berkeley, 1980.

———. *Sixteenth Century North America: The Land and the People as Seen by the Europeans*. Berkeley, 1971.

Severin, Timothy. *The Brendan Voyage*. London, 1978.

Skelton, R. A. *The European Image and Mapping of America: A.D. 1000–1600*. James Ford Bell Lectures No. 1. Minneapolis, 1964.

Skelton, R. A., Thomas E. Marston, and George D. Painter. *The Vinland Map and the Tartar Relation*. New Haven, 1965.

Smith, Thomas Buckingham, trans. *The Relation of Alvar Núñez Cabeza de Vaca*. Ann Arbor, 1966.

———, ed. and trans. *Narratives of de Soto in the Conquest of Florida*. 1866. Reprint, Gainesville, 1968.

Stefansson, Vilhjalmur. *The Three Voyages of Martin Frobisher*. 2 vols. London, 1938.

Story, G. M., ed. *Early European Settlement and Exploration in Atlantic Canada*. Saint John's, Newfoundland, 1982.

Taylor, E. G. R. *Tudor Geography, 1485–1583*. London, 1930.

Vigneras, Louis-André. *The Discovery of South America and the Andalusian Voyages*. Chicago, 1976.

Wagner, Henry R. *Juan Rodríguez Cabrillo: Discoverer of the Coast of California*. San Francisco, 1941.

———. *Spanish Voyages to the North West Coast of America in the Sixteenth Century*. San Francisco, 1929.

Weddle, Robert S. *Spanish Sea: The Gulf of Mexico in North American Discovery, 1500–1685*. College Station TX, 1985.

Wheat, Carl I. *Mapping the Trans-Mississippi West, 1540–1861*. 5 vols. San Francisco, 1957.

Williams, Gwyn A. *Madoc: The Making of a Myth*. London, 1979.

Williamson, James A. *The Cabot Voyages and Bristol Discoveries under Henry VII*. Hakluyt Society, 2d ser., no. 120. Cambridge, U.K., 1962.

———. *The Voyages of the Cabots and the English Discovery of North America under Henry VII and Henry VIII*. London, 1929.

Winship, George Parker. *The Coronado Expedition, 1540–1542*. Chicago, 1964.

Winsor, Justin, ed. *Narrative and Critical History of America*. 8 vols. Boston, 1884–89.

Wroth, Lawrence C. *The Voyages of Giovanni da Verrazzano, 1524–1528*. New Haven, 1970.

Contributors

John L. Allen is a professor of geography at the University of Connecticut. He is the author of several books, including *Passage through the Garden: Lewis and Clark and the Images of the American Northwest* and *Jedediah Smith and the Mountain Men of the American West*, and numerous articles in scholarly periodicals, edited volumes, and conference proceedings. Dr. Allen is also the editor of *Annual Editions: Environment*. He has served his academic department as its first head (1976–81) and as acting head (1986–87) and has held many other administrative and committee posts at the University of Connecticut, where he has spent his entire academic career. Dr. Allen has served as a National Councilor of the Society for the History of Discoveries and as a member of the Editorial Board of *The Journal of Historical Geography*. He is an authority on the role of images in exploration. Dr. Allen holds academic degrees from the University of Wyoming (B.A. and M.A.) and Clark University (Ph.D., 1969) and was an NSF Post-Doctoral Fellow at Clark University in 1970–71.

Robert H. Fuson is professor emeritus of geography at the University of Southern Florida. He has also held academic appointments at Louisiana State University and the University of Miami. Dr. Fuson is an authority on the Columbian voyages and Caribbean exploration and has published extensively in the field, including *The Log of Christopher Columbus* and numerous other books and scholarly articles. He has extensive experience as a lecturer and in 1986, won the prestigious Webb-Smith Essay Award at the University of Texas–Arlington for a lecture given as part of the Walter Prescott Webb Lecture Series. In addition to his teaching and lecturing experience, Dr. Fuson served as chairman of the Geography Department at the University of Southern Florida for over twenty years. Dr. Fuson received his undergraduate degree at Indiana University and his graduate degrees at Florida State University (M.A.) and the Louisiana State University (Ph.D., 1958).

Oakah L. Jones Jr. is professor emeritus of history at Purdue University. He is an authority on the Spanish frontier in North America (Spanish Borderlands) and Latin American colonial and national history. Dr. Jones is the author of a number of books in the field of Spanish Borderlands history, including *Pueblo Warriors and Spanish Conquest* and *Nueva Vizcaya: Heartland of the Spanish Frontier*; in addition, he has edited several books and has contributed over a dozen articles to the scholarly literature. He has served on the editorial board for several important journals, including *Journal of the West*, *Pacific Historical Review*, and *New Mexico*

Historical Review, and was chairman of the editorial board of Purdue University Press in 1986–87. Dr. Jones attended the University of Tulsa and the University of Arkansas before receiving his B.S. degree from the U.S. Naval Academy at Annapolis. His graduate degrees are from the University of Oklahoma (M.A., 1960, Ph.D., 1964).

Karen Ordahl Kupperman is a professor of history at the University of Connecticut. She is the author of several scholarly books, including *Roanoke: The Abandoned Colony* and *Settling with the Indians: The Meeting of English and Indian Cultures in America, 1580–1640,* as well as a number of articles in the professional literature. Dr. Kupperman is an authority on the history and historical geography of the colonial period in the United States and is particularly noted for her work on the relationships between colonization and the climatic environment. She has held fellowships from the National Humanities Center, the American Council of Learned Societies, and the American Philosophical Society; she also was a Mellon Faculty Fellow at Harvard University and held a Woodrow Wilson Fellowship at Harvard. She received her baccalaureate from the University of Missouri, her master's from Harvard University, and her doctorate from Cambridge University (1978).

G. Malcolm Lewis is retired from a position as senior lecturer in geography at the University of Sheffield (England), where he served throughout his academic career. He also has held visiting professorships at a number of American institutions, including Pennsylvania State University, the University of Nebraska, and the University of Denver. Recognized as an authority on the cosmography and cartography of North American Indians, Mr. Lewis has also contributed extensively to the literature on the early exploration of the American Great Plains. He currently serves as a coeditor of The History of Cartography project. Mr. Lewis has also had considerable experience in applied geography and has served in several consulting capacities in England. Mr. Lewis holds his academic degrees from the University of Sheffield (1952, 1954) with postgraduate work at the University of Wisconsin–Madison in 1954–56.

Alan G. Macpherson is a professor of geography at Memorial University of Newfoundland, St. John's. One of Canada's leading authorities on the Norse voyages and settlement in North America and the historical geography of Atlantic Canada, Dr. Macpherson has published widely in scholarly periodicals and has edited several major works, including *The Natural Environment of Newfoundland, Past and Present* (to which he also contributed chapters) and *The Atlantic Provinces.* He has held a number of academic positions at McMaster University, the University of Manitoba, the University of Rochester, and Memorial University. At Memorial he has also served as director of research at the Institute of So-

cial and Economic Research. He has served on the editorial board of the Historical Atlas of Canada project and was a Councillor of the Executive Committee of
the Canadian Association of Geographers. Dr. Macpherson's graduate degrees
are from the University of Edinburgh (M.A.) and McGill University (Ph.D., 1969).

W. Michael Mathes is professor emeritus of history at the University of San Francisco, where he spent most of his academic career, interrupted by visiting professorships both in the United States and abroad. Long recognized as an authority
on the exploration and settlement of the Pacific coastal region (particularly Baja
and Alta California), Dr. Mathes is the author or coauthor of over thirty books,
including *Vizcaíno and Spanish Expansion in the Pacific Ocean, 1580–1630; The Conquistador in California*; and *Spanish Approaches to the Island of California, 1628–1632*,
along with several articles in American, Mexican, and Spanish scholarly literature. He is the recipient of numerous awards for his research and writing, including
the Henry R. Wagner Memorial Award of the California Historical Society.

Dennis Reinhartz is a professor of history and Russian at the University of Texas at
Arlington. An authority on the early cartography of Texas and the Southwest,
Dr. Reinhartz is the editor of a number of books, including *The History of North
American Discovery and Exploration, The Mapping of the American Southwest*, and *Entrada: The First Century of Mapping the Greater Southwest*, and the author of many
articles in professional journals. Dr. Reinhartz has served as both National
Councilor and President of the Society for the History of Discovery and is a past
president of the Western Social Science Association. He received his education
at Rutgers (B.A. and M.A.) and New York University (Ph.D.).

David Beers Quinn is emeritus professor of modern history at the University of Liverpool, England. He is recognized as the leading authority on the early exploration of eastern North America and has written many books on that topic, including *England and the Discovery of America* and *North America from First Discovery to
Early Settlements: The Norse Voyages to 1612*. With his wife, Alison Quinn, and
S. Hillier, he edited the massive five-volume collection *New American World: A
Documentary History of North America to 1612*. His publications also include many
papers in learned journals. Dr. Quinn has received numerous awards for his
scholarly contributions and holds a number of honorary doctorates from institutions in the United States, Canada, and Great Britain. In 1987 he gave a lecture
tour in the United States as a Distinguished Fulbright Visiting Professor. Most of
his academic career was spent at the Universities of Wales and Liverpool, but he
has held numerous visiting professorships and research fellowships in North
American universities. Dr. Quinn received his undergraduate degree from
Queen's University (Belfast) and his doctorate from King's College, London, in
1934.

Robert S. Weddle is a journalist, author, and historian who has worked as an editor, newspaper editor, and publisher; in university and state government public information; in book publishing; and in management and consulting work. Since 1976 he has been self-employed in research and writing. A specialist in Spanish and French colonial history of the Southwest and Gulf Coast, Mr. Weddle is the author or coauthor of nine scholarly books and numerous articles for both scholarly journals and popular magazines. His research has included work in the principal Spanish archives and site study in Mexico. His most recent works, done with the assistance of a research grant from the National Endowment for the Humanities, are *Spanish Sea: The Gulf of Mexico in North American Discovery, 1500–1685* and *La Salle, the Mississippi, and the Gulf: Three Primary Documents.* Mr. Weddle was educated at Texas Tech University (B.A., 1947).

Index